BRITISH ENVOYS TO THE KAISERREICH

1871–1897

VOLUME II: 1884–1897

BRITISH ENVOYS TO THE KAISERREICH

1871–1897

VOLUME II: 1884–1897

edited by
MARKUS MÖSSLANG

CAMDEN FIFTH SERIES
Volume 56

CAMBRIDGE
UNIVERSITY PRESS

FOR THE ROYAL HISTORICAL SOCIETY IN ASSOCIATION WITH
THE GERMAN HISTORICAL INSTITUTE LONDON
2019

Published by the Press Syndicate of the University of Cambridge
University Printing House, Shaftesbury Road, Cambridge CB2 8BS, United Kingdom
One Liberty Plaza, Floor 20, New York, NY 10006, USA
477 Williamstown Road, Port Melbourne, VIC 3207, Australia
C/Orense, 4, Planta 13, 28020 Madrid, Spain
Lower Ground Floor, Nautica Building, The Water Club,
Beach Road, Granger Bay, 8005 Cape Town, South Africa

First published 2019

A catalogue record for this book is available from the British Library

ISBN 9781108484961 hardback

SUBSCRIPTIONS. The serial publications of the Royal Historical Society, *Royal Historical Society Transactions* (ISSN 0080-4401) and Camden Fifth Series (ISSN 0960-1163) volumes, may be purchased together on annual subscription. The 2019 subscription price, which includes print and electronic access (but not VAT), is £205 (US $342 in the USA, Canada, and Mexico) and includes Camden Fifth Series, Volumes 56, 57 and 58 and Transactions Sixth Series, Volume 29 (published in December). The electronic only price available to institutional subscribers is £172 (US $286 in the USA, Canada, and Mexico). Japanese prices are available from Kinokuniya Company Ltd, P.O. Box 55, Chitose, Tokyo 156, Japan. EU subscribers (outside the UK) who are not registered for VAT should add VAT at their country's rate. VAT registered subscribers provide their VAT registration number. Prices include delivery by air.

Subscription orders, which must be accompanied by payment, may be sent to a bookseller, subscription agent, or direct to the publisher: Cambridge University Press, University Printing House, Shaftesbury Road, Cambridge CB2 8BS, UK; or in the USA, Canada, and Mexico: Cambridge University Press, Journals Fulfillment Department, One Liberty Plaza, Floor 20, New York, NY 10006, USA.

SINGLE VOLUMES AND BACK VOLUMES. A list of Royal Historical Society volumes available from Cambridge University Press may be obtained from the Humanities Marketing Department at the address above.

Printed in the UK by Bell & Bain Ltd.

CONTENTS

ACKNOWLEDGEMENTS

This second and final volume of *British Envoys to the Kaiserreich, 1871–1897* marks the conclusion of an editorial enterprise that saw its first publication nineteen years ago with Volume one of the preceding series *British Envoys to Germany, 1816–1866*. Together, the two series cover Anglo-German history from the resumption of diplomatic relations in 1816 to the year 1897, when Germany's new aspirations in and beyond Europe affected already volatile relations. This period corresponds, roughly and possibly quite tellingly, with Otto von Bismarck's lifespan (1815–1898). Yet while Bismarck and many other statesmen on both sides of the channel feature prominently in the reports that were filed to the Foreign Office, this editorial enterprise aimed, from the outset, to include perceptions of Germany that were as diverse as possible, and in particular the diplomatic reports from the smaller German courts and capitals. What was initiated with the aim of contributing to the historiography of Anglo-German relations gradually coincided with a renewed and widened interest in the history of diplomacy and of international relations. Thanks to the multitude of topics, and the mostly subtle nature of reporting, the selection of dispatches from the British missions in Germany and their compilation in individual instalments, six in all, proved to be a challenging but always enjoyable task. The years 1867–1870, which so far – for the sake of a balanced selection – have been omitted from the project, will be the subject of a future supplement volume.

As with the previous volumes, the publication of this book would not have been possible without the constant support of many people. Special thanks go to the Literary Directors of the Royal Historical Society, Andrew Spicer and Richard Toye, and the RHS publications committee for accepting this edition for publication in the Camden Fifth Series and thus continuing the co-operation with the German Historical Institute London (GHIL). It seems appropriate that *British Envoys to the Kaiserreich* is published under the terms of a Creative Commons licence and can be freely shared electronically in 'gold' open access. Melanie Howe and Daniel Pearce, from Cambridge University Press, and especially Miranda Bethell saw the book through the printing process with great expertise and professionalism. Thanks are also due to the anonymous readers.

I have been privileged to be involved in this project since I joined the GHIL in 1999. For the long-standing institutional and personal endorsement I should like to thank the Institute's advisory board and its current chairperson, Andreas Fahrmeir, and the present and past directors of the GHIL, Christina von Hodenberg and Andreas Gestrich. It is sad that their predecessors, Peter Wende and Hagen Schulze, did not live to see the conclusion of this edition which they initiated and shaped in its crucial stages.

Again, I am especially grateful to my colleagues and friends at and beyond the GHIL, who supported me over the years and never tired of critically debating the project, its scope and its editorial principles. Jane Rafferty, Angela Davies, and Emily Richards as well as generations of GHIL interns were of invaluable help, as were the staffs of archives and libraries in both the UK and Germany. As with the previous volumes, the vast holdings of the National Archives, the British Library, and the Bavarian State Library, as well the ever-growing resources and collections on the internet, were indispensable in the search for the sometimes obscure details that often make editing historical documents as fascinating as it is unpredictable.

During the various stages of the two *Kaiserreich* volumes I had the pleasure of sharing my enthusiasm for British envoys – and a good deal of editorial pragmatism – with my then colleagues, Chris Manias and Helen Whatmore. Chris delved into the diplomatic correspondence from Germany in a crucial first round of selection and Helen, co-editor of volume one, made sense, among others things, of the often hastily penned initials and notes on the reverse side of the dispatches and helped to bring this volume to a successful completion. Naturally absorption in the depths and shallows of nineteenth-century Anglo-German history was not always understood by my family, but Alex and our sons, Lorenz, Peter, and Benno, provided welcome distractions in the editor's workshop; my thanks to them for constantly reminding me that there is life outside the diplomats' world.

London, January 2019
Markus Mösslang

INTRODUCTION

In 1897, the concluding year of this editorial project, British envoys posted to the *Kaiserreich* remained as watchful as ever of Germany and were duly attentive to changes and developments in its constituent states. In this respect their correspondence differs only by degrees from what had been reported by earlier generations of diplomats. In 1816, the first year of the preceding series *British Envoys to Germany, 1816–1866*,[1] as well as in 1871, the starting point of *British Envoys to the Kaiserreich, 1871–1897*, Anglo-German-relations had been similarly marked by apprehensions about what lay ahead. Yet at the end of the nineteenth century the shift to global politics, Germany's increasing economic power, aspirations in terms of *Weltpolitik* and plans for a fleet – reinforced by ministerial appointments, and accompanied by an Anglophobic press and public opinion – heralded a new quality of bi-lateral and international relations. Indeed, almost forty years ago Paul M. Kennedy, in his classic study *The Rise of the Anglo-German Antagonism*, pointed out that 'in 1897, despite the confused political scene which confronted contemporaries, it is possible for the historian – aided quite unashamedly by the benefit of hindsight – to detect the most significant pointers to the future'.[2]

While many historians have argued that the fate of Anglo-German rivalry was not inevitable and the years to 1914, in fact, saw many elements of rapprochement, the significance of the chronological caesura in 1897–1898 is still widely recognized.[3] It is no coincidence that the two long-standing editions of British diplomatic reports from Germany before 1914 start – as is the case with *British Documents on the Origins of War* – in 1898 and likewise concentrate – as in the case of *British Documents on Foreign Affairs* – on the years after 1897.[4] This book,

---

[1] *British Envoys to Germany, 1818–1866*, Royal Historical Society, Camden Fifth Series, 4 vols (Cambridge, 2000–2010).

[2] Paul M. Kennedy, *The Rise of the Anglo-German Antagonism, 1860–1914* (London, 1980), p. 223.

[3] For more recent historiography on Anglo-German relations before 1914, see Jan Rüger, 'Revisiting the Anglo-German Antagonism', *The Journal of Modern History*, 83 (2011), pp. 579–617.

[4] *British Documents on the Origins of War, 1898–1914*, 11 vols (London 1926–1938); *British Documents on Foreign Affairs: Reports and Papers from the Foreign Office Confidential Print: Part I, Series F, Europe*, 35 vols (Frederick, MD, 1987–1991). The Foreign Office correspondence

the second installment of a two-volume mini-series, presents a selection of diplomatic correspondence sent from Germany in the years 1884 to 1897 that complements this traditional and often teleological focus on Anglo-German relations before the First World War. As part of the *British Envoys* editorial project as a whole, that is, from 1816 to 1897,[5] it is integrated into a broad chronological framework and thus challenges any attempt to explain the volatile Anglo-German history of the long nineteenth century as a linear story of deteriorating relations, and estrangement between formerly close cousins.

As material records from the past, the handwritten dispatches of 1897 – with a margin on the inner side of the page, folded three times (when sent), and inscribed with a docket on the wider side of the back – look much the same as those sent eighty years earlier and are collected in thick, worn, and sometimes crumbling leather bound volumes, which can be consulted in the National Archives at Kew.[6] Although Her Majesty's Stationery Office supplied the Berlin embassy with a Remington typewriter in 1892, lack of able junior secretaries or attachés meant that this innovation caught on only slowly, and, until 1905, fair copies of dispatches in typescript retained the traditional folio format and layout.[7] The understaffed missions at the smaller German capitals did not, initially, participate in this technological progress and in 1907 the Foreign Office responded to the request of the British representative at Munich, that 'one typewriter ought to be amply sufficient for the work of the Legation'.[8]

The formal conventions of dispatch writing demonstrate the persistence of traditional ways of operating in the Foreign Office bureaucracy, but the dispatches from the German *Kaiserreich* also reveal more important continuities in terms of content and substance. This applies to the patterns of perception and the mindsets of British diplomats – for example regarding the general superiority of British political institutions or the global approach to international affairs

---

on Germany is available on microfilm from 1906 onwards: *Confidential British Foreign Office Political Correspondence: Germany, Series 1, 1906–1925: Part 1, 1906–1919* (Bethesda, MD, 2005).

[5] The omission of the contested years 1867 to 1870 is intended to enable the publication of a substantial selection of dispatches on the *Kaiserreich* (1871–1897) in two coherent and balanced volumes, an aim that would have been compromised by the inclusion of the extensive reportage that was produced on the Franco-Prussian War of 1870. This gap will be closed in an additional volume.

[6] See Michael Roper, *The Records of the Foreign Office, 1782–1968* (Kew, 2002), pp. 15–18.

[7] Malet to Rosebery, 25 September 1893, The National Archives, Kew (TNA), FO 64/1294 [unless otherwise stated dispatches of the years 1884 to 1897 are printed in this volume].

[8] Note, dated 7 April 1907, TNA, FO 371/900/10715.

– and no less importantly to the wide thematic scope of their reportage.[9] Just like their predecessors in 1816, who were instructed to provide information about 'the events as they arise at the Court at which you reside' and 'to convey home whatever further information you may judge likely to prove useful to H.R. Highness' Government',[10] British envoys to the *Kaiserreich* reported on an astonishing array both of inner-German events, and of facets of Anglo-German entanglements and encounters which are not normally taken into account in thematically focused narratives. Examples include the repercussions of an incident which took place on a Dresden lawn-tennis court in 1885,[11] or, in the same year, a query made by a German 'sub-officer' 'on what conditions he would be admitted to serve in the British army […], if possible, in the present Egyptian campaign'.[12] While this edition of documents allows only for a small selection from the diplomatic coverage of seemingly secondary topics, anecdotal observations form a substantial part of the diplomatic correspondence and shed light on everyday and more mundane diplomatic activities, as well as on those more out of the ordinary occasions. Arguably, reports by British envoys thus make more entertaining reading than the, sometimes, technocratic reportage from their German counterparts.[13]

Central to the diverse and often colourful testimonies from Germany is the fact that Great Britain, in addition to the embassy at Berlin, was individually represented at four smaller German capitals of the twenty-seven constituent states of the empire.[14] These second-tier, not second-ranking, missions were located in

---

[9] For a detailed account of the mind-set and principles behind foreign policy before 1914, see T.G. Otte, *The Foreign Office Mind: The Making of British Foreign Policy, 1865–1914* (Cambridge, 2011). For perceptions of Germany, see Richard Scully, *British Images of Germany: Admiration, Antagonism & Ambivalence, 1860–1914* (Basingstoke, 2012) and the chapter 'British Views of Germany, 1815–1914', in James Retallack, *Germany's Second Reich: Portraits and Pathways* (Toronto, 2015), pp. 44–85.

[10] Castlereagh, Circular No 2, 1 January 1816, TNA, FO 244/6.

[11] Strachey to Salisbury, 7 July 1885, FO 68/169.

[12] Barron to Granville, 7 February 1885, FO 82/170.

[13] See, for example, Hans Philippi, *Das Königreich Württemberg im Spiegel der preußischen Gesandtschaftsberichte: 1871–1914* (Stuttgart, 1972); Hans-Jürgen Kremer, *Das Großherzogtum Baden in der politischen Berichterstattung der preußischen Gesandten 1871–1918*, 2 vols (Stuttgart, 1990–1992); Winfried Baumgart, *Ein preußischer Gesandter in München: Georg Freiherr von Werthern: Tagebuch und politische Korrespondenz mit Bismarck 1867–1888* (Berlin, 2018). For German diplomatic documents between 1885 and 1897, see also Vols 4, 8, and 11 of *Die Große Politik der europäischen Kabinette 1871–1914: Sammlung der diplomatischen Akten des Auswärtigen Amtes*, 40 vols (Berlin, 1922–1927).

[14] The British ambassador to Berlin was simultaneously accredited as minister plenipotentiary to Mecklenburg-Schwerin, Mechlenburg-Strelitz, Saxe-Weimar-Eisenach, Oldenburg, Anhalt-Dessau, and Brunswick.

Darmstadt (Grand Duchy of Hesse, whose representative was simultaneously accredited to the Grand Duchy of Baden), Dresden (Kingdom of Saxony), Munich (Kingdom of Bavaria), and Stuttgart (Kingdom of Württemberg, until 1890, when the mission was amalgamated with that of Munich).[15] A further post at Coburg, where Britain had been represented by a chargé d'affaires since Queen Victoria's marriage to Albert, was upheld until 1897, when the legation was finally merged with that at Dresden. As in the years before 1884, the correspondence remained thin on the ground and largely trivial; it is not included in this volume.

The distinct feature of multiple diplomatic representations had its roots in the Holy Roman Empire and then the foundation of the German Confederation in 1815; it outlasted the creation of the German nation state in 1871 and continued to exist up to August 1914. Over time, the diplomats in their respective capitals became increasingly detached from the power centre and high politics of Berlin, but they fulfilled a symbolically charged role as a reminder of their host states' former independence and dynastic glory. It is their focus on individual state affairs as well as their provision of local perspectives on German and international affairs that prove to be of particular historical value. This is why, along with the hitherto unpublished dispatches from Berlin, an edition of diplomatic papers such as this can still add to our knowledge of the well-researched field of Anglo-German history.

I

After the German Empire was founded in 1871, British multi-representation in Germany continued, but with a smaller number of diplomats and reservations towards its utility and longevity.[16] Notwithstanding an acknowledgment of the value of the legations 'in the present condition of Europe', in its final report of May 1871 the Select Committee on Diplomatic and Consular Services – was 'of opinion, that there is a reasonable likelihood, at a not very distant date, that there may cease to be any good grounds for maintaining

---

[15] For information on British missions and diplomats, see *The Foreign Office List and Diplomatic and Consular Yearbook* (London, 1852–1914); and *A Directory of British Diplomats*, compiled by Colin Mackie. Available at http://www.gulabin.com/britishdiplomatsdirectory/pdf/britishdiplomatsdirectory.pdf (accessed 26 July 2018).

[16] See *British Envoys to the Kaiserreich, 1871–1897*, Vol. I, pp. 2–6.

some of them'.[17] Two months later, in the House of Commons debate about the civil service estimates, it became clear that this matter was still open for discussion when Peter Rylands, Liberal MP for Warrington, saw 'now no reason why the small German Missions should be continued'.[18] Over the next forty years, until 1914 when World War I put an end to diplomatic relations with Germany, reference was repeatedly made to the anomaly of having several diplomatic missions in Germany, including twice before Royal Commissions (in 1889 and 1914) and twice more in Parliament. In 1895 the former editor of *Vanity Fair* magazine and Conservative MP, Thomas Gibson Bowles – renowned for his insights and ironic take on the diplomatic establishment – thought it 'absurd to maintain diplomatic arrangements with the smaller German Courts',[19] and in 1913 the Liberal MP Joseph King concluded: 'To my mind they are absolutely useless, except that they are gentlemen of high social position and no doubt very agreeable personalities, but they are not wanted at all.'[20]

A first indication that the Foreign Office itself was thinking seriously about a further reduction in the service to Germany can be found in 1884 in the *Estimates for Civil Services*. Here a footnote to the table of salaries and rent allowances – compiled by the Foreign Office chief clerk – stated that '[i]t is proposed on the occurrence of vacancies to amalgamate the Missions at Munich, Stuttgardt, and Darmstadt, so as to reduce the cost'.[21] In 1884 the total annual budget for British representations in Germany was £13,700, of which £7,900 was allocated to the Berlin embassy and £5,800 to the rest of Germany. With the salaries of the temporarily seconded

[17] First Report from the Select Committee on Diplomatic and Consular Services; together with the Proceedings of the Committee, Minutes of Evidence, Appendix, and Index, 18 May 1871 [238] (1871), p. vi. On the select committees and on the development of the diplomatic service and the Foreign Office in general, see Raymond A. Jones, *The British Diplomatic Service, 1815–1914* (Gerrards Cross, 1983); Thomas Otte, 'Old Diplomacy: Reflections on the Foreign Office before 1914', *Contemporary British History*, 18, 3 (2004), pp. 31–52; for the missions in Germany, see Markus Mösslang, 'Gestaltungsraum und lokale Lebenswelt: Britische Diplomaten an ihren deutschen Standorten, 1815–1914', in Hillard von Thiessen and Christian Windler (eds), *Akteure der Außenbeziehungen: Netzwerke und Interkulturalität im historischen Wandel* (Cologne and Vienna, 2010), pp. 199–215.
[18] Speech in House of Commons, 28 July 1871, *Hansard's Parliamentary Debates*, Ser. III, Vol. 208 (1871), col. 440.
[19] Speech in House of Commons, 30 August 1895, *Hansard's Parliamentary Debates*, Ser. IV, Vol. 36 (1895), col 1270.
[20] Speech in House of Commons, 29 May 1913, *Hansard's Parliamentary Debates*, Ser. V, Vol. 53 (1913), col 445.
[21] Estimates for Civil Services for the Year Ending 31 March 1885, House of Commons Sessional Papers 1884 (57), LII.i., p. 414.

junior secretaries this latter amount roughly corresponded to the cost of the British representation in the USA, or the costs of the missions at Columbia, Uruguay, and Venezuela combined.[22] In the winter of 1889–1890, when the diplomatic service came under the scrutiny of the Royal Commission on Civil Establishments, the total cost of the smaller missions had risen to £6,845.[23] In his testimony before the commission the permanent under-secretary of state for foreign affairs, Sir Philip Currie, defended the outposts in Germany but cautiously and not entirely convincingly. Confirming that 'Berlin is the only place where we should, of course, carry on negotiations', Currie struggled to explain fully the raison d'être of the legations at Munich, Darmstadt, Stuttgart, Coburg, and Dresden when asked: 'What political information can be needed from a centre of that sort beyond gossip?'[24] While the representation at Coburg – due to the close ties with the British royal house – was 'a separate affair altogether',[25] as far as the other cases were concerned Currie did little more than point to the fact that the respective host states had independent sovereigns and that Britain's practice of maintaining legations was also mirrored by other European powers. Yet, as the members of the committee rightly objected, Russia was the only country, with a total of five legations at the 'lesser German Courts', that roughly matched Great Britain's six (including Coburg). France and Italy, on the other hand, both had only a representative at Munich. Tellingly, in its final report of July 1890, the commission stated that it was 'not in a position to judge as to any further reasons, political or otherwise, which may exist for maintaining these missions'.[26]

One reason for the committee's hesitation to recommend any radical steps might have been that, in the meantime, the secretary of state for foreign affairs, Lord Salisbury, had decided to go ahead with the long-planned amalgamation of the missions (though not including Darmstadt). Against the protests of the Stuttgart chargé d'affaires, Sir Henry Barron, who had been forcibly pensioned off, and much to the displeasure of the Württemberg court, the Stuttgart legation was abolished and in May 1890, the British minister resident at Munich, Victor Drummond, was accredited at

---

[22] Ibid., pp. 413–416.
[23] Fourth Report of the Royal Commission Appointed to Inquire into the Civil Establishments of the Different Offices of State at Home and Abroad [C.6172] (1890), Appendix, p. 183.
[24] Evidence, Currie (27 November 1889), Fourth Report of the Royal Commission, qq. 27152–3.
[25] Ibid. q. 27078.
[26] Fourth Report of the Royal Commission, p. 11.

Stuttgart as well.[27] As a concessionary gesture to the King of Württemberg a junior diplomat (with the rank of second secretary) remained in Stuttgart, officially as part of the Munich mission.[28] Whether the king subsequently kept in touch with 'his' British envoy, who had left the diplomatic service two weeks earlier to spend his retirement in Stuttgart, is not known.

Barron's role as a foreign socialite and slightly eccentric bachelor, and diplomat resident at Stuttgart (both active and retired) epitomizes the anachronistic societal role of British diplomats in the political backwaters of Europe. However, his career also hints at another, more structural, element in British diplomacy, i.e. 'the famous block in promotion'.[29] Since October 1887, Barron, who had entered the service as an attaché in 1840, had been 'the senior member of the Diplomatic Service on the Active List'.[30] Not only was '[h]is a case', as a magazine article on 'Our Diplomatists' pointed out, 'of exceptionally slow promotion, for it took him forty-three years to become a Minister-Resident',[31] his post at Stuttgart proved to be his final one. The same applied to George Strachey, who from 1873 was secretary of legation with 'the additional character of Chargé d'Affaires while resident at Dresden',[32] whose annual additional allowance of £250 (i.e. £750 instead of £500) was justified by his 'length of service'.[33] Strachey's promotion to minister resident in December 1890, after thirty-eight years in the service, was initially purely nominal; it was only in 1893, nineteen years after he first appealed to the foreign secretary 'to consider the propriety of my receiving an addition to my small salary', that Strachey was awarded a pay rise of £150 per year, commensurate with the position of minister resident.[34]

For critics of the multiple diplomatic establishments in Germany, such as Sir Charles Dilke, parliamentary under-secretary of state for foreign affairs from 1880 to 1883, these postings exemplified the unsatisfactory state of affairs, as they were unattractive for aspiring diplomats – 'you cannot hope to be permanently represented at

---

[27] Barron to Currie, 12 March 1890, FO 82/175 (not included in this volume).

[28] King Karl II was also invested with the Order of the Garter on 23 April 1890 – possibly a further source of consolation. See *The London Gazette*, 9 May 1890, p. 2688; Philippi, *Das Königreich Württemberg*, pp. 59–60.

[29] Jones, *Diplomatic Service*, p. 147.

[30] 'Our Diplomatists', *Temple Bar, A London Magazine for Town and Country Readers*, 84, 335 (1888), pp. 179–198, at p. 184.

[31] Ibid.

[32] *The Foreign Office List* (1876), p. 9.

[33] *Estimates for Civil Services* (1884), p. 414.

[34] Estimates for Civil Services for the Year Ending 31 March 1894, House of Commons Sessional Papers 1893 (59), LVI.1, p. 401. See also Jones, *Diplomatic Service*, pp. 147–148.

those courts by your best men – you cannot expect that your best men will be anxious to represent you at these small places'.[35] Yet the question of who were the 'best men' was highly subjective. For instance, the author of the above-cited article in the *Temple Bar* magazine reflected on the fate of Drummond, chargé d'affaires at Munich from 1885 and also accredited to Stuttgart from 1890 until his retirement in 1903: 'Why he has not yet been appointed Minister is a mystery, for he is universally popular and strikes everybody as a type of the accomplished, genial and kind-hearted English gentleman.'[36] George Strachey was similarly unable to comprehend why he was, despite some support in the senior ranks of the service, 'on no one occasion [...] ever offered a post'.[37] In contrast to what he himself had assumed many years earlier the smaller missions were not 'valuable nurseries for agents of a lower rank'.[38] With the two exceptions of Sir Hugh Guion MacDonell, Drummond's predecessor at Munich, and more prominently George W. Buchanan, who took over Darmstadt in 1892 and was ultimately made ambassador in 1910, first to St Petersburg, and then until 1921 to Rome, appointment to one of the smaller German courts proved to be a career move of dubious distinction.[39]

Of course, the opposite was true of the three ambassadors who served at Berlin between 1884 and 1897.[40] While they had not, like some of their predecessors, previously worked in one of the other German capitals, all three of them had first-hand knowledge of Germany or its political establishment when they arrived at their post. The appointment of Lord Odo Russell, later Baron Ampthill, in 1871 can, among other things, be attributed to his close contacts with Wilhelm I and Bismarck when he was on a special mission to the headquarters of the German Army at Versailles from

---

[35] Evidence, Dilke (6 March 1890), Fourth Report of the Royal Commission, qq. 29046.

[36] 'Our Diplomatists', *Temple Bar*, p. 197.

[37] Strachey to Russell, 17 December 1883, FO 918/63 (not included in this volume).

[38] Evidence, Strachey (30 May 1861), Report from the Select Committee on Diplomatic Service; together with the Proceedings of the Committee, Minutes of Evidence, Appendix, and Index 23 July 1861 [459] (1861), q. 2701.

[39] MacDonell, after his three year stint in Bavaria, was promoted to envoy extraordinary at Rio de Janeiro (1885), Copenhagen (1888), and Lisbon (1893–1902). For Buchanan's diplomatic career, see George W. Buchanan, *My Mission to Russia, and Other Diplomatic Memories*, 2 vols London, 1923); for his time at Darmstadt, see Vol. 1, pp. 26–37; and Meriel Buchanan, *Diplomacy and Foreign Courts* (London, 1928), pp. 18–33.

[40] See Hans Philippi, 'Die Botschafter der europäischen Mächte am Berliner Hofe 1871–1914: Eine Skizze', in Oswald Hauser (ed.), *Vorträge und Studien zur preußisch-deutschen Geschichte* (Cologne and Vienna, 1983), pp. 159–250, here pp. 163–175.

November 1870 to March 1871.[41] His successor Edward Malet, who took over after Ampthill's early death in 1884, had also previously encountered Bismarck during the Franco-Prussian War of 1870, when he was secretary of legation at Paris and likewise sent on a special mission to the German headquarters.[42] Malet also profited from the friendship of his father, Alexander Malet, with Bismarck, which dated back to their time together as representatives to the Diet of the German Confederation in Frankfurt in the 1850s.[43] Lastly, Frank Lascelles, who succeeded Malet in 1895, had served as third secretary of legation at Berlin between July 1867 and January 1870, during which time he established valuable contacts in Berlin society. What is more Lascelles, when minister to Romania, had also befriended Bernhard von Bülow, the future German chancellor.[44]

In contrast to diplomats at the smaller missions in Germany, whose appointment was more or less based on Foreign Office internal politics (the question of seniority being just one factor among others), promotion to the Berlin ambassadorship was highly politicized, and involved both government and court on both sides. The question of Lord Ampthill's successor was a case in point. Queen Victoria favoured the greatest expert on German politics at the time, Sir Robert Morier, who, before becoming ambassador to St Petersburg, had been stationed at Berlin, Darmstadt, Stuttgart, and Munich, but who was not acceptable to Bismarck due to personal differences between the two men.[45] Edward Malet, on the other hand, had only just been accredited as envoy extraordinary and minister plenipotentiary at Brussels and lacked seniority. In the end, however, he prevailed as not only the most promising but also, to the German side, the most acceptable candidate.

---

[41] For Odo Russell's ambassadorship, see Winifred Taffs, *Ambassador to Bismarck: Lord Odo Russell, First Baron Ampthill* (London, 1938); Karina Urbach, *Bismarck's Favourite Englishman: Lord Odo Russell's Mission to Berlin* (London, 1999); Paul Knaplund (ed.), *Letters from the Berlin Embassy: Selections from the Private Correspondence of British Representatives at Berlin and Foreign Secretary Lord Granville, 1871–1874, 1880–1885* (Washington DC, 1944); and *British Envoys to the Kaiserreich*, Vol. I.

[42] Edward Malet, *Shifting Scenes or Memories of Many Men in Many Lands* (London, 1901), pp. 233–255. For Malet's ambassadorship at Berlin, see also Willem Alexander van't Padje, 'At the Heart of the Growing Anglo-Imperialist Rivalry: Two British Ambassadors in Berlin, 1884–1908', DPhil thesis, University of Oxford, 2001; for his appointment, see ibid., pp. 15–28; Jones, *Diplomatic Service*, pp. 182–183.

[43] Willem Alexander van't Padje, 'Sir Alexander Malet and Prince Otto von Bismarck: An Almost Forgotten Anglo-German Friendship', *Historical Research*, 72 (1999), pp. 285–300.

[44] James Bourne, 'Sir Frank Lascelles: A Diplomat of the Victorian Empire, 1841–1920', PhD thesis, University of Leeds, 2010, pp. 13–18, 110–130. For Lascelles's ambassadorship at Berlin, see also Van't Padje, 'Two British Ambassadors'.

[45] For Morier's relationship with Bismarck, see Agatha Ramm, *Sir Robert Morier: Envoy and Ambassador in the Age of Imperialism 1876–1893*, Oxford 1973, pp. 270–304.

Despite the almost impossible challenge of following the popular and, according to Prince Bismarck, irreplaceable Lord Ampthill,[46] Edward Malet's old-school approach to diplomacy allowed him to navigate through the complexities of Anglo-German relations until 1895, when, apparently weary of his duties, he applied for early retirement. His irritation with Germany's colonial policy and her conduct in the Transvaal question overshadowed the last months of his tenure – especially during the so-called 'Malet incident' in October 1895.[47] It did not, however, affect the search for a suitable successor. After Sir Edmund Monson, the ambassador to Vienna, had declined the position and Wilhelm II's attempts to secure a military general as ambassador had been thwarted, the embassy was offered 'by default'[48] to the ambassador to St Petersburg, Frank Lascelles. Lascelles kept the post for thirteen years, two years longer than his predecessor, until 1908. Like his old friend Malet (both had served at Paris during the turbulent year of 1870)[49] Lascelles was endowed with courteous manners and a positive disposition towards Germany, though these were to become increasingly difficult to sustain in the months and years to come.

Having 'passed through the "Lyons school" of diplomacy'[50] in their junior years, Malet and Lascelles were well prepared for the position of ambassador, both inside the embassy in handling junior staff and outside the embassy in their dealings and contacts with their host country. They also had few illusions with regard to the demands on their loyalty, professionalism, and perseverance at one of the most important and most prestigious posts that the diplomatic service had to offer. The total of 6,174 'diplomatic' dispatches addressed to the foreign secretary between 1884 and 1897 alone illustrate that ambassadors Ampthill, Malet, and Lascelles were playing in a completely different league from the other British heads of missions in Germany, whose combined output of official dispatches was well under half that of Berlin – not counting the many additional

[46] 'England might give a successor to the Ambassador that she had lost, but could not expect to replace him.' Bismarck quoted in Scott to Granville, 30 August 1884, FO 64/1051 (not included in this volume); see Taffs, *Ambassador to Bismarck*, p. 394.

[47] Willem-Alexander van't Padje, 'The "Malet Incident", October 1895: A Prelude to the Kaiser's "Kruger Telegram" in the Context of the Anglo-German Imperialist Rivalry', in Geoff Eley and James Retallack (eds), *Wilhelminism and its Legacies: German Modernities, Imperialism, and the Meanings of Reform, 1890–1930* (New York and Oxford, 2003), pp. 138–153.

[48] Otte, *Foreign Office Mind*, p. 190.

[49] Bourne, 'Lascelles', pp. 18–30.

[50] Otte, *Foreign Office Mind*, p. 156; Jones, *Diplomatic Service*, p. 183.

telegrams from Berlin and the correspondence marked 'Commercial'.[51] In the last decade of the nineteenth century Berlin became even more dominant, especially after the Stuttgart mission was closed in 1890, and George Strachey retired in spring 1897. In this year only one fifth of the diplomatic dispatches did not come from Berlin – just thirty-three from Darmstadt, fifty-seven from Munich (including the last reports from Stuttgart), and eleven from Dresden. It is consistent with this that, from 1898 onwards, the correspondence from the German rump missions is collected under one single class mark (FO 30).[52]

The dispatches selected for this edition show clearly that quantity and quality are two quite different things, but it should also be borne in mind that these statistics reflect completely different material circumstances, local environments, diplomatic tasks, and social obligations, and at times, also, different degrees of professionalism.[53] Diplomats at Darmstadt, Dresden, Munich, and Stuttgart, who tended to conduct their business from their private quarters, usually situated in exclusive residential areas,[54] more or less ran a one-man show. As the legation records and the *Foreign Office List* show, they were only occasionally assisted or deputized by a junior secretary. In stark contrast the Berlin ambassador was in charge of a minimum of eight further diplomatic officials (1897), and they worked at the Palais Strousberg at No. 70 Wilhelmstrasse, only a short walk from the epicentre of German politics, the imperial chancellery at No. 77 Wilhelmstrasse.[55]

The selection of dispatches from Berlin in this volume highlights the significance of the British embassy in the German capital and its proximity to power, both governmental and royal. Yet confronted

---

[51] In most cases reports on economic issues were largely based on German statistics and other official publications. These dispatches, marked 'Commercial', are not included in this selection.

[52] The number of dispatches is based on the listings of TNA's online catalogue and the FO 9, 30, 64 (including 'Africa'), 68, and 84 series, consulted for this volume.

[53] See, in general, Mösslang, 'Gestaltungsraum'.

[54] See, for example, the following entries in municipal directories: George Strachey, Bürgerwiese 16, Dresden (*Adreßbuch, Wohnungs- und Geschäfts-Handbuch der königlichen Residenz- und Hauptstadt Dresden* (Dresden, 1895), part 1, p. 751), George Buchanan, Wilhelmstrasse 17, Darmstadt (*Adressbuch der Haupt- und Residenzstadt Darmstadt* (Darmstadt, 1895), p. 19), and Victor Drummond, Barrerstrasse 15 (*Adreßbuch für München, 1893* (Munich, 1893), p. 77).

[55] In 1897 the diplomatic staff in Berlin consisted of one secretary of embassy, one military and one commercial attaché, three second secretaries, one third secretary, and one attaché. See *The Foreign Office List* (1898), pp. 8–11; the *Adressbuch für Berlin und seine Vororte* (Berlin, 1897), p. 12 lists nine diplomatic officials for the year 1897. For embassy life in Berlin, see Vincent Corbett, *Reminiscences: Autobiographical and Diplomatic* (London, 1927), pp. 58–90.

with the complex tasks of following, and deciphering, politics and political life, and the delicate business of weighing up the words and sentiments of imperial royalty and officials, the ambassador to Berlin was also to some extent more restricted than his colleagues at the smaller courts. This applies to his perceptions, since his choice of what to report on was often influenced by the obligations of the fast-paced world of Berlin diplomacy, and also affected by the exclusivity of the ambassadorial position; but it also applies to what he found the time for and thought worth sending to London. Thus reports from Berlin and those from the less constrained posts at Darmstadt, Dresden, Munich, and Stuttgart complement each other. Their simultaneous perspectives on Germany were not only defined by geography and local environment, but by the points of view of the individual diplomats.

II

It is one of the specific characteristics of diplomatic correspondence that the reports, in their continuous sequence, form a chronicle of the host states and their foreign relations. Depending on whether dispatches were written just before, during, or in the aftermath of an event, they often differ greatly in terms of depth, insights, and interpretation. Topics appear and disappear, and very much as in diaries, the often unrelated proximity of observations filed side by side makes it possible to experience and reimagine historical processes in their temporal context, indeed, almost as if in 'real time'. This is especially true when new topics (and historical actors) emerge and begin to dominate the reportage, but also when they then disappear from the diplomats' agenda.

In the decade after 1871, which is covered by the first volume of *British Envoys to the Kaiserreich*, diplomats reflected and commented widely on how the new nation-state was coming to terms with German unity and the empire's role in the European concert of powers. Prominent topics of these early *Kaiserreich* years, such as the allocation of power relations between the empire and its constituent states; national integration and anti-Prussian resentments; the relationship of church and state, and the consequences of the anti-Catholic *Kulturkampf*; the repressive measures against the Social Democrats; and, in the realm of foreign affairs, Germany's policy towards France, Germany's alliances and changing relationships with Austria and Russia, and Germany's role in the so-called Eastern Question still feature throughout the years to 1897 and continued to have repercussions on British perceptions of and relations with

Germany. What is distinctly new from 1884 onwards, however, is that in the wake of Germany's unexpected colonizing activities British envoys to Germany widened their horizons of observation towards non-European parts of the world, especially Africa, and, in their interpretations of the imperialist drive, disbanded their long-held assumption that Bismarck simply wished to consolidate German power and maintain the status quo.[56] With Germany's colonial enterprise in full swing, it became apparent that German and British interests could be diametrically opposed. In this respect Bismarck left no room for speculation when he told Edward Malet 'that at every point at which Germany had endeavoured to found a Colony England had closed in, making new acquisitions so as to restrict Germany's power of expansion'.[57]

With the historian's benefit of hindsight, aspirations for a German colonial empire can be detected in diplomatic reports from Germany well before 1884.[58] However, as two of Ampthill's dispatches from Berlin in April 1884 indicate, the real shift in British perceptions came about rather more abruptly. The first dispatch in question reported on the foundation of the Society for German Colonization, on 28 March. This was deemed to be no more significant than a series of similar initiatives that had emerged in recent years and caused neither Ampthill nor London any disquiet: 'There is no reason to suppose that the German Government will be more disposed to lend its countenance to the efforts of this Society than it has been in the case of similar movements in the past.'[59] The second dispatch dealt with the appointment of Gustav Nachtigal as imperial commissioner for West Africa, which took place only one day after the Society for German Colonization was founded, on 29 March. Based on a newspaper article it was one of the many unspectacular reports that elicited no further comment or interpretation from Berlin. At the Foreign Office in London, however, the senior clerk of the Consular and African Department, Henry P. Anderson, appears to have been more alert to the steps Germany was about to take when he noted on the dispatch's docket: 'This is a movement that must be watched'. '[T]his and any subsequent dispatch on the same subject', he instructed his junior clerk,

[56] See in general Kennedy, *Antagonism*, pp. 167–183; Axel T.G. Riehl, *Der 'Tanz um den Äquator': Bismarcks antienglische Kolonialpolitik und die Erwartung des Thronwechsels in Deutschland 1883 bis 1885* (Berlin, 1993); Michael Fröhlich, *Von Konfrontation zur Koexistenz: Die deutsch-englischen Kolonialbeziehungen in Afrika zwischen 1884 und 1914* (Bochum, 1990).

[57] Malet to Granville, 24 January 1885, FO 64/1146.

[58] See *British Envoys to the Kaiserreich*, Vol. I, pp. 86; 105; 128–129; 160; 184–185; 307; 357.

[59] Ampthill to Granville, 8 April 1884, FO 64/1102.

were to be 'number[ed] [...] in the African Section'.[60] In fact, from April 1884 onwards, the importance of colonial affairs within Anglo-German relations was reflected in the filing system. Henceforth dispatches marked 'Africa' were separated from other political dispatches from Berlin and, while still being part of the Berlin series, were subsequently collected in special volumes.

While Germany's entry into the 'Scramble for Africa' found expression at this bureaucratic level, the British ambassador to Berlin and his government at home were taken by surprise by the fact that Bismarck had 'secretly embarked upon an imperialist course'.[61] Until the spring of 1885 this new course saw the successive establishment of the German protectorates and colonies of German South West Africa, Togoland, German Cameroon, German New Guinea, and German East Africa. Ampthill's dispatches reveal little about the political motives underlying these actions, however, in private correspondence, he left no doubt that Bismarck, '[c]ompelled by the Colonial mania, [...] has discovered an unexplored mine of popularity in starting a Colonial policy, which Public Opinion persuades itself to be anti-English'.[62] One of the last official dispatches he sent before his untimely death, on 25 August 1884, reveals Ampthill's irritation and his concern about developments, especially as they directly affected Anglo-German relations: 'The feeling in Germany respecting these Colonial Questions is so strong, as Your Lordship is aware, that the publication of the above-named correspondence can only tend to confirm the General suspicion that England opposes the Colonial Aspirations of the people of Germany, and the impression of disappointment it must produce will be painful and lasting throughout Germany.'[63] Indeed, as diplomatic reportage of the various disputes that occurred over the next thirty years confirms, there were few issues between Germany and Britain as emotionally charged as the colonial question.

It has been said 'that in a very literal sense the colonial question killed' Lord Ampthill, who due to the developments in spring and summer of 1884 had cancelled the planned period of rest and recuperation in Marienbad he so desperately needed.[64] Speculations of this kind rightly hint at the diplomats' increasing responsibilities in times of crisis, both as observers and interlocutors, and (in the

---

[60] Docket, Ampthill to Granville, 23 April 1884, FO 64/1102.

[61] Kennedy, *Antagonism*, p. 179.

[62] Ampthill to Granville (private), 2 August 1885, quoted in Knaplund (ed.), *Letters from the Berlin Embassy*, p. 339.

[63] Ampthill to Granville, 18 August 1884, FO 64/1103.

[64] Urbach, *Russell*, p. 201.

particular case of the ambassador to Berlin) as negotiators. It is no coincidence, then, that during the years 1884 and 1885, but also in 1895 and 1896, when the Transvaal question and the Kruger telegram dominated Anglo-German diplomacy, diplomats wrote more frequently. At the same time they also wrote more briefly and – in an attempt not to omit anything of potential importance – in more detail. Intense discussions, diplomatic negotiations, and the rapid sequence of events also left less time for general observations and comments. This was especially true of Edward Malet who started his new post at Berlin as delegate to the Berlin West Africa Conference, in November 1884.[65] One of Malet's few comprehensive and opinionated dispatches written during this conference was based on a confidential conversation with Prince Bismarck, in January 1885. Its subsequent publication in a British *Blue Book*, in February, led to indignation in the suspicious German press, and reminded diplomats of the delicate role they had to play under increasing public scrutiny, both in their host states and at home.[66]

In the course of 1885, after Berlin had managed to push through its colonial programme in spite of London's objections, Europe once again became the focal point of Bismarck's foreign policy interests, and consequently that of his British observers.[67] Despite the serious nature of the Bulgarian crisis, the increasingly strained relations with Russia, and renewed tensions between Germany and France, the diplomats found themselves back on familiar territory. What is more, since 1887 Britain had herself become involved in Bismarck's complex system of alliances through the Mediterranean Agreements with Austria and Italy. The fact that Edward Malet clearly felt less compelled to reflect on the principles of German foreign policy than his predecessor, Ampthill, is probably attributable to his more remote relationship with Bismarck who was now often absent from Berlin. In August 1886, for instance, shortly after the coup against Alexander of Bulgaria, Malet remarked: 'As long as Prince Bismarck is away from Berlin it is impossible to form any

---

[65] For the conference, see Stig Förster, Wolfgang J. Mommsen, and Ronald Robinson (eds), *Bismarck, Europe, and Africa: The Berlin Africa Conference 1884–1885 and the Onset of Partition* (Oxford, 1988).

[66] Scott to Granville, 4 March 1885, FO 64/1149.

[67] For 'Anglo-German' foreign policy, see, in general, Kennedy, *Antagonism*, pp. 157–222; Gordon Martel, 'The Limits of Commitment: Rosebery and the Definition of the Anglo-German Understanding', *Historical Journal*, 27 (1984), pp. 387–404; David Steele, 'The Place of Germany in Salisbury's Foreign Policy, 1878–1902', in Adolf Birke et al. (eds), *An Anglo-German Dialogue: The Munich Lectures on the History of International Affairs* (Munich, 2001), pp. 57–76; Jörg Femers, *Deutsch-Britische Optionen: Untersuchungen zur internationalen Politik in der späten Bismarck-Ära* (Trier, 2006).

distinct notion of the views of the German Government upon passing events.'[68] The appointment of Bismarck's son, Herbert von Bismarck, as state secretary for foreign affairs did little to improve this situation. Malet made but sparse references to times when he had successfully 'pressed Count Bismarck to acquaint me with the views of the Chancellor'.[69] Although this did not cut Malet off from the power centre in Berlin – and his access to Bismarck was arguably still better than that of most of his colleagues in the Berlin diplomatic corps – the number of conversations that provided greater insights into Bismarck's thinking declined.

Apart from the discussions on German colonial policy already mentioned, the dispatches selected for this volume document, among other things, confidential or even secret exchanges on the Afghan border dispute in 1885, the Bulgarian Question in 1886, and the consequences of Wilhelm II's accession for Anglo-German relations in 1888.[70] In these conversations – as in those with Bismarck's successor Leo von Caprivi and the state secretaries of the Berlin foreign office, Herbert von Bismarck and Marschall von Bieberstein – the increasing complexity of Anglo-German relations becomes clear. The dispatches provide an abundance of material on the anti-British implications of German imperialism, the asymmetry of interests between the two powers, and on 'Germany's ability to cause disruptions'.[71] What becomes equally clear, however, are areas of mutual interest and understanding, and Germany's strategic importance for Britain, particularly as regards Russia and France. This applied to Russia's policy in the East as well as to France's interest in Egypt and other British spheres of interest. Compared to these threats to the British Empire, German policy not only caused the Foreign Office less immediate concern, but reassuring accounts, and also suggestions for an Anglo-German Alliance, were still being received from Germany into the 1890s. Shortly before Bismarck was dismissed in March 1890, for instance, Malet wrote: 'It is every where felt that Prince Bismarck is a guarantee of peace. He seeks no more victories. His only aim is to consolidate what he has made.'[72] The diplomats' anxiety during the chancellor crisis of 1888 and after Bismarck's dismissal in 1890 can thus be explained by the uncertainty it brought to the future of German policies.

---

[68] Malet to Iddesleigh, 21 August 1886, FO 64/1117.

[69] Malet to Salisbury, 9 January 1886, FO 64/1113.

[70] Malet to Granville, 7 May 1885, FO 64/1077; Malet to Iddesleigh, 12 November 1886, FO 64/1119; Malet to Salisbury, 25 May 1887, FO 64/1157; Malet to Salisbury, 14 July 1888, FO 64/1187.

[71] Otte, *Foreign Office Mind*, p. 223.

[72] Malet to Salisbury, 8 February 1890, FO 64/1234.

Indeed, the dispatches show that, 'British diplomats had viewed Anglo-German relations through the lens of Bismarck's dominant personality.'[73] While Bismarck still featured prominently in diplomatic reports after 1890 (his journeys, speeches, birthdays, and reconciliation with the emperor provided ample opportunity for commentary) the focus of attention shifted towards the young emperor and the beginnings of his personal regime and, in matters of foreign policy, increasingly towards the press.[74] British envoys outside Berlin in particular, excluded from the arcane world of diplomatic negotiations, seized every opportunity to report on newspaper articles covering matters of national and, especially, international importance. A dispatch which was appraised by the foreign secretary, Rosebery, as 'the best thing we have had from Munich', for example, dealt with a press comment on the Triple Alliance between Germany, Austria-Hungary, and Italy.[75] In fact, in this case and many others, summaries of articles printed in German newspapers and journals were forwarded to other British embassies and legations throughout Europe for perusal.

Certainly, British envoys to the *Kaiserreich* had witnessed the ramifications of newspaper articles on foreign relations prior to this time, during the 'War-in-Sight' crisis of 1875, for example, and in a similar fashion during another war scare in 1887, when aggressive French nationalism (Boulangism) was exploited for the domestic objective of securing the military budget.[76] As their reports indicate, such vociferous press campaigns had been characteristic of both Bismarck's foreign and his domestic policy. George Strachey's countless condemnations of the 'reptile press' demonstrate this particularly clearly and it is thus quite telling that in 1891, he also identified Leo von Caprivi's 'New Course' in the latter's handling of critical voices. As he wrote, on the 'hectoring, browbeating, manner in politics, on which, although in Germany its use gives great weight to the

---

[73] Otte, *Foreign Office Mind*, p. 182.

[74] See Otte, ' "The Winston of Germany": The British Foreign Policy Élite and the Last German Emperor', *Canadian Journal of History*, 36 (2001), pp. 471–504; Lothar Reinermann, *Der Kaiser in England: Wilhelm II. und sein Bild in der britischen Öffentlichkeit* (Paderborn, 2001); Dominik Geppert, *Pressekriege: Öffentlichkeit und Diplomatie in den deutsch-britischen Beziehungen (1896–1912)* (Munich, 2007).

[75] Drummond to Rosebery, 15 August 1893, FO 9/267.

[76] Strachey to Iddesleigh, 24 August 1886, FO 68/170; Jocelyn to Salisbury, 25 October 1886, FO 30/264; Drummond to Iddesleigh, 4 January 1887, FO 9/258; Malet to Her Majesty's Principal Secretary of State for Foreign Affairs, 15 January 1887, FO 64/1155; Scott to Salisbury, 20 April 1887, FO 64/1156; Scott to Salisbury, 9 July 1887, FO 64/1158; Strachey to Salisbury, 19 January 1889, FO 68/174. See *British Envoys to the Kaiserreich*, Vol. 1, pp. 98–108, 217–219.

authority of public men, General Caprivi has turned his back'.[77] However, this positive assessment remained an exception. One reason for this was Wilhelm II's autocratic political style which could be followed in newspaper reports on a daily basis; another – and here the press acquired a new significance – was that greater attention started to be paid to public opinion, especially with regards to Anglo-German relations. In the smaller missions, in particular, the diplomats' daily business was increasingly marked by flare-ups of Anglophobia that they observed with irritation and reported upon in detail. This applies, for instance, to the accusations against Sir Robert Morier in 1888, the so-called 'Morier incident',[78] and to the criticism directed against Morell Mackenzie, British physician to the crown prince and Emperor Friedrich III,[79] but above all to the German press campaign during the Transvaal crisis of 1895–1896, which erupted into a veritable Anglo-German press war after Wilhelm's congratulatory telegram to Paulus Kruger, president of the Transvaal Republic, on 3 January 1896. Yet in contrast to the openly chauvinist sentiments in public opinion, Frank Lascelles maintained his conciliatory attitude towards the German government. Not only was he, as he told the state secretary of the Foreign Office, Adolf Marschall von Bieberstein, on 11 January, '[p]ersonally […] surprised at the excitement caused by the Emperor's Telegram', he also had few doubts 'that this question should be amiably settled'.[80]

III

In spite of their close attention to German public opinion and the news coverage of current affairs, British diplomats at the smaller German capitals were aware that, as George Buchanan put it, 'one was naturally entirely outside politics'.[81] Ironically, Buchanan, posted to Darmstadt from 1892, made this remark in an audience with the Russian emperor, Tsar Nicholas II, on 6 October 1897 in which he discussed the benefits of 'reading the foreign papers',[82] but also

---

[77] Strachey to Salisbury, 4 December 1891, FO 68/176.

[78] Malet to Salisbury, 5 January 1889, FO 64/1211; Strachey to Salisbury, 19 January 1889, FO 68/174. See Ramm, *Sir Robert Morier*, pp. 288–304.

[79] Drummond to Salisbury, 29 October 1887, FO 9/258; Strachey to Salisbury, 2 March 1888, FO 68/173.

[80] Lascelles to Salisbury, 11 January 1896, FO 64/1386. See also Bourne, *Lascelles*, pp. 184–194.

[81] Buchanan to Salisbury, 6 October 1897, FO 30/287.

[82] Ibid.

touched upon the affairs of Greece, India, and Afghanistan. This was probably the only instance of a lower-rank British diplomat in Germany having an extended interview with a non-German sovereign ruler, between 1884 and 1897, and given the elusive nature of such encounters, the next best thing was an audience with a deposed foreign ruler. It was again at Darmstadt that the chargé d'affaires had occasion to meet Alexander of Battenberg, former *kynast* of Bulgaria.[83] On both of these occasions the family bonds of the House of Hesse had led to royal or imperial sojourns at the court of Darmstadt: Alexander of Battenberg was the second son of Prince Alexander of Hesse and by Rhine; and Nicholas II was married to Princess Alix, daughter of Alice, the late Grand Duchess of Hesse, and Queen Victoria's grandchild. Despite the potential political dividends from Hessian connections with Russia, it was these family connections with the royal house of Saxe-Coburg-Gotha that really made Darmstadt 'an important listening post'.[84]

William Nassau Jocelyn's and George Buchanan's 'court dispatches' not only drew the Queen's attention but made for a welcome change in the Foreign Office, as 'there is a grave humour about them which is refreshing after some of the other reading'.[85] Nevertheless, the particulars from the German courts did also concern serious matters. This is true, for example, of the numerous reports sent from Munich about the eccentricities of King Ludwig II of Bavaria, and especially his increasingly troubled financial situation. As for the unexpected deaths of Ludwig and Dr Gudden, on 13 June 1886, Victor Drummond's dispatch adds little to our knowledge of the mysterious drowning of the two men; but it is a remarkable document, no less, as Drummond was most likely the first diplomat, if not foreigner, to be informed of the incident. By sheer coincidence he had been staying 'in a Country Inn, on Lake Starnberg, […] only twenty minutes from the Schloss Berg'.[86] The unorthodox behaviour of Ludwig had piqued British curiosity since the 1860s, and left little doubt about his predilection for young men. However, the scandal of the King of Württemberg's relationship with Charles Woodcock, which was publicized by a newspaper article in 1888, challenged the British representative to find an appropriate mode for conveying the

[83] Jocelyn to Iddesleigh, 25 October 1886, FO 30/264.

[84] Zara Steiner, 'Buchanan, Sir George William (1854–1924), diplomatist', in *Oxford Dictionary of National Biography* (online ed.), 2008, retrieved 20 July 2018, https://doi.org/ 10.1093/ref:odnb/32150. See Jonathan Petropoulos, 'The Hessens and the British Royals', in Karina Urbach (ed.), *Royal Kinship: Anglo-German Family Networks 1815–1918* (Munich, 2008), pp. 147–159.

[85] Helyar to Rosebury, 2 January 1893, FO 30/278 (not included in this volume).

[86] Drummond to Rosebery, 14 June 1886, FO 9/256.

news back to Britain. Notwithstanding Henry Barron's contradictory and reassuring interpretation of the Woodcock affair, which circumnavigated the issue of King Karl's homosexuality, in this case, his 'despatches respecting the "unpleasant discussions" were not sent to the Queen'.[87]

From time to time dispatches which concerned British royal interests, and close personal relations, were also of a delicate nature. The succession to the throne of Saxe-Coburg-Gotha by the Duke of Edinburgh was just such a case, Queen Victoria's disputed marriage project between her granddaughter, the Prussian princess, Viktoria, and Prince Alexander of Battenberg another, along with the fate and subsequent standing of the Queen's daughter 'Vicky' (Empress Friedrich) following the death of her husband, Friedrich III, who was German Emperor for just ninety-nine days.[88] Together with assessments of Queen Victoria's grandson, Wilhelm II, these reports demonstrate that the dynastic dimensions of Anglo-German relations were highly symbolically charged. Among other things, for example, envoys reported on celebrations to mark the Queen's Golden and Diamond Jubilees (in 1887 and 1897), the reactions to the Victoria's visit to Berlin in 1888, and Her Majesty's appointment as honorary colonel in 1889, but also on Wilhelm II's feelings towards England after his accession to the throne, and his attendance of the Cowes Week regattas.[89]

While endeavouring to have confidence in 'The Emperor's friendly disposition towards England',[90] British diplomats were nevertheless apprehensive about political stability, especially after Bismarck's dismissal in 1890, and this continued against the background of Russo-French rapprochement from 1891 onwards. In this respect they conveyed mixed news about Germany's 'New Course'. They did not expect to be 'exposed to a policy of surprises'[91] under Leo von Caprivi's chancellorship, but they were increasingly irritated by Wilhelm's II erratic behaviour and, consequently,

---

[87] Barron to Salisbury, 14 November 1888, FO 82/173.

[88] Malet to Salisbury, 28 April 1888, FO 64/1186; see Eleanor L. Turk, 'The Battenberg Affair: Chancellor Crisis or "Media Event?" ', *German Studies Review*, 5 (1982), pp. 233–255.

[89] Malet to Salisbury, 12 June 1887, FO 64/1157; Drummond to Salisbury, 22 June 1887, FO 9/259; Strachey to Salisbury, 26 June 1887, FO 68/172; Malet to Salisbury, 14 July 1888, FO 64/1187; Strachey to Salisbury, 10 August 1895, FO 68/180; Lascelles to Salisbury, 1 July 1897, FO 64/1411. See John C. G. Röhl, 'The Kaiser and England', in Birke et al. (eds), An Anglo-German Dialogue, pp. 97–113. Roderick R. McLean, 'Kaiser Wilhelm II and the British Royal Family: Anglo-German Dynastic Relations in Political Context, 1890–1914', *History*, 86 (2001), pp. 478–502; Otte, ' "The Winston of Germany" '; Reinermann, *Der Kaiser in England*.

[90] Malet to Salisbury, 14 July 1888, FO 64/1187.

[91] Malet to Kimberley, 14 July 1894, FO 64/1325.

uncertain about future developments. In the second year of Wilhelm's reign, for example, Edward Malet observed that 'even in Germany it is thought that ambition in every direction is latent in his character and that if it does not find vent in a peaceful direction it would do so in another and more dangerous one'.[92] Malet's colleagues from the other missions likewise filed reports on the 'extraordinary activity of mind of His Imperial Majesty'[93], and were puzzled that 'one of the family virtues of the Hohenzollerns – tact – has not been inherited by the Emperor William'.[94] Opportunities for outspoken assessments of his personality included the emperor's birthday, the unveiling of monuments, his attendance at army manoeuvres, and his various speeches. In fact almost every 'public utterance of the young Emperor'[95] had repercussions throughout Germany.

Perspectives from Baden, Bavaria, Hesse, Württemberg, and Saxony are of especial value with regards to the emperor, and particularly at times when he visited their respective capitals. As had been the case with Wilhelm II's grandfather, Wilhelm I, visits to different parts of the empire served as a barometer for the emperor's popularity, but also held up a mirror to the state of Germany unity.[96] Diplomats suggested that imperial visits helped to 'strengthen the bond of union'[97], as they revealed 'a considerable mastery by the young Emperor of the arts of popularity, as well as the progressive extinction of regional sentiment under the growth of the German idea'.[98] Comparable assessments concerning the matter of unity can be found on other occasions such as the annual Sedan Day celebrations, and are perhaps at their most explicit in George Strachey's assessment of this event in 1895: 'The attitude of the Saxon public has again demonstrated what, perhaps, required no further proof – namely, than in none of the 26 States of the Empire is the new pan-Germanic spirit stronger than it is here. Particularism is dead: the people may almost be described as Germans first, Saxons afterwards.'[99]

Although such emphatic assessments of Germany unity are markedly clearer in the reports filed after 1884, the dispatches still reveal strong feelings of allegiance to the individual states of the *Kaiserreich* and their ruling houses. The federal dimensions of the empire

[92] Malet to Salisbury, 8 February 1890, FO 64/1234.
[93] Drummond to Kimberley, 21 February 1895, FO 9/270.
[94] Strachey to Salisbury, 27 October 1891, FO 68/176.
[95] Scott to Salisbury, 18 August 1888, FO 64/1188.
[96] See *British Envoys to the Kaiserreich*, Vol. 1, pp. 241, 311–313, 384, 495, 528.
[97] Drummond to Salisbury, 12 September 1891, FO 9/264.
[98] Strachey to Salisbury, 13 September 1889, FO 68/174.
[99] Strachey to Salisbury, 3 September 1895, FO 68/180.

were particularly apparent in matters where the rights of individual states seemed to be curtailed, such as those involving taxation, school policy, or imperial military reforms,[100] or, as in the case of the so-called subversion bill, when the states made 'complaints [...] against the growing predominance of Prussia'.[101] The negotiations in the *Bundesrat* (Federal Council, at which all the states were represented) often provided an opportunity to discuss things from a regional perspective. So, too, did the numerous dispatches dealing with the run-up to *Reichstag* elections and with their outcomes, especially in the years 1887 and 1893 when the army bill was rejected and, accordingly, snap elections were called. Local newspapers (of which there were many, often with strong political ties) were particularly useful to the diplomats and enabled them to follow developments within the fragmented German party political system as well as within the parties themselves, as these varied considerably from state to state.[102]

Yet the relationship of the federal states to the German Empire – and their integration into it – was only one aspect of political life in Germany as seen through diplomatic eyes. What happened in the imperial chancery and the *Reichstag*, for example, for all its repercussions on the individual states of Germany, was a matter of prime importance for the embassy in Berlin. Here, junior diplomats were tasked to provide a 'weekly summary of Parliamentary Proceedings',[103] and countless enclosures of laws, rescripts, and other official papers ensured that the Foreign Office could keep up with the finer points of detail concerning German internal affairs. The ambassador himself largely dealt with the 'grand topics'. Dispatches on the septennial army bill in 1887 and 1893, the political fates of Bismarck and Caprivi in 1890 and 1891, or the accession of the Emperors Friedrich II and Wilhelm II in 1888, in particular, all affected British interests.

Observations on internal politics made by diplomats based in the smaller capitals were naturally more limited in scope. If we compare the dispatches of the years 1884 to 1897 to the correspondence of earlier decades, it is noticeable that, apart from periods of political crisis (for example the year 1886 in Bavaria), the number of such reports

---

[100] Strachey to Salisbury, 12 December 1890, FO 68/175; Drummond to Rosebery, 9 December 1893, FO 82/178; Drummond to Rosebery, 15 May 1893; FO 9/267; Drummond to Rosebery, 23 December 1893, FO 82/178; Drummond to Salisbury, 13 October 1897, FO 9/272.

[101] Boothby to Salisbury, 10 November 1895, FO 9/270.

[102] Strachey to Salisbury, 18 February 1887, FO 68/171; Drummond to Rosebery, 15 May 1893, FO 9/267; Buchanan to Rosebery, 7 June 1893, FO 30/278.

[103] Scott to Salisbury, 30 January 1886, FO 64/1113.

decreases, as does their level of detail. At the same time the correspondence still reveals that each state had its own specific political particularities, such as the role of Catholicism in Bavaria, or, in Saxony, the condition of the Social Democrats and the constraints on them. These concerns can often be followed in the diplomatic reports over decades. In a dispatch selected for this volume, Victor Drummond in Munich, for example, left little doubt of his attitude towards 'bigoted'[104] Catholics and the 'prejudices of the Ultramontanes, who are always inclined to determine State matters by permeating them with an overflow of religious dogma'.[105] Strachey in Saxony, on the other hand, discussed 'the phantom of Social Democracy' with relative impartiality. His claim that he did not 'easily pass from facts to speculation'[106] holds true of his reports on the continued measures instigated by, and the effects of, the imperial Anti-Socialist Laws of 1878, which were periodically extended until 1890. Back in London, the Home Office, to which many of his dispatches concerning elections, strikes, and 1 May demonstrations were forwarded, was left in little doubt that while 'Social Democracy had been silenced its vitality was unimpaired'.[107] The British interest in policies to combat socialism reminds the reader, at least to some extent, of the attention which was paid to the *Kulturkampf* in the 1870s, when anti-Catholic measures were interpreted in the light of the Irish Home Rule movement.[108] With the end of the *Kulturkampf* the former link between the two strains of German 'radicalism' (Ultramontanism on the one hand, and socialism on the other) had all but disappeared – only in Bavaria was socialist electoral success still interpreted as an anti-Catholic referendum.[109]

---

[104] Drummond to Rosebery, 26 July 1886, FO 9/256.

[105] Drummond to Salisbury, 23 April 1890, FO 9/263.

[106] Strachey to Salisbury, 18 October 1889, FO 68/174.

[107] Strachey to Granville, 7 May 1884, FO 68/168; see similar assessments from Darmstadt and Munich; Jocelyn to Granville, 31 October 1884, FO 30/258; MacDonell to Granville, 19 November 1884, FO 9/252; with various references to Strachey's reports, see James Retallack, *Red Saxony: Election Battles and the Spectre of Democracy in Germany, 1860–1918* (Oxford, 2017), pp. 131–184, 230–317.

[108] In one instance, Irish Home Rule still affected how German affairs were perceived, when, on 9 December 1893, George Strachey described German centralization and the decline of the state legislatures as 'the result of that gradual extinction of Home Rule which is the feature of the German political evolution'. Strachey to Rosebery, 9 December 1893, FO 68/178 (not included in this volume); see Strachey to Rosebery, 4 January 1894, FO 68/179.

[109] MacDonell to Granville, 19 November 1884, FO 9/252. See *British Envoys to the Kaiserreich*, Vol. 1, p. 13.

Beyond such focal points, what most diplomats had in common was their belief in supposedly more timeless, universal English principles and deep-rooted convictions, to which reference was often made in discussions of German political and constitutional life and legal practice. This is especially obvious in George Strachey's frequent tirades on the inadequacies of German political culture. In 1891, in a particularly harsh evaluation, he stated 'that it is idle to measure the behaviour of the disputants in this controversy by standards taken from English or French history. The Germans are in the political nursery, and they are now less near to the possession of a recognized constitutional morality, and to the conquest of the virtues of tolerance, magnanimity, and self-assertion than they were 40 years ago.'[110] Indeed, most diplomats alluded to the anachronistic or at least – to an English observer – peculiar features of the German political landscape. This was the case, for example, when the creation of an imperial ministry, responsible to the *Reichstag*, was suggested in 1884, or in view of the interminable discussions on constitutional reform in Württemberg. Here, Henry Barron, in fact, took a pragmatic stance when writing that the 'Constitution of Wurttemberg, now unique in Europe, and resting on a combination of the feudal and Democratic principles, has hitherto worked fairly well'.[111] Yet while the diplomats still measured German political affairs against British yardsticks, in comparison to the constitutional and moral impetus which had moved so many of the reports from the time of the German Confederation and during the early *Kaiserreich* years, their increasing apathy towards more liberal and progressive forces in these later years, not least in the middling German states, is remarkable.[112]

*

In general the reports on Germany met the Foreign Office's expectations. British envoys all had varying personal experiences of Germany and, particularly in times of Anglo-German tension, were confronted with a plethora of newspaper articles of which to make sense. Yet rather than write lengthy, rambling reports, the representatives of Britain increasingly prioritized their observations of their host country, and confined themselves to shorter assessments. Their occasional, detailed reports on Baden and Hesse, Bavaria, Saxony, and Württemberg, and also on the Kingdom of Prussia or

---

[110] Strachey to Salisbury, 21 February 1891, FO 68/176.
[111] Barron to Salisbury, 23 February 1888, FO 82/173.
[112] See Retallack, *Germany's Second Reich*, pp. 49–50. This also corresponds with the lack of commentary on the liberal predilections of the crown prince and future emperor, Friedrich III, which, at least in their official dispatches, envoys only occasionally addressed.

one of its twelve provinces, were of real interest to the Foreign Office only when they concerned the empire and its political stability as a whole. Nevertheless, as part of a larger repository of perceptions, the diplomatic reports produced between 1884 and 1897, each in their own specific context and taken together over a longer period of time, provide a comprehensive British account of Germany and Anglo-German diplomatic practice and relations, just as they do in earlier years. As can be seen in the previous volumes of this editorial project, British envoys to Germany left a treasure trove of observations to future readers, which is singular in the history of British diplomatic relations. Arguably, nineteenth-century Foreign Office officials and the respective foreign secretaries were better informed about Germany than any other country. To what extent this affected the collective mind-set of the foreign policy establishment, the 'Foreign Office Mind', is open for discussion.[113]

What is clear is that British envoys to Germany, despite the constraints of their posts and their limited agency in the ever more complex ' "engine room" of international relations',[114] often found their own tone and manner of expression, and thus left distinct traces in Anglo-German history. Between 1884 and 1897 one diplomat in particular, George Strachey at Dresden, stands out for this. Strachey's highly opinionated reports, which were not always to the taste of his superiors in the Foreign Office, now make for extremely useful, and, at times, amusing reading. After his death, in February 1912, an obituary in the *Pall Mall Gazette* described Strachey as 'one of those erratic geniuses who should have made a brilliant career in the Diplomatic Service' had it not been for 'his whimsical sense of the limitations of other people' and 'his trenchant wit [used] in the wrong direction'.[115] From a historian's point of view Strachey's stagnant career at Dresden is a stroke of luck as it resulted in his continuous and direct communication from Germany with various foreign secretaries for over twenty-four years. Comparison of his reports with simultaneous reportage emanating from the other missions shows that Strachey not only followed German politics far beyond his host state, but he also showed growing expertise in topics beyond the more traditional subjects covered by his colleagues, for instance

[113] See, in general, Otte, *Foreign Office Mind*.
[114] Raymond Cohen, 'Putting Diplomatic Studies on the Map', *Diplomatic Studies Programme Newsletter*, May 1988, p. 1.
[115] *Pall Mall Gazette*, 28 February 1912. The obituary also quotes Lord Ampthill with the words: 'Strachey would wreck a dynasty to make an epigram.'

on German monetary policy or agricultural tariffs.[116] Yet, despite his widened authorial scope, the dispatches from Dresden almost always reflected his 'special Saxon horizon'.[117]

Certainly Strachey, just like the other diplomats, does not always measure up to the historian's expectations when it comes to his analysis of German society. It has been noted that they 'failed to untangle the many ties that linked Germany's liberal and nationalist movements',[118] and similar shortcomings can also be identified regarding the rise of political anti-Semitism or the Polish question in East Prussia.[119] Yet while diplomats struggled to bring together their various observations, let alone foretell the implications of an unfurling nationalism in wider society, the juxtaposition of many and various issues in the correspondence from Germany (in its entirety, as in the selection in this book) often provides the context for interpretation of these matters. With regard to the question of German nation building and the unity of the German Empire, for example, the dispatches vividly illustrate that the provincialism of the German federal states and German nationalism were two sides of the same coin.[120] Up to 1897, at least, ambiguous accounts from the various envoys do not confirm the view that 'Germany is what it is, in virtue of having become Prussianized', a judgment made by the leading Foreign Office expert on Germany, Eyre Crowe, in January 1907.[121] Rather, pre-1900 British envoys would have approved of a later statement made by Eyre Crowe in 1914 to a Royal Commission, enquiring once again into the need 'to maintain such missions as those at Darmstadt and Dresden'. On 3 July, only a few weeks before the out-

---

[116] Strachey to Salisbury, 28 October 1887, FO 68/172; Strachey to Salisbury, 27 April 1890, FO 68/175; Strachey to Salisbury, 5 June 1891, FO 68/176; Strachey to Rosebery, 17 December 1892, FO 68/177, Strachey to Rosebery, 25 February 1893, FO 68/178.

[117] Strachey to Kimberley, 10 March 1894, FO 68/179.

[118] Retallack, *Germany's Second Reich*, p. 50.

[119] Malet to Salisbury, 5 September 1885, FO 64/1079; Scott to Salisbury, 30 January 1886, FO 64/1113; Jocelyn to Salisbury, 8 November 1890, FO 30/272; Strachey to Rosebery, 10 December 1892, FO 68/177; Gosselin to Salisbury, 19 June 1896, FO 64/1377.

[120] See, in general, Dieter Langewiesche, *Nation, Nationalismus, Nationalstaat in Deutschland und Europa* (Munich, 2000), pp. 55–81; Siegfried Weichlein, *Nation und Region: Integrationsprozesse im Bismarckreich* (Düsseldorf, 2002).

[121] Note, 21 January 1907, based upon a minute by Mr Crowe which was attached to Cartwright's dispatch to Grey, 12 January, FO 371/257, printed in *British Documents on the Origins of War*, Vol. 6 (1930), p. 11. For Crowe's, now renowned, view of Germany, see also his 'Memorandum on the Present State of British Relations with France and Germany', published three weeks earlier, on 1 January 1907, in ibid., Vol. 3, pp. 402–406.

break of the First World War, Crowe responded in favour of the multiple British envoys to the *Kaiserreich*: 'They are very useful. I should be sorry to part with them. They give very useful information from a point of view that we do not get elsewhere. Germany is a very peculiar country, and Berlin is not the centre of Germany in the same sense that Paris is the centre of France.'[122]

[122] Evidence Crowe (3 July 1914), Royal Commission on the Civil Service. Appendix to Fifth Report of the Commissioners. Minutes of Evidence, 29th April 1914–16th July 1914 [Cd. 7749] (1914)], q. 43463.

EDITORIAL PRINCIPLES AND
TECHNICAL DETAILS

Volume II of *British Envoys to the Kaiserreich* comprises a selection of official reports on Germany and Anglo-German relations sent to the Foreign Office from the diplomatic missions in Berlin, Darmstadt, Dresden, Stuttgart, and Munich between 1884 and 1897. All originals are held in the National Archives, Kew.[1] As in the preceding volume, the selection is based on the quality, originality of perspective, and informative value of the dispatches as well as on a balance between the individual missions. While not aiming to present a representative selection of letters from each mission, the edition is intended to cover the major developments of the period 1884 to 1897 and present as multifaceted a picture of British perceptions of Germany as possible.

The dispatches are ordered chronologically for each mission. This also applies to dispatches marked 'Africa', and filed in separate volumes of the FO 64 series (Berlin), and dispatches marked 'Treaty' which can be found either in separate sections of the 'diplomatic' volumes, or in separate volumes of the individual missions. After the amalgamation of the missions in Munich and Stuttgart, in May 1890, dispatches on Württemberg were mostly sent from Munich and are filed both in the FO 82 (Württemberg) and FO 9 (Bavaria) series. In this volume they are all printed in the Stuttgart section.

Each dispatch is provided with a standardized heading giving archive class mark (e.g. FO 68/179 = Foreign Office, general correspondence Saxony, volume 179), author, addressee, number of dispatch, place, and date of origin, and, in squared brackets, further information which has been taken from the dockets (found on the reverse side of the letters). This usually comprises the date the dispatch was received at the Foreign Office, the name of the messenger, the distribution list (government departments, individuals, other legations), recipients' initials, initials of Foreign Office clerks, the permanent under-secretary, and, lastly, the initial of the incumbent

---

[1] For a comprehensive introduction to the Foreign Office record series see Michael Roper, *The Records of the Foreign Office, 1782–1968* (Kew, 2002).

secretary of state for foreign affairs. As far as possible, in-house acronyms have also been retained including 'Qy', meaning 'Query', i.e. refer to relevant department, minister, or other authority; 'X', which, in the Western Department of the Foreign Office, had multiple meanings including (specifically for the dockets) 'put by'; 'UFS' which stood for 'under flying seal', i.e. senior diplomats were authorized to open dispatches sent via their legation before forwarding them on to their final destination.

Each dispatch is preceded by a brief summary in italic, composed on the basis of the original dockets. The transcribed reports are printed in their entirety in order to maintain the authenticity of the sources, although the standardized salutation and concluding formula are omitted. Enclosures to the original dispatches, which can be voluminous, are not reproduced, but listed in footnotes.

With the exception of 'ß' (which has been transcribed as 'ss'), the orthography (including capitalization and abbreviations), punctuation (including dashes, hyphens, apostrophes, mixed use of single and double quotation marks, and the usage of 'it's' as a possessive pronoun instead of 'its'), emphases (underlining), and superscript of the original are retained. Notes made in the margins of dispatches by recipients are transcribed in square brackets. Errors or deviations in the original which might be mistaken for mistranscriptions are marked '[sic]'. Placeholders, line breaks or pagination are not considered.

Annotations to the dispatches, in the form of brief footnotes, aim to provide the information required for an understanding of the document which does not become apparent from the document itself. German, French, and Latin expressions and terms are all translated. Treaties, legislation, and publications mentioned in the reports are specified in the footnotes, and explained where necessary. In many cases, reference is made to other annotations and documents in this volume. All individuals mentioned are identified, as far as possible, and listed with brief biographies in the annotated index of names.[2]

A subject index, including place names, completes the volume. A combined subject and biographical index of the series (also including the volumes of *British Envoys to Germany, 1816–1866*) is available online at https://www.ghil.ac.uk/envoys.html.

---

[2] Please note that the Queen, and the incumbent prime ministers and foreign secretaries are not indexed each time they appear on the dockets.

GERMAN EMPIRE

(BERLIN)

BERLIN

FO 64/1050: Lord Ampthill to Earl Granville, No 91, Berlin, 7 April 1884

[Received 10 April by post. For: The Queen / Gladstone / X, Ch.W.D. [Charles Wentworth Dilke]; Prince of Wales; G[ranville]]

State governments oppose suggestion to create an imperial ministry responsible to the Reichstag

I have the honour to enclose to Your Lordship herewith in original and translation a Report given in yesterday's official Gazette of the proceedings in a plenary meeting of the Federal Council which took place on the 5th Instant, at which The Imperial Chancellor[1] was present in person.[2]

As reported in my Despatch N° 53 of the 6th ultimo the newly formed Parliamentary free minded fraction[3] advocate in their programme the formation of a responsible Ministry for the Empire.

This seems to have excited the apprehension of some of the Federal Governments, and Saxony and Wurtemberg instructed their Representatives[4] to make a declaration on the subject to the Federal Council on the 24th ultimo and invite an interchange of views from the Prussian and other Governments.

At the meeting of last Saturday the Prussian Representatives[5] handed in a declaration on the part of their Government, which is given "in extenso" in the enclosed Report.

The Prussian Government agrees with the Saxon Government in considering it absolutely necessary that the Federal States should

---

[1] Otto von Bismarck.

[2] Enclosures: article (untitled) in *Deutscher Reichsanzeiger und Königlich Preußischer Staatsanzeiger*, 6 April 1884 and translation.

[3] The liberal *Deutsche Freisinnige Partei* (German Free-Minded Party) was founded on 5 March 1884 as a merger of the *Reichstag* factions of the *Deutsche Fortschrittspartei* (Party of Progess, founded in 1861) and the *Liberale Vereinigung* (Liberal Union or 'Secessionists'), a group that had broken away from the National Liberal Party in 1880. Their programme was disclosed on the same day.

[4] Oswald von Nostitz-Wallwitz and Fidel Baur von Breitenfeld.

[5] The sitting of the Federal Council of 5 April was attended by ten Prussian representatives.

place on record, beyond the possibility of a doubt, their firm intention to maintain in their entirety the terms of the Federal engagements on which the union of the German States rests, considering that any step which would shake the confidence of the States in the stability of those engagements would be fraught with danger.

The Prussian Government is firmly convinced not only that a system of Imperial Government by responsible Ministers could not be introduced without sacrificing some of the essential rights of Government secured by Treaty to the Separate States[6] but also that Parliamentary Government, subordinating Ministers to the decisions of changeable majorities in the Reichstag would inevitably lead to the dissolution of the Union and the Downfall of the Empire.

Under the circumstances it is of opinion that the scheme should be strenuously opposed whenever and wherever advanced.

The Representatives of Bavaria[7] and all the other States having expressed agreement with these views the Council unanimously resolved to adhere to the terms of the Prussian Declaration.

FO 64/1102: Lord Ampthill to Earl Granville, No 92, Berlin, 8 April 1884

[Received 14 April by Messenger Cavendish. For: The Queen / X, Ch.W.D. [Charles Wentworth Dilke] / African Department; Qy: Colonial Office, 15 April 1884; T.V.L. [Thomas Villiers Lister]]

Society for German Colonization founded in Berlin

With reference to my despatch No. 59 February 14th 1883, and to Sir John Walsham's No. 254 of August 31. 1883, I have the honour to report to Your Lordship that a new colonization Society[8] has just been started at Berlin with the avowed object of Founding German Agricultural and Trading Colonies.

The Chief promoters of this Society which has apparently no connection with the Frankfurt Society or the Bremen Firm,[9] whose efforts in the same direction were reported on in the despatches above referred to, appear to be Count Behr Bandelin the President, Major von Mechsow [*sic*] the African traveller, Doctor

---

[6] This declaration alluded to the North German Confederation Treaty of 18 August 1866 and the 'November Treaties' of 1870.

[7] On 5 April Bavaria was represented by Emil von Xylander and Ferdinand von Raesfeldt.

[8] *Gesellschaft für deutsche Kolonisation*, founded on 28 March 1884.

[9] Ampthill is referring to the *Deutscher Kolonialverein* and the trading firm owned by Adolf Lüderitz.

Peters, and the African Missionary Doctor Merenski who spoke at the Inaugural meeting of the Society on the 4th instant.

Africa was indicated as the most suitable and available field for German Colonization, and the Aims to be embodied in the Statutes were unanimously decided on as follows: –

1. To collect funds for the object of the Society.
2. To discover and acquire suitable districts for colonization.
3. To direct the stream of German emigration to these districts.

It was stated that the number of German Emigrants to the United States of America in 1883 was 194,490. Of this number 25,190 belonged to the commercial and industrial classes.

There is no reason to suppose that the German Government will be more disposed to lend its countenance to the efforts of this Society than it has been in the case of similar movements in the past.

FO 64/1102: Lord Ampthill to Earl Granville, No 102, Berlin, 23 April 1884

[Received 28 April by Messenger Taylor. African Department; Print; Copy to: Colonial Office / Admiralty, 8 May][10]

Nachtigal's mission to improve German trading interests on west coast of Africa

With reference to my Despatch N° 93 of the 9th instant I have the honour to inform Your Lordship that the semi-official Nord Deutsche Zeitung of the 21st instant,[11] gives some further information respecting the object of Dr Nachtigal's Mission to the West Coast of Africa.[12]

The Nord Deutsche states that the happy increase in the commercial relations of Germany with the West Coast of Africa, and the evident need felt that the interests of German Commerce should not be left to the protection of trading-consuls[,] have induced the Foreign

---

[10] Notes on docket: 28 April 1884: 'This is a movement that must be watched and I think no time should be lost in deciding what we tell to our Consulates [.] Copy (Conf^d) to Admiralty asking that Admiral Salmon may be asked to ascertain & report what the Germans are doing. Copy to Colonial Office with copy of letter to Admiralty; Shew to Consul Hewett, Drafts, 9 May. Print (Congo <u>and</u> Oil Rivers). Write with compliments to Head of Berlin Chancery and tell him to number this and any subsequent dispatch on the same subject in the African Section.' H.P.A. [Henry Percy Anderson]; G[ranville]].

[11] *Norddeutsche Allgemeine Zeitung.*

[12] On 29 March 1884 Nachtigal was appointed imperial commissioner for West Africa (*Reichskommissar*) and ordered to Lisbon to await further instructions.

Office to send out Dr Nachtigal to those parts, a person particularly suited for such a duty, to further German interests there and to report upon a scheme for consular appointments on that Coast. Dr Nachtigal takes with him, at this own request, the African traveler Dr Buchner, and likewise Herr Moebius now a Secretary at the German Consulate-General in London.

It is intended, at the suggestion of the Foreign Office, to station permanently some war vessels on the West Coast of Africa, and for the present the Gunboat "Möwe" has been placed at the service of the Commission. The "Möwe" left Kiel on the 15th instant and is expected at Lisbon towards the end of the month, where it will take on board Dr Nachtigal and his staff.

FO 64/1102: Lord Ampthill to Earl Granville, Confidential, Africa, No 5, Berlin, 30 May 1884

[Received 2 June by Messenger Taylor. For: The Queen / X, Ch.W.D. [Charles Wentworth Dilke]; Copy to: Colonial Office, 10 June 1884; G[ranville]]

False reports in British press regarding German takeover of Angra Pequena

With reference to Your Lordship's despatch No. 142 of the 22nd instant, enclosing copies of despatches relative to the question of the right of Sovereignty over Angra Pequeña as well as to my despatch No. 4 Africa, of the 27th instant, I have the honour to state that the report in the Standard of May 14th respecting the alleged assumption of the Sovereignty of that Territory by the German Government is unfounded.[13]

The German Government are still awaiting an answer from Your Lordship to Count Münsters Letter of the 31st of December last[14] and the premature reports in the Press about the taking possession of Angra Pequeña by the German Government are due to the great and growing impatience of the German people for the inauguration of a Colonial policy by Prince Bismarck, who has hitherto shewn no inclination to satisfy their cravings for colonies; beyond sending Doctor Nachtigall on board the "Moewe" to report generally on the West Coast of Africa as reported to you in my despatches Nos: 93 and 102 of the 9th and 23rd of April last, respectively.

[13] In a telegram of 24 April 1884 Bismarck instructed the German consul at Cape Town to declare that the coastal area of Angra Pequena, acquired by the Bremen merchant Adolf Lüderitz in 1883, was under German protection.

[14] In his note to Granville of 31 December 1883, Münster enquired whether Britain claimed sovereignty over Angra Pequena.

FO 64/1103: Lord Ampthill to Earl Granville, No 225, Berlin, 18 August 1884

[Received 21 August by post. For: Lord Derby; X, Ch.W.D. [Charles Wentworth Dilke]; G[ranville]]

German press reports about British expansion on African west coast; concern that this might affect German colonial aspirations

The "Nord Deutsche Allgemeine Zeitung" of today republishes from the "Cape Times" of the 16th Ultimo, the Correspondence which has passed between Her Majesty's Government and Sir Hercules Robinson,[15] respecting the German Protectorate of Angra Pequēna and the extension of British Authority on the West Coast of Africa.

By way of comment, the "Nord Deutsche Allgemeine" reproduces an article from the "National Zeitung" of the 12th instant, on the same subject of which a translation is herewith enclosed.[16]

The feeling in Germany respecting these Colonial Questions is so strong, as Your Lordship is aware, that the publication of the above-named correspondence can only tend to confirm the General suspicion that England opposes the Colonial Aspirations of the people of Germany, and the impression of disappointment it must produce will be painful and lasting throughout Germany.

FO 64/1051: Charles S. Scott to Earl Granville, No 231, Berlin, 25 August 1884

[28 August by post; For: The Queen / Gladstone; X, Ch.W.D. [Charles Wentworth Dilke]; Qy: 'Any comments to Mr Scott?', T.G.S. [Thomas G. Staveley]; 'Answered', 4 September]

Report detailing the death of Ampthill; sympathies of German imperial family and press

I have the melancholy duty to report to Your Lordship the death of Her Majesty's Ambassador, Lord Ampthill, which took place this morning at eleven o'clock at his country residence at Potsdam.

[15] Telegram from Lord Derby to Robinson, dated 15 July 1884. This stated that the British government was 'not in a position to oppose' German protection for German subjects, but 'where no British jurisdiction already exists' it 'will be prepared to proclaim under British protection and authority any other places [...] to which British subjects have claims'.

[16] Enclosures: article 'Politischer Tagesbericht' in *Norddeutsche Allgemeine Zeitung* and translation, both dated 18 August 1884.

His Excellency although for some time past in delicate health had apparently recovered strength and spirits from the country air, and even so late as Tuesday last transacted business at the Ministry for Foreign Affairs, and neither complained of nor exhibited any unusual symptoms likely to create uneasiness on his account. – It appears that on returning to Potsdam in the evening severe pains set in in the region of the liver, similar to those from which His Excellency suffered in the beginning of last May. Medical assistance was at once called in but it was not until Thursday morning that he was so unwell as to be quite unable to attend to business, and accordingly requested me to act for him, expressing a hope that he might be sufficiently recovered to come up to town on Saturday to sign the despatches. – Lady Ampthill having expressed more uneasiness on Friday I went to Potsdam on Saturday and found that Lord Ampthill had suffered greatly during the night, and was very weak; the illness however seemed to be running a favourable course and no serious alarm was entertained.

His Excellency was so far recovered in the morning as to be able to take notice of some private communications which I had brought him and to give me his instructions through Lady Ampthill. On Sunday morning the accounts were more favourable, but in the evening what proved to have been an abscess burst, perforating the intestines and violent vomiting ensued, causing serious alarm. – Her Majesty the Empress[17] despatched her personal physician[18] to assist Lord Ampthill's medical attendant,[19] and he then pronounced the case a dangerous one, but this news only reached the Embassy at 10 this morning, and on arriving at Potsdam we found our worst fears realised.

His Excellency, after six hours of almost complete absence of pain and, except during a slight interval in full possession of his consciousness, passed peacefully away at 11 oclock [*sic*] in the presence of Lady Ampthill and all his family.

Their Imperial Majesties had been unremitting in their enquiries ever since the commencement of the illness, and The Empress, arriving at the villa to make personal enquiries, a few minutes after its fatal termination had herself assisted into the house from the carriage and was the first to offer her sympathy to Lady Ampthill. – The Emperor who has been deeply affected by this sad event has expressed to Colonel Swaine his concern at the loss of a respected personal friend.

[17] Augusta.
[18] Carl Velten.
[19] Name not traceable.

From every quarter private and Official expressions of sympathy have been presented both at Potsdam and at Her Majesty's Embassy, and the Press, of every shade of opinion testifies to the great loss which the two countries have sustained by the death of a diplomatist, whose unremitting efforts have during 13 years been directed to strengthening and maintaining the friendly relations between the two Governments.

I lost no time in officially communicating the melancholy intelligence to the Imperial Minister of Foreign Affairs, and in requesting His Excellency to permit me to carry on the necessary official communications of the Embassy with him until Your Lordship's instructions have been received.

Dr Busch, in the absence of Count Hatzfeld, who left Berlin today has promptly replied, agreeing to my proposal and assuring me of the deep sympathy which the Imperial Government feel in the loss which The Queen has sustained of so eminent a diplomatist as Lord Ampthill.

Lady Ampthill who is prostrated with grief, has expressed a desire that His Excellency's remains should be conveyed to England, but no arrangements will be concluded until the arrival of Colonel Villiers and other members of the family who are expected tomorrow. – In the meantime there appears to be a very general desire here to pay some public mark of respect to His Excellency's Memory.

FO 64/1051: Charles S. Scott to Earl Granville, No 242, Berlin, 30 August 1884

[Received 1 September by Messenger Powell. For: The Queen; X, Ch.W.D. [Charles Wentworth Dilke]; Qy: 'Mr Scott to take an opportunity of expressing satisfaction of H.M. Government, at the marks of respect & affection thus shewn by the Emperor; the Crown Prince & Princess and the Royal Representatives of Foreign Countries on the occasion referred to.' T.G.S. [Thomas G. Staveley]; G[ranville]]

Ampthill's remains sent from Potsdam to England; ceremony attended by diplomatic corps, the emperor and royal family

I have the honour to report that the Remains of Lord Ampthill, as stated in my telegram N⁰ 11 of the 27th instant, left Potsdam yesterday morning for England.

On the afternoon of the preceding day His Imperial and Royal Highness the Crown Prince,[20] who only returned that morning from South Germany, paid a visit of condolence at the villa, and

---

[20] Friedrich Wilhelm.

placed with his own hands two wreathes [*sic*] on the Bier, as a last mark of the affections felt for Lord Ampthill by His Imperial Highness and by the Crown Princess[21]. Wreaths were also sent by Her Majesty the Empress,[22] and by Their Royal Highnesses the Princess Christian of Sleswig Holstein,[23] Princes William and Henry of Prussia and the Princess of Saxe Meiningen.[24]

By His Majesty's orders a Royal Hearse, followed by two of the Royal Carriages in full state was sent early yesterday morning to convey the Coffin from the Villa to the Potsdam Railway Station, and every attention and mark of respect, compatible with Lady Ampthill's wish to maintain throughout the strictest privacy, was paid to His Excellency's memory. At the Potsdam Station Prince Radziwill and Count Königsmark were in waiting to represent the Emperor and Empress.

On the arrival of the train at Charlottenburg at about 7.30 a.m., the funeral carriages were detached, and waited there for the morning Express Train to Flushing.

The Ambassadors of Italy, Austria-Hungary and France,[25] the Staff of Her Majesty's Embassy, and the whole of the Diplomatic Body now in Berlin were present at the Charlottenburg Station, as well as D[r] Busch, Acting Minister for Foreign Affairs, and Count Radolinski, Comptroller of the household of His Imperial and Royal Highness, the Crown Prince.

FO 64/1104: Charles S. Scott to Earl Granville, No 307, Berlin, 9 October 1884

[Received 13 October by Messenger Wynter. Extends telegram No 19. Copy to: Colonial Office; Print (South West Coast of Africa); G[ranville]]

Appeal to German minister for foreign affairs concerning Lüderitz's actions in Angra Pequena

On receipt of Your Lordship's telegram N° 25 of yesterday I at once called on the Acting Minister of Foreign Affairs, and made a strong representation to His Excellency in the sense of Your Lordship's instruction in regard to the action of Mr Lüderitz at Angra Pequeña requesting that instructions might be sent to that Gentlemen to desist from advancing claims to the possession of the

---

[21] Victoria.
[22] Augusta.
[23] Helena.
[24] Augusta (Saxe-Meiningen).
[25] Edoardo de Launay, Emmerich Graf Széchényi and Alphonse Chodron de Courcel.

islands lying off the West Coast of Africa between 26° South Latitude and the Grange River, and from interfering with those islands or with the British Lessee.[26] Dr Busch at once admitted that these islands were the ten referred to by Baron Plessen,[27] as claimed by the Government of the Cape Colony to which the German Protectorate would not extend, and promised to attend to my representation at once and let me know the result as soon as possible.

His Excellency said, that as there was at the present moment no German Consul or Authority within easy access to Angra Pequeña, Mr Lüderitz had probably acted without full knowledge of the latest views and intentions of the Imperial Government in regard to the recently established Protectorate.

FO 64/1145: Edward Malet to Earl Granville, Very Confidential, No 331, Berlin, 23 October 1884

[Received 27 October by Messenger Leeds. For: The Queen / Prince of Wales / Gladstone / Circulate / Approve Language / Copied for Print (South West Coast of Africa); Query: Copy to Colonial Office – very confidential / Embassies – very confidential; Qy: 'Mr Anderson to see'; G[ranville]]

Conversation with Bismarck concerning Anglo-German relations and German colonization

With reference to my Despatch N° 36, Africa, of this date, I have the honour to inform Your Lordship that I took the opportunity of Prince Bismarck's visit to me this morning to endeavour to speak to His Highness on the general question of the relations between England and Germany, and stated to his Highness that I was authorised by Your Lordship to say that it would give you great satisfaction to be fully informed of his Highness' views, and to act with His Highness in the most friendly spirit on the points on which the common interest of the two countries were engaged.

His Highness replied that he was sure that if he had only to deal with Your Lordship these friendly relations would easily maintained,

---

[26] The coastal area of Angra Pequena (see n. 13 in this section) was proclaimed a German protectorate on 7 August 1884. On 6 October Lüderitz claimed that the hoisting of the German flag on mainland Africa meant that the islands in question came into German possession, and called upon the lessee to vacate them.

[27] Busch was probably referring to the German chargé d'affaires' interview with Earl Granville at the Foreign Office on 20 September. The ten islands (Ichaboe, Long Island, Seal Island, Penguin Island, Halifax, Possession Island, Albatross Rock, Pomona, Plum-pudding and Roast Beef [Sinclair] Island) had been formally annexed to the Cape Colony in 1874.

but that unfortunately Your Lordship did not rule the Colonial Office, and that there he met with a spirit of disregard for all but the exclusive interests of England. He said that the Colonial Office, although it was aware of the aspirations of other countries, and of the advantages which such aspirations must afford to civilization, treated each question, as it arose, within the narrow circle of English commercial advantage, and ignored the larger view of friendly relations and benefit to the world.

I observed to His Highness that latterly this had really been not the case; that Her Majesty's Government had recently, in the various questions which had come up for settlement with Germany, done all in their power, consistently with State rights and obligations, to meet His Highness' wishes; and I referred notably to the question of New Guinea, where we had restricted our protectorate simply in consequence of his Highness's observations.[28]

Prince Bismarck went on to say that the Colonial question in Germany had taken a hold on the sentiment of the German People greater than that to which it was entitled, but that for the moment there was no restraining it. He said that the Emperor Napoleon on one occasion,[29] speaking about an ambition of the French which had recently taken shape, that the Mediterranean should approach the condition of a French Lake, had observed that the French, who did not shine as a nation by their horse-riding, nevertheless were always endeavouring to excel in a circus, and considered the superiority of Franconie as a legitimate ambition. So, though they were mighty in arms on land, and might have been satisfied with that, they must needs now prove their powers at sea, for which they had never shewn great aptitude.

Something of the same sort, said Prince Bismarck was occurring in Germany at present with regard to colonisation, and the sentiment had so entangled itself with the electioneering question, that it had to be treated with greater deference and circumspection than in the beginning had appeared to be necessary.

I should add, that although Prince Bismarck made use of no words which could wear the appearance of being designed to attenuate his recent attitude on the colonial and other questions towards Her Majesty's Government, his manner was eminently friendly and

---

[28] On 19 September 1884 Scott informed the German government of the British intention to extend British authority in New Guinea; on 9 October Scott communicated the British restriction to the south coast; on 6 November 1884 the Territory of Papua, the south-eastern part of New Guinea, became a British protectorate.

[29] Bismarck was referring to Louis-Napoleon Bonaparte's speech at Marseille on 26 September 1852.

cordial, and gave me the impression that that which I may be allowed to call his past ill-humour has been rather the result of political calculation than personal sentiment.

This, however, increases the gravity with which it should be regarded, as it may prove to be a carefully prepared excuse for a more complete understanding with France than we are aware of.

FO 64/1052: Edward Malet to Earl Granville, No 407, Berlin, 27 December 1884

[Received 29 December by Mr Taylor. Immediate: Print – Egypt (Finance) / Embassies; G[ranville]]

German government's policy towards Egyptian debts; public opinion increasingly anti-English

With reference to Your Lordship's Despatch N° 391^A of the 10th Instant, recording a Conversation with Count Münster on that date, in which Your Lordship urged upon His Excellency the pressing character of the question of Egyptian Finance, I have the honour to inform Your Lordship that I have lost no opportunity of speaking in the same sense here.

I regret to say that I have found no disposition on the part of the German Foreign Office to use any pressure on other Powers to give a speedy answer to the proposals of Her Majesty's Government, nor has it pronounced its own opinion with regard to them.[30]

It regards the question as one to be settled in the first instance between England and France, and I am led to believe that any agreement which is come to by them will be followed by the adhesion of Germany[,] Austria and Russia.

On the other hand, if no understanding is arrived at with France, Germany and the Powers which accept her lead are certain not to consent to English proposals.

There remains to be considered the attitude which Germany would assume in the event of the failure of the present negotiations and the consequent necessity of England acting without European sanction.

---

[30] The British proposal, based upon a modification of the Law of Liquidation of July 1880, provided details for the financial settlement between Egypt and its international creditors. It was submitted to the German government on 29 November 1884. In his conversation with the German ambassador to London, on 10 December, Earl Granville stated that further delay would render the proposal insufficient; therefore he hoped for a favourable reply at an early date. The British – as well as the German – negotiating position on the Egyptian question was largely affected by the fact that two-thirds of the debt was held by French creditors. The British role in Egypt – de facto a British protectorate since 1882 – was also affected by the Mahdist revolt against Egyptian rule in Sudan.

Public feeling in Germany has for the last six months been encouraged in the direction of hostility towards England; the friendly attitude which we have assumed on the Colonial question has effected no appreciable change.[31] Our manifest desire to meet the wishes of Germany as far as is compatible with our rights and obligations have met with so little response that it would seem as though the German Foreign Office were deliberately maintaining ill-feeling towards us for some ulterior purpose after the original cause has been obliterated.

It is not necessary to be possessed of an unduly suspicious nature to suspect that there is a direct connection between the maintenance of this irritation on the Colonial question and the future policy of the German Government towards England in case the Egyptian question enters upon a more acute phase.

The way, at least, is thus prepared for a coalition of the Great Powers, with the exception of Italy, against us, which would not have been possible a year since. At that time German public feeling would have sided with England in such an emergency, and the coalition, including Italy, would have been against France.

As matters are at present, probabilities point to Germany, Russia, Austria and France being arrayed against us, if we do not come to terms with the last named Power; and I fear that our exceeding weakness in Egypt, in consequence of the expedition to Khartoum[32] has been taken into account in calculating the means which we should have at our disposal to withstand such a coalition.

FO 64/1146: Edward Malet to Earl Granville, Confidential, No 45, Berlin, 24 January 1885

[Received 26 January by Messenger Callander. Print (Pacific)]

Conversation with Bismarck regarding German colonial policy

With reference to my Despatch N° 55, Africa of today's date, I have the honour to inform Your Lordship that, after I had finished reading to

---

[31] Malet is referring to Britain's concessions in colonial matters, including the formal recognition (on 22 September 1884) of German policy with regard to South West Africa (in particular, the declaration of Angra Pequena (Lüderitz Bay) as a German protectorate) and her conduct during the Berlin West Africa Conference, which opened on 15 November 1884 and aimed to regulate European trade and colonization in Africa.

[32] The British Nile Expedition was sent to relieve General Gordon and his troops at the besieged city of Khartoum, Sudan. However it arrived on 28 January 1885, two days after the city had fallen to Mahdist Sudanese forces.

Prince Bismarck Your Lordship's Despatch N° 29 African of the 20th Instant, he spoke to me at length on the circumstances leading to the present political estrangement between the two countries.

He said that at every point at which Germany had endeavoured to found a Colony England had closed in, making new acquisitions so as to restrict Germany's power of expansion. He proceeded to the question of New Guinea, and he asserted that he had understood from Mr Scott's Note of the 9th October that we had accorded him free hand with regard to the north; that to his understanding, the words "without prejudice to any territorial question beyond these limits" gave him such liberty.[33]

I argued with the Prince on both points to the effect that we had not extended our Protectorates in the order stated; that we had on the contrary, been going even to the Cameroons before we were in any way aware that Germany intended to establish a Protectorate there;[34] that in regard to New Guinea, when first Count Münster had spoken about it, Your Lordship had informed him that steps towards annexation had already gone farther than was known; as to the words, "without prejudice",[35] conveying such a meaning as the Prince attached to them, I assured him that the only meaning which could be attached to them in the English language was that the question with regard to the rest of New Guinea remained as it was before, and that, in any case, the words were followed by the statement of opinion that questions regarding territories beyond those which we had annexed should be dealt with diplomatically. The Prince persisted that he had understood the words in an entirely different sense, and had considered that he was free to annex that which we had not annexed.

He proceeded to say that in order to show me how different were our relations only a year ago, and how much he had desired that the good relations then subsisting should continue, he would read me a Despatch which he had addressed to Count Münster on the 5th of last May.

He must believe that Her Majesty's Government had entirely failed to appreciate the importance which his Government attached to the Colonial Question, as he could not suppose that, if Your

---

[33] For Scott's note of 9 October 1884 and the British protectorate in New Guinea see n. 28 in this section.

[34] The German protectorate of Cameroon was declared by Gustav Nachtigal on 14 July 1884.

[35] In his conversation with Münster of 8 August 1884 Granville stated that 'the extension of some form of British authority in New Guinea [...] will only embrace that part of the island which specially interests the Australian colonies, without prejudice to any territorial questions beyond those limits'.

Lordship had understood it, the successive annoyances to which Germany had been exposed would not have been averted.

This Despatch of the 5th May to Count Münster was a very remarkable one.

It stated the great importance which the Prince attached to the Colonial question, and also to the friendship of Germany and England.

It pointed out that in the commencement of German Colonial enterprise, England might render signal service to Germany and said that for such service Germany would use her best endeavours in England's behalf in questions affecting her interests nearer home. It pressed these considerations with arguments to show the mutual advantage which such understanding would produce, and it then proceeded to instruct Count Münster to say that if it could not be effected the result would be that Germany would seek from France the assistance which she had failed to obtain from England, and would draw closer to her on the same lines on which she now endeavoured to meet England. The Despatch was a long one, and the Prince read it to me in German, but the above was the gist of it.

Prince Bismarck went on to say that, not being satisfied with the result, and attributing it in part to the Ambassador not having stated the points with precision, he sent his son, Count Herbert Bismarck, to England,[36] in the hope that he might succeed where Count Münster had failed; but that he, unfortunately, had only succeeded in obtaining those general friendly assurances of good-will which were of little value in the face of subsequent occurrences.

The Prince then read to me a Draft of a Despatch which he is now sending to Count Münster,[37] in which he takes up a remark, which His Excellency attributes to Your Lordship, in a report[38] on the Egyptian Question, to the effect that the attitude of Germany on the Colonial Question makes it difficult for Your Lordship to be conciliatory on other points.[39]

The Prince next reverted to what he termed our closing-up system, and he mentioned Zululand, observing that the Boers claimed a cession dating from 1840 with King Panda.[40]

---

[36] Talks between Herbert von Bismarck and Earl Granville took place on 14, 17, and 22 June 1884.

[37] Bismarck to Münster, 24 January 1884 (sent on 26 January).

[38] Münster to Bismarck, 21 January 1885.

[39] For the Egyptian question see n. 30 in this section.

[40] Bismarck was probably referring to the cession of territory to the Natal Boers – in exchange for the support of the proclamation of Mpande as king of the Zulus in 1840. Another cession to the Boers – land on the border between the Zulu Kingdom and the Transvaal Republic – took place in 1854.

I said that I feared the Prince's good faith had been imposed upon, as no such State as the Transvaal had existed at that date,[41] and that the only Boers who could have obtained a cession of territory, if such existed, were our own subjects. The Prince replied that it was not a question which a law-suit would settle.

I then said to the Prince that the whole situation was undoubtedly a very unsatisfactory one, and that it gave me great pain, as it had been my hope and endeavour, under instructions from Your Lordship, to bring about a more cordial understanding between the two Powers; that I knew that it had never been the intention of Her Majesty's Government to thwart the Colonial aspirations of Germany, and that in my opinion, our action had repeatedly shewn this desire; but I said that it would be impossible for us to act so as to meet his wishes, even where it was easy for us to do so, unless we knew what those wishes were, and I therefore begged him to tell me what now, at this moment, he wanted: was it the parts of New Guinea which we were now annexing? Was it Zululand? I said that the knowledge of his wishes, whatever they might be, was better than that we should go on mutually acting in the dark, and consequently running against each other.

The Prince replied that the understanding which he had arrived at with France[42] in consequence of his failure to come to one with us put it out of his Power to take up the question now, as he had expounded it to us in May. The long conversation came to an end, by his saying that he had been anxious to explain to me the series of circumstances that had preceded the present phase of the political relations between the two countries, which he was sure I must regret as much as he did.

FO 64/1149: Charles S. Scott to Earl Granville, No 107, Berlin, 4 March 1885

[Received 6 March by post. For: The Queen / Gladstone / X, Ch.W.D. [Charles Wentworth Dilke]/ Print (Pacific) / Consular Department; G[ranville]]

German press reactions to revelations in Blue Books about colonial negotiations between Britain and Germany

I have the honour to enclose, with translations, copies of two further Articles directing somewhat violent charges against her Majesty's

[41] The South African Republic (Transvaal) was founded in 1852.

[42] Bismarck was referring to Germany's approval of the French scheme of 8 January 1885 to financially reorganize Egypt, and the French support of the Russo-German request to send representatives to the Public Debt Commission (Caisse de la Dette Publique), which supervised the repayment of Egyptian debts to foreign creditors.

Government for alleged indiscretions committed in the publication of the recently issued Parliamentary Papers on questions under negotiation between the two Governments.[43]

These Articles appeared in the semi-official Norddeutsche Zeitung of last night and this morning, and like their predecessor in yesterday's edition of the same paper bear the impress of official inspiration.

The first Article is devoted to Your Lordship's Note to Count Münster of the 21st ultimo on the subject of recent occurrences in the Cameroon Protectorate, and the charges preferred against English officials by the German Government, which the Article asserts have in the Note referred to met with a rude dismissal at Your Lordship's hands, – by the notification of counter claims against the German Government on the part of English Subjects for losses occasioned during the same occurrences, of which, it says, it is impossible Your Lordship could have received sufficient proofs at the time the Note was penned.[44]

The Article concludes by referring, as a parallel case, to the alleged Bombardment and destruction of Alexandria by Her Majesty's Naval forces,[45] and the losses thereby occasioned to German and other subjects; and says that England seems to deal out unequal measures in regard to the two cases, asserts that a country pledged for international obligations; and instead of taking upon herself the compensation of the Alexandria losses, throws it upon the Bondholders; but it states its conviction that Germany will insist on the proceedings of England in Egypt and those of Germany in the Cameroons being considered on the same lines of justice.

The second Article deals with Sir E. Malet's Despatch N° 45 to Your Lordship of the 24th January,[46] and states that it's publication constitutes the gravest of all the indiscretions, that the revelation to the public of observations made by Prince Bismarck to Her Majesty's Ambassador in the course of a confidential conversation which was prompted by the footing of personal friendship on

---

[43] Enclosures: extracts from *Norddeutsche Allgemeine Zeitung*, 3 March 1885 and *Norddeutsche Allgemeine Zeitung*, 4 March 1885 and corresponding translations.

[44] Charges were brought against British traders and the acting British vice consul for stirring up the natives; against Captain Campbell and Consul Hewett for international discourtesy and disrespect towards the German authorities; and, lastly, against English missionaries, who were suspected of giving aid to rebellious natives. These German measures led to the destruction of English mission buildings and storehouses in Hickory Town.

[45] The bombardment of Alexandria by the British Mediterranean Fleet (11–13 July 1882) took place during the Anglo-Egyptian War.

[46] Malet's No 45 (see pp. 44–47) was published in *Further Correspondence respecting New Guinea and Other Islands in the Western Pacific Ocean*, in February 1885.

which the Chancellor stood to His Excellency, and the late Lord Ampthill, will in the future preclude the possibility of similar confidential intercourse between the Statesmen of the two Governments. The tone of this Article is especially significant in the suspicion thrown out that the publication of this Report was meant to sow the seeds of distrust between France and Germany, and in the strange rendering of Sir Edward Malet's very clear request to know what were the precise Colonial aims of Germany, into an attempt to loosen the political relations of Germany with France.

FO 64/1149: Charles S. Scott to Earl Granville, No 112, 7 March 1885

[Received 9 March by Messenger Newton. For: The Queen / X, Ch.W.D. [Charles Wentworth Dilke]; Qy: Print dispatch and extract[47] for inclusion / Copy to Colonial Office / Print (Pacific); G[ranville]]

Debates on colonial policy in Reichstag *and Prussian* Landtag; *Social Democrats defend English position*

With reference to my despatch No: 100 of the 28th ultimo I have the honour to transmit a summary of the proceedings on the German Reichstag and Prussian Landtag during the past week,[48] which has been carefully drawn up by M[r] Gosselin, and to which I would venture to invite special attention as the Reichstag has this week been almost exclusively occupied with the votes for Colonial purposes on which the Government lay much stress, and some very interesting and remarkable speeches were delivered.

One of these, that of the Imperial Chancellor, I have already had the honour to transmit in full text and translation to Your Lordship in my despatch no: 104 of the 3rd instant.[49]

The remarks of M. de Kusserow, the Representative of the Department of the German Foreign Office specially occupied in Colonial questions, are interesting as explaining among other matters

---

[47] Extract from Granville to Scott, No 96 A, Secret, 9 March 1885 (on his conversation with Herbert von Bismarck about his father's speech in the *Reichstag*).

[48] Enclosures: summary of *Reichstag* proceedings, 2–6 March, by Mr Gosselin, 7 March 1885; summary of *Landtag* proceedings 28 February–6 March, by Mr Gosselin, 7 March 1885.

[49] In his speech of 2 March 1885 Bismarck deplored the lack of support for his colonial policy and criticized the obstruction of his endeavours by the British press and government. He also denied encouraging Earl Granville to annex Egypt.

the genesis and development of the new Colonial movement in South Africa, and the South Sea, and the mission of Dr Nachtigal.[50]

The Government, as Your Lordship will perceive, carried the Cameroon vote, but were defeated on the vote for increasing the Consular salaries at Samoa and Corea.[51]

It is unfortunate that the part of defending England against certain attacks in the course of this debate should have been taken up solely by the Social Democratic member, Herr Liebknecht, and by the Free Trade Deputy Herr Richter, both of them inveterate opponents of the Imperial Chancellor as well as of his Colonial policy.

This may possibly account for some of the displeasure which, strange to say, was manifested by the factions sitting on the right side of the house at Herr Richter's quotation of the Times article[52] advocating the cultivation of friendly relations between England and Germany.

FO 64/1077: Charles S. Scott to Earl Granville, Secret, No 161, Berlin, 11 April 1885

[Received 13 April by Messenger Cavendish. For: The Queen / Mr Gladstone / Cabinet; G[ranville]]

German public and political views on the Afghan border crisis; financial markets affected by Russo-British tension; conversations with Hatzfeld and Turkish ambassador

The German Government and public are following with intense interest the action of the English and Russian Governments in regard to Central Asia.

Already on the 7th instant before receiving Your Lordship's Secret telegram of that day I ascertained privately that the general purport of the Russian reply to Your Lordship's despatch of the 13th March and of the light in which it was regarded by the English Cabinet was known to Prince Bismarck and in certain other influential quarters here, and that in spite of the serious turn which the negotiations seemed to be now taking Prince Bismarck could not bring himself

---

[50] Kusserow, on 2 March 1885, stated that the German government's policy was 'to follow with assistance private undertakings'. On Nachtigal's mission see nn. 12 and 34 in this section.

[51] The *Reichstag* passed the supplementary budget for the German protectorates in Africa on 2 March 1885; the recommendations concerning the consulates in Corea and Samoa were rejected on 4 March.

[52] On 4 March Richter (after being informed by a telegram from the Wolff News agency) referred to the *Times* editorial of that same day.

to believe that they would end otherwise than in a peaceful arrangement between the two Governments.[53] In the course of the following day a rumour to the effect that the Russian troops had advanced and occupied Pendjeh had been received by one influential Banking house here, and a slight fall took place on the Bourse in Russian securities which had already been sensibly affected by the news that a tax was to be levied on the coupons of the later Russian loans, but the German Foreign Office had received no intelligence tending to confirm it. When the official telegram of the Engagement was received from St. Petersburgh the following day, a panic, such as has not been known for years, ensued on the Bourse, Russian securities falling five and English Consols one per cent.

Considering that Russian Stock to the extent of I believe fifty millions sterling are held in Germany alone, the interest of this country in the maintenance of a peaceful policy by Russia is self-evident, and this fact is, I am informed, not lost sight of by the German Chancellor who is as anxious for a peaceful solution of the present difficulty as Her Majesty's Government can be. I am privately informed that even so late as last night the Prince professed a confident hope that serious conflict would be avoided. The information which he had received from St. Petersburgh as well as from London shewed the two Governments to be equally animated by an ardent desire for peace and that they were approaching the discussion of a most serious incident, in regard to which the reports from their respective officials on the spot sensibly differed, in a moderate and statesmanlike spirit.

I may add that Count Hatzfeld spoke to me yesterday in a similar sense, and that on my shewing him the report of M[r] Gladstone's statement in the House of Commons on Thursday which I had just received by telegraph from Your Lordship,[54] His Excellency expressed his sincere appreciation of its calm and dignified tone and said that it strengthened his hopes of a peaceful solution, as the same spirit seemed to prevail at present at S[t] Petersburgh, and he believed the Russian Government had already made more acceptable proposals to Your Lordship.[55]

[53] The Russian reply to the British memorandum on the Afghan border question of 13 March was dated 29 March. The British proposal for a frontier in north-west Afghanistan was rejected and the Russians insisted on their original proposal made in January that year. The British government deemed it impossible to proceed on this basis and on 30 March Russia occupied the Panjdeh district, which belonged to the Emirate of Afghanistan.

[54] On 9 April 1885 Gladstone informed the House of Commons about the Afghan frontier negotiations with Russia, and in particular his knowledge of the Panjdeh incident.

[55] Hatzfeld was probably referring to new proposals which had been sent by telegraph to the Russian ambassador to London, Baron Staal, on 7 April 1885 which were communicated to the Foreign Office on 8 April.

His Excellency admitted the possibility of the Russian Generals having exceeded their instructions, though he could not avoid suspecting that the Afghans must on their side have given some provocation.

I have been privately informed in strict confidence by the same gentleman[56] to whom I was indebted for the information contained in my despatch N° 145 Secret of the 28th ultimo, that on his making a suggestion to Prince Bismarck that his powerful influence might now be exerted with good effect at St Petersburgh to induce the Russian Government to offer some satisfaction to England for an incident for which the excessive military ardour of her generals seemed to be mainly responsible, the Prince replied that it was entirely impossible for him to take the slightest action in this sense: – His feeling for England was more friendly now than it had ever been, this fact was known at St Petersburgh, and any step he might take there was sure to be misconstrued. Up to the present moment he had not received a hint either from St Petersburgh or London that his good offices were desired, but they would be gladly given on the first intimation of such a desire from the two Governments. He still looked forward to a peaceful issue of direct negotiations between the two Governments without the necessity of help from a third party, and in the meantime his policy was and would continue to be one of absolute neutrality. He was satisfied of the sincere desire for peace of the Emperor of Russia and his Government and also of Mr Gladstone and his colleagues but his whole efforts would be directed to securing by every means in his power that if hostilities did unhappily break out between those two powerful nations, they should not endanger the peace of the rest of Europe but be localized as strictly as possible.

With this view I am positively assured on authority entitled to considerable credit that very strong pressure is, at the present moment being put by Prince Bismarck, and at his instigation by the Austrian Government on Turkey to hinder any act, engagement or attitude on her part which might eventually involve the East of Europe in the conflict.

This action, I am assured is being taken not with any desire to hamper or paralyze the action of England in case of an Anglo Russian war, or to secure an unequal advantage to Russia in the struggle, but simply because the peace of Europe was a paramount necessity both for Germany and Austria who had entered into formal engagements at Skierniewicz[57] to use their influence to keep Turkey

---

[56] Name not traceable.

[57] Malet is referring to the three emperors' meeting at Skierniewice from 15–17 September 1884.

quiet on the slightest symptom of her adopting an attitude likely to endanger that peace.

I am the more inclined to attach credit to this information since a conversation which I had with the Turkish Ambassador[58] this afternoon. His Excellency took the opportunity of a visit which I paid to him to discuss the general political situation and to express his conviction that although he was inclined to believe matters would be patched up at present between us and Russia, a conflict must eventually ensue between the two Powers in Central Asia, and he then repeated to me at great length his views of the policy which had led up to the present situation[,] the advantages which we had on several occasions let slip of meeting a Russian advance with a preponderance of chances in our favour and ended by an opinion that in view of a strong coalition of the European Powers anxious to secure the Peace of Europe by every means in their power, the task which we should eventually have to undertake was becoming every day a more difficult one.

FO 64/1077: Edward Malet to Earl Granville, Secret, No 205, Berlin, 7 May 1885

[Received 11 May. Extender Telegram No 34; X; G[ranville]]

Conversation with Bismarck on matter of German arbitration in relation to Anglo-Russian difficulties

I have the honour to inform Your Lordship's [*sic*] that I have enquired of Prince Bismarck whether, if the Governments of Her Majesty the Queen and His Imperial Majesty the Emperor of Russia were to ask his Imperial Majesty the Emperor to arbitrate, His Majesty would accept.[59]

The Chancellor replied that he would immediately submit the point but that he was doubtful as to whether the Emperor could consent, or as to whether he himself could advise His Majesty to do so.

He stated that the position of Germany was extremely delicate, and should the result of the arbitration prove to be adverse to

---

[58] Said Pasha Kurd.

[59] Anglo-Russian tensions revolved around the rivalry for supremacy in Central Asia, and in particular the Afghan border question (see previous dispatch). At the time of the dispatch it was proposed to the German Emperor to act as arbiter and judge whether Russia had departed from Nikolai de Giers' verbal assurances of 16 March (reported to Earl Granville by Edward Thornton on the same day) that Russian forces would not advance from their positions, 'provided the Afghans [...] do not advance or attack, or unless there should be some extraordinary reason [...], such as a disturbance in Penjdeh'.

Russia, the ill-feeling which had been created by his policy at the Congress of Berlin might be kindled afresh.[60] Should he be justified in risking this danger? He was of opinion that a sovereign of less prominence would be preferable and more especially His Majesty the King of Denmark on account of his consanguinity to the Royal Families of the two Countries.[61]

He remarked that in any case it would be desirable to delay the award of the arbitration until the delimitation of the frontier had taken place, lest its promulgation should wound susceptibilities and endanger the negotiations.

The Prince enquired of me what was the precise point on which arbitration was sought as much must depend upon the text and it was settled between us that he should not call upon His Majesty for a final reply until Your Lordship had furnished me with an answer to this question. He wished to know the text of the agreement of the 16th March.[62]

I was able to reply to the Chancellor in general terms but I stated that I had not yet received instructions from Your Lordship as to the text of the matter to be submitted to arbitration.

I have the honor to request that Your Lordship will furnish me with precise instructions on these points.

The Chancellor and I agreed that, in case His Majesty declines, the proposal should be treated as "non-avenu"[63], as another Sovereign might be disinclined to accept if it were known that the Emperor considered the matter too thorny a one to undertake, and that the conversation which had taken place between us was to remain secret.

FO 64/1078: Charles S. Scott to Marquess of Salisbury, Confidential, No 290, Berlin, 4 July 1885

[Received 6 July by messenger. For: The Queen / Munich / Prince of Wales / Duke of Cambridge; S[alisbury]]

Bavarian press reports on Brunswick succession; Federal Council seeks to disqualify Ernst August's claims

In compliance with the instructions of Your Lordship's Despatch N° 280 to Sir E. Malet of the 1st instant, I have the honour to return

---

[60] The Berlin Congress of 1878 aimed to settle territorial claims on the Balkans and restore the balance of power after the Russo-Turkish War of 1877–78.

[61] Christian IX's first daughter Alexandra was married to Edward, Prince of Wales; his second daughter Dagmar (Maria Feodorovna) was Empress of Russia.

[62] Bismarck was referring to the Russian assurances of 16 March.

[63] French 'nul et non avenu': not having happened.

herewith Mr Macdonell's Confidential Despatch N° 15 of the 15th ultimo on the Action of Bavaria in the Brunswick Succession Question which was forwarded for His Excellency's perusal.[64]

With regard to the Comments of the Bavarian Press on the action of Prussia in proposing to the Federal Council to declare His Royal Highness The Duke of Cumberland disqualified from succeeding to the Crown of a Federal State of the German Empire, I would venture to remark that no apprehensions seem to be entertained here that the decision taken by the Federal Council in the Case of The Duke of Cumberland can by any possibility be used, as a precedent such as the Bavarian press seems to anticipate, for altering the legitimate order of succession in other States of the Empire.[65] The position of the Duke of Cumberland is unfortunately a peculiar and essentially exceptional one. The State to the Crown of which His Royal Highness is heir presumptive has already recognized by treaty the Sovereignty of Prussia in Hanover, The Duke is understood to question it, and this is the ground on which, so far as is yet known, the Federal Council has expressed an opinion that he is disqualified from acting as Sovereign in the Federal Union, the members of which have mutually recognized the respective rights of the Confederate Sovereigns to the territories in virtue of which they act and vote in the Federal Council.

Prussia, it is argued, has as a directly interested Party a constitutional right to invite an opinion on this point from the Council, and the latter an equal right to give it.[66]

It is not likely that a similar pretext could be found for invoking the intervention of the Council in any of the Succession questions indicated in Mr Macdonell's Despatch as possible to raise in the future.

---

[64] See MacDonell's dispatch of 15 June 1885, pp. 473–475.

[65] After the death of the childless Duke Wilhelm on 18 October 1884, Ernst August, Duke of Cumberland and son of the deposed Georg V of Hanover, proclaimed himself Duke of Brunswick. On 2 July 1885, following the Prussian motion of 18 May 1885, the Federal Council declared the rule of Ernst August, who was next in the succession, to be incompatible with the principles of the treaties of August 1866 and November 1870, and the imperial constitution of 1871. The background to this was Prussian mistrust of Ernst August due to the latter's claim to the throne of Hanover, which had been annexed by Prussia in 1866. On 25 October 1885, the Brunswick diet elected Prince Albrecht of Prussia as regent.

[66] The original motion of 18 May referred to Article 76 of the imperial constitution, according to which disputes between states of the confederation were to be settled by the Federal Council, at the request of one of the parties.

FO 64/1078: Charles S. Scott to Marquess of Salisbury, No 315, Berlin, 18 July 1885

[Received 20 July by messenger. For: The Queen / Lord Iddesleigh / Prince of Wales / Duke of Cambridge; S[alisbury]]

Press coverage of the Brunswick succession

With reference to the various rumours which have recently appeared in the public press in regard to the probable solution of the Brunswick Succession Question, I have the honour to state that I have good reason for believing them to be all based on simple conjectures & to have no foundation, as yet, in fact.[67]

The Norddeutsche Allgemeine Zeitung whose utterances are generally supposed to be more or less officially inspired, has lately commented in two leading Articles[68] on the apparently irreconcilable sentiments expressed in the two letters of His Royal Highness The Duke of Cumberland written respectively to The Queen and the late Duke of Brunswick in 1878,[69] the purport of which, as reported in my Despatch N° 294 of the 8th instant, was communicated to the Brunswick Diet by the Minister of State,[70] – the one letter upholding His Royal Highness's claims to an eventual Succession in Hanover, while the other professed His readiness to respect in the event of his Succession in Brunswick all the treaties concluded by that State with Prussia & other Federal States of the Empire.

The Norddeutsche Zeitung observes that the evident mental reservation with which The Duke of Cumberland wrote his professions to the late Duke of Brunswick is entirely in accordance with the known views of the Guelph political party, and adds that a Guelph Sovereign in Brunswick would naturally always remain a pretender to Hanover, consequently the ally of Prussia's enemies both at home and abroad, for this reason he would be unacceptable both to Prussia and to Germany.

Commenting on a statement in the Brunswick press[71] that Prince Bismarck had in 1878 assured Lord Beaconsfield that no objection would be offered to the Succession of the Duke of Cumberland in Brunswick, provided that His Royal Highness formally renounced

---

[67] On the Brunswick succession question see n. 65 in this section.

[68] On 15 and 18 July 1885.

[69] The letters in question are dated 18 September 1878 (to Victoria) and 14 January 1879 (to Wilhelm).

[70] Hermann von Görtz-Wrisberg, on 30 June 1885.

[71] The *Norddeutsche Allgemeine Zeitung* was referring to the *Hannoversche Kurier*.

His claims to Hanover, and in reply to the charge that this assurance was difficult to reconcile with the statement of opinion in the Prussian Motion recently submitted to the Federal Council to the effect that even a renunciation by the Duke of his claims to Hanover would not render his position in Brunswick more acceptable to Prussia, The Norddeutsche says that, even if it should prove to be a fact that Prince Bismarck gave such an assurance in 1878, it would not be inconsistent with his holding a different opinion in 1885 on reading the letters referred to and after The Duke of Cumberland had distinctly asserted, in reply to advice offered to him by His Relations, that he would never under any circumstance renounce his claims to an eventual succession in Hanover.

I should add that the German press had stated that on Lord Beaconsfield receiving the assurance referred to from Prince Bismarck, Her Majesty the Queen wrote to the Duke of Cumberland advising His Royal Highness to comply with the conditions specified by the Prince, and that The Duke's Letter to Her Majesty, a copy of which His Royal Highness had sent to the Duke of Brunswick, was his reply to the advice thus offered to him.

FO 64/1079: Edward Malet to Marquess of Salisbury, No 388, Berlin, 5 September 1885

[Received 7 September by messenger. For: The Queen / Lord Iddesleigh / St Petersburgh / Vienna; S[alisbury]]

Account of expulsion of Poles from East Prussia

The alleged wholesale expulsion of Poles from the Eastern Provinces of Prussia to which the Foreign Press is apparently devoting some attention is, I understand, taking place not as has been asserted, in virtue of any special decree, but of Police measures which the Prussian Government has a legal right to put in force in case of necessity.[72]

The Poles who have received notice to quit are of foreign, chiefly Russian and Austrian, nationality, who in recent years have, in gradually increasing numbers, been crossing the frontier and establishing themselves for purposes of trade on Prussian soil without acquiring

---

[72] On 26 March 1885, the Prussian minister of the interior, Puttkamer, in his rescript to the *Oberpräsidenten* of the eastern provinces ordered all Russian subjects of Polish nationality who resided in Prussia illegally to be expelled. On 26 July this order was extended to all alien residents of Polish provenance, in particular Poles from Galicia. Altogether about 32,000 people were affected.

German nationality. This appears to have been especially the case in the Province of Posen.

The object of the Government in trying now to check the movement by steps which in many cases will no doubt entail great individual hardship is to prevent the gradual denationalization of a German Province by an undue increase of a Polish element of foreign nationality.

As many of the Poles in question are of Jewish extraction whose business habits and pursuits are uncongenial to their German competitors, the Government is no doubt also acting in what it believes to be the commercial interests of their own subjects in the province in question.

I believe that neither the Russian nor Austrian Government has as yet questioned the right of this Government to inforce [sic] this Police measure, but that the former Government is acting in a similar manner in regard to Prussian Poles settled in the frontier province of Russia.

The expulsions appear to be taking place only after due notice has been given to admit of the sufferers making their necessary arrangements and the measure as far as I can learn is not an entirely general one but carried out with some degree of discrimination in regard to the particular cases selected.

FO 64/1079: Edward Malet to Marquess of Salisbury, Secret, No 436, Berlin, 22 September 1885

[Received 28 September by [Messenger] Taylor. For: The Queen / Cabinet; S[alisbury]]

Bismarck on leadership of Austro-German policy in the East

I asked Prince Bismarck today whether Germany or Austria took the lead in deciding questions of policy regarding the East. He replied that he left all minor questions to Austria, giving her free swing as long as the tranquillity of Europe was not endangered, but that if he saw that she was moving too quickly or without sufficiently foreseeing consequences he took the reins into his own hand and was able to hold them.

FO 64/1079: Edward Malet to Marquess of Salisbury, No 527, Berlin, 29 October 1885

[Received 2 November. Recording telegram No 99]

Colonel Swaine suggests free passage for all German officers wanting to attend Indian army manoeuvres

I had the honour to forward to Your Lordship this day at 11 AM the following telegraphic dispatch Cypher: – N° 99.

Colonel Swaine hears he is to be sounded as to the extent to which hospitality will be offered to the Foreign Officers invited to the Indian Manœuvres.[73] He thinks that as English officers have for so many years enjoyed the hospitality of Foreign Governments at their autumn manœuvres we should do nothing that would risk a refusal of our invitation by any one county on the plea of expense. He suggest that a passage free of all expense be given them in a troop-ship from Egypt to Bombay and back, and that while at Delhi they should be the guests of the Governor General.[74] Colonel Swaine asks for an early reply.

FO 64/1113: Edward Malet to Marquess of Salisbury, Very Confidential, No 17, Berlin, 9 January 1886

[Received by [Messenger] Goodyear, undated. For: The Queen; Copy secret to: India Office / Teheran; Print (Asia)]

Discussion with Herbert von Bismarck about Baron Reuter's concession; Bismarck unwilling to commit to scheme of an international company for railway construction in Persia

With reference to Your Lordship's Despatches N° 371 of the 2nd of September last and N° 550 of the 22nd ultimo, and to my Despatch N° 389 of the 5th of September, on the subject of Baron Reuter's concession, I have the honour to inform Your Lordship that I have recently pressed Count Bismarck to acquaint me with the views of the Chancellor[75] on the project.[76]

Count Bismarck now informs me that the Chancellor is unable to entertain the suggestion that Germany should join England and other Powers in starting the scheme as a "Compagnie Internationale des Chemins de Fer de Perse," under a guarantee. Such a step would require the consent of the Reichstag which it would not be possible to obtain, or advisable to ask.

On the other hand, if German Capitalists were to combine with English Capitalists and to start a Company on their own responsibility, Count Bismarck said that the Chancellor would not discourage

---

[73] Manoeuvres were scheduled for January 1886.
[74] The Earl of Dufferin.
[75] Otto von Bismarck.
[76] On 5 September 1885 Malet presented an unofficial memorandum to Herbert von Bismarck which outlined Reuter's proposal for a railway, stretching from Rasht to the Gulf, which was to be set up under the protection of 'certain powers'. He inquired whether the German government was disposed to join Britain in encouraging the scheme. The proposal went back to Reuter's concession of 1872 which was subsequently annulled by the shah as a result of domestic and Russian pressure.

it or throw obstacles in its way. He should merely decline to give it official support.

Count Bismarck went on to give the reasons which led to this decision.

He reminded me of the general desire of the Chancellor to cooperate with Her Majesty's Government so long as such co-operation did not imperil his friendly relations with Russia, which, for motives, with which Your Lordship is cognizant, he is compelled to endeavour to maintain. To enter into the project submitted to him would be regarded as a direct combination against Russia; but apart from this he was of opinion that it would entail responsibilities which Germany would not be able to fulfil. The position of the State of Persia was, according to the accounts which he received from Tehran, already somewhat precarious and its danger could not but be enhanced by the prosecution of a scheme which contained so much that would provoke the fanatic feeling of the country. He finally returned to the cardinal objection that it would not be possible for him to obtain the consent of the Reichstag to a guarantee involving a new departure in general policy and future responsibilities.

Under all these circumstances The Chancellor was not disposed to join Her Majesty's Government in giving encouragement to Baron Reuter in the promotion of his present scheme, or to suggest to what extent or in what form assistance should be given to him.

FO 64/1113: Charles S. Scott to Marquess of Salisbury, No 60, Berlin, 30 January 1886

[Received 1 February by Messenger Seymour. For: The Queen / Prince of Wales / Sir W. Harcourt / Vienna / Mr Childers; S[alisbury]]

Federal Council contests Prussian measures to expel Poles; debates in Prussian parliament; noteworthy speeches by Bismarck explaining reasons for policy

The Debates of the Second Chamber of the Prussian Parliament have this week acquired an unwonted interest from the remarkable speeches delivered by Prince Bismarck on Thursday and Friday night, for a fuller account of which I have the Honour to refer Your Lordship to the weekly summary of Parliamentary Proceedings by Mr Corbett inclosed in my Dispatch N° 62 of this day.

As these speeches have caused no little sensation here, I venture to recall Your Lordship's attention to the circumstances which gave rise to them.

The Question on the orders of the day was the political necessity of recent measures taken by the Prussian Government for expelling a large number of non-Prussian Poles from the Provinces of Posen, Silesia and Prussia.[77]

From the weekly summaries of the Reichstag Debates transmitted by Sir E Malet, Your Lordship will have learnt that when these measures were first brought before the notice of the Reichstag, Prince Bismarck refused to allow an interpellation on the subject to be addressed to him in his character of Chancellor of the Empire, and cut short any attempt of this kind by leaving the House accompanied by the Representatives of all the Federal States in the Bundesrath.[78]

The Reichstag,[79] however, in the exercise of what is considered its undoubted right, proceeded to discuss a form of petition on the same subject to the Bundesrath[80] and this form was eventually voted by a majority of that Assembly, constituting, so to speak, a vote of Censure on the Policy represented by the Prince as Minister president of the Prussian Government. When this petition was brought up to the Bundesrath, that Body[81] refused to entertain it, on the ground that the measures complained of were internal measures passed by a federal state in the exercise of its independent Sovereignty and, therefore, beyond the cognizance of the Federal Council.

In order to give Prince Bismarck the opportunity he desired to explain the policy of his Government in adopting measures which had given rise to such bitter attacks on the part of the National Representation of Germany, a motion was tabled in the Prussian Chamber[82] expressive of Confidence in Prince Bismarck, and thanking the Royal Government for their active defence of the Frontiers of the Kingdom and of the independence of its nationality.

Prince Bismarck[83] has taken advantage of this opportunity to explain and defend his policy in one of the longest speeches on record in the Parliamentary annals of this Kingdom, and he has

---

[77] See n. 72 in this section.

[78] Sitting of 1 December 1885; the interpellation, which was sustained by 155 deputies, was filed by the Polish faction on 26 November.

[79] On 15 and 16 January 1886.

[80] Federal Council.

[81] On 23 January 1886.

[82] On 23 January 1886.

[83] On 28 January 1886.

done so with a frankness and disregard of popular criticisms which has taken the whole chamber by surprise.

While maintaining that the measures of expulsion hitherto adopted have simply been those which the Prussian State has, by ordinary law, a perfect right to enact, and have been applied solely to foreign Poles who had not acquired Prussian Citizenship, he does not hesitate to express his opinion that the open avowal by representative Poles of their aspiration for a separate Polish nationality, as distinct from that of their German fellow subjects, constitutes such a danger to the safety of the frontier of the Kingdom and Empire at large as would justify a Prussian Ministry in appealing to parliament for still larger powers.

He went on to say that he would regard such a Minister as an arrant coward were he to be deterred by any amount of resolutions in the Reichstag arrayed against him from adopting on his own responsibility any measures which he thought absolutely imperative for preserving the unity of the Kingdom and defending its frontiers from encroachment by a foreign nationality.

He indicated as measures of this kind which might become necessary – the voluntary or even compulsory appropriation by the State by the purchase at their full value of the properties of Polish Landowners in the German provinces, and their resettlement by a thoroughly loyal German population which should be restrained from intermarriage with Poles.

The Prince supported his arguments by reviewing at great length the whole history of the Polish Question, reading to the House a great deal of official correspondence on the subject which had not yet seen the light, to shew the impossibility of thoroughly amalgamating the Polish with the Prussian Element and maintaining that the incorporation of the Polish provinces with the Kingdom of Prussia was not based upon any compact between two contracting Powers, but on a proclamation of the recognized Sovereign, and that the promises made in that Declaration were not irrevocable, but liable to modification, if the results which it had desired to effect were not realized.[84]

The character of the encounter which followed this speech between Prince Bismarck and Herr Windthorst, the leader of the Centre,[85] who boldly supported the Poles on this occasion, may be judged from the summary of the two debates to which I have

---

[84] Bismarck was referring to the 'occupation manifesto' (*Besitznahmepatent*) of 15 May 1815 and proclamation of the same date in which Friedrich Wilhelm III assured his 'new' subjects that they would not have to relinquish their nationality.

[85] *Zentrumspartei* (Catholics).

referred. I have referred to the Princes own speeches in a separate dispatch, as I cannot help thinking that the remarkable stress which he laid upon the danger of the situation in the Eastern provinces of the Empire may throw some light on the international policy of the Imperial Chancellor, and the considerations which have guided him in his relations with the Governments of neighbouring Empires.

FO 64/1116: Edward Malet to Earl of Rosebery, No 257, Berlin, 18 June 1886

[Received 21 June by messenger. For: The Queen / Prince of Wales; R[osebery], 21 June 1886]

Unfounded rumours in press regarding Malet's removal as ambassador to Berlin

In the course of an interview which I had on the 12th instant, with Count Berchem, acting Secretary of State for Foreign Affairs, he remarked to me that the German newspapers had been busying themselves with me of late. I understood that he referred to an idle report which has gained currency, foreshadowing my transfer from Berlin to another post, not content with merely stating this, the "National Zeitung" had in a recent article[86] ascribed the course of my approaching removal, to the fact that my position as Ambassador has been shaken through the attitude which I assumed last year during the political differences between England and Germany.

Count Berchem went on to say that the Imperial Government has noticed these statements and intended to put a stop to them by a communication to the Cologne Gazette, the paper often used for inspired utterances.

An article in refutation of them has accordingly appeared and I have the honour to enclose copy and translation herewith.[87]

I am not able to throw any light on the concluding sentence of the paragraph which hints at the source of these rumours being known. I am inclined to regard them as mere journalistic elaborations of a rumour which appeared some time ago in the English Press.

---

[86] On 9 June 1886.
[87] Enclosures: extract (untitled) from *Kölnische Zeitung* and translation, 15 June 1886.

FO 64/1116: Charles S. Scott to Earl of Rosebery, Confidential, No 291, Berlin, 17 July 1886

[Received 19 July by messenger. For: The Queen / Gladstone / Paris for perusal, P.L. [printed letter], No 521; R[osebery], 20 July; Copy to keep]

No danger of war between France and Germany at present

I read with much interest Sir E. Monson's despatch N° 70 of the 9th ultimo on the relations between France and Germany and the comments on its contents contained in Lord Lyons' Confidential despatch N° 337 of the 25th ultimo transmitted for my perusal in Your Lordship's Confidential despatch N° 347 of the 14th instant.

Relying on the best information at the command of the Embassy I feel little difficulty in reechoing Colonel Villier's remarks that there is no more immediate or exceptional danger to be seen in the present state of relations between the two Governments than there has been any time in the last twelve or eighteen months: –

It is impossible to deny that relations between the two Governments are far less cordial than they were during the administration in France of Monsieur Ferry,[88] and that Prince Bismarck has evidently finally abandoned many hopes which he had founded on the incipient good understanding effected at that time, but between this fact and actual danger there is a very great distance to be traversed.

No doubt the strict mot d'ordre to keep all irritating expressions and topics quiet has since been tacitly relaxed, and it may often serve the Chancellor's purpose when dealing with the question of Imperial Finances and the party of retrenchment, to keep the mind of the Parliamentary majority alive to the importance of not remitting any measures of defensive precaution, but it is impossible to conceive that Prince Bismarck, who keeps the foreign policy of the country firmly in his own hands, and has nothing more to gain for Germany or his own reputation by a successful, and everything to lose by an unsuccessful war, would allow the alarmist rumours, circulating chiefly in military circles in the provinces, to reach a point which would endanger a rupture between the two countries.

This, I feel confident, he would only do if absolutely convinced that the safety of the Empire was actually imperilled by any act of provocation on the part of France. If he really distrusts the Government at present in power in that country it is only because

---

[88] Jules Ferry's second term as prime minister was from February 1883 to April 1885.

he distrusts its ability to keep popular clamour and agitation within the bounds of safe control.

FO 64/1117: Edward Malet to Earl of Iddesleigh, Confidential, No 332, Berlin, 21 August 1886

[Received 23 August by messenger. For: The Queen / Lord Salisbury / Circulate / Embassies – confidential / East Department to see; F.B. [Francis Bertie]; I[ddesleigh]]

German government circles uneasy about Eastern events; desire for Britain to engage in bold policy to compensate for enfeebled three emperors' alliance

As long as Prince Bismarck is away from Berlin[89] it is impossible to form any distinct notion of the views of the German Government upon passing events, but since my return[90] I have ascertained that there is a considerable feeling of uneasiness in Government circles regarding the future of events in the East. The sudden hostile effervescence of the Russian Press towards Germany has induced the presumption that the alliance of the three Emperors[91] is weakened and this presumption is strengthened by the advances of France towards a better understanding with Russia being received in the Russian Press with favour.[92] The general situation has caused the keenest attention to be paid to the attitude which would be assumed by Her Majesty's Government and the announcement by Lord Salisbury,[93] that the traditional policy of the maintenance of the integrity of the Ottoman Empire will be followed has caused the liveliest satisfaction.

It is asserted that it is only necessary that this should be thoroughly understood at St Petersburg for all danger to be allayed. Russia feels that England would have Austria[,] Germany and Italy as allies in a war to defend Turkey. On the other hand

---

[89] Bismarck left Berlin for Gastein on 31 July and returned on 28 August 1886.

[90] Malet returned to Berlin from leave of absence on 14 August 1886.

[91] The League of the Three Emperors, founded in 1873 but abandoned through the Dual Alliance of 1879 (see n. 489 in this section), was renewed in the Three Emperors' Treaty of 18 June 1881, albeit not as a formal alliance. In this, Austria, Germany and Russia agreed to maintain benevolent neutrality in the event of one signatory being at war with a fourth power, and to take into consideration their respective interests in the Balkans. Territorial changes in the European part of Turkey were subjected to prior agreement.

[92] The anti-German press reports were based upon the Bulgarian crisis, in particular the alleged German support of Alexander of Bulgaria, Russia's closure of the port of Batumi, which had been declared a free port by the Treaty of Berlin in 1878, and, more generally, nationalist and economic issues with regard to Russia's role in the Balkans.

[93] On 19 August 1886, in the House of Lords.

Germany will be unable to help Austria if England holds back because were she to do so, an active alliance would at once take place between France and Russia.

Austria therefore knowing that she cannot count on Germany if she engages war singlehanded with Russia will be compelled to look on quietly whatever Russia may do with regard to Bulgaria and Eastern Roumelia, consequently unless England's policy is unmistakable that of Austria will be weak and vacillating.[94]

There are many, who imagine that England is content because Egypt is in her group and that she will no longer hazard war to defend Constantinople, that at all events, she may consider that she may stand aloof at first and allow Austria to draw the chesnuts out of the fire or at least to bear the brunt of the first shock of war. Should this be the view held at St Petersburg it is believed that war or, in any case events which would lead to war, were Austria not afraid to engage in it, would be near at hand.

England it is said need not enter into any alliance at present with Austria or Germany to avert the prospect, she has merely to show a bold front to let it be known that she will act in case of necessity and Russia will recognize that the present is not her opportunity.

FO 64/1118: Charles S. Scott to Earl of Iddesleigh, No 382, Berlin, 18 September 1886

[Received 20 September by messenger. For: The Queen / Lord Salisbury / Lord R. Churchill; I[ddesleigh]; S[alisbury]]

Social Democrats seek explanation of government policy regarding Bulgarian Question; political and public feeling over treatment of Prince Alexander in press; lack of sympathy for Bismarck's policy in the East

The National Zeitung, which is generally well-informed on such matters, states that the Socialist Party in the Reichstag held a meeting yesterday to discuss the possibility of forcing in the present extraordinary session an explanation from the Imperial Foreign Office of its action in the Bulgarian Question and a parliamentary discussion of its policy.[95]

To compel a reply from the Government the motion must have the support of at least thirty members, and when the explanation of

[94] For the unification of Bulgaria and the Ottoman province of Eastern Rumelia see n. 15 in Darmstadt section.

[95] The Social Democratic faction intended to enquire whether Bismarck, in his consultations at Kissingen and Gastein that summer, had agreed to the deposition of Prince Alexander of Bulgaria and consented to the strengthening Russian influence in the Balkans. For the Bulgarian crisis see nn. 15, 25, and 27 in Darmstadt section.

policy has been given it cannot be discussed unless a motion for leave to that effect is supported by fifty members of the House.

The Socialists in the House at present can only number twenty four votes and the National Zeitung doubt their being able to secure the necessary six votes from any other party. The same paper states that although the House will in all probability have no opportunity to hear or discuss publicly the foreign policy of the Chancellor, the reassembly of the Parliament[96] has enabled the members of the legislature to discuss and exchange news privately, with the result that the confidence of the National Liberal Party in the wise guidance by Prince Bismarck of the foreign policy of the Emperor has been unanimously confirmed, that this feeling of confidence, however, does not exclude the existence of a very strong and general condemnation of the manner in which the semi-official press has dealt with Prince Alexander personally. The National Zeitung learns that the Liberalist and Free Conservative fractions on the contrary are far from unanimous in regard to their apprehension of Prince Bismarck's policy in the present crisis.

This description of the state of feeling of political parties corresponds with the general impression as to the public feeling of the country, and, although public opinion has not the same power to influence the foreign policy of the Empire as it has in other countries, it may be safely conjectured that Prince Bismarck is anxious not to provoke a parliamentary discussion of the Bulgarian question at the present moment. At no period in the history of the Empire has the feeling of the public and army been so much out of sympathy with the policy adopted by the Chancellor as in this question.

Conservative organs of the highest respectability and generally in touch with the Chancellor's political views have characterized the complacency with which the official and semi-official press viewed the treatment of a popular and heroic prince[97] and compatriot as more than unfeeling, and have expressed their conviction that the reasons of state policy and the danger must have been extreme indeed to induce Prince Bismarck to do violence to feelings which, in his heart, he must personally share.

The apparent victory along the whole line of the Slav party which was but lately so rabid in its attacks on the German Chancellor and nation has been a bitter pill for the German public to swallow, and the high decoration conferred on Monsieur Katkow by the Emperor

---

[96] The *Reichstag* reconvened on 16 September 1886.
[97] Alexander I of Bulgaria.

of Russia for his service in educating the public opinion of his country has increased this bitterness.[98]

With regard to this incident Count Bismarck[99] admitted to me that it was rather a strange step to take at the present moment, but that it was probably only a "sop thrown to Cerberus"[100] as it was quite possible that the Emperor Alexander privately did not view without apprehension the growing power of a party, some of whose proceedings were somewhat akin to those of the Nihilists.

FO 64/1118: Edward Malet to Earl of Iddesleigh, No 416, Berlin, 9 October 1886

[Received 11 October by messenger. For: The Queen / Prince of Wales / Lord Salisbury; I[ddesleigh]]

German press desirous of knowing whether there is a political objective in Randolph Churchill's private visit to Germany

Much comment has been made in the newspapers this week on the visit to Berlin of Lord Randolph Churchill travelling as M[r] Spencer and the inquiries of newspaper correspondents at the Embassy have been unceasing during the last three days.[101] To these applicants it was easy enough to state that nothing was known here regarding it, but to others I have been obliged to be a little more explanatory, especially to Count Bismarck,[102] who was good enough to say, on reading in the English newspapers of the intended visit, that he should see Lord Randolph with much pleasure.

I have explained that His Lordship merely came abroad for the sake of relaxation from his arduous duties and that he was particularly anxious that no political significance should be attached to his journey. Had he come to see me during his stay here, it would have involved his either making other visits or refusing to make them, both of which courses would have been open to misinterpretation by newspaper correspondents who watched all his movements. It therefore appeared to me that he exercised a sound discretion in

[98] Katkov, editor of the *Moskovskiye Vedomosti*, was awarded the Order of Saint Vladimir, 2nd class, on 10 September 1886.

[99] Herbert von Bismarck.

[100] Cerberus was the three-headed watchdog who guarded the gates of the underworld. Virgil's *Aeneid* relates how he was distracted by a sop, or drugged cake, that was given to him in order to let Aeneas slip safely past on his journey to visit his father's spirit.

[101] On his way to Vienna via Dresden and Prague, Randolph Churchill also visited Berlin on 6 and 7 October 1886. He returned to London via Paris on 21 October.

[102] Herbert von Bismarck.

remaining completely aloof, and that his doing so was the only sure means of securing the rest which he desired and of avoiding the supposition that his journey had a political object. I may add that I abstained on the above grounds from intruding on Lord Randolph's privacy during his stay here. Under other circumstances it would have given me great satisfaction if I could have contributed in any way to promoting the comfort or interest of his visit.

FO 64/1118: Edward Malet to Earl of Iddesleigh, Confidential, No 419, Berlin, 14 October 1886

[Received 18 October by [Messenger] Woodford. For: The Queen / Prince of Wales / Lord Salisbury / Constantinople / ~~Intelligence Department~~; H.B. [Henry Brackenbury]; S[alisbury]; I[ddesleigh]]

German foreign office has adopted Daily Telegraph'*s correspondent to Berlin as its mouthpiece*

It may be useful for Your Lordship to know that the German Foreign Office, which is usually not only reticent but dumb towards foreign newspapers correspondents, has recently taken under its wing Mr Bashford, correspondent of the Daily Telegraph at Berlin, and supplies him with news which it wishes to circulate. A curious instance of this was related to me yesterday by this gentleman. He has been placed in communication for the purpose of obtaining information, with Herr Tchiersky[103] of the Foreign Office, who acts in some respects as Private Secretary to Count Bismarck.[104] Two days ago he asked Herr Tchiersky whether there was any truth in a rumour that the Russian Government were endeavouring to obtain from the Sultan[105] an island in the sea of Marmora. Herr Tchiersky replied in the negative, but in the evening Mr Bashford received a message asking him to call again in the morning. At the interview which took place in consequence, Herr Tchiersky told Mr Bashford that he knew nothing about the rumour concerning the island, but that it was certainly the case that the Russian Government was using its utmost endeavours to bring the Sultan under Russian influence, and would probably make considerable promises to gain their end; that what the Russians desired was to induce the Sultan to permit the fortification of the Dardanelles under their supervision. He told Mr Bashford that he might make any use he liked of this information provided he did not divulge its source.

[103] Heinrich von Tschirschky und Bögendorff.
[104] Herbert von Bismarck.
[105] Abdul Hamid II.

He appears generally to communicate very freely on all subjects with Mr Bashford so that if Your Lordship should desire to learn what news the German Government wishes the English newspapers to give, it can be found in the letters in the Daily Telegraph from its correspondent at Berlin.

FO 64/1119: Edward Malet to Earl of Iddesleigh, Most Confidential, No 455, Berlin, 12 November 1886

[Received 15 November by messenger. 'Important'. For: The Queen / Prince of Wales / Lord Salisbury / Lord R. Churchill / Circulate to Cabinet in M.S. / Copy for Print (South East Europe) / Secret to: Embassies / Sofia; S[alisbury]; I[ddesleigh]]

Bismarck's views on Bulgarian Question; his belief that Austria should not go to war with Russia; Germany to attack France if French invade England

Prince Bismarck, who returned the day before yesterday to Berlin, requested me to come to see him this afternoon, and, at the interview which resulted, he spoke to me at length upon the situation in Bulgaria.

He said that the conduct of General Kaulbars[106] was not to be attributed to his personal character, that he was quiet and gentlemanlike in his intercourse with all except the Regents, the members of the Government and their adherents, to whom he had behaved like a ruffian, that this bearing was the result of direct instructions from the Emperor, who regarded the Regency[107] as the legacy of the Prince of Bulgaria to whom His Majesty was still implacably indisposed. General Kaulbars, however, must bear his share of responsibility, for he had made false reports to The Emperor and had misled him. Prince Bismarck said that he had proof of this in an incident with which he had had to deal. General Kaulbars had informed the Emperor that Mr. Thielmann, the German Agent at Sophia, had written to him an insulting letter regarding the firing in the direction of the German agency on the occasion of the elections,[108] Mr. Thielmann was consequently instructed to send a copy of the letter which he had written, and it proved to be one such as

---

[106] Kaulbars was sent as special commissioner to advise the Bulgarian government and represent Russian interests. He arrived at Sofia on 25 September 1886 and was withdrawn – alongside all Russian consular officers in Bulgaria and Eastern Rumelia – on 17 November.

[107] On 7 September 1886, the day that Alexander abdicated as prince (*knyaz*) of Bulgaria, he appointed a regency comprised of three members.

[108] On 11 October, the second day of the elections to the national assembly, peasants from the neighbourhoods of Sofia, incited by the speech of a Russian representative, attempted to obstruct proceedings. Shots were apparently fired from the Russian consulate

one gentleman would write to another, and contained nothing which could give the slightest grounds for the accusation of insolence. Prince Bismarck had therefore instructed the German Ambassador at S[t] Petersburgh[109] to inform M. de Giers that the Russian Agent was a liar. M. de Giers had not dared to communicate this to The Emperor, and the Prince had therefore taken an opportunity to inform the Grand Duke Vladimir, who has recently been here, of the incident, and had begged him to relate it accurately to The Emperor on his return to S[t] Petersburgh.[110]

Prince Bismarck then spoke of the candidature of the Prince of Mingrelia and I said that I was permitted to inform him confidentially and unofficially that Her Majesty's Government were of opinion that it was contrary to the plain intention of the Treaty of Berlin, which excluded members of the Dynasties of the Great Powers of Europe, and that a Prince, who was a vassal of one of them, seemed to be equally objectionable.[111]

Prince Bismarck replied that this objection was too sweeping, that all candidates were either vassals or subjects of one or other of the Great Powers, but, waiving the argument, he reverted to the candidature of the Prince of Mingrelia,[112] and observed that he thought that Russia would be no better off if that Prince were in Bulgaria than she was when Prince Alexander was there, that the Prince of Mingrelia was not a Russian, that he was not likely to entertain strong feelings of gratitude towards the Power which had deprived him of his inheritance, and that his marriage with the elderly daughter of Count Adlerberg[113] showed that his ideas of honour were not high-strung. He would probably begin as Prince Alexander had begun, and, eventually be swayed by the Bulgarian popular current.

Prince Bismarck proceeded to speak about Austria. He said that, as far as he could judge at present, the Emperor of Russia did not intend to occupy Bulgaria, but that, should he change his mind,

after they sought refuge there, which hit the walls of the British and German consular agencies.

[109] Hans Lothar von Schweinitz.

[110] The Grand Duke Vladimir visited Berlin on 30 November 1886 on his way to Weimar.

[111] Niko I Dadiani was the last ruling prince of the Georgian principality of Megrelia which was abolished by Russia and annexed to the latter in 1866. He remained close to the Russian court and in early November 1886 Russia suggested that he be nominated for the election of Prince of Bulgaria. Article 3 of the Treaty of Berlin of 1878, which established Bulgaria as an autonomous principality of the Ottoman Empire, stipulated that no member of the reigning houses of the great European powers should be elected Prince of Bulgaria.

[112] Niko Dadiani.

[113] Maria Alexandrovna.

and were an occupation to take place, Austria would in the Prince's opinion be wrong to oppose it. "At all events", he said, "we should not assist her were she to do so: our relations with Austria do not bind us to that – we wish that she should maintain herself as she is. Her existence is necessary to us for the European Equilibrium. We cannot allow her to disappear or to be essentially weakened. This was my view in 1866,[114] and I carried it against my King, who was of the contrary opinion. But, in the present situation, Austria has placed herself on a new platform. She seems to consider that she must contend against Russia regaining the influence in Bulgaria, contemplated by the Treaty of Berlin. There we cannot follow her. Besides she would be ill-advised in her own interest to do so. She will be much more powerful as an adversary of Russia the day that the occupation takes place. At present Russia can attack her on the coterminous frontier and wars go rapidly. There is now-a-days no question of winter quarters. A fortnights campaign decides the fate of an empire, and Austria is not prepared. We have bad accounts of her organisation, of her cavalry and of her artillery. In these matters she has been the victim of Parliamentary exigencies, seeking retrenchment where expenditure is the patriotic policy. In this respect she resembles England. We do not want her to go to war, because we should be obliged to interfere to prevent her from being essentially weakened. We cannot permit the vacuum in Europe which such an event would create. But the Emperor and I are old and we wish that peace should continue until we go."

My policy with regard to England is the same as it is with regard to Austria. In the case of a war between England and France, if the English Fleet were to be destroyed, and a French invasion of England became imminent, we should at once make war on France, because we could not permit the power of England to be destroyed."

I asked the Prince whether he considered that the reasons which reder [Note in margin: '? render'] it unadvisable for Austria to oppose the occupation of Bulgaria by arms applied equally to England, whether such an event would not open the door for Russia to Constantinople, whenever she chose to take advantage of it? The Prince somewhat evaded the question. He said that he considered it to be of extreme importance to England to gain the confidence of the Sultan[115] and that, by alienating that confidence, Mr Gladstone had done incalculable, perhaps irreparable, harm to his

[114] During the course of and after the Austro-Prussian war.
[115] Abdul Hamid II.

country.[116] He said that he was extremely glad that Sir William White was at Constantinople, because he was a clever man and would do what lay within the means of an Ambassador to bring the Sultan round. I spoke of a Russianised Sultan being a great danger to England. The Prince was of opinion that the Sultan could not go far in this direction. His obsequiousness to Russia even now caused him to be in danger. The native Mussulman feeling was strongly opposed to it, and were he to pursue the policy to extremes he would disappear like Sultan Abdul Aziz.[117]

I should add that when speaking previously of a possible Russian occupation of Bulgaria, Prince Bismarck had said that Austria ought not to interfere, even if Russia went to Constantinople; for that the day Russia effected this, she would be so weakened that Austria would become comparatively powerful.

At the conclusion of the interview, I thanked Prince Bismarck for informing me of his views. He replied, "I have spoken to you frankly, but you must regard what I have said as quite confidential."

FO 64/1155: Edward B. Malet to Her Majesty's Principal Secretary of State for Foreign Affairs,[118] No 13, Berlin, 15 January 1887

[Received 17 January by messenger. For: The Queen / Prince of Wales / Circulate / Eastern Department; S[alisbury]]

Vote on the army bill in the Reichstag; *speeches by Bismarck on his policy with regard to other European Powers*

The Vote on the Army Bill was taken yesterday in the Reichstag, and resulted in the adoption of Freiherr von Stauffenberg's amendment, limiting the duration of the grant to three years instead of seven, as demanded by the Government, by 186 Votes against 154. There were 28 abstentions, the number of deputies present 368.[119]

[116] Bismarck was generally referring to Gladstone's engagement with the 'Eastern Question' before and during his second premiership (1880–1885), and especially with regard to the question of the Ottoman Empire's territorial integrity.

[117] Abdülaziz was deposed by his ministers in May 1876.

[118] The Earl of Iddesleigh died on 12 January 1887; he was succeeded by Lord Salisbury on 14 January, who as well as being foreign secretary also held office as prime minster.

[119] Stauffenberg proposed the amendment to the bill (introduced on 25 November 1886) on 11 January 1887. The original bill was reintroduced after the convocation of the newly elected *Reichstag*; it was passed on 11 March 1887 and enacted in the Imperial Military Law of 11 March 1887. It allocated supplies for a peacetime army of 468,406 men until 31 March 1894.

The speeches made by Prince Bismarck in the course of the debate[120] have reviewed the political situation of Germany with regard to other Powers, but what he has said has thrown no new light upon it, and has had no surprises to those who have lived in the atmosphere of his political views and conversations.

The aim of his policy is peace, in order that there may be time for the complete consolidation of the German Empire. This consolidation is the one object which he has in view, and he considers peace to be the primary condition of its attainment.

He believes, however, that the best way to preserve peace is to be strong enough to inspire other Powers with the conviction that Germany is able not only to hold its own, but to inflict chastisement on any Power that attacks it. He will not be turned aside from maintaining the most friendly relations with Russia, but he has taken the opportunity to deny that there is any truth in recent rumours to the effect that there is a special alliance between the two countries. "I do not know" he said "how Herr Windhorst [*sic*][121] comes to know that Russia is our ally. If he has secret intelligence that Russia wishes to conclude an alliance with us against France, ·I shall be thankful to him to communicate it to me ..."

I have stated my conviction that Russia will not attack us, will not conspire with other Powers, and seeks no alliance against us. But we can reckon on no alliance with her if we should be at war with France. The report is, therefore, erroneous and I am constrained to give it a timely contradiction"[.]

With reference to Austria he dwelt upon the success of his efforts to be on the most friendly terms with her. "In regard to Austria our relations are firmer and more intimate than they ever were, either at the time of the Confederation or in the days of the holy Roman Empire, as all the questions which were the cause of strife for centuries between us have been settled through mutual confidence and good will"[.]

Prince Bismarck's distrust of France is too well known for his statements in support of it to have caused any surprise, and the effect of the vigour of his language in describing his apprehensions seems to have been discounted beforehand, and to have given rise to no feeling of resentment or surprise.

On the whole, the general effect of his speeches has been to tranquillize the public mind with regard to the danger of war.

[120] On 11, 12, and 13 January 1887.

[121] Bismarck made this speech on 11 January and was referring to Windthorst's *Reichstag* speech of the same day.

After the vote was announced, Prince Bismarck read an Imperial message, dissolving the Reichstag, and so ended the beginning of a Parliamentary struggle of which the result cannot at present be foreseen.

FO 64/1155: Edward B. Malet to Marquess of Salisbury, Confidential, No 25, Berlin, 29 January 1887

[Received 31 January by messenger. For: Eastern Department / The Queen / Prince of Wales / Print (S.E. Europe) / Embassies; Qy: War Office / Intelligence Department; S[alisbury]]

Reflections on Bulgarian crisis; Bismarck's views and his policy on this matter; Bismarck's insistence on Septennate for army bill

The sensational reports which have appeared from some time past in the papers, coupled with the taking of measures indicative of insecurity, such as the prohibition[122] to export horses from Germany, have produced a state of apprehension in the public mind which lead me to submit some remarks upon the situation.

For more than a year Europe has been kept in agitation by the Bulgarian Crisis.[123] When it began, Prince Bismarck, though he would not overtly aid the aspirations of the two Bulgarias, was not sorry to see them united. He could watch this union with complacency because it formed part of the Russian programme, and with satisfaction, because he knew that it would be a barrier to Russian aggrandisement. The downfall of Prince Alexander was a blow to his policy, because it forced him in a moment to decide whether he would support Russia or England. Austria did not count. For the sake of German interests Prince Bismarck would have been compelled at any hazards to restrain her, if Great Britain was not prepared to send her fleet into the Black Sea, that is to declare war on Russia. Whether we would do so or not was doubtful. The consequences of our not doing so would have been the defeat of the Austrian forces and a war forced upon Germany, at a tremendous disadvantage, to retrieve the disaster. That, at least, was the view taken here by the authorities acquainted with the military resources of Austria.

---

[122] Imperial decree of 25 January 1887. The reports in question which, in part, were stirred up by Bismarck's *Reichstag* speech of 11 January (see preceding dispatch), referred to the French threat to peace, and in particular to the French war minister's (Georges Boulanger) anti-German policy.

[123] For the Bulgarian crisis see pp. 70–73 and nn. 15 and 25 in Darmstadt section.

Prince Bismarck embraced certainty, and supported, Russia, but his bitterest regret was that Prince Alexander did not defy Russia and say, "J'y suis, j'y reste."[124] [Note in margin (Thomas Sanderson): 'Prince B. showed no signs of wishing or encouraging such a decision']

What was the situation at the moment that the Prince abdicated? The Emperor of Russia had said, "as long as you remain, there can be no issue to the question between Russia and Bulgaria." But it is known that the military Authorities of Russia were against occupation and that the pacific tendencies of the Emperor are extreme. He would have sulked, and the consolidation of the Bulgarias under the Prince would have become an accomplished fact.

Prince Bismarck said to me in the course of a conversation in which he declared that he could not understand why the Prince had abdicated; "it was the moment for a great man."

Meanwhile Prince Bismarck had decided on his own policy. Bulgaria was nothing to Germany. Russia might do with it as she chose. It quickly appeared, however, that the voice of Prince Bismarck was no longer all powerful. Public opinion in Germany blamed him. Notwithstanding his advice to the contrary, Count Kalnoky found that he was compelled to use vigorous language to the Delegations, and the tension which from that moment sprang up between Austria and Russia fortified by Your Lordship's speech at the Mansion House, because it was supposed to be prompted by an understanding between the Austrian and the British Governments, has never been allayed.[125]

Prince Bismarck knows that the real danger of war lies in the East. He is therefore endeavouring to divert the attention of the whole of Europe to the fear of a war between Germany and France. By this means he believes that the Bulgarian question may drop into insignificance. Before the tremendous results which may spring from a war between France and Germany and the efforts which would be made to prevent it, the fate of Bulgaria would pale and no longer trouble the peace of Europe.

He is assured that France will not make war, [Note in margin: 'Mr Waddington's language is to the same effect.' T.H.S. [Thomas Henry Sanderson]] however provocative may be his attitude. He counts upon the alarm and agitation which he intends to excite to

[124] French: 'Here I am, here I remain.'

[125] Malet is referring to a speech that Count Kálnoky, the Austro-Hungarian minister for foreign affairs, made to the Hungarian Delegations at Budapest on 13 November 1886 in which he stated Austria-Hungary's readiness to act in the event of a Russian military occupation of Bulgaria. In his speech at the Lord Mayor's Banquet on 9 November 1886, Salisbury stressed the importance of the Berlin Treaty for Bulgaria's independence and stated that 'Austria's policy will to a great extent govern that of England'.

procure the passing of the Army Bill, and his extraordinary tenacity in insisting on the Septennate is to be ascribed to the one dominant aim of his life, which is to leave the Empire which he has created, safe from all attack and so to ensure to it time, as far as human foresight can, for self-consolidation.[126]

It has been considered that his insistence on the Septennate when the Reichstag was willing to vote the Bill for three years, was a sign of obstinacy arising from the plenitude of success in the course of his great career. This is not so; he knows that with the life of the Emperor the actual order of the state politic in Germany, as it exists at present, closes, and that a new order of things will arise in which the Imperial Government will have the most serious Parliamentary difficulties to face. He regards the efficiency of the Army as indispensable to the safety of the country and he desires to render its dependence on the Parliamentary troubles, which are certain to ensue upon a change of Sovereign, as remote as possible.

The tone of German Officers is, for the moment, exceedingly warlike, but that need give no apprehension. In assuming such a tone they are probably obeying a hint, and the Army is under perfect control; the danger, if there is one, comes from France, but I presume that the reports which Prince Bismarck receives convince him that that Power will not be moved to action by defensive precautions on the part of Germany.

FO 64/1156: Edward B. Malet to Marquess of Salisbury, Confidential, No 90, Berlin, 12 March 1887

[Received 14 March by messenger. For: The Queen / Prince of Wales / Paris; S[alisbury]]

Bismarck's ways and means of manufacturing and moulding public opinion

In my Despatch No 33, Secret of the 1st of February I mentioned what Prince Bismarck said to me with regard to the duty of a statesman to endeavour to create public opinion. The remarks did not seem to me at the time to be particularly apposite to the point he was endeavouring to urge which was the advantage of an alliance between England and Italy,[127] but he laid so much stress upon them that I could not but insert them in their place in recounting the Conversation.

---

[126] For the army bill (Imperial Military Law) see preceding dispatch and n. 119 in this section.

[127] An agreement to maintain the status quo in the Mediterranean was concluded between Britain and Italy – through German mediation – on 12 February 1887.

Looking back at the events of the last few weeks inclines me to think that he was, at that time, engaged, to the fullest extent, in putting in practice what he was inculcating as the duty of the head of a Government. He was in fact leaving no stone unturned in inducing the public to believe that war was imminent, and that the only means to stave it off was to return a majority to the Reichstag in favour of the Septennate.[128] I do not say that this was not his own honest opinion. I would merely call attention to the variety of levers which he used to bring the people of Germany to share his own view and to the marvellous success with which he himself practised the lesson which he preached.

During what may be called his campaign on public opinion, hardly a day passed without some fresh incident occurring to pile up the agony of apprehension, most of them indeed were molehills, but so successfully manipulated as to appear like mountains to the anxious Electors. He said to me that it was the duty of a Minister to colour the Government stream. He was certainly dyeing it with the deepest hues. Nothing was met in Government circles with a sterner rebuke than an insinuation that the war scare was being raised for electioneering purposes, but the calm which has succeeded the elections goes a long way to confirm the faintly uttered suspicion.[129]

Were Prince Bismarck to speak to me again on the subject, he could point triumphantly to what has occurred in this instance as illustrating the possibility and utility for Government purposes of creating public opinion.

FO 64/1156: Edward B. Malet to Marquess of Salisbury, No 118, Berlin, 29 March 1887

[Received 4 April by messenger. For: The Queen (returned from Aix unmarked)[130] / Circulate / Copy to: Rome/ Paris, P.L. [printed letter], 6 April; S[alisbury]]

New Prussian church bill to cease state conflict with Catholic Church; Bismarck's remarks on nature of past conflict and present circumstances as being favourable for peace

In my Despatch N° 117 of the 28th instant I had the honour to submit to Your Lordship a report of the discussions in the Prussian Parliament on the 1st reading of the New Church Bill, the object of which is to terminate the long contest between the Prussian

---

[128] For the army bill (Imperial Military Law) see n. 119 in this section.

[129] Elections to the *Reichstag* were held on 21 February 1887.

[130] Victoria stayed in Aix-les-Bains from 6 to 28 April 1887.

State and the Roman Catholic Hierarchy, and to consolidate peaceful relations between the Governments of Berlin and the Vatican.[131] This Bill has in some quarters been characterized as an inglorious Surrender by Prince Bismarck of principles which he formerly held to be essential, and he is accused of having at last done penance at Canossa[132] in order to secure the assistance of the Vatican in questions of purely internal German Policy.

Prince Bismarck has boldly refuted this charge in the able speech summarized in the report of Parliamentary Proceedings above referred to, and in an article of evidently official inspiration in yesterdays Norddeutsche Allgemeine Zeitung[133] to which are appended extracts from the official correspondence which took place between Berlin and the Vatican in 1871 previous to the commencement of the War waged with the Roman Catholic Hierarchy.

Prince Bismarck's speech and the correspondence quoted, clearly explain the nature and object of that War and of the May laws.

The "Centre",[134] most of whose members owed their election to Clerical influence, had, from the very commencement of the work of consolidating the German Empire, assumed a policy of Obstruction; – as the Chancellor maintains, – with the object of compelling the Imperial Government to interfere actively in defence of the Pope's territorial position at Rome.[135] This obstruction was offered on questions of a purely political interest without reference to Church matters, e.g. the framing of the Imperial Constitution, the Incorporation of Alsace Lorraine, the Polish and Guelph Questions: the Catholic members of the "Centre" on each of these questions taking the side of the anti-national and anti-unionist Malcontents.

Prince Bismarck[136] urged the Vatican to express openly its disapproval of this line of action or, at any rate, to prove that it discountenanced it. Cardinal Antonelli was favorably disposed to listen

[131] The bill which amended the anti-Catholic legislation (May Laws; see n. 17 in Munich section) of 1873, 1874, and 1875, as well as the Third Mitigation Law of 11 July 1883 and the First Peace Law of 24 May 1886, was debated and passed in the Prussian upper house on 23 and 24 March 1887; the chamber of deputies followed suit on 27 April. The Second Peace Law came into effect on 29 April 1887.

[132] Bismarck's speech of 1872, in which he refused to submit to Catholic influence in German affairs and used a reference to Heinrich IV's submission to the pope at Canossa in 1077 as an illustration of secular powers deferring to the Catholic Church, became renowned as the 'we will not go to Canossa' speech.

[133] *Norddeutsche Allgemeine Zeitung*, 27 March 1887.

[134] *Zentrumspartei*.

[135] Malet is referring to the demands for the reestablishment of temporal papal sovereignty following the takeover of the Papal States by the Italian kingdom in 1870.

[136] Bismarck to Tauffkirchen, 17 April 1871.

to this request, but the Catholic Party in Germany eventually prevailed over his influence, sent a Deputation to the Pope, headed by Prince Löwenstein,[137] who finally induced Pope Pius IX to bluntly refuse to interfere in any way with the action of the German Catholics in Parliament.[138]

Hereupon Prince Bismarck instructed the Prussian Chargé d'affaires[139] to warn the Vatican that it must accept the consequences of any severe measures which the Prussian Government might be obliged to take in self protection.

The May Laws, as Prince Bismarck reminds the Parliament and public, were especially described by him at the time as a warlike weapon to be used to obtain an object; and were not a permanent institution fitted for a time of peace.

Pope Pius IX persisted in his hostile attitude, but in 1878 his Successor Pope Leo evinced a more conciliatory disposition, and from that time it had been the Chancellor's desire to facilitate a re-establishment of peaceful relations.

He hoped that peace had now been firmly established. Pope Leo had consented to do what Pope Pius refused, and discountenanced the Anti-national political Agitations of the German Catholics, and the Prussian Government could therefore safely lay aside the weapons which they had used in the war. The Prussian Government had always been desirous of securing to the Roman Catholic Church in Prussia all the rights and privileges to which it attached value, and which were not incompatible with the preservation of any of the essential Sovereign rights of the Prussian Crown.

The present Bill secured all this.

He would hesitate to assert of any peace that it was a permanent one, but he had perfect confidence in the wise and peaceful disposition of the present Pope, and if the peace was at any time broken, they could always take the weapon out of the armoury again.

I have been induced thus shortly to summarize the pith of the Chancellor's explanations, as it seems to me singularly characteristic of the mode in which Prince Bismarck treats political difficulties, and because the effects of the policy he has adopted ?/is [sic] likely to exert an influence beyond the question it has been applied.

---

[137] In June 1871, on the occasion of Pius IX's 25th anniversary as pope (16 June).

[138] Malet is referring to Antonelli's conversation with Tauffkirchen on 23 June 1871.

[139] Bismarck to Tauffkirchen, 22 (telegram) and 30 June 1871.

FO 64/1156: Charles S. Scott to Marquess of Salisbury, Confidential, No 146, Berlin, 20 April 1887

[Received 20 (25) April by messenger. Extends telegram No 22. Print (Western Europe); S[alisbury]]

Various opinions with regard to the impact of German military preparations on relations between France and Germany

In reply to Your Lordships telegram N° 68 of this days date inquiring whether I considered that there was any imminent danger of a rupture between Germany and France, I have the honour to report that in the course of a conversation which I had with Count Bismarck[140] today I mentioned to His Excellency that I had heard that a good deal of uneasiness existed at present at Paris on account of the continued military preparations in Germany. He replied that the uneasiness manifested by the French Government was all fictitious and that their object was to maintain the apprehensions of the people in order to have pretext for their own Armaments. Count Bismarck added that there was not the remotest intention on the part of Germany of attacking France.

In Colonel Swaine's opinion the military preparations that are being made in Germany are of such a nature as to lead to the supposition that a war with Russia is deemed more likely than one with France. The nature of the transport which is being prepared points to its use in Russia rather than in France.

Monsieur Herbette, the French Ambassador, told me today that he had just returned from a visit to Stettin, and that there, war between Germany and Russia was talked of as imminent. He seemed however to have no apprehension of a rupture between Germany and France at present.

FO 64/1156: Charles S. Scott to Marquess of Salisbury, Very Confidential, No 150, Berlin, 23 April 1887

[Received 25 April by messenger. For: The Queen / Prince of Wales / Print (Western Europe) / Embassies / Intelligence Department; 2nd: Confidential to War Office; S[alisbury]]

Franco-German tension; report by Colonel Swaine; supplementary war budget

I have the Honour to enclose, herewith, a confidential report[141] which Colonel Swaine [Note in margin: 'Col. Swaine No. 34 of 20 April

---

[140] Herbert von Bismarck.
[141] Enclosure: confidential report No 34 by Colonel Swaine, Berlin, 20 April 1887.

1887'] has made for Her Majesty's Ambassador[142] of a conversation which he recently had with a high Military Authority here.

In view of the renewal of uneasiness which Lord Lyons reports as existing at Paris in regard to the intentions of Germany, I venture to invite Your Lordship's special attention to the information which Colonel Swaine has elicited from an exceptionally well-informed source.

This information confirms the impression which I have derived from other sources, that Germany has neither the desire nor intention to provoke hostilities in any quarter, but that the uncertainty of the political situation at St Petersburgh, and the effect of this uncertainty on certain political parties at Paris,[143] renders it imperative on the German Government to be prepared for all contingencies, to strengthen good relations with other Powers, and at the same time to show the world that she is in a position to repel attack or resist pressure on her Eastern as well as Western frontier.

It is with this object that her military preparations are being hurried on, – the Supplementary War Budget necessitated by the New Military Septennate has just been published, the amount required, one hundred and seventy two millions of marks, [Note in margin: 172,000,000] which will have to be raised by a further loan, – is larger than the public had expected, and I have little doubt that in order to secure its passing the Reichstag, the dangers of the political situation will be somewhat accentuated in the official and semi-official utterances of the next few weeks, but it would, I think, be a mistake to infer from this that the situation has, at present, become more menacing in any quarter than it was a month ago.[144]

---

[142] Edward Malet.

[143] Scott is referring to the struggle between the Russian foreign minister, Nikolai de Giers, and the conservative publicist Mikhail Katkov for primacy in Russian foreign policy. Katkov's anti-German agitation was paralleled in France by the minister of war, General Boulanger.

[144] The bill was introduced on 22 April and passed by the *Reichstag* on 20 May 1887. For the underlying Imperial Military Act of 11 March 1887 see n. 119 in this section.

FO 64/1156: Charles S. Scott to Marquess of Salisbury, No 157, Berlin, 28 April 1887

[Received 2 May by messenger. Print (Western Europe) / Embassies; S[alisbury]]

Schnæbelé incident politically contained; summary of events and suppositions

The general impression in all well-informed circles here, is that the Schnaebele incident[145] will not be allowed to assume a dangerous Character, but that a settlement satisfactory to the 'amour propre'[146] of both countries will soon be arrived at between the two Governments.

Monsieur Herbette has had several interviews on the subject with Count Bismarck,[147] and has furnished His Excellency with all the documents in support of the French side of the case, which reached him by special Messenger from Paris on Sunday night.

Count Bismarck was good enough to show me yesterday two of these documents – photographic facsimiles of two letters[148] addressed by the German Police Officer, Herr Gautsch to his "Cher Collègue" Monsieur Schnaebele inviting him to meet him on the frontier for the purpose of examining a disputed question in regard to a frontier post, and begging him to come unattended.

Count Bismarck admitted that these letters would at first sight throw a suspicion on the code of honour, regulating international relations between colleagues of the police force, as it looked like very unhandsome treatment of Monsieur Schnaebele by his "cher Collègue" on the German side of the frontier.

His Excellency said that he had, however, pointed out to Monsieur Herbette that the Charge against Monsieur Schnaebele was not one of a common offence, but a very serious criminal charge of high treason.

From other sources I learn that there is good reason to believe that Herr Gautsch acted in perfect good faith, and had no knowledge, when he wrote to his French Colleague, inviting him to meet him, that detectives, acting under secret instructions from the Judge at Strassburg, were lying in wait to arrest the French Commissioner on the first occasion of his crossing over the frontier.

---

[145] Guillaume Schnæbelé, an Alsatian-born French railway police officer, was arrested for crossing the Franco-German border on suspicion of espionage on 20 April 1887. He was subsequently released on 28 April.
[146] French: 'self-respect'.
[147] Herbert von Bismarck.
[148] Dated 13 and 16 April 1887.

The Strassburg Court, set in motion by the High Court of Justice at Leipzig is understood to have most damning proofs of Monsieur Schnaebele's complicity with treasonable intrigues against the safety of the German Empire. German Courts of justice are excessively jealous of any intervention on the part of the Government with the course of justice in it's earlier stages, hence possibly the delay in furnishing the French Government with the full dossier of the preliminary enquiry into the circumstances attending the arrest, which seems clearly to have taken place on German Soil, although it has been asserted by some that, during the struggle which ensued, the French Commissioner at one time dragged part of his person across the frontier line into French territory.

The general impression however seems to be that Monsieur Schnaebele will be eventually set at liberty, if it is shown that he was treacherously induced to cross the frontier by an invitation to confer on frontier questions with the German official.

There seems to be no ground whatever for suspecting the German Government of being privy to Monsieur Schnaebele's arrest by means of a stratagem, the discredit of which, if proved, would only attach to the subordinates of the police court charged with the arrest.

FO 64/1157: Edward B. Malet to Marquess of Salisbury, Secret, No 192, Berlin, 25 May 1887

[Received 30 May by messenger. For: The Queen; S[alisbury]]

Bismarck's concerns over ill health of crown prince

I have reported in my Despatch N° 191 of today, that Prince Bismarck called upon me yesterday to present his congratulations on the occasion of the Queen's birthday. His principal subject of conversation was the illness of the Crown Prince,[149] which, he said, caused him deep anxiety, and had prevented him from sleeping at night. He had learnt that the Physicians, who attended His Imperial Highness, prepared to perform an operation of a very serious nature, for the purpose of extracting a growth which was forming itself in his throat, and Prince Bismarck had felt that such an operation ought not to be performed without the sanction of the Emperor, and he was also of opinion that His Imperial Highness should himself be made acquainted with the nature of the operation, to which it was

---

[149] Friedrich Wilhelm had cancer of the larynx. The operation (thyrotomy) was originally scheduled for 21 May, subsequently postponed and ultimately cancelled.

proposed to subject him. He had found it necessary to remind the Physicians that they were dealing with the Heir to the Throne, and that his life was too precious to be considered like that of an ordinary man. Prince Bismarck showed much emotion in speaking on the subject to me. It is now hoped that the operation may prove to be unnecessary and in any case no precaution which art or form can suggest will be neglected.

FO 64/1157: Edward B. Malet to Marquess of Salisbury, No 218, Berlin, 12 June 1887

[Received 14 June by post. For: The Queen / Prince of Wales; S[alisbury]]

Long and friendly article in Deutsche Allgemeine Zeitung *on Queen Victoria's Golden Jubilee; general praise for Britain and her policies*

The Semi-official Nord Deutsche Allgemeine Zeitung publishes this morning a long leading article couched in the most friendly tone on the approaching Jubilee of Her Majesty The Queen.[150]

The article commences by saying:

"Within the next few days a festival will be celebrated in a country bound by ties of friendship to our fatherland, which having regard to the term of human life must be acknowledged an uncommon one, but which on other grounds is sure of the lively sympathy of Germany. Our readers will divine that we refer to the 50th Jubilee anniversary of the reign of the Queen of England and will recognize from the fact that His Imperial and Royal Highness the Crown Prince and His Royal Highness Prince William are starting today for London to take part in it, how essential our Ruling house esteems it that the German Empire should be most worthily represented on this festal occasion. It is not only the many ties of blood which have long united the two monarchies, but in a no less degree the kindred origin of the two nations and their common work in the cause of culture and civilisation which will be recognised by the world as finding significant record in the visit above referred to."

The article then goes on to resume the efforts of the last fifty years in England towards internal progress and reform and the energy displayed in remedying social deformities, and expresses the hope that the present crisis in Parliamentary development[151] will be brought to as satisfactory an issue. It glances rapidly over the history of

---

[150] The 50th anniversary of Victoria's accession as queen was on 20 June 1887.

[151] The *Norddeutsche Allgemeine Zeitung* was alluding to the unresolved question of 'Home Rule' after the rejection of the Government of Ireland Bill in 1886.

Englands more important colonies and concludes that Her Majesty's reign has witnessed the firm establishment of our colonial empire under a high principled administration. The article concludes with these words.

"We can only hope that the bond, founded on the mutual confidence of the two Governments in one another, which derives yet stronger support from the union of the Princess Royal of England[152] with the Prussian Prince Frederick William, will be upheld in the future, and we take this opportunity of expressing the feelings of sympathy which the German nation offers especially at this moment to the British Empire, and the liberal recognition which we pay to the achievements of the English national spirit, by wishing the Royal Lady who rules over Great Britain many more years to dispense the blessings of her reign to her people.["]

FO 64/1158: Charles S. Scott to Marquess of Salisbury, No 261, Berlin, 9 July 1887

[Received 11 July by messenger. For: The Queen / Prince of Wales; Qy: Print (Western Europe) / Embassies / Intelligence Department; S[alisbury], 13 July]

Treason trial at Leipzig; feelings among German press and public towards France

I have the honour to transmit herewith a short summary by M[r] Lister of the Newspaper Reports of a further remarkable treason trial which has been taking place this week before the High Court of Leipzig.[153] This Summary gives very fully the remarks of the Public Prosecutor[154] when stating the case for the Crown, and these will be found to constitute a very open and serious charge against the French Government.

This trial has a special interest, as being intimately connected with the recent arrest of the French Commissaire de Police, Schnaebele.[155]

Although, as Your Lordship has already learnt from the reports of the Military Attaché to Her Majesty's Embassy, Colonel Swaine, the German War Office has for many months past been in possession of facts clearly showing that a wholesale system of 'Spionage' has for some years been going on in the Western frontier of France, under

---

[152] Victoria.
[153] The trial against three citizens from Alsace-Lorraine took place from 4 to 8 July. Two defendants, Tobias Klein and Martin Grabert, were sentenced to imprisonment for five and six years respectively; the third was acquitted. Enclosure: memorandum on treason trials at Leipzig, 9 July 1887.
[154] Hermann Tessendorf.
[155] For the Schnæbelé incident see pp. 83–84.

the direction of the French War Office, the General public was, until very lately, not aware of the manner in which this system was being carried on, or of the extent of the danger to which the Empire was exposed.

There were consequently to be found, even in Germany, a few persons and newspapers to maintain that the German Government had attached unnecessary importance to rumours of hostile designs on the part of General Boulanger, and to the agitations of the French patriotic League.

The Revelations made in the Course of this trial, appear to have completely dissipated these doubts, and judging from the present tone of the German press of all shades and colours it would be difficult to exaggerate the prevalent feeling of general irritation and indignation directed not so much against the Alsatian spies who have fallen into the clutch of German justice, but against the French Government, who instigated and employed them.

It is argued that most military Governments have their Intelligence Departments, and are often obliged to have recourse to Secret sources of information, but that the system which the French Government has been employing – using officials of the War office, and of the Ministry of the Interior (such as the frontier police who are entitled to claim special confidence from the neighbouring state) to seduce German subjects from their allegiance, and to employ them as paid spies against their country is unparalleled in the history of the relations between two States in time of peace.

In alluding to this trial yesterday, Count Bismarck[156] spoke very strongly, and very much in the above sense; – he said that Monsieur Herbette had naturally not ventured to allude to the subject in conversation with him and he could not conceive how the French Government could justify their action even in their own eyes.

His Excellency said that the German Government had been forced to court the utmost publicity for the Leipzig trials, by the tone and temper of the French press and public when commenting on the Schnaebele incident and the trial of the Members of the Ligue Patriotique.[157]

Not only in the French press, but in other quarters unfriendly to Germany, efforts have been persistently made to represent Germany as endeavouring to provoke a quarrel with France, and irritating her by unnecessarily persecuting French sympathizers in

---

[156] Herbert von Bismarck.
[157] The trial against members of the *Ligue Patriotique* (a nationalist league founded in 1882) took place from 13 to 18 June at Leipzig and led to the conviction of four of the eight defendants (all from Alsace Lorraine).

Alsace Lorraine; it was therefore absolutely necessary to show the world at large the extent of the danger to which the German Empire had been exposed for some time past, and the manner in which the French Government employed their frontier officials in time of peace.

The feelings of the German public towards France have not been improved by hearing of the proposals in the French Chamber to adopt so-called measures of retaliation against German residents in France and the Norddeutsche Allgemeine Zeitung commenting this week on the proposal to levy a tax in lieu of Military Service on foreigners in France, not only contests to the legality of such a measure, but utters a distinct warning that Germany may at last lose patience, and be obliged to recur to severe measures of retaliation against French subjects especially in Alsace Lorraine.[158]

Count Bismarck, with reference to this subject told me that the Commercial Treaty Engagements of Frankfort[159] clearly prevented the French Government from levying any tax from Germans not similarly imposed on French subjects.

I have thought it my duty to report the state of feeling produced here by the trial of Klein and his associates – taken together with the feeling which the Leipzig trials appear to have evoked in France, the situation would, under ordinary circumstances, appear so serious as to justify alarm for the relations between the two Countries, but at present no apprehension of serious consequences appears to be entertained here.

The whole German press appears to be unanimous in regard to the necessity of treating the Anti-German outbursts of the French Chamber and public with the same calm indifference as the German Foreign office.

As one German Newspaper puts it, the only guarantee that we possess for the preservation of peace between the two countries is the firm conviction on both sides that a fresh appeal to arms could now only terminate in the complete extinction of one or other of the two combatants, but this guarantee is a very solid one, and will doubtless have the desired effect.

---

[158] The tax on foreign residents in France – on which *the Norddeutsche Allgemeine Zeitung* commented on 6 July – was discussed in the committee of the French chamber of deputies. It was proposed that foreigners pay a tax comparable to the fee for exemption from military service for French citizens.

[159] Bismarck was referring to Article 11 of the Treaty of Frankfurt of 10 May 1871.

FO 64/1158: Charles S. Scott to Marquess of Salisbury, Confidential, No 273, Berlin, 16 July 1887

[Received 18 July by messenger. Print (Western Europe). For: The Queen / Prince of Wales / Mr W.H. Smith / Embassies / Eastern Department (last paragraph); S[alisbury], 18 July]

Boulanger's noisy departure from Paris increases public anxiety about Franco-German relations; German political attention focused on France at expense of Eastern Europe

The Paris telegrams of yesterday morning reporting that the Fête of the 14th had passed off without serious disturbance or incident have caused a very general feeling of relief here, for it is impossible to disguise the fact that the past week at Berlin has been one of very grave anxiety and suspense.

As I had the honour to report in my Confidential Despatch N° 261 of the 9th instant, I understood that, notwithstanding the bitter feelings aroused in both countries by the late Leipzig trials,[160] serious apprehensions of immediate danger were not entertained here, as the recognized gravity of the situation was in itself a guarantee that no rash step would be taken on either side.

When, however, the news of the disorderly scene at General Boulanger's departure from Paris, and of the inaction or impotence of the French authorities on that occasion reached Berlin, a great change took place in public feeling, and the possibly exaggerated reports of the occurrences sent to the local press by their Paris Correspondents, caused very real alarm both on the Berlin exchange and among the General public, and this alarm was not allayed by the appearance of warnings of danger in organs generally credited with official inspiration, such as the Norddeutsche Allgemeine Zeitung, Post and other papers.[161]

Count Berchem told me yesterday that the German Foreign Office had been so absorbed by the gravity of the situation in France, that he had paid but little attention to what was going on in the East of Europe: he felt however that as the French Government had shown their ability to cope with the party of disorder on the 14th, and had gained a decided victory over the Radical Section of the Chamber, serious apprehension might be dismissed for the present.[162] He

---

[160] See the preceding dispatch.

[161] Boulanger who, to the embarrassment of the French government had polled 100,000 votes in the Seine by-election despite not being a candidate, was appointed commander of an army corps in Clermont-Ferrand (on 28 June). About 10,000 of his supporters tried to prevent the departure of his train from Gare de Lyon on 8 July.

[162] Berchem was referring to the preventive measures which had been taken against demonstrations in support of Boulanger on 14 July, and the failed interpellation regarding

admitted, however, that the situation, after the demonstration at the Lyons railway station, had been very alarming.

It was, he said, just possible that the French Government may have acted wisely in allowing the outburst to waste it's force on this occasion, instead of at the Military Review, where the consequences might have been more serious, and, in fact, it seemed as if the Boulanger party had lost instead of gaining ground by their demonstration.

'At all events', he added, 'let us hope that things will remain quiet at least till the Autumn.'

I may add that among the reports from Paris, which caused most alarm, was one stating, on what professed to be high authority that Panslavist agents had been the chief instigators of the Boulanger demonstration, and that their object was to provoke a war between France and Germany, as Russia was only waiting to move in the East, until Germany was seriously occupied in the West of Europe.

FO 64/1158: Charles S. Scott to Marquess of Salisbury, No 298, Berlin, 6 August 1887

[Received 8 August by messenger. Copy. Qy: 'Admiralty for observations'; Adm [iralty], 10 August; S[alisbury], 8 August]

Difficulties in obtaining information about German naval manoeuvres near Danzig

In compliance with the instructions of Your Lordship's Despatch No: 339 of the 18th ultimo, I have been endeavouring to obtain as much information as possible with regard to the German Naval Manoeuvres now going on in the Baltic off the Coast of Dantzig.[163] I have also instructed Mr Consul Hunt at Königsberg, whose Consular District includes Dantzig, to supply every information in his power, and I shall eventually have the honour to report as fully as I can to Your Lordship.

In the meantime, I would venture to point out to Your Lordship the difficulty which Mr Hunt and I experience in carrying out Your Lordship's instructions.

The German Admiralty are, I understand, desirous that the greatest part of these naval manoeuvres, and probably that very part, which would be most interesting to Her Majesty's Admiralty, should be kept secret from Foreign Powers, and I presume that Your

the government's general attitude and its position towards the royalist and clerical movements on 11 July 1887.

[163] Naval manoeuvres in the Baltic took place until mid September.

Lordship would not wish Her Majesty's diplomatic and Consular officers in Germany to expose themselves to the charge of employing secret means to obtain the desired information.

The British Vice-Consul at Dantzig, Mr Durège, although I believe recently naturalized as a British Subject, is a German by origin, and for other reasons I should doubt the propriety of entrusting to him the duty of collecting the information in question.

Königsberg being at a considerable distance from the scene of them, Mr Hunt does not seem to think that it will be possible for him to supply much valuable information to the Admiralty.

I therefore fear that my Report will have to be confined to the reports of the Manoeuvres which are given in the local press and to any information which I may be able to pick up from private friends, eyewitnesses of the manoeuvres from the shore.

FO 64/1159: Charles S. Scott to Marquess of Salisbury, No 360, Secret, Berlin, 30 September 1887

[Received 3 October by messenger. For: The Queen; Qy: Print (Western Europe); Secret to: Embassies, P.L. [printed letter], 8 October / War Office / Intelligence Department; Prince of Wales; S[alisbury], 6 October 1887]

Franco-German tension increased by border incidents; military attaché's concerns about possible conflict; diplomatic view of continued peace

I have the honour to forward herewith to Your Lordship a Secret Memorandum referring to the dangers of a possible conflict between Germany and France, which has been submitted to me by Colonel Swaine, Military Attaché to Her Majesty's Embassy, in continuation of the information forwarded by Sir E. Malet in His Excellency's despatch number 328 of the 3rd instant.[164]

Colonel Swaine, as Your Lordship will perceive, takes a rather alarming view of the present situation in the West, and indicates certain military preparations and strategical considerations which give colour to a surmise that the German Military Authorities would prefer that a war with France, if inevitable, should be brought about in the coming winter.

This military view of the situation is one which should certainly not be lost sight of, but at the same time I understand that in the highest

---

[164] Swaine's memorandum of 3 September 1887, enclosed in Malet's No 328, dealt with the German War Office's plans to order 1,000 large huts which would provide accommodation for an additional 50,000 men. According to Swaine's secret memorandum of 26 September (enclosure to No 360) this number was raised to 2,000 huts.

diplomatic and political quarters here a much more sanguine view of the prospects of peace is generally entertained.

It is admitted that the recurrence of irritating frontier incidents,[165] and the ferment which these have naturally provoked in the minds of the populations on both sides of the frontier, have made the situation somewhat a critical one, and that the maintenance of peace is at the mercy of any untoward event, but fresh confidence has been inspired here by the more moderate views prevailing in the present French Cabinet and by the repeated assurances of the German Foreign Office that no effort will be spared to avoid wounding French susceptibilities, and that it is not only the desire but the interest of Germany to refrain from giving the slightest provocation to France.

On the other hand, if the French Government were induced by overweening confidence in the success of their late experiment at mobilization,[166] to take any action on the frontier such as Colonel Swaine has indicated and a rumour of such an intention has, I believe, already reached the German Foreign Office – there can be no doubt but that it would be promptly met by some German counter move, and the dangers of the situation would be greatly increased. Moreover, if it was clearly established here that a war with France was inevitable and impending in a near future, the general consensus of opinion is that even the ardent desire of the Emperor and Prince Bismarck for the maintenance of peace would give way to the general desire to secure that the conflict should take place under the most favourable conditions possible to Germany.

While venturing to submit to Your Lordship the impression which I find prevalent in diplomatic quarters here on the subject touched on in Colonel Swaine's Memorandum, I may mention the fact that the Austrian Chargé d'Affaires[167] told me a few days ago in confidence that he had observed in the last despatches from the Austrian Ambassador at St Petersburg which had passed through his hands on their way to Vienna, that Count Volkenstein [sic] had reported a conversation with Monsieur de Giers, in which the latter laid stress on the greater dangers to peace in the West of Europe, and, had observed that it might be impossible for the Emperor

---

[165] A border incident occurred near Raon-sur-Plaine on 24 September 1887 when a German soldier fired at a French hunting party; a servant was killed and an officer severely wounded. See also pp. 83–84 and 86–88.

[166] Scott is referring to the test mobilization of the Seventeenth Army Corps, which was conducted in Toulouse on 1 September 1887.

[167] Arthur Ritter von zu Eissenstein-Chotta.

and himself to withstand a popular cry for action by Russia, when the inevitable and impending conflict between Germany and France broke out. I observe that Sir R. Morier reports that Monsieur de Giers has held very similar language to him, and it is probable that Monsieur de Giers has derived his apprehensions from military information received from Berlin similar to that supplied by Colonel Swaine.

FO 64/1159: Edward B. Malet to Marquess of Salisbury, Confidential, No 405, Berlin, 29 October 1887

[Received 21 October by messenger. For: The Queen / Prince of Wales / Confidential to Embassies in M.S.; S[alisbury], 30 October]

Deterioration in relations between Germany and Russia; tsar's probable visit to the emperor

I enquired of Count Bismarck[168] yesterday whether there was now reason, to suppose that the Emperor of Russia would visit the Emperor of Germany. His Excellency replied that no communication on the subject had, as yet, reached the German Court, but that it looked, at present, as if the Czar would be compelled to go back to Russia through Germany and that in that case it was almost natural that His Majesty should pay a visit to the German Emperor; indeed it was difficult to arrange the journey with the necessary comfort without the Imperial train passing through Berlin.[169]

According to the latest advices the Czar, he said, would not leave Copenhagen before the 16th of November.

I gather that such a visit would be regarded rather as an embarrassment than as a satisfaction, but that it is looked upon now as almost unavoidable unless the Czar should himself take the measles which would give His Majesty a valid excuse for not coming to see the Emperor of Germany although passing through his dominions.

The general relations between Germany and Russia grow less and less cordial, and it is not desired here that the effect produced by the alliance between Germany and Italy should be in any way diminished.

---

[168] Herbert von Bismarck.

[169] Alexander III had been staying in Denmark since 26 August. On his return journey to Russia he visited Berlin, on 18 November 1887.

FO 64/1160: Edward B. Malet to Marquess of Salisbury, Very Confidential, No 442, Berlin, 19 November 1887

[Received 21 August by messenger. For: The Queen / Prince of Wales / Cabinet / Copies to: Embassies (M.S.); S[alisbury], 22 August]

Count Bismarck's conversation with General Čerevin about European uneasiness at Russia risking European peace; no secret alliance between the two countries

Count Bismarck informed me today that the Chancellor[170] had had a long interview with the Emperor of Russia yesterday and that he, Count Bismarck, had spoken at length on the general situation to General Tcherévin, who was in attendance on the Emperor, and was one of the few people who enjoyed His Majesty's Confidence, and was in a position to tell His Majesty the truth.[171]

Count Bismarck said that he used to him the same language which he had used to Count Shouvaloff,[172] as related in my Despatch No: 414, of the 5th instant, and had gone on to say that the uneasiness at present felt throughout Europe with regard to the future was directly attributable to Russia, and that it lay with Russia to appease it. The French, he said, were only courageous because they believed that they had Russia at their back. The "Revanche"[173] was a mere balloon inflated by Russian Gas. If Russia allowed it to be known that she had no intention of coming to the assistance of France, if she would withdraw her troops from her Western Frontier, if the Emperor would forbid the Russian press to indulge in calumnies against foreign nations, all insecurity would instantly pass away and Europe would be able to breathe; Commerce would progress and prosperity return.

The alliances which had been formed in Central Europe were only designed to preserve peace: there was not a Power in Europe about whose intention to maintain peace, a doubt could be entertained except Russia and France, and France, if she no longer had hope of Russian aid, would be completely powerless. Treaties prevented her from attacking Germany, Austria or Italy without engaging all three.[174] England was equally safe from her because Germany could not permit the diminution of her power.

---

[170] Otto von Bismarck.

[171] Alexander III visited Berlin on 18 November 1887.

[172] In his conversation of 1 November 1887.

[173] French: 'revenge'.

[174] Herbert von Bismarck was referring to the Triple Alliance between Germany, Austria-Hungary and Italy of 1882 (renewed in February 1887). It pledged Austro-German support for Italy in the case of an attack by France.

Russia had at present forfeited the confidence of Germany – for a hundred years the two Countries had been in friendly alliance, but of late Russia had thrown all these pleasant traditions to the winds, had only sought to vilify her and misinterpret her motives.

The result was a drawing together of the other Powers, who no longer felt confidence in Russia's policy, and it was only by a complete change of front on the part of Russia, that confidence could be restored.

Count Bismarck said to me that he was able to speak thus frankly to General Tcherévin because he had known him very intimately before in Russia.[175]

The General had listened with attention, and had promised to use such influence as he possessed with the Czar in the direction indicated.

Count Bismarck said that the Chancellor had spoken in the same sense to the Czar, though, perhaps, not with the same bluntness and want of form, and that His Majesty had given him the most pacific assurances as to the future, so far as regarded Russia – but Count Bismarck remarked that time only could show what these assurances were worth, and he recalled the saying that the road from the Caspian to Merv was paved with Russian assurances.

He said finally that he wished to give Your Lordship the assurance through me that no understanding, agreement or arrangement of any kind had been come to on this occasion, and he summed up by saying that not withstanding all that Prince Bismarck had urged and all that the Emperor had replied, the feeling of confidence in the future which had been destroyed by Russian action was not in any particular degree restored by the Imperial Visit, although, as between the two Sovereigns, it has been most cordial and affectionate.

FO 64/1186: Edward B. Malet to Marquess of Salisbury, No 86, Berlin, 15 March 1888

[Received 19 March by messenger. For: The Queen / Prince of Wales / Circulate; S [alisbury], 10 March]

Friedrich III's imperial rescript and address to the people; analysis of press responses – generally very favourable

In my despatches Nos 22 and 23 Treaty of the 13th instant, I had the honour to transmit to Your Lordship copies and translations of The

---

[175] Herbert von Bismarck – while retaining his post as first secretary in London – was attached to the embassy at St Petersburg from January to May 1884.

Emperor Frederick's address to his people, and of the Imperial Rescript addressed to the Chancellor.[176] These documents, and more especially the latter which is fuller in detail, and which I was informed by Prince Bismarck himself was entirely composed by the hand of His Majesty, have evoked expressions of the most lively satisfaction from the Press of all shades of opinion. Journals of the most opposite tendencies have joined hands in approving them, and the chorus of appreciation is not merely such as might naturally be prompted by consideration for the trying position of the new Sovereign, but bears the stamp of genuine sincerity.

The extreme Conservative "Deutsche Tageblatt" calls the address a most attractive one, calculated to win confidence, and to reach the hearts and sympathies of the Prussian nation and of the whole of Germany no less. The United German nation will respond with gratitude and loyal devotion to the address of the heir of The Emperor William[.] Especial satisfaction is expressed at the confidence reposed by His Majesty in the Imperial Chancellor, a confidence which indicates the lines his policy will follow.

Similarly the "Conservative Correspondenz" welcomes the assurance given that the Imperial Government will continue to work in the lines in which the Prussian State has been developed. It dwells on the Conciliatory attitude adopted towards the various shades of religious thought, and notices with satisfaction the encouragement promised to Art and Science.

The "National Zeitung", a journal of liberalist tendency, and generally considered to represent the views of the financial party, says that the two documents will make a deep impression throughout Germany, and convince the world that The Emperor William has been succeeded by a Prince who looks upon it as his first duty to maintain peace and prosper the arts of Peace. The substance of the two documents may be thus summed up, "First and foremost The Emperor Frederick's programme of peace is animated with a genuine National spirit; it is loyally constitutional; it contemplates no rupture with the former internal policy, but nevertheless its' utterances with regard to internal affairs are characterized by a distinct individuality." Not even The Emperor William could have insisted more imperatively than is here done in the necessity of keeping the defensive forces of the Empire up to their utmost strength. The paragraph in which The Emperor declares he will maintain Universal Tolerance in matters of religion was evidently, the Journal continues,

---

[176] The address and the rescript to Otto von Bismarck are dated 12 March 1888; Wilhelm I died on 9 March.

written "con amore"[177] and while promising peace to the Catholic
Church it administers an implied rebuff to the militant protestants
of the school of Herr Stöcker. On points of social, financial and
administrative policy, the two documents point to a continuance of
tried methods, while they discountenance an undue interference of
Government in coping with all social ills. The Programme is a thoroughly moderate one. Anyone who imagined that the Emperor
Frederick intended to introduce a system of Government by
Parliament will realize his mistake.

The "Börsen Courier" points out that the Rescript Contains a
warning against legislative overproduction, and welcomes the principle of religious toleration upheld.

The "Germania", the organ of the Catholic Party, expresses itself
in words of warm appreciation, and finds the general constitutional
tendency of these utterances best characterized by the clause, requiring a loyal respect for the Rights of the Emperor from all those concerned, in return for the Emperor's guarantee that the rights of the
Federal Governments and those of the Reichstag shall be loyally
respected by His Majesty.

The semi-official North German Gazette[178] has hitherto confined
itself to collecting the favourable notices published in the contemporary press; but the inspired "Post" and "Cologne Gazette"[179] have
both recorded their sincere approval; while the "Freisinnige
Zeitung" the journal of the radical party,[180] founded by their leader
Herr Richter, says that these two state papers are sure to awake a
loyal echo in the German Nation: the Paragraph referred to above
by the "Germania", dealing with the mutual confidence which
The Emperor and the Federal Governments as well as the
Reichstag must repose in one another's loyal observance of the rights
of Each, can leave no room for dictatorial ambition, and the promise
of absolute religious tolerance is no less satisfactory, it is no party programme and all honest efforts, from every point of view, on behalf of
the Fatherland, may hope to win His Majesty's appreciation.

The opinions of the provincial papers, as far as they have yet come
in, are in a similar key. The "Hannoversche Courier" rejoices in the
fact that The Emperor Frederick will have at His side His Father's
faithful Councillor, Prince Bismarck. From Hamburg, from Stettin,
from Magdeburg and from the Rhine Provinces, the most appreciative notices are quoted in the North German Gazette, and generally

[177] Italian: 'with love'.
[178] *Norddeutsche Allgemeine Zeitung.*
[179] *Kölnische Zeitung.*
[180] *Deutsche Freisinnige Partei* (see n. 3 in this section).

the two first documents which The German Emperor has published to His people have evoked a chorus of approval from the organs of all opinions which is a good augury for the New Reign.

FO 64/1186: Edward B. Malet to Marquess of Salisbury, Confidential, No 101, Berlin, 6 April 1888

[Received 9 April by messenger. For: The Queen / Circulate / Prince of Wales; S [alisbury], 11 April]

Crown prince's speech at a dinner to mark Bismarck's birthday has aroused much public comment

At a banquet which took place at the Chancellor's residence on the occasion of his birthday on the first instant, His Royal And Imperial Highness The Crown Prince[181] proposed the toast of the evening in a brief speech which has excited considerable comment here. The speech, as it first appeared in the papers here, contained nothing but a metaphor, in which the nation was compared to a regiment, whose commander had fallen, leading the attack. "The next officer", the Prince continued, according to the report first published, "lies severely wounded. In this critical moment forty six millions of loyal Germans turn their eyes to the colours and to their bearer, as to the one on whom all depends. The bearer of this banner is the Prince, our great Chancellor. Let him lead the way, we will follow him. Long live the Chancellor."

This somewhat slighting notice, the only one, as the speech was first reported, of the reigning Emperor, as "the second officer lying severely wounded" gave rise in many quarters to the most lively criticism, and it was soon discernible that these criticisms had reached official ears by the appearance of a paragraph in the Cologne Gazette, stating that the speech had been submitted to and been approved by His Majesty.

This morning, however, the semi-official "Norddeutsche Allgemeine Zeitung" gives as the actual text a somewhat different version of the speech, with a view, it says, to correcting various inaccuracies and omissions in previous reports.

I have the honour to transmit copy and translation[182] of the text of the speech as given in this morning's North German Gazette. Your Lordship will observe that this version opens with expressions of loyalty and devotion to the Emperor, who in the metaphor of the battle,

---

[181] Wilhelm.

[182] Enclosures: extract (untitled) from *Norddeutsche Allgemeine Zeitung* and translation, 6 April 1888.

is described as, though wounded, still bravely riding on. It concludes as follows:

"Long may you (the Chancellor) be spared us, that is our heartfelt wish, to hold on high the Imperial banner, at the side of our beloved Emperor – God bless and guard both Him and you."

FO 64/1186: Edward B. Malet to Marquess of Salisbury, No 117, Berlin, 14 April 1888

[Received 23 April by messenger. Qy: Direct Sir E. Malet to thank German government / Enclosure to War Office and inform[183]; S[alisbury], 23 April; Drafts Sir E. Malet & War Office, 26 April]

Press opinions on chancellor crisis; press notification that Queen Victoria supports Bismarck's views of the inappropriate union between Princess Viktoria of Prussia and the former Prince of Bulgaria

The political storm which is termed by the Press "The Chancellor-crisis" has filled the newspapers during the week and has dealt with by them according to their respective political leanings without much regard to fact in any quarter. What is termed the inspired Press has taken side with the Chancellor while the opposition sheets blame him and ask for his retirement.

It seems to be generally agreed that the conflict has passed out of it's acute phase, and that the project of marrying Princess Victoria of Prussia to Prince Alexander of Battenberg has been either abandoned or postponed.[184]

On the whole I am inclined to think that the Chancellor's reputation has been tarnished by the manner in which he has conducted the campaign or at all events has allowed the battle to be fought. It is well known that the newspapers which support the Government are so far practically under control that when they take a line, they do so from official inspiration. These newspapers have teemed with paragraphs indirectly attacking The Emperor and dragging in the name of The Queen.

---

[183] No enclosure in FO 64/1186.

[184] Princess Viktoria and Alexander of Bulgaria became engaged in 1883. Despite dynastic and diplomatic objections concerning German relations with Russia, the marriage plan was renewed after Alexander's abdication as Prince of Bulgaria, in 1886, and again after the accession of Friedrich III. The matter was brought to public attention in April 1888 by newspaper articles which were largely directed against the German Empress, Victoria, who supported the marriage. The *Kölnische Zeitung* of 5 April, on the other hand, reported of rumours of Bismarck's resignation.

Prince Bismarck must look for approval for this method of warfare to those who are compelled to support him from interested motives, for none who are chivalrous or loyal can uphold it. I am glad to say that a contradiction of the rumour that The Queen advises the Marriage, is now going the round of the Press. It is much to be regretted that Her Majesty's name should ever have been mentioned in the matter, but it was shameful that, without a shadow of foundation, a course of action should be ascribed to Her Majesty which might have envenomed public feeling against Her on the Eve of Her Majesty's projected visit to Berlin.[185]

The following appears in this morning's edition of the National Gazette:[186]

"The Berlin correspondent of the Press [sic] Correspondence[187] writes as follows: Queen Victoria will come at the end of this month to Berlin. We are assured by well informed persons that, in opposition to the view generally propagated, The Queen of England is entirely on the side of the Imperial Chancellor in the question of the opportuneness of a marriage between Her Grandchild and the former Prince of Bulgaria, and fully realizes the force of the objections which are raised against this marriage from a political point of view! We reproduce this communication, the correctness of which is difficult to control, because it is clearly being spread intentionally, and has found its way into a great number of newspapers".

FO 64/1186: Edward B. Malet to Marquess of Salisbury, No 124, Berlin, 28 April 1888

[Received 30 April by messenger. For: The Queen / Prince of Wales / Circulate; S[alisbury], 1 May]

Success of Queen's visit to Berlin; Battenberg affair

There is no doubt that The Queen's visit to Berlin has been a political success.[188]

The circumstances, under which Her Majesty's journey was undertaken, had induced a vague apprehension that it might be

---

[185] Queen Victoria was expected to visit Berlin on her return journey from Italy, and did so from 24 to 26 April 1888.

[186] *National-Zeitung*, 14 April 1888.

[187] *Politische Korrespondenz* (semi-official news agency from Vienna). The name of the correspondent is not traceable.

[188] Victoria visited Berlin from 24 to 26 April 1888.

more prudent for Her Majesty not to come. Acting on a complete misapprehension with regard to the attitude of Her Majesty in connection with an anticipated betrothal of Princess Victoria of Prussia to Prince Alexander of Battenberg, the portion of the press which is supposed to write in accordance with inspiration from the Government had denounced foreign influence in the internal affairs of Germany and although the fundamental Error of the argument had been almost officially exposed, the flood of insolent writing which had been let loose did not quickly subside, and it was feared that the greeting which might await Her Majesty on arrival would not be cordial and that, on this account, the feeling between England and Germany already somewhat estranged through misrepresentations of the Press might be further embittered.[189] It is therefore with no common degree of satisfaction that I am able to record that the exact reverse has taken place. The breach, such as it was, has been closed not widened. The hearty cheers with which Her Majesty was greeted by dense crowds during her drive through Berlin, proved how little effect the venom of the Press had upon the people, and the general feeling with regard to the result of the visit is that it has done great and, it is to be hoped, lasting good.

I may say that this view is shared by many with whom I have spoken, of whom it cannot be said that their opinion is the result of the wish being father to the thought.

It is believed that the interchange of personal communication of The Queen with The Empress Augusta, The Crown Prince,[190] and Prince Bismarck, has been of the highest value in freely brushing away industriously woven cobwebs, and the spiders, of which unfortunately there are too many, have had to retire to their holes.

Prince Bismarck has openly expressed the great satisfaction which he derived from his Conversation[191] with The Queen, and has said that if the action of England should correspond with the sound sense and practical character of the views held by Her Majesty, the danger of a European War would be minimised.

The graceful tribute to the Queen, which appeared in last night's North German Gazette of which I have the honour to enclose a copy and translation,[192] is a fitting Epilogue to the Royal Visit, which has ended so happily and shown that good will and cordial relations

---

[189] This refers to the 'Battenberg affair', on which see preceding dispatch.

[190] Wilhelm.

[191] On 25 April 1888.

[192] Enclosures: original (untitled cutting), *Norddeutsche Allgemeine Zeitung*, 27 April 1888 and translation.

between England and Germany are once more the order of the day with the inspired Press.

FO 64/1187: Edward B. Malet to Marquess of Salisbury, Confidential, No 139, Berlin, 11 May 1888

[Received 14 May by messenger. For: The Queen / Prince of Wales / Print (S.E. Europe) / Embassies; S[alisbury], 14 May]

Storm in German press over new foreign loan for Russia; Bismarck intends depreciation of Russian credit even if German interests affected

I have the honour to acknowledge the receipt of Your Lordship's Despatch No: 130, Confidential, of the 9th instant, transmitting to me a copy of Lord Lytton's despatch No: 278 Confidential of the 4th instant, respecting rumoured negotiations for a loan between Russia and the Comptoir d'Escompte of Paris.[193]

In connection with this subject, the recent reopening of the attack on the financial credit of Russia by the Cologne Gazette and other Organs of the German Press, generally considered to be in touch with official views, deserves attention.

The real secret of this onslaught of the press appears to be a desire on the part of Prince Bismarck to put every possible difficulty in the way of Russia obtaining a fresh loan in the Money markets of Europe, so long as there is any fear of such a financial reinforcement being employed to the detriment of European peace.

I learn from Herr v. Bleichröder confidentially that although it is quite true that the Comptoir d'Escompte offered to negotiate a loan with the Russian Government, the terms of the offer were such as no Power, having a regard for it's financial dignity could entertain. The Comptoire d'Escompte proposed to take up only one fifth of the loan itself, and intended to offer the remaining four fifths for subscription in the public market.

As long as Herr v. Bleichröder of Berlin, who took up the last loan for Russia,[194] does not feel himself at liberty to undertake a fresh one, it is quite certain that Messrs Rothschild[195] will not come forward, because it is known that Herr Bleichröder's attitude is guided by the will of the Chancellor.

---

[193] Negotiations for a loan of 500 million roubles were entered into at St Petersburg in early April 1888. A smaller loan of 125 million roubles was finally agreed on in November 1888 between the Russian government and a French-led bank syndicate.
[194] In 1885 as part of an international consortium.
[195] N.M. Rothschild & Sons.

Were it not for the political objections to a new Russian loan, the German Money Market has more direct interest than any other foreign country in keeping up the financial credit of Russia as long as that Empire contains any element of solvency. In spite of the panic caused here by the first attack on Russian Credit in the inspired press, the amount of Russian stock still held in this country is enormous, the bulk of it being held by the very numerous class of small Capitalists.

Moreover, agricultural interests in Germany, already in a very depressed condition, have sustained a serious additional blow from the reduction of the exchange value of the rouble which has caused the German Grain market to be overflooded with Russian produce.

The 'Börsen Courier'', a paper professing to give the impressions of the Berlin Money Market, has recently been at some pains to restore confidence in Russia's credit by an attempt to refute, on the authority of figures which it pronounces to be absolutely trustworthy, a recent assertion of the 'Cologne Gazette'[196] that unless Russia can raise a new foreign Loan, she will within a measurable distance of time, be unable to provide the requisite amount of gold to meet the annual interest on her foreign loans payable in that currency.

The same paper also expresses its' conviction that the next Russian loan will be effected in Germany, but only when Russia has given solid hostages to peace.

I understand that Prince Bismarck is quite aware of the injury which the depreciation of Russian Credit is doing to important interests in this country, but that his invariable reply to representations on this score is that the maintenance of European peace is the paramount interest of Germany at present, and that private interests whether of investors or of landlords must give way to it.

A point which should also be noted is that the policy of Prince Bismarck with regard to the alliance of the Central Powers is assisted by the depreciation of Russian Credit. The Italian Ambassador[197] tells me that he considers that the maintenance of the value of Italian 'Rentes' has been mainly due to their purchase in Germany by investors who have sold out of the Russian funds, and this view is also applicable to Austrian Securities.

[196] *Kölnische Zeitung.*
[197] Eduardo de Launay.

FO 64/1187: Edward B. Malet to Marquess of Salisbury, Secret, No 207, Berlin, 14 July 1888

[Received 16 July by messenger. For: The Queen / Prince of Wales; Secret to: St Petersburg / Vienna / Constantinople; S[alisbury]]

Remarks on general state of affairs and Bismarck's position following deaths of Wilhelm I, Friedrich III and accession of Wilhelm II; importance of emperor's friendly feelings towards England

Before quitting Berlin on leave of absence, I venture to lay before Your Lordship some remarks upon the altered state of things consequent on the deaths of The Emperors William and Frederick and the Accession of The present Emperor.[198]

In the month February 1885 The Emperor William's health was waning and Prince Bismarck spoke to me about his own position in the event of His Majesty's decease. He said that when this occurred he should retire into private life, that it had taken him twenty years to obtain His Majesty's confidence and that at the age at which he had himself arrived he had neither the inclination nor the strength to go through the same labour again with a new master. I remarked that I thought that he would find that, whether he wished it or not, it would be impossible for him to relinquish his post and that he could surely count upon The Crown Prince's confidence. He replied that that was not the case: No doubt The Crown Prince would retain him in his post at the beginning of his reign but, "if ever I make a mistake, and we all do that, I should not be able to count upon his support. My methods of Government may be old fashioned, perhaps they are out of date, but I am too old to go to school again and to learn other systems. The unity between my Master and me would cease. It is better that I should forestall this situation. The best thing that could happen to me would be that I should be shot by some assassin when The Emperor dies."

The melancholy circumstances[199] under which the Emperor Frederick came to the throne prevented Prince Bismarck from carrying out the intention which he thus announced to me, but, although the reign only lasted three months, it was long enough to prove the accuracy of the Chancellor's judgment in regard to his own position. It is certain that if the reign had continued, and The Emperor had been in the enjoyment of good health, the Chancellor would not have retained his post many months.

---

[198] Wilhelm I died on 9 March; Friedrich III died on 15 June 1888 and was succeeded by Wilhelm II.

[199] Malet is referring to Friedrich's advanced stage of cancer of the larynx.

In saying that he had gained the confidence of The Emperor William, he did not exactly express the situation. He would have been more precise if he had said that it took him twenty years to gain the mastery over his Sovereign. Prince Bismarck's is not a character in which one can place confidence as we accept the term. The Emperor may have had confidence in his intellect, his foresight, his relentless perseverance and his patriotism, but The Emperor himself was high minded[,] chivalrous and disinterested and the lack of these qualities in the chancellor must have prevented mutual confidence in its best sense. The stronger nature only gained the upper hand.

The Chancellor therefore, foresaw that a similar struggle waited him on the accession of The Emperor Frederick who inherited all His Father's finer qualities in a higher degree and stimulated to vigour and intensity by the intellect of his wife.[200]

The scene has changed: A young Prince has come to the throne, and I have only touched upon the past in order to impress the point that the power of Prince Bismarck is dependent upon the will of The Emperor[.] And that whereas in all the latter years of The Emperor William's reign we had only to consider the intentions of Prince Bismarck, we should now in a considerable measure turn our attention to the Emperor, who has just succeeded.

It has, as Your Lordship is aware, been asserted that He is anti English in his feelings and that he leans towards Russia. I am anxious to place on record that I believe this assertion to be unfounded. All the straws in the air which I have been able to detect, blow the other way, and, besides straws, I have from Count Bismarck[201] a positive assurance given by Prince William himself in November last, at a time when the supposed anti-English proclivities of His Royal Highness were the subject of newspaper gossip, that it is not true.

But herein lies a danger: Although His Majesty is nearly thirty years of age, it is not to be supposed that His likes and dislikes are matured, while on the other hand it is probable that events at the outset of His reign may have an enduring influence upon them, and nothing is more calculated to change his feelings with regard to England than the suspicion that all His efforts to show friendliness towards us in the reception which he has given to English Officers,[202] and other minor matters, which have alone been hitherto within His power, have been unavailing to correct the false impression which has got abroad regarding His views. He is a high mettled Prince, and He has Given His Royal word that we are mistaken. The fear

---

[200] Victoria.
[201] Herbert von Bismarck.
[202] On 9 July 1888.

is that a continued show of want of confidence in him at this especial period of his life may produce a revulsion of the feelings which have hitherto weighed the balance, that he may renounce the effort to prove himself friendly to England as a task beyond his attainment and cease his friendliness at the same time.

If we were dealing with a country in which the foreign policy was guided by the Government and not by the Sovereign this would be a matter of small moment, but that is not the case, and we already know by unpleasant experience that, although at the present moment the Chancellor's policy is to court the most friendly relations with Her Majesty's Government, we can never feel sure from one day to another how long that policy may continue. It is therefore of special importance that the Emperor should be on our side. His sentiments will count as a strong factor in the policy which may be adopted towards us. The Chancellor's position is no longer as strong as it was during the reign of The Emperor William, and he will have to humour the Young Sovereign in order to maintain his own power.

I do not know that there is any special thing to be done at present, in furtherance of the views which I have ventured to submit, but I believe that much may be effected by adopting a general tone of confidence in The Emperor's friendly disposition towards England and in allowing it to be known that that Confidence exists.

FO 64/1188: Charles S. Scott to Marquess of Salisbury, No 250, Berlin, 18 August 1888

[Received 20 August by bag. For: Print (Western Europe) / The Queen; S[alisbury]]

Ceremonial unveiling of statue of Friedrich Karl of Prussia; great attention paid to emperor's speeches

The Emperor William on the occasion of unveiling the Statue which has just been erected at Frankfort on the Oder of His late Royal Highness Prince Frederick Charles of Prussia – a ceremony which took place with marked honours the day before yesterday – replied to the speech with which His Majesty's health was proposed by the Ober-bürgermeister of the City[203] in words which have not failed to create a deep impression.

At the outset of the new reign every public utterance of the young Emperor is seized upon as an indication for the future and there must always be the risk of attributing a greater importance to the Royal words than they were meant to convey.

[203] Mayor Hermann von Kemnitz.

On the present occasion the Imperial speech which is singularly characteristic of the ardent and enthusiastic temperament of the young Monarch, bears every mark of an improvised utterance inspired by the military surroundings and associations of the ceremony.

No authentic official report of His Majesty's words has as yet been published, but I have the honor to enclose copy and translation of the report which has appeared in the "Post"[204] the best informed of the unofficial daily Papers.

His Majesty alluding to the seriousness of the present time takes occasion to dispel any illusions in regard to the firm determination of Germany never to relinquish an inch nor a stone of the possessions which She has won by her Sword, and indignantly repudiates the suspicion of His Majesty The Emperor Frederick having ever harboured a contrary view.

It is not easy to discover the immediate motive for this last declaration, as The Emperor Frederick's Proclamations on ascending the Throne were clear and unequivocal on this point, but possibly it may have been prompted by certain utterances in the French press, when reviewing the Acts and Character of the late Emperor, and also by a recent allusion in the Belgian "Nord" to the possibility of Germany cementing her friendship with Denmark by the retrocession of North Schleswig.[205]

FO 64/1188: Charles S. Scott to Marquess of Salisbury, Confidential, No 265, Berlin, 31 August 1888

[Received 3 September by messenger. For: The Queen; S[alisbury]]

Appointment of Bennigsen as Upper President of Hanover; remarks on political state of Germany and role of Junker party

The appointment of Herr von Benningsen [*sic*], the Parliamentary Leader of the National Liberal Party, to the Post of Upper President of Hanover, the Province which has been the chief scene of his political career and activity, was announced in the

---

[204] Enclosures: original cutting of emperor's speech printed in *Post*, 18 August 1888 and translation.

[205] *Le Nord*, a Russian controlled newspaper from Brussels, reported on 14 August 1888, that, according to the Danish press, a full reconciliation between Denmark and Germany was dependent on a plebiscite in the northern districts of Schleswig (as stipulated in Article 5 of the Peace of Prague of 1866).

Gazette[206] of the 29th instant, and is regarded here as a significant indication of the principles by which the new reign will be guided.

Although differing on many internal political questions from the Chancellor of the Empire, the eminent leader of the National Liberals has always retained the personal friendship and respect of Prince Bismarck with whom he has lately been staying at Friedrichsruhe [sic].[207]

On more than one occasion in the last ten years it has been rumoured that Herr von Benningsen would be given a portfolio in the Prussian Government, but the negotiations always fell through owing, it is said, to marked divergence of opinion in regard to economical questions between the Liberal Leader and the Prussian Premier.

On the questions of national union and defence, Herr von Benningsen has always been a staunch supporter of the Views of the Chancellor, and it was in a great measure due to his instrumentality that the union of the National Liberals with the Imperial and Conservative factions into the so-called Cartel Party was cemented last year and secured the majority in the present Reichstag which passed the recent Army Bills.[208]

At the onset of the new reign the continued existence of this Union seemed for the moment in some danger. The Reactionary or Junker party, represented in the Press by the "Kreuz Zeitung",[209] discounting in their own favour the prevailing uncertainty as to the personal political bias of the new sovereign, began very prematurely to agitate the question of reforming the Union by the exclusion of the National Liberal element, and of forming a new majority for the Government out of exclusively Conservative elements, the immediate pretext for Union being certain imminent questions in the Prussian Landtag connected with denominational Education.[210]

This party seems to have based its hopes of success on the effects of the heated controversy which ensued on the retirement from office

---

[206] *Deutscher Reichs-Anzeiger und Königlich Preußischer Staats-Anzeiger.*

[207] Bennigsen stayed at Friedrichsruh from 7 August 1888.

[208] For the army bill (Imperial Military Law) of 1887 see n. 119 in this section. The 'Cartel' (*Kartell der Ordnungsparteien*), a coalition and electoral alliance consisting of the *Deutschkonservative Partei* (*Junker* party), *Freikonservative Partei* (*Reichspartei*), and *Nationalliberale Partei*, was formed in February 1887.

[209] *Neue Preußische Zeitung (Kreuz-Zeitung).*

[210] The disputed question of denominational elementary schools was postponed until after the elections of the Prussian *Landtag*, which were to be held in October and November 1888. The suggestions to end the Cartel were made in the run-up to these elections.

of its chief champion Herr von Puttkamer, during the short reign of The Emperor Frederick,[211] and by the attempt which was then made to identify that large minded Sovereign with the more extreme views of the Freisinnige party[212] and with unqualified opposition to the internal policy of the Chancellor.

Possibly also the fact of The New Emperor having, when Prince, devoted himself almost exclusively to regimental and military matters may have induced the Junker party very unjustifiably to associate His Majesty with the extreme political views of His Messroom Associates, of whom a great number are connected with that Party by family ties.

The grounds for their false confidence in His Majesty's support, whatever they may have been, betrayed the Party into overstepping the bounds of common prudence, and we have for the last two months seen the "Kreuz Zeitung" gradually developing more and more reactionary schemes for the new regime.

With scarcely concealed triumph over the pretended discomfiture of hopes built upon the known liberality of view of the Emperor Frederick, the reactionary organ began to hint that the return to office of Herr Puttkamer was only a question of time, and began to interpret according to its own narrower views those passages in The present Emperor's Manifesto to His People[213] which proclaimed principles of religious and political tolerance similar to those of His Majesty's Royal Predecessor on the throne, and only a few days ago[214] it went so far as to openly advocate a renewal of the Anti-Semitic Crusade, and a reversal of the measure which secured the political emancipation and equality of the Jews.

A recent speech[215] of The Emperor William II in the Chapter of the Knights of St John, of which varying versions have been published, was interpreted as encouraging the presumption that the present sovereign looked to the Junker Party for His chief support.

One version represented His Majesty as saying that in His endeavours to advance the material and moral well-being of His People, "he relied on the support of the noblest part of it, the high nobility represented in that order" – the other version ran "the support of the noblest part of the Prussian Nobility."

The hopes of the Kreuz Zeitung Party have now received a severe shock from the first political appointment of the new reign, which is

[211] Puttkammer was dismissed as minister of the interior on 8 June 1888.

[212] *Deutsche Freisinnige Partei;* see n. 3 in this section.

[213] Proclamation of 18 June 1888.

[214] On 25 August 1888; the author of the article in question was Adolf Stoecker.

[215] Speech at Sonnenberg on 23 August 1888.

admitted to have been in a great measure due to the personal initiative of the sovereign, and also by the selection of Herr von Leipziger, the former Upper President of Hanover, for the similar post in East Prussia for which appointment Herr von Puttkamer was supposed to be the favoured Candidate.

The appointment of Herr von Benningsen indicates the continuance of the Cartel Party, and a renewal of confidence in the support of the National Liberals on the part of the Government. It is also an unmistakable reply to the Agitation of the Reactionary Conservatives for the overthrow of the Liberal Leader's political influence in Hanover, and gives colour to a remark which The Emperor William is commonly reported to have recently made to a rising Prussian Statesman, that His Majesty was firmly resolved to know no distinction of political parties among those of his subjects who were animated by patriotism and a desire for healthy national development, and that He would never countenance a reactionary policy, or the Agitation of class against class.

Utterances like these, so thoroughly in harmony with the liberal views of the Beloved Sovereign, whose premature loss this country is now mourning, will be hailed as of good augury for the opening reign by every liberal minded man both in and out of Germany.

FO 64/1188: Edward B. Malet to Marquess of Salisbury, No 276, Berlin, 11 September 1888

[Received 13 September by messenger. For: The Queen; S[alisbury]]

Press article accusing Queen Natalie of Serbia of being ill-disposed towards Germany; might have broader political purpose

I have the honour to transmit herewith in original and translation an article from the North German Gazette of last night which, for certain reasons is specially deserving of attention. It relates to the attitude of the German Authorities towards Queen Natalie of Servia when Her Majesty was recently at Wiesbaden.[216]

The Article after imputing to the Queen Natalie unfriendliness to Germany says that it is an old principle of policy that one must be a

---

[216] Enclosures: untitled extract from *Norddeutsche Allgemeine Zeitung*, 10 September 1885 and translation. The article was published in response to allegations made by the Russian press. Natalie had stayed in Wiesbaden from 17 May to 13 July 1888 when, against her will, her son was sent back to Belgrade upon the request of King Milan. Natalie was asked to leave 10 hours after the departure of the crown prince.

friend to one's friends and an enemy to one's enemies and that it makes no difference if among the latter there should be Royal ladies with Kingly title "The rule of political duty renders it necessary to allow us no distinction in regard to sex or rank"[.]

There are indications that the Chancellor[217] is renewing a tilt against feminine influence in politics and that the article which is clearly inspired is intended to be of wider application than to Queen Natalie.

FO 64/1189: William N. Beauclerk to Marquess of Salisbury, Very Confidential, No 315, Berlin, 13 October 1888

[Received 15 October by messenger. X (See minute inside)]

Remarks on theft of the late Friedrich III's cypher book

Most of the German newspapers have this morning reproduced a paragraph from the semi official "Berliner Politische Nachrichten"[218] to the effect that "a Cypherbook formerly given to the late Emperor Frederick for secret communications with the higher Officers of State, and which His Majesty had by him even on his deathbed, has been lost and has vanished leaving no trace behind."

The paragraph concludes by asking whether the Chief of the secret Police[219] has only just learned of this, and, remarks that the whole affair is "exceedingly strange".

I mention this matter only because about a month ago I heard from an indubitably trustworthy source of the loss of these cyphers and was informed in addition that (as has been usual of late when any documents of importance have been lost, stolen, or published contrary to the inclination of the Chancellor) Her Majesty The Empress Frederick[220] has been accused of the theft and that the insinuation was added that the cypher had no doubt been given to England.[221]

---

[217] Otto von Bismarck.
[218] 12 October 1888.
[219] Ernst Wilhelm Schütte.
[220] Victoria.
[221] The cypher book was eventually found in the *Kronprinzenpalais* at the end of October.

FO 64/1189: William N. Beauclerk to Marquess of Salisbury, Confidential, No 317, Berlin, 15 October 1888

[Received 22 October by messenger. For: The Queen; S[alisbury]]

Morell Mackenzie's book published in Germany and promptly confiscated in Berlin; imprisonment of Dr Geffcken

A German Edition of Sir Morell Mackenzie's book[222] was published this morning at Styrum and Leipsig. It is said that a truckload of some 25.000 copies arrived at Berlin early in the morning and the work was hawked about the streets for sale at the price of 1 mark 50 Pfennigs until noon when it was confiscated by the Police.

I should not trouble Your Lordship with noticing this matter, but for the fact that the reason of the seizure is stated to be that the publication of contradictions of official statements amounts in Germany to the crime of High Treason, and Sir Morell Mackenzie's refutation of the official report of the German Physicians[223] is held to come under this category. The above event in connection with the arrest of Doctor Geffcken,[224] under a similar capital charge, has caused some slight consternation in Berlin; for the citizens are commencing, as I am informed, to fear lest their most well meant and innocent actions may not bring down upon them the wrath of judgment of the supreme Authorities.

I have the honour to inclose a copy of the confiscated volume.

[...]

P.S. Since writing the above I learn that 130.000 copies of Sir Morell Mackenzie's pamphlet have been printed in this country, in German, and that the Editor[225] has already appealed to the Courts of Law against the confiscation. According to German Law the prosecution for an offence of this nature must commence within a fortnight, otherwise the case falls to the ground, and in the instance of Doctor Geffcken judicial proceedings have already begun by his examination before the Juge d'Instruction[226] at the Moabit prison in Berlin.

---

[222] *The Fatal Illness of Frederick the Noble (1888);* the German edition (enclosure to dispatch) was published as *Friedrich der Edle und seine Ärzte (1888)*. It was confiscated following an order of the court at Mühlheim of 14 October 1888.

[223] The official report was published in July 1888 as *Die Krankheit Kaiser Friedrichs III.*

[224] Geffcken was arrested on 29 September 1888 and prosecuted for high treason because he had published extracts of Friedrich III's diary written during the Franco-Prussian War.

[225] Adolf Spaarmann.

[226] French: 'investigating magistrate'. Here, Georg Hirschfeld.

FO 64/1189: William N. Beauclerk to Marquess of Salisbury, Confidential, No 323, Berlin, 19 October 1888

[Received 22 October by messenger. Qy: The Queen / Prince of Wales; S[alisbury]]

Press article on late Friedrich III's political views potentially intended to encourage present emperor to desist from excessive opinions

With reference to my despatch No: 319 Confidential of yesterday's date, on the subject of the Political views of The late Emperor Frederick, and the article published in the "North German Gazette" thereupon, I have the honour to mention that there is another light in which the meaning of the said Article may be viewed.[227]

The political elections to the Reichstag and Landtag are coming on in a few days and are expected to be unfavourable to the Government,[228] who have wished in the publication of the Article in question to show indirectly that the reigning Emperor can no longer, as such, entertain or put in practice the ultra Conservative opinions which he is supposed to have held as Prince William of Prussia and Crown Prince of Germany.

Such opinions are believed to have included a great enmity to the Jewish race as well as to the Roman Catholic population, very important elements in the German Nation, and considerable factors in political affairs in this country.

It is to prove this proposition that the theory is so strongly put forward that The Late Emperor could not – had his reign been prolonged – have maintained or given further development to the very liberal views which are known to have animated His Majesty.

It is argued in this connection that the whole history of the Royal House of Brandenburg tends to prove that all excessive opinions held by the occupant of the Throne must, in practice, be modified to suit the traditions of the Nation and the exigencies of the time.

---

[227] The article disputed that Friedrich's disagreements with the policies of Wilhelm I when he was crown prince had any political implications. It was published in the *Norddeutsche Allgemeine Zeitung* on 15 October 1888.

[228] By-elections took place in three electoral districts before the re-opening of the *Reichstag* on 22 November; elections for the Prussian house of deputies were held on 30 October 1888.

FO 64/1211: Edward B. Malet to Marquess of Salisbury, Confidential, No 4, Berlin, 5 January 1889

[Received 7 January by bag. For: The Queen / Prince of Wales; Qy: approve language; not to St Petersburg; S[alisbury]; Draft Sir E. Malet, 10 January]

Conversation with Count Bismarck about Kölnische Zeitung's *publication of his correspondence with Robert Morier concerning the latter's alleged warning to Colonel Bazaine during Franco-Prussian War*

I have the honour to inform Your Lordship that Count Bismarck spoke to me today about the publication which has taken place in the newspapers of the correspondence between himself and Sir Robert Morier on the subject of the charges brought against the latter by the "Cologne Gazette".[229] He said that he considered that he had just reason to complain of Sir Robert's transmitting the correspondence to the Press without going through the usual form of inquiring whether he, Count Bismarck, consented. If Sir Robert had made this inquiry, Count Bismarck would certainly have raised no objection to the publication. He had been greatly surprised at the tone of Sir Robert Morier's first letter, which in his opinion was rather that of a chief to a subordinate that that of one gentleman to another. Sir Robert made use of a phrase in it which showed that he misapprehended the bearing of the case. He seemed to think that he was charged with betrayal towards the Emperor Frederick and his Army. In the first place the Emperor Frederick was far away at the time of the alleged revelation to Marshall Bazaine and in the second place the charge against Sir Robert Morier was founded on the report of Major Deines,[230] which did not preclude the explanation that the intelligence, if originally given by Sir Robert, might have reached Bazaine without Sir Robert's complicity.

I said to Count Bismarck that I regretted most sincerely the publicity which had been given to the allegations against Sir Robert Morier by the Cologne Gazette because it was impossible to suppose for an instant that Sir Robert had done what was insinuated and because the attack was calculated to cause an acrimonious polemic

---

[229] On 16 December 1888 the *Kölnische Zeitung* accused Robert Morier of having betrayed Prussian military movements to Marshal Bazaine in August 1870. In his letter to Herbert von Bismarck of 19 December 1888, Morier demanded a public refutation. Bismarck, on 24 December, answered in the negative, whereupon Morier, on 31 December, declared his intention of publishing the correspondence. It was published in *The Times* and the *Daily Telegraph* on 4 January 1889.

[230] Report of 2 April 1886. The report had been privately communicated to Morier by Herbert von Bismarck in March 1888.

between the Press of the two Countries which might have an evil influence on the friendly feelings between them. Count Bismarck urged that it was owing to Sir Robert Morier that the matter had got into the papers.

He said that Sir Robert had written on the subject to Herr Hinzpeter, formerly tutor to the Emperor inclosing copies of the correspondence between him and Marshall Bazaine,[231] that Herr Hinzpeter had forwarded Sir Robert's letter to the Emperor, that in reply Herr Hinzpeter had been furnished with Major Deines' reports[232] – that Herr Hinzpeter lived at Bielefeld, which was close to Cologne, that very likely he had talked about the affair and that so the Editor[233] of the Cologne Gazette had come to hear it and had then revealed what he knew imperfectly to the Public.

It was a mistake, he said, to consider that what appeared in the Cologne Gazette necessarily emanated from the Government. It was the most influential paper in that part of Germany and the Government occasionally gave it intelligence. In the present instance when Sir Robert Morier's denial appeared,[234] the Editor certainly claimed the help of the Government in substantiating the statements already made and had urged that unless it was given, the character of the paper for trustworthiness would be lost. Upon this he had been furnished with the reports made by Major Deines. Count Bismarck then proceeded to comment on the article in the Times of the 4th instant: and said that he was surprised that so serious a newspaper should not think it below its dignity to found a charge against Prince Bismarck in connection with the matter which was in fact untenable and to read him a lecture on the manner of treating foreign officials, when Prince Bismarck had done nothing in this case which could justify such an attack. The only document relating to the matter which had emanated from a member of the Government was his (Count Bismarck's) letter to Sir Robert. The Times styled it "crude". Count Bismarck thought that considering the tone of the letter to which it was an answer, it was remarkable for its moderation.

---

[231] Copies of Morier's letters of 25 July and 28 August 1888 (the latter containing Bazaine's denial) were sent to Hinzpeter on 5 October.

[232] Reports of 2 April 1886 and 12 November 1888; they were published by the *Kölnische Zeitung* on 2 January 1889.

[233] August Schmits.

[234] *The Times*, 21 December 1888.

FO 64/1211: Edward B. Malet to Marquess of Salisbury, Secret, No 51, Berlin, 3 February 1889

[Received 6 February. Qy: The Queen / Washington (secret) / Admiralty (secret); S [alisbury]; Paris; P.L. [printed letter], 16 February; L[ister]]

Report of a German shipbuilder receiving an American order for warships; Count Bismarck on need for England to strengthen her fleet and a united front between England and Germany

Count Bismarck[235] told me yesterday very confidentially that he had received a report from Count Münster, the German Ambassador at Paris, to the effect that an agent[236] of the ship building firm of Schichau at Elbing had been to him and told him that the United States Government had proposed to his firm to build for the Government six torpedo boats at once, and had made inquiries as to the time which his firm would take to furnish the Government with cruisers and men of war. Messrs Schichau had refused the order for reasons which Count Bismarck did not state to me, but His Excellency said that he was anxious that Your Lordship should know of the circumstances which he said, to his mind, pointed more than ever to the necessity of England strengthening her fleet, and the utility of its being thoroughly understood in the United States that the Governments of England and Germany were in complete understanding, and that there was no chance of dividing them upon questions where the interests of the United States were antagonistic to one or the other.

He said that politics in the United States were always dominated by electioneering considerations, and that the vote of English and German naturalized Americans were weighty factors. These factors would be united if the policy of Germany and England were united, and such an union would exercise a wholesome influence over the executive, and compel it to moderate its aggressive tone.

FO 64/1212: Edward B. Malet to Marquess of Salisbury, No 106, Berlin, 22 March 1889

[Received 25 March by bag. Qy: Express satisfaction, 30 March; Copy to: War Office, P.L. [printed letter], 1 April; S[alisbury]]

Expression of regret at the departure of Colonel Swaine as military attaché to Berlin; qualities required of someone in this position

While I was absent from my post Colonel Swaine C.B, who has been military Attaché at this Embassy since 1882, with an interval of

---

[235] Herbert von Bismarck.
[236] Name not traceable.

service in Egypt,[237] quitted Berlin on being appointed to the command of the 2nd Battalion of The Rifle Brigade. I desire to take the earliest opportunity on my resuming my post to record my high sense of the manner in which Colonel Swaine has discharged the duties of his office during the period which he has served under me.

The performance of these duties at Berlin require[s] great tact and circumspection on account of the suspicious eye with which all inquiries are regarded, and Colonel Swaine succeeded in completely winning the confidence of those with whom he came in contact by his straight forwardness, his soldierlike qualities, and his ability. He was regarded with friendship by The Emperor Frederick and the present Emperor, and was always treated with exceptional courtesy by the military authorities. He was in every way the model of what a military attaché should be, and I sincerely regret that the withdrawal of his services from Her Majesty's Embassy should have become unavoidable.

FO 64/1213: William N. Beauclerk to Marquess of Salisbury, No 231, Berlin, 17 August 1889

[Received 19 August by messenger. For: The Queen / ~~Circulate~~; S[alisbury]]

Banquet to celebrate Her Majesty's appointment as honorary colonel of Queen Victoria's Regiment; celebration of Anglo-German solidarity

I beg to report to Your Lordship that I had the honour yesterday of attending the Banquet of "Queen Victoria's Regiment", the 1st Dragoon Guards, on the occasion of Her Majesty the Queen having accepted the honorary Colonelcy of the Regiment.[238]

The Adjutant, Count G[.] Waldersee, had called at the Embassy about ten days ago and, on behalf of the Colonel[239] and Officers, invited our entire staff to be present at the banquet.

The invitation was originally for dinner at 6 P.M., but at the command of His Imperial Majesty the Emperor, who specially desired to be present, the arrangements were altered to suit His Majesty's engagements, and a luncheon was given at 1 P.M.

---

[237] Swaine was military secretary of the expeditionary force to Egypt in 1882.
[238] The honorary colonelcy was conferred on Victoria on 2 August 1889 on the occasion of Wilhelm II's visit to England.
[239] Oberleutnant von Kotze.

The entertainment happened to coincide with the annual regimental festival commemorating the battle of "Mars la Tour",[240] where the Corps so highly distinguished itself, at great sacrifice of life, in coming to the rescue of two Regiments of Infantry which were sorely pressed by the enemy.

The banquet was thronged with Royal and distinguished guests.

On his arrival, the Emperor was received by a deputation of veterans of the Regiment, survivors of the campaign in which it has taken part.

His Royal Highness Prince Albrecht of Prussia, Regent of Brunswick, proposed the health of Her Majesty the Queen, as the new Chief of the Regiment, in a terse and appropriate speech. The health of Her Majesty was received with the utmost enthusiasm, the Emperor and all present cheering vociferously and standing whilst the band played "God save the Queen".

The Colonel of the Regiment next gave the health of the Emperor, as head of the German Army. He said that the motto of the Regiment in peace and in war, was "Long live the King": – he trusted that they might in any future campaign shout "Victoria" in every sense.

His Majesty the Emperor responded in a feeling speech, lauding the brotherly sentiments which had always existed amongst the troops of the Empire, and which even more than their devotion to the throne had led them to perform the valorous feats of which they were so justly proud.

I then had the honour to address the company present in the following words:

"Your Imperial Majesty and Gentlemen! My Colleagues of the British Embassy and I myself will never forget the honour which we have had today, in attending this banquet commemorating an incident which may well be regarded as pregnant with importance in the History of our own times."

Germany and England united by the most ancient bonds of race and kindred, have marched together in unbroken alliance from the earliest period of their national existence. By land and by sea they proceed hand in hand with the common object of preserving international Peace and furthering the progress of civilization in every quarter of the Globe.

The close ties of family relationship between the Imperial Houses have today been accentuated by the honorary distinctions exchanged between Our Sovereigns.

---

[240] Battle of Mars-La-Tour of 16 August 1870.

Gentlemen I esteem it a high privilege to be permitted to thank you in the name of my great and gracious Queen for the cordial manner in which you have welcomed Her as your chief, and for giving to us the opportunity of making the personal acquaintance of the officers of "Queen Victoria's Regiment."[']

Colonel Russell also expressed the honour and pleasure felt by the British army in being more closely connected with the Imperial forces by the event celebrated on this occasion.

The whole proceedings were marked by excessive courtesy and cordiality towards ourselves on the part of His Imperial Majesty the Emperor and all the donors of the entertainment.

His Royal Highness Prince Albrecht was good enough personally to compliment me most graciously on my small oration, and I venture to say that the occurrences of the day may be regarded as having given a distinct and marked proof of friendship, unison and alliance between Great Britain and the German Empire.

FO 64/1214: Edward B. Malet to Marquess of Salisbury, No 269, Berlin, 4 October 1889

[Received 7 October by messenger. For: The Queen; S[alisbury]]

Emperor has officially repudiated claims that he shares the views of the Junker party

I have the honour to inclose herewith copy and translation of an article[241] which has appeared in the Official Gazette stating that the Emperor disapproves of the views expressed by the "Kreuz Zeitung" in a certain article[242] which it mentions and that His Majesty does not permit any party to indulge in the pretence of possessing The Imperial ear.

The appearance of this statement in the official Gazette has caused much sensation among German politicians.

Ever since the accession of the present Emperor the old conservative formerly styled "Junker" party have striven not only to draw His Majesty within their fold but to cause it to be believed that the Imperial views are already in consonance with theirs.

Their organ the "Kreuz Zeitung", has recently in a series of articles put forward this pretension with so much arrogance that The Emperor has deemed it necessary to disclaim such partizanship

---

[241] Enclosures: untitled extract, *Deutscher Reichsanzeiger und Königlich Preußischer Staatsanzeiger*, 2 October 1889 and translation, 4 October 1889.

[242] On 26 September 1889.

officially less by repeated reiteration it should gain credence among the masses. The step has given great satisfaction to the moderates who form the cartel party[243] and are the section of the Reichstag upon which the Government rests for support. There is no doubt that the Emperor and Prince Bismarck deemed such a public utterance to be necessary in order to retain the support of this party and there is equally no doubt that its appearance has had tranquilizing effect upon all Germany, as the supposition that The Emperor was impregnated with the antiquated and arrogant views of the old feudal party might have a serious effect on the conduct of the moderates in the coming session of the Reichstag and on the next elections.

FO 64/1214: Edward B. Malet to Marquess of Salisbury, Secret, No 282, Berlin, 13 October 1889

[Received 16 October. For: The Queen; Secret to: St Petersburg / Vienna / Constantinople; S[alisbury]]

Czar's visit to Berlin; reassured by Bismarck of Germany's peaceful aims towards Russia; England dismissed as unable to form an alliance against Russia due to complex parliamentary institutions

I had this evening an opportunity of speaking to the Emperor about the visit of His Imperial Majesty the Czar who left for Schwerin at four o'clock in the afternoon.[244]

His Majesty said to me that the visit had done great good, that the Czar came to Berlin with much misgiving, as, however strange it might seem, he really harboured the idea that Germany intended to make war upon Russia.

He had, however, had an interview of an hour and a quarter with Prince Bismarck,[245] who had gone over the whole political situation with him, and had really succeeded in dispelling the strange cloud of anxiety which seemed to oppress His Majesty. He had assured the Czar that Germany desired nothing but peace, and had quieted his mind respecting the existence of hostile alliances. The Emperor said to me that the Czar came back from the interview a changed man and had afterwards been quite cheerful and pleasant, and had invited Him to the military manoeuvres next summer in Russia, an invitation which His Majesty had at once accepted.

[243] Malet is referring to the National Liberals and the Free Conservatives; originally the *Deutschkonservative Partei* was part of the 'Cartel' party. See n. 208 in this section.
[244] Alexander III visited Berlin from 11 to 13 October 1889.
[245] On 11 October.

Immediately afterwards I spoke to Count Bismarck[246] on the same subject telling him what the Emperor had said, and His Excellency entirely confirmed it. He said that in conversation with his father the Czar had shown particular apprehension on two points, an alliance concluded with England, and alliance projected with Turkey, both of an offensive nature towards Russia.

Prince Bismarck had reassured him on both points. He had said that, although there was an excellent understanding with Her Majesty's Government, and that the general lines of policy between the two Governments was similar, that these only tended towards the preservation of peace, they had no aggressive nature, and that, although Your Lordship was the strongest Prime Minister that The Queen had had for twenty years, the traditions and the complex nature of the British Parliamentary institutions made it impossible for you to conclude an alliance of the kind which His Majesty seemed to apprehend.

With regard to Turkey, Prince Bismarck had said that the visit of the Emperor of Germany to Constantinople[247] was only prompted by a love of travel and that the timid and vacillating character of the Sultan[248] rendered it impossible to entertain the idea of contracting serious engagements with him; at the same time Prince Bismarck assured the Czar that no design of this kind formed part of the programme of the Emperor of Germany's intended journey.

FO 64/1234: Edward B. Malet to Marquess of Salisbury, Confidential, No 36, Berlin, 8 February 1890

[Received 10 February. For: The Queen / Prince of Wales / Circulate; S[alisbury]]

Emperor suggests international conference on Labour Question; Bismarck unwilling to adopt more liberal stance; reflections on relationship between Bismarck and emperor

The Emperor's letters to the Chancellor and the Ministers of Trade and Public works giving instructions that invitations should be issued to certain Foreign Powers to join in a conference on the labour question continue to be the absorbing topic of the moment.[249]

---

[246] Herbert von Bismarck.

[247] Wilhelm II left Potsdam for Athens and Constantinople on 18 October and returned on 15 November.

[248] Abdul Hamid II.

[249] The rescript addressed to Bismarck demanded the convocation of an European conference on social reform; the second proclamation of 4 February instructed ministers Berlepsch and Maybach to prepare legislation on social insurance, the regulation of working hours and conditions, and the representation of labour.

The public tendency is to believe that the Emperor and the Chancellor are not agreed as to the wisdom of the step which His Majesty has taken and I fancy that there is no doubt that this view is correct.

Five years ago Prince Bismarck spoke to me generally on the subject of liberal legislation with a view to courting popularity. It was at a time when there was grave apprehension that the Emperor William's end was near and it was supposed that the accession of the Emperor Frederick would inaugurate an era of liberal reforms. The Chancellor then said to me alluding to the repressive and autocratic Government of which he was the administrator that it might be an antiquated system not fitted to modern ideas, but that he was too old to try a new one and that he should retire into private life rather than endeavour to adapt himself to the new state of things.

I believe that the Chancellors views have not changed and that he only remains in office at the earnest request of the Emperor and on condition that he should have nothing to do with the working of the Emperor's project.

To insure this he has resigned[250] the Portfolio of the Ministry of commerce and he has disengaged his responsibility by refusing to countersign the Royal Rescript.

It might be expected that so decided a difference of opinion between the Sovereign and his first Minister would lead to the latter's retirement, but it must be remembered that the Emperor must have paramount reasons for wishing to retain his services and that they are of a nature to carry most serious weight with the Chancellor also.

In the first place he is the creator of the Empire and the Captain of the Ship, his disappearance from the helm would be a matter of most serious importance affecting not only internal affairs, but in a far graver manner the external relations of the Empire.

It is every where felt that Prince Bismarck is a guarantee of peace. He seeks no more victories. His only aim is to consolidate what he has made. No such feeling prevails with regard to the young Emperor. On the contrary even in Germany it is thought that ambition in every direction is latent in his character and that if it does not find vent in a peaceful direction it would do so in another and more dangerous one.

The Emperor is well informed as to the opinions which have been formed of him and he knows that public confidence would be shaken if Prince Bismarck were to cease to be at his side.

---

[250] On 31 January 1890.

These considerations probably operate strongly on the Chancellor. He feels that it would not only be unchivalrous to abandon the young Emperor but that it might also be unsafe.

On the other hand his displeasure at the Emperor's liberal effort may be tempered by the conviction that it will ultimately prove abortive, while in the meantime it may again gain votes in the approaching election for the Reichstag.[251]

Some go so far as to consider that the whole matter is an electioneering manoeuvre; but I believe that the Emperor is perfectly sincere and that he thinks it is his duty and his interest to grapple with the great problem of the age.

FO 64/1234: Edward B. Malet to Marquess of Salisbury, Confidential, No 70, Berlin, 22 March 1890

[Received 24 March by messenger. For: The Queen / Circulate / Confidential to Embassies; S[alisbury]]

Bismarck's enforced resignation and its effects

Although in the letter from The Emperor accepting Prince Bismarcks resignation His Majesty speaks of the uselessness of attempting to induce him to withdraw it, it is an open secret that The Chancellor finally resigned at His Majestys reiterated request.[252]

The Prince first announced his intention of resigning when The Emperor decided to invite the labour Conference.[253] He then proposed however to remain as Chancellor and only give up the office of Prussian Prime Minister. He subsequently decided that this was not a workable scheme and he determined to retire altogether but he certainly intended to await the meeting of the Reichstag, after Easter and to attend its first debates.

I believe however that the prospect of retirement exercised an injurious effect upon his nervous system and that the Doctors were of opinion that to prevent a serious illness it was advisable that he should give up all work as soon as possible. The Emperor acted upon this advice and requested the Chancellor[254] to send in at once the resignation which he intended for a later period.

---

[251] Elections for the *Reichstag* were to be held on 20 February 1890.

[252] Bismarck handed in his letter of resignation on 18 March 1888. It was accepted by Wilhelm II on 20 March.

[253] See preceding dispatch.

[254] On 17 March 1890 (medical reasons were irrelevant).

But patients are not always of the same opinion as the medical advisors and Prince Bismarck absolutely denies that the state of his health precluded him from discharging the duties of his office.

Hence unfortunately his final retirement has been accompanied by a good deal which his conspicuous services and great position made it desirable to avoid.

Count Bismarck has also resigned[255] but the Emperor has as yet refused to accept his resignation. I believe that His Excellency will maintain it and that the Emperor will be obliged to give way.

All the other Ministers remain but it is doubted whether the cabinet thus composed will long hold together. The new Chancellor, General Caprivi, is a strong conservative while Herr v. Botticher [*sic*] his principal Minister has well marked liberal tendencies which were only held in control by the powerful will of Prince Bismarck.

FO 64/1234: Edward B. Malet to Marquess of Salisbury, Confidential, No 74, Berlin, 27 March 1890

[Received 31 March by messenger. For: The Queen; S[alisbury]]

Resignation of Count Bismarck; diplomatic corps wish to see Bismarck take leave of Berlin without offending the emperor

As I foreshadowed in my Despatch N° 70 of the 22nd instant, The Emperor has not been able to prevail upon Count Bismarck to remain in office and the post of Minister for Foreign Affairs has been offered by His Majesty to Count Alvensleben, German Minister at Brussels, who, however, is very unwilling to accept it.[256]

A story has appeared in the papers to the effect that a heated discussion took place at Her Majesty's Embassy between The Emperor and Count Bismarck after the dinner which I had the honour of offering[257] to Their Majesties and the Prince of Wales and that the discussion ended in The Emperors abruptly accepting His Excellency's resignation.[258]

---

[255] Herbert von Bismarck offered his resignation on 21 March; he was dismissed on 26 March.

[256] On 22 March Herbert von Bismarck suggested Alvensleben to be his successor but the latter declined, ultimately due to his lack of parliamentary and oratory skills. See also previous note.

[257] On 24 March 1890.

[258] Edward visited Berlin from 21 to 28 March 1889, then proceeded to Coburg. The dinner at the British embassy took place on 24 March.

There is absolutely no foundation in this report. I can affirm from personal information and observation that the Emperor's communications with Count Bismarck on this subject have been characterised by perfect self restraint on both sides and that His Majesty sought by kindness of manner and delicate persuasion to induce him to relinquish his determination to resign.

Count Bismarck assures me that his health obliges him to seek repose and that The Emperor's offer to allow him to go on leave for six months is impracticable because it would prevent the absolute rest of which he has need.

The Ambassadors were anxious to ascertain whether it would be displeasing to The Emperor if they were to go to the Station when Prince Bismarck leaves[259] in order to bid him farewell and they deputed me to sound His Majesty on the subject. I therefore asked His Majesty whether he would mind my seeing the Prince off and I said that I asked, because, if I went to the station there was no doubt that my colleagues would do the same and that we were anxious lest such a step might be looked upon as a demonstration and so in some degree annoy His Majesty. The Emperor replied that he had not the slightest objection and that I might take my whole staff with me if I liked and he further authorised me to tell the other Ambassadors the answer which He had made to me so that they might have no hesitation on the subject.

FO 64/1235: Edward B. Malet to Marquess of Salisbury, No 100, Berlin, 3 May 1890

[Received 5 May by bag. For: The Queen / Prince of Wales / Mr Matthews / Commercial Department to see; S[alisbury]]

Report on the quiet nature of socialist demonstrations on May Day

I have the honour to report that no disturbances took place in Berlin on the first Instant in connexion with the Socialistic movement, that work was carried on in most of the manufactories and workshops and that the number of men who absented themselves on that day was small.

Special precautions had been taken by the police to endure the maintenance of order in the quarters of the town inhabited by workmen; but it is stated that no special orders were given to the troops and that the usual exercising took place on the Tempelhof Fields.

---

[259] Bismarck left Berlin for Friedrichsruh on 29 March 1890.

Some difference, however, was noticed in the workman's [*sic*] trains arriving in Berlin in the morning which were strikingly empty, and during the day small bands of workmen were seen proceeding to places of amusement in the suburbs. In general, however, the meetings announced to take place at various beer-gardens on the morning of the 1st were very poorly attended.

One or two attempts were made to nail red flags to the telegraph and telephone posts during the night, but these were taken down at dawn by the police.

Over 200 manufactories and workshops granted a holiday to their men voluntarily, but the total number of men employed by these does not appear.

At the Central Office of the Association of Berlin Iron foundries, Engineering works and allied Industries it was announced that, in 48 establishments with a total number of 10,769 men, only 2,034 or about one fifth had not appeared at work.

The accounts which have come in from other parts of Germany are much of the same nature. A certain number of men appear to have abstained from work, but no riots are reported.

FO 64/1235: Edward B. Malet to Marquess of Salisbury, No 116, Berlin, 24 May 1890

[Received 20 May by bag. For: The Queen / Prince of Wales / Circulate; Qy: Copies to Embassies, bag 28 May; (Interesting); S[alisbury]]

Interview with General Caprivi à propos Bismarck's problematic statements and foreign press reports about them; assurances of good relations with England

General Caprivi asked me to come to see him today at three o'clock, and, on my presenting myself, His Excellency said that he desired to speak to me regarding the recent utterances of Prince Bismarck as recorded in the press of different countries.[260] I was aware, he said, of the great respect and regard which he entertains for Prince Bismarck, but it really looked as if the moment had come, when he must distinguish between the Prince Bismarck of the past and the Prince Bismarck of the present.

He could not regard Prince Bismarck's recent remarks to correspondents as wise, justifiable or even true and he confessed that they caused him much pain and even anxiety, lest they might prejudice the confidence which he hoped that foreign Governments

---

[260] Caprivi was referring to Bismarck's interviews published in the Russian *Novoye Vremya* (10 May 1890) and French *Le Matin* (18 May 1890). See n. 316 in Dresden section.

would repose in the policy of the Emperor and of His Majesty's Government. As long as Prince Bismarck confined himself to talking about German Affairs and his own retirement, no great harm could be done; but when he began to speak about the policy of Germany towards other countries and to hint at the view that the moment had come for Germany to rally to Russia, it was time to speak out plainly and for the Imperial Government to dissociate itself from all complicity in the utterance which came from Friedrichruh [*sic*].

The Government was unfortunately unable to take any public step in this direction, a contradiction in the newspapers would only awaken fresh controversy. It might become a question whether, if the evil became more serious, the clause of which Prince Bismarck was himself the author and which had been inserted in the penal Code to meet the case of Count Arnim,[261] should not be invoked against the Prince himself; that was, however, for future consideration.

In the meantime the Emperor had desired him to say to me that there was not the remotest foundation for the insinuation which Foreign newspapers had based upon the disclosures of the Prince, to the effect that the existing alliances[262] were considered to have run their day and that Germany proposed now to draw more closely to Russia.

General Caprivi went on to say that Prince Bismarck had talked to him about Foreign Policy,[263] and had said that he (the Prince) had been like a juggler throwing balls from one hand to another and ringing the changes upon them. General Caprivi had replied that that might be possible for the Prince; but that if he himself were to attempt it, he should merely let the balls fall and be regarded as incompetent. He only knew of one policy and that was the one which he had announced on assuming office,[264] and which was to continue the situation to the best of his ability as he found it; and General Caprivi finished by saying that the Emperor and he both held especially to being on the best terms with England and that he had invited me to see him at the Emperors desire in order to dispel any doubts which might possibly have been engendered in Your

---

[261] Article 335a, which prohibited the unauthorized disclosure of official documents, was introduced into the Imperial Criminal Code in 1876. It was a reaction to the Arnim affair of 1874 in which the former ambassador to Paris was charged of illegally retaining diplomatic documents, and subsequently sentenced to nine months imprisonment.

[262] This is referring to the Triple Alliance (see n. 174 in this section).

[263] Most probably on 21 March; the day after Bismarck's dismissal.

[264] Caprivi was referring to his speech in the Prussian house of deputies of 15 April 1890.

Lordship's mind by the reports of the interviews which had occurred at Friedrichsruh.

FO 64/1253: Power Henry Le Poer Trench to Marquess of Salisbury, No 25, Berlin, 7 February 1891

[Received 9 February. For the Queen / Prince of Wales / Print (Western Europe) / Eastern Department; S[alisbury]]

Downfall of Crispi in Italy; concerns for Triple Alliance; Marschall hopes that King of Italy will not cut expenditure for military and navy forces due to financial crisis

The news of the fall of Signor Crispi's Cabinet was received in this capital with much surprise and the Leading Papers express regret at what they term the temporary defeat of a statesman who was not only friendly towards Germany but an ardent supporter of the Triple alliance.[265]

The "North German Gazette"[266] attributes Signor Crispi's defeat to the position he took on the financial question, now the vital question, and says it now remains to be seen where the statesman is to be found capable of rehabilitating the finances of Italy.

In the opinion of "National Zeitung"[267] Signor Crispi's downfall need cause no anxiety; he did not form the Triple Alliance, all he did was to carry on the policy of his predecessors, which the elections of last November show is approved by a very large majority of the electors.[268] His disappearance for a while will in no way alter or endanger the Triple Alliance, but it is certain that the interests of Italy all point to the desirability of an early return to Power of such an eminent Statesman. Baron von Marschall told me, in the course of a conversation I had with him this morning, that the Imperial Government had heard of the fall of Signor Crispi with sincere regret and that, in his opinion, the King will have great difficulty in finding a statesman strong enough to form a Cabinet which will satisfy all parties, and considers Crispi's return to Power merely a question of Time. He attributes Crispi's defeat partly to his financial policy, which was his weak-point, but mainly to his want of tact and brusque manner in dealing with the Chamber, and also to his violent

---

[265] The Italian government, under Francesco Crispi, handed in its resignation after a parliamentary defeat over a financial bill on 31 January 1891. It was succeeded on 6 February. For the Triple Alliance see n. 174 in this section.

[266] *Norddeutsche Allgemeine*, 2 February 1891.

[267] On 4 February 1891.

[268] The elections of 23 and 30 November saw the victory of the ministerial party, the *Sinistra Storica*.

language. The Triple Alliance he believes to be in no way imperilled, but fears that Signor Crispi's successor[269] may seek a way out of the financial difficulties by asking the Chamber to consent to a considerable reduction in the expenditure for the Army and Navy. This Germany would greatly deprecate as weakening Italy's powers of defence and leaving her more open to an attack from France. Germany, Baron von Marschall added, is fully alive to Italy's present financial difficulties and would not go so far as to protest against such reductions. But from the tone of His Excellency's language I think it not impossible that were such a reduction proposed, the Imperial Government might, in a friendly way, counsel Italy to make economies in some other direction and advise her not to reduce her army and navy.

Baron Marschall, however, thinks and hopes that the King will resist any attempt to cut down the naval and military budgets and believes him to be as fully alive as Germany is to the importance of maintaining peace in Europe and that the best way to do this is not to invite attack by weakening the naval and military forces of Italy.

FO 64/1253: Power Henry Le Poer Trench to Marquess of Salisbury, Secret, No 40, Berlin, 28 February 1891

[Received 2 March. For: The Queen / Prince of Wales; S[alisbury]]

War of words between semi-official press and newspapers supporting Bismarck's criticisms of the emperor

Much excitement has been caused here of late by the war of recrimination which has been carried on between the semi-official German papers and those papers which are said to encourage and support Prince Bismarck in his constant attacks against, and severe criticisms of, the policy of the Imperial Government.

It is an open secret that the ex-Chancellor already controls the "Hamburger Nachrichten", and it is generally believed that he has also succeeded in winning over the "Münchener Allgemeine Zeitung". Many of the hostile articles which appear in these papers are supposed to be inspired, if not written, by the ex-Chancellor, who is said to be also organizing a party opposition to the Court and the Government.

It is asked: how long will The Emperor submit to these attempts of the ex-Chancellor to thwart him on all sides? Baron von Marschall,

---

[269] Antonio Starabba di Rudini.

who spoke to me very confidentially on this subject last week, said that these constant endeavours to discredit The Emperor's policy were most galling to His Majesty. The ex-Chancellor was trading on his popularity and prestige; it was true that Germany owed much to him, but there were also limits to the forbearance of The Emperor and the country. The Emperor would be extremely loth to resort to severe measures, such as prosecuting the ex-Chancellor. The Government hoped therefore to be able to confine their action to refuting in the official and semi-official papers any statements of the ex-Chancellor seeking to resist or discredit The Emperor's policy, as well as all false reports that might be spread by his supporters.

I enclose copy and translation of an Article from the North German Allgemeine Zeitung contradicting a report supposed to have been circulated by Prince Bismarck's friends.[270]

At a dinner given the other day[271] by General von Caprivi, The Emperor, who spoke on almost every subject, including even socialism, stated very clearly that should the social Democrats overstep the bounds of legality they will meet with the most decided repression. This was also considered as a warning to the ex-Chancellor. Again at the annual dinner given here by the members of the Provincial Diet of Brandenburg,[272] His Majesty severely condemned the attempts that were being made to instil anxiety into the minds of the people and to foment a spirit of discontent, if not, of insubordination. These words were likewise considered as directed against the ex-Chancellor.

From the tenor of his remarks it was quite evident to me that Baron von Marschall is greatly incensed against the ex-Chancellor, and should the latter go so far as to lay himself open to a charge of high treason or carry out the intention imputed to him of publishing Documents which, though his own property, are of a very confidential nature, it would not surprise me if he were to meet the same fate that overtook Count Arnim.[273]

On the other hand Prince Bismarck expresses great indignation at being made responsible for all the political articles in the "Hamburger Nachrichten", though he does not say that they do not on the whole reflect his opinions. But he absolutely denies that

[270] The article disputed reports that the Prussian ministerial council (*Ministerrat*), on 15 February 1891, had deliberated on measures against Bismarck's press activities. Enclosures: untitled cutting and translation from *Norddeutsche Allgemeine Zeitung of* 20 February 1891.

[271] On 13 February 1891.

[272] On 20 February 1891.

[273] See n. 261 in this section.

he is seeking to discredit the policy of The Emperor or is trying to throw difficulties in the way of the Government. What are imputed to him as attacks against The Emperor are merely words of warning which he considers he has a right to address to the people when he thinks the country is menaced by danger. As proof of his desire not to meddle in politics or to re-enter political life, his defenders instance his having refused the offer of a mandate for the Reichstag and his declining the pressing invitation of his supporters to take his seat in the Herrenhaus.[274]

It is difficult to arrive at the real truth, but there can be no doubt that a general feeling of uneasiness prevails throughout the country, and thinking men are of opinion that Germany has more to fear from internal dangers than from foreign enemies.

FO 64/1253: Edward B. Malet to Marquess of Salisbury, Very Confidential, No 53, Berlin, 13 March 1891

[Received 16 March. For: The Queen / Prince of Wales; S[alisbury]]

Summary of political events during Malet's absence from Berlin: Waldersee's retirement as chief of staff; Shuvalov's visit to Bismarck; empress dowager's unfortunate visit to Paris

The chief incidents of interest which have taken place during my absence[275] from Berlin are the retirement of Count Waldersee from his post of Chief of the Staff, the visit of Count Schouvaloff to Prince Bismarck and its supposed connexion with the latter's attitude towards the Government, and the visit of The Empress Frederick[276] to Paris. It may be of interest to Your Lordship if I divest them of the entanglements which the numerous versions of newspaper reports have woven round them.

Count Waldersee, who succeeded Field Marshal Count Moltke as Chief of the Staff, owes his fall to somewhat the same cause as brought about the fall of Prince Bismarck.[277] He had been the military mentor of The Emperor for many years, and like Prince Bismarck he fancied that his personal influence with His Majesty was so great that he could do pretty much what he chose. He had

[274] Bismarck stood for the by-election in Kehdingen and Neuhaus (Province of Hanover) and was elected member of the *Reichstag* in April 1891. As with his seat in the Prussian upper house (of which he had been a member since 1849) he did not attend the sittings.

[275] From 16 January to 10 March 1891.

[276] Victoria.

[277] Waldersee tendered his resignation at the end of January; he was dismissed on 2 February 1891.

indeed urged The Emperor to get rid of Prince Bismarck and there is little doubt that he aspired to the post of Chancellor himself. No sooner did The Emperor become aware of his aspirations to supreme influence than His Majesty began to cool towards him, and in the autumn he made a remark which was supposed to show the way the wind was blowing. His Majesty said "Count Waldersee is endeavouring to thrust himself between me and the Chancellor."

A dispute had arisen between General Caprivi and Count Waldersee in regard to the duties of Military Attachés abroad. General Waldersee claimed that they should address their reports direct to him without submitting them to their diplomatic chiefs, and he is said even to have proposed that the military attachés should take charge of the missions in the absence of their chiefs. The resolute refusal of the Chancellor to yield to these demands brought about the critical moment in which the victory of either involved the fall of the other. The Emperor stood by the Chancellor.

In the meantime General Leszcynski [*sic*], who commanded the 9th Army Corps, had fallen into disgrace for receiving Prince Bismarck with high honour as he passed through Altona on his way from Varzin to Friedrichsruh, and he had been relieved of his command.[278] This gave a vacancy which enabled The Emperor to confer a post upon General Waldersee involving no loss of rank or position.

I am inclined to dismiss without much attention a rumour that The Emperor could not forgive General Waldersee's criticism of His Majesty's management of the troops under His Command at the autumn manoeuvres,[279] though many aver that that was the beginning of his loss of Imperial favour.

General Waldersee has borne his reverse with dignity and The Emperor has since taken pains to make it appear that his personal regard for him has not diminished

.//.

The visit of Count Schouvaloff to Friedrichsruh had been long projected, for the invitation had been made and accepted at the time of Prince Bismarck's retirement from Berlin at the end of last March and the Emperor has long been aware that it was likely to take place nor has His Majesty shown any displeasure at the Ambassador's intentions, who however felt that, as time went on, the matter became somewhat delicate owing to the Prince's general

---

[278] Leszczynski – who had invited Bismarck for dinner on 9 January – was dismissed on 2 February; he was succeeded by Waldersee on the same day.

[279] On 19 September 1890.

attitude and to the articles in the "Hamburger Nachrichten" which were attributed to his inspiration.[280] He therefore found excuses to put off the visit, but towards the close of the year he was again pressed by the Prince to redeem his promise. He then mentioned the matter to Baron von Marschall, who said that a mere visit, considering the intimacy which had existed for years between the two, could not offer ground for objection or unfriendly comment. But no date was mentioned and when, on the 13th of February,[281] Count Schouvaloff did actually go to Friedrichsruh, it was without the Knowledge of the authorities. He merely spent a few hours there and he has assured a Colleague that the Prince did not touch upon politics of any kind during the whole time they were together.

Two days afterwards The Emperor called first on Madame Herbette and then went on to call on Countess Schouvaloff. His Majesty was at once admitted at the Russian Embassy but the Countess was not at home and Count Schouvaloff received His Majesty, who then heard for the first time from His Excellency himself of his visit to Friedrichsruh. There is therefore no truth in the report current at the time, that the Ambassador took a message from The Emperor to the Prince. Nor is there, as far as I can learn, any reason for supposing that His Majesty was particularly annoyed at the visit. Count Schouvaloff is a "persona" as "grata" as a Russian Ambassador can be at Berlin. He is a gentleman and a conservative of the old Russian party, without the fads and ambitions of the younger generation of his countrymen, and I imagine that The Emperor would much regret his removal from the post which he holds.

.//.

The result of The Empress Frederick's visit to Paris has caused recriminations all round.[282] It was undertaken with the consent and approval of The Emperor and his advisers. Monsieur Herbette, the French Ambassador, who has honestly striven, during his tenure of office, to ameliorate the relations between France and Germany, had achieved a real success in inducing several French Painters of eminence to promise to send pictures to the coming international Exhibition of Art at Berlin,[283] and The Emperor, who undoubtedly

---

[280] See previous dispatch.

[281] The visit actually took place on 12 February 1891.

[282] Victoria visited Paris on her way to London from 18 to 27 February 1891.

[283] The international arts exhibition – celebrating the 50th jubilee of the *Verein Berliner Künstler* – was opened on 1 May under the patronage of Wilhelm II and Victoria.

wishes for peace and desires that a cordial feeling should exist between all the European Powers, thought that the moment had come when he might evince this feeling especially in regard to France. I suspect that there is truth in the suspicion that if The Empress Frederick's visit to Paris had passed off successfully He would himself have endeavoured to go there not long afterwards. This is however now strenuously denied. Unfortunately one mistake followed upon another in carrying out the project which was undertaken with such laudable objects.

In the first place no warning was given to the French Government. They had no time either to prevent the visit to Paris or to prepare the Paris public for it. Secondly The Empress' veil of incognito was not maintained with sufficient reserve. If Ambassadors and Ministers were received, some step should have been taken in regard to the Chief of the State. This was only done when the error become clear and on the fourth day after The Empress' arrival. The overture was declined. In the interval the drive to Versailles through the Park of St. Cloud had given a handle to the "patriots".[284] When The Empress left Berlin it was settled that the visit should last at most three days. Now that all is over, it is maintained by those who were responsible here that if this programme had been maintained success instead of failure would have been the result. In any case it is now clear that the experiment was a perilous one, for the bitterness of feeling caused here by the conduct of Monsieur Déroulède and his party and the disinclination or powerlessness of the French Government to keep it within bounds,[285] was so strong that it was within an ace of leading to a rupture involving the recall of Monsieur Herbette and Count Münster and a state of tension between the two countries of which the ultimate result might have been most serious.

Count Münster indeed has I believe only been saved by the declaration of Moniseur Herbette that he would himself be compelled to resign if the Count were recalled.

[284] Victoria visited the ruins of the Château de Saint-Cloud and the Palace of Versailles on 24 February. This was seen as a provocation due to the symbolism associated with their role in the Franco-Prussian War, and the subsequent proclamation of Wilhelm I as German Emperor in 1871.

[285] During Victoria's visit adherents of the *Ligue des Patriotes* decorated the Strasbourg statue at La Place de la Concorde with French flags and also placed a wreath on the monument of Henri Regnault, a painter who had fallen during the siege of Paris in January 1871. The wreath was removed by the government for bearing the initials of the banned *Ligue* (L.D.P.), but was subsequently replaced after Déroulède threatened to interpellate in the National Assembly.

The Decree reimposing obstructive passport regulations on the Alsace-Lorraine frontier has been strongly criticized as an act of petulance involving grave inconvenience to people who had nothing to do with the events in Paris.[286] Baron Marschall upholds it as a logical sequence of what has taken place. He says that they were originally imposed by Prince Bismarck as a demonstration on the part of Germany against Boulangeism. At that time the French Government was so weak that General Boulanger and his party were sweeping all before it. Diplomatic representations to the Government were worse than useless. The passport regulations were introduced to rouse the better thinking people in France from their apathy and to show them the consequences of their allowing themselves to be overridden by a reckless minority. It is believed by the German Authorities that the overthrow of Boulangeism[287] was due to the measure in question as it opened the eyes of the French to the precipice before them. A precisely similar situation showed itself at the time of The Empress Frederick's visit. The noisy minority again cowed the Government and the restoration of the obnoxious Passport rules was the best way of recalling the people of France to their senses. It is already asserted to be a success, as the Patriotic league is being credited with the inconvenience caused and a deputation from Alsace to The Emperor is, today, to present a loyal address disclaiming all connexion with the party of revenge.

FO 64/1254: Edward B. Malet to Marquess of Salisbury, No 155, Berlin, 22 August 1891

[[No date] For: Board of Trade, 26 August / Commercial Department; S[alisbury]]

Effects of Russia's ban on rye exports to Germany; press campaign for abolition of corn laws versus government intention to maintain them; prospects for German harvests unclear

The Decree issued by the Russian Government[288] prohibiting the export of Rye from Russia has been made a pretext by a large portion

[286] On 28 February 1891, the imperial ministry for Alsace-Lorraine decreed the strict implementation of the passport regime which had been introduced on 22 May 1888 but subsequently relaxed. Amongst other things, the regulation imposed visa requirements on all French citizens who crossed the border to Alsace-Lorraine, but this was abrogated in September 1891.

[287] The Boulangist movement declined in 1889 after Boulanger, fearing arrest for conspiracy and treason, fled to Brussels and then London. He was tried in absentia for treason later that year.

[288] The imperial *ukase* prohibiting the export of rye, rye flour, and bran was issued on 11 August and came into effect on 27 August.

of the German Press to get up an agitation for the abolition of the corn duties which in Germany are very high amounting to fifty marks per tonne (a German tonne equals nineteen hundredweights two quarters, twenty pounds ten ounces). [Note in margin: '£2–10 – 0. Cwt: 19; qts: 2; lbs: 20; oz: 10']

The subject was discussed by the Council of Ministers[289] under the Presidency of the Imperial Chancellor and it was decided neither to abolish nor reduce the existing duties on Corn.

The Government consider that the amount of Rye imported from Russia, which is comparatively small, can be replaced by consignments from America or other large grain growing countries and they are also of opinion that, pending negotiations with Austria and Italy for the renewal of commercial Treaties,[290] it would be very inexpedient and impolitic to make any change in the existing laws.

The reports too, received by the Government from various parts of the country are not on the whole discouraging and show that the harvest of Rye and wheat, though not a very good one, is likely to be only very little below average.

The policy of the Government has been severely condemned by a large section of the Press, its figures as regards the prospects of the Harvest are disputed and the agitation instead of diminishing seems to be on the increase. The Government while still determined neither to abolish nor alter the corn duties has decided[291] to lower the railway rates for the conveyance of grain and mill produce for distances of over two hundred Kilometers. The reduction in the rate will come into force on the 1st proximo and the Chancellor will urge the smaller German States to follow the example of Prussia in this respect.

The present agitation has naturally led to enormous speculation in Rye which has risen considerably but the prices quoted are merely nominal and fluctuate according as the "Bulls" or the "Bears" get control of the market.[292] It is likewise impossible to arrive at anything approaching correct data in regard to Harvest prospects. If the figures of the "Reichsanzeiger"[293] which are not only disputed but even ridiculed, are correct the Rye Harvest this year should amount to 6,256,136 tonne[s] or nearly as much as in 1887.

---

[289] Sitting of the Prussian state ministry (*Staatsministerium*) on 15 August 1891.

[290] The commercial treaties with Austria-Hungary and Italy were signed on 6 December and passed by the *Reichstag* on 18 December 1891.

[291] On 15 August 1891.

[292] A bull market being a buoyant period when prices rise; a bear market being when prices fall and financial pessimism sets in.

[293] *Deutscher Reichs-Anzeiger und Königlich Preußischer Staats-Anzeiger* of 14 August 1891.

By the recently contracted commercial treaty with Austria the duty on cereals coming into Germany was reduced from 5 marks to 3½ marks and in return for this reduction Austria decreased the tariff on numerous articles of German export.[294] If the German Government were to reduce the tariff on cereals generally the advantage gained by Austria in its commercial negotiations would be cancelled and the treaty would run the risk of not being accepted by the Austrian Parliament and the German Government feel that they would be exposed to a suspicion of bad faith. The duty is imposed from political as well as economic motives and the former weigh heavily in the consideration of the question the political object being to enable Germany to be self providing in cereal in the event of war.

FO 64/1273: Edward B. Malet to Marquess of Salisbury, Secret, No 17, Berlin, 13 January 1892

[Received 18 January. For: The Queen; S[alisbury]]

Wilhelm II receives new Archbishop of Posen; Kulturkampf *consigned to history as emperor seeks reconciliation between Germany and papacy*

I have the honour to inform Your Lordship that Monseigneur Stablewski, the new Archbishop of Posen, was received by the Emperor on the 11th instant. His Majesty tells me that He has great hopes that this appointment may be fruitful of good results, and that He had spoken to the Archbishop at length, and had explained to him that the principal difficulty which he would have to encounter in his diocese would be the democratic tendencies of the lesser clergy.

He had remarked that the Pope[295] was equally interested with Monarchs in combating this tendency, and he expressed his regret that His Holiness should sometimes coquette with republican and democratic ideas.

Monseigneur Stablewski had replied that this action on the part of the Pope was only for show; and that, at heart, His Holiness was entirely conservative.

The Emperor went on to say that he was on the best of terms with the Pope: He had let it be known that the "Culturkampf" was for

---

[294] The reduction in tariffs was agreed during the negotiations for the new commercial treaty in March and April 1891 at Vienna. The draft treaty to which Malet is referring to was concluded on 3 May; the final treaty was signed on 6 December 1891.

[295] Leo XIII.

Him a matter of history only; and that His desire was, to enter on a path of conciliation in all matters in discussion between the Papacy and Germany. The Pope had received these overtures in a very friendly spirit, and His Majesty thought that the nomination of Monseigneur Stablewski, who was a man of high education and good family, would not only be agreeable to the Pope, but would prove His Majesty's solicitude for the spiritual wants of the population of Prussian Poland.

FO 64/1273: Edward B. Malet to Marquess of Salisbury, No 88, Berlin, 26 March 1892

[Received 28 March by bag. For: The Queen / Prince of Wales / Mr Balfour; S[alisbury]]

Ministerial crisis; resignation of Zedlitz over elementary school bill

The Ministerial crisis through which the Government has just passed came upon the public as a complete surprise and there is little doubt that it was equally unforeseen by those principally concerned, for if the Emperor and General Count Caprivi had a prescience of what was coming, it is to be presumed that they would have taken their measures accordingly, and have made such arrangements as would have prevented the public from knowing the dilemma into which they had fallen until it was smoothed.

When the School bill was first submitted to the Prussian Chamber it was approved by the Emperor, but I am assured that His Majesty always held that it must be so modified as to conciliate the moderate party in the Landtag.[296] In the debates which ensued, the bill encountered naturally the violent opposition of the socialist party and the Chancellor considered himself bound as Prussian Prime Minister to come to the assistance of Count Zedlitz,[297] the Minister of Public Instruction, who introduced the Bill. He did so with a chivalrous warmth which it is not unfair to say did more credit to his heart than this head, because he shared the opinion of the Emperor that it would be unwise to force the bill upon the country by the sole vote of the clericals and the conservatives. The opposition in the country became louder but the Government continued to think they would be able to make such modifications in the bill that a part of the opposition would be disarmed. It was however at last

---

[296] The elementary school bill made significant concessions to clerical and Catholic interests; it was introduced in the Prussian house of deputies on 15 January 1892.

[297] Malet is here referring to Caprivi's speeches in the house of deputies on 22 and 29 January 1892.

perceived that this could only be done by divesting the bill of the clauses which alone made it acceptable to the majority.

Under these circumstances the Emperor presided on the 17th at a crown council. Many rumours have been afloat as to what took place at it – one report says that His Majesty complained that the ministers had not kept him properly informed of the strength of the opposition in the country, and that he spoke with such warmth that Count Zedlitz considered himself personally aggrieved. On the other hand I am assured that His Majesty spoke with perfect moderation but that he said that it would be useless to pass the bill if it only received the votes of the clericals and conservatives as he would not sign it, and that those present apparently acquiesced in the prospect of either abandoning it or changing it. At all events at the conclusion of the council there were no indications of the crisis which followed and the questions of the resignation of any member of the Government was not mooted.

Count Zedlitz however the same evening sent in his resignation and told all his friends that he had done so, and once more Count Caprivi's feelings of chivalry gained the upper hand, for he wrote to the Emperor to say that if Count Zedlitz persisted in his intention he also must resign as he was too far committed to his support of the Count to withdraw it.[298] The Emperor endeavoured to prevail upon Count Zedlitz to remain by sending him the Chancellor's letter and expressing the hope that such a crisis might be averted – unfortunately no more discretion was exercised with regard to this communication than over the resignation of Count Zedlitz and the crisis at once became of public notoriety.

With regard to the present arrangement by which Count Caprivi lays down the position of Prussian prime Minister and retains the office of Chancellor of the Empire and Prussian Minister for Foreign Affairs, it is to be observed that the post of Prime Minister in Prussia cannot be said to correspond to that of a Prime Minister in England. He does not form his Government as with us. He presides at the cabinet councils, but at these councils matters are decided by a majority of votes and the Prime Minister has only one vote so that he is not more powerful in the deliberations of the cabinet than any of his colleagues. The new arrangement will have one decided advantage and that is that the position of the Chancellor of the Empire will not be affected by the difficulties of the Prussian prime Minister and that there cannot again be a question of his

---

[298] Caprivi handed in his resignation as Prussian minister president and foreign minister, as well as German chancellor, on 18 March 1892. On 24 March he was dismissed as minister president but retained his two other posts.

falling through the mismanagement of matters alone affecting the Kingdom of Prussia.

FO 64/1273: Power Henry Le Poer Trench to Marquess of Salisbury, Very Confidential, No 117, Berlin, 29 April 1892

[Received 2 May. For: The Queen / Mr Balfour / Print (Western Europe) / Embassies; S[alisbury]]

Irritation caused by Times *article on Triple Alliance; Marschall claims financial cuts in Italy preferable to a bankrupted state; visit by Italian sovereigns of no political significance*

Baron Marschall told me this afternoon that his attention had been called to a Telegram from Berlin, a copy of which is enclosed, which had appeared in yesterday's "Times" regarding the Triple Alliance and the coming of the Marquis di Rudini to Berlin.[299] It was, he said, a pure invention of the acting correspondent of the "Times"[300] and was almost too ridiculous to contradict. He was annoyed, however, that such a report had been spread, and that a leading English Journal should give credence to such absurd rumours; and expressed a hope that, when "The Times" had a regular correspondent here, the information sent to it would be founded on fact, and not on fiction.

Italy and Austria, Baron Marschall said, were entirely free to increase or diminish, according to the state of their finance, their military and naval forces, and although Germany would be sorry to see any serious reductions in the armaments of those countries, such as might tend to raise the warlike hopes of France and Russia, she would rather have Italy cut down her Army to half its present strength than see her become bankrupt.

The financial condition of Italy was most serious; Signor Crispi had spent far too much money on the Army and Navy, and on railways and other public works; – small economies would now avail nothing: some other means must be found to establish an equilibrium between Revenue and Expenditure; and this, he found, could only be

---

[299] The article dated 27 April (Enclosure: 'The Triple Alliance', *The Times*, 28 April 1892) reported a rumour that the Italian prime minister 'will intimate ... that Italy can no longer support the burden of armaments ... and the consent of the German Government would be necessary before any reduction could be carried out without a breach of Italy's written engagements'. Furthermore, the Italian proposal would be followed by a similar one from Austria. For the Triple Alliance see n. 174 in this section.

[300] Name not traceable. The last correspondent, J.B. Richards, died on 5 April 1892.

accomplished by a serious reduction of her Army, and even the weakening of her Navy.

Baron Marschall referred to various other rumours which had appeared in the Press, in regard to the coming visit of the King and Queen of Italy, and to the political importance attached by some Papers to the meetings between the Sovereigns of Germany and Italy.[301] The approaching visit, Baron Marschall assured me had no political significance. It had been arranged early in March, and is made in return for the one paid by the German Emperor and Empress[302] to the King and Queen of Italy at Monza in October 1889.

FO 64/1274: Power Henry Le Poer Trench (in the absence of Sir Edward Malet) to Marquess of Salisbury, Confidential, No 181, Berlin, 6 August 1892

[Received 8 August by bag. For: The Queen / Prince of Wales; S[alisbury]]

Speeches by Bismarck critical of imperial government

I have the honour to enclose herewith, in translation, Précis of the Speeches made by Prince Bismarck at Jena on the 30th and 31st ultimo.[303] These speeches, which have been commented on by the entire German Press, are regarded in Government circles as the most important yet delivered by the Prince, and great has been the surprise of the nation at large at hearing that the Ex-Chancellor, who when in power rode roughshod over the Reichstag and expressed the utmost scorn for Parliamentary institutions, should now come forward as the champion of a Parliamentary regime and of constitutional Government and should claim the right to express the sharpest criticism on the advisors of the Emperor.

The Prince, as in his former speeches, again attacks the Chancellor, and the Government have answered these attacks to an article which appeared in the "Norddeutsche Allgemeine Zeitung" of the 4th. instant, copy and translation of which I have the honour to enclose.[304]

---

[301] Umberto I and Margherita visited Potsdam and Berlin from 20 to 24 June 1892.

[302] Auguste Viktoria.

[303] Enclosures: original cuttings '*Fürst Bismarck in Jena*', *Post*, 1 August 1892 and untitled extract from *Norddeutsche Allgemeine Zeitung*, 2 August 1892; précis of Prince Bismarck's speeches at Jena on 30 and 31 July 1892.

[304] Enclosure: untitled extract, *Norddeutsche Allgemeine Zeitung*, 4 August 1892 and translation.

The constant reflections and attacks by the Prince on the Centre or Catholic Party have given the latter, who on account of the withdrawal of the School Bill in March last[305] had refused to support some Government measures, an excuse, they have eagerly desired, for returning to their former allegiance, and they will now give their entire support to Count von Caprivi and to the Government of the Emperor.

FO 64/1274: Power Henry Le Poer Trench (in the absence of Sir Edward Malet) to Marquess of Salisbury, Confidential, No 186, Berlin, 15 August 1892

[Received 22 August by bag. For: The Queen / Commercial Department; R[osebery], 25 August 1892][306]

Proposal for International Exhibition in Berlin rejected by broad swathes of German society

I have the honour to transmit herewith copies and translation of a report made by the Imperial Chancellor[307] to the Emperor, in consequence of which His Majesty has decided not to adopt the project of holding an International Exhibition in Berlin.[308]

This project was started some months ago and at first met with but little support, except from the class of people who expected to benefit from a large influx of foreigners into Berlin, and the press took very little notice of it. When, however, it became known that France contemplated holding an International Exhibition in Paris in 1900, the scheme was at once taken up and warmly supported by the Anti-French Party and by those Papers which are hostile to France. On the other hand the more influential and moderate portion of the Press, setting aside politics and sentiment, discussed the matter dispassionately and solely in the interest of German Industry. The Chancellor, in a circular,[309] referred the project to the several Federal States, when it was ascertained that there were 40 votes against it, 7 for it and 11 neutral. Opinion is of course divided as to the wisdom of the Chancellor's decision, but it meets with the general approval of the leading newspapers. The majority of the German leaders of Industry, the great employers of labour,

---

[305] See pp. 138–139.
[306] Archibald Primrose, the 5th Earl of Rosebery, became foreign secretary on 18 August 1892.
[307] Leo von Caprivi.
[308] Enclosures: untitled cutting from *Deutscher Reichsanzeiger und Königlich Preußischer Staatsanzeiger*, 13 August 1892 and translation.
[309] In early July 1892.

and especially the more important manufacturers were either against the project or gave it but a lukewarm support, and on all sides it was considered that the State would in all probability have to bear the greater part of the expense. In short, the intelligent classes and the leading newspapers, after due reflection, came to the conclusion that Germany would gain nothing by adopting the scheme, and recognised that Paris was in every way more suitably situated than Berlin for an International Exhibition.

FO 64/1275: Edward B. Malet to Earl of Rosebery, Confidential, No 227, Berlin, 22 October 1892

[Received 24 October. For: The Queen / Prince of Wales / Mr Campbell Bannerman / Confidential to Intelligence Division War Office, 11 November 1892; 'The secrecy has broken down', R[osebery]]

Forthcoming army bill designed to close loophole in recruitment of army reserves and draw more young men into military service

On my return to Berlin, on the 18th instant, I went to see Baron von Marschall, and His Excellency told me that nothing had occurred in Foreign Affairs to give any anxiety to Germany during my absence.[310]

The news of a rupture of relations between Greece and Roumania had just come in, and although the subject which led to the rupture was not of particular importance, the fact that Greece had confided the protection of her Subjects in Roumania to Russia was a circumstance which might produce further complications.[311]

His Excellency went on to say that in Germany the public mind was occupied by the Military Bill, which would be presented to the Reichstag on its assembling.[312] It would lead to serious discussion but the Chancellor Count Caprivi was of opinion that it would pass.

By the Constitution[313] every male subject was liable to conscription, but as the strength of the peace establishment was fixed at a certain number, this provision of the Constitution had never been carried out. The result was that, as the populations had increased, the

---

[310] Malet was on leave of absence from 15 July and stayed at Homburg until 10 September when he left for England.

[311] Diplomatic relations were interrupted on 16 October 1892 in the course of the 'Zappa Affair', a dispute over the will of a Greek merchant who had resided and died in Romania in 1865, and to whose estate the Greek government laid claim.

[312] The army bill stipulated a reduction in military service from three to two years (infantry) and allocated supplies for a perpetual peacetime army of 492,086 men (an increase of 72,037 men) for seven years. It was introduced in the *Reichstag* on 23 November 1892.

[313] Article 57 of the imperial constitution of 1871.

number of men escaping service had steadily increased also, until it had attained the large figure of 100,000 yearly.

The consequence of this would be, that, in case of war, the Government would in the first instance have to call out men who were in reserve and who were mostly married and established in professions; while vast numbers of young men, who were the proper material for the army, were hurriedly being trained to be fit for duty. It was hoped that the alleviation which the bill would bring to the prospects of the Reserve men would render it popular to the masses, and that it would be recognised that the present state of things created an anomaly which ought to be abolished.

The crux would arise through the necessity of finding funds to pay for the large increase of men, but the Chancellor hoped that the patriotism of the Germans was sufficiently strong to enable a majority of their Representatives in the Reichstag to vote them.

I had a conversation with Count Caprivi on the following day, and His Excellency confirmed Baron von Marschall's statement that he hoped and thought that the measure would pass.

The Bill was presented yesterday to the federal Council but its clauses will remain a secret until it is submitted to the Reichstag.

FO 64/1293: Edward B. Malet to Earl of Rosebery, No 5, Berlin, 3 January 1893

[Received 9 January. For: Chief Clerk / Copy to: War Office; Seen by Chief Clerk [stamped]; 'This is a very important question. Might not the Desp. and Encl[.] 1 be printed for: Cabinet / War Office / Admiralty / Treasury / Post Office', T.H.S. [Thomas Henry Sanderson]; 'Yes – let me see the Reports in print', R[osebery]; [Printed] 19 January]

Colonel Swaine's report on civil employment of German military; remarks on far-reaching positive effects of military training on working life

I have the honour to inclose herewith a report from Colonel Swaine on the system under which civil employment is guaranteed to soldiers and sailors in Germany on the completion of a certain number of years military or naval service.[314]

The question of adopting a system of this kind in the United Kingdom has already been the subject of attention in Parliament,[315]

---

[314] The 'civil employment' of German soldiers and sailors was regulated by decrees of 10 September 1882 and 20 June 1885. Enclosure: report No 1 by Colonel Swaine on the state employment of all soldiers and sailors, Berlin, 3 January 1893.

[315] On 10 June 1892.

and, as it is one of grave importance, I venture to draw Your Lordship's special attention to Colonel Swaine's report.

Being a civilian I shall not be suspected of prejudice if I bear testimony to the wholesome effect which military training has upon the classes from which soldiers are drawn. In Germany this effect is constantly before one's eyes. In all branches of labour men who have served are preferred by employers on account of their habits of discipline and regularity.

It would be beyond the scope of the subject of Colonel Swaine's report to urge evidence that the military system in Germany gives back-bone to the Empire in the field of trade and industry in peaceful progress and prosperity, but it is allowable to deduce from what is patent here, that if State Employment in the United Kingdom were assured to soldiers of good conduct after the completion of a certain number of years of service, the general public would gain largely through the increased efficiency of the service in those departments to which such soldiers were admitted.

FO 64/1294: Power Henry Le Poer Trench to Earl of Rosebery, Confidential, No 116, Berlin, 19 May 1893

[Received 22 May. For: The Queen / Prince of Wales; R[osebery]]

Publication of a letter written by Prince Albrecht of Prussia in favour of reconciliation between Bismarck and the emperor; not the right moment for this course of action

On the 13th Instant the "Vorwärts", the chief organ of the Social Democrats, published a letter dated Blankenburg, May 9, 1893, alleged to have been written by Prince Albrecht of Prussia, and addressed to an Excellency whose name was not stated. The Prince, in this letter, of which I have the honour to enclose a translation,[316] says that Herr von Witzleben, being of opinion that a reconciliation between the Emperor and Prince Bismarck would have a favourable effect on the internal situation in Germany, has asked him to use his influence to get the Prince invited to the ceremony of unveiling the monument to the Emperor William I at Görlitz[317] and thus afford him an opportunity of meeting the Emperor. Prince Albrecht adds that, while he cannot himself interfere officially, he fully recognizes the importance and advisability of such a step and

---

[316] Enclosure: translation of letter by Albrecht of Prussia which appeared in *Vorwärts* on 13 May 1893.

[317] The monument was unveiled by Wilhelm II on 18 May 1893.

trusts His Excellency will see his way to giving effect to Herr von Witzleben's suggestion.

The "Vorwärts", alarmed at the prospect of such a reconciliation, publishes in the same paper in which appears the letter, an earnest appeal to the Socialists throughout Germany to do their utmost to prevent Prince Bismarck's return to power.

I deferred writing to Your Lordship about this letter before assuring myself of its authenticity, and until I was able to say more about it than was to be found in the Press. I have now ascertained from a thoroughly trustworthy source, that the letter was really penned by Prince Albrecht and was destined for General von Winterfeldt, now commanding the Garde Corps, and who was formerly chief of the Staff to Prince Albrecht. The letter, it is said, never reached its destination, and is supposed to have been stolen at Blankenburg. The "Vorwärts" got it without an envelope and only learnt the day before yesterday for whom it was intended. It tells us nothing new as regards Prince Albrecht's sympathies, for it is well known that he has always been in favour of a reconciliation between the Emperor and Prince Bismarck. His Royal Highness thinks, like many other Germans, that it is much to be regretted that the Emperor should appear to be ungrateful and unfriendly to the founder of the Empire, but forgets that a reconciliation during the present crisis would be humiliating for His Majesty, and prejudicial to the prestige of the Throne. Indeed, Prince Bismarck is reported to have admitted to a friend that, supposing a reconciliation were possible, this would certainly not be the moment to seek to bring it about. The Emperor is not in the least annoyed at such a letter having been written and published, but he has given orders that every effort shall be made to discover who stole it, and the Imperial Secretary of the Post Office[318] and the Police are taking the necessary steps to trace the thief.

In connection with the above letter it is to be remarked that, for some little time, Prince Bismarck's Papers have ceased to attack the policy of the Emperor.

As Your Lordship is aware, there has always been a Party in Germany who would rejoice to see Prince Bismarck once more at the helm of the State, and there can be no doubt that there is now also a Party, though a small one, which includes even some supporters of the Government, which would welcome the downfall of Caprivi and Miquel. The Chancellor's policy of making Commercial Treaties at the expense,[319] as they consider it, of the

---

[318] Heinrich von Stephan.

[319] Commercial treaties were concluded with Austria-Hungary, Italy, Belgium, Switzerland (all December 1891 and put into effect from February 1892), with Servia

agriculturalists, has incensed a large number of Conservative Landowners. It is an open secret that many of these Conservatives, though willing to support the Army Bill voted with alacrity for the closure, thus signing the death warrant of the late Reichstag.[320] They hope the next Reichstag will, while favourable to the Army Bill, be strongly protectionist and prevent the conclusion of any more Commercial Treaties on the basis of those already in operation, which they consider so detrimental to their special interests.

FO 64/1294: Edward B. Malet to Earl of Rosebery, No 126, Berlin, 27 May 1893

[Received 29 May by messenger. For: The Queen / Prince of Wales; R[osebery]]

Unease about composition of future Reichstag; political implications of army bill

Nothing but the most general surmises are as yet afloat as to what will be the composition of the future Reichstag and the result, as is constantly the case in general elections, may upset all calculations.[321] The general opinion seems to be that the coming chamber will pass the military bill,[322] but, although this may be counted as a victory for the Emperor and the Government, it will be to some extent counterbalanced by a defeat of their policy in another direction. A Reichstag which will vote the Military Bill will oppose the commercial policy of the Government. The Treaties recently concluded with Roumania and Servia will probably be rejected and the negotiation of a Treaty with Russia will have to be abandoned.[323]

The split in the "Central" or clerical party is complete. A very influential member of it, Freiherr von Schorlemer = Alst, who was the foremost fighter in the Cultur Kampf next to Windthorst, has

(August 1892, effected in January 1894), Spain (August 1893, but not ratified by Spain), Rumania (October 1893, in effect from January 1894), and Russia (February 1894, effected in March 1894). All treaties were based on a most favoured nation clause and set to last until 31 December 1903.

[320] The *Reichstag* was dissolved on 6 May 1893. For the rejection of the army bill see n. 322 in this section.

[321] Elections to the *Reichstag* were held on 15 June 1893.

[322] The army bill (see n. 312 in this section) and the 'Huene compromise' proposed by Karl von Hoiningen-Huene (which reduced the intended increase of army strength from 72,037 to 59,198 men) were rejected by the *Reichstag* on 6 May 1893. A revised bill was introduced in the newly elected *Reichstag* on 7 July and passed on 14 July.

[323] The treaty with Serbia was signed on 21 August 1892; the treaty with Romania was initialled on 9 April and signed on 21 October 1893. Negotiations with Russia started in October 1893. For the commercial treaties see also n. 319 in this section.

refused to accept the rejection of the Military Bill as a plank of the "Central" platform. He is a large landed proprietor in Westphalia where he is styled the "King of the peasants", and his example in maintaining his candidature for his former electoral district,[324] and proclaiming his support of the Bill will be followed by many Catholics.

When I was in England I observed an impression that the crisis in Germany was of so serious a nature that it might be the prelude to great events, tending even towards some Imperial Coup d'État or revolution. There does not appear to be any apprehension of this kind in Germany. The Emperor and the Government have taken the steps which they deemed best calculated to secure the passing of the Bill. They have acted strictly within the limits of the Constitution and there seems to be no sort of apprehension that, if they fail, they will attempt to gain their object by means which would constitute an infringement upon it.

FO 64/1294: Edward B. Malet to Earl of Rosebery, No 185, Berlin, 31 August 1893

[Received 4 September. For: The Queen / Prince of Wales; R[osebery]]

Duke of Edinburgh's accession to the throne of Saxe-Coburg and Gotha is generally welcomed

Your Lordship will doubtless have received from Her Majesty's Chargé d'Affaires at Coburg,[325] reports as to the way in which public opinion in the Duchies has regarded the accession of His Royal Highness The Duke of Edinburgh to the Ducal Throne.[326]

Here in Berlin the public press has, with but few exceptions, hailed the event as yet another tie binding together the two Empires, and has greeted the accession of the new Sovereign with every mark of sympathy and respect.

As a notable exception to this attitude I may refer to an Article published in the Conservative "Reichsbote",[327] with which it is unnecessary to trouble Your Lordship as it has already been translated by the English Press. [Note in margin: See "Times" of Aug. 26. 1893']

The "National-Zeitung", one of the principal Berlin Liberal Organs, published on the 27th Instant a leading Article on the

---

[324] Schorlemmer-Alst was candidate for the electoral district Bochum-Witten.

[325] Alexander Condie Stephen.

[326] Alfred succeeded as Duke of Saxe-Coburg and Gotha on 22 August 1893.

[327] On 26 August the *Reichsbote* stated that the thought of a foreigner on a German throne was intolerable.

same subject. The writer points out that by the Constitution of 1852[328] the English Sovereign or Heir Apparent would, in the event of there being no other descendant of His Royal Highness The Prince Consort, be entitled to rule over the United Duchies "and for this purpose to appoint a Lieutenant Governor or Stadholder, until such time as the Government could be undertaken by a Prince of the special line of Prince Albert, of age and capable of reigning." After pointing out that the possibility of a personal Union of the Duchies to the British Crown might under certain circumstances still occur, the writer declares that "this possibility must be considered as a political impossibility: the new German Empire is a national self-contained commonwealth, a state of things which excludes the personal union of any part of the Empire with foreign Powers."

Baron von Rotenhan, the Acting Secretary of State for Foreign Affairs, assured me the other day that The Emperor had been very pleased to be able to testify, by His Majesty's presence on the occasion of the taking of the Oath to the Constitution by the Duke of Edinburgh,[329] that His Majesty upholds the order of Succession to the Throne of the Duchies; and another distinguished Member of the Government stated in the course of conversation yesterday that the accession of The Duke of Edinburgh will be an additional assurance of practical sympathy between two Empires who have so great an interest in the maintenance of the European peace.

FO 64/1294: Martin Gosselin to Earl of Rosebery, No 197, Berlin, 9 September 1893

[Received 11 September by messenger. For: The Queen; Confidential to: Paris / War Office; 20 September; R[osebery]]

Wilhelm II's visit to Alsace-Lorraine appears to have made a good impression

The visit of the German Emperor to the Reichsland[330] appears from all accounts to have passed off without a hitch of any sort, and the German press of all shades of opinion are unanimous in recording the good impression produced by His Majesty's presence in Alsace Lorraine. [Note in margin: 'Confidential memo: by Colonel Swaine: 5 Sept: 1893']

---

[328] Article 9 of the constitution of 1852 (*Staatsgrundgesetz für die Herzogtümer Coburg und Gotha*).

[329] Alfred took the oath on 23 August at Reinhardsbrunn Castle. See pp. 152–153.

[330] Wilhelm visited the Imperial Territory of Alsace-Lorraine from 3 to 9 September 1893.

Baron von Rotenhan told me yesterday that the Government were greatly gratified at the cordial reception given to the Emperor and the other German Princes in Lorraine, and specially at Metz, which the Party of Protest have hitherto regarded as their stronghold: and Colonel Swaine, the Military Attaché of this Embassy, who has been residing at Metz all this week, writes word that the enthusiasm of the French-speaking peasantry has been most remarkable wherever and whenever the Emperor has shewn himself.

The Mayor of Ogy,[331] an old man of 85 years of age, long known for his French sympathies, speaking in French, welcomed His Majesty to Lorraine, and expressed the hope that His Majesty during his short stay in the province would learn "the certainty of our true and loyal feelings, and that God might grant long life to our August Sovereign, and so enable us often to welcome His Majesty to our dear Lorraine".

The Government are specially pleased with the address of Bishop Fleck of Metz,[332] as indicating that for the future they can count on the cooperation and support of the clergy of the Province.

On the other hand, the speech delivered by the Emperor at the banquet given to the civil authorities of Metz on the 5th instant struck a chord which has reechoed to the furthest limits of the Fatherland:

"Germans you are, and with the help of God and our German Sword, Germans you shall remain."

Following the example of the King of Belgians, the Grand Duke of Luxemburg sent his Minister of State, Herr Eyschen, and the Luxemburg Chargé d'Affaires at this Court, Comte de Villers, to Metz on the 5th instant, to greet His Majesty on his arrival at the frontier fortress.

In my despatch N° 189 of the 2nd instant, I alluded to the absence of Colonel Meunier, the French Military Attaché at this Court, from this year's autumn manoeuvres on the French frontier; I have the honour to enclose a Confidential Memorandum for which I am indebted to Colonel Swaine, showing how this silent protest on the part of the French Government is regarded by His Majesty and public opinion in the German Army.[333]

This morning's papers announce that the Prince of Naples[334] will accompany the Emperor to South Germany and attend the Autumn Manoeuvres of the Wurtemburg Army Corps at

---

[331] Monsieur Dory, on 3 September.
[332] On 3 September.
[333] Enclosure: confidential memorandum by Colonel Swaine, Metz, 5 September 1893.
[334] Vittorio Emanuele.

Ludwigsburg on the 16th instant. His Royal Highness will be lodged
at the Royal Palace. The foreign Military Attachés have been also invited by the King
of Wurtemburg to attend these manoeuvres.

FO 64/1294: Edward B. Malet to Earl of Rosebery, No 216, Berlin, 25 September 1893

[Received 28 September. For: Chief Clerk (see separate minute); Copy to Treasury
(with Lord Dufferin's No 408), 4 October; R[osebery]]

Report on use of Remington typewriter at the embassy

In reply to Your Lordship's dispatch No 229 of the 19th Instant, I
have the honour to report that the Remington Type-writer supplied
by the Stationery Office has been in constant use at this Embassy for
a period of over 18 months.

It is used for signature copies of Despatches and Notes as well as
for copies of enclosed documents; and the Imperial Secretary of
State for Foreign Affairs[335] has repeatedly expressed to me his satisfaction at Notes which being addressed to him in type-writing, the clear-
ness of which greatly facilitates the reading and translation.

Although the junior Secretaries have not, of course, attained the
speed and proficiency of professional typists, it is nevertheless
found that the use of the machine involves a considerable saving of
time and labour, and also obviates the possible mutilation of proper
names resulting from illegible handwriting.

The staff of Secretaries has not been constant during the above-
mentioned period, but in spite of this the type-writer has never
been entirely neglected; and I am of opinion that with good-will
and application anyone may learn it sufficiently in a fortnight
to effect a saving of time. The machine has been used by
Mr Whitehead, Mr Wyndham and Mr Ian Malcolm, and each of
these were soon able to type-write with greater rapidity than they
could have copied in a good and clear handwriting.

If I may venture to make a suggestion, however, I would advise that
type-writers should only be supplied to Embassies and larger Missions
where there are several junior Secretaries, of whom one at least may be
expected to familiarize himself with the use of the machine. At the same
time I should wish to point out that the machine supplied to this
Embassy is apparently inferior to that used in the Foreign Office, the

---

[335] Adolf Freiherr Marschall von Bieberstein.

latter having much larger and clearer type, better suited to official correspondence; and I would suggest that machines similar to the Foreign Office type-writer should in future be supplied to Her Majesty's Missions abroad. Whether the Remington is the best machine for official use is a question which can no doubt be fully determined by experience at home, and Her Majesty's Stationery Office is doubtless cognisant of all the most recent improvements.

To illustrate how useful the type-writer has proved, I may mention that a second machine, the property of a member of staff, has also been in use in the Chancery of this Embassy for the last six months.

FO 64/1295: Martin Gosselin to Earl of Rosebery, No 238, Berlin, 14 October 1893

[Received 16 October by messenger. For: The Queen; Copy to Admiralty with reference, 16 October 1893; C.B.R. [Charles B. Robertson]; R[osebery], 19 October]

Accession of Alfred to throne of Saxe-Coburg-Gotha; reflections on oath and absence of allegiance to empire in all sovereign oaths; explanations concerning sovereigns' ties to the constitution

With reference to [Note in margin: 'Anzeiger, 26 Augt 1893'] Your Lordship's despatch N° 251 of the 9th instant respecting the form of oath [Note in margin: 'Translation'] taken by Duke Alfred of Saxe-Coburg-Gotha on the occasion of His Royal Highness' accession to the ducal throne, I have the honour to enclose copy and translation of the oath taken by the Duke on the 23rd of August last,[336] before the Saxe-Coburg-Gotha Ministers of State and officially communicated by the Minister of State, Herr Strenge, to the Common Diet of the two Duchies on the 25th that month.[337]

By this Oath, His Royal Highness swore to observe and defend the Constitution of the Duchies, but no reference whatever is made therein to the relations of the Ducal Government to the Empire.

The Oath, it is true, was taken in the presence of the Emperor, but His Majesty assisted at the ceremony merely as a spectator, and as a mark of affection and respect towards his uncle, the new Sovereign of the Duchies.

No oath of Allegiance is taken either by the King of Prussia or by any of the German Sovereign Princes to the Empire; each German

[336] Alfred succeeded as Duke of Saxe-Coburg and Gotha on 22 August 1893. Enclosures: oath taken by Duke Alfred of Saxe-Coburg-Gotha upon his accession to the ducal throne printed in *Deutscher Reichs-Anzeiger*, 26 August 1893 and translation.

[337] Both Saxe-Coburg and Saxe-Gotha each had their own *Landtag*; the joint *Landtag* consisted of the members of the two assemblies.

Ruler enjoys an absolutely independent position as far as his individual Sovereignty is concerned, the King of Prussia, as German
Emperor, being simply primus inter pares.

According to the Constitution of the German Empire, – dated
April 16, 1871 – , the German Sovereigns concluded "an everlasting
Confederation for the protection of the territory of the Confederation
and the rights thereof",[338] under the Presidency of the King of
Prussia, who, as such, bears the name of German Emperor; and
this Engagement is held to bind the successors of all the original parties to the Constitutional Act.

FO 64/1295: Martin Gosselin to Earl of Rosebery, No 246, Berlin, 20 October 1893

[Received 23 October by messenger. For: The Queen / Confidential to Embassies;
'Pleasant', R[osebery], 23 October]

*Marschall on Franco-Russian fêtes; Czar's visit to French ships in Copenhagen seen as a significant
gesture; growing Franco-Russian amity*

Baron von Marschall, referring today to the Franco-Russian fêtes,
said that there was no cause for complaint in the tone of the many
speeches which were being made all day long by the French and
Russian Orators, and that he hoped that the visit of the Russian officers to Paris would pass off without any untoward incident.[339]

He was much struck by the telegraphic correspondence exchanged
between Monsieur Carnot and the Russian Emperor, the former
congratulating His Majesty on the profound sympathies uniting the
two nations, and receiving in reply a mere expression of the pleasure
felt by His Majesty that the Russian Fleet had been able to return the
Cronstadt visit.[340]

"On voulait, à ce qu'il parait, mettre pas mal d'eau dans le vin
français."[341]

I asked His Excellency what was thought here of the visit[342] paid by
the Czar to the French Ships at Copenhagen.

He replied that this step was in his opinion far more "significant"
than anything which had occurred either at Toulon or Paris. It was

[338] Preamble of the imperial constitution of 1871.

[339] The festivities referred to took place on the first day of the visit of a Russian naval
squadron at Toulon from 13 to 28 October; a delegation of 50 Russian officers visited
Paris from 17 to 27 October.

[340] The French naval squadron visited Kronstadt between 23 July and 8 August 1891.

[341] French: 'One wished, so it would seem, to water down the French wine.'

[342] On 13 October 1893.

well known that during his annual outing in Denmark, the Emperor always abstained as much as possible from taking part in public demonstrations, and his visit therefore to the French Ship – and the Salute given to the French Vessels by the Imperial Yacht in a foreign port are the more remarkable. [Note by Rosebury in margin : 'Yes, but all this was not contemplated but forbidden by H.I.M [His Imperial Majesty]]

Baron von Marschall considers that this step on His Majesty's part shows "une habileté hors ligne"[343] on the part of Monsieur Mouraview, the Russian Minister, and Monsieur Pasteur, the French Chargé d'Affaires at Copenhagen.

He has, however, been given to understand that the Danish Court is anxious to dissociate itself from this philo-French Demonstration and that neither the King nor the Crown Prince[344] accompanied the Emperor on board the French Ship.

"It remains to be seen", the Baron added, "whether Germany or England will be the first to suffer from this Franco-Russian foregathering."

FO 64/1295: Edward B. Malet to Earl of Rosebery, Confidential, No 306, Berlin, 20 December 1893

[Received 25 December by bag. For: The Queen / Print / Western Europe / Paris / Rome; Qy: Admiralty – secret / Lord Spencer; R[osebery], 27 December]

Bülow's appointment as ambassador in Italy due to emperor's intervention; Holstein's views on Italian question; Italy may turn to Russia and France if England unwilling to protect her

The appointment of Herr von Bülow to be German Ambassador at Rome has caused some surprise, as he is junior to nearly all the Chiefs of Mission in the German diplomatic Service.[345] It is said that his nomination is due entirely to the Emperor and that it was prompted, on His Majesty's part, by the feeling that the state of affairs in Italy is critical and that it was necessary to send thither a man of marked ability to represent Germany at the present juncture.

Monsieur de Bülow is married to a daughter of Madame Minghetti, the widow of the Italian Statesman by her first husband.[346] She may, however, encounter difficulty in making her position at Rome, as she is the divorced wife of Count Doenhoff, now German Minister at Dresden.

---

[343] French: 'outstanding acumen'.
[344] Frederick.
[345] Bülow was appointed on 20 December 1883.
[346] Maria von Bülow was the daughter of Domenico Beccadelli di Bologna.

The recall of Count Solms the late Ambassador, has been in the air for some time. I am told that his favour with the Emperor was much shaken by the blunder, intentional or otherwise, of not informing His Majesty of Lord Vivian's Garden Party during the Imperial visit to Rome on the occasion of the silver wedding.[347]

Baron Holstein, the Chief of the diplomatic department at the German Foreign Office, met me in the Street this morning and spoke to me about Italian affairs. He is a man of great intelligence and a very keen politician. In Count Bismarck's time,[348] I used often to see him, and got a good deal of news from him, as he talks very openly; but since Baron von Marschall's advent to office he has ceased to receive visits from all heads of missions.

He remarked to me that affairs in Italy were very critical, and that although Signor Crispi came into office with the most reassuring declarations, it was difficult to have complete confidence in the continuity of Italian policy, while it was under his control.[349] All would depend upon the attitude of Great Britain. Italy had always two policies open to it: – the triple Alliance with its burthens,[350] or the irredentist programme[351] with the alluring prospects held out to it by France and Russia, if it would abandon the triple Alliance.

The crucial test was confidence in the safety of its coasts from attacks. Signor Crispi would retain this confidence as long as he could believe that Great Britain would come to Italy's assistance if they were attacked. He would probably soon begin to sound our Foreign Office to see what he had to expect; and Baron Holstein hoped that he might at least receive courteous and not altogether discouraging replies, for he could not help fearing that the day that Signor Crispi was convinced that he had nothing to hope for in that quarter, he would turn his face towards France and Russia.

"But", I said, "Italy is bound by the treaties with Austria and Germany, which have some years to run: she cannot escape from the obligations which these treaties impose." Baron Holstein rejoined that he had not much faith in the efficacy of treaties of this nature if a country did not wish to be bound by them. "If a treaty is to die, it is very useless during the time that precedes its decease".

---

[347] Wilhelm II visited Rome from 20 to 27 April 1883. Umberto I and Margherita of Savoy's wedding anniversary was on 21 April; the garden party at the British embassy was on 24 April.

[348] Herbert von Bismarck.

[349] Francesco Crispi took office as prime minister on 15 December 1893.

[350] For the Triple Alliance see n. 174 in this section.

[351] The Italian irredentist movement demanded the cession of the Italian speaking parts of Austria-Hungary to the Italian kingdom.

FO 64/1325: Edward B. Malet to Earl of Rosebery, Secret, No 25, Berlin, 3 February 1894

[Received 5 February. For: The Queen / Lord Spencer J.; ~~Print (Brazil) vol only~~; R[osebery]]

Meeting with Wilhelm II at opera ball; emperor threatens Brazilian minister that German war vessels will fire on Rio if threatened again

With reference to my Despatch N° 24 of this day's date reporting that Baron von Marschall had spoken to me about the situation at Rio de Janeiro,[352] I have the honour to inform Your Lordship that, at the Opera Ball last night, The Emperor, during his usual visit to the box allotted to the Ambassadors and Ambassadresses, in the course of conversation with the former (we were all standing round His Majesty) fell upon the same subject, and he told us that he had spoken "carrément"[353] about it to the Brazilian Minister, Baron Itajuba, at the Court Ball which took place on the 31st Instant. His Majesty said that he had told the Minister that the German war vessels would blow the town of Rio to pieces if the Brazilian Government batteries fired again upon their boats, and, His Majesty added laughing, that he thought he had given the Minister a good fright.

In this assumption I fancy that His Majesty was correct, for it has come to me from another source that, after the Ball, Baron Itajuba stayed up till three in the morning telegraphing to his Government.

FO 64/1325: Edward B. Malet to Earl of Kimberley, Secret, No 53, Berlin, 24 March 1894

[Received 26 March by bag. For: Lord Rosebery / Chancellor of the Exchequer / Commercial Department; K[imberley]]

Conversation with Baron von Marschall on advantages and implications of Russo-German commercial treaty

With reference to Your Lordship's Despatch No. 83 Secret of the 20th inst, requesting me to ascertain the opinion of members of the German Government as to the relative advantages gained by Russia and Germany by the Commercial Treaty and the object of Russia in making one from which it could derive so little benefit, I

---

[352] Malet is referring to the second Brazilian naval revolt against the central government in Rio de Janeiro which broke out in September 1893 and was suppressed in March 1894. Wilhelm II was sympathetic to the allegedly royalist insurgents.

[353] French: 'bluntly'.

have the honour to inform Your Lordship that I spoke to Baron von Marschall on the subject to day.[354] He is the member of the Government who is most qualified to speak on the subject, as he defended the Treaty in the Reichstag[355] and in conjunction with the Chancellor[356] has borne the burthen of the fight and reaped the spoils of victory, the Emperor having bestowed upon him[357] the Grand-cross of the Red Eagle.

He acknowledged that he honestly considered that the advantage was nearly all on the German side. I then asked His Excellency what was the motive which induced the Russian Government to conclude it. He replied that a large preponderance of public opinion in Russia considered that Russian grain would find its market in Germany and that the leading object of the Russian Government was to conciliate those who held this view.

I said the prices of grain in Germany rendered this hope illusory. His Excellency replied that in the case of wheat and barley it was so, but that oats would find a ready and immediate market here.

I then asked His Excellency whether general political consider-ations might not have something to do with it; whether the Russians had not acted in the interests of peace; whether they had not wished to make a counterpoise to the French-Russian Rapprochament, feeling that the latter might carry them further than was intended. His Excellency said that he had not heard any-thing to lead him to suppose that this had entered into the calculation of the Russian Government, but that he was of opinion that the Russians and the Emperor especially were somewhat out of conceit with their French friends.

I then suggested another possible motive to His Excellency; I asked whether if the negotiations had not been brought to a successful issue it would not have been a very serious outlook for both countries? To this Baron von Marschall assented. He said that continuance of the tariff war would have been frought [sic] with dangers for both – the customs duties being so onerous gave rise to smuggling on a large scale. As long as the negotiations were going on, the customs author-ities on both frontiers were, as it were, authorised to be lax in the observance of its most rigorous terms. If the negotiations had been broken off, continuous frontier trouble would have been the result,

---

[354] The commercial treaty with Russia – based on a most favoured nation clause – was concluded on 10 February 1894 and passed by the *Reichstag* on 16 March. It came into effect on 20 March.
[355] On 26 February 1894.
[356] Leo von Caprivi.
[357] On 20 March 1894.

armed collisions would probably have taken place and the ill-will of the two nations towards each other would have grown apace. He considered that the continuance of the customs war would have been distinctly dangerous to peace between Germany and Russia. He added that it would have ruined the German Ports on the Baltic and that he was grateful to these towns, Dantzig, Lubeck etc. for their attitude during the negotiations, for had they proclaimed their danger it would have been a strong weapon in the hands of Russia to win further concessions from Germany.

FO 64/1333: Edward B. Malet to Earl of Kimberley, Africa, No 47, 14 April 1894

[Received 16 April by bag. Print (Niger I); 17 April][358]

Colonial affairs in Cameroon's hinterland causing thorny Anglo-German relations; draft note for German government; useful relationship between German head of colonial department and secretary of embassy

I have the honour to acknowledge the receipt of Your Lordship's Despatch N° 36 [Note in margin: 'Africa'] of 11th instant on the questions arising out of Agreements lately concluded by Germany with Great Britain and France affecting the Cameroons Hinterland.[359]

Your Lordship instructs me to be guided generally in my communications on the subject by the terms of this Despatch, and Your Lordship empowers me to communicate to the German Government the revised regulations for the navigation of the Niger which are inclosed in it.[360]

---

[358] Notes on docket: 'This draft note is good and civil, but it would be certain to be answered, perhaps unpleasantly. Our real object is to anticipate a joint attack by Germany and France resp[ecting] the Niger Navigation. It might be best that Sir E. Malet should send the regulations with a note in the sense of the bracketed passages of the draft and speak in the sense of the remainder when he thinks it advisable.' H.P.A. [Henry Percy Anderson]; 'I quite agree. The note would only irritate and produce a long winded reply in the "best" German Chancery style.' K[imberley], 18 April; 'Dft [draft] accordingly', 21 April].

[359] Malet is referring to the German agreement with Great Britain of 14 April and 15 November 1893 respecting the borders of the German Cameroon colony, and the agreements with France of 4 February and 15 March 1894.

[360] The revised regulations for the Royal Niger Company were issued on 19 April 1894. According to Kimberley, in his dispatch to Malet of 11 April 1894, these regulations were 'at least as favourable to foreign trade as those [that] apply to any other river open to general navigation'. Notwithstanding German accusations against the Niger Company and complaints that navigating the Niger was 'next to impossible', 'Great Britain as the riparian Power, has done its utmost to assist the passage of vessels engaged in peaceful commerce'.

The action of the German Government has been so little frank or friendly in the matter of the French negotiations, that I am inclined to think that it would be well to place our appreciations of the course they have chosen to pursue on record in a Note to Baron von Marschall with such reticence as becomes a State Paper, and bearing in mind that we prefer cooperation with Germany in Africa to continued rejection of proposals which one Government may make to the other, and that therefore the general design of the note should rather be to disarm future opposition than to widen the breach by the exposure of the naked truth.

I venture to submit herewith to Your Lordship a draft of a Note which I have drawn up on these lines, and to submit it for Your Lordship's emendation in case You should agree in the advantage of writing such a Note at all.[361]

I have omitted all mention of Dr Kayser and his remarks.[362] The position in regard to this gentleman is a difficult one. The Ambassador can only communicate with Baron von Marschall, the Secretary of State, but as His Excellency practically leaves the whole direction of African Affairs to Dr Kayser, who is the head of the Colonial Department, it has been found convenient that Her Majesty's Secretary of Embassy should have access to the latter, and, as Dr Kayser is tolerably communicative, the system has been useful in keeping us to some extent in touch with the views prevailing [in] German Colonial policy. If however the information gained in this manner were brought up against Dr Kayser, it is probable that he would decline to see Mr Gosselin any more, and we should lose a very convenient medium of communication on colonial affairs – the only one, in fact, which we possess, for my conversations on these matters with Baron von Marschall are usually treated by His Excellency as ad referendum[363] to Dr Kayser.

If Your Lordship does not approve of engaging in a polemic with the German Government which may be the result of sending in such a Note as I have drafted, I would propose to send to Baron von Marschall a draft of the revised regulations of the Niger Navigation without comment beyond such as I may make verbally in speaking of the matter to His Excellency.

---

[361] Enclosure: Draft, Malet to Marschall, Berlin, April 1894.

[362] Malet is probably referring to Kayser's complaints about the attitude of the Royal Niger Company, which he made in a conversation with Martin Gosselin on 6 April 1894.

[363] Latin: 'for further consideration'.

FO 64/1333: Martin Gosselin to Earl of Kimberley, Africa, No 63, 26 May 1894

[Received 28 May. For: The Queen / Lord Rosebery / Chancellor of the Exchequer; Cabinet; Print / Paris, P.L. [printed letter], No. 179, 31 May / Brussels; P.L. [printed letter], No 56, 30 May][364]

Reflections of Paul Kayser on Anglo-Congolese agreement

Doctor Kayser having asked me a few days ago whether I had yet received the text of the Agreement between Great Britain and the Congo State, signed at Brussels on the 12th inst., I called on him yesterday and showed him the text which I had received the night before in Your Lordship's Despatch No. 18 Treaty of the 23rd inst.[365]

He thanked me but added that he had received the document that morning from the German Embassy in London, and had evidently lost no time in studying its contents, as I noticed that the new boundaries were pencilled out on the map hanging up in his room.

Doctor Kayser remarked that the agreement had come upon him as a surprise; and that at first sight it seemed to involve a novel principle in international law. Would it be possible for Belgium or Switzerland to "Lease" part of their territories which had been neutralized under an international guarantee?[366] Yet this is what apparently has been done by King Leopold.

As for the novel system of leasing territories for "a period to be hereafter determined", Doctor Kayser said that in his opinion it would be difficult to differentiate it from a cession, but added that he had not had time as yet to master all the details of the Anglo-Congo[l]ese Agreement.

We then proceeded to discuss other matters, but on rising to take leave of me, he went to the map, and pointing to the strip of territory

[364] Note on docket: 'Sir E. Hertslet as to the point of international law. As reflecting the views of the Colonial Office the articles are not satisfactory.' C.Ll.H. [Clement Lloyd Hill]; 'We must await what the German Govt may say after more mature reflection. The point of international law is not made officially. There are two mistakes. The frontiers of the Congo State have not been settled by international agreement. The frontier with the German sphere will not be altered unless our road runs along it which is unnecessary. It should be an interior road.' H.P.A. [Henry Percy Anderson], 20 May; 'The Germans did not consult us when they gave the French access to the Niger.' K[imberley], 29 May.

[365] The treaty with Leopold II of 12 May 1894 settled the limits of the Congo Free State. It granted the Congo access to the Nile valley (while recognizing British sovereign rights) and stipulated the lease to Britain of a corridor of land from Lake Tanganyika to Lake Edward, thus linking British 'possessions' in southern Africa and Uganda.

[366] On the basis of the Final Act of the Berlin West Africa Conference (26 February 1885) Leopold II declared the Congo Free State to be permanently neutral; its neutrality, however, was not internationally guaranteed.

extending from Lake Tanganyika to Lake Albert Edward, said: "Your Government wish to be our neighbour here as elsewhere – but who knows whether the plan can be carried out?"

I think it right to report Doctor Kayser's observations to Your Lordship, though made, as he expressed it, merely as to a friend; the more so as the newspapers which have as yet referred to the new agreement generally concur in considering that German interests have been thereby injured. Even the <u>Vossische</u> Zeitung, which always adopts a moderate tone in colonial matters, ends up an anti-English article[367] by saying that the creation of an English "girdle" northwards from Tanganyika has brought German interests nearer to France with whom Germany has never yet had any dispute in Africa.

I have the honour to enclose precis of two articles in the National Zeitung,[368] which I have reason to believe reflect very faithfully the views of the Colonial Department on the subject.

FO 64/1325: Edward B. Malet to Earl of Kimberley, Secret, No 117, Berlin, 14 July 1894

[Received 16 July by bag. For: The Queen / Lord Rosebery / Chancellor of the Exchequer / Cabinet / Paris; K[imberley]]

Remarks on Caprivi's chancellorship; emperor's compassionate release of imprisoned French officers following the assassination of President Carnot of France

I have said in my Despatch No. 116 Secret of this day's date that as long as General Caprivi is Chancellor, I do not think that we shall be exposed to a policy of surprises on the part of Germany.

A rapprochement with France would however certainly be a surprise and the recent action of the Emperor on the occasion of Mr Carnot's assassination has been considered by some to indicate a desire of His Majesty in this direction.[369]

I am not inclined to take this view. I regard His Majesty's feeling telegraphic messages[370] as the genuine and spontaneous expression of horror at the crime and sympathy with the widow.

In regard to the liberation of the French officers imprisoned at Glatz, I am informed by Monsieur Herbette, the French

---

[367] On 25 May 1894.

[368] Enclosures: précis of article 'England's agreement with the Congo State', *National Zeitung*, 25 May 1894; précis of article 'Germany, England and the Congo State', *National Zeitung*, Evening Edition, 25 May 1894.

[369] On 24 June Carnot was stabbed by an Italian anarchist and died the following day.

[370] Telegram to Cécile Carnot of 25 June 1894.

Ambassador, that this act of clemency was due to His Excellency's intercession and did not emanate from the Emperor's own inspiration.[371] Monsieur Herbette was ordered to Kiel[372] to thank His Majesty for his messages of condolence and he took advantage of a private audience to urge upon His Majesty the opportunity of releasing the two French officers on the occasion of Monsieur Carnot's funeral. At first the Emperor said it was impossible, but he was gradually persuaded by Monsieur Herbette who spoke of the unhappy circumstance of an aged mother of one of the officers[373] who could not travel and feared that she would never see her Son again. The Emperor's heart was touched. He promised to telegraph to General Caprivi to come to him immediately. The Chancellor arrived at Kiel the following morning which was Saturday. Having decided with the Chancellor that the thing should be done, the Emperor did not neglect the "mise en scène"[374] and sensibly extracted all the advantage possible from his Imperial act of clemency which was announced the next day to President Casimir Perier immediately before the funeral.[375]

The action of the Emperor has undoubtedly produced a diminution of tension between France and Germany, but it was not the result of a settled policy and will probably not have a lasting effect.

FO 64/1326: Martin Gosselin to Earl of Kimberley, No 147, Berlin, 10 September 1894

[Received 13 September. For: The Queen / Prince of Wales / Lord Rosebery; K[imberley]]

Conservative Kreuzzeitung *on emperor's appeal to nobility in his speech at Königsberg; Prussian nobles proclaim loyalty to throne but persist in opposition to Caprivi's commercial policy*

The "Kreutz Zeitung", the organ of the extreme Conservative Party, took two days to consider the pronouncement made by His Majesty at Koenigsberg on the 6th Instant, before venturing to do more than to reproduce the text of the speech.

---

[371] On 1 July Wilhelm II pardoned Robert Degouy and Jacques Delguey de Malavas – two French naval officers who, in December 1893, had been sentenced to six and four years imprisonment respectively for espionage.
[372] Herbette visted Wilhelm II on 28 June 1894.
[373] Jacques Delguey de Malavas.
[374] French: 'staging'.
[375] The funeral was on 1 July.

After the lapse of 48 hours, and, it may be presumed, after consultation with the Agrarian leaders, the Conservative organ publishes a leading article in the following sense:

The Conservatives, whether nobles or commoners, have never yet opposed their King: this would indeed be "an absurdity". They have merely voted against the responsible servants of the Crown, when convinced of the harmfulness of the Ministers' policy. Such a course is the right and the duty of the most faithful of subjects. It is not so much the attitude of the nobility towards the Commercial policy of the Government, as the form which this opposition has taken, which has grieved His Majesty; and the "Kreutz Zeitung" is fain to admit that "in the heat of the fray" this may have here and there overstepped the bounds of propriety. His Majesty is pleased himself to recognize the "heavy cares" which weigh on agriculture, and the "Kreutz Zeitung" must add, "with all loyalty," that the manners "and method adopted by the Imperial Chancellor and other responsible servants of the Emperor towards this "heavy care" has not been calculated to temper or render more moderate the complaints on the subject."

If the above should turn out to be the last word of the Agrarians, the Sovereign's conditional promise to let bye-gones be bye-gones will certainly not be realized.

The Prussian Constitution of 1850,[376] it is true, proclaims the equality of all in the eye of the law; but the feelings and customs of centuries are not be wiped out by even so solemn a document as a Constitution. The Kings of Prussia have ever regarded their Nobles as forming a privileged Class apart, closely bound to the fortunes of the House of Hohenzollern; this feeling has hitherto been fully reciprocated, and in no part of the Monarchy are feudal traditions and aspirations so thoroughly rooted amongst all classes of the population as in the Provinces of East and West Prussia.

It cannot be gainsaid that exceptional privileges have been reserved to the Prussian Aristocracy; the Army List, the Civil Service, the Protection, even under the regime of the new Commercial Treaties,[377] still accorded to the landed interest, all testify to this; and His Majesty clearly indicates that in return for these privileges He expects that the beneficiaries will cease their opposition, and loyally support a policy which is for the benefit of the whole Community. The "professional" opposition of the various political parties in the State is only what is to be expected; it is their right, and they legally exercise it; but the "Monarchy by Divine Right"

---

[376] Article 4.
[377] For the commercial treaties see nn. 319 and 354 in this section.

expects that those standing nearest to the Throne will give a loyal support to measures judged necessary for the Common Weal.

His Majesty has now once more solemnly warned the Prussian Nobles that Count Caprivi's Commercial policy is His own: and that it is His wish that Germany should enter into closer Commercial relations with her neighbours; yet in spite of this solemn warning the "Kreutz Zeitung" after 48 hours' cogitation, has nothing else to reply than that the Conservatives have never opposed the Sovereign, but only His Ministers, and incorporates in the answer another attack on Count Caprivi.

It remains to be seen whether the leading Conservatives will submit with a good grace to the clearly expressed wish of their Sovereign, or whether they will continue their opposition to the Chancellor and all his works and hostility to the Imperial Government, which is apparently the policy still upheld by the most influential organ of their party.

FO 64/1326: Martin Gosselin to Earl of Kimberley, No 188, Berlin, 28 October 1894

[Received 30 October by post. For: The Queen / Lord Rosebery / Chancellor of the Exchequer; K[imberley]]

Hohenlohe-Schillingsfürst set to be new imperial chancellor and Prussian prime minister; remarks on his career to date; Caprivi glad to be moving on from Berlin

In continuation of my Despatch N. 186 of yesterday, I have the honour to state that it appears certain that Prince Hohenlohe-Schillingsfürst, the Statthalter of Alsace-Lorraine, will be appointed Imperial Chancellor and Prussian Prime Minister, and that Herr von Köller, who has for some time past been His Highness' right hand man as Under Secretary of State for the Reichsland, will receive the seals of the Prussian Ministry of the Interior, hitherto held, together with the Premiership, by Count Eulenburg.[378]

There can be no doubt that the Emperor had these appointments in view when His Majesty summoned, on Friday evening, the Prince and Herr von Köller from Strasburg to Potsdam, and, though no official announcement has yet been made, the fact that Prince Hohenlohe called this morning at the Ministry for Foreign affairs and visited, among others, Baron Holstein, the Political Director of

---

[378] Hohenlohe-Schillingsfürst and Köller were appointed on 29 October 1894. For Caprivi's resignation as chancellor see the following dispatch.

that Department, tends to show that His Highness has accepted the charge which His Majesty desires to entrust to him.

Prince Chlodwig Hohenlohe, who is now in his 76th year, has had a long experience of public life. From January 1867 to March 1870 he was Bavarian Minister President in the Liberal administration, and as first Vice President of the Customs Parliament and of the German Reichstag from 1867 to 1874, has acquired considerable Parliamentary experience.

In 1874 he succeeded Count Harry Arnim as German Ambassador in Paris, and, during the eleven years which he held that post, he did much to improve the official relations of the two countries.

For some months in 1880, during Prince Bismarck's illness, he took over the work of the Imperial Foreign Department, and acted on behalf of the Chancellor in the Government and in Parliament.

For the last nine years he has held the important post of Statthalter of Alsace-Lorraine, and has done much to reconcile the population to German rule in the Reichsland.

Colonel Swaine informs me that he met Count von Caprivi in the street this afternoon, who stopped him to say goodbye, adding "I am going at once to Switzerland to rest and recruit. I am glad to get away from this atmosphere and these surroundings. They were too much for me".

FO 64/1326: Martin Gosselin to Earl of Kimberley, Very Confidential, No 191, Berlin, 30 October 1894

[Received 1 November by post. For: The Queen / Lord Rosebery / Chancellor of the Exchequer; K[imberley]]

Conversation with Bavarian minister Lerchenfeld on Caprivi's resignation and Hohenlohe's nomination as imperial chancellor

I called yesterday on Count Lerchenfeld, the Bavarian Minister in Berlin, and asked him whether he could give me any details of the recent Chancellor crisis.

His Excellency, who, by his position as Representative of the second largest German State, by his long residence here and by his personal capabilities, has quite exceptional opportunities of knowing what is going on, told me that Count von Caprivi's resignation[379] came to him, as to all the rest of the world – as a complete surprise.

---

[379] Caprivi handed in his resignation on 23 October and was dismissed on 26 October 1894.

The Chancellor, had only last Wednesday, submitted to the Bundesrath[380] his programme for strengthening the hands of the Executive against the "Parties of Disorder", – submitted, not as a Prussian proposition, but as one emanating from himself as President (a "Präsidial-Vorschlag" as it is called here): this proposition had been discussed and unanimously agreed to by the Bundesrath, and was, moreover, Count Lerchenfeld added, approved by a large majority of the Prussian Cabinet.[381]

When the Representatives of Bavaria, Saxony, Wurtemberg and Baden[382] were summoned by His Majesty to the Schloss on Friday afternoon,[383] immediately after the Emperor's interviews with Count von Caprivi and Count Eulenburg, he, Count Lerchenfeld, had no idea that the Chancellor had resigned, much less that his resignation had been accepted: and it was from the Emperor's own lips that they were made acquainted with the fact.

His Majesty took pains to explain to the four Ministers that He entirely approved of Count von Caprivi's draft proposal, already sanctioned by the Bundesrath, – that it was simply a change of Ministers that had occurred, rendered necessary by the dissentiments [note above in pencil: 'dissensions'] which could no longer be tolerated, and that the internal policy of the Imperial Government would in no way be modified.

Count Lerchenfeld said that, of course, it would depend on the new Chancellor whether the proposed programme would be presented intact to the Reichstag – with or without modification, – but he answered me that Count von Caprivi's scheme was entirely endorsed by himself and his colleagues in the Bundesrath.

In reply to my enquiry whether Prince Hohenlohe, if nominated,[384] was of an age to support the double burden of the Chancellorship and the Premiership, which had proved almost too much for Prince Bismarck, His Excellency replied that he thought, under the circumstances, no better appointment could be made: he trusted that the new Chancellor would hold himself more "à l'écart"[385]

---

[380] Federal Council, on 24 October 1894.

[381] The so-called 'subversion bill' (bill for the amendment and amplification of the Criminal Code, the Military Penal Code, and the Press Law), drafted by the Imperial Office for Justice and more moderate than Eulenberg's proposal, was discussed in the Prussian council of ministers (*Staatsministerium*) on 19 October and found approval in the Federal Council on 25 October 1894. It was introduced in the *Reichstag* on 5 December 1894 and subsequently rejected on 11 May 1895.

[382] Hugo Graf von Lerchenfeld, Wilhelm Graf von Hohenthal, Axel Freiherr Varnbüler, and Eugen von Jagemann.

[383] On 26 October 1894.

[384] Hohenlohe was appointed on 29 October.

[385] French: 'at a distance'.

than his predecessor; Parliamentary Government was not the same here as in England: there is no necessity for the Chancellor to be continually interfering in the Reichstag debates, he should rather keep himself in reserve for cases of extreme necessity. If Prince Hohenlohe adopted this practice, he thought, he could very well undertake, even at his age, the supreme direction of the Imperial and Prussian Governments.

The Emperor has been severely criticized in more than one quarter for having thrown overboard a public servant, with whose policy His Majesty is still supposed to have been in entire agreement, but, if the state of affairs is examined dispassionately, it seems to me that, on the supposition that the Chancellor and the Premier[386] could no longer work together, no other course could have been adopted.

Had His Majesty determined to stand at all risks by his Chancellor, and accepted Count Eulenburg's resignation alone, all the agrarian party, and the Conservative forces in East and West Prussia, would have been up in arms at what would have rightly been considered the abandonment of their champion in the Councils of the Sovereign.

Had His Majesty, on the other hand, accepted the Chancellor's resignation without that of the Prime Minister, it would have been regarded throughout all Germany as a sign that a strong reactionary policy was again to be adopted. Moreover, by accepting the resignation of both Ministers, His Majesty is enabled to do away with the dualism which has, during the last six months, become almost a public scandal.

The successor to Prince Hohenlohe in the Statthalership of Alsace-Lorraine has not yet been gazetted. It was the Emperor's intention, I am told, to offer it to Count Eulenburg, but difficulties have since arisen with regard to His Excellency's nomination, and it is now rumoured that Prince Hohenlohe-Langenburg, is the probable candidate for the post.

Other changes in the Prussian Cabinet are spoken of, but nothing is yet known positively on the matter.

I do not like to close this Despatch without informing Your Lordship that the Press of all shades of opinion, official, Catholic, Liberal and Radical, with the single exception of the extreme agrarian organs, bear hearty testimony to the honesty of purpose and singleness of mind which have been the distinguishing marks of the late

---

[386] Eulenburg, who, in contrast to Caprivi, was prepared to impose anti-socialist measures and advocated a coup d'état against the *Reichstag*, resigned as Prussian minister president on 24 October and was dismissed on 26 October.

Chancellor during the four years he has held the post of Imperial Chancellor.

FO 64/1334: Martin Gosselin to Earl of Kimberley, Africa, No 134, Berlin, 7 November 1894

[Received 9 November by post. For: Lord Rosebery / Colonial Office; 'It has been from the first in this direction that there is hope of better African relations with Germany', H.P.A. [Henry Percy Anderson], 9 November; 'Satisfactory', K[imberley], 11 November]

Positive reports of cooperation between German and British directors of the South West African Company

The papers announce that the question of improving the landing place at the Swakop Mouth in German South West Africa has been discussed this week at the Ministry for Foreign Affairs[387] by Representatives of the Colonial Department, the South West African Colonial Society, the Hanseatic Land, Mining, and Trading Society for South West Africa, the South West African Emigration Society, and the South West Africa Company, the latter Company being represented by Mesrs. George Cawston, Davis and Gaill[*sic*].[388]

It was eventually decided that a technical engineer, to be appointed by the Foreign Office, should be sent to South West Africa by the Foreign Office to draw up a report on what had best be done in the matter, the expenses being met half by the Government and half by the Societies interested in the Colony.

The Kreuz Zeitung of yesterday, in announcing this decision says that the moderation displayed by the English Representatives is another proof that "the fears connected with the establishment of the South West African Company went too far.[389] The English Members of the Company have from the very beginning proved themselves uniformly loyal, and admit without reserve the German Sovereignty and Administration, and take the liveliest interest in all improvements in the Territory, even when such entail on them expenditure. So much cannot be said of many other entirely German Companies."

It is not often that the Conservative organ bestows such unstinted praise on anything connected with British undertakings in Africa,

---

[387] On 5 November 1894.

[388] Probably H. Gale, director of *Railway and Works Contractor Ltd.*

[389] The South West Africa Company Limited, an Anglo-German joint venture in German South West Africa, was founded in 1892 under English law and had its headquarters in London.

and I am therefore the more pleased to place on record the success which has attended the visit of Mr Cawston and his friends to Berlin.

It may reasonably be hoped that the harmonious cooperation of the British and German Directors of the South West Africa Company may tend to bring about a more cordial feeling in this country towards British Colonial enterprise, and so unite the interests of the two countries in South Africa.

Mr Cawston, who seemed well pleased with his reception by Dr. Kayser, told me this morning he meant to return direct to London, and will doubtless cause Your Lordship to be informed of the result of his negotiations.

FO 64/1326: Edward B. Malet to Earl of Kimberley, Confidential, No 256, Berlin, 8 December 1894

[Received 10 December by bag. For: The Queen / Lord Rosebery; Print (Samoa); Qy: Cabinet; K[imberley]]

Conversation with Marschall about colonial matters; article in the Standard *on Germany's isolation in international affairs has rankled*

I have the honour to inform Your Lordship that I saw Baron von Marschall yesterday and had my first conversation with him on general matters since my return from England.[390] His Excellency's language was couched in an entirely different tone from that of Doctor Kayser, reported in my despatch N°150, Africa, confidential, of the 2nd instant. He began by saying that the situation reduced itself to a journalistic war, in which, to his mind, neither party conceded enough to the relative internal exigencies of either country and he attributed the violence of the German press to the extreme irritation caused by the article in the Standard on the isolation of Germany.[391]

I have no doubt that this is in a great measure true. The article was like putting a finger into a secret wound which Germany felt but hoped to keep concealed.

I replied that the Standard was a Conservative organ and could not be supposed to represent the views of Her Majesty's Government. Baron von Marschall acknowledged this but said that the article was looked upon as a sign of the feeling in England regarding Germany and therefore produced extreme annoyance.

[390] Malet was on leave from 16 October to 26 November 1894.
[391] Marschall was referring to the editorial in the Standard of 12 November 1894. It pointed to the imminent isolation of Germany on the basis of Rosebery's Guildhall speech on foreign policy of 9 November, and the Anglo-Russian agreement on Central Asia.

He then touched lightly on the three points of Delagoa Bay, Samoa and Togo. What he said in regard to the latter Your Lordship will find in my Despatch N° 152 of today, of the African series.

In regards to Delagoa Bay, he said that the German Government only desired the maintenance of the Status quo; they objected to encroachments of Mr Cecil Rhodes on the sovereignty of Portugal, or the commercial independence of the Port or of the Railway.[392]

In regard to Samoa, he went over the old ground, and said that Germany had always hoped that Her Majesty's Government would have regarded the matter in the same light as Lord Salisbury did in 1887, when the opposition of the United States was the only bar to the Islands being placed under a German Administration as long as German interests there remained preponderant.[393]

The opposition of the United States was now withdrawn,[394] and he could not see that the situation was changed so as to render it impossible to follow the course now, which, in the opinion of Her Majesty's Government at that time, offered the best chance of a satisfactory solution of the question.

In regard to what passed in 1887, it may be useful to refer to the confidential print containing the "bases of arrangement approved by the Governments of Great Britain and Germany in relation to Samoa, signed by the Marquis of Salisbury and Baron von Plessen, April 23. 1887", (Memorandum by Mr Cockerell N° 17 Page 7, Confidential print February 1889: Further Correspondence respecting the Navigators' Islands, Part III.)

Lord Salisbury's despatch of the 30th of April 1887, transmitting these bases to Sir Lionel West, set forth the views, which Her Majesty's Government then held.

Baron von Marschall's tone was conciliatory and he was at special pains to say that the German Government looked upon the better feeling which had sprung up between Great Britain and Russia only as a further guarantee or European peace, and he said that personally he did not share the view which was entertained in some quarters that it would induce Russia to bring forward the question of the opening of the Dardanelles, or the further apprehension that this question might be dealt with separately by England, France and Russia to the exclusion of other Powers.

---

[392] Rhodes, prime minister of the Cape Colony, had attempted to buy Delagoa Bay (Maputo Bay) – the terminus of the railway line from Pretoria – from Portugal.

[393] Marschall was referring to the failed Samoa conference at Washington in 1887.

[394] On 3 December 1894 Grover Cleveland, in his State of the Union address, signalled American intentions to withdraw from the condominium governing the Samoan Islands (composed of Germany, the United States, and Great Britain) which had been created by the Treaty of Berlin in 1889.

FO 64/1357: Edward B. Malet to Earl of Kimberley, Africa, No 10, 1 February 1895

[Received 4 February by bag. For: The Queen / Lord Rosebery / Lord Ripon; Colonial Office – confidential; Print (South Zambezi); See No. 11 Africa, 22 February; Approve language, 4 February; [approved] 19 February]

Conversation with Marschall on Transvaal question; Rhode's designs on Transvaal might have severe consequences for Anglo-German relations

On my going to see Baron von Marschall this morning, His Excellency opened the conversation by reverting to what had passed between us regarding the Transvaal, as recorded in my Despatch N° 6ᴬ Africa of the 26ᵗʰ ultimo,[395] and said that Mʳ Rhodes had recently amply justified the apprehensions of the Imperial Government as to his intentions with regard to the Republic.[396] He had openly announced his intention to take it. I said I thought His Excellency must be in error: that I had carefully read what Mʳ Rhodes had said and I had seen no statement of that kind. Baron von Marschall spoke in a very animated manner and with great anger at Mʳ Rhodes' interview with the "Kreuz Zeitung" correspondent,[397] and I did not see any way to contesting that what he was reported to have said was in the highest degree offensive to Germany. His Excellency said that it was outrageous that the Prime Minister of a Colony[398] should speak in that way of a friendly nation, and that it rendered the task of endeavouring to moderate the language of the Colonial party in Germany hopeless. Baron von Marschall said that I had spoken of the coquetry of Germany with the Transvaal; what was this in comparison with the overtly aggressive tone of Mʳ Rhodes towards that country.

By this time the reports of Mʳ Rhodes' interview and of Dʳ Jameson's speech,[399] which His Excellency had sent for, had arrived, and I was at pains to point out to His Excellency that neither the one nor the other contained language which could be construed to a

---

[395] In their conversation of 26 January Malet and Marschall discussed the implications of the German 'tendency to coquetry with the Government' of the South African Republic (Transvaal) and Germany's plan to send a naval ship to Delagoa Bay for the opening of the railway line to the Transvaal. From Marschall's point view this was a 'mere act of courtesy'; however, it could not, in Malet's opinion, 'fail to raise hopes in the mind of President Krüger which might do harm'.

[396] Marschall was referring to Rhodes's undisguised ambition to incorporate the South African Republic into the Cape Colony.

[397] The account of the interview was published in the *Neue Preußische Zeitung (Kreuzzeitung)* of 27 January 1895. The correspondent's name is not traceable.

[398] Cape Colony.

[399] Speech at the Imperial Institute, London, on 28 January 1878.

menace. Both only dealt with the natural progression of events. I said that it seemed to me that no objection could be taken to the remarks regarding the progressive increase of the English population and its eventual result.

Baron von Marschall held that it distinctly pointed to an eventual alteration of the status quo which both Her Majesty's Government and the German Government proposed to maintain, and he said that the effect of these utterances on public feeling in Germany was intense.

I said that my great fear was that it would become so also in England if the German Government continued to allow the Transvaal Government to rely upon it as aiding it against England; that I was glad that His Excellency had opened the question with me again, because it so happened that Your Lordship had written to me privately on the subject and that in order that he might know exactly what you felt, I would read it to him. I then read to him Your Lordship's private letter of the 30th ultimo.[400]

I will not say that the reading of the letter moderated His Excellency's vivacity. He strongly asserted that nothing had passed between Germany and the Transvaal which should give us umbrage; that he knew the wording of our Treaty and that there could be no question of an Alliance.[401]

Here I remarked that there were various forms of Alliance; that for instance there was no Treaty Alliance between Great Britain and Italy, but that Italy doubtless hoped that the strong friendship which existed between the two countries would be of valuable assistance to her in case she were attacked. Were we to announce suddenly that we would under no circumstances raise a finger to save her from aggression, her position would be greatly changed, and this I said was what I feared in regard to the Transvaal; the ostentatious friendship of Germany might lead to further demonstrations of hostility towards us, and might precipitate the very state of affairs which Germany desired to ward off – "After all", I said, "surely the commerce of the Transvaal is not so serious an interest to Germany as the continued existence of the present European equilibrium."

---

[400] In his private letter of 30 January Kimberley referred to President Kruger's toast to the Kaiser on the occasion of Wilhelm II's birthday (on 27 January 1895) and addressed the ambivalent German position towards the South African Republic.

[401] Article 4 of the London Convention of 27 February 1884 stipulated that the 'South African Republic will conclude no treaty or engagement with any State or nation other than the Orange Free State ... until the same has been approved by Her Majesty the Queen.'

Baron von Marschall asked me in what way the Transvaal has ever shown hostility to us. I said that I could but consider as a feather in the air showing which way the wind blew, that the Transvaal Minister accredited to this Court, Herr von Blokland, had never got introduced to me. How did His Excellency account for this want of common courtesy? Baron von Marschall said it merely showed that he was a "Monsieur mal élevé".[402]

The discussion had now drifted into quieter waters. I readily acknowledged that His Excellency had a right to be indignant at the way in which Mr Rhodes had spoken about Germany and her colonies, but I said that, as to the progress of events in South Africa tending towards a Commercial Union[403] at some future time, there was no means of hindering it. The 50,000 Englishmen in the Transvaal would probably be 100,000 within twenty years: could it be otherwise than that they would impress their views in the end on the numerically insignificant minority of Boers. His Excellency said that Commercial Union means the annihilation of German trade with the Transvaal. It would be exactly the alteration of the status quo which was against Germany's interest. It was juggling with words to express an intention to maintain the status quo and at the same time to desire a Commercial Union. I said that I was extremely sorry that there should be such warm feeling in regard to the Transvaal on either side and that I regarded the question as a "point noir".[404] His Excellency said – "prevent Mr Rhodes from speaking about Germany. The two Governments can get on amiably on the basis of the status quo; but if Mr Rhodes thunders in public about never relinquishing Walfisch Bay,[405] for which we never asked, and twits us with maladministration and the poverty of our possessions, how is it possible to expect things to go on smoothly?"

The discussion which had begun stormily ended quietly with the mutual expression of the general desire which animates both Governments to work in harmony.

There is no doubt that Mr Rhodes' remarks were intolerably galling and that, if he continues to hold language of this nature, the desire of the two Governments to keep up friendly relations, so far as the Press and public feeling are concerned, will be frustrated.

---

[402] French: 'badly brought up gentleman'.

[403] Malet was referring Jameson's idea of a future 'commercial union, amalgamation, or federation of all South African States' as brought forward in the speech of 28 January.

[404] French: 'black spot'.

[405] Walvis Bay was an enclave in German South West Africa which had been in British hands since 1878, before being formally annexed to the Cape Colony in 1884.

FO 64/1350: Martin Gosselin to Earl of Kimberley, No 74, Berlin, 29 March 1895

[Received 1 April by bag. For: The Queen / Prince of Wales / Lord Rosebery; K[imberley]]

Political implications of a rejected bill authorizing the Reichstag *president to congratulate Bismarck on his 80th birthday*

In my Despatch No. 69 of the 23rd instant, I had the honour to report to Your Lordship the rejection by the Reichstag[406] of the proposal that the President should be empowered to convey to Prince Bismarck the official congratulations of the House on the occasion of the 80th anniversary of his birthday.

The Emperor, on hearing of the result of the vote, lost no time in telegraphing to the Prince that the decision of the Reichstag was diametrically opposed to the sentiments of all German Princes and their peoples; and I am informed that, had it not been for the advice tendered by Prince Hohenlohe, the telegram, significant as it is of the position of parliamentary government in this country, would have been yet more strongly worded.

The intended parliamentary demonstration in favour of the old Chancellor, which undoubtedly ought to have been treated as an entirely non-political question, has been seriously mismanaged. The Centre[407] would probably have acquiesced in, or at least have abstained from opposing a mere message of congratulation, had not the Conservative Press done their best for the last fortnight to capture the demonstration for their own agrarian purposes, and shut the door to any compromise by loudly proclaiming the Radical and Socialist Parties as "hostile to the Empire," for opposing the repressive legislation which is now being considered by the Reichstag.[408]

The rumour that the Emperor intends to dissolve the Reichstag is discredited in all well-informed circles here; if the elections could take place at once, when the country is under the impression of the recent vote, it is possible that the Conservatives and National Liberals might improve their position; but in view of the work which still remains to

---

[406] On 23 March 1895. The proposal was made by the president of the *Reichstag*, Albert von Levetzow. Bismarck's birthday was on 1 April.

[407] *Zentrumspartei* (Catholics).

[408] Gosselin is referring to the 'subversion bill' (*Umsturzvorlage*) which had been introduced in the *Reichstag* on 5 December 1894. See n. 381 in this section.

be done, before the present session can be closed, two months must elapse before the new elections could be held, and long before the expiration of that period, the Nation would have forgotten the unfortunate incident of last Saturday, which after all was not technically a defeat of the Government, and the electorate would in all probability be under the influence of other and more dangerous cries.

In consequence of the rejection of the proposal, not only the President, Dr. von Levetzow, but Dr. Bürklin, the second Vice President, belonging to the National Liberal Party, both resigned their offices;[409] and the Reichstag met the day before yesterday to elect two of their members to the vacancies.

Baron von Buol-Berenberg, formerly the Senior Vice President, belonging to the Centre Party, was elected President by 183 out of 291 votes; the first Vice Presidency falling to Herr Schmidt, the Radical Member for Elberfeld, and the second to Herr Spahn, the Catholic Member for Cologne.

The Socialists, who number forty-five in the present Reichstag, and, after the Centre, formed the most numerous group in the heterogeneous majority of the 23rd, declined to exercise their right to be represented on the Presidency, on the ground that their freedom of action would be fettered, if one of their members were elected Vice President.

The Conservative and National Liberal Parties, who formed the minority on Saturday, handed in blank voting papers as a protest against the action of the majority.

The new President has gained a long experience of his duties in the Chair as Senior Vice President, and made favourable impression by the readiness with which he stilled the storm which broke out, when the result of the Bismarck vote was announced; unfortunately he is somewhat deaf.

In the interest of the smooth working of the Parliamentary Machine, it is none the less to be regretted, that the new President owes his election to the support of the Socialists, and that neither the Conservatives nor the National Liberals, – the so-called Cartell Parties,[410] – are responsible for the election of the Speaker or of either of his Substitutes.

[409] On 23 March 1895.
[410] See n. 208 in this section.

FO 64/1350: Martin Gosselin to Earl of Kimberley, No 76, Berlin, 30 March 1895

[Received 1 April by bag. For: The Queen / Prince of Wales / Lord Rosebery; K[imberley]]

Bismarck's 80th birthday; Reichstag and Prussian Landtag deputations visit Friedrichsruh; Bismarck's speech; emperor's congratulatory visit and bestowal of honours

In my Despatch No 74 of the 29 instant, I have related the untoward incident which occurred in the Reichstag on the 23 instant, with regard to the refusal of the House to authorize the President to convey to Prince Bismarck their congratulations on his 80th birthday.[411]

As a counter-demonstration to this vote, the members of the upper and lower Houses of the Prussian Diet and the Conservative and National Liberal members of the Reichstag, to the number in all, of some four hundred, went to Friedrichsruh on the 25 instant to offer to the old Chancellor their best wishes on his birthday, Herr von Levetzow, the ex-president of the Reichstag, in his address taking an opportunity of expressing his personal regret that he was enabled to speak in the name of only some 150 members of the House.

Prince Bismarck, in his reply, urged his hearers to follow, not a local Brandenburg, nor even a Royal Prussian, but an Imperial German Policy; a piece of advice, which in view of the known Agrarian sympathies of many of his hearers, was the more remarkable; and he further urged the legislators present to hold fast to their loyalty to the Sovereign Houses of Germany.

With a very pardonable allusion to the Reichstag Vote, His Highness said, "I can truly say that the Confederated States, their Governments and Dynasties are better people ("leute") than the Political factions. The latter place above the national interests every political ill-humour, every rivalry, every clean and unclean emulation; whereas our reigning families place national interests to the fore. Compare and weigh the bearing of our dynasties and our political factions, and learn a lesson therefrom."

Prince Bismarck repeated the same idea on the following day in his speech to the Emperor. "Outside of attachment to the dynasties, there is no salvation in Germany."

His Majesty, who was fully alive to the bad effect which the refusal of the Reichstag to join in the national celebration of Prince Bismarck's birthday would make throughout Germany, determined to do all that was possible to enhance the effect of His visit to

---

[411] See preceding dispatch.

Friedrichsruh on the 26 instant, being accompanied by the Crown Prince,[412] the Minister of War,[413] and the heads of the military, naval and civil Cabinets.[414]

In a military country such as Germany the significance of the attention paid by His Majesty to the ex-Chancellor, in holding a review of troops in his honour, – an honour which, as far as I am aware, has never yet been paid by a Sovereign to a subject, – is brought home to the whole nation; and the fact that the arms of Alsace-Lorraine were engraved on the golden sword of honour presented to the Prince by the Emperor in the presence of the troops, and still more the words in which the Emperor alluded to the part played by him in the events of 1870 –71, will strike not only a responsive chord throughout the Fatherland, but will, it may be surmised, make a serious impression beyond the Vosges.

I am informed that the Prince was quite overcome by His Majesty's gracious words, and stooping down, kissed the Emperor's hand.

On the 27th, Prince Bismarck received a visit from Prince Henry of Prussia, the Grand Duke of Baden and Prince Hohenlohe, the present Chancellor, who conveyed to his illustrious predecessor the congratulations of the Bundesrath and the Prussian Ministry.

The chief political greetings are now over, but a whole series of deputations and excursionists from all parts of Germany intend to visit Friedrichsruh during the course of the next week.

Prince Bismarck is said to be none the worse for the fatigues naturally incident on this long series of receptions.

FO 64/1350: Edward B. Malet to Earl of Kimberley, No 151, Berlin, 24 June 1895

[Received 30 June. For: The Queen / Admiralty, 8 July; S[alisbury]]

Celebratory opening of the North Sea and Baltic Canal at Hamburg and Kiel

I have the honour to inform Your Lordship that the official fêtes for the opening of the North Sea and Baltic Canal[415] came to an end on Saturday the 22nd instant.

The number of ships representing the various maritime Powers of the world which were together on the occasion in Kiel harbour

---

[412] Wilhelm.
[413] Walther Bronsart von Schellendorff.
[414] Wilhelm von Hahnke, Gustav von Senden-Bibran, and Hermann von Lucanus.
[415] The Kiel Canal (Kaiser Wilhelm-Kanal) linked Brunsbüttel and Kiel.

surpassed, I believe, any international gathering of the kind which has ever taken place. Vessels of the following nations were present:

United States of America,	4 vessels
Denmark.............................,	6 "
Great Britain.........................,	10 "
Germany.............................,	48 "
France................................,	3 "
Italy....................................,	9 "
Holland...............................,	2 "
Austria................................,	4 "
Portugal..............................,	1 "
Roumania............................,	2 "
Russia................................,	3 "
Sweden and Norway.............,	5 "
Spain..................................,	3 "
Turkey................................,	1 "
	101,

in all, one hundred and one ships belonging to the various navies of 13 nations. The nations not represented were not invited.

The Banquet given by the Emperor on the 21st instant numbered 1,160 guests.

The speeches made by His Majesty at Hamburg and Kiel[416] were chiefly remarkable for the manner in which His Majesty dwelt upon the blessings of peace and his desire to maintain it.

The whole of the Reichstag was invited and was present, with the exception of the socialists. A large number of the deputies probably saw the sea for the first time, and it no doubt entered into the calculation of the Government that the impressive sight would render them more pliant in future in regard to Naval estimates.

Some comment was excited by the refusal of the French officers to attend the Banquet at Hamburg, but they came to the ball and the Banquet at Kiel. The French sailors did not go on shore. The Emperor spoke to the two French Admirals[417] for some time after the Banquet, and the French Ambassador[418] told me that they were much impressed by His Majesty's extraordinary mastery of the details of naval matters and his power of expressing the minutest technical points in correct French.

---

[416] On 19 and 21 June 1895.
[417] Only one French admiral, Rear Admiral Ménard, was present.
[418] Jules Herbette.

A newspaper correspondent informed me that the only official injunction which had been issued by the bureau of the Press at the German Foreign Office was that if any disagreeable incident should unfortunately arise in connection with the presence of the French it was not to be reported.

The arrangements for the comfort and convenience of the guests were admirable. As an instance of how far these were carried, it is worth mentioning that the telephone was laid to all the principal ships, so that it was possible for those on board to communicate with each other as well as with the principal towns of Germany.

The Diplomatic Corps was treated with the greatest hospitality and attention, and at the last repast on board the "Augusta Victoria" I rose at the request of my colleagues and proposed the health of Baron Marschall, Minister for Foreign Affairs, and expressed our grateful thanks for the attention which we had received.

FO 64/1359: Martin Gosselin to Marquess of Salisbury, Africa, No 139, 29 October 1895

[Received 31 October by post. For: Print (South Zambezi) / Mr Balfour / Duke of Devonshire / Colonial Office; S[alisbury]][419]

Marschall's response to Amatongaland protectorate; resumption of conflict in South-Eastern Africa; German activities in Southern Africa seen as serious threat to Anglo-German relations

The answer of Baron von Marschall to the notification announcing the Amatongaland protectorate (copy of which is enclosed in my immediately preceding Despatch of today's date)[420] is but the latest of a whole series of steps taken by the German Government to show their sympathy with the Boers and their anxiety to increase the political and commercial influence of this country in the South African Republic and in the Portuguese province of Lorenzo Marques.

---

[419] Note on docket: 'Thank for interesting resumé', C.Ll.H [Clement Lloyd Hill]; 'The various communications between Lord Kimberley and Count Hatzfeldt might be added. On one point Mr Gosselin is mistaken. The arrangement between the steamship companies allows the British Companies to run to Lorenzo Marques but not north of it. Mr Donald Curne tells me that both his line and the Union line will continue to trade in Delagoa Bay. This might be explained.' H.P.A. [Henry Percy Anderson], 31 October. 'Done', 11 November; S[alisbury].

[420] British sovereignty over Amatongaland (Tongaland) was proclaimed on 23 April and publicly announced on 11 June. Marschall's answer is dated 25 October and contained, apart from the customary acknowledgements, the observation that the South African Republic had protested against this annexation of territories.

It may be of interest to recapitulate the various incidents of this campaign in South East Africa, the first of which dates from a little more than a year ago.

(1.) When the Kaffirs were threatening Lorenzo Marques in October of last year,[421] the German men-of-war "See-adler" and "Condor" were despatched to Delagoa Bay, to safeguard, as Baron von Marschall stated, "the large German interests involved both on the coast and in the Transvaal." [Note in margin: 'See my Desp 121 Africa of Oct 19. 1894']

So serious did the German Government then consider the situation that, as Baron von Marschall explained to the Reichstag,[422] when the naval estimates were being discussed, [Note in margin: 'See my Desp. 46 Africa of April 2. 1895'] the "See-adler" was hurriedly despatched from Kilwa to Delagoa Bay, though at the time Kilwa itself was being threatened by the insurgent Arabs; while the "Condor" was ordered out to the same destination all the way from Kiel.[423] Simultaneously with the despatch of the two German ships to Delagoa Bay, Jonkherr Beelaerts von Blokland, the Transvaal Minister accredited here and to the Portuguese and Netherlands Governments, arrived in Berlin.

(2.) The next incident bearing on Germany's relations with the Transvaal was Mr Rhodes' interview with the "Kreuz Zeitung's" London correspondent[424] (reported in the "Times" of the 28th of January last) which created quite a storm of indignation in the German Press, and was the subject of somewhat acrimonious observations on Baron von Marschall's part, as reported in Sir E. Malet's Despatch No 10 Africa of the 1st February last.[425]

(3.) [Note in margin: 'See Sir E. Malet's 26 Africa of March 12. 1895'] In the following month the German Government replaced the trading Consul Herr W. Joost, who had hitherto represented German interests at Delagoa Bay, by a "consul de carrière", and appointed Count Markus Pfeil to the post,[426] a step which was greeted with undisguised satisfaction in Colonial circles, [Note in margin: 'My

---

[421] The revolts and attempted attacks by the population, here derogatively called 'Kaffirs', on Lourenço Marques (Maputo), a Portuguese port in Delagoa Bay, stemmed from resistance to Portuguese taxation and interference in a succession dispute.

[422] On 1 March 1895.

[423] The cruiser *Seeadler* was ordered from Kilwa on 15 October 1894; *Condor* left Germany on 16 October and arrived at Lourenço Marques on 15 December.

[424] Walter Freiherr von Bissing.

[425] See pp. 171–173.

[426] Pfeil was appointed commissary consul at Lourenço Marques on 29 January 1895.

Desp No 33 Africa of March 16. 1895'] as tending to mark the Empire's independent policy in South Africa inaugurated last Autumn, and as a means towards the maintenance of the balance of Power in that part of Africa.

(4) [Note in margin: 'My Desp 68 Africa of June 10. 1895] At the annual general meeting of the German Colonial Society, held at Cassel under the Presidency of Duke John Albert of Mecklenburg-Schwerin, on the 6th of June, a resolution was adopted in favour of "all measures calculated to promote friendly relations with the Transvaal people and to strengthen their independence", and it was currently reported at the time that during the discussion of this resolution the hope was expressed that the German Government would refuse to recognize the annexation of the three Amatongaland States.

(5) [Note in margin: 'Sir E. Malet N° 89 Africa of July 20.1895] The return of the "Condor" to Delagoa Bay[427] and the visit of the Germans to Pretoria on the occasion of the opening of the Delagoa-Pretoria Railway.[428]

(6) The telegram[429] of congratulation addressed by the Emperor William to President Kruger on the occasion of his visit to the "Condor", in which the opening of the railway is alluded to, as a "means of drawing the bonds which connect the two countries".

(7) Lastly, the Agreement of April last, between the Portuguese Government and the German East Africa Line,[430] whereby the mail-packet service between Portugal and her possessions on the South East Coast of Africa passed from British into German hands, [Note in margin: 'Sir H. Macdonell N° 41 Africa May 20. 1895. Sir E. Malet N°ˢ 86 & 116 Africa of 12ᵗʰ July & 30 Oct. 1895.'] an arrangement, which must inevitably strengthen Germany's position and prejudice English trade on that portion of the African Littoral.

All these several incidents, capped as they are by Baron von Marschall's reply with regard to Amatongaland, are symptoms of an intention on the part of the German Government to adopt a forward, not to say aggressive line of action with regard to the

---

[427] On 27 June 1895.
[428] The Delagoa-Pretoria Railway was opened at Pretoria on 8 and 9 July. A deputation of German naval officers from the *Condor* visited Pretoria on 8 July 1895.
[429] Dated 17 July 1895; Kruger visited the *Condor* on the same day.
[430] Convention of 10 April 1895.

Transvaal; and I would venture to point out that none of the incidents alluded to above were the handiwork of Colonial Chauvinists and excited explorers, like Dr. Peters of yesterday or Dr. Gruner of today, who, full of their achievements, enjoy nothing so much as to put forward claims to the regions of their exploits.

Nor, as far as I can discover, are they to be attributed to the advice of the Colonial Department, which, I believe, has nothing whatever to say to German relations either with the Transvaal or the Portuguese Colonies.

The policy of this country in the Transvaal would seem to be inspired from the highest source; and, if this surmise is correct, it undoubtedly demands all the closer attention on the part of Her Majesty's Government.

As illustrating the rapidity with which the idea of Germany's interests in the Transvaal is spreading, I may mention that in an article published by Dr. Georg Schweinfurth, the noted African traveller, in the "Berliner Rundschau" for last July, entitled the "New Birth of Egypt",[431] which breathes throughout a very friendly spirit to the British occupation in Egypt, it is expressly laid down that Germany's price for a free hand for England on the Lower Nile is, amongst other things, "the Independence of our South African friends".

I am not, of course, aware whether it is the intention of Her Majesty's Government to enter into any negotiations for the settlement of the Colonial questions still outstanding with this Empire; but if any such idea should be entertained, I would venture to call attention to this new "dark spot", which threatens to become, unless taken in time, a danger to the good relations of the two countries, far otherwise serious than any possible disputes as to Togoland, Damaraland, Witu or even Samoa.

In conclusion, I would observe that all the incidents referred to above have taken place since Count von Caprivi's resignation,[432] and that the present Chancellor[433] is known to be personally in favour of a forward policy in all Colonial matters.

---

[431] 'Die Wiedergeburt Ägyptens im Lichte eines aufgeklärten Islam', *Berliner Rundschau*, No 24, 10 July 1895.

[432] See n. 379 in this section.

[433] Chlodwig zu Hohenlohe-Schillingsfürst.

FO 64/1351: Martin Gosselin to Marquess of Salisbury, Secret, No 278, Berlin, 25 November 1895

[Received 29 November by messenger. For: The Queen / Mr Balfour / Duke of Devonshire; S[alisbury]]

Discussion with Prussian minister of war, rumours of possible alliance with Russia

Some fortnight ago one of the best informed of my colleagues met the Minister of War, General Bronsart von Schellendorff, and the conversation turned on the question of the possible alliances of this country.

General Bronsart said that, come what might, it was essential for this country to do everything possible to reestablish a good understanding with Russia.

Why, asked my informant: would it not be well, before speaking so positively, to think of England? Every penny advanced to Russia, every concession made to her in the near or the far East, weakens pro tanto[434] the influence of England, who, next to Austria, is after all Germany's nearest blood-relation.

The War Minister answered that it was all very well to talk of an English Alliance, but even if England had the will, she hadn't the men to make it worth while for this country to sacrifice for her good will the possibility of a Russian Alliance.

At Sea she is a great Power, – "too great a Power, I had almost said", – but she would be of little use to Germany in a European war. Russia, England, France, all Europe is looking to the East, while, as for Austria, her axis has already been moved from Vienna to Pesth, and in this Eastward movement, our own Eastern neighbour will assuredly play a great part – so that Germany, whatever might be wished, cannot afford to neglect Russia for the platonic good will of Great Britain. It is hoped, too, said His Excellency, that the marriage of the Russian Emperor with a German Princess[435] will tend to draw nearer the relations of the two Empires.

Besides this, England cannot be counted: she has treated us in the East African business in a quite scandalous manner; ("Man hat uns in dieser Ost-Afrikanischen Angelegenheit ganz miserabel behandelt;") and is always opposing any extension of German influence in the Colonies.

Well, said the diplomatist, I know little of Africa, but surely there should be room for all, and most of all for England and Germany,

---

[434] Latin: 'to that extent'.
[435] Nicholas married Alix of Hesse (Alexandra Feodorovna) on 26 November 1894.

who are the two great civilizing (Kultur) powers of the day in that part of the world.

General Bronsart expressed the wish that this happy state of things could be realized; it might in the future, but certainly had not been so yet.

As General Bronsart von Schellendorff is one of the most important members of the Prussian Cabinet, and is perhaps more frequently in contact with the Emperor than any of his colleagues, I venture to record His Excellency's observations as related to me.

The Statement about East Africa is singular, and illustrates the height to which the feeling about Zanzibar is rising in this country: the cession by Her Majesty's Government of Heligoland appears to be entirely forgotten by the German Colonial Party: people look at the Map of German East Africa, and see the adjacent islands of Zanzibar and Pemba marked with another colour, and straightway fly to the conclusion that England has robbed the Fatherland of her fairest flowers in that region.[436]

There can be little doubt, that His Excellency's remarks as to the urgency of a good understanding with Russia reflect very faithfully the views of the Emperor.

To take only the last month, His Majesty has given within that time three proofs of his anxiety to be well with his Russian Neighbour: –

1 – The despatch to St Petersburg by an Aide de Camp,[437] of the famous Allegorical picture, designed by His Majesty, representing the European crusade against Buddha, in which (as a glance at the enclosed print will show)[438] the wish for intimate relations with Russia is clearly indicated by the grouping of the figures.

2 – The presence of the whole Court at the Russian Embassy Chapel at the Requiem sung on the anniversary of the late Emperor Alexander's death.[439]

---

[436] On 1 July 1895 the territory that had been claimed by the British East Africa Company in 1888 was placed under the protectorate of Great Britain (East Africa Protectorate). Zanzibar and Pemba had already become a British protectorate, following the Anglo-German agreement of 1 July 1890, known as the Heligoland-Zanzibar Treaty, which amongst other things, regulated the frontiers of East Africa. In return for the recognition of British interests in the Zanzibar region Britain ceded the islands of Heligoland to Germany.

[437] Helmuth von Moltke; the picture was presented to the tsar on 30 September.

[438] Enclosure: cutting of image entitled *Völker Europas wahrt eure heiligsten Güter* (*Peoples of Europe, Protect Your Most Sacred Possessions*), designed by Kaiser Wilhelm II; lithograph by Hermann Knackfuss, 1895.

[439] On 1 November 1895.

3 – The invitation to the Grand Duke Vladimir to join in a shooting party last week near Potsdam.

These incidents, which are merely the latest of a whole series of similar attentions on the part of His Majesty, show clearly enough the importance which is attached here to a good understanding with Russia.

FO 64/1351: Martin Gosselin to Marquess of Salisbury, No 296, Berlin, 7 December 1895

[Received 9 December by bag. For: The Queen / Prince of Wales / Mr Balfour; S [alisbury]]

Resignation of Prussian interior minister; purported reasons include repression of socialists, bad relations with other ministers, Agrarian Party opposition

A ministerial crisis has during the last week declared itself in the Prussian Cabinet, and it is reported positively that Herr von Köller, Prussian Minister of the Interior, has tendered his resignation to His Majesty.[440]

Herr von Köller, who came into Office simultaneously with the present Chancellor[441] in November of last year, has not been a successful Minister; his manner in the Reichstag has been anything but conciliatory, and the failure of the Government to pass the anti-Socialist Bills last Session[442] is generally attributed as greatly due to His Excellency's want of tact and Parliamentary experience.

During the last two months severely repressive measures have been taken against the Socialist leaders. The chief socialist committees in the Capital have been dissolved;[443] private residences have been searched by the Police; the editors of Newspaper Articles have been prosecuted; and the policy of repression culminated a short time ago in the action taken by Herr von Köller against Professor Delbrück, the Editor of the "Preussische Jahrbücher", Professor of History at the Berlin University, and formerly attached to the Household of the Emperor Frederick, when Crown Prince.[444]

---

[440] Köller handed in his resignation on 2 December 1895; he was dismissed on 8 December.

[441] Chlodwig zu Hohenlohe-Schillingsfürst.

[442] See n. 381 in this section.

[443] On 29 November 1895 the Berlin police dissolved 11 social democratic associations (*Vereine*), including the executive committee of the Social Democratic Party.

[444] Delbrück, in an article entitled 'Politische Korrespondenz', dated 20 September 1895, which appeared in the October issue of *Preußische Jahrbücher*, termed the measures against

It was subsequently announced that the proceedings against the Professor for insulting the Police had been quashed,[445] on the ground that he had assured the Minister of the Interior that he had no intention of inciting the Public against the guardians of public order; but the mistake has none the less damaged the position of the headstrong Minister.

It is also asserted that Herr von Köller had last week a violent dispute with the Minister of War, General Bronsart von Schellendorff, on the subject of the Army Discipline Bill, which may perhaps be the immediate cause of the Ministerial Crisis.[446]

I asked Baron von Marschall yesterday whether it was true that Herr von Köller had resigned, and, if so, who would be his probable successor at the Home Office.

Baron von Marschall replied that if he had not actually resigned the seals of Office, he was "un Ministre démissionaire",[447] but that nothing would be known as to His Excellency's successor, until His Majesty's return from Hanover this evening.

In reply to my enquiry whether the Crisis would involve, any further changes in the Prussian Cabinet, His Excellency said that he really could not say; "now that Count Caprivi is no longer here, all the force of the agrarian attack will doubtless be levied at me, and I expect to have many a scene in the coming Session of the Reichstag".

As illustrating the length to which the Agrarian Party are prepared to go in opposing the Imperial Government, I may mention that the Agrarian League have – it is stated – addressed a letter[448] in the following terms to the Imperial Secretaries of State for the Home and Foreign Departments (Herr von Boetticher and Baron von Marschall): –

"You have never ceased to fight us. You will therefore be considered and treated by us as enemies".

If this is true it would seem to indicate that the policy of concentration urged on the parties of order by His Majesty has not yet found much favour amongst those who have hitherto been regarded as the most loyal supporters of the Throne.

Social Democrats 'Thorheiten der Polizei' (the foolishness of the police). At Köller's instigation he was charged with defamation on 2 November.

[445] On 30 November 1895.

[446] Köller was the only Prussian minister who opposed the reform of military criminal procedure, in particular the introduction of public trials. The dispute culminated when Bronsart von Schellendorf, in the sittings of the war ministry of 13 and 18 November, accused Köller of indiscretions and suspected him of leaking internal matters to the press.

[447] French: 'an outgoing minister'.

[448] *Bund der Landwirte*. Details of the letter could not be established.

FO 64/1359: Frank C. Lascelles to Marquess of Salisbury, Africa, Confidential, No 166, 13 December 1895

[Received 16 December by bag. Where is enclosure?; For: Colonial Office; 'Herr Vohsen used much the same language as Dr Sieveking when over here in the summer, but it did not prevent the support of the Grüner and Togo claims.' C.Ll.H [Clement Lloyd Hill]; S[alisbury]]

Differing approaches to colonial administration of England and Germany

I have the honour to enclose a confidential memorandum by Mr Spring-Rice, 2nd Secretary of Her Majesty's Embassy, recording a conversation he recently had with Doctor Sieveking, the President of the Hanseatic Supreme Court at Hamburg on Anglo-German Colonial Matters.[449]

Hamburg is the great centre of the Colonial trade of this country, and the opinion of so competent an authority as the President of the Hanseatic Court on the Colonial relations of the two Empires may be of interest to Your Lordship. As illustrating the different systems of administration in vogue in the British and German possessions in Africa, I may mention that Mr Gosselin was told only today by an eye-witness that some years ago, Major v. Wissmann during his first Governorship of German East Africa met one of the Directors of the British East Africa Company at dinner at the British Agency at Zanzibar.

After dinner, the Conversation turned on the different systems adopted in the neighbouring Protectorates, and the Major, speaking perhaps more openly than he would have done before the banquet, said,

"My good friend, what is the use of our discussing these matters? We adopt an entirely different method of rule than that which prevails with you. If a nation chief comes to you with a grievance, you give him a length of cloth, and try to put him in a good temper, whereas if a chieftain comes to me with a complaint, he is simply shot."

Allowing for a large amount of after dinner exaggeration in the above remark, it shows how little the then Governor, (who has just returned in the same capacity to Dar-es-Salaàm) had tried to understand the natives entrusted to his charge, and may explain many of the difficulties with which he had to contend.

---

[449] Enclosure: confidential memorandum by Cecil Spring-Rice recording his conversation with Dr Sieveking, undated.

FO 64/1386: Frank C. Lascelles to Marquess of Salisbury, Africa, Confidential, No 1, 2 January 1896

[Received 6 January by bag. For: The Queen / Cabinet, 7 January; Colonial Office (confidential); Print; S[alisbury]]

Crisis in Transvaal; Marschall disconcerted by 'Jameson Raid'; state of affairs in South Africa

At the New Year's reception at Court yesterday I had an opportunity of a short conversation with Baron von Marschall who told me that he had received very bad news from the Transvaal. A band of 800 men belonging to the Chartered Company had crossed into the Transvaal and it was evident that a conflict was imminent even if it had not already taken place. Our conversation was interrupted by the entry of the Emperor who after having spoken to the other Ambassadors addressed me with great cordiality and after expressing the extreme pleasure which the Queen's New Year's present had given him, began to talk about the events in the Transvaal.[450]

His Majesty characterized the armed force under Dr Jameson as a band of filibusters who he hoped would all get shot as they deserved to be, and said that he was anxious to see what steps Her Majesty's Government intended to take. He could quite understand that this incident would cause embarrassment to Her Majesty's Government, who he hoped would send more ships to the Cape. His Majesty concluded by saying that his concern in this question was caused by the vast German Commercial Interests in that part of the world.

On my return from the Palace I found Your Lordship's Telegram N° 9 Africa of which I at once took a paraphrase to Baron von Marschall.[451] His Excellency who was in a state of considerable excitement, said that he did not doubt Mr Chamberlain's pacific intentions, but that the invasion of the Transvaal by an armed force of English soldiers constituted so grave a violation of Treaties and International Law that the German Ambassador in London had been instructed[452] to ask Your Lordship what steps Her Majesty's Government intended to take in the matter. This armed attack on a Power with whom Her Majesty's Government were at peace was

---

[450] The crossing into the Transvaal ('Jameson Raid') started on 29 December 1895 and ended on 2 January 1896 when the invading force, under Jameson, the administrator general of the chartered company for Matabeleland, surrendered. It aimed to incite an uprising among the foreign (and especially British) residents of the South African Republic (Uitlanders) who, amongst other things, demanded citizenship and voting rights.

[451] The telegram, dated 31 December 1894, stated Chamberlain's intention 'to avert violence and restore tranquillity' in South Africa.

[452] Telegram of 31 December from Marschall to Paul von Hatzfeldt.

all the more unjustifiable because it took place at the very moment when the Transvaal Authorities were considering the concessions they could make to the Uitlander population. If the Chartered Company were to be permitted to attack a friendly state with impunity, there could be no security for Foreign Interests in South Africa, and they might even take it into their heads to attack the German possessions.

I called again this morning on Baron von Marschall who had received from Count Hatzfeldt a telegraphic account of his conversation with Your Lordship.[453] His Excellency was calmer than he had been yesterday, but still took a very serious view of the matter. He doubted whether the orders of Her Majesty's Government to Dr Jameson to retire could reach him in time to prevent a conflict, and he did not feel sure that they would be obeyed. His Excellency then referred to the tone of the English press which had become very unsatisfactory more especially the "Times" which said that England could not permit any foreign interference in the Transvaal. Such a statement could only apply to Germany and could not fail to increase the very great irritation which was now entertained against England. Germany could not admit that England had greater rights over the Transvaal than any other Power except in so far as the 4th Article of the Convention of 1884[454] provided that any Treaties which the South African Republic might make with other Powers would be submitted to Her Majesty's Government who had a right of objecting to them within a given period. In all other respects, His Excellency said Great Britain had recognized the South African Republic as an independent State. His Excellency again referred to the commercial interests of Germany and said that the railway[455] from Pretoria to the Portuguese frontier had been built almost entirely with German capital. There was a feeling that the commercial interests of Germany had not been sufficiently protected by the Government and he could not conceal from me that the serious consequences which he apprehended from the conflict which now seemed imminent, would seriously impair the friendly relations, which, ever since he had been in office it had been his constant effort to maintain between our two Countries.

---

[453] Telegram of 1 January 1896 on Hatzfeld's conversation with Salisbury of the same day.

[454] See n. 401 in this section.

[455] Delagoa Bay railway line, opened on 8 July 1895.

FO 64/1386: Frank C. Lascelles to Marquess of Salisbury, Africa, Confidential, No 7, 6 January 1896

[Received 8 January by post. For: Print (S. Zambezi) / Colonial Office / The Queen / Cabinet; S[alisbury]][456]

Marschall surprised by attitude of English press towards Kruger telegram; German position on South African independence

On the 4th instant, I met Baron von Marschall at dinner and had the opportunity of conversing with him in the course of the evening.

His Excellency showed me a telegram which had been addressed to the Emperor by the Editor[457] of the "Pall Mall Gazette", asking His Majesty's permission to publish a statement to the effect that His Majesty's telegram to President Kruger[458] was not to be considered as an act of hostility towards Great Britain. Baron von Marschall said that no answer would be returned to this telegram and that that the view taken of His Majesty's language could be gathered from the utterances of the German Press.

His Excellency then went on to say that he was astonished at the attitude taken by the English Press and he was at a loss to understand how a congratulatory telegram addressed to the Chief of an independent State for having defeated an armed band which Her Majesty's Government had themselves declared to be outlaws could possibly be regarded as an act of hostility towards Great Britain. In His Excellency's opinion there could be no question as to the independence of the Transvaal which was fully secured by the convention of 1884, subject only to the limitation contained in Article 4 of that convention.[459]

I replied that however much I might regret the tone adopted by the English Press, I must confess that it did not astonish me. I reminded His Excellency that there had been a previous convention between Her Majesty's Government and the Transvaal by which the suzerainty of Great Britain was acknowledged, of 1881[460] and I was not prepared without referring to the documents to say how far the convention had been superseded by the Convention of 1884.

---

[456] Enclosure: untitled extract from the *Norddeutsche Allgemeine Zeitung* of 5 January 1896.

[457] Henry Cockayne-Cust; telegram of 4 January 1896.

[458] In his telegram of 3 January 1896 Wilhelm II congratulated the president of the South African Republic, Kruger, on repelling the 'Jameson Raid' (see n. 450 in this section), on restoring peace and maintaining the independence of the country without appealing to the help of friendly powers.

[459] See n. 401 in this section.

[460] The Pretoria Convention (3 August 1881) was the peace treaty between the South African Republic and the United Kingdom which ended the First Boer War.

Baron von Marschall said that he also would require to refer to the document before expressing a decided opinion, but that he was under the impression that the suzerainty had been completely abolished, and, if this was so, the German Government were perfectly in their right in making any communication they thought fit to the Chief of an independent State. The German Government had certainly no intention or desire to encroach upon any right of Her Majesty's Government but he was under the impression at present that the English press were unjustifiably claiming a right which did not exist and which would certainly be resisted by Germany.

I had a further interview with Baron von Marschall this morning who told me that he had compared the two conventions and had also read the correspondence which had been presented to Parliament on the subject in 1884. His Excellency laid great stress upon the fact that all the articles of the Convention of 1881 which gave effect to the principle of suzerainty had been omitted in the Convention of 1884, and called my attention to Lord Derby's despatch to the Transvaal Deputation of the 15th February 1884 in which the following words occur:

"Your Government will be left free to govern the country without interference and to conduct its diplomatic intercourse and shape its foreign policy subject only to the requirements embodied in the 4th Article of the new draft etc".

I replied that I had also been reading the Blue Book[461] to which His Excellency referred and that, while admitting that the passages he had quoted strongly supported the view taken by the German Government, there was also another view of the question. The limitation contained in Article 4 proved that the independence of the Transvaal was not quite complete, and I reminded His Excellency that a draft submitted by the Deputation, the first article of which provided for the full independence of the South African Republic, had been rejected by Her Majesty's Government.[462]

Baron von Marschall said that he was still of opinion that the suzerainty had been abolished. In any case Germany had no wish to encroach upon rights we might have and was very sensible to a reproach of that nature; he therefore protested against the attitude of the English press which was likely to embitter the question by putting forward claims which appeared to be in direct contradiction to international treaties.

---

[461] *Correspondence respecting the Convention Concluded with the South African Republic on the 27th February 1884*, March 1884.

[462] The draft was submitted on 26 November 1883; it was rejected by the Earl of Derby in his letter to the Transvaal deputation of 29 November 1883.

His Excellency then repeated the language which he had held to me on the 4th instant with regard to the Emperor's telegram to President Kruger, and I at once drafted my Telegram to Your Lordship, the wording of which was changed more than once in consequence of His Excellency's suggestions before it attained its final form.[463]

Baron von Marschall was at pains to explain that he did not seek to interpret the Emperor's language which, in his opinion needed no justification, but he wished to protest against the interpretation which had been put upon it by the English press.

I thanked Baron von Marschall warmly for this communication which I felt was dictated by a friendly spirit towards Her Majesty's Government although he had been careful to explain that it was not to be considered as an explanation of the Emperor's language. I of course accepted at once his assurance that it was not intended as a hostile act towards England but observed that, considering the wording of the telegram, it was not astonishing that it should have given rise to the idea that it had been dictated rather by animosity towards England than by friendship for the Boers.

Baron von Marschall said that he would admit that there had been considerable suspicion of the action of the Chartered Company and that, even as it was, he did not feel sure that the reports that they were moving more troops were absolutely unfounded. He feared that the Company and more especially Mr Rhodes might give a good deal of trouble to Her Majesty's Government, and he could not conceal from himself that, if Doctor Jameson's attempt had been successful, the Company would have been encouraged to go to greater lengths even against the wishes of Her Majesty's Government. A strong feeling of animosity and distrust certainly did exist in Germany towards the Chartered Company, but this feeling certainly did not extend to Her Majesty's Government.

FO 64/1386: Frank C. Lascelles to Marquess of Salisbury, Africa, Confidential, No 13, 11 January 1896

[Received 13 January by bag. For: Print / The Queen / Cabinet / Colonial Office – confidential; S[alisbury]]

Discussion of Anglo-German relations with Marschall in the wake of the Kruger telegram

In a conversation I had this morning with Baron von Marschall, His Excellency alluded to the tone which was still adopted by the English

---

[463] Frank C. Lascelles' Telegram No 3 to Salisbury, marked Africa, 6 January 1896, was drawn up in consultation with Marschall.

Press, more especially the "Times" and the "Standard" towards Germany which would seem to show that public opinion in England was animated by hostile sentiments towards his country. His Excellency could not understand what had caused this feeling and he could assure me that no sentiment of animosity was entertained in Germany, except perhaps in Colonial circles, where we were not popular, towards England, and he was glad to recognize that there had never been a shadow of dissension between the two Governments.

His Excellency added that the Emperor had informed him that he had received a very friendly letter from the Queen[464] at the end of which Her Majesty had alluded to the unfortunate effect which His Majesty's Telegram to President Krüger [*sic*] had produced in England.[465] The Emperor had replied that he was astonished at the view taken in England of his Telegram which certainly was not intended to be in any way offensive and he was still at a loss to understand how such an interpretation could have been put upon it.

I replied that I was sincerely glad to hear from His Excellency, who I was sure was convinced of my sincere desire that this question should be amiably settled. Personally I had been surprised at the excitement caused by the Emperor's Telegram, which I had been told had been greater than anything known in London since the outbreak of the Crimean War, and I sincerely hoped that the incident might now be considered as terminated.

Baron von Marschall said that everything now depended on President Krüger. If he maintained his moderate and conciliatory attitude, which was probable, as it was palpably his interest to do so, it was not likely that any further incident would arise to prevent a satisfactory solution.

FO 64/1386: Frank C. Lascelles to Marquess of Salisbury, Africa, Confidential, No 58, 24 April 1896

[Received 27 April by messenger. For: Print / Mr Balfour / Duke of Devonshire / Mr Chamberlain; S[alisbury]]

Marschall's complaint about misleading British press portrayals of German relations with the Transvaal

In conversation with Baron von Marschall this morning I alluded to the language recently held by the Emperor to Colonel Grierson at

---

[464] Victoria to Wilhelm II, dated Osborne, 5 January 1896.
[465] For the so-called Kruger telegram see n. 458 in this section.

Coburg which formed the subject of my Despatch N° 112 of this day's date.[466]

His Excellency said that he could quite understand the Emperor's complaints against the English Press, which appeared to be animated by a desire to excite public opinion in England to such an extent as to render war with the Transvaal inevitable. His Excellency alluded to the alarmist telegrams which had recently appeared in the "Times" and which were absolutely inaccurate, the evident object of which was to create the impression that Germany was actively interfering in the Transvaal: His Excellency especially referred to the telegram with regard to the arrival of the German Steamer "Bundesrath" in Delagoa Bay, which formed the subject of my Despatch N° 55 Africa of the 23rd instant.[467]

Baron von Marschall went on to say that these alarmist telegrams had produced a great effect in England and he had observed that M[r] Chamberlain in a recent speech[468] had thought it necessary almost to declare war against any Power who should interfere in the Transvaal. His Excellency did not see the necessity for this remark of M[r] Chamberlain's, and he thought that the publication of the White Book[469] and his own speeches in the Reichstag would have had the effect of convincing people in England that there had been no interference on the part of Germany. His Excellency believed that the Transvaal Government were prepared to consider the legitimate grievances of the Outlander[470] population which, it was generally admitted, ought to be redressed. The rapid and increasing development of Johannesburg, which had completely outgrown the administrative arrangements of Boers, was one of the difficulties which would have to be dealt with; and it was evident that it would be impossible to confer political rights upon persons who had merely gone out in the hope of making their fortunes without any intention of permanently remaining in the country, many of whom would not be desirable citizens. But however this might be, His Excellency could not but think that the tone adopted by the majority of the English Press, and even M[r] Chamberlain's remarks about the

[466] Lascelles is referring to Grierson's conversation with Wilhelm II as they attended the wedding of Princess Alexandra of Saxe-Coburg and Gotha and Ernst II, Prince of Hohenlohe-Langenburg, which took place on 20 April 1896.

[467] According to a report from Barberton, printed in the *Times* of 20 April 1896, uniforms and other military equipment had been found in the luggage of German passengers on board the *Bundesrath*, which had landed at Delagoa Bay on 14 April.

[468] Marschall was referring to Chamberlain's speech at the Constitutional Club, London, on 22 April 1896.

[469] *Aktenstücke betreffend die Südafrikanische Republik*, published on 12 February 1896.

[470] Outlander or Uitlander; Afrikaans for 'foreigner' (see n. 450 in this section).

corruption of the Transvaal Government[471] were scarcely calculated to bring about an amicable understanding.

FO 64/1377: Martin Gosselin to Marquess of Salisbury, No 185, Berlin, 19 June 1896

[Received 22 June by messenger. For: African Department; S[alisbury]]

Dispute between Daily Telegraph's *correspondent to Berlin and a clerk of the Imperial Telegraph Office; politicized by Anti-Semites in* Reichstag

A dispute which arose last month between M[r] Bashford, the Berlin correspondent of the Daily Telegraph, and one of the Imperial Telegraph Office clerks has for some days past been discussed in the Berlin newspapers, and was brought before the notice of the Reichstag yesterday.

I have the honour to enclose copy and summary of a statement published by Mr Bashford on the subject, together with a précis by Mr Spring Rice of the statement made in the Reichstag[472] by D[r] von Stephan, the Postmaster General on the incident.[473]

The motion brought forward by Herr Liebermann and supported by 30 Anti-Semites was to the following effect:

(1) Does the Imperial Chancellor[474] know that the Telegraph Clerk Kaiser on the 10th of May last was, while engaged in his work in the Post Office, abused and insulted by the English newspaper correspondent Bashford; and (2) Is the Chancellor aware that the insulted official was induced, through the influence of the Postmaster General, to forego bringing an action, the offender having merely to pay Mks. 100 compensation [Note in margin: 'Mks. 100 = £5'] and to make a verbal apology.

After hearing the Postmaster General's explanation of the incident, the House declined to allow the motion to be discussed, and the question was dropped.

Baron von Marschall told me this morning that the motive of the attack made on M[r] Bashford was the belief that he is a Jew, "whereas he is, I believe, an excellent Christian"; that there could be no doubt that the clerk was in the wrong, in declining to forward the telegram

---

[471] In his speech of 22 April Chamberlain characterized the Transvaal government as 'defective and corrupt'.

[472] On 18 June 1896.

[473] Enclosures: 'Reichstags- Verhandlungen' ('Reichstag proceedings'), *Norddeutsche Allgemeine Zeitung*, 19 June 1896. Report entitled 'The Bashford Case' based on an uncited *Norddeutsche Allgemeine Zeitung* article of 17 June 1896. Précis by Spring-Rice entitled 'Interpellation of the Antisemites on the subject of Mr Bashford', 18 June 1896.

[474] Chlodwig zu Hohenlohe-Schillingsfürst.

till paid for; a proceeding which His Excellency explained by the fact that the clerk in question was not the ordinary official for the Despatch of Press Telegrams, but an extra hand employed on Sundays; that very possibly Mr Bashford had been somewhat hasty in his remarks; but that there was no idea (as suggested by Herr Liebermann) of ordering him to leave Berlin.

My own impression is, that the Anti-Semites availed themselves of the somewhat trumpery incident to attack the Postmaster General, in the hopes of being able to oust him from his post, an official who though one of the ablest in the Imperial Service, has more than once found himself in opposition to the policy advocated by Agrarian and Anti-Semite Agitators.

It is, however, somewhat unfortunate that Mr Bashford should be the Berlin Agent of the South African territories Company Limited, which, as reported in my despatch N° 92 Africa of the 3rd instant, got into trouble only the other day by the appointment of Mr Fort as their Local Manager at Warmbad, in German South West Africa.[475]

FO 64/1387: Martin Gosselin to Marquess of Salisbury, Africa, No 124, 15 July 1896

[Received 20 July by bag. Print (East Africa); 'Consult Mr Hardinge, Sir H. Johnston and India Office', C.Ll.H. [Clement Lloyd Hill]; S[alisbury]; 'Answered No 132', 17 August][476]

Conversation with Paul Kayser on the establishment of game reserves in East Africa

With reference to my despatch No 104 Africa of the 22nd ultimo, respecting the protection of big game in German East Africa, I

---

[475] On 2 June G. Seymour Fort resigned from his post as managing director at Warmbad as a result of an article on the 'Jameson Raid' (see n. 450 in this section), published in the June issue of *The Nineteenth Century*, In this he insinuated secret understandings between Germany and the Transvaal.

[476] Notes on docket (also printed as official Minutes on Berlin No 124, Africa, July 15 1896). 'See typed copy of following: The subject is one that requires very careful consideration. I will submit an expression of my views separatly [*sic*], or rather a compromise between my own views & those of Mr Alfred Sharpe, as I find there is some divergence between them and that Mr Sharpe in his recent private correspondence can adduce good reasons for not following me more than a certain distance in my desire to control the destruction of certain animals.' H.H.J. [Henry Hamilton Johnston]; 'I have not read Major von Wissmann's proposals, but in principle I think it very desirable that a sort of "park" should be marked out, within which certain animals should be sacred. I have discussed this question with several Officials at Mombasa & think we should reserve a certain district in Kikuyu and another in Ukambani and perhaps another on the Tana. We should have to have 3 European rangers whose business it would be to see that our regulations were observed. When the railway is made, Africa will be flooded with Sportsmen making

have the honour to report that I enquired this morning of Dr Kayser how Major von Wissman meant to enforce respect for his proposed sanctuaries, without incurring any considerable expense.[477]

Dr Kayser replied that he had put this very question to Major von Wissman on his return here the other day to Berlin.[478]

Major von Wissman had explained that the nearest stations to the reserves would be charged with the carrying out of his game regulations, and that as far as European sportsmen go, he did not anticipate any insuperable difficulties; with native hunters it will of course be more difficult to deal; but the Major is of opinion that if the system of sporting licences is strictly enforced, and the first few offenders duly punished, it will be quite possible to ensure a considerable amount of respect for the game reserves.

Major von Wissman is himself in favour of some international agreement being come to between all the Powers on the East African littoral for the protection of game in the interior.

Dr Kayser said that while he personally entirely sympathised with this suggestion he foresaw difficulties in carrying it out; for instance the Portuguese might agree to the plan on paper, but they had no means, even with the best will in the world, for carrying it out on the Mozambique coast.

Dr Kayser had no doubt that the British and German authorities would heartily co-operate in the effort to protect elephants and other big game from extermination; but that if the natives found that by

---

for the Athi plains. We should not lose in B.E.A. [British East Africa] by the diversion of trade to Portuguese Africa – our ivory hunters would not go so far South. There is already a Company's regulation prohibiting the killing of cow-elephants & I believe the tusks can be distinguished from the bulls', so there ought to be no difficulty in enforcing it. I would suggest sending Major von Wissmann's proposals to Mr Crawford & asking him to draft a set of regulations for B.E.A. following the German lines wherever practicable or advisable.' A.H.H. [Arthur Henry Hardinge]; 'Sir John Kirk thinks that we should do better by keeping sportsmen out of certain large areas than by attempting to control what foes are within them. He would strictly enforce against sportsmen the regulations of the Brussels Act as to stamping arms & the regulations as to licenses already existing. He thinks the areas should not be traversed by a main road, shd not be near a foreign frontier & shd not be in too thickly inhabited districts & that they shd be large. He suggests that one might be near the Tana, and then in the Kenia ranges, & a third on the Man heights, but agrees in asking local advice. We have already called special local attention to the matter & might now, as suggested by Mr Hardinge, tell Mr Crawford to draft regulations for approval.' C.Ll. H. [Clement Lloyd Hill], 3 August; S[alisbury]; Draft, 14 August & Draft, Sir F. Lascelles, No 132, 17 August].

[477] On 7 May 1896 Hermann von Wissmann, governor of German East Africa, issued a wildlife ordinance which stipulated restrictive regulations for hunting. A *Runderlaß* (circular directive) of the same day justified these measures and proposed the establishment of game reserves; the first two were to be west of Mount Kilimanjaro and on the Rufiji River.

[478] Wissmann had left Africa on 11 May 1896 and visited Berlin in early July.

crossing the Rovuma they could find a ready market for their ivory, all the ivory trade on the east coast would be diverted to the Portuguese possessions; England and Germany would be the losers; while no protection would be afforded to the African elephant.

The only means he could see by which the depredations of sportsmen (both European and native) could be checked would be for the Powers to fix, by international agreement a close time for elephants and hippopotami, and to authorise the confiscation by the authorities on the littoral of all tusks under a certain weight.

Dr Kayser said he would be glad if I would mention this suggestion to Your Lordship as a possible solution of the question, though he feared that it would be very difficult to ensure the adequate carrying out of any such a measure by the Portuguese authorities on the Mozambique coast.

If the British authorities concerned have any suggestion to make on the subject, Dr Kayser assured me he would gladly give them his earnest consideration.

In view of the fact that a question was asked in the House of Commons on the 30th ultimo, respecting the establishment of a reserve or sanctuary for elephants within the British Somali Land Protectorate, I venture to report Dr Kayser's observations to Your Lordship for the information of the India Office.

FO 64/1387: Martin Gosselin to Marquess of Salisbury, Africa, No 133, 23 July 1896

[Received 27 July by messenger. For: Colonial Office with No 128, P.L. [printed letter], 4 August; S[alisbury]]

Discussion with Paul Kayser on penal settlements in German colonies

With reference to my despatch N° 128 Africa of the 20th instant, I have the honour to enclose a summary by Mr Whitehead of a leading article in last night's "Norddeutsche" on the subject of the establishment of penal settlements in German Colonies.[479]

I asked Dr Kayser today whether the German Government had any immediate intention of adopting the scheme, which has met with warm support in the Colonial Society's recent meetings.[480]

Dr Kayser replied that the Colonial Department saw no reason to prevent an examination of the question, which was favoured by the

---

[479] Enclosure: précis of a leading article in the *Norddeutsche Allgemeine Zeitung* of 22 July 1896 on the question of deporting criminals to South West Africa.

[480] On 30 May 1896 the general meeting of the Colonial Society referred the question of penal settlements to the society's standing committee.

Professors and the Parsons – two powers in the State whom he could not afford to neglect; he had consequently a few days ago given a letter of introduction to an acquaintance in Paris for a gentleman who was about to visit France, on behalf of the supporters of the scheme, to investigate into the French system of transmarine penal settlements; but he did not anticipate that anything would come of the movement.

In the first place it was a question about which the Department of Justice would have a weighty word to say; and Dr Starke, one of the leading officials of that Department in criminal matters, was strongly opposed to the scheme. It was calculated that each prisoner in Prussia costs the State one Mark a day – (including general prison expenditure and maintenance); if the criminals were transported, the average expenditure would be tenfold that amount: this alone, said the Doctor, would be sufficient to damp the ardour of the Government.

Then, the Department of Justice would never sanction "a slow death sentence" by the deportation of criminals to unhealthy Colonies: a German Cayenne would be an impossibility;[481] the only colony which could ever be used for such a purpose would be South West Africa; and the Government, if they had funds at their disposal, would prefer to assist free immigration there than to embark on a large expenditure on behalf of the criminal classes of the country.

In reply to my enquiry whether it is a fact, as stated in the "Norddeutsche's" Article, that the French Government have established penal settlements at Obok and Gaboon, Dr Kayser said he had never heard of them, and thought the statement incorrect.

FO 64/1379: Frank C. Lascelles to Marquess of Salisbury, Confidential, No 310, Berlin, 15 October 1896

[Received 19 October by messenger. For: The Queen / Prince of Wales / Duke of Devonshire / Mr Balfour / Mr Chamberlain / Eastern Department / African Department; S[alisbury]]

Hatzfeldt apologetic about the sorry state of Anglo-German relations; blames Britain's unclear policy towards Turkey; discussion of colonial matters

Count Hatzfeldt, who is staying for a few days in Berlin,[482] was good enough to call upon me today. His Excellency spoke to me very openly about the relations between England and Germany, and

---

[481] Kayser was referring to the Bagne de Cayenne (Devil's Island), a penal colony in French Guiana.

[482] Hatzfeldt was on leave of absence from 1 September. He returned from Sommerberg to London in mid November 1896.

regretted that they were no longer on their former satisfactory footing. His Excellency considered that this was due to the change which
took place some years ago in English policy with regard to Turkey.[483]
Before then, it was a recognized axiom that England would do all in
her power to maintain the integrity of the Turkish Empire. There
was now however considerable doubt as to the line which England
would take if the Eastern question were reopened, and it was evident
that under these circumstances there must be some hesitation on the
part of other Governments until they knew the line which Her
Majesty's Government might decide to adopt.

His Excellency personally did not attribute much importance to the
differences with regard to Colonial questions which had arisen between
the two countries. They were not of sufficient importance to bring
about a permanent estrangement between the two countries. With
regard to the case of Said Khalid,[484] His Excellency said that he was
convinced that in similar circumstances England would have refused
to give him up, and in proof of this he cited the case of Witbooi who
had given great trouble to the German Authorities in South West
Africa, and who had not only not been given up by the Cape
Authorities, but had been allowed sufficient liberty to be able to
enter German territory and create trouble, and then to take refuge
in the territory of the Chartered Company.[485] His Excellency thought
that the action of the German Government with regard to Said
Khalid would compare favourably with that of the Cape Authorities
with regard to Witbooi, but however this might be, there was no
doubt that the relations between England and Germany were far
from being on a satisfactory footing, and he had considered it his
duty to inform the Emperor that there were people in England, and
even influential people, who contemplated the possibility of a war
with Germany. His Majesty had expressed the greatest astonishment
that this should be the case, and His Excellency himself did not believe
that the irritation which no doubt existed on both sides would lead to
war, but the change which had taken place in recent years with regard

[483] Hatzfeldt was referring to Britain's policy towards Turkey since 1895. As he understood it, Great Britain – in light of the Turkish policy towards the Armenian people and
the Hamidian massacres – was considering the division of the Ottoman Empire and thus
abandoning the leading principle of her Eastern policy.

[484] Khalid succeeded to the position of Sultan of Zanzibar without British consent, on
25 August 1896. On the day of the one-day Anglo-Zanzibar War, on 27 August, he took
refuge at the German consulate. On 2 October he was brought to Dar es Salaam
(German East Africa) where he sought political asylum.

[485] British South Africa Company (founded 1889). Hatzfeldt was referring to conflicts
with the German colonial authorities in German South West Africa (Namibia) from
1888, when Hendrik Witbooi became chief of the |Khowesin (Witbooi) people. He condi-
tionally surrendered in 1894.

to the policy of England on the Eastern question had given rise to grave
doubts as to the line she would adopt if the question were reopened. His
long residence in England had given him an insight into English character, which was little understood on the Continent, and, although he
was perfectly aware that the recent movement in England with regard
to the Armenian massacres had been dictated solely by disinterested
and humanitarian motives,[486] he found it almost impossible to convince
people here that England ever acted except from selfish motives, or
allowed her political action to be influenced by sentimentality.

FO 64/1379: Frank C. Lascelles to Marquess of Salisbury, No 321, Berlin, 27 October 1896

[Received 2 November by bag. For: Print (West Europe) / The Queen / Prince of
Wales / Mr Balfour / Duke of Devonshire; Confidential to: St Petersburg / Vienna
/ Rome; Cabinet; S[alisbury]]

*Surprising press reports on secret Reinsurance Treaty and Russia; Russo-German relations during
reign of Alexander III*

I have the honour to enclose to Your Lordship, herewith, copy and
translation of a notice which has appeared in the "Reichs Anzeiger"
relative to an Article published in the "Hamburger Nachrichten",[487]
which is generally supposed to be Prince Bismarck's organ.

In this article it was stated that ["]soon after the accession of the Czar
Alexander III[488] good relations were established between Germany and
Russia, which lasted till 1890. Till that date both nations had a full
understanding that if one was attacked without provocation the other
would maintain an attitude of friendly neutrality. This understanding
came to an end with Prince Bismarck's retirement not because of
Russia's unwillingness to renew it but because Count Caprivi refused
to prolong the mutual policy of insurance". This, says the writer, was
the origin of Russia's friendship for France, for her isolation, in consequence of Germany's changed attitude left her no other choice.

The Article has excited a very great amount of interest in
Germany, which has resulted in the official notice, which I have

---

[486] Lascelles is referring to the Hamidian massacres against the Armenian population of
the Ottoman Empire; see also n. 557 in Dresden section.

[487] The secret Reinsurance Treaty between Germany and Russia of 18 June 1887 – and
its non-renewal in 1890 – was exposed in the *Hamburger Nachrichten* of 24 October 1896. The
notice in the *Deutscher Reichs-Anzeiger und Königlich Preußischer Staats-Anzeiger* was published on
27 October. Enclosure: clipping entitled 'Deutschland. Die Hamburger Enthüllungen',
and translation (both undated).

[488] 13 March 1881.

the honour to enclose to the effect that the Government has no statement whatever to make on a subject which belongs to the domain of official secrecy, where any disclosure whatever would entail injury to state interests of the gravest kind.

The statement apart from general considerations is of a sufficiently surprising nature. Alexander III succeeded to the throne in 1881. The history of the ensuing years is full of the antagonism between Russia and Germany. The Imperial Bank took hostile action against Russian securities. The army was increased in 1887 precisely on account of the alleged danger of a Russian attack: the German-Austrian Treaty was ostentatiously published in 1888[489] and on the 6th of February of that year Prince Bismarck made his famous speech[490] in which he said that Russia had turned her old friend Germany out of doors, and concluded with the famous words – "We Germans fear God but nothing else in the world"[.]

But the most remarkable aspect of the statement is the fact that the Treaty was concluded with Austria in 1879 and that, if what is alleged is true, an understanding was made shortly afterwards[491] with Russia to the knowledge of which Austria does not appear to have been admitted.

FO 64/1379: Frank C. Lascelles to Marquess of Salisbury, Secret, No 339, Berlin, 5 November 1896

[Received 9 November by bag. For: The Queen / Mr Balfour / Duke of Devonshire; Secret to: Paris / St Petersburg / Peking; 'It is not Mickie but Michie. He is or was a merchant at Tientsin: & is a well informed and far sighted authority.' G.N.C. [George N. Curzon]; S[alisbury]]

Similarity of German and British interests in China; need for cooperation to guard against internal and external threats

I have the honour to inclose an interesting Memorandum by M[r] Spring-Rice of a conversation he has had with M[r] Detring, who is about to resume his duties in China.[492]

---

[489] In the secret treaty of 7 October 1879 (published on 3 February 1888), which brought about the so-called Dual Alliance, Austria and Germany pledged to aid one another in the case of an attack by Russia, or in the event of an attack by a Russian-supported power. In all other cases it was agreed to observe benevolent neutrality.

[490] See pp. 303–304.

[491] The date of the Reinsurance Treaty (1887) was not disclosed by the *Hamburger Nachrichten* and still unknown at the time of the dispatch.

[492] Enclosure: secret memorandum recording conversation between Spring-Rice and Mr Detring, undated.

I have had an opportunity of conversing with Mr Mickie [*sic*][493] to whom allusion is made in the Memorandum, and who is strongly of opinion that English and German interests are identical in China and that it is of the utmost importance that the two nations should act, if not in cooperation, at all events on parallel lines. If France and Russia were to encroach on China the one from the South and the other from the North, the Commercial interests both of England and Germany would be fatally affected. Mr Mickie pointed out that there were two dangers which threatened the present Chinese Dynasty.[494] One was a popular rising such as the Taiping rebellion,[495] and the other was an intrigue against the present Emperor, whose right to the throne had been contested and who was popularly supposed to be incapable of leaving a direct heir.[496] An attack against the Dynasty either in the shape of a Palace intrigue or of a popular rising would probably, if successful entail a long period of anarchy in China, of which it was probable that France and Russia would take advantage to the detriment of the commercial interests of England and Germany. It was only natural that each of the two latter countries should strive to push their own interests, but it would be of great advantage to both if they could be brought to understand that they were both threatened by the same dangers, and that they should act together in order to avoid them.

FO 64/1379: Frank C. Lascelles to Marquess of Salisbury, Confidential, No 356, Berlin, 20 November 1896

[Received 23 November by bag. For: The Queen / Prince of Wales / Duke of Devonshire / Mr Balfour; Confidential to: Paris / Vienna / St Petersburg / Rome / Constantinople; African and United States departments to see; Print for Cabinet; S[alisbury]]

Debate on disclosed Russo-German Reinsurance Treaty; conversation with Marschall regarding anti-English feeling in Reichstag debate and different parts of the German political spectrum

With reference to my despatch No. 349 of yesterday's date, I have the honour to report that I took an opportunity this afternoon of congratulating Baron von Marschall on the favourable impression which had been produced by the debate in the Reichstag on the

---

[493] Alexander Michie.

[494] Qing dynasty.

[495] The Taiping Rebellion of 1850–1864 was a civil war between the Qing government and the religious-social movement of the Heavenly Kingdom of Peace in southern China.

[496] Guangxu Emperor; he was enthroned as emperor despite belonging to the same generation as his predecessor and cousin, Tongzhi Emperor.

Bismarck revelations.[497] I said that I was also glad to hear that His Excellency's speech had caused satisfaction at Vienna and Rome.

Baron von Marschall thanked me and said that his task had been a most difficult one, as it had been impossible for him to speak openly on the subject, and he was glad to say that the favourable impression which had been created in Austria and Italy was shared also to a certain extent in Russia, although Count Osten Sacken had urged to maintain complete secrecy with regard to the Treaty which expired in 1890. He had explained to Count Osten Sacken that although he would certainly not make any revelations on the subject, it was impossible for him to contradict Prince Bismarck, who had himself signed the Treaty, and the very fact of his not denying the existence of the Treaty could not fail to be taken as a tacit avowal of its having existed. Count Osten Sacken had agreed that this was the case, and had apparently been satisfied with the speech, which had not been unfavourably received by the Russian Press.

I went on to say that while I rejoiced that the Government had extricated themselves from the very difficult position in which they had been placed by Prince Bismarck's revelation, I could not but regret the Anti-English feeling which prevailed in the Reichstag.

His Excellency answered that the Bismarckians were certainly Anti-English. It had in fact invariably been Prince Bismarck's habit to proclaim hostility to England, although in his political action he had frequently shown that he was not unfriendly to her, but he doubted whether the other sections of the Reichstag entertained any Anti-English sentiments, while the Left were decidedly Anglophil[e].

I observed that the Centre[498] appeared to me to have shown a decidedly Anti-English tendency, and His Excellency's speech itself contained two statements which I could only regard as being directed against England. At His Excellency's request, I quoted the two passages to which I drew Your Lordship's attention in my above-mentioned despatch.

Baron von Marschall replied that his allusion to the joint action of Germany with Russia and France last year in the Far East[499] was a

---

[497] Lascelles is referring to the *Reichstag* debate of 16 November 1896. For the disclosure of the existence of the Russo-German Reinsurance Treaty, and its non-renewal in 1890, see n. 487 in this section.

[498] *Zentrumspartei* (Catholics).

[499] The so-called Triple Intervention of 23 April 1895 demanded the return of the Liaodong Peninsula from Japan to China, which had previously been ceded by China in the peace treaty of Shimonoseki of 17 April 1896. In his *Reichstag* speech Marschall stated that German overseas interests would probably provide future opportunity for the co-operation of the three powers.

confirmation of his statement that the relations of Germany and Russia were on a satisfactory footing, and his expression of the desire of the German Government to maintain friendly relations with other Powers and to recognize their rights to the same extent as they recognized the rights of Germany was merely an amplification of the remarks he had made in an earlier part of his speech, that good relations between Germany and Russia must depend upon reciprocity.[500]

Baron von Marschall added that he did not consider that the Centre was animated by Anti-English sentiments. He thought that it was rather Anti-Russian, but Prince Bismarck's revelations had done enormous harm in two respects. They had in the first place given rise to the suspicion that the Emperor allowed himself to be guided by the influence of the Empress Frederick[501] to follow a policy which might not be in accordance with the true interests of Germany, and on this point all Germans were particularly sensitive, and in the second place they had asserted that the Franco-Russian understanding had been brought about by the refusal of Prince Bismarck's successor[502] to renew the secret Treaty with Russia. In a Bismarckian Newspaper which he had just received it was stated that, although the Treaty with Russia may not have been officially communicated to the English Government, there existed family relations by which communications could be made without the knowledge of the responsible Ministers. Such statements, which were no doubt inspired by Prince Bismarck, were most perfidious and would excite animosity against the Empress Frederick, and through her against England, and he could not conceal from me that the action of Her Majesty's Government with regard to Said Khaled [*sic*][503] had produced a most unfavorable impression in Germany.

I did not think it necessary to prolong the discussion, as I thought I had done enough in showing His Excellency that the remarks in his speech against England had not passed unnoticed, but I asked him whether Prince Bismarck's adherents did not perceive that the revelations were more damaging to the Prince's reputation than to anyone else.

Baron von Marschall replied that the majority of Bismarckians had such faith in the Prince that in their eyes he could not be wrong, but that he had every reason to believe that Count Herbert Bismarck, who had attended the sitting of the Reichstag no doubt with the

---

[500] In his speech Marschall expressed the general German desire for friendly relations with 'other powers with that respect for their rights which they may accord to ours'.

[501] Victoria.

[502] Leo von Caprivi.

[503] Sayyid Khalid; see n. 484 in this section.

view of defending his Father if necessary, deplored the action which the Prince had taken, and strongly disapproved of the revelations.

FO 64/1379: Frank C. Lascelles to Marquess of Salisbury, Confidential, No 368, Berlin, 28 November 1896

[Received 30 November by messenger. For: The Queen / Duke of Devonshire / Mr Balfour / Secret to Home Office (with reference H.E. Telegram No 4, 28 November 1896), P.L. [printed letter], 2 December; S[alisbury]]

Discussion with emperor about Hamburg strike; suspected British support; dangers of increasing anti-English feeling in southern Germany

At a quarter before eight this evening I received a visit from Baron von Senden Bibran the head of the Emperor's Naval Cabinet who told me that His Majesty who was on his way back to Potsdam desired to see me as soon as possible. I told the Admiral that I should at once obey His Majesty's commands by taking the train which left Berlin for Potsdam at five minutes past nine, and shortly afterwards I received a Telegram from His Majesty requesting me to come to Potsdam immediately.

I had the honour in my Telegram No 49, to report to your Lordship the principal points of His Majesty's remarks with regard to the Hamburg strike which evidently had deeply impressed His Majesty as being not merely a local outbreak, but a carefully organized international movement.[504] There had been no justification for the strike. The dock labourers were receiving wages which would command the services of skilled artizans, and the strike appeared to be collapsing when it suddenly revived on the appearance of Mr Tom Mann in Hamburg.[505] There were 45000 workmen in Hamburg of whom 10,000 were on strike. Their places were filled up by importations from other ports of Germany, and even from England, but it was to be expected that the men on strike would oppose the employment of imported labour, and that disturbances might ensue. There was no danger of serious disorder as General von Waldersee who was in command would certainly repress any disturbance with severity and the Socialists would probably receive a lesson which would keep them quiet for the next twenty years, but incalculable harm would be done if Hamburg and the Elbe which

[504] The Hamburg dock strike began on 21 November 1896 and ended, unsuccessfully, on 6 February 1897.

[505] Tom Mann, a British trade unionist, who had been evicted from Hamburg on 15 September, returned on 23 November. He was arrested on 26 November.

had hitherto been friendly to England began to believe that English capital had supported the Hamburg strike with the object of damaging German commerce.

I told The Emperor that I would not fail to report to Your Lordship the observations which His Majesty had made, but I remarked that although Socialists all over the world might act together it was inconceivable that English commerce should seek to win Hamburg with whom it had such vast interests.

His Majesty replied that the Anti English feeling which was prevalent in South Germany seemed to be increasing, and that if it extended to Hamburg and the Elbe the relations between the two countries would become so embittered that there would be an estrangement between them, which would last for at least fifty years, of which no doubt both France and Russia would take full advantage.

FO 64/1409: Frank C. Lascelles to Marquess of Salisbury, Confidential, No 41, Berlin, 12 February 1897

[Received 15 February by bag. For: The Queen / Prince of Wales / Duke of Devonshire / Mr Balfour / Commercial Department / Admiralty – confidential / Cabinet; S[alisbury]]

Political effects of Germany's growth in industrial production and foreign trade; weak naval power renders Germany precarious in times of war

I venture to draw Your Lordship's attention to the speech recently delivered in the Reichstag by Baron von Marschall, reported in my despatch No 38 Commercial of the 10th instant, and to the communication of the Emperor to the Reichstag of which I sent a translation in my despatch No 39 of this series of today's date.[506]

The gist of these statements appears to be that this Government is deeply impressed with the changed conditions brought about by the great development of German industry.

Germany is no longer a country living on its own resources; it is fed from abroad and it pays for its food by the products of German industry which from year to year take more decidedly the character of elaborately manufactured products, the raw material of which comes from foreign countries. In the mean while the urban population of Germany is increasing at a far more rapid rate that the population of the country districts and the proportion of the German people who are engaged in the production of food stuffs is yearly diminishing.

---

[506] Lascelles is referring to Marschall's speech of 8 February 1897 which dealt with future German trade policy and commercial treaties. For the communication of the emperor see n. 508 below.

This tendency has a two-fold effect on German politics.

On the one hand it has produced the agrarian movement the main strength of which lies in the sentiment expressed in the article from the Norddeutsche[507] which I had the honour to transmit in my despatch No 40 of this series of today's date. This is, in brief, firstly that Germany must, as far as possible, provide her own food, and secondly that the fighting strength of Germany lies in a prosperous country population. Hence arises the desire which is constantly apparent in the public utterances and the legislative proposals of the Government to do all that is possible for the landed interest, landlords and farmers.

But this tendency has another and a more striking consequence. Germany depends for part of her food supply on foreign countries, and, for the pecuniary resources which enable her to meet her military expenses, on foreign trade. And, as is apparent from the tables communicated by the Emperor to the Reichstag,[508] Germany disposes of a sea power greatly inferior to that of France and Russia. The sea approaches of Germany are at the mercy of a combination between France and Russia or of France alone. And Germany accepted the doctrine of sea law advanced by France at the time of her hostilities with China, that the necessaries of life were contraband of war.[509] In case of a war with France the food supply of Germany would be drawn (as they are now drawn in yearly increasing proportion) from Russia. But if she were at war with both France and Russia for any length of time the economical and political position of Germany, with the enormous number of socialists in her midst, would be indeed perilous.

In the report recently published by the Board of Trade[510] it is stated that the tendency noticed, – of the development of the industrial activity of Germany, – it is likely to continue if peace is assured. I venture to think that peace is not only a condition of German prosperity but is regarded in many quarters as almost a condition of her existence.

---

[507] Lascelles is referring to the editorial titled *Unsere Handelspolitk* (Our Trade Policy) in the *Norddeutsche Allgemeine Zeitung* of 11 February 1897.

[508] On 11 February 1897 Wilhelm II presented the *Reichstag* library with tables that he had drawn up himself, which compared the naval strength of Germany, France, Russia, the United States, Japan, and France.

[509] Lascelles is referring to the Sino-French War when, in February 1885, France declared rice as contraband. Unlike Great Britain, Germany did not protest against this measure.

[510] Board of Trade, *Memorandum on the Comparative Statistics of Population, Industry, and Commerce in the United Kingdom and some Leading Foreign Countries, presented to both Houses of Parliament by Command of Her Majesty*, January 1897 [C.8322].

FO 64/1410: Frank C. Lascelles to Marquess of Salisbury, No 134, Berlin, 14 May 1897

[Received 17 May by bag. For: The Queen / Prince of Wales / Duke of Devonshire / Mr Balfour, A.J.B. [Arthur James Balfour]; S[alisbury]]

Public feeling exasperated by repeated ineptitude of administration

The recent debate on the subject of the law of High Treason and the publication of the bill respecting the right of association and public meeting have directed the attention of the press and public opinion to the principles under which the present Government is administered.[511]

So far as comments are possible under the severely restrictive laws of Germany, it would appear that public feeling has been deeply stirred by the recent irresponsible utterances of the crown[512] and by the obstacle which would seem to be encountered by ministers in carrying out their pledges to the peoples' representatives.

Reiterated promises have been made to the Reichstag that the military penal laws will be reformed, and after the retirement of one minister[513] and numerous rumours of Cabinet crises [Note in margin: '(See No 3 Jan 1)'] (as to which the Tausch trial offered an interesting commentary)[514] a bill in the above sense has only now been submitted to the Bundesrath.[515]

A year ago the Reichstag[516] consented to the withdrawal of a resolution for the abolition of the restriction on the right of association on the receipt of a pledge from the Government that a bill in that sense would shortly be presented. Such a bill has only been published, and contains provisions which make its rejection almost certain.[517]

[511] Lascelles is referring to the *Reichstag* motion by August Bebel of 12 May 1897 to abolish the classification of lèse-majesty as criminal offence and to the bill respecting the right of assembly and association, introduced in the Prussian house of deputies on 13 May 1897.

[512] Lascelles is probably referring to Wilhelm's telegram to his brother Heinrich of 20 April, in which he reprimanded the *Reichstag* and insulted its deputies for having rejected large parts the navy budget. The letter's content was leaked to the public after having been read out by Heinrich to the crew of his cruiser.

[513] Walther Bronsart von Schellendorff; on 14 August 1896.

[514] Lascelles is referring to a trial against two journalists at the end of which, on 7 December 1896, Eugen von Tausch, superintendent of the political police, was arrested for perjury. Tausch, who had sold confidential information to the press and disseminated political misinformation, was on trial from 24 May to 4 June 1897 and was ultimately acquitted.

[515] The Military Penal Code was presented to the Federal Council by Prussia on 8 May 1897. See n. 186 in Munich section.

[516] On 27 June 1896.

[517] Lascelles is referring to the bill respecting the right of assembly and association introduced in the Prussian house of deputies on 13 May 1897. It was rejected on 24 July.

And while the Government thus appears to be continually hampered by a hidden opposition, statements are publicly made by the highest authority reflecting on the representative body as a whole, or on individual parties; or, as in the case of the naval estimates, proposals from the same source are submitted to the Reichstag, which the Ministers have never even seen.[518] [Note in margin: 'No 89 March 26']

The socialists have been branded as "enemies of their country";[519] even the Conservatives have been characterized as "grumblers";[520] The Reichstag as a body has been described as a set of men "who did not know what patriotism meant"[521] and [Note in margin: No 136; May 14] as a "crew unworthy of the name of Germans".[522] No minister can be made responsible for these statements, and language in self defence comes under the law of high treason.

The position of the Ministers themselves can be judged by the action of the Chancellor[523] above quoted and by recent events in the domain of foreign policy.[524]

Under these circumstances it is not surprising if, at the present moment, the rumours of a ministerial crisis are renewed, and if, from almost every quarter, expressions of discontent are making themselves heard.

FO 64/1410: Frank C. Lascelles to Marquess of Salisbury, No 141, Berlin, 20 May 1897

[Received 23 May. For: Duke of Devonshire / Mr Balfour, A.J. B. [Arthur James Balfour] / Intelligence Division (War Office) / Commercial Department / African Department; S[alisbury]]

Discussion of emigration bill; no formal emigration policy but attempts to direct migrants to colonies

I have the honour to inform Your Lordship with reference to my Despatch N⁰ 121 of the 8th Instant that the Emigration Bill has been read a third time in the Reichstag.[525]

---

[518] The navel estimates, which reflected Wilhelm II's intention to expand the German navy, were decreased by the budget committee and passed by the *Reichstag* on 28 March 1897.

[519] Wilhelm II on 14 May 1889, at an audience with a delegation of striking coal miners.

[520] Wilhelm II, in a speech to the members of the provincial diet of Brandenburg, on 24 February 1894 .

[521] Wilhelm II, in a telegram to Prince Heinrich of 20 April 1897.

[522] Not a literal quote. Lascelles is referring to Wilhelm's telegram to Bismarck of 23 March 1885, after the *Reichstag* refused to congratulate Bismarck on his 80th birthday.

[523] Chlodwig zu Hohenlohe-Schillingsfürst.

[524] Lascelles is referring to anti-Greek policy (and Wilhelm II's plan to blockade Greece) in the run-up to, and during, the Greco-Turkish War (5 April to 8 May 1897).

[525] The bill was passed on 19 May 1897; it came into effect (as the law of 9 June 1897) on 1 April 1898.

In addition to the Bill, resolutions (drawn up by the special committee to which the bill had been referred) were passed, one urging the appointment of Consuls in the harbours frequented by German Emigrants in order to look after their interests and the other advocating measures to make it easier for Germans born, or living, abroad to perform their military service.

The House then considered two further resolutions proposed by a private member.[526] The first urged the Government to use the means at their disposal in order to "guide the stream of emigration, as much as possible, to those countries where in addition to finding means of earning a livelihood German Emigrants have the best chance of maintaining their nationality (Deutschtum) as well as good relations with their old home."

After a favourable statement on the part of the Government this resolution was passed.

A second resolution asking the Government to lay a bill before the House for the Colonization of the German Protectorates was however rejected.

It was stated that the only Protectorate suitable to Colonization was South West Africa and that experiments with a view to discovering whether or not it was suitable for small farmers were now being made. The Government was taking the necessary practical measures and no further steps were required at present.

I have already had the honour to draw Your Lordship's attention to the importance of the principle embodied in these resolutions. Although the Government Representatives did not formally give expression to an emigration policy (which appears, however, to have been communicated to the Committee) having for its object the establishment under foreign flags, of bodies of Colonists owing allegiance to Germany, performing services for the Mother Country, such a policy has been for long advocated in Germany; and, from the terms of the Government Bill and from Baron von Marschall's speech on the objects of a navy (See my Despatch N° 92 of the 27th March)[527] appears to have been fully adopted by the Government.

---

[526] Paul Förster.

[527] Lascelles is referring to Marschall's *Reichstag* speech in the second reading of the navy estimates on 18 March 1897.

FO 64/1411: Frank C. Lascelles to Marquess of Salisbury, No 180, Berlin, 1 July 1897

[Received 5 July by bag. Seen by the Chief Clerk [stamped]; For: The Queen / Prince of Wales / Brussels / Admiralty; S[alisbury]]

Banquet in honour of Queen Victoria's diamond jubilee on board Hohenzollern *at Kiel; emperor's affectionate speech*

On the 27th ultimo The Emperor gave a banquet on board His Majesty's Yacht "Hohenzollern" at Kiel in commemoration of the Queen's Jubilee,[528] to which all the members of Her Majesty's Embassy at present at Berlin had the honour of being invited, as well as the owners of the English yachts who had come to take part in the Kiel Regatta.

The German Ships of War in the Harbour were all flying the White Ensign.

During the Dinner The Emperor rose and speaking in German welcomed The King of the Belgians who was present and announced that he had appointed His Majesty an Admiral "à la suite"[529] of the German Navy. He expressed the hope that the friendly relations between the two countries which were of a commercial rather than a political character might be still further developed, and concluded by asking His Majesty's permission to propose the toast of The Queen.

Then, speaking in English, His Majesty bade a cordial welcome to his English guests to whom he was glad to give an opportunity of drinking The Queen's health, a toast which could nowhere be more appropriately honoured than on board a ship on blue water. In touching terms he described his admiration of The Queen, to whom he alluded as the wisest Sovereign in Europe and said that every German Officer in command of [a] ship felt honoured that day by flying the White Ensign in celebration of Her Majesty's Jubilee. In conclusion His Majesty called for three cheers for The Queen which he led himself.

The King of the Belgians expressed his thanks for the honour which The Emperor had conferred upon him, expressed the hope that German ships would come in greater numbers to Antwerp and concluded by proposing the health of The Emperor and Empress.[530] The effect of His Majesty's speech was somewhat marred

---

[528] Victoria celebrated the 60th anniversary of her reign (her Diamond Jubilee) on 22 June 1897.

[529] 'In the entourage of'; an honorary military title with no official position.

[530] Auguste Viktoria.

by its being delivered during the firing of the Royal Salute in honour of the Queen.

FO 64/1411: Frank C. Lascelles to Marquess of Salisbury, No 184, Berlin, 2 July 1897

[Received 5 July by bag. For: The Queen / Prince of Wales / Duke of Devonshire / Mr Balfour, A.J.B. [Arthur James Balfour]; S[alisbury]]

Marschall replaced by Bülow as foreign minister; new incumbent a triumph for Agrarian Party

I have the honour to enclose a translation of a notification published on the 28th ultimo by Wolff's Telegraphic Bureau and reproduced by all the German Newspapers to the effect that the state of Baron von Marschall's health has made it necessary that he should be replaced at the Ministry for Foreign Affairs and that Herr von Bülow has temporarily been charged by The Emperor with the direction of that Office.[531]

It has been generally known for several months past that Baron von Marschall had fallen out of favour with The Emperor, and His Majesty is reported to have said at the conclusion of the Tausch Trial, that the acquittal of von Tausch made it impossible that Baron von Marschall should remain in Office.[532]

I have been informed that Baron von Marschall's health has greatly improved since he left Berlin,[533] and at that time he had certainly no intention of resigning his Office. He told me on the very day of his departure that he expected to return to Berlin about the middle of August and that he hoped to obtain a further leave of absence in September.

The state of his health therefore can only be regarded as a pretext for his dismissal, and I am informed that it was only through the newspapers that he became aware of any intention on the part of the Emperor to remove him from Office.

In speaking to me on this subject this morning, Baron von Rotenhan told me that Baron von Marschall had written a letter to the Chancellor[534] placing himself entirely in his hands in case it should be found advisable, in order to avert a crisis, to entrust the Ministry for Foreign Affairs to some other Minister, but there is

[531] Marschall was officially dismissed on 19 October 1897. Enclosure: translation of Wolff's telegraphic correspondence, Kiel, 28 June 1897.

[532] For the Tausch trial see n. 514 in this section.

[533] Marschall was on leave of absence from 4 June 1897.

[534] 24 June 1897.

reason to believe that this letter was written after Baron von Marschall had learned from the Public Press that his position was threatened.

The want of consideration with which Baron von Marschall has been treated is also evidenced by the fact that Herr von Bülow will only take possession of his post after The Emperor's return to Berlin about the middle of August, at the very time when Baron von Marschall had intended to resume his duties.

Herr von Bülow's appointment is generally considered as a triumph of the Agrarian Party and to indicate the adoption of a reactionary policy, an opinion which has been strengthened by a visit[535] which Prince Hohenlohe and Herr von Bülow paid to Prince Bismarck on their return from Kiel.

FO 64/1411: Frank C. Lascelles to Marquess of Salisbury, No 259, Berlin, 27 September 1897

[Received 4 October by bag. For: Duke of Devonshire / Mr Balfour / Admiralty, 8 October; S[alisbury]]

Kölnische Zeitung *on naval bill*

With reference to my despatch No 253 of the 17th instant, I have the honour to report that the Cologne Gazette, in its issue of the 24th instant, publishes an article on the subject of the naval construction Bill which is to be presented to the Reichstag,[536] in which it condemns the agitation against the measure in which Herr Eugen Richter the leader of the Radical Party[537] has for some time been engaged.

The Article points out that even the more moderate sections of the German Press had previously been somewhat alarmed, because words spoken in the highest places had led to the belief that the Government desired to create a fleet equal to that of France, but that the appointment[538] of Admiral Tirpitz to be Secretary of State for the Navy had removed these apprehensions, as his moderation could be relied upon.

It goes on to say that according to information obtained from sources in touch with the Federal Council, the new bill will make

---

[535] On 28 June 1897.

[536] The naval bill, which authorized the maintenance of nineteen battleships and the building of seven vessels, was introduced in the *Reichstag* on 30 November 1897 and passed on 28 March 1898. It became law on 10 April 1898.

[537] *Deutsche Freisinnige Partei*.

[538] On 18 June 1897.

no excessive demands but will merely be designed to restore the fleet to its former level of efficiency. Experience has shown that the vessels of the "Siegfried" class although excellent ships in themselves are not suitable as a uniform type, which is a necessity for the German navy.[539] The type required is one which does not exceed 12,000 tons, as a larger size would not be convenient for the Kaiser Wilhelm Canal or the general conditions of the German Coast. Accordingly a uniform type for battleships of about the above tonnage is proposed. The programme extends to the year 1905[540] and on an average the annual expenditure will not greatly exceed that demanded this year. The estimate for ship- building in the first year of this programme will be about 2½ million sterling, in the following years somewhat more than 3 millions in each year. To this must be added a permanent increase of annual expenditure of about £500,000 for the necessary increase of the personnel.

FO 64/1412: Frank C. Lascelles to Marquess of Salisbury, No 301, Berlin, 13 November 1897

[Received 15 November by messenger. For: The Queen / Prince of Wales / Duke of Devonshire / Mr Balfour, A.J.B. [Arthur James Balfour]; S[alisbury]]

Last Reichstag *session before elections; fortunes of the major political parties since the last sitting in June*

I have the honour to inform Your Lordship that it is stated in the Reichs Anzeiger[541] that the Reichstag is summoned to meet on the 30th instant. It is generally believed that immediately on its reassembly the Government will communicate the proposals for the increase of the navy and the reform of the military judicial procedure.[542] The present Reichstag meets for the last time and preparations are being actively made for the elections which must take place next year.[543]

The recess[544] has been marked by an evident growth of "particularism", – anti-Prussian or anti-imperial sentiment – in various parts of Germany. The debates in the Bavarian parliament have been strongly tinged with anti-Prussian feeling; the national Liberals

---

[539] The eight Siegfried class vessels, built between 1888 and 1896, were coastal defence ships (displacement of 3,500 tons).

[540] The final law stipulated the fiscal year 1903.

[541] *Deutscher Reichsanzeiger und Königlich Preußischer Staatsanzeiger*, 11 November 1897. The imperial rescript was dated 10 November.

[542] For the imperial naval bill see n. 536 in this section; for the German Military Penal Code see n. 186 in Munich section.

[543] Elections were held on 16 June 1898.

[544] The last sitting of the *Reichstag* was on 25 June 1897.

have for the first time lost control of the legislature of Baden; and the agitation in Brunswick for the restoration of the legitimate dynasty has assumed considerable proportions.[545]

With regard to the movement of parties it would seem that the long continued struggle in connection with the military Jurisdiction bill had increased the forces of the left; but on the other hand a fierce dispute has broken out between the adherents and opponents of Herr Eugen Richter which must end by impairing the strength of the party and has already resulted in disaster at the polls.[546]

The Social Democrats hitherto a model of discipline, have also developed an internal question which is causing the party considerable difficulty. At a recent party meeting it was decided to take part in the Prussian [sic] elections but under the condition that the Socialist voter should only vote for Socialist candidates.[547] This resolution was strongly opposed on the ground that it would only tend to strengthen the forces of the Conservatives and will undoubtedly have this effect at the next Prussian elections which are also to take place next year.[548] The attitude of the centre which holds the balance of the Reichstag and which is a perfectly organized party is still doubtful. A demand has recently been made on the Chancellor by the leader of this party for the abrogation of the law still in force against the Jesuits.[549] This demand has been refused.

The chief losers during the present Reichstag have been the Conservative party. They have already lost ten seats since the last election[550] and recently they have lost a seat in a district[551] where they had hitherto undisputed control. This latter defeat appears to have been due, not to an increase of the liberal vote but to the revolt of the extremists of their own party who preferred to vote for a

---

[545] Lascelles is referring to the elections of the Baden *Landtag* on 28 October 1897. For the events in Bavaria see pp. 550–552; for the Brunswick succession question, which was kept in discussion by the Guelph *Braunschweigisch Landes-Rechts-Partei*, see n. 65 in this section.

[546] Lascelles is referring to the *Landtag* elections in Saxony of September and October 1897 when all candidates of the *Freisinnige Volkspartei* failed to win seats. The dispute was brought about by Richter's refusal to cooperate with the liberal *Demokratische Volkspartei* (Progressives) in order to avoid competing candidatures in the *Reichstag* elections of 1898.

[547] Lascelles is referring to the conference of the *Sozialdemokratische Partei* at Hamburg from 3 to 9 October 1897; the resolution concerning the candidacy for *Landtag* elections was passed on 6 October.

[548] The elections for the Prussian house of deputies were held on 3 November 1898.

[549] In a conversation with Hohenlohe on 28 October Ernst Lieber – in exchange for the *Zentrum*'s support of the navy bill – demanded that Article 2 of the Anti-Jesuit Law (of 4 July 1872) be rescinded. This made it possible to restrict freedom of residence for Jesuits and to banish foreign members of the Jesuit order from Germany.

[550] Elections took place on 15 June 1893.

[551] By-election in the electoral district of Westprignitz on 8 November 1897.

radical rather than to support their former leaders. The augury for the next election is not encouraging and it is the more unfortunate for the Government as in the last two years the Government has initiated legislation in the interests of this party which has left a deep feeling of animosity in industrial and financial circles, which cannot fail to bear fruit in the coming elections.

But while the general tendency of party movement is a trend to the left the recent reconstitution of the Government is considered to show that in the highest circles the trend is in the opposite direction.[552]

[552] Lascelles is referring to the replacements of Boetticher as vice chancellor and state secretary of the imperial office of the interior, Hollmann as state secretary of the naval office, and Marschall as state secretary for foreign affairs.

BADEN and HESSE

(DARMSTADT)

DARMSTADT

FO 30/258: William Nassau Jocelyn to Earl of Granville, No 24, Darmstadt, 26 March 1884

[Received 31 March by messenger. For: The Queen / Gladstone / Berlin; G[ranville]]

National Liberals meet at Frankfurt and Heidelberg to galvanize support ahead of elections

The prospect of the Elections for the German Diet[1] has determined the Leaders of the National Liberal Party in South Germany to endeavour to arouse their adherents from the condition of apathy into which they had lately fallen, and to define more accurately the characteristic attributes which should distinguish the Party as a whole, and as freed from those minor divisions which have so lamentably weakened it during the last few years.

In order to do this effectually, it was determined to make a stand against the recently formed Free thinking Party (freisinnige Partei) which had risen from the fusion of the Socialists [*sic*][2] with the Party of Progress, and threatened to entice into its ranks many of those whose principles were known to be in reality opposed to its extreme opinions.[3]

The meetings were therefore convened at Frankfort and at Heidelberg, in order to exchange opinions and to express the determination of the genuine National Liberals of South Germany to continue on the path of patriotism and loyalty in legislation for the Empire.

The more important meeting was held at Frankfort on the 23rd Instant, and was chiefly composed of Hessians from the three Provinces,[4] represented by One Hundred and twenty delegates.

After a debate of four hours, in which the speakers were unanimous in rejecting any compromise with the new Party, the following Resolutions were carried.

[1] Elections to the *Reichstag* were due to take place on 28 October 1884.

[2] Secessionists.

[3] On the *Deutsche Freisinnige Partei*, see n. 3 in Berlin section.

[4] Provinces of Oberhessen, Rheinhessen, and Starkenburg. The meeting in question was the *Landesversammlung* of the Hessian *Fortschittspartei* (Hessian Progressive party), the regional branch of the National Liberal Party.

The Hessian Party of Progress refuses to join the German free-thinking Party. It sees in the fusion forming this party, the strengthening of the German Party of Progress in an evil sense, – that of a systematic opposition to the Policy of the Imperial Chancellor,[5] and to the consolidation of the Empire contemplated by him by means of the promotion of Industrial and Agricultural Independence.

At the close of the meeting the Committee were entrusted with the formation of a Programme to be subsequently submitted to the Electors.

The second Meeting took place in Heidelberg on the same day, and was well attended by delegates from Bavaria, Wurtemberg, Baden, and the Bavarian Palatinate. The results of this gathering were essentially similar to those obtained in Frankfort and pointed more especially to the maintenance of the national liberal programme of May 29. 1881.[6]

These indications would seem to prove that the intentions now proclaimed by Prince Bismarck[7] of consulting more especially the agricultural interests of the nation are likely to receive efficient support from the National liberal party in both the Grand Duchies, and indeed throughout Southern Germany.

FO 30/258: William Nassau Jocelyn to Earl of Granville, No 80, Darmstadt, 31 October 1884

[Received 3 November by messenger. For: The Queen / Gladstone / Sir W. Harcourt / X, Ch.W.D. [Charles Wentworth Dilke]; G[ranville]]

Provisional Reichstag election results; increase in Social Democrat representation; remarks on electoral success of Social Democrats and their more moderate outlook

The Elections for the German Diet took place throughout the Grand Duchies of Hesse and Baden on the 28th Instant, but the definite Result of them is not yet known, owing to the delay in obtaining the Polling-Papers from the outlying Villages of the Districts; and, besides this, the last Elections (Stichwahle [*sic*])[8] which are still in abeyance, will not be taken before the 11th of November.

---

[5] Otto von Bismarck.

[6] The meeting resulted in the 'Heidelberg Declaration' which adhered to the programmatic Berlin declaration of 29 May 1881. The National Liberal Party had sought to reinvigorate itself through this declaration following the secession of the Liberal Union in 1880.

[7] Jocelyn is probably referring to Bismarck's *Reichstag* speech of 20 March 1884.

[8] Run-off vote.

The present aspect, however, of the result in Hesse and Baden is on the whole favorable to the National Liberals, but a very great increase in the Socialist Democratic element has become evident and this unexpected augmentation in the Rank of that Party through the Grand Duchy of Hesse, and especially near the Rhine is causing the present concern.

In the Electoral District of Darmstadt alone, whereas, on the last occasion about fourteen hundred Socialists went to the Poll, there are now upwards of 4000. It is calculated that in Bessungen, a suburb of Darmstadt, one half of the adult males belong to the Party and in the large manufacturing town of Offenbach the proportion can scarcel[y] be smaller, and here the Ultra Socialist member Liebknecht has been chosen by an overwhelming majority.

The sudden accession of members has been obtained in a very quiet and unobtrusive manner. All public meetings for the propagation of socialist doctrines are prohibited, the agitation has therefore been carried on through the house to house visitation of Agents and through their mixing with the workmen at the factories in the large towns – a certain number being told off by the leaders to engage themselves as skilled hands for this purpose.

The Political objects set forth by the Party have also been considerably modified, and the violent and subversive doctrines which prevailed some years ago have given way to more moderate counsels. Hence the Votes of many have been secured, who would have recoiled from the revolutionary and anarchical programme of the former propagandists.

Whatever may be the case, there is no doubt that a great accession of strength has accrued to the Party throughout Germany, whose Leaders having shewn their skill in obtaining adherents in the teeth of arch opponents, may, it is feared, extend their influence indefinitely.

FO 30/262 [*sic*]: William Nassau Jocelyn to Earl of Granville, Confidential, No 8, Darmstadt, 5 February 1885

[Received 9 February by messenger. For: The Queen; G[ranville]]

Prussian government conniving to purchase Hessian railway; political consequences

Your Lordship will doubtless recollect that a few years ago the Main-Weser Railway, which connects Frankfort-on-the Main with Cassel, was purchased by the Prussian Government at a very favorable rate, after considerable opposition on the part of the Hessian population, who viewed with apprehension the interference of their powerful neighbour in what they considered their internal concerns.[9]

Ever since that time it has been the ambition of the Prussian Minister of Public Works M. Maybach, to become if possible the possessor or at least the comptroller of the Hessische Ludwigs'bahn, a private Railway Company, whose lines run almost exclusively through Hessian territory, whose interests are likewise entirely concerned with the transit traffic from the Rhine to Switzerland, Italy, Bavaria, South Germany, and Austria, besides being the shortest route from England and Belgium to the above named countries.[10]

In order to effect this, and to compel the company to sell their property at a lower price than it would naturally fetch, M. Maybach has not scrupled to employ means, which would not be tolerated by any fairly trading firm – or company.

The first attack upon the Hessian Railway, was made some years ago,[11] when the Prussian Government, owning the line on the right Bank of the Rhine between Coblenz and Frankfort, asked the Rhenish Railway Company to let all goods addressed to Frankfort and beyond, from the Lower Rhine and the Moselle, pass the bridge at Coblenz thence to be forwarded over the Government line from Coblenz to Frankfort instead of by the direct route viâ Bingen, offering to carry them at the same rates as were charged by the other way, and to indemnify the Rhenish Railway Company for the loss they would sustain on freights between Coblence and Bingen, where the Hessian Railway begins. This was to be done by paying them the full charges from Coblence to Bingen, they themselves carrying the goods for nothing from Coblence to Rudesheim opposite Bingen, the sacrifice in question being intended solely to deprive the Hessian Railway of its share in the carriage of goods from Bingen to Frankfort, and by thus reducing its trade profits to force it ultimately to accept the Minister's conditions.

To the credit of the Rhenish Railway Company, however, it must be recorded that they indignantly refused to become a party to any such unfair arrangement, and for the time, therefore, the design of the Minister failed, until, the Rhenish Railway becoming itself a Prussian Government Road,[12] M. Maybach was at liberty to carry

[9] Hesse and Prussia, as the legal successors to Hesse-Nassau and the Free City of Frankfurt, were co-owners of the Main-Weser railway, and agreed on the acquisition of the remaining shares by Prussia on 20 November 1878. The transfer of ownership was effected on 1 April 1880.

[10] The privately owned Hessische-Ludwigs-Eisenbahngesellschaft was founded in 1845.

[11] In 1879.

[12] The Rheinische Eisenbahn-Gesellschaft (founded in 1836), was nationalised by the Prussian law of 14 February 1880.

out his project, whereby a loan of about £30,000 per annum is sustained by the Hessian Railway.

Subsequently similar negotiations were opened with the Bavarian Government, in order to induce them to send their goods to Frankfort and the Rhine from Gemünden over the Prussian State Railway viâ Elm, instead of, as at present, viâ Aschaffenburg and the Hessian line to Frankfort or Mayence – the Prussian Minister offering a similar compensation to the Bavarian Government for the loss incurred on their line between Gemünden and Aschaffenburg, as had previously been held out to the Rhenish Railway Company.

This proposal was met by a decided refusal on the part of Bavaria, who declined to inflict in favor of Prussia, a gratuitous injury upon the Hessian Railway, which had always fulfilled its engagements, besides being by many miles the shortest route for traffic.

Towards the close of last year the Prussian Railway administration notified to the Hessian Railway[13] the cessation after next April of the through traffic from Prussia over its line, thus compelling consigners of goods to send them by a longer route though at the same rate as formerly.

The animus of this proceeding was so obvious, that a notification was issued on December 31st by the Directors of the Hessian Railway requesting the Public to label their goods "to be sent viâ Bingen or Aschaffenburg" as the case might be. The Prussian Administration, however, lost no time in issuing a counter-notification,[14] in which they endeavoured to establish the monstrous proposition that consigners of goods have no right to determine the route by which they shall be sent, and that in the case of consignments from Prussia such a proceeding would be illegal.

Every attempt having hitherto failed to bring about an understanding between the Hessian Railway and the Prussian Government, with a view to induce the latter to reconsider its decision, it is feared that the Private Company will eventually succumb to the designs of its powerful and unscrupulous rival, who will then be enabled to step in and purchase this valuable property at a moderate price, and to the great detriment of the present Bondholders. Should the designs of the Prussian Government be successful it is estimated that a further annual loss of Two millions of Marks will be suffered by the Hessian Line, that is, nearly one quarter of its Revenue for the gross traffick.

The Dividend hitherto paid has been four per cent, the shares being chiefly in the hands of the peasants and small landed proprietors in the neighbourhood, and almost entirely in Hesse.

[13] On 30 September 1884.
[14] Notification of the Königliche Eisenbahndirektion zu Frankfurt, 4 January 1885.

In future a dividend of three per cent would scarcely be possible, and a heavy loss will fall upon the shareholders, while there is every fear that M. Maybach will then attain his object, and purchase the line at a very low rate.

The Political consequences of the sale and transfer of the line to Prussia will be disastrous to the independence of the Grand Duchy, for, with this purely Hessian road in her hands, Prussia will be enabled to use means, hitherto impossible, for undermining the loyalty of the Hessian people, and for rendering them less than ever averse to forming before long part of the Prussian Nation.

The officials and others employed on the line in the pay of Prussia will, moreover, exercise an undoubted influence upon the Elections, most decisively in her favor: and, considering the forces already at work in this direction, it is to be deplored, that the creation of one, more formidable than the rest should be imminent.

FO 30/261: William Nassau Jocelyn to Marquess of Salisbury, No 81, Darmstadt, 21 November 1885

[Received 23 November by messenger. For: The Queen / Eastern Department / Copy to Sofia; S[alisbury]]

Hessian sympathies towards Bulgaria; creation of Bulgarian Assistance Association at Darmstadt

Recent events in the Balkan Peninsula culminating in the War between Bulgaria and Servia, have called forth an amount of feeling, and sympathy among the population of this Grand Duchy which was hardly to be expected.[15]

The deeply rooted affection existing between the Grand Ducal family and the people of Hesse has been displayed in the intense interest taken with regard to all that concerns The Prince of Bulgaria[16] – his present critical position – and his uncertain future: and no stronger proof of this could have been given than the establishment of the Bulgarian Assistance Association[17] which has just been founded in this town under the auspices of many of the

[15] The Serbo-Bulgarian War, triggered by the proclamation of unification between Bulgaria and the Ottoman province of Eastern Rumelia on 18 September, took place from 14 to 28 November 1885. The Bulgarian victory over Serbia led to the recognition of the status quo; in April 1886, on the basis of the Tophane Agreement, Abdul Hamid II appointed the Prince of Bulgaria as Governor-General of Eastern Rumelia.

[16] Alexander I was the second son of Alexander of Hesse.

[17] Jocelyn is referring to the provisional *Hilfs-Comité* for the relief of wounded Bulgarian soldiers; the collecting point in the palace of Prince Alexander was established on 17 November 1885.

most influential members of the community and of all classes of society.

The committee holds its sittings daily at the Palace of Prince Alexander of Hesse: and the Association has already been very successful in obtaining assistance in money and in kind to be sent without delay to meet the requirements of the unhappy victims of the War.

Although it is generally feared that Bulgaria will eventually succumb to the unprovoked hostility of her superior and better equipped antagonist, it is equally felt that the bravery and moderation displayed by the Prince under trying circumstances have won for him a position in the subsequent settlement of affairs by the council of Europe, which His Highness might otherwise not have been entitled to claim.

FO 30/264: William Nassau Jocelyn to Marquess of Salisbury, No 4, Darmstadt, 13 January 1886[18]

[Received 18 January by messenger. For: Consular ? [*sic*] Department; 'I think this has been given due scrut[iny] and recommend that it sh[oul]d be done. Alston concurs in this recommendation', H.P.A. [Henry Percy Anderson], 21 January; Qy: Appoint Mr Goldbeck Consul accordingly, 8 February; S[alisbury]]

Proposal to raise vice consul Goldbeck at Frankfurt to rank of consul; benefits of such an arrangement

I trust Your Lordship will pardon my troubling You upon a subject, which, although but indirectly affecting the countries to which I am accredited, is one with which the efficiency of the recently established Consulate General at Frankfort on the Main is concerned.[19]

The business of that Consulate, under the active Superintendence of Mr Oppenheimer has acquired very considerable proportions, and besides the duties undertaken by the Consul General it occupies the entire time of the Vice Consul, Mr Goldbeck.

This is more especially the case during the travelling season, when Frankfort is full of English visitors, either passing through, or resorting to the City from the neighbouring watering places, but especially from Homburg, with requests on matters of business involving only too frequently applications to the local Authorities.

---

[18] This dispatch is not marked 'Consular' but is included in the consular section of the volume FO 30/264.

[19] The British consulate at Frankfurt was raised to the status of consulate general for Frankfurt, the Province of Hesse-Nassau, the Grand Duchy of Hesse, and the Grand Duchy of Baden in October 1882.

Moreover, on the occasions of the absence of the Consul General on leave, it is the duty of M[r] Vice Consul Goldbeck to take sole charge of the Consulate General, and in discharging the duties which the post requires, he is frequently brought into very close contact with the local Authorities.

It has been shewn by two well known cases which occurred last summer, that M[r] Goldbeck, as holding the rank and Authority of British Vice Consul only, is placed at some disadvantage in maintaining these interests, and the difficulties which were then experienced in bringing matters to a favorable termination, owing to M[r] Goldbecks inferior rank, were only partially surmounted by the energy and excellent judgment he displayed.[20]

It might be, therefore, a matter for consideration, whether, as such a step would involve no public expenditure whatever, it would be advisable that M[r] Goldbeck should hold the rank of Consul, a position, in which he would doubtless be more free to act in support of British interests, and, moreover, in discharging the delicate and often unpleasant duties which the peculiar nature of his instructions involves, he would be enabled to apply there to the persons with whom he has to deal, with greater authority than he can as a mere Vice Consul.

M[r] Goldbeck is a hardworking and energetic public servant, and would, I feel sure, be much gratified were it possible to give effect to the above suggestion.

I have also every reason to believe that the arrangement would be acceptable to M[r] Oppenheimer.

FO 30/264: William Nassau Jocelyn to Earl of Rosebery, No 43, Darmstadt, 17 July 1886

[Received 20 July by messenger. For: The Queen; R[osebery]]

Decision to appoint Dr Haffner as Bishop of Mainz has met with widespread satisfaction

The appointment of D[r] Paul Leopold Haffner as Bishop of Mayence has been received throughout the Diocese with real satisfaction. The Episcopal See had been so long vacant,[21] and the consequent difficulties attending ecclesiastical preferments had so increased, that it was

---

[20] In his capacity as acting consul throughout July and August 1885 Goldbeck had provided a statement for the German authorities about the marriage of the British consul general for Borneo, and took steps to secure the release of five British subjects who had been arrested in Frankfurt.

[21] Since Bishop Ketteler's death in 1877.

with a feeling of relief that the news was received of the Roman Curia having decided upon naming a Bishop sure to be approved of by the Grand Ducal Government. Dr Haffner, tho' a native of Wurtemberg, has for many years past formed part of the Cathedral Chapter, and has lately filled the post of dean. He is well known for his moderation and peaceable disposition, so that there is a prospect of a satisfactory solution of the Catholic Question in the Grand Duchy being attained.

The Consecration of the new Bishop is fixed to take place on the 25th instant in the Cathedral of Mayence, and is to be carried out upon a scale of unusual pomp and ecclesiastical splendour.

The Seminary for the Education of Priests at Mayence, which has remained closed by the Hessian Government ever since the promulgation of the May Laws against the Curia,[22] will, I am informed, be shortly reopened; but, in a conversation which I had with Monsieur Finger on this subject a few days ago, His Excellency declared that its scope was to be strictly limited to the theological training of persons about to enter Holy Orders, and not, as in former times to undertake the education of the Catholic Youth of the country, who will continue, by law, to attend the Government schools equally with their Protestant fellow subjects.

FO 30/264: William Nassau Jocelyn to Earl of Iddesleigh, No 58, Darmstadt, 10 September 1886

[Received 13 September by messenger. For: The Queen; I[Iddesleigh]]

Alexander of Bulgaria enthusiastically received in Darmstadt

The Prince of Bulgaria, accompanied by his brother Prince Francis Joseph of Battenberg, arrived at Darmstadt this afternoon from Sofia, having performed the journey without stopping.

Although but short notice had been given of His Highness' arrival, the authorities of the town and the inhabitants had prepared for him a most enthusiastic reception, and several thousand persons had arrived to bid him welcome.

His Highness was met by His Grand Ducal Highness Prince Alexander of Hesse, and Prince Louis of Battenberg; and his sister the Countess of Erbach-Schönberg.

---

[22] After the promulgation of the Hessian church laws of 23 April 1875, and especially the *Gesetz betreffend die Vorbildung und Anstellung der Geistlichen*, no new candidates were admitted to the seminary. It was not, however, formally closed. For the Prussian May Laws of 1873–1875, see n. 17 in Munich section and n. 131 in Berlin section.

I had also the honour of being present, and had been charged by The Queen to make special enquiries after His health, and that of Prince Francis Joseph, and at the same time to deliver to the Prince of Bulgaria a Bouquet from the Queen.

His Highness, though appearing much worn and fatigued by his long journey, and by all that he had lately undergone, was otherwise well in health, and evidently felt highly gratified at the warmth and enthusiasm with which he was greeted by the very large assembly at the station.

He proceeded, after half an hour, to Jugenheim by a special train. I have reported the above to Your Lordship by telegraph.

FO 30/264: William Nassau Jocelyn to Earl of Iddesleigh, Confidential, No 62, Darmstadt, 25 October 1886

[Received 1 November by messenger. For: The Queen / Prince of Wales / Lord Salisbury / Lord R. Churchill / Print (South East Europe); I[ddesleigh]]

Conversation with Prince of Bulgaria; his remarks on changeable attitudes of German press and developments in Bulgarian governance

During a conversation which I had this morning with Prince Alexander of Bulgaria, His Highness expressed much astonishment at the unfriendly attitude lately taken up by the semi official Press of Berlin towards Him and at the unfair tone of the North German Gazette,[23] in blaming Him for quitting Bulgaria, and in attributing to His conduct the present general feeling of insecurity, whereas, upon His return to Sofia some weeks ago; the German Consul[24] there had been incessant in urging Him to abdicate, and to quit the Country forthwith, as the only means of averting a Russian occupation.[25]

His Highness could only account for this abrupt change, on the supposition that, the conditions upon which Germany had at the time agreed to forego interference with the action of Russia – namely the cessation of the hostile attitude of the Russian Press – not having

[23] Alexander was referring to the *Norddeutsche Allgemeine Zeitung* of 27 September 1886, which alleged that Alexander had left Bulgaria in a cowardly fashion and out of self-interest.

[24] Conrad von Saldern.

[25] After the successful counter-revolution against the Russian controlled provisional government (which had assumed power on 21 August 1886) Alexander returned to Bulgaria on 28 August and to Sofia on 3 September. Ultimately, Alexander, the return of whom was disapproved of by Russia, left Bulgaria on 8 September 1886, one day after his abdication as prince (*knyaz*) of Bulgaria.

been fulfilled – Prince Bismarck had sought this way of displaying his irritation at Russia's want of good faith.

Prince Alexander assured me that if he were reelected by the Sobranje,[26] he would not return to Bulgaria, unless satisfied of the approval of the Powers,[27] and especially of that of the Porte.

His Highness was inclined to believe that some Republican form of Government was that best suited to the country, and to the character of the people – the constitution[28] moreover, being eminently favorable to such a development.

The present Government[29] were placed in a serious dilemma, for even if they yielded to Russian demands, they would probably be driven from power by their own troops.

He anticipated serious trouble should General Gourko be appointed Russian Commissioner, an eventuality which appeared not unlikely to occur.

His Highness appears to be in good health, and to have recovered from the fatigue and trials which he had undergone.

FO 30/266: William Nassau Jocelyn to Marquess of Salisbury, Confidential, No 5, Darmstadt, 22 January 1887

[Received 24 January by messenger. For: The Queen / Circulate; Copies confidential to: Paris / Berlin / Brussels, P.L. [printed letter], 26 January; S[alisbury]]

Concerns about a French attack on the Alsatian frontier

I was informed by an officer of high standing who had just returned from Strasbourg that considerable apprehension is felt in that neighbourhood, shared in even by The Governor Prince Hohenlohe, and the Commanding General[30] at the continued concentration of French troops near that frontier.

He said that the numbers now occupying the district are far in excess of what is required to garrison the frontier fortresses, and that not only are these overflowing with men, but a large camp is in course of formation, the object of which can only be to insure

---

[26] *Narodno sybranie*, the National Assembly of Bulgaria.

[27] Signatory powers (Britain, Austria-Hungary, France, Germany, Italy, Russia and the Ottoman Empire) of the Treaty of Berlin (1878) through which Bulgaria became an autonomous principality of the Ottoman Empire.

[28] Tarnovo Constitution of 1879.

[29] The incumbent government, under Minister President Vasil Radoslavov, had taken power on 28 August 1886.

[30] Wilhelm von Heuduck.

the success of a sudden coup de main[31] directed against that part of the German frontier.

Altho' this information does not directly refer either to Hesse or Baden, I venture to trouble Your Lordship with it, and I am also unable to report for its accuracy, but the apprehension of a French attack at no very distant period is doubtless felt in military circles here, and the possibility of a rush upon the Alsatian frontier simultaneously with a principle attack on the Rhine through Belgium gives rise to grave fears.

FO 30/266: William Nassau Jocelyn to Marquess of Salisbury, No 9, Darmstadt, 11 February 1887

[Received 14 February by messenger. Circulate; S[alisbury]]

Minor state of siege declared at Offenbach following exodus of socialists from Frankfurt; electoral prospects in Hesse

During a conversation which I had with Monsieur Finger yesterday, His Excellency informed me that the Hessian Government had on the previous day proclaimed the Minor State of Siege at Offenbach on the Main.[32]

This measure has become necessary owing to the number of Socialist Democrats recently expelled from Frankfort and its neighborhood in virtue of a similar proclamation made there some weeks ago.[33]

Many of these have taken refuge in Offenbach, and have received a cordial welcome from the Socialist Operations in that democratic centre.

The Elections for the Diet being now near at hand,[34] disturbances were not unlikely to occur, and it was considered expedient to place in the hands of the Authorities, the means of at any moment ridding the town of its obnoxious visitors.

His Excellency seems to be sanguine as to the results of the Elections and hoped to win two Seats for the Government.

Of the Nine Members contributed by Hesse to the last Diet, six had been National Liberals. One seat at Friedberg then held by a

---

[31] French: 'surprise military attack intended to take out opposing forces in one swift manoeuvre'.

[32] Section 28 of the Anti-Socialist Law of 1878 (see n. 10 in Dresden section) authorized federal governments, with prior approval of the Federal Council, to impose a minor state of siege (*Kleiner Belagerungszustand*) in towns and districts where activities of the Social Democrats jeopardised public safety. The measures restricted the freedom of assembly and dissemination of publications, allowed for the expulsion of persons suspected of endangering public security, and imposed a general ban on weapons.

[33] On 16 December 1886.

[34] The *Reichstag* elections took place on 21 February 1887.

Social Democrat, is now almost certain to be gained by Dr Miquel, the former Burgomaster of Frankfurt, and at Mayence, either a National Liberal or a Clerical Conservative will be returned in the place of the Social Democrat last elected.[35]

FO 30/266: William Nassau Jocelyn to Marquess of Salisbury, Confidential, No 26, Darmstadt, 9 April 1887

[Received 11 April by messenger. For: The Queen / Print (South East Europe); Embassies / Sofia – M.S.; S[alisbury]]

Prince Alexander's views of situation in Bulgaria; Stoilov's mission to European powers; Bulgarian affection for prince

The Newspapers both English and German have been very full of rumours lately as to the mission of Monsieur Stoiloff to Vienna, his projected visit to Darmstadt, and the possibility of Prince Alexander being invited by him to return to the throne of Bulgaria.[36] It may interest Your Lordship to learn something of His Highness' views in respect of the situation: I have obtained my information from an excellent source.

The Prince looks upon the present action of the Regents, and the journey of Monsieur Stoiloff, as due to the difficulties which these gentlemen experience in the Government of the Principality. They find themselves unable to control the military element in the country, and, knowing the devotion of the Army to the Prince, would endeavour to induce His Highness to return, not so much because they wish to reinstate him on personal grounds, as because they consider that his restitution would be the easiest means of solving the present difficulties of the situation. They cannot manage the horse themselves, so they would place a rider on his back whom he knows, in the hopes of a better result, not quite regardless of whether the horseman should experience another fall or not.

The Prince has however no inclination to risk his fate a second time: he will return to Bulgaria on one condition only, namely, that he does so as the mandatory of the Great Powers, or at any rate of a sufficient combination of them, and with a guarantee that

---

[35] The serving candidate at Friedberg was a *Freisinnig* Liberal, while the serving candidate at Mainz was a member of the Catholic *Zentrumspartei* (Centre). The only socialist elected in the previous elections of 1884 was Wilhelm Liebknecht at Offenbach. Miquel was simultaneously elected in three electoral districts.

[36] The Bulgarian minister of finance, Konstantin Stoilov, arrived at Vienna on 30 March 1887 on a special mission to the European powers. For Alexander's abdication in 1886, see n. 25 in this section.

his position, should he accept the mission, will be secured to him. His Highness is fully aware of the continued antipathy of Russia, and of the relentless personal animosity of the Czar against him. As an illustration of the latter I may mention that I am informed that the Emperor of Russia has himself headed a subscription list for the families of the officers recently executed at Sofia, and has provided their widows and children with pensions.

In the meantime Prince Alexander loses no opportunity of exhorting the Bulgarian Government to maintain a peaceful demeanour, and discourages all attempts to excite popular demonstrations in favour of his recall. On the occasion of his birthday,[37] a few days ago, the Prince received some one hundred and fifty telegrams from Bulgaria, not merely congratulating him on the anniversary but encouraging him to return to his people, and he receives daily letters and Newspapers couched in the same language. To all these His Highness has replied in the sense sketched above, He has even endeavoured to discourage Monsieur Stoiloff from seeking an audience of him here, and, should that Gentleman persist in coming to Darmstadt, it is very uncertain that the Prince will receive him.

FO 30/266: William Nassau Jocelyn to Marquess of Salisbury, No 60, Carlsruhe, 10 September 1887

[Received 19 September by messenger. For: The Queen; J. P. [Julian Pauncefote]]

Grand Duke of Baden's birthday; speech by Turban in which he admonishes hostile attitude of Catholic party

Yesterday being the Birthday of the Grand Duke of Baden, I was invited to take part in the official Banquet presided over by The Minister of State, Monsieur Turban in celebration of the Day.

His Royal Highness being at the Castle of Mainau on the Lake of Constance, the Congratulations of those present were despatched to Him by telegraph, and a gracious Reply was received before the guests had separated. The Health of His Royal Highness was proposed by Monsieur Turban in a Speech of which I have the honor to annex a short translation,[38] because under the present circumstances it assumes an interest, which in general it would not possess.

The attitude of the Ultramontane party has lately been becoming more openly hostile to the Government, and the influence of The

---

[37] Alexander's 30th birthday was on 5 April 1887.
[38] Enclosure: translation of speech by Ludwig Karl Friedrich Turban, undated.

Archbishop of Freiburg,[39] from whose apparently loyal and pacific disposition, the best results had been expected, has unfortunately not been exercised in the right direction.

The character of that Prelate is weak, and his disposition yielding: while some of the Members of the Chapter, influenced, no doubt, by instructions from the Vatican, are endeavouring again to create dissension, and to regain for the Catholic Clergy the ascendancy which was lost to them eight years ago.[40]

The Badische Beobachter – the organ of the Party, has lately displayed considerable acrimony and hostility in its articles, by stirring up the Catholic fraction in view of the coming elections to the Second Chamber;[41] venturing even to introduce the name of The Grand Duke, representing His Royal Highness as being at variance with His Government, and disposed in their favor.

It was, consequently, against these attacks that Monsieur Turban in unmistakable language protested, maintaining that The Grand Duke, instead of being led by His Government into paths of intolerance, has even striven to promote the welfare of the State, by upholding freedom of thought, and religious equality among His subjects.

Had the Minister failed to notice the present state of things, and the calumnies of which his Government has been the object on such an occasion, his silence might have been misinterpreted, and he therefore was at some pains to shew that on this question The Head of the State and His political advisers were entirely agreed.

FO 30/268: William Nassau Jocelyn to Marquess of Salisbury, Confidential, No 5, Darmstadt, 13 January 1888

[Received 16 January by messenger. For: The Queen / Prince of Wales / Print (South East Europe), by Wednesday / Constantinople / Sofia; S[alisbury], 18 January]]

Prince Alexander approached by Albanian chieftain; proposition to unite Albania and part of Macedonia in a new principality under Alexander's rule

During a Conversation which I recently had with Prince Alexander of Battenberg, His Highness took the opportunity of informing me that overtures of a very singular nature had recently been made to

---

[39] Johann Christian Roos.

[40] Jocelyn is referring to the reconciliation between the Baden government and the Catholic Church in 1879–1880 and the so called 'Peace Law' (*Friedensgesetz*) of 5 March 1880.

[41] The elections took place later in October 1887.

a former private Secretary[42] of His now at Sofia, by certain Albanian chieftains of high position.

These Persons had come to him, and had requested him to propose to His Highness to place Himself at the head of a movement for the Union of Albania with part of Macedonia – to form a Principality under His Rule, and subject to the Sultan as Suzerain.

They declared themselves able and willing should the Prince consent, to bring about a general movement throughout the Provinces in this direction, and expected that when the first part of the Programme has succeeded, the Bulgarian People would not be slow in following and annexing themselves to the New Principality.

His Highness appeared amused at this wild proposition, which, of course, he could not entertain for a moment, or do otherwise than entirely discourage, but He told it to me as a touching proof of the undiminished anxiety felt by the Bulgarians for His return under any circumstances, as He felt sure that Bulgarian influence was at the bottom of the whole scheme.

FO 30/268: William Nassau Jocelyn to Marquess of Salisbury, No 22, Darmstadt, 21 April 1888

[Received 23 April by messenger. Copy, inclosure in original, to Education Department, P.L. [printed letter], 25 April; T.V.L. [Thomas Villiers Lister]]

Regulation to preserve eyesight of Hessian school pupils

It has been generally observed that in some parts of Germany the eyesight of young persons belonging to the middle and better educated classes, is apt to become defective, so as to necessitate the use of glasses at an early age – a circumstance which has in a great measure been attributed to the manner in which school work is carried on.

In the Grand Duchy of Hesse, where premature failure of sight is of frequent occurrence, the Minister[43] who presides over the School System has endeavoured to do all in his power to mitigate this evil, and various rules have been framed with a view to the preservation of the eye sight of the Students.

A regulation has recently been promulgated, which has received the approval of the oculist faculty, and from which successful results are expected: I venture therefore to transmit a Copy of it to Your Lordship accompanied by a Translation.[44]

---

[42] Most probably Aleksandr F. Golovin.
[43] Jakob Finger.
[44] No enclosures included in FO 30/268.

FO 30/268: William Nassau Jocelyn to Marquess of Salisbury, Confidential, No 36, Darmstadt, 23 June 1888

[Received 25 June by messenger. Mr Charles Heneages' views are not of great moment. Qy: Approve; Consular Department for observations; 'Appointment quite unnecessary', T.V.L. [Thomas Villiers Lister]; H.P.A. [Henry Percy Anderson]]

Reasons why a resident consular officer at Baden-Baden is unnecessary

I have the honor to inform Your Lordship that some time ago Mr. Charles Heneage, brother to Mr. Edward Heneage M.P. wrote to me, urging the necessity of a Consular officer being appointed to reside at Baden-Baden, during the season, for the convenience of British residents and Visitors.

I pointed out to him, in reply, that a British Vice Consul[45] was already established at Mannheim – at a comparatively short distance, and that I myself made frequent visits to Karlsruhe – in the immediate neighbourhood, offering, as it appeared to me – sufficient opportunities for transacting any official business required by Visitors to Baden.

As Mr Heneage has now renewed his representations, I have thought it advisable to bring the matter to the knowledge of Your Lordship in case of any question being asked with regard to it in Parliament.

Any person leaving Baden at 11.30 can reach Mannheim at 1.40 and return in the course of the evening, whereas, by leaving Baden at 9.30 he would be at Mannheim at 12.45 viâ Heidelberg; and, returning viâ Schwetzingen at 2.30, would reach Baden at 4.30.

With these facilities, I venture to submit to Your Lordship whether a resident Consular Officer at Baden would be required.

On the occasion of my own visits to Karlsruhe, where I generally spend two clear days, I have frequently had occasion to transact business for persons coming from Baden and even from Freiburg.

FO 30/270: William Nassau Jocelyn to Marquess of Salisbury, Confidential, No 41, Carlsruhe, 3 July 1889

[Received 8 July by messenger. For: The Queen; Circulate; Qy: Copies to: Berlin / Berne; Print (Western Europe); S[alisbury]]

Turban's views on the Bismarck's punitive policy towards Switzerland; effects on Baden

During a conversation which I had with Monsieur Turban yesterday, His Excellency appeared much depressed at the serious character of

---

[45] Ferdinand Ladenburg.

relations now existing between Germany and Switzerland, and more especially so, as in case of puntive [*sic*] measures being resorted to by the Imperial Council, the duty of carrying them out would principally fall upon the Government of the Grand Duke...[46]

I could plainly perceive that his Excellency was very far from satisfied with the course adopted by the German Chancellor in this affair, regarding it rather as the consequence of an unfortunate outburst of temper, than as a stroke of statesmanlike policy.

His Excellency stated that the number of Subjects of Baden alone at present living and domiciled in Switzerland, exceeded Forty Thousand, and that upwards of One Hundred Thousand Germans would be ruinously affected in case of retaliatory measures being adopted against Switzerland.

At the same time he said that not Eight Thousand Swiss citizens were domiciled in Germany, so that the injury inflicted upon the latter would be enormously greater than any corresponding disadvantage sought to be applied to the country which it was intended to punish.

He portrayed very strongly the serious consequences which would be brought upon general traffic and railway communication by such a catastrophe, and the sudden cessation of the intercourse between the Grand Duchy and Switzerland at Basle and Constanz alone, where it is of the most intimate character; besides which, it must not be forgotten that many miles of the Baden State railway run through Swiss territory...

He told me that he had, with the consent of The Grand Duke, represented these facts very strongly to the Federal Council,[47] and, though declaring himself and his Government prepared to execute any orders given them, which might be considered necessary for the safety of the Empire, on the maintenance of its Dignity abroad, he deprecated in the strongest manner any step being rashly taken to bring about a state of things so obviously disadvantageous to the Country itself, and so likely to perpetuate a feeling of intense irritation and hatred towards Germany on the part of a nation so independent and sensitive as that of Switzerland.

His Excellency promised on my taking leave of Him to inform me of the nature of the reply which he might receive to his representation from Berlin.

---

[46] Bismarck's campaign against Switzerland concerned German and European socialists and radicals residing in that country, and the arrest of a German police inspector (who had been investigating the smuggling of socialist newspapers into Germany) by Swiss authorities in April 1889. At the time of the dispatch – in addition to tighter border controls and rigorous customs inspections – closing the frontier to the canton of Aargau and the abrogation of the Swiss German treaty on settlement rights of 1876 were being deliberated.

[47] Turban was referring to the instructions of 11 and 19 June 1889 he gave to the Baden plenipotentiary to the Federal Council, Adolf Freiherr Marschall von Bieberstein.

FO 30/270: William Nassau Jocelyn to Marquess of Salisbury, No 69, Carlsruhe, 21 November 1889

[Received 25 November by messenger. For: The Queen; S[alisbury]]

Opening of Baden chamber; only small gains of Ultramontane party; importance of principle of indirect elections

The Session of the Baden Legislature was opened today by Monsieur Turban, the Minister President, acting as Commissioner for His Royal Highness The Grand Duke, and I have the honor to enclose herewith a Copy and Translation of the Speech which His Excellency delivered on the occasion.[48]

In a conversation which I had with him yesterday, Monsieur Turban said he was not dissatisfied with the result of the recent elections.[49] They had, it was true, given five Seats to the Ultramontanes, but, considering the exertion the party had made in order to overthrow the National Liberal Majority, the gain was comparatively small.

In a former despatch I had reported to Your Lordship the apparent preponderance of the Ultramontane Electors chosen by the people.

It appears, however, that, during the interval which elapsed between their own Election, and that of the Members, the views of many were considerably modified, with the result that these had voted for National Liberals even in such constituencies as that of Freiburg, hitherto, a stronghold of the Papacy.

This His Excellency said, shewed the importance of maintaining the principle of indirect Elections, – the crude opinions of the ignorant uneducated Masses being modified by the more mature judgment of the Electors themselves.

FO 30/270: William Nassau Jocelyn to Marquess of Salisbury, No 56, Carlsruhe, 10 September 1889

[Received 17 September by post. For: The Queen; Berne, 30 September; S[alisbury]]

Grand Duke of Baden's Sedan Day speech to military association at Überlingen; unusually forthright on dangers within German society

On the 3rd Instant The Grand Duke of Baden, who is at present residing at the Mainau [palace] on the Lake of Constance, went to Überlingen, the principal town of the district, to be present at a

---

[48] Enclosures: original (clipping) from *Karlsruher Zeitung* and translation, both undated.

[49] Elections of the Baden *Landtag* took place on 9 (electoral delegates) and 23 October 1890.

meeting of the Military Association (Kriegerverein),[50] organized for the purpose of celebrating the anniversary of the Victory of Sedan.[51]

This Society had formed part of the great assembly of Veterans which, on the occasion of the Visit of the German Emperor to Karlsruhe some weeks before,[52] had welcomed His Imperial Majesty to the Capital, as I reported in my despatch N° 54 of the 22nd ultimo.

The Grand Duke was received with great enthusiasm – an Address being presented by General von Deimling who presided at the Festival.

His Royal Highness replied in a Speech, of which I have the honor to enclose a translation,[53] containing expressions of much significance, with reference to the internal dangers which appeared to Him to threaten the Peace and well being of Society.

To anyone who knows the somewhat reticent style of His Royal Highness when speaking in public, the words He used on this occasion will carry the conviction that He felt most strongly on the subject, and was determined that his hearers should not remain unwarned of the hidden dangers which He considered to exist in their midst.

On the occasion of the Grand Duke`s birthday on the ninth instant, I was present at the annual Ministerial dinner given in His honor, and in the course of conversation Monsieur Turban expressed to me how entirely he approved of the words spoken by His Royal Highness.

Moreover, it may be presumed, that the Speech delivered, as it was, close to the Swiss frontier, will have produced an impression not only upon the immediate hearers, but also have had a beneficial effect in the neighbouring country.

FO 30/272: William Nassau Jocelyn to Marquess of Salisbury, No 11, Darmstadt, 12 February 1890

[Received 17 February by messenger. Chancellor of the Exchequer; Commercial Department to see; S[alisbury]]

Financial relations between imperial and federal exchequers

At the sitting of the Upper Chamber of the Baden Legislature on the 8th Instant, during a Debate upon the Report of the Financial Committee, some unexpected light was thrown upon the financial

[50] The meeting of the *Seegau Kriegerbund* took place on 1 September, not on 3 September as stated in the dispatch.

[51] For Sedan Day (2 September), see n. 50 in Dresden section.

[52] On 19 August 1889.

[53] Enclosure: translation of speech by the Grand Duke of Baden in which he referred to an 'internal Foe, – a concealed enemy, going about closely veiled, and who must be overcome'.

relations of the Minor German States to the Empire by The Minister of Finance Monsieur Ellstätter.

His Excellency explained that the financial condition of each separate State depended upon that of The Imperial Exchequer,[54] and not vice versa, as was very generally believed.[55]

For, said he, with the increase or decrease of the contribution of each State to the Imperial Treasury the financial condition of such State is materially altered.

This somewhat unpleasant condition of affairs would continue until the Separate State had sufficiently consolidated its finances to render it independant [sic] of its Imperial contribution.

The Government were exerting themselves to bring about this most desirable result, which could only be done by a constant Augmentation of the Sinking Fund which now amounted to Twelve Millions of Marks, – Six Hundred Thousand Pound[s].

The Speaker, in conclusion, declared himself decidedly opposed to further construction of State Railways, and the Government would decline to entertain any Proposal which might be laid before them by those interested.

The Chamber then adjourned until after the Elections for the Imperial Diet.

FO 30/272: William Nassau Jocelyn to Marquess of Salisbury, No 14, Carlsruhe, 8 March 1890

[Received 17 March by messenger. For: The Queen / ~~Circulate~~ / Qy: Home Office for perusal; S[alisbury]]

Reichstag election results in Hesse and Baden; Ultramontane gains

The Elections for the Imperial Diet in Hesse and in Baden took place on the 20th of February, but so many second Ballots became necessary, that the final Result remained unknown until their termination on the 28th.

In the Nine Electoral Districts of the Grand Duchy of Hesse there were elected Two Socialist Democrats, Three Radical Progressists, One antisemite, and the remainder National Liberals.[56]

---

[54] Helmuth von Maltzahn.

[55] According to Article 70 of the imperial constitution of 1871, the federal states paid per capita contributions to the empire (*Matrikularbeiträge*) in order to balance the deficit of the imperial budget. The federal states, for their part, received indirect taxes and tariff revenues that exceeded 130 million *Reichsmark* ('Franckenstein Clause' of 1879).

[56] The final results for Hesse were: two anti-Semites, two Socialists, two Progressives and three National Liberals.

Three years ago the District of Mainz returned an Ultramontane,[57] who has now been replaced by a Socialist[58] – a remarkable result, considering the purely clerical nature of the Electorate, and the fact that no other opponent save an Ultramontane[59] was in the field.

The other Socialist[60] was elected in the district of Offenbach, a large manufacturing centre, the representation of which remains unchanged,

The fourteen Elections in the Grand Duchy of Baden have been less favorable to the Imperial Government.

Altho' only one Socialist[61] was elected in Mannheim, no fewer than nine Ultramontanes will represent their respective districts. Two conservatives were chosen at Heidelberg and Bretten, and not a single national liberal member has been returned from the Grand Duchy.[62]

This unexpected result is no doubt to be traced to the energy with which the Clerical Party have been organising their forces since the rejection by the National Liberals of the measure in the Chamber in favor of the employment of brothers of the monastic orders as assistants to the permanent clergy in the cure of souls.

This proposal, which was supported by the Government, and considered by them of importance as supplying a want severely felt throughout the country, was violently opposed by the majority in the Chamber, and, in spite of all explanations on the part of Ministers, finally rejected.[63]

Hereupon the clerical element, urged on by the Archbishop[64] and Chapter of Freiburg – and doubtless with the Sanction of the Vatican, organised a regular crusade against the National Liberals, and persuaded the Ultra Socialist party to join with them against the common enemy…

Monsieur Turban, whom I saw this morning though foreseeing an unfavorable result, was evidently much depressed at the signal victory gained by the clericals, and attributed entirely to the cause I have above stated, a defeat, which might have been averted had greater moderation prevailed in the ranks of the Liberal party on a question, which the Government well knew to be a vital one to the Catholics of

---

[57] Nicola Racke.

[58] Franz Jöst.

[59] Philipp Wasserburg.

[60] Carl Ulrich.

[61] August Dreesbach.

[62] The final results for Baden were: eight members of the Catholic *Zentrum*spartei, three Conservatives; one left liberal; one Progressive; and one Socialist.

[63] The proposal was part of the government bill to revise the Baden church laws (Article 4); it was rejected by the *Landtag* on 17 April 1888.

[64] Christian Roos.

the Grand Duchy, and should have been left to their better judgment to decide.

FO 30/272: William Nassau Jocelyn to Marquess of Salisbury, No 64, Darmstadt, 8 November 1890

[Received 10 March by messenger. For: The Queen / S[alisbury]]

Jews petition Grand Duke for protection against anti-Semitic treatment

The Public feeling against the Jews which has assumed such formidable proportions in some parts of Germany, has not failed to shew itself in the Grand Duchy of Hesse, and more especially so in the Province of Upper Hesse and the towns of Giessen and Mayence where on the occasion of the last Election for the Diet an Antisemitic member was returned for each constituency.[65]

In Upper Hesse the Cattle trade is almost entirely in Jewish hands, and no doubt the hostility against them which has now assumed a very aggravated form, was to some extent owing to the usurious terms exacted and the hard bargains driven by the Jews with the farmer in selling cattle – much exclusive dealing being employed on both sides, and the Jews, being in the minority, suffering severely from the continued and increasing bitterness of their opponents.

Matters at length reached such a stage, that an application was made to the Grand Duke by a Deputation from the three Provinces[66] of the Grand Duchy and headed by the Chief Rabbi[67] of Mayence, recounting in glowing, and, as I am informed not altogether justifiable terms, their wrongs, and imploring His Royal Highness to extend His protection to the exercise of their lawful rights and occupations.

The Deputation was received by The Grand Duke, and the written petition of its Members taken into consideration.

The Minister of Justice, Monsieur Finger received orders, on the first Instant to address to them the Reply of which I have the honor to enclose herewith a Copy and a translation.[68]

This Answer, while expressing His Royal Highness['] horror and detestation of the treatment received by one portion of His Subjects at the hands of another, and the Royal injunction that

[65] Wilhelm Pickenbach and Oswald Zimmermann.

[66] See n. 4 in this section.

[67] Siegmund Salfeld; on 29 October 1890.

[68] Enclosures: original newspaper clipping, Finger to Salfeld (undated), and translation, 1 November 1890.

such proceedings should speedily cease, does not fail, as will be observed, to admonish the petitioners to be more careful in future not to give cause for complaint to those who are so ready to use it as justifying a fresh attack and persecution.

The Document has been criticized by the Press much in accordance with the Principles upheld by each journal, but the qualification attached to the Grand Ducal censure of the Antisemitic party throwing some of the blame upon their opponents, has, tho' in general approved, not been very palatable to the Jewish part of the community.

Monsieur Finger informed me that the Petition, as presented to the Grand Duke, has been withheld from publication owing to its somewhat exaggerated statements and intemperate language.

FO 30/274: William Nassau Jocelyn to Marquess of Salisbury, No 31, Carlsruhe, 2 August 1891

[Received 5 August by post. For: The Queen / Prince of Wales; S[alisbury]]

Death of Baroness Bos du Thil

A Person of considerable interest connected with the Court of the Grand Duke of Hesse – and almost the last remaining link with the period of Napoleon's rule in Germany, passed away a few days ago – the Baroness Bos du Thil, who for many years held the Post of Obersthofmeisterin or Mistress of the Robes to Her late Royal Highness The Grand Duchess,[69] and, previously, to The Grand Duchess Mathilda.

She was the widow of The Baron Bos du Thil, who, as Minister of State to The late Grand Duke for upwards of a quarter of a century, filled that high office during a time of exceptional agitation in Germany, ending with the Revolution of 1848, after which His Excellency, in company with many other German Ministers, was compelled to resign His Post.

During the earlier part of his career, the very existence of Hesse as a State was owing to his exertions, – for, after the Battle of Leipsic,[70] when Hesse was fighting on the side of Napoleon, Du Thil, with consummate ability, succeeded in convincing the Allied Sovereigns that the apparent friendship of the Grand Duchy for the French Emperor had been forced upon her at the swords

[69] Alice.
[70] Battle of the Nations, 16–19 October 1813.

point, and that the loyalty of The Grand Duke to the German cause was in truth unquestionable.

The funeral of the Baroness, who died at the age of 82, on the 28th Ultimo, took place two days ago, and was attended by The Grand Duke and the members of the Grand Ducal family, who took part in the procession to the grave, and remained to the end of the Service.

FO 30/274: William Nassau Jocelyn to Marquess of Salisbury, No 38, Carlsruhe, 10 September 1891

[Received 14 September by messenger. For: The Queen; S[alisbury]]

Grand Duke of Baden's 65th birthday; speech by Turban discreetly urges political loyalty to royal figurehead

Yesterday being the sixty fifth anniversary of the Birthday of The Grand Duke of Baden, I was, as usual, invited to to [*sic*] take part in the festivities and dinner given by the Ministers in honor of His Royal Highness.

Owing to the absence of almost the entire garrison of the town at the military maneuvres, the attendance was comparatively small, and my Russian Colleague[71] and myself were the only representatives of the Diplomatic Body at the dinner.

Monsieur Turban, whose health has recently become much impaired by overwork, proposed the Health of His Royal Highness in a speech containing no direct allusion to the actual unsettled condition of public feeling, in the Grand Duchy; but dwelling with considerable meaning upon the essentially patriotic and wise character of the Sovereign, and thus tacitly urging, which he did not express in words, the duty of every loyal subject to rally round the Leader in the present emergency.[72]

This was perfectly well understood by the majority of the guests, who received the toast with the greatest enthusiasm.

In view of the present political agitation prevailing in the country, the Ministers have thought it desirable to present an address of congratulation to The Grand Duke, containing a short summary of His Royal Highness' and their own conduct of affairs during the last few years.

---

[71] Vladimir Alexandrovich Fredericks.

[72] In his address, which was sanctioned by the Grand Duke, Turban hinted at the struggles of the Baden government with the Democratic and Catholic parties in the run-up to the elections of the Baden chambers. Contested fields of policy included constitutional and electoral reforms and further revisions of church laws, especially the admission of religious congregations and male religious orders.

I have the honor to inclose a Translation of this address, and also of the Reply which it elicited from His Royal Highness, in which He expresses a wish that it might be published, and that both His own, and His Governments['] views on subjects now being discussed, might be widely known.[73] As might have been expected, the Ultra Radical party with the "Frankfurter Zeitung" at their head, do not hesitate to criticize this somewhat unusual step of the Ministry, declaring it to be not only an Electioneering desire, but an unmanly attempt to make The Grand Duke responsible for what they themselves had failed in, and to compel Him to side with the Government Party on questions, with regard to which He should remain altogether unbiased.

FO 30/277: William Nassau Jocelyn to Marquess of Salisbury, No 8, Carlsruhe, 31 January 1892

[Received 2 February by post. For: The Queen / Prince of Wales; S[alisbury]]

Debate in chamber respecting appointment of Eisenlohr to new ministerial department; opposition on grounds of misuse of public money

As I had the honor to inform Your Lordship at the time, the Elections for the Second Chamber of the Grand Duchy of Baden resulted in a majority of one vote for the National Liberal Party; and the opposition, consisting of the clerical and Socialistic fractions, had determined to lose no opportunity of placing the Government in a minority.[74]

Owing to declining health, and pressure of work, the Prime Minister, Monsieur Turban had in the month of August withdrawn himself from the presidency of the Ministry of the Interior, and of several minor Departments, and had with the Consent of the Grand Duke created a new Department[75] over which Monsieur Eisenlohr had been called upon to preside.

The step was one which could only be of benefit to the country, and at the same time by relieving the Prime Minister of one of the most onerous of his functions enable him to devote increased energy to those which he still retained.

The Salary attached to the New Ministers' post was to be paid out of the very considerable Surplus in the hands of the Exchequer[76] so

---

[73] Enclosures: translations of Turban's address (8 September) and Friedrich I's reply (9 September1891).

[74] Elections took place on 24 September (electoral delegates) and 2 October 1891.

[75] An independent ministry of the interior.

[76] Moritz Ellstätter (minister of finance).

as to be – for the present at any rate – independent of the Legislative Vote.

The change was, however, made during the recess, and previous to the Elections and of course without consulting the Chamber.

While the Elections were going on, the matter was much discussed, and was used by the Opposition party as a powerful Lever against the alleged misappropriation of the Public Money, – independently of the Representative Body. [*sic*] and, as might have been expected several Votes were lost to the Government in consequence.

A few days ago, when the Chamber reassembled after the Christmas Vacation an attack was at once directed against the Ministry on this ground and after a very hot discussion the motion, which was virtually one of want of confidence, was finally rejected by only six votes, twenty eight voting against, and thirty two in favour of the appointment of the new Minister.[77]

During the debate which was on the attacking side, of an exceptional violent character, grave accusations were brought against the Government for tampering with the freedom of Election, which, however, were triumphantly disproved by Monsieur Turban and his colleagues.

The Government appear to be fully aware of the formidable nature of the forces arrayed against them, and, on the Question of the Education of Priests at Catholic Seminars, and the admission of the Monastic Orders into the Grand Duchy which will, before long, come on for discussion, it will require all their skill and tact to avert a defeat which might drive them from Office, and place the Ultramontane party in power.[78]

FO 30/277: William Nassau Jocelyn to Marquess of Salisbury, No 43, Darmstadt, 26 July 1892

[Received 30 July by post. For: The Queen / Prince of Wales; S[alisbury]]

Six thousand people from Hesse and Baden attend demonstration at Kissingen in support of Bismarck

An imposing demonstration took place on the morning of the 24th Instant, when more than six thousand persons from the Grand

---

[77] The Landtag reconvened on 18 January 1892; the debate (including the vote on the motion of the *Zentrum* faction) took place on 26 January.

[78] The education of priests was regulated by the laws of 5 March 1880 and 5 July 1888 which, amongst other things, stipulated attendance at a university. New religious orders were, as regulated by the Church Law of 9 October 1860, subject to approval of the Baden government.

Duchies of Hesse and Baden and from the Bavarian Palatinate set out for Kissingen in order to express the assurance of their regard to Prince Bismarck before His Highness' departure from that town.

Special trains were organised and started from Mannheim, Heidelberg, Darmstadt, and Frankfort, at an early hour, arriving before noon at Kissingen, and returning the same evening.

The Deputation[s], including many Ladies, were very cordially received by the Prince, who was quite overcome by the magnitude of the assembly, and responded to the several speeches, which were delivered by the Representatives of the different countries, expressing his thanks and passing in review the principal events which had marked his administration – alluding also to the recent circumstances connected with his visit to Vienna,[79] which had led to the expression of feeling so forcibly manifested by those whom he was addressing.

Your Lordship will probably have received a report of His Highnesses speech on this occasion from Her Majesty's Legation at Munich, but some expressions contained in the address of M. Eckhard, the veteran leader of the National Liberal party in Baden are deserving of special notice.

After referring to the work which Prince Bismarck had achieved in the unification of Germany in 1870, the Speaker said:

"I say, therefore, that what happened in the year 1890[80] and much of what occurred later was quite unintelligible to our South German feelings and understandings, and what is more it remains to this day unintelligible to us. For we feel that it is the Duty and the honorable Duty of a Nation to be proud of its greatest Statesman, and we also know that it is a Shame for a Nation to depreciate and seek to weaken the work of her great men. Against this Kind of National Education and teaching we do here this day protest most loudly and energetically, and I trust that we shall not be alone in doing so."

These words were received by the thousands present with thunders of applause sufficiently indicating the sentiments which animated the whole assembly.

---

[79] Bismarck visited Vienna on the occasion of his son's wedding from 18 to 22 June 1892. His audience with the Austrian emperor was impeded by the intervention of Leo von Caprivi and Wilhelm II.

[80] Eckhard was referring to Bismarck's resignation from office on 18 March 1890.

FO 30/277: Horace Augustus Helyar to Earl of Rosebery, [unnumbered], Darmstadt, 14 November 1892

[Received 16 November by post. For: The Queen; R[osebery]]

Sadness of Grand Duke at Jocelyn's death

I had the honor of being received in audience this morning by His Royal Highness The Grand Duke of Hesse Darmstadt.

His Highness, who was very gracious, expressed his deep regret and sorrow at the lamented death of the late Mr Jocelyn, for so many years Her Majesty's Representative at this Court.[81]

His Royal Highness said that the death of Mr Jocelyn had come as an unexpected blow on all who knew and liked him, and that is was difficult for those to realise that he was taken away who had seen him in full health and strength only the day before.

I begged respectfully to thank His Royal Highness for the magnificent wreath which he had sent in token of regard to the late Minister.

His Royal Highness concluded by reiterating his feeling of the loss which Darmstadt had sustained and of the universal popularity of Mr Jocelyn.

Lord Powerscourt[82] likewise had the honour of being received in audience, and His Royal Highness expressed to him His sincere sympathy with the family in their grief.

FO 30/278: George W. Buchanan to Earl of Rosebery, No 46, Baden Baden, 7 June 1893

[Received 9 June by post. For: The Queen; R[osebery]]

Grand Duke of Baden's speech at Offenburg; endorses army bills

At a Meeting of a Society of Old Soldiers held a few days ago at Offenburg the Grand Duke of Baden took occasion to deliver a Speech on the Army Bills, copy and translation of which I have the honour to enclose,[83] which has attracted considerable attention in the Press.

---

[81] Jocelyn died on 11 November 1892.

[82] Mervyn Wingfield, 7th Viscount Powerscourt, represented the family at Jocelyn's funeral on 14 November.

[83] Friedrich I attended the meeting of the *Badischer Militärvereinsverband* on 4 June. Enclosures: original (clipping) from *Karlsruher Zeitung* of 6 June 1893 and translation.

After referring to the misconstructions which had been placed on his Speech at Heidelberg, reported in my despatch No 40 of the 16th ultimo, His Royal Highness proceeded to say that, in order to avoid any similar misconceptions of his meaning, he had preferred to commit his Speech to writing.[84]

Everyone, He said, ought to ask himself what was the real issue of the pending Elections[85] and ought only to vote for those Candidates who placed the honour and safety of the Empire above the interests of party and who recognised in the Army Bills a safeguard against a possible humiliation of their country.

The step which the Grand Duke has thus taken in making a direct appeal to the Baden Electorate in favour of the Army Bills has been severely criticised by the Opposition Press, and, although the National Liberal and official organs are loud in their praises of His Royal Highness['] Speech, some Members of the Government, as I have reason to believe, do not entirely approve His Royal Highness' action in entering thus personally into the Electoral contest.

FO 30/280: George W. Buchanan to Earl of Kimberley, No 26, Darmstadt, 21 May 1894

[Received 22 May by post. X; K[imberley]]

Constitutional revision in Baden; lower chamber in favour of electoral reform and direct elections; upper chamber and government favour indirect elections; ongoing discussions

The question of the Revision of the Constitution[86] of the Grand Duchy of Baden, in the sense of the substitution of a Direct for the present Indirect Electoral System, has for some time past engaged the attention of the Second Chamber of the Landtag.

As far back as the years 1871 and 1876 motions in favour of Direct Elections were introduced, though without success, in the Chamber. In the year 1883 a Resolution to the same effect was, in spite of the strenuous opposition of the National Liberals and of the Government, actually carried by a majority of one; but it remained inoperative in consequence of the opposition of the Upper Chamber.

A similar resolution, coupled, however, with a proposal for the total revision of the Constitution and for an increase of the powers

---

[84] In press reports on the speech of 14 May, the Grand Duke reportedly said that it was not the number but the quality of soldiers upon which Germany must rely. For the army bill (Imperial Military Law), see nn. 312 and 322 in Berlin section.

[85] Elections to the *Reichstag* took place on 15 June 1893.

[86] Constitution of 22 August 1818.

of the Upper Chamber, was again carried during the Session of the late Landtag,[87] but no effect was given to it by the Government.

The Revision Committee of the Lower Chamber has now,[88] by a unanimous vote, expressed itself in favour of the adoption of Direct Elections based on a system of Proportional Representation. Though all parties have thus joined in recommending this reform of the Electoral System, it is more than doubtful whether any immediate result will follow from the decision of the Committee. The Government have, indeed, expressed themselves as not absolutely and unconditionally attached to the existing system of Indirect Elections, and have thus departed from their former irreconcileable [*sic*] attitude towards this question. They do not, however, according to the Ministerial statement,[89] consider that the guarantees offered by the Proportional Representation are sufficient in themselves to guard against the dangers apprehended from the proposed change in the Constitution. It remains to be seen, therefore, whether, in the event of their embodying the suggestions of the Committee in a Bill, the further safeguards which they may propose, will be such as to recommend themselves to the acceptance of the majority of the Chamber.

FO 30/281: George W. Buchanan to Earl of Kimberley, No 33, Darmstadt, 29 June 1894

[Received 2 July by post. X; K[imberley]]

Debates at closing session of Baden Landtag on admission of religious orders, progressive income tax and revision of constitution

The Session of the Baden Landtag was closed yesterday by the Grand Duke in person, the Speech from the Throne, copy and translation of which I have the honour to enclose, being read by His Royal Highness.[90]

Apart from the many important measures discussed during its course, the Session attracted unusual interest from the fact that at the Elections,[91] which preceded it, the National Liberal Party lost the absolute majority which they had for more than twenty years

---

[87] On 14 May 1892.

[88] The committee which discussed the two diverging motions of 24 November (Democrats) and 15 December 1893 (*Zentrum* faction) presented its report to the second chamber on 6 June; it was passed on 22 June 1894.

[89] Declaration by minister Eisenlohr before the committee on 17 May 1894.

[90] Enclosures: *Rede seiner Königlichen Hoheit des Goßherzogs bei dem Schluß der Ständeversammlung am 28 Juni 1894* (printed copy and translation).

[91] The elections took place on 20 (electoral delegates) and 27 October 1893.

possessed in the Lower Chamber. They still formed indeed the largest and more important party in the House, numbering thirty out of a total of sixty three members, and could, when the two Conservative members voted with them, defeat any combination of the Centre,[92] Radicals and Social Democrats. On more than one occasion, however, they were not only defeated by this coalition, but had the additional mortification of seeing proposals, to which they were bitterly opposed, accepted and supported by the Government.

Of the measures alluded to in the Speech from the Throne that on the subject of the holding of Missions by Members of Religious Orders[93] gave rise to a long and very heated debate. The discretionary powers[94] possessed by the Government to sanction or refuse the admission of Religious Orders have at present only been made use of in the case of two Female Orders; – a fact which, the Centre maintain, proves that the Catholic Church in Baden is not treated as it ought to be in a country so equally divided between the Catholic and Evangelical Confessions. They accordingly submitted three Resolutions to the Chamber, demanding the free admission and right of settlement of Religious Orders, the right of such Orders to hold Missions and a relaxation of the regulations which prescribe, among other conditions, a three years residence at a German University of all Candidates for Holy Orders. These proposals encountered the strongest opposition on the part of the National Liberals, and in the five days' debate,[95] which ensued the violent and abusive language used on both sides has seldom, if ever, been surpassed in the worst days of the "Culturkampf" debates. The occupants even of the Visitors['] Galleries, which were densely crowded throughout, made repeated demonstrations for one side or the other and were more than once threatened with expulsion by the Speaker.[96]

The Government, whose conciliatory attitude towards the Centre was in marked contrast to that of the National Liberals, accepted the Second Resolution, which sanctions the holding of Missions by Members of Religious Orders subject to the provisions of the Common Law, but they declined, as regarded the other two Resolutions, to do more than promise to grant dispensations whenever they could safely do so.

---

[92] *Zentrumspartei* (Catholics).

[93] The law which readmitted missions in Baden was passed by both chambers on 19 and 26 June 1894 and was promulgated on 28 June.

[94] Law of 5 March 1880.

[95] 13 to 17 February 1894.

[96] Albert Gönner.

The second Resolution was eventually carried by 34 to 27 votes, three National Liberals and the two Conservatives voting with the Centre, the Radicals and the Social Democrats. The first and the third Resolutions were defeated respectively by 32 to 30 and 31 to 30, the National Liberals voting in a body against them.

Among the other measures referred to in the Speech from the Throne may be mentioned the reform of the Income Tax in a progressive sense.[97] The old Income Tax was in a manner also progressive, inasmuch as, while all Incomes of £1500 and over paid the full tax, those under that amount paid it at a graduated degressive rate. According to the law now passed Incomes between £1000 and £1250 will pay the full tax, the old abatements below £1000 being retained, while with Incomes of £1250 the real progression will begin.

This is to take the form of Surtax on the amount of the tax paid, rising by successive gradations of 5% till with incomes of £10,000 a year the maximum surtax of 40% is reached. Thus when the rate of the Income Tax is 4%, an Income of £10,000 will, in addition to the £400 formerly levied, have to pay a surtax of £160.

The Bill also enacts severe penalties against any fraudulent evasion of the tax.

As regards the question of Constitutional Revision, reported in my despatch No 26 of the 21st of May last, the Landtag[98] before separating adopted a resolution in favour of the introduction of Direct Elections based on a system of Proportional Representation.

The Government, however, who fear that the influence of the middle classes and the representation of local interests will suffer by the proposed reform, have, while accepting in principle the decision of the Chamber, declared[99] that they cannot allow the minority of the educated and propertied classes to be overridden by the masses, nor the representation of local interests in the Landtag to be imperilled. The measure, therefore, which they have promised to prepare for the next Session of Parliament, will endeavour to combine the system of Proportional Representation and its large Electoral Districts with a system of smaller Districts returning but one member in places where there are special local interests to be represented.

The Landtag will not meet again till November 1895, previous to which date the usual biennial elections for the partial renewal of the Lower Chamber will take place.

[97] Law on the modification of income tax of 26 June 1894, passed by the second chamber on 21 May.

[98] On 22 June 1894.

[99] Buchanan is referring to August Eisenlohr's speech in the Baden *Landtag* of 22 June 1894.

FO 30/283: George W. Buchanan to Earl of Kimberley, No 9, Darmstadt, 2 April 1895

[Received 5 April by post. For: The Queen / Prince of Wales / Lord Rosebery; K [imberley]]

Bismarck's birthday celebrated in grand style at Karlsruhe and Darmstadt; speech by Grand Duke of Baden extolling the patriotic virtues of Bismarck and his legacy

Prince Bismarck's Birthday was celebrated yesterday with great enthusiasm both at Darmstadt and at Carlsruhe. All the public and most of the private buildings were decorated with flags, the schools were closed and numerous Banquets were held, at which the great services rendered by the Prince to United Germany were extolled in a series of patriotic speeches.

The Grand Duke of Hesse sent Prince Bismarck a cordial letter of congratulations, and the Grand Ducal Government in a congratulatory letter assured His Serene Highness that the Hessian people – in common with all Germans – were deeply conscious of the debt of gratitude which they owed him.

The Grand Duke of Baden, who had already, on the occasion of his recent visit to Berlin, personally conveyed his congratulations to Prince Bismarck,[100] gave yesterday a further proof of his admiration for the old Chancellor by presenting the Municipality of Carlsruhe with the Prince's Portrait, to which the following inscription was attached:

"In commemoration of the never to be forgotten services of Prince Bismarck, and in the hope that future Generations as they look upon his picture may be stirred to deeds of patriotism."

At a Banquet held in the evening in the Town Hall the Grand Duke made a lengthy and important speech. After referring to all that the first Chancellor had done for Germany and to the recent speech,[101] in which the Prince had remarked that, without the Emperor William I and the army which He had created, the German Empire would never have been founded, His Royal Highness said that the great and noble qualities of the Emperor William I should ever serve as a pattern to all those who were called on to cooperate in the task of maintaining and developing the greatness of the Empire.

"The States of Germany", His Royal Highness continued, "must work loyally together to this end. We must, moreover, keep a careful

---

[100] Friedrich I stayed at Berlin from 21 to 29 March; on 27 March he visited Bismarck at Friedrichsruh.

[101] Friedrich I was referring to the speech Bismarck gave to members of the first and second Prussian house and the German *Reichstag* at Friedrichsruh on 25 March 1895. See also n. 107 in this section.

watch so as to preserve the foundations of the Constitution intact and to protect them against any attempts to bring destructive and disorganising germs into our Institutions."

After having for a period of forty years steered the Ship of State, I feel myself entitled to speak these words of warning: Let us be on our guard against the disturbing tendencies of unpatriotic ideas and utopian schemes, which would introduce under the guise of liberty an arbitrary and selfish tyranny.

It is for us to preserve to our country the fruits of more than thirty years labour in the field of social legislation, so that its further development may advance the highest interests of our land and tend to its lasting welfare.'"

FO 30/283: George W. Buchanan to Earl of Kimberley, No 13, Darmstadt, 3 May 1895

[Received 6 May by post. For: The Queen / Prince of Wales / Lord Rosebery; K [imberley]]

Political views in Hessian Landtag *regarding anti-revolutionary bills*

I have the honour to report that the Second Chamber of the Hessian Landtag has for the past two days been engaged in a discussion of the Anti Revolutionary Bills. The debate was occasioned by a resolution moved by a Member[102] of the National Liberal Party, requesting the Government to oppose these Bills in the Bundesrath,[103] should they be passed, by the Reichstag either in their original shape or in the form in which they had been amended in Committee.[104] The Members of the Centre[105] announced their intention of voting for this Resolution, while the Social Democratic Party proposed that its terms should be extended to any Anti Revolutionary measure that might receive the sanction of the Reichstag.

Eventually, after a prolonged debate, the House passed by a large majority an amendment moved by another National Liberal Deputy,[106] to the effect that the Government should be requested to strenuously oppose the Anti Revolutionary Bills if passed in the amended form which they had received in Committee.

[102] Ignatz Metz.

[103] Federal Council.

[104] For the 'subversion bill' (*Umsturzvorlage*), see n. 381 in Berlin section; the bill was dismissed by the *Reichstag* in its second reading on 11 May 1895.

[105] *Zentrumspartei* (Catholics).

[106] Alexander Friedrich.

The Debate has attracted some attention in the German Press on account of the attitude adopted by the Hessian Ultramontanes in this question being in striking contrast to that of their party in the Reichstag, and also because the Hessian Landtag, in occupying itself with a question appertaining to the competence of the Reichstag, has been the first of the Parliaments of Germany to follow the advice recently given in this sense by Prince Bismarck.[107]

FO 30/283: George W. Buchanan to Marquess of Salisbury, No 31, Darmstadt, 5 November 1895

[Received 6 November by post. For: The Queen / ~~Prince of Wales~~; S[alisbury]]

Electoral results to the Baden Landtag; no party majority

The Elections, which have first been concluded for the partial renewal of the Second Chamber of the Diet of the Grand Duchy of Baden, have not brought about any great change in the position of parties.[108] The National Liberals, who up to 1893 had for more than twenty years possessed an absolute majority in the Chamber, have gained one Seat, while the Ultramontanes have lost two and the Antisemites have for the first time succeeded in returning a Representative to the Diet. The strength of the other parties remain[s] unchanged, the composition of the Chamber being as follows: –

National Liberals	31
Ultramontanes	21
Democrats & Radicals	5
Socialists	3
Conservatives	2
Antisemites	1

The chief feature of the Elections was antagonism to the National Liberals: a striking illustration of which was afforded by the return of an Antisemite[109] in the place of a National Liberal at Weinheim,[110] in consequence of the support which he received at the Second Ballot

---

[107] Buchanan is referring to the speech of 25 March (see n. 101 in this section) in which Bismarck stated that he was happy when imperial policy was criticised by state parliaments as it proved their shared interest in German affairs.

[108] Elections took place on 12 October (electoral delegates); the second ballots were concluded on 30 October 1895.

[109] Georg Philipp Pfisterer.

[110] Albert Klein.

from the Democratic Party. The Antisemite Candidate was, the Democrats considered, the lesser of the two evils which they had to choose between. He had declared himself in favour of Direct Elections to the Diet and of various social reforms, and as the solitary Representative of Antisemitism he could not be regarded as a source of danger. The National Liberal Candidate on the other hand had refrained from pledging himself to any Electoral Reform and would, had he been returned, have given his Party the absolute majority in the Chamber.

The campaign thus opened against the National Liberals is likely to be followed up in the approaching Session of the Diet, but, as their party is still by far the strongest in the Chamber, it will be necessary for the Ultramontanes, the Conservatives, the Democrats, the Socialists and the Antisemite to join their forces in order to bring it to a successful issue.

The fact that there is no party commanding an absolute majority in the Chamber is not altogether displeasing to the Government. The National Liberals have indeed for a number [of] years been regarded as the Government Party, but now that they no longer dispose of the absolute majority of the Chamber, the Government is relieved of the pressure which they often brought to bear on it, and is able to adapt its policy to what it considers best for the general interests of the country rather than to the wishes of a particular party.

FO 30/285: George W. Buchanan to Marquess of Salisbury, No 11, Darmstadt, 24 June 1896

[Received 29 June by messenger. For: The Queen / Mr Balfour; S[alisbury]]

Closure of Baden Landtag *by Grand Duke; constitutional revision still outstanding with regards to electoral reform*

The Session of the Landtag of the Grand Duchy of Baden was yesterday closed by the Grand Duke in person, the Speech from the Throne being read by His Royal Highness.

After thanking the Chambers for the readiness with which they had agreed to the measures submitted to them by his Government, for the generous manner in which they had passed the Budget without alteration and for their acceptance of the Government proposals for relieving the distress caused by the serious inundations of last winter,[111] the

---

[111] On 16 June the second chamber of the Baden *Landtag* granted 3.3 million marks to remedy the damage caused by the floods of March 1896, which had affected areas west and south-west of the Black Forest.

Grand Duke expressed his satisfaction that an increase of taxation had been rendered unnecessary in consequence of the favourable condition of the finances of the Empire. His Government was, however, he remarked, still convinced of the necessity of an organic reform in the matter of Imperial Finance, and would, in conjunction with the Allied Governments, continue its efforts to bring about a satisfactory solution of this question in the Reichstag.

After citing the various measures passed by the Landtag – among which may be mentioned a Bill for connecting Carlsruhe by a Canal with the Rhine[112] – His Royal Highness concluded by expressing the hope that the new Code of Civil Procedure would become law during the present Session of the Reichstag.[113]

The late Session of the Landtag has been barren of results so far as regards the question of Constitutional Revision. In the preceding Session of 1894 the Second Chamber adopted a Resolution[114] in favour of the introduction of Direct Elections based on a system of Proportional Representation, and the Government, while declining to be bound by the terms of this Resolution, promised nevertheless to prepare a measure of Constitutional Revision before the next Session of the Landtag.

During the Session, which has just closed, several Resolutions in favour of Direct Elections were discussed, but, in consequence of the state of parties in the Second Chamber, where the National Liberals are in a majority of one, not one of them was supported by an absolute majority. The National Liberals, in the hope of disarming the opposition of the Government, did, indeed, withdraw their proposal that the Direct Elections should be based on a system of Proportional Representation.[115] The Government, however, who are opposed to any radical reform of the present system of Indirect Elections, declined, in view of this want of unanimity, to lay any measure of their own before the Chamber.

[112] In his speech the Grand Duke referred to the construction of the Karlsruhe Rhine Port (opened in 1901); on 20 May the second chamber approved the payment of the first instalment (200,000 marks) to the city of Karlsruhe.

[113] The Civil Procedure Code of 1877 was amended in May 1898. At the time of the dispatch the Imperial Office for Justice (*Reichsjustitzamt*) adjusted the provisions of the bill to the new German Civil Code which was passed in July 1896 (see n. 456 in Dresden section).

[114] On 22 June 1894.

[115] The motion by the National Liberal faction was passed on 15 June 1895; it requested the Baden government to present a bill on the election of the *Landtag*, and for directly and indirectly elected members to be in equal proportion.

FO 30/285: George W. Buchanan to Marquess of Salisbury, Confidential, No 30, Darmstadt, 21 October 1896

[Received 26 October by messenger. For: The Queen / Duke of Devonshire / Mr Balfour; Confidential to: Berlin / Paris / Vienna / St Petersburg; S[alisbury]]

Exchange of visits between German Emperor and the tsar

The recent exchange of visits between the German and the Russian Emperors has given rise to so many comments in the Press, that I venture to report what I have heard on the subject in Darmstadt.[116]

The initiative in the matter was taken by the German Emperor, who considered that the vicinity of Wiesbaden, where His Majesty happened to be staying, rendered a meeting with the Emperor Nicholas an act of ordinary courtesy. The necessary steps were therefore taken and an exchange of visits was ultimately arranged.

In proposing to visit the Emperor of Russia at Darmstadt the German Emperor acted, and I hear on very good authority, entirely on his own responsibility and even contrary to advice which was actually tendered Him. Influential personages of His Majesty's Suite have even, I am informed, expressed their regret that the Emperor did not abandon his visit to Wiesbaden altogether, rather than allow himself to be suspected of having forced an interview on the Emperor of Russia.

That the Emperor Nicholas would have preferred to have enjoyed an uninterrupted rest at Darmstadt is evident from the very plain language of several Russian officials here, who have all along hinted that a second meeting of the Emperors was unnecessary. Some newspapers have even attempted to draw certain inferences from the facts that His Majesty did not go to the Station to meet the German Emperor, as he did on the arrival of the Empress Fredrick,[117] and that, in returning the visit at Wiesbaden, His Majesty wore the uniform [of] the Hessian Regiment, of which the Colonelcy in chief has first been conferred on Him by the Grand Duke, instead of that of His Prussian regiment.[118]

The German Empress did not accompany the Emperor William to Darmstadt, on the grounds, I believe, that it was of the Empress of Russia to pay Her Majesty the first visit.

---

[116] Wilhelm visited Nicholas II, who stayed at Darmstadt from 11 to 29 October, on 19 October. The tsar returned the visit the following day (at Wiesbaden).

[117] Victoria arrived 22 October 1896.

[118] From 19 October 1894 Nicholas II was *Regimentschef* (colonel-in-chief) of the 24th (2nd Grand Ducal Hessian) Life Dragoon Regiment. On 17 November 1894 he was likewise made *Regimentschef* of the 8th (1st Westphalian) Hussars, known thenceforth as the Emperor Nicholas II of Russia's.

FO 30/287: George W. Buchanan to Marquess of Salisbury, Confidential, No 24, Darmstadt, 6 October 1897

[Received 11 October by post. Interesting. For: The Queen / Prince of Wales / Duke of Devonshire / Mr Balfour, A.J.B. [Arthur J. Balfour] / Eastern Department; S[alisbury]]

Audience with tsar; his views on international affairs

I had this morning the honour to be received in Audience by the Emperor of Russia.

After referring to matters of local interest and to his recent visit to Poland,[119] the Emperor spoke of the Greek Question and of the new Greek Ministry. The exclusion of Monsieur Delyannis from the Ministry was, His Majesty said, a very good thing, while the mixed character of the Government would enable the King to exercise greater control over their policy – a decided advantage for Greece. He had, His Majesty continued, seen a good deal of Greek politicians during His visit to Athens, and the opinion which he had formed both of them and of the working of the Greek Constitution was not high.[120]

Alluding next to the disturbances on the Indian Frontier,[121] the Emperor expressed His satisfaction at the progress being made by our Troops, adding that, where a civilized Power was the neighbour of a semi barbarous State,[122] such disturbances must occasionally occur.

In the course of our further conversation the Emperor spoke of the policy of "Buffer States", remarking that to be of real service such States must be strong and independent. The idea of Russia and England ever becoming neighbours in Asia was, He believed, regarded with some apprehension in England, but, in His opinion, such an eventuality, were it even to take place in the distant future, would rather tend to improve than to endanger the relations of the two countries. Russia, His Majesty added, had no desire to increase her existing possessions, which were quite as large as she could administer with advantage.

From some remarks made by the Emperor respecting Afghanistan, His Majesty would appear to regard that country as fulfilling the conditions of a strong Buffer State, while He spoke of Persia, of the ill

[119] The tsar visited Warsaw from 31 August to 4 September 1897.

[120] Nicholas, as tsarevich, visited Athens in November 1890. Theodoros Deligiannis was dismissed as premier in April 1897 in the course of the Greco-Turkish War. By the time of the dispatch Deligiannis' successor had been replaced as well.

[121] Buchanan is referring to the rebellion of Pashtun tribes in the Tirah valley which led to the Tirah Campaign of 1897–1898.

[122] Afghanistan.

health of the Shah[123] and of the weakness of the Government, as if that country did not possess the strength and vitality essential to an independent State.

In the course of the conversation which lasted over half an hour I ventured to remark to His Majesty that at Darmstadt one was naturally entirely outside politics, but that an Englishman, who lived in Germany and read the German Papers, had opportunities of learning a great deal that was new to him respecting the aims and policy of his Government.

The Emperor laughed, and said that he always made a point of reading the foreign papers, as it both amused and interested Him to know what others thought of Him and of His Government.

FO 30/287: George W. Buchanan to Marquess of Salisbury, Confidential, No 30, Darmstadt, 27 October 1897

[Received 11 October by post. For: The Queen / Prince of Wales; Confidential to: Berlin, 2 November / St Petersburg; S[alisbury]]

Grand Duke of Baden's proposed visit to the tsar declined; press speculation rife

The announcement made in the Carlsruhe Court Circular[124] respecting the proposed visit of the Grand Duke of Baden to the Emperor of Russia, on which I had the honour to report in my despatch No 29 of the 24th instant, has given rise to a series of sensational stories in the German Press. While some Journals hint that the Emperor's refusal of His Royal Highness' visit is to be attributed to political motives, others explain it by laying the blame for what has happened on the Hessian Court, and by raking up old stories to prove that the relations between the Courts of Carlsruhe and Darmstadt are far from friendly.

The Grand Duke of Baden occupies such an exceptional position among the Sovereign Princes of Germany,[125] that it is but natural perhaps that anything like a slight on His Royal Highness should be generally resented. The only motive, however, which led the Emperor to decline His Royal Highness' visit was His Majesty's desire to keep his annual stay at Darmstadt[126] as quiet and as private as possible. A

---

[123] Mozaffar ad-Din Shah Qajar.

[124] *Karlsruher Zeitung*, 24 October 1897. The Grand Duke's request to visit the imperial couple on 23 October was declined on 22 October.

[125] Friedrich I's position among the German princes was distinguished by his long reign and marriage to Princess Luise of Prussia, aunt to Wilhelm II of Germany.

[126] From 2 to 28 October 1897.

similar proposal on the part of the Grand Duke of Saxe Weimar had, I am confidentially informed, been already declined by His Majesty, without any notice whatsoever being taken of the refusal, and the curt and somewhat unfriendly manner in which the Carlsuhe Court Circular has given publicity to the present incident has caused much pain and surprise in official circles here. The Emperor's reply to the Grand Duke's Telegram was, I am assured, couched in much more cordial terms than those given in the Court Circular, and was moreover followed by a Letter, written on the same day by the Empress to the Grand Duchess of Baden, to which Her Majesty has received a most friendly reply.[127]

One report, which is credited by many persons here, has not as yet found its way into the Newspapers – namely that the Grand Duke of Baden's proposal to visit Darmstadt was made at the instigation of the German Emperor. His Royal Highness' Telegram to the Emperor of Russia was sent very shortly after the Emperor William's departure from Carlsruhe,[128] and during the latter's short stay in Darmstadt a hint was dropped by one of His Majesty's Suite that a visit from the Grand Duke of Baden might be expected.[129]

Though I cannot vouch for the truth of this report, I have reason to believe that the initiative as to the exchange of visits between the German and Russian Emperors came from the former, and that the Empress of Russia was especially invited to accompany the Emperor Nicholas to Wiesbaden. The fact that Her Majesty declined to do so and that the Emperor Nicholas again appeared on this occasion in His Hessian, instead of in His Prussian Uniform,[130] is said to have caused the Emperor William much displeasure, to which, I believe, His Majesty gave expression in conversation with some of the Court Officials here, whom he appears to have held responsible for what has taken place.

The Emperor and Empress of Russia will leave Darmstadt early tomorrow morning.

---

[127] The letters from Alexandra Feodorovna and Luise are dated 22 and 23 October 1897 respectively.

[128] On 21 October; Wilhelm II departed for Darmstadt.

[129] Nicholas II visited Wilhelm II at Wiesbaden on 20 October; the visit was returned on 21 October 1897.

[130] See n. 118 in this section.

SAXONY

(DRESDEN)

DRESDEN

FO 68/168: George Strachey to Earl Granville, No 1, Dresden, 4 January 1884

[Received 9 January by post. For: The Queen / X, Ch.W.D. [Charles Wentworth Dilke]; G[ranville]]

Press views of Bismarck's foreign policy and Germany's leading role in Europe; England's marginal role

On the occasion of the New Year, the Saxon Press has spoken in very optimist language of the state of Europe, as guaranteeing a continuance of peace. The Germans seem to have a belief in the existence of a separate diplomatic faculty, to whose agency they ascribe events due more to the natural evolution of affairs than to the forethought and contrivance of statesmen. Prince Bismarck is credited with the monopoly of this force, with which he regulates at will the European alliances, bringing the continent into an international system controlled by Germany. The feeling that the Reichskanzler has created a German hegemony in Europe, is expressed in the 'Dresdner Nachrichten'[1] in some remarks of which the following is the purport.

'With admirable moderation and self-restraint, Prince Bismarck has so used the military and diplomatic preponderance of Germany, as to establish a certain moral order amongst the European states, which is maintained against all interrupters by the menace of the interference of the Empire. This gives it's importance to the German-Austrian Alliance of 1883.[2] Originally directed against France and Russia, the central European League of Peace has grown to be "the sole decisive factor and regulator of Europe".

Furthermore, around the central sun it has been possible to gather a circle of satellites. Into this European system even Russia herself has now been drawn, and France, standing aloof, is held to peace by the absorption of her energies in distant enterprises.

---

[1] On 1 January 1884.
[2] In the protocol of 22 March 1883 Austria-Hungary and Germany prolonged their Dual Alliance of 7 October 1879 (see n. 489 in Berlin section).

It is characteristic of such articles in the German press, that they generally efface England from the international map. We may be named as exercising a certain indirect influence on Europe, through some Egyptian, or Chinese, incident, but, on the whole, the diplomatic position assigned to us is that indicated in the well-known line of Virgil

'penitus toto divisos orbe Britannos'.[3]

FO 68/168: George Strachey to Earl Granville, No 14, Dresden, 23 February 1884

[Received 25 February by post. For: The Queen; X; G[ranville]]

Spirited participation of Social Democrats in Saxon Landtag *debates; other politicians beginning to tire of it*

The Social-Democrats in the Landtag are discharging their assumed duties as Tribunes of the People with an activity not shewn by them in any previous session. They intervene in every sitting with questions, motions, remonstrances, and explanations, denouncing things and persons in language which, but for the privilege of Parliament would involve them in endless prosecutions for libel and sedition.

Lt. von Vollmar is a ready & incisive debater: Liebknecht would be an ornament to the most illustrious of Assemblies: and such is the eloquence of Bebel, that no topic is so mean that he cannot raise it in a few sentences to first-rate interest and importance.

Hitherto the combined majority of Conservatives (42), National-Liberals (15), and Progressists (19), has heard them with attention and tolerance, the President,[4] who is a Conservative, shewing himself admirably impartial, and a determined stickler for the liberty of debate.

However the daily Philippics of this 'fourth Party' – their defiant manner, interruptions, and altercations with the chair – their invectives against officials – their hardly covered appeals to eventual Revolution – (I am using the language of Saxon politicians) – all this which, in effect, if not in intention, is obstruction, is tiring the Chamber.

Accordingly, the majority are beginning to resort to the clôture,[5] for which justification might be given on other grounds. I find, for

---

[3] Latin: 'The Britons, separated from all the world' (Virgil, Ecl.1.66).
[4] Ludwig Haberkorn.
[5] French: 'close' (of session).

instance, that of 54 speeches delivered in certain recent debates, 25 were made by the 3 Social-Democrats. The other 76 members can hardly be expected to go on submitting to this, especially, as the torrent of Bebel's and Liebknecht's eloquence far overflows the limits of time traditional for parliamentary speaking here. Their oratory can never influence the house: its' object is the utilisation, for the benefit of their partizans out of doors, of the only place except the Reichstag where Social Democracy is not gagged.

FO 68/168: George Strachey to Earl Granville, No 27, Dresden, 11 April 1884

[Received 15 April by post. For: The Queen / Qy: Berlin; G[ranville]]

General Fabrice on Saxon initiative in the Federal Council against suggestion to form an imperial ministry

General Fabrice told me yesterday, in reply to a question of mine as to the real authorship of the debate in the Bundesrath[6] on the responsible Imperial Ministry, that this step had been provoked by himself and his colleagues on their own initiatives.[7] They had not acted on suggestions from any other quarter, but on their own sense of the necessity and policy of some such interchange of ideas between the Governments of Germany. The interpellation had not been preceded by any correspondence with other Courts: the only preliminary was, that the King's agents in the Bundesrath had, to a certain extent, felt the pulse of some of the other representatives before moving in the matter.

When the General went on to speak of the motives of Saxony for taking this step, his expressions were so chaotic and incoherent, and his delivery was so ejaculatory and intermittent, that I could only obtain glimpses of his meaning. He talked with a certain emphasis of the necessity of shewing the German public, on the eve of the forthcoming election,[8] that the allied Governments took their stand on Treaties, and were determined to resist the encroachments of the Democrats and Socialists. By 'Democrats' His Excellency meant Liberals in general, and, in particular, the new liberal party[9] whose programme was next door to Socialism. The Democrats

---

[6] Federal Council.

[7] For the debate in the Federal Council on 5 April 1884, see pp. 33–34.

[8] Elections to the *Reichstag* were to be held on 28 October 1884.

[9] *Deutsche Freisinnige Partei*. See n. 3 in Berlin section.

were giving trouble in Prussia, and Saxony thought it desirable to keep the cause of Government and order in the way supposed.

I remarked, that the ostensible accusation against the United Liberals was, that they wanted to centralize, whereas His Excellency had now been denouncing them as Democrats: must I, then, understand, that the Saxon move in the Bundesrath was, after all, a mere electioneering manoeuvre designed in view of the coming appeal to the constituencies? The General replied – 'well! not absolutely that:' – but, nevertheless, refrained from claiming for his policy that higher political purpose affirmed in the Bundesrath as the basis of the whole proceeding.

FO 68/168: George Strachey to Earl Granville, No 31, Dresden, 7 May 1884

[Received 9 May by post. For: The Queen; X, Ch.W.D. [Charles Wentworth Dilke]; G[ranville]]

Conditions and constraints on the Social Democrats in Germany; attitudes of crown adherents towards this party

General Fabrice expects the Reichstag to pass the Bill for renewing the repressive measures of 1878 against Social-Democracy.[10] In Germany the persons in the service of the Crown form a caste apart, no individual of which dares, or desires, to differ from the opinions which they all profess. The views of every one about everything political or administrative are absolutely identical with those of every one else in the given State, and of this rule the question on which I am writing is a signal exemplification. There is a perfect consensus of official opinion here, not only that under the law of 1878 Social Democracy has been silenced, but that the influence of Bebel and Liebknecht has been partly broken, and that the numbers and enthusiasms of their followers have diminished. Not long ago, the Saxon employé[11] who is best versed in the subject assured me that the Catiline restlessness,[12] the obstructive parliamentary tactics,

[10] The Anti-Socialist Law (Law against the Publicly Dangerous Endeavours of Social Democracy) of 21 October 1878 banned social democratic and socialist societies, associations, meetings, and publications which aimed at 'the overthrow of the existing political or social order'. The law, which was originally limited to two and a half years, was prolonged by the *Reichstag* on 12 May 1884. It was renewed a total of four times until 1890.

[11] Hermann von Nostitz-Wallwitz.

[12] Strachey is referring to the Catiline conspiracies to overthrow the Roman Republic in the 1st century BC.

the aggressive language, of the Socialists in the Landtag indicated their consciousness that they were now the generals of a diminished and demoralized army – a description of Bebel and Liebknecht from which the King, who was present at the conversation, visibly dissented.

It is a natural consequence of the application of the coercive law, that the materials on the ground of which propositions of this sort might be safely affirmed or denied are no longer available. No Saxon newspaper propagating the obnoxious doctrines now survives. Permission to hold meetings for discussion of topics likely to provoke the utterance of their peculiar opinions is systematically refused to prominent agitators or adherents of the party. Public meetings proper very seldom occur in North Germany, and any speaker who ventured to enunciate Socialist ideas, in however diluted a shape, would be immediately silenced by the Police. Last winter, however, Bebel and others were allowed to lecture in Dresden on neutral topics, such as strikes, commercial crises, the condition of the Bricklayers, the Arabian Culture-period in History &c, &c.

The control of writings is very strict. Even the stupidity of Russian censorship has been equalled here. There has been a prohibition of the 'Quintessence of Socialism',[13] a scientific and conservative work, by the Ex-Austrian Minister Schäffle: also of Bebel's recent book on 'Woman',[14] an interference which the King (who is not affected by Caste views), thought absurd: but these prohibitions did not originate in Saxony.

I see in the English London periodicals "To day" and "Justice", the statement that "the principal townships in Germany are in a state of siege". In Leipzig the so-called "lesser state of siege" is still in force.[15] This institution looks very formidable in the text of the anti-Socialist law, but in Leipzig, (as in Hamburg and Berlin), the authorities have only taken advantage of the paragraph which enables them to withdraw the right of residence to persons whose presence may be considered to endanger the public peace.

In 1882–3 there were 13 cases of such removal under the Act, and 65 of the usual requests for temporary leave to return from partizans previously expelled. Last year the persons who now assert that Socialism is in process of extinction were desirous to arouse a belief

---

[13] *Die Quintessenz des Sozialismus* (Gotha, 1874).

[14] *Die Frau und der Sozialismus* (Zurich, 1879) [*Die Frau in der Vergangenheit, Gegenwart und Zukunft* (Zurich, 1879)].

[15] At Leipzig the minor state of siege was imposed on 27 June 1881; it was annually renewed until 1890. For Section 28 of the Anti-Socialist Law which underpinned these measures, see n. 32 in the Darmstadt section.

in its increase, and the above figures were quoted in proof that there had been a local augmentation of the enemy's forces, and that the old agitators of Leipzig were pertinaciously adhering to their former plans and connections.

One of the individuals who returns at intervals by permission of Herr von Nostitz-Wallwitz to his former head-quarters is Bebel. The Socialist leader, who was originally a working turner, & is joint owner (with a Conservative partner)[16] of a small manufacturing of door-handles, frequently asks for leave of absence to attend to his affairs in Leipzig. The Minister of the Interior recently told me that the great orator's door-handles are nearly as excellent as his speeches, and that he should not think it fair to prevent Bebel from time to time looking after his interests in that department.

The coercive system having driven the party to earth the police are gradually losing sight of its wire-pullers and organization. But for the Reichstag, and the Saxon Landtag, German Social-Democracy would be a secret conspiracy like that of the 'Carbonari', or 'Mary-ann'.[17] When the Saxon Government had to show reason last year in the Bundesrath[18] for the continuance of the 'lesser state of siege' in Leipzig, the following statistics were all they could add to the figures above given.

On 3 occasions in the previous annual period, there were seized packets of the Zurich 'Social-Democrat'[19] which contained copies of that periodical far in excess of the wants of the local market. The inference was natural, that Leipzig is still a centre of Socialist agitation, from which numerous sympathizers, undeterred by risks, disseminate the literature of the party. Again: – the reports in Socialist journals on provincial Saxon incidents connected with the movement shew a familiarity with details of things and persons which proves how deeply the connexions of Social-Democracy ramify into the various circles of Society. Further: the two leading personages of the party (Bebel and Liebknecht), after their expulsion from Leipsic [*sic*], established themselves in a small village[20] on the immediate boundary of the proclaimed district, where they were joined by two other agitators,[21] in view, as might be surmised, of subterranean study and Encouragement of the Socialist propaganda.

---

[16] Ferdinand Ißleib.

[17] The *Carbonari* was an Italian secret society which existed in the first decades of the nineteenth century; *Marianne* was the name of a republican secret society during the Second French Empire.

[18] Federal Council.

[19] *Der Sozialdemokrat* (weekly periodical, established in 1879).

[20] Borsdorf; on 2 July 1881.

[21] Theodor Otto Burkhardt and Max Preißer.

What, then, could be plainer, than that if Social Democracy had been silenced its vitality was unimpaired?

This seems a very meagre minimum of fact to set forth by a Government which disposes of such a highly disciplined army of local administrators and such an inquisitorial police. Their proper interpretation is doubtful, and equally ambiguous, I think, is the information yielded by the electoral statistics of the periods previous, and subsequent, to the passing of the Act of 1878. As the present despatch has already attained an inconvenient length, I will defer to another opportunity my observations in this point, which it will be in my power to elucidate by some local figures prepared for my use at the Ministry of the Interior.

FO 68/168: George Strachey to Earl Granville, No 46, Dresden, 1 November 1884

[Received 3 November by post. For: The Queen / Gladstone / Sir W. Harcourt / X, Ch.W.D. [Charles Wentworth Dilke]; G[ranville]]

Increased votes for Social Democrats in Reichstag *elections*

The elections have rudely dissipated the illusions wh [= which], as my Correspondence has shown, have been entertained here on the subject of Social Democracy.[22]

It has been a cardinal point of Conservative and official faith, that Socialism was being stamped out by the coercion initiated six years ago,[23] and that it's diminished followers were beginning to contrast the empty promises of demagogues with the philanthropic realities of State-Socialism. Tuesday's polls show, that what has been happening is the reverse of this.

The Social-Democrats have completely emerged from the eclipse into which they temporarily fell after the Proscription of 1878, and have made a new departure in energy and enthusiasm, which is as obviously a consequence of the political persecution that was to intimidate them, as their improved party organisation and discipline is the undoubted result of the attempt to draw them, by the offer of official nostrums, from the leadership of Bebel and Liebknecht.

Complete figures cannot be given until after the casting elections, when the socialist vote may be largely augmented. I can say at present that whereas after the dissolution of 1881, that vote in Saxony was

[22] Elections to the *Reichstag* were held on 28 October 1884.
[23] For the Anti-Socialist Law of October 1878, see n. 10 in this section.

80,000, on Tuesday it reached nearly 127,000, the highest mark yet attained in the Kingdom.

As special examples of the increase I will take the cases of Leipzig, and Leipzig county, and the manufacturing city of Chemnitz, which is the German Manchester and Newcastle combined: (of Dresden nothing definite can yet be said). Leipzig, and Leipzig county, as I have often reported, have enjoyed an extra touch of the repressive screw. In order that Bebel and Liebknecht might be got rid of, both the city and district have been kept under the so-called "Little State of siege".[24] The utility of that measure may be judged from the circumstance that Bebel has just polled 9,676 votes, while in 1881 the Candidate[25] of his party only received 6,482 votes. In Leipzig county the effects of the 'Little State of siege' have been still more remarkable. The seat was held by a popular National-Liberal manufacturer, or capitalist, to whose enterprise and intelligence the district had been largely indebted. Doctor Heine[26] has lost it to a Social-Democrat,[27] and it is noteworthy that his defeat has been the most crushing in the particular villages where his opportunities for personal influence were the greatest. Connecting these two Saxon facts with the portentous growth of Socialism revealed in Berlin and Hamburg, which have been under the same regime as Leipzig, I cannot resist the belief that the cause in each case has been the "Little State of Siege".

On the instance of Chemnitz I will not dwell further than to say, that in 1881, with a much lower poll, the "Parties of Order"[28] received a much larger vote than now, while the Socialist (an editor from Stuttgart)[29] who, at the first election then was in a minority, has now obtained on the first trial a vote far in excess of the prescribed "absolute" majority. (More than half of the entire poll.)

This large increase of votes has effected no corresponding change of seats. The Saxon contingent of the Socialist faction in the Reichstag will hardly be above it's former strength of four members. It is characteristic of the Dresden press, that it persistently ignores the statistics above given, which I have had to compile for myself, and makes the shameless assertion, that this favoured Kingdom offers

---

[24] For the 'minor state of siege', see n. 15 in this section.

[25] The candidate in 1881 was also August Bebel – who stood simultaneously in thirty-five constituencies.

[26] Heine was *Reichstag* deputy for Leipzig (county) from 1869 to 1880; in 1884 the defeated incumbent was Johann Gottfried Dietze.

[27] Louis Viereck.

[28] *Kartell der Ordnungsparteien*, i.e. the National Liberals and the conservative parties. See n. 208 in Berlin section.

[29] Bruno Geiser.

an exception to the alarming growth of the Social-Democracy throughout the Empire!

Of the other parties, I can only say at present that the New Liberals (Freisinnige)[30] appear to have suffered the same ill-fortune which has overtaken them everywhere. Official spheres will see in the collapse of this party a perfect compensation for the alarming advance of Social-Democracy.

FO 68/168: George Strachey to Earl Granville, No 54, Dresden, 17 December 1884

[Received 19 December by post. X; G[ranville]]

Saxon press attacks on British colonial policy and diplomacy regarding Angra Pequena

The publication of the 2nd part of the German 'White Book'[31] has elicited in the Press, and otherwise, a renewal of the bitter comments on British policy and diplomacy with which the various steps in the acquisition of Angra Pequena have been received here. The sentiment from which they proceed scarcely rises to the importance of hostility: it is rather simple contempt. The 'Dresdner Nachrichten'[32] puts, as usual, a stronger point upon it than many other journals, but its' expectorations[33] do not depart in essentials from average German feeling. That paper believes, as Germans frequently do, in the existence of a separate Diplomatic black art of which the higher secrets are at present possessed by Prince Bismarck alone. The Reichskanzler's superior energy, endurance, finesse, and tact are described as having frustrated our equivocations, frauds, and greed, and as benefiting the whole world by scattering to the winds, once for all, our pretension that all the unoccupied lands of the globe are England's natural inheritance, to deprive her of which is robbery. The feints and subterfuges of Her Majesty's Government were unmasked and baffled, till, in the end, the presumptuous power that swaggers on the strength, not of might, but

[30] See n. 3 in Prussia section.
[31] The so called *Weißbuch*, a collection of diplomatic papers on Angra Pequena submitted by Bismarck to the *Reichstag* on 11 December, was published on 12 December 1884 . The first *Weißbuch* on colonial policy – pertaining to the Togo area and Biafra Bay – was presented to the *Reichstag* on 4 December. On the Angra Pequena question, see pp. 36–37 and n. 26 in Berlin section.
[32] *Dresdner Nachrichten*, 16 December 1884.
[33] This word is underlined in pencil in the dispatch and accompanied by '!!' in the margin.

of the pretence of might, was driven to creep to the cross with excuses, and congratulations to the new neighbour of the British Colony at the Cape.

I need not pursue the writer's amenities, – (the original is more stinging than my abridgement) – or repeat his compliments to Count Münster, who is called 'a phlegmatic Anglican'. It may be affirmed, without risk of error, that the transactions relative to Angra Pequena have opened a new depth within the old deeps of German ill-feeling towards Great Britain.

FO 68/169: George Strachey to Earl Granville, No 1, Dresden, 1 January 1885

[Received 3 January by post. For: The Queen / X, Ch.W.D. [Charles Wentworth Dilke]; Qy: Colonial Office, P.L. [printed letter], 5 January; G.Dl. [George E. Dallas]; G[ranville]]

Demonstrations in favour of Bismarck as sole director of Berlin foreign office; colonial protectorates behind his increased popularity

The movement provoked by the vote of the Reichstag on the Foreign Office incident[34] has extended to Saxony. The unusual, and indeed, hitherto unseen spectacle has been witnessed of corporate bodies, societies and private persons, spontaneously coming forward, in English fashion, with emphatic expressions of their opinions on a topic of the day. Small towns have forwarded addresses and telegrams to the Reichskanzler; Dresden and Leipzig have been conspicuous in their sympathy with Prince Bismarck, and demands for a reversal of the adverse vote in question.

Such a movement, arising without official suggestions on a public question, is doubly interesting: as it shows that political education is advancing, and that the old Saxon particularism has nearly vanished under the growth of the new German spirit. As regards Prince Bismarck, this sudden blaze of popularity is, without doubt, to be ascribed to his having laid the beginnings of what German imagination magnifies into a Colonial Empire. There are not wanting those who remark that possibilities of trade have been mistaken for opportunities of emigration, and that these new possessions are likely to involve the Empire in difficult and costly enterprises, but the dominant statement is strongly and indeed enthusiastically in favor

---

[34] On 15 December 1884 the *Reichstag* refused to grant the post of an additional director in the Berlin *Auswärtiges Amt*.

of the Protectorates.[35] This is tantamount to saying, that the feeling of Germany is now unfriendly to ourselves. It is unnecessary for me to enlarge again on the illiberal interpretations of British policy current in the German press, which in Foreign Affairs, is largely prompted by the "Kölnische Zeitung", and also by the less malignant, but, as far as we are concerned unfriendly lithographic "National-Liberal" correspondence sheet.[36]

FO 68/169: George Strachey to Earl Granville, No 9, Dresden, 9 March 1885

[Received 12 March by post. Qy: X; G[ranville]]

Frequent impertinent reports about British policy in the Saxon press; German self-exaltation

Today's "Anzeiger"[37] has an article on our policy, apparently derived from the National-Liberal lithographed sheet,[38] and being therefore representative of the views of that party, or even, as is constantly the case, having been written by one of its leaders, has more than local significance.

The mere language is not offensive, but it overflows with the national self-exaltation which now possesses the Germans – or, at least, their journalists, and speaks of us in a supercilious and dictatorial style more appropriate for the subjects of King Bell[39] than for the people of Great Britain.

The purport of the article is, – that we have been false, that we have been insolent, that we have made the humblest apologies possible, that we are forgiven on probation of future good behaviour – "Laudabiliter se subjecit"[40] – says the writer "would have been Count Herbert Bismarck's proud telegram yesterday, announcing the grand success of his London mission."[41] And it goes on to speak of complete recantation under pretext of "error", of "misunderstanding altogether", and consequent triumph of Prince

[35] At the time of the dispatch German protectorates were Angra Pequena (Lüderitz Bay; from 1885 German South West Africa), Kamerun (German Cameroon), and Togoland.

[36] *Nationalliberale Korrespondenz*, Berlin.

[37] *Dresdner Anzeiger*.

[38] *Nationalliberale Korrespondenz*, Berlin.

[39] Ndumbé Lobé Bel, leader of the Duala.

[40] Latin: 'laudably he has submitted himself'. The phrase *Auctor* (the author) *laudabiliter se subiecit* refers to the Roman Congregation of the Inquisition.

[41] On 3 March Herbert von Bismarck was sent to London in consequence of ongoing colonial disputes between Great Britain and Germany (see pp. 44–49 in Berlin section). The 'grand success' refers to Granville's conciliatory statement in the House of Lords on 6 March.

Bismarck and this nation, over a statesman[42] who has hitherto set such remarkably little store on his relations with Germany.

It would be idle to reproduce further samples. The "Nachrichten"[43] has been dwelling on the same subject day after day, with the disregard of truth and fact, and the insolent brutality and vulgarity of language, which characterizes this influential organ of the "Philistine" elements of the ornamental upper class and the lower middle social strata.

In pursuance of one of the objects for which I am placed here, I forward from time to time controversial extracts from this paper, but their [*sic*] are limits imposed by respect for Your Lordship, and they would be passed if I were to transmit some of the recent utterances, or I should say, war[w]hoops, of the "Nachrichten".

The semi-official and Conservative "Journal"[44] has no great weight, and official persons cannot be held responsible for its mild assaults on our policy, which are never personal, and usually see in our domestic and foreign troubles examples of the calamaties [*sic*] which befall nations which have lost all reverence for the Throne and Altar, and delivered up their destinies into the hands of radical doctrinaires.

FO 68/169: George Strachey to Marquess of Salisbury, No 26, Dresden, 28 June 1885

[Received 30 June by post. For: The Queen / Berlin; S[alisbury]]

Rumoured appointment of Count Fabrice as Governor-General of Alsace-Lorraine; no progress with Germanisation of province under Manteuffel

Rumours have been connecting the name of the Saxon Minister President General Count Fabrice, who holds the portfolios of War and Foreign Affairs, with the vacant Government of Elsass-Lothringen. His Excellency asserts that these are mere newspaper stories, and no one who knows the General would be likely to ascribe to him the capacity for originating the new departure which is said to be desirable in the Reichsland.

The policy of the late Statthalter[45] is generally thought to have been a failure. It was the belief of the previous administrator, Herr von Müller [*sic*],[46] that all attempts to conciliate the elder generation of Elsassians would, in the nature of things, be fruitless, and that

---

[42] Earl Granville.
[43] *Dresdner Nachrichten.*
[44] *Dresdner Journal.*
[45] Edwin von Manteuffel died on 17 June 1885.
[46] Eduard von Moeller.

Germany must be contented to wait for the result of that natural process of transformation which is silently converting the youth of the province into loyal subjects of the Empire.

For the ambitious mind of General von Manteuffel this attitude was too passive, and he imagined that he could hurry on by contrivance the solution which his predecessor proposed to leave to time. His plan was to neglect the Autonomists and peasantry, as being already half-converts to Imperial sympathies, and to pay court to the Notables, and higher Catholic clergy, with whom his conservativism and ultra-orthodoxy seemed calculated to keep him in favour. This broke down. The autonomists grew suspicious and sullen: the protest-Party[47] were not to be complimented out of their hatred to their new masters: and collisions occurred with the intransigentes, in which authority was so sternly asserted as to suggest the comparison of the whips and scorpions.

On the whole, the Manteuffel period cannot be said to have been marked by any obvious progress in the Germanisation of Elsass-Lothringen. Many think that it would be wise to revert to an idea entertained in Berlin some years ago, viz. the annexation of the Reichsland to Baden by personal union.[48] The population have always entertained very friendly sentiments towards their neighbours in the Grand-Duchy, and the Grand Duke being – (I do not know if the reasons are other than geographical) – persona grata in the Province, would enter on its' government with advantages which no 'Prussian' would possess.

These remarks may not be quite in agreement with current Press judgments. But I have gathered them from authoritative and unprejudiced sources.

FO 68/169: George Strachey to Marquess of Salisbury, No 28, Dresden, 7 July 1885

[Received 9 July by post. 'In a private letter Mr Strachey asks for an answer by tel [egraph]: as the case comes on Friday, tomorrow.' G.Dl. [George E. Dallas]; Sir J. Pauncefote; Qy: Tel[egraph] to Mr Strachey, 9 July]

Lawn tennis court incident; request for information about English law in cases of simple assault to aid charges against English offenders

A difference having arisen between the marker of the Dresden lawn-tennis court and two English youths (brothers, aged 15–17), as to the

---

[47] *Elsass-Lothringische Protestpartei.*

[48] The amalgamation with Baden, which had been dismissed in 1871, was discussed in 1879 in connection with the imperial law concerning the constitution and administration of Alsace-Lorraine, promulgated on 4 July 1879.

duration of a game, the marker made an offensive observation, to which one of the youths replied by a blow in the face. The marker's father, who owns the court, then interposing in his son's favour, was attacked by the second youth. The result of these collisions was, that both Germans were knocked down, and that the youths, with a companion who was not concerned in the affray, were taken into custody, and, after three days detention, bailed out on security for £500 being given for each of them. The Germans were not seriously injured, and were attending to their avocations as usual next day.

So extravagant is the severity of the new Imperial penal code,[49] that the youths may not impossibly be sentenced to imprisonment for six or eight weeks, especially as the assaults were, in the eye of German law, "combined".

The advocate retained to defend the case informs me that he can advantageously urge explanation of the offence on two grounds. Firstly: Striking with the fists ("das boxen") does not indicate on the part of an Englishman malice prepense, for he is only acting under the impulsion of a natural national instinct. Secondly: English law minimizes the importance of trifling assaults, and punishes them with fines of two or three pounds, or with a few hours incarceration.

In these circumstances it would be useful to the defence that an authoritative statement should be available in regard to English practice in cases of simple assault, and I should be glad to be informed how an incident similar to the above would be dealt with in our Police Courts.

FO 68/169: George Strachey to Marquess of Salisbury, No 29, Dresden, 3 September 1885

[Received 5 September by post. For: The Queen / Lord Iddesleigh / Paris / Berlin; S[alisbury]]

Sedan Day celebrations

The Sedan fête has been kept in the customary manner.[50] Its' observance has always a strictly private character; official participation in the rejoicings of the day being rigorously limited to the display of a few flags from public buildings.

The brilliant part played in 1870 by the Crown Prince – now King – of Saxony, and his troops, gives this anniversary a special

---

[49] *Strafgesetzbuch für das Deutsche Reich* of 15 May 1871 (newly edited in 1876).

[50] Sedan Day was on 2 September. It was (semi-officially) intended to commemorate the German victory in the Battle of Sedan, which took place on 1 and 2 September 1870 during the Franco-Prussian War, and the capitulation of the French emperor, Napoleon III.

significance here. Yet the 'Military Moment,' as the Germans express it, was but slightly touched in the postprandial and newspaper eloquence of the day. Sedan as a battle-field, as a source of German power and glory, as a witness to German science and valour – was kept in the background. But Sedan as the symbol of the End of the humiliation of Germany, of the crowning of the national Unity, of the deliverance of the country from the dangers of foreign invasion and dominion – this was the central idea on which stress was mainly laid.

Count Fabrice observed to me yesterday that he thought the annual holiday was somewhat of a nuisance. The Government had always thrown cold water on it, and the army held aloof, but the Liberal party insisted that the yearly dining and speechifying must go on. No doubt people were careful in what they said, but French susceptibilities were very keen and, added the General, I wish, on all grounds, to see the celebration dropped.

FO 68/169: George Strachey to Marquess of Salisbury, No 33, Dresden, 3 October 1885

[Received 7 October by post. For: The Queen / Lord Iddesleigh / Sir R. Cross / Prince of Wales; J.P. [Julian Pauncefote]]

Social Democrats accused of breaching law on secret societies on trial at Chemnitz

A great trial of Social-Democrats is in process before the Chemnitz Landgericht.[51] Amongst the accused are Bebel, Vollmar, and other members of the Socialist party in the German Reichstag. They are charged under Sections 128 and 129 of the Criminal Code,[52] relative to Secret Societies and associations for hindering the execution of the law, and of administrative measures.

The present phase of German Socialism dates from the Congress of Gotha in 1875, when, as explained in detail in my correspondence of the time, Bebel and Liebknecht effected a fusion of the two factions in which Social-Democracy had fallen after the death of Lassalle.[53] The so-called "German socialist workmen's party" attained wide ramifications and had an elaborate machinery of

[51] The trial took place from 28 to 30 September 1885 and resulted in the acquittal of all nine defendants on 7 October. On 4 August 1886 the court of appeal at Freiberg sentenced them to six and nine months imprisonment respectively.

[52] *Strafgesetzbuch* of 15 May 1871.

[53] The Gotha Congress of 22 to 27 May 1875 resulted in the foundation of the *Sozialistische Arbeiterpartei Deutschlands*.

committees, secretaries and wire-pullers, rules for admittance, sub-scriptions, and a recognized press organ, the Leipzig "Vorwärts". The Socialist Law[54] suppressed the visible corporate existence and action of this body, but the proceedings of the Congress of Wyden, in 1880, and the Congress of Copenhagen, in 1883, favored the belief that the penal legislation of 1878 had failed to reach the Social Democratic propaganda and organization.[55] Occasional proofs of this fact might also be derived from the results of the elections, which could hardly be ascribed to a mere spontaneous development of the proscribed creed, and some significance might be attached to certain articles in the Zurich 'Social Democrat',[56] the partly esoteric character of which plainly shewed that they were addressed to the sectaries of a subterraneous society.

Saxony has always been a chief centre of the socialist evolution, but the police, as I happen to be aware, have hitherto been almost entirely ignorant of the inner life of Social-Democracy, their knowledge has been mainly inferential, derived, that is, from such sources as those named above. The Chemnitz trial has not added a single new fact to what was known before: the Indictment only travels over the old Crambe repetita.[57]

Its' point of departure is the participation of Bebel and others in the Congresses of Wyden and Copenhagen, which are described as having charged the socialist members of the German Reichstag with the direction of the administrative and pecuniary affairs of the party. Under this authority, contends the Public Prosecutor,[58] the defendants formed a junta, which has exercised a variety of functions, such as organizing districts, calling meetings, empowering and controlling expenditure, expelling obnoxious partizans, &c.

The Indictment says: – "their presence at the Congress of Copenhagen is to be considered as proving their complicity as delegates in deliberate activity in consolidating, spreading, developing, and strengthening the Socialist party connexion – an activity completely adequate to the conception of membership in a party combination in the sense of §§ 128 and 129 of the Criminal Code." In the course of the usual interrogatory, the prisoners were asked by the Court how they understood the statements in the protocols of the Congress, and in the 'Social-Democrat', that the

[54] For the Anti-Socialist Law of October 1878, see n. 10 in this section.

[55] Strachey is referring to party conferences at Wyden, Switzerland (21–23 August 1880), and Copenhagen (29 March–2 April 1883).

[56] *Der Sozialdemokrat* (established 1879).

[57] Based on a Greek proverb (Juvenal), it literally means 'warmed up boiled cabbage' and was used as a metaphor for wearisome, repeated arguments.

[58] Christian Julius Schwabe.

Directory of their party had established "a new and effective organisation": also, what meaning was attached to expressions like "party-district", "Central-Committee", "Conferences", Confidential agents", "employés", "archives-fund", and the like.

The more important replies were made by Bebel, who observed that it was a matter of notoriety that the Socialists were animated by a community of principles and aims, and that their tactics consisted in the intimate relationship of man and man. This constituted the force of their Propaganda, which no law could prohibit; it was a survival from the earlier, unproscribed, days of Social-Democracy, and might reasonably be called an "organization". Bebel further requested the Court to observe, that in spite of the Law of 1878 the Berlin Police had for some time systematically tolerated an effective Social-Democratic "organization" for the elections, trade-societies, friendly and sick funds &c. As regards the expressions from which the prosecution sought to evolve the existence of a secret association, he need only say that they were for the most part mere survivals of an earlier jargon, and that the allusions incriminated were to arrangements for the elections, or for the support of partizans and their families who had been expelled from their places of residence by the Police.

Observing that the case was altogether one of constructive crime Bebel asked: – "how is it, with their unlimited command of pecuniary means, that the police have been unable to discover any positive facts incriminating us, and are driven to try to establish our membership of their illegal secret society by mere argumentative deductions of the thinnest description."?

As far as can be judged from the miserably imperfect accounts of the trial published in the local papers, Bebel displayed in his answer all the dialectical power, the subtlety, and resource, of which he is so unrivalled a master. The harangues of the public prosecutor, and of the advocates of the Socialists, were expansions of the arguments given in outline above. Bebel judiciously refrained from making a general defence. The oratorical faculty of the German tribune of the people is as suited to a forensic as to a parliamentary occasion, but in the present disposition of Saxon judges his eloquence would probably have been less persuasive than his silence.

Sentence will be given in a few days; it is thought here that a conviction is inevitable.

FO 68/170: George Strachey to Earl of Rosebery, No 7, Dresden, 5 June 1886

[Received 7 June by Berlin. Seen at Berlin. For: The Queen / Gladstone / Paris for perusal, 16 June; R[osebery]]

Reports about project to increase size of French army received calmly; German confidence in own military prowess

The local press is devoting considerable space to the new project for the augmentation of the French Army.[59] The facts are stated with a calmness as unruffled as if they concerned, not Germany but some distant planet. There is not a single bitter comment, not a word of recrimination escapes. The situation is treated as a natural phase in the evolution of a neighbouring people, which must be followed with attention, and not by a watchful maintenance of the defensive attitude hitherto observed by the Empire. France, it is pointed out, is sedulously preparing for revenge and reconquest, and the rising generation of the Republic are growing up in irreconcilable hatred of Germany, which is fermented by a party amongst the commercial class by whom the belief is entertained, that the advances of Germany to the industrial hegemony of the continent can be best interrupted by war. On the other hand, it is remarked that there will be a reluctance to assume, at any rate for a continuance, the crushing personal and financial burdens which would be entailed by such measures as the addition of 118,000 men to the peace effective, and the formation of 51 new line regiments. And, it is urged, the instability of the institutions and policy of France are likely to continue to impede for the present the adoption of a definite military organization.

This pacific temper is not mere journalistic prudence. The expression 'Public Opinion' is, as a rule, inapplicable to German questions, and it would be an abuse of language to speak of a feeling deserving that description as existing here with respect to France. But such sentiments as may be discovered entirely conform to the language of the press. In Saxony, at any rate, there is not – has not been of late years – a vestige of ill-feeling against the Republic. The habitual tone of conversation, and of literature, periodical and other, is, as regards the French, sympathetic. I have seldom, if ever, heard or read any malignant remarks on their national or personal character, and I suspect that they are generally preferred to ourselves.

---

[59] Strachey is referring to the army bill presented by the French minister of war, Boulanger, to the chamber of deputies on 25 May 1886.

The imperturbability of the Germans in presence of the perpetual menace that overhangs them, and of the various provocations from time to time addressed to them from France, is, in part, to be ascribed to temperament. Confidence is, however, inspired by the knowledge that the overwhelming numbers of France would be met by a machinery of war which is being perpetually improved and tested at every point, so as to guarantee the attainment of the highest perfection in matériel, mobility, and power. The people of Germany have complete self-reliance: they believe that they are competent to defend their territory themselves. But they entertain little doubt that under the present management of the Imperial Foreign Office[60] their efforts would be supported by allies.

FO 68/170: George Strachey to Earl of Rosebery, No 13, Dresden, 17 July 1886

[Received 19 July by Berlin. For: The Queen; R[osebery]]

Diminishing German hostility towards British liberal administration and foreign policy

Our elections have been exciting less than the average degree of interest here.[61] The fact has been noticed by the local press, and has been interpreted, not without probability, as indicating an abatement of the old antipathy to Her Majesty's actual Government. It has for some years past been the belief of the majority of Germans, that the presence of a liberal administration in Downing Street was a standing menace to the European equilibrium, being, in particular, incompatible with the maintenance of cordial relations between this Empire, with its' Austrian ally, and Great Britain. Accordingly the announcement of each successful political crisis at home was hitherto accompanied by the expression of a strong German desire for the retention, or resumption, of office by the Tory party.

On the present occasion, this feeling has not been apparent. The verdict of Germany on the Irish bills has,[62] no doubt, been hostile – the authorship of the measures was sufficient to secure that: – but the

---

[60] At the time of the dispatch Herbert von Bismarck, as state secretary for foreign affairs, was in charge of the *Auswärtiges Amt* (Foreign Office).

[61] The general elections to the House of Commons took place from 1–27 July 1886; the results returned the Conservatives to government.

[62] Strachey is referring to the failed First Home Rule Bill which was introduced by Gladstone on 8 April 1886; it subsequently led to the split of the Liberal Party and the dissolution of parliament.

usual angry partizanship has been absent, and the eventuality of a change of Ministry has been treated as a domestic British question in which the German Empire was not directly concerned.

During the absence of Count Fabrice, the Saxon Foreign Office is represented by Herr von Watzdorff, the virtual head of the department, who made some observations to me yesterday on the above topic. That gentleman, whose views are always representative of average German sentiment, observed that he thought the unpopularity of our liberal statesmen had been giving way. The 'hands off',[63] and the tendencies indicated by that phrase – in particular the Russian proclivities of Mr Gladstone – had caused considerable irritation and jealousy in Germany. Then the liberal foreign policy viewed in itself, and without reference to German interests, had not been calculated to arouse much enthusiasm in foreign countries. The common German notion had been, that with Lord Salisbury in office sympathetic relations between England and the Austro-German alliance were a matter of course, which was not so when Mr Gladstone was in power. However, last February a new departure appeared to have been taken by our Foreign Office.[64] Your Lordship was animated by very cordial feelings towards Germany, and it had become evident that the action of Downing Street was now the expression of a specific plan. There was no longer any rambling about in the dark, but there was a definite system, with vigour to carry it out. The Greek settlement was mainly Your Lordship's performance,[65] and reliance could be placed on the hand which guided it, the more so as the sinister influences[66] which had formerly been so potent, appeared to be no longer influencing our foreign policy. These impressions, derived from realities, had been strengthened amongst the general public by others of a personal kind, which perhaps, were partly of mythical origin; but the net result was, that the old German grounds of suspicion and dislike were felt to have been removed, so that the Empire had no reason to desire a change of men in England.

[63] This refers to Gladstone's warning to Austria-Hungary after the occupation of Bosnia and Herzegovina in 1878.

[64] On 6 February 1896 Rosebery took over as the new foreign secretary in the brief Liberal administration under Gladstone (1 February to 20 July 1886).

[65] This is referring to the ultimatum and subsequent naval blockade of Greek ports in May 1886, which the signatory powers of the Berlin Congress had imposed as a result of Greek attitudes towards Turkey in the ongoing frontier dispute. The blockade was lifted after Greek demobilization on 7 June.

[66] This is probably referring to the Earl Granville's policy.

FO 68/170: George Strachey to Earl of Iddesleigh, No 15, Dresden, 24 August 1886

[26 August by post. For: The Queen / Lord Salisbury; I[ddesleigh]; S[alisbury]]

Press responses to Bulgarian coup d'état *and Prince Alexander's deposition; anti-British and anti-Russian sentiments rife*

The first announcement of the Bulgarian Coup d'État was published here simultaneously with the Sunday's articles in the Berlin 'Post', and the 'Kölnische Zeitung'. The former journal is subject to the influence of the official 'Reptile Fund':[67] the second named, according to public notoriety and to internal evidence, is in the pay of Russia. As the articles in question were the earliest authoritative comments on the deposition of Prince Alexander which happened to be available, their opinions were adopted by the local press. Owing to this accident, the accounts of the transactions at Widdin given here have been coloured by malicious interpretations of recent British policy.[68]

For instance: the Prince was a wedge, to be driven in by us between Austria and Russia: he was our tool, but we abandoned him: it was our device to make Bulgaria an apple of discord between Austria and Russia, so that Austria might pull our chestnuts out of the fire: &c. &c. &c.

Owing to our disrepute in this Empire, the press is, of course, always ready with malignant appreciations of our actual proceedings, and of those which editorial imagination ascribes to us. But while Great Britain is the object of a passive German dislike, towards Russia a deadly national hatred prevails, and there can be no doubt that this sentiment will be stirred and intensified by the deposition of Prince Alexander. The remark may be made, that it was better for the Prince to be sacrificed, than for the peace of Europe to be endangered by the revengeful ill-humour of the Emperor of Russia

---

[67] The secret 'reptile fund' or 'Guelph fund' consisted of the confiscated assets of King Georg V of Hanover. It was administered by a Prussian commission and, amongst other things, used for influencing the Prussian and German press. The expression 'reptile' was originally coined by Bismarck to describe the agents of the likewise dethroned prince elector of Hesse, but the meaning was quickly deflected back onto its originator. Accordingly, journalists and press in the service of the Prussian government and its *Literarische Büro* were termed 'reptile press'.

[68] On 21 August 1886 a group of pro-Russian military officers carried out a plot against the knyaz of Bulgaria, and forced him to abdicate; Alexander was subsequently deported to Russia. According to the erroneous newspaper reports to which Strachey referred he was brought to Vidin. In an article of 22 August the *Cologne Gazette* accused Britain of having abandoned Alexander to his fate.

and the wire-pullers of Moscow. But it is not forgotten that the Prince is a German, that he exhibited the chivalry and qualities of his race, that he represented the civilisation of Germany, and that he has fallen before a Slav plot.

FO 68/170: George Strachey to Earl of Iddesleigh, No 30, Dresden, 15 October 1886

[Received 18 October via Berlin. For: The Queen. Seen at Berlin. I[ddesleigh]]

Speculation as to Randolph Churchill's visit to Germany

The capacity of the German mind for hypothesis has been well illustrated by the local comments on the journey of "Mr Spencer".[69] Nearly all the statements of fact which happened to be genuine, were set aside by the press and public as irreconcilable with the idea of a British Cabinet Minister as evolved by the moral consciousness of Germany, and the most amazing deductions were drawn from the details accepted as true.

A representative of some of the chief Austrian and German papers, who is full of the sagacity which borders on stupidity, informed me that the identity of "Mr Spencer" with Lord Randolph Churchill was not properly established. "Mr Spencer" had occupied a pit stall at the Theatre, instead of a box seat, which was just the behaviour for a notability wishing to pass incognito; but then he had visited a minor place of entertainment, and witnessed a performance of learned geese, with other pastimes unsuited to the solemn leisure of a Cabinet Minister.

My interviewer received with deep distrust my assertion that, if so, "Mr Spencer" had done exactly what Pitt, or Lord Palmerston, or Mr Gladstone, would have done in his place, and that if Her Majesty's Government contemplated any special negotiations with Germany, their proposals would be made in the recognized way, and not through the channel of subterraneous diplomacy, an instruction which, I said, like other survivals of state-craft still in favour on the Continent, had been discarded in Downing Street, as out of harmony with British 19th Century ideas and practice.

The suspicion is now dawning, that the journey which seems likely to equal in celebrity the expedition of the two Mr Smiths to Spain[70]

---

[69] For Randolph Churchill's incognito journey, see n. 101 in Berlin section.

[70] Strachey is referring to the Prince of Wales (later Charles I) and George Villiers, Duke of Buckingham, who travelled to Madrid in 1623 to negotiate Charles' marriage with the Infanta of Spain, Maria Anna; they were not successful.

was, perhaps, undertaken for the mere vulgar purposes of recreation. However the semi-mythical element in the Spencerian evolution has just been augmented by the discovery that "Mr Spencer" or "Mr Trafford"[71] were met by the Prince of Bulgaria in this neighbourhood, as well as by the accounts from Vienna, where those gentlemen have "conferred" with "General Sir Smiths", and are awaiting the arrival of Sir E. Malet. On the whole, I might say, that if all the hatred which Germany can feel is at present concentrated on General Kaulbars and his master,[72] the most popular figure in the Empire, next to the august head of the nation, is the dubious "Mr Spencer".

FO 68/171: George Strachey to Earl of Iddesleigh, No 2, Dresden, 1 January 1887

[Received 4 January by Berlin. Seen at Berlin. For: The Queen / Lord Salisbury; I [ddesleigh]]

German views on Churchill's resignation from the cabinet

Although it is mere newspaper sensationalism to describe the resignation of Lord R. Churchill as 'the topic of the day in Germany', that incident is receiving some discussion, at least in the Press, on account of its presumed bearings on our foreign policy.[73] The following is abridged from the 'Nachrichten'.

'The many cases which will dog the friends of peace into the new year are augmented by doubts as to the future policy of England.

*** Whatever the grounds of Lord R. Churchill's resignation, Europe is now again utterly in the dark as to what England may do. With a strong Salisbury Government, Russia had to reckon with England as an adversary on the road to Bulgaria and Constantinople. The new Cabinet, patched up as it may be, will not enjoy the confidence of the continent in respect to reliability. The danger is not excluded, that Gladstone may sooner or later return to office. It is unnecessary to enlarge on the significance of the accession to power, at such a moment, of this sworn partizan by Russia. Neither Austria nor Germany can count on England's support. That country has ceased to be a factor in European politics on which we can reckon'.

---

[71] Churchill's companion 'Tommy' [William Henry] Trafford.
[72] Alexander III.
[73] Randolph Churchill resigned on 20 December 1886.

The anxiety betrayed in regard to our action is not quite consistent with the new German fashion of speaking of our power, national spirit, and prestige, in the past tense. The fact is, that although young Germany is accustomed to think of Great Britain as a quantité négligeable, the historic past has not yet faded from the minds of the older generation, there being a vague sense that British influence will probably be felt in the next European struggle. In these circumstances there is a natural desire that our foreign policy may continue to be guided by the party[74] which is thought to be pledged to resistance to the encroachments of Russia, and that its' control may not revert to a statesman who is not credited with good-will towards Germany, who is believed to be actively hostile to her ally – Austria-Hungary – and to be disposed to be the accomplice of M. M. Katkoff and Kaulbars.[75]

FO 68/171 George Strachey to Marquess of Salisbury, No 9, Dresden, 28 January 1887

[Received 31 January by post. Seen at Berlin. For: The Queen / Prince of Wales / Circulate / Paris for perusal – in original, 9 February; S[alisbury]]

Liberals do not support Conservative view that Bismarck intends a coup d'état to carry through the army bill

In reply to Herr Windhorst [*sic*] in the Prussian Landtag, Prince Bismarck repelled, as a mere calumny of the opposition, the idea that if the new Parliament did not give a majority for the military Septennate, the Imperial Government would abrogate the Electoral Law,[76] and, in violation of the Constitution, order fresh elections on an arbitrary basis.[77]

It is inconceivable that Prince Bismarck should be unacquainted with the real authorship of the rumours in question, which, in fact, arose amongst his own partizans, and not in the Catholic and freisinnig'[78] camps. Immediately after the Dissolution, the Conservative Press, and, in a lesser degree, their National-Liberal allies, began to hint that if the electorate failed in its duty the confederated Governments would do theirs. The semi-official Dresden 'Journal'

---

[74] Conservative party.

[75] Katkov was editor of the *Moscow Gazette*; for Kaulbars, see n. 106 in Berlin section.

[76] Electoral Law of 31 May 1869 – adopted by the imperial constitution of 1871. The *Reichstag* was directly elected by universal suffrage for men aged 25 years or older.

[77] The debate took place on 24 January 1887. On the failed army bill (military septennate) and the dissolution of the *Reichstag* on 13 January, see pp. 73–75.

[78] *Deutsche Freisinnige Partei*. See n. 3 in Berlin section.

quoted Prince Bismarck as saying: 'the elections can have <u>no influence whatever</u> on the attitude of the Governments, which have plainly shewn that <u>they will not be guided by the wishes of the Reichstag, or by the result of the elections</u>: a renewed refusal by the Reichstag <u>will not alter their policy</u> the duty entailed on them will be unchanged. "It is impossible," said the Journal "to characterize the policy of the Governments in plainer and more elevated language."

Insinuations that Prince Bismarck would have to "take away that bauble" were frequent in the "Reptile" press:[79] I spoke to many Conservatives on the subject, and the reply in every case was 'There will be a Charte Octroyée,[80] and a Reichstag will be elected which will pass the Army Bills, and Bismarck's other favorite measures.' Their belief was universal, that the Reichskanzler would be troubled by no doubts or scruples, and it is questionable if his recent parliamentary professions of constitutional orthodoxy will alter their conviction.

The Liberals have not put this malignant interpretation on Prince Bismarck's words. Far from believing him to be plotting an eventual Coup d'État, they have argued that the constituencies have the issues in their own hands. Like the bulk of the Conservatives, the Liberals think that though the dissolution may have been a formal result of the vote on the Septennate, it was really prompted by the conviction that "the army in danger" would be a telling electoral cry. Prince Bismarck's threats, they say, are brag: if a subservient Reichstag is not returned, he will give way as on other occasions.

The alacrity of the Conservatives in attributing to the Prince such nefarious designs, arises to a great extent from their own sympathy with the reactionary programme which they suppose him to entertain.

I am personally unable to see that, because a Minister has not the constitutional morals of Sir R. Peel, or Pitt, or Walpole, he is capable of proposing to the 25 German Governments schemes more infamous than the publication of the Ordinances of July.[81] It is true that a German Polignac would be encouraged by the knowledge, that there is in the Empire no Thiers, no 'National', and that if the existing institutions were subverted, hardly a word would be uttered, and not a shot fired, in their defence.

---

[79] See n. 67 in this section.

[80] French: 'imposed constitution'. This expression particularly refers to *La Charte Octroyée* which established a constitutional monarchy in France in 1814.

[81] The July Ordinances were a were a series of repressive decrees instituted by Charles X which led to the July Revolution of 1830 and his subsequent abdication.

FO 68/171 George Strachey to Marquess of Salisbury, No 10, Dresden, 28 January 1887

[Received 31 January by Berlin. Seen at Berlin. For: The Queen / Prince of Wales / Circulate / Paris for perusal – in original 9 February; S[alisbury]]

Rumours of war with France; German press cast aspersions on exaggerated war rumours in English press

The independent press is engaged in a controversy with the 'Reptiles'[82] respecting the war rumours. The former alleges that the Kölnische-Zeitung, Wolff's Telegraph-Bureau,[83] &c are doing their utmost to disturb the public mind with tendentious stories of French orders for picric acid and sulphuric-aether, (said to be ingredients of melinite), of French purchases of boards for frontier barracks, of impending mobilisations, and the like, in the hope that they may influence the constituencies in favor of candidates pledged to the military Septennate.[84] On the other hand, Prince Bismarck's organs, and their allies, are arguing that it requires the peculiar baseness of the anti-national (Reichsfeindlich) parties to minimize the import of such serious facts, and to accuse the Imperial Government and its friends of such infamous political practises.

These reports and discussions have aggravated the sense of insecurity created by the sensational parliamentary pictures of France and Germany 'bleeding to death', with which Prince Bismarck met the arguments of the opponents of the Septennate.[85] In vain the liberals urge that the visible European symptoms are pacific, that Russia and Hungary are arranging large financial operations which hostilities would upset, that General Boulanger and M. Déroulède are not the French people, and so forth. The universal talk is of war: persons high in office say, without being able to give any definite reasons, that it will break out "in the spring": the military of all ranks say the same.

In Germany such feelings do not assume an excited shape; but the public is sensibly perturbed. The idea that it might be wise to anticipate the coming danger by an attack on France, is, as far as I can judge, abhorrent to the national sentiment; and the 'Daily News' story of Monday was, after a moment of alarm, instinctively rejected

---

[82] See n. 67 in this section.

[83] *Wolffs Telegraphisches Bureau*, Berlin news agency founded in 1849.

[84] For the army bill (the military septennate) which led to the snap elections for the *Reichstag* on 21 February 1887, see n. 119 in Berlin section.

[85] For the debates, see pp. 73–75.

as an obvious fable.[86] The 'Nachrichten'[87] remarked, that this particular lie of Mr Gladstone's hack organ was a stock-exchange trick,[88]
but that the persistency with which the English press exaggerates
war rumours, and their suspicious reiteration of advice to
Germany to arm to the teeth, shews our anxiety for a conflict
between the two neighbours, when, true to the brutal traditions of
British policy, we shall proceed to fish to our own advantage
in the troubled European waters. The 'German-Conservative'
semi-official 'Journal',[89] which is always ready with malignant interpretations where we are concerned, last night used similar language,
saying that some of the recent alarms arose from "the impure hope
of certain English circles" for a war in which they may find their
account.

The Editor[90] of one of the leading German Reviews tells me, that
according to a letter which he has just received from a particularly
reliable French Senator, the war party in France is a very small
minority, who are looked on by all reasonable men as incendiaries
and maniacs. I gather from various indication that the authority
quoted is M. Barthèlemy [*sic*] de St. Hilaire, who, according to my
recollections of that eminent person, is very likely to underrate the
strength of the imaginative political forces.

FO 68/171 George Strachey to Marquess of Salisbury, No 17, Dresden, 18 February 1887

[Received 21 February by Berlin. Seen at Berlin. X; S[alisbury]]

Nostitz's circular explaining the meaning of military septennate; press reactions

Some years since, the Minister of the Interior replying to a question
of mine – was he putting pressure on the constituencies? – replied
that in Saxony no Government dared to do this; "not even Baron
Beust" had been charged with such practises. His Excellency yesterday issued what is virtually an electioneering placard. He states,
with the usual Teutonic amplitude of style, that whereas "by a

---

[86] On 24 January the *Daily News* reported that war was imminent between France and
Germany and that Germany was about to demand explanations from France, regarding
the movements of French troops on the German frontier.

[87] *Dresdner Nachrichten*, 27 January 1887.

[88] Prices on the London and other European stock exchanges fell on the day that the
Daily News article was published.

[89] *Dresdner Journal*, 27 January 1887.

[90] Name not traceable.

reprehensible agitation and erroneous comments", the idea has been disseminated that 'Septennate' signifies Seven years active service with the colours (instead of 2 ¼ years as now), the Department of the Interior makes known, that the sole point for the decision of the new Reichstag is this – 'shall the military augmentation be voted for seven years certain'?[91]

Herr von Nostitz is, judged by our standards, a narrow minded statesman, but he would not lightly put his name to the charge on which his Circular is based. The 'freisinnig'[92] 'Zeitung'[93] remarks, however, with truth, that the 'Reptiles'[94] have been repeatedly challenged, but in vain, to give chapter and verse for their allegation that the opposition has been explaining the Septennate to mean 'seven years with the colours'. In this Empire, a Ministerial Circular must be delicately handled, if the critic wishes to escape half a dozen actions for libel; but the 'Zeitung' is courageous and rash enough to observe, that the accusation has been trumped up by the so-called 'patriotic' coalition, and propagated by the 'Reptile' press as an effective electioneering lie. Looking to the high educational standard attained in this Kingdom – to the fact that the classes with the lowest degree of political instruction principally read Conservative newspapers – and to the practical knowledge of military topics possessed by every German family – it is altogether improbable that the opposition would attempt to impose on the electorate in the gross manner supposed.

The Ministerial Manifesto is in the modest form of a rectification, and no hint is given how a patriotic elector ought to vote. Still, authoritative commentary is suggestion veiled, and, in a country where servility is so rampant, this placard cannot fail to stimulate the civil servants of all grades, clergy, schoolmasters, and the like, to work against the opposition candidates. I have no doubt that the Circular which bears the signature of Herr von Nostitz will turn out to be, in substance and initiative, a Prussian concoction, and that it is the substitute for the Imperial proclamation of which so much has been lately said.

---

[91] On the army bill (military septennate) which led to the snap elections for the *Reichstag* on 21 February 1887, see n. 119 in Berlin section.

[92] See n. 3 in Berlin section.

[93] *Dresdner Zeitung*, 18 February 1887.

[94] See n. 67 in this section.

FO 68/171 George Strachey to Marquess of Salisbury, No 25, Dresden, 25 March 1887

[Received 28 March viâ Berlin. Seen at Berlin. For: The Queen; S[alisbury]][95]

Fawning celebrations to mark Wilhelm I's birthday; high praise for his achievements as German Emperor; remarks on diminishing particularism and Wilhelm's significance in unifying Germany

The Emperor's birthday[96] has been kept here, and in the provinces, with extraordinary demonstrations of loyalty. I doubt if a similar local anniversary would be commemorated with so much civic decoration and illumination, by so many convivial and ceremonial assemblages of societies[,] clubs and corporations of every description, by such effervescence of patriotic oratory, and such deluges of complimentary biographies[,] articles and odes.

On these occasions German enthusiasm invariably slides into servility and caricature. Some of the most accomplished of the representatives of learning and science lauded the amicable object of the national veneration in superlatives too strong for Alexander, or Julius Caesar, or Edward I, or Frederic. A very distinguished person[97] reviewed the series of the successors of Karl the Great, and comparing the present occupant of the Imperial throne with Henry the Fowler, Otto I, Barbarossa, and Frederic II, declared that as kings of men the place of all of them was lower than that of the Emperor William. A leading divine[98] described the German sovereign as "the first monarch of the world, who governs not only Germany but Europe as well," and "in his wisdom and goodness desires only peace for mankind", although it lay in him "as representative of the mighty German race, and as hero laden with glory, to enforce obedience on the universe." In more than one other public harangue the fact was stated, that now for the first time the wearer of a crown was adorned with piety, moderation, humility, and self control. At the principal meeting here, an orator[99] categorically asserted that "never on any throne had sat a ruler with such self denial and sense of duty."

---

[95] Additional note to No 25: 'Sir Julian, There are some expressions in this despatch which I think may not be favorably viewed by the Queen, especially those marked in P.P. 2 & 7. I have some doubt as to the expediency of sending the despatch to H.M.' H.H. [Henry Hervey], 28 March; I[ddesleigh]. 'It is rather an amusing skit on the hysterical enthusiasm of the Germans for their glorious selves. Qy.'

[96] On 22 March.

[97] Karl Woermann, director of the Saxon picture gallery.

[98] Clemens Peter.

[99] Superintendent Ernst Julius Meier.

An introductory article in the National-Liberal 'Anzeiger',[100] which is not addicted to the Chauvinistic style, commenced, "Great are the Lords' marvels for us! Glory be to God in the highest:" viz for the act 'of divine grace whereby to the German people has been vouchsafed the unexampled happiness of beholding the close of the 90th year of their glorious Kaisers' life."

The language of Byzantism and Versailles seems to be rivalled, when the virtues and powers of Pericles, Marcus Aurelius, Alfred and Napoleon, are gravely said to be united in a single ruler. That such disfigurements of loyal sentiment should be received in Dresden with universal applause shews how great a revolution in feeling has been accomplished since the establishment of the Empire. The old 'particularism', so rampant here within my own memory, has been entirely obliterated, and its place has been taken by a genuine pan-Germanic sentiment. "Deutschland über alles" is now a household Saxon word and thought, by the side of which regional patriotism could hardly continue to subsist, but for the remarkable – I may say, Oriental – susceptibility of the Germans to the fascinations of the monarchical idea. There is no doubt whatever that the Emperor William has been the principal agent in affecting this change. The popularity of the "Mehrer des Reichs"[101] has strengthened the foundations of the Empire. The not inconsiderable position of the German public which craves for an authoritative exercise of sovereignty – or for its semblance – has been gratified by His Imperial Majesty's occasional announcements of his royal will and pleasure, and his other assumptions of the autocratic style. His mastery of the arts of conciliation, his moderation, his unfailing tact, have done much to quench the antagonisms, and jealousies provoked by the growth of the Central power, while his patriarchal dignity, his courtesy, and the irresistible charm of his caressing Hohenzollern manner, have been largely instrumental in subduing and reconciling to the Reich many of the most venomous enemies of the new order of things. Kaiser Wilhelm is not a Charlemagne, or a Barbarossa – of his Prussian ancestry, several have surpassed him in unaided capacity for government and war. But the services which he has rendered to United Germany could not have been performed except by a ruler of his sympathetic personality and his venerable age.

---

[100] *Dresdner Anzeiger*, 22 March 1887.

[101] German: 'enlarger of the empire'; as in *semper augustus*, one of the appellations of the Holy Roman Emperor.

FO 68/171 George Strachey to Marquess of Salisbury, No 28, Dresden, 15 April 1887

[Received 18 April viā Berlin. Seen at Berlin. For: Treaty Department; J.P. [Julian Pauncefote]; The Queen / Prince of Wales; S[alisbury]]

Succession to the throne of Saxe-Coburg-Gotha; problem of foreign dynasts on German thrones

With reference to Lord Granville's 'Secret' Despatch No 11, of December 15, 1884 (Treaty) on the Saxe-Coburg-Gotha succession,[102] I have the honor to report that the National Liberal 'Anzeiger'[103] thus alludes to the Duke of Edinburgh's alleged renunciation of his claims in favor of His Royal Highness Prince Alfred.[104]

"This news, which, however, requires confirmation, will be received all through Germany with satisfaction. The German nation, now come of age, would certainly have disliked the accession to power on their soil of a Prince out and out foreign, and strange to German ways and ideas. The youthful Prince Alfred, who is to be brought up amongst us, has ample time, let us hope, to become a German man before he is called to mount a German throne." This note is apparently a so called "washing bill", or communiqué of the Berlin Government 'Literary Bureau'.[105] But it expresses with accuracy the national feeling on the point involved. Notoriously, the foreign alliances of certain German dynasties have given rise to malignant local comment, and have entailed unpopularity on some of those who have formed them. As in these cases the collision between the imported beliefs, ideals, and habits, and those of Germany, has been so marked, the devolution of actual sovereignty here on a foreigner would naturally be viewed as a probable source of antagonism rather than of concord. As regards ourselves, the political and educational influences under which young Germany is growing up, are not such as to suggest the belief that the antipathies of the Bismarckian era will be followed by a revival of the feelings which animated the generation of Bunsen.[106]

---

[102] Note in margin: 'I think the Desp[h] in question was addressed also to other of H.M.R.R. [Her Majesty's Royal Representatives] but will probably be found under Germany[.]' J.H.G.B. [John Henry Gibbs Bergne].

[103] *Dresdner Anzeiger*, 10 April 1887.

[104] The Duke of Edinburgh, Alfred, succeeded to the ducal throne of Saxe-Coburg and Gotha in 1893; his son Alfred was hereditary prince from 1893 until his early death in 1899.

[105] Strachey is referring to the news service of the Prussian *Literarisches Büro*. *Waschzettel* (literally 'laundry list', given here as 'washing bills') was the derisive name for semi-official information passed to the loyal press.

[106] Christian Karl Josias von Bunsen was Prussian envoy to London from 1842–1854.

FO 68/171 George Strachey to Marquess of Salisbury, No 30, Dresden, 29 April 1887

[Received 2 May by Berlin. Seen at Berlin. Print (Western Europe); S[alisbury]]

Schnæbelé affair in the German press

The Bismarckian press always welcomes every opportunity for pouring out the vials of their hatred and contempt on us. The 'Anzeiger',[107] alluding to the remarks of the 'Standard' on the Schnäbele affair, says: – "we do not desire, and we do not need, England's goodwill under any circumstances whatever.[108] For little states, like Egypt, Greece, Hayti, which cannot move, its possessions may have a value. In the councils of the great powers, the rôle of England, which was for long decisive, often the detriment of other nations, is played out. In case of another war with France, we shall know how to defend ourselves, and more energetically than before, against British benevolence, which in 1870–71, for it's own benefit, furnished our enemies with coals, arms, and military stores, and tried by backstair tricks to rob us of part of the fruits of our victories."

The article which I quote is probably derived from the Berlin 'National Liberal' lithographic circulars,[109] or it may have been inspired by one of the 'washingbills'[110] of the official Prussian 'Literary Bureau'.

The Conservative 'Nachrichten'[111] has been using language of similar import, arguing that the aim of England is to hound on France against Germany. This paper, like others, discusses the Schnäbele incident with moderation, observing that if German officials have committed international irregularities, the Government of the Empire will at once disavow them. The 'Nachrichten' remarks, that the circumstances connected with this policeman's arrest, and the hysterics into which it has thrown the Paris press, prove the relations of France and Germany to be in a state of tension such that war may at any moment arise from some utterly trivial incident. The "circonstances actuelles"[112] named as the ground of the prohibition of 'Lohengrin',[113] are assumed to indicate the fear, that the expected

---

[107] *Dresdner Anzeiger*, 26 April 1887.

[108] The editorial in the *Standard* of 23 April 1887 stated that 'unless the German authorities can clearly justify their action, public opinion throughout Europe will loudly condemn their proceedings'. For the Schnæbelé incident, see pp. 83–84.

[109] *Nationalliberale Korrespondenz*.

[110] See n. 105 in this section.

[111] *Dresdner Nachrichten*, 27 April 1887.

[112] French: 'present circumstances'.

[113] Strachey is referring to the *Dresdner Nachrichten* of 28 April 1887.

demonstration against the music of Wagner might be the signal for an outburst of Parisian fury against the 'Prussiens'.[114]

FO 68/171 George Strachey to Marquess of Salisbury, No 31, Dresden, 29 April 1887

[Received 2 May by Berlin. Seen at Berlin. See separate minute inside.[115] X]

Celebrations in honour of Saxon king's birthday; visit of Prussian Prince Wilhelm; Saxon Conservatives would prefer emperor's grandson as successor to imperial throne

The King's 59th birthday[116] was kept throughout Saxony with warm demonstrations of attachment to the sovereign and the dynasty. The German capacity for monarchical feeling is boundless, so that the new sentiment of devotion to the head of the Empire has not been developed at the cost of the local loyalty. Far from the recent commemoration of the Emperor's jubilee[117] having exhausted the popular disposition to do honour to such anniversaries, the customary homage to the domestic ruler was almost more strongly accentuated than in previous years.

Leipzig, which is nothing if not 'National-Liberal', and, a few years ago, used to be described by Dresden courtiers and officials as more Prussian than Saxon, was prominent in its' utterances of allegiance. The Germans are a servile people, and the respects and good wishes of the authorities and leading citizens of Leipzig were conveyed in terms of exaggerated submission.

The Royal family of Saxony maintain a cordial intimacy with the Court of Berlin, and on the 23rd Instant the King and the residence were agreeably surprised by the congratulatory visit of Prince William of Prussia, who was accompanied by the Hereditary Grand Duke and Duchess of Saxe-Meiningen.[118] An assembly held by Count Fabrice was attended by His Royal Highness, on whom the German nobility and conservatives build their hopes for the

---

[114] The first night of *Lohengrin* at the Paris Éden-Théâtre, scheduled for 26 April 1887, was postponed after the intervention of the French government. The only performance of the opera, originally scheduled for ten performances, took place on 5 May.

[115] Separate minute in FO 68/171 reads: 'Mr Strachey's No 31. Qy: 'Send this to the Queen – "The Germans are a servile people", see p. 3, may not be agreeable to H.M.' H.H. [Henry Hervey], 2 May. 'The Queen would not lose much by the suppression of this desp[atch].' T.V.L. [Thomas Villiers Lister]; 'I agree.' S[alisbury].

[116] On 23 April 1887.

[117] The emperor's 90th birthday was on 22 March 1887. See pp. 293–294.

[118] Bernhard and Charlotte.

political future. Their argument is, that it would be a happy day for Germany, if the Emperor William were succeeded by his grandson, whose tendencies and character promise a vigorous assertion of the prerogatives and authority of the Crown: while the accession of the Emperor's son would presumably be followed by a lamentable surrender to liberal demands, and by the intrusion of an influence known to be entirely antagonistic to Hohenzollern traditions and ideals.

FO 68/171 George Strachey to Marquess of Salisbury, No 34, Dresden, 13 May 1887

[Received 16 May by Berlin. Seen at Berlin. Qy: X / Mr Goschen; G.J.G. [George Joachim Goschen]; S[alisbury]]

German opinions on Irish Home Rule

The Chancellor of the Exchequer[119] is reported as having lately observed, that Home Rule for Ireland was deprecated by our continental friends, and desired by our ill-wishers, who foresaw the calamities which its adoption would entail on Great Britain.

This can scarcely be said of Germany. In the Empire we are objects of dislike, rather than of sympathy. And average German public opinion, in so far as British questions occupy it at all, is hostile to Home Rule in whatever edition, and favorable to the Crimes Bill.[120] Our ill-wishers are Unionists, not Home Rulers; whereas the German defenders of Home Rule are to be looked for amongst our friends.

The feelings of the majority towards us lie on the surface. They are visible, or audible, in society, in the oratory of the day, in the inspired and the independent press, in political and learned literature (particularly the historical,) and in the language of the representatives of commerce, industry, and colonial enterprise. In such quarters, the condemnation of Home Rule is, as far as I know, emphatic. 'Non sic fortis Etruria crevit'[121] is the judgment commonly passed on the long British toleration of Irish agitation and crime, which, with other circumstances of our recent history, is occasionally quoted by official scribes as a warning example of the political disintegration

---

[119] George Goschen made these comments on 4 May 1887 at a Unionist banquet held at the Bow and Bromley Institute in London.

[120] The disputed Irish crimes (coercion) bill, directed at the non-payment of rents, was introduced in parliament in March 1887 and became law on 19 July that year.

[121] Latin: 'not thus mighty Etruria grew' (Virgil, *Georgics*, Book II).

and collapse inseparable from democratic and parliamentary government.

On the other hand the 'freisinning' party,[122] who hold up British institutions and ideals for admiration here, may have betrayed a certain sympathy with the Parnell-Gladstone programme.[123] My knowledge of this point is not direct, but, unless I mistake, any liberal leanings that way are chiefly significant of the habit of the party to accept M[r] Gladstone's competence on such English questions of the day as are specifically domestic. Herr Richter and his following may desire the dissolution of the Union, (which I do not affirm) but their motives have not a malignant origin, and, if persuaded that Home-Rule would endanger the power and influence of the British Empire, they would become staunch Unionists.

FO 68/172: George Strachey to Marquess of Salisbury, No 41, Dresden, 26 June 1887

[Received 11 July by Berlin. X. See minute within][124]

Queen Victoria's Golden Jubilee celebrated by British community in Dresden

The British community in Dresden celebrated the Jubilee[125] by a Banquet at the Belvedere, which was attended by about 100 persons. The Consul and Vice Consul[126] of the United States were invited as guests, and several private Americans were present. There are some English artisans in the employ of a local Lace and Curtain Mill: on my expressing the wish that they could share in our festivity, the Directors at once furnished our countrymen with tickets for the dinner.

The following toasts were settled by the Committee, and proposed by me from the chair: the King of Saxony and the German Emperor: the Queen: Prince and Princess of Wales:[127] President of the United

---

[122] *Deutsche Freisinnige Partei.* See n. 3 in Berlin section.

[123] This is referring to the self-government of Ireland within the United Kingdom (home rule).

[124] Additional note (minute) to dispatch: 'The last sheet of this Despatch is peculiar. Shall it be marked and sent on to The Queen in the ordinary course.' [unclear initials], 4 July. 'Lord Salisbury, Shall Mr Strachey be called on to explain the last para[graph] of this peculiar Despatch? He perhaps refers to himself & his Vice Consul. If so I think the Crown is the real sufferer.' J.P. [Julian Pauncefote] 'Take no notice. It is not worth while sending on Mr. Strachey's despatches.' S[alisbury], 5 July.

[125] The 50th anniversary of Victoria's reign was on 20 June 1887.

[126] Joseph T. Mason and Wilhelm Knoop.

[127] Edward and Alexandra.

States[128] and his representatives: the ladies. The call to drink Her Majesty's health was received with unbounded enthusiasm: the cheering was vociferous and prolonged, and the National Anthem was sung with an accent and tunefulness which would have done credit to a professional chorus.

The dinner was followed by a dance. Before the close of the proceedings an Address to the Queen was read, and signatures were taken: this document will be forwarded hereafter.

As I am lodged on a 3rd floor, it was impossible to light up the exterior of the Legation, but a display of gas flames in appropriate devices was made on the pavement below.

Owing to peculiarities in the composition of our Dresden community, which, moreover, in summer shrinks to very small dimensions, the idea of a collective commemoration of the Jubilee was, at first, coldly received. A young Irish landlord,[129] who appears to be a Jacobite, declined to rejoice over the reign of a sovereign who had permitted the virtual confiscation of the property of the local landowners of Ireland!! Another recalcitrant was a strong English Conservative, who objected to meeting "mixed" society, even to do honour to the Queen! That the various difficulties of the situation were finally overcome, was chiefly owing to the loyal activity of two gentlemen not belonging to the higher social spheres – a tutor, and an engineer employed on the Dresden tramway – and to two persons more or less connected with the public service, from whom no such active interference was to be expected, as neither of them has had any reason to congratulate himself on the results of his employment under the Crown.

FO 68/172: George Strachey to Marquess of Salisbury, No 58, Dresden, 28 October 1887

[Received 31 October viâ Berlin. Qy: Commercial; Qy: Lord Salisbury / Circulate; C.M.K. [Charles M. Kennedy], 1 November; S[alisbury], 2 November]

Conversation with Nostitz on new German grain duties

Yesterday I asked Herr von Nostitz if he expected the new grain duties to pass the Reichstag.[130] His Excellency replied that,

---

[128] Grover Cleveland.

[129] The names of the remaining people referred to in the dispatch are not traceable.

[130] The grain tariff bill was introduced in the *Reichstag* on 1 December and passed on 17 December 1887.

abstractedly [*sic*] considered, there would be a majority against the augmentation.

But that if Prince Bismarck made it, so to speak, a personal question, his influence would, no doubt, carry the measure.

Herr von Nostitz did not say if the allied governments had decided on the particular figures which would be named in the Tariff 'Novel'; but he expressed his belief, that the duty on wheat would, in the end, be raised (from 3 Marks) to 5 Marks per double cwt, that is, from about 7^s/6^d to 12^s/ per quarter.

In the course of our conversation His Excellency observed, that he had a strong objection to food duties. Some years ago he had publicly committed himself to the opinion that they were inadmissible for Germany, and he could now only justify them as a temporary expedient calculated to give some little relief to the corn-growers. The question was not so vital in this kingdom as, for instance, in Pomerania. Still, not only his own class, that of the large landholders – but also the so-called 'peasant' proprietors of Saxony were clamorous for more protection against foreign cereals, and it was necessary to come, or seem to come, to their assistance.

I remarked that the growers would be fortunate if they pocketed half the additional tax, which would be a mere fraction of the amount requisite for making the price of corn renumerated. And this small advantage would vanish with the opening of a new railway in the Punjab, cheaper freights, or a fu[r]ther fall in the Rupee. Herr v. Nostitz, said there was no disputing that; but the higher duty would, no doubt, act for a time as a parachute to German corn prices.

FO 68/173: George Strachey to Marquess of Salisbury, No 7, Dresden, 2 February 1888

[Received 6 February by Berlin. For: The Queen / Prince of Wales / Mr Matthews; S[alisbury], 7 February]

Opinions on renewal of Anti-Socialist Laws; servility of public officials; repressive instincts of German public outweigh democratic notions of freedom of speech

No one who attaches precise meanings to words would speak of a German "public opinion" on the Bill against Social-Democracy; but I may say that the feeling is probably in favor of a simple renewal of the existing law.[131]

---

[131] The Anti-Socialist Law of 1878 (see n. 10 this section) was renewed for the fourth time on 17 February 1888 (effective until 30 September 1890).

The independent press of all parties denounces the banishment clause[132] as theoretically indefensible, and as calculated to aggravate class hatreds, and to turn agitators into martyrs. Doubts are expressed whether, in a country with the advanced political civilisation of Germany, a minority can be permanently kept under the gag of an exceptional law. While the question is raised, if there are, in fact, any visible signs of that efficacy in repressing Social-Democracy which persons in office profess to discover in the present system of proscription.

The mental servitude which is the mark of all Germans in public employments makes it impossible to allow any weight whatever to their views. Their rule is, to "say ditto to M[r] Burke"[133] as often and as loudly as possible. All of them profess belief in coercion, as being itself an admirable instrument of Government, and they declare in chorus that its results have, in the present case, been excellent. When the objection is raised, that under the law of 1878 the proscribed party has grown portentously in numbers and vigor, the reply is vaguely made that but for repression things would have been worse.

The Germans have little of our repugnance to silencing & persecuting obnoxious minorities, and far from persons of average enlightenment being unfavorable to the imposition of the restraints in question, there are many who would like the law against Social-Democracy to be extended so as to reach the left wing of the liberal party. I have no doubt that a plebiscite taken in Dresden would give a strong vote in favor of the banishment clause: according to an opinion given me by the President[134] of the lower house of the Saxon legislature, a majority of that body would possibly be on the same side. However, the head Burgomaster[135] of the city, who may be called a National-Liberal, considers that moderate men disapprove the idea of expatriation.

The general subject has been frequently illustrated in detail by the facts and figures given in my correspondence. These new discussions have confirmed me in my belief that the propaganda of Bebel and Liebknecht has had an active auxiliary in Prince Bismarck.

---

[132] The clause allowed the denaturalization of Social Democrats; it was rejected by the *Reichstag* on 17 February.

[133] This catchphrase had originated in an anecdote about Edmund Burke, meaning 'I agree'.

[134] Ludwig Haberkorn.

[135] Paul Alfred Stübel.

FO 68/173: George Strachey to Marquess of Salisbury, No 8, Dresden, 9 February 1888

[Received 13 February by Berlin. For: The Queen; S[alisbury], 14 February]

Incongruous reactions to Bismarck's speech in Reichstag

The moderation and sense of proportion for which the Germans are usually conspicuous, seem to have abandoned them since Monday last. Prince Bismarck's appearance in the Reichstag is described in superlatives which might be suitable for an account of the career of Alexander or Napoléon. Not only will the 6th of February "mark [*sic*] with the most noteworthy days in the annals of the fatherland", but it is to be "an epoch in the history of the world".[136]

The Reichskanzler has never possessed the physical or rhetorical conditions of eloquence, and the defects of his ejaculatory, uncouth, and prolix, style were as palpable on Monday as on some other occasions. Yet the current estimates of his speech are in the terms commonly reserved for the great masterpieces of ancient and modern oratory.

Within my horizon here, it is always hard to distinguish between real enthusiasm and the servile devotion of parasites. But the existence of genuine excitement is, no doubt, indicated by the circumstance that a number of leading personages, chiefly merchants and traders of Dresden, have appealed to their fellow citizens to join in an address of thanks and adhesion to Prince Bismarck: and that although the document itself has yet to be written, signatures, as it seems, are coming in by thousands.

The promoters describe themselves as "overpowered by the overwhelming effect of the world-historical speech of our Reichskanzler", and this is probably a fairly accurate account of the feelings of the public. There is a confused sense of something great having happened, but the anxieties of the community with respect to the preservation of peace do not appear to have been sensibly relieved. The prevalent estimate of the European situation is nearly what it was a week ago, except that there is now a dismissal of the doubts, entertained in some quarters, of the solidity of the alliance with Austria-Hungary,[137] which connexion is, on all grounds, highly popular here. If the public wish is decisive, a collision between Russia and the Monarchy of the

---

[136] Bismarck made the speech on the state of foreign affairs at the first reading of the military loan bill.

[137] See n. 489 in Berlin section.

Danube will be followed, whether a <u>casus foederis</u>[138] has arisen or not, by the armed interposition of Germany.

The Reichskanzler's review of the relations of Prussia and Germany, may possibly be comparable, as the Reptile-Press considers,[139] to the best pages of Thucydides or Ranke; but its' spirit is in some respects antagonistic to the national feeling. The new Germany does not possess the sensibilities of the age of Novalis and Fichte, but there exists in men's minds what is called an "ideal conception of the Universe", which involves something of that recognition of the rights and duties of nations, some of that sympathy with aspirations to independence and progress, which have been so prominent amongst ourselves.

Prince Bismarck's realistic, almost cynical, account of his attempts – defeated as it happened – to make Prussia or Germany, the international associate of Russia, shews his incapacity, or contempt, for the range of ideas in question. And many, even amongst German Conservatives, will ask if some of the dangers which now hang over Germany and Europe might not have been averted, if the Reichskanzler, and his predecessors, had not made it their object to qualify, as Prince Bismarck humorously puts it, for the highest Russian order in diamonds.

Similar remarks apply to the persistency with which the Bulgarians and their ruler are trampled under foot[140] – where the Prince is entirely out of touch with his countrymen. Curiously enough, the assertion that the Germans fear the Deity, has been much applauded by this highly agnostic nation.

FO 68/173: George Strachey to Marquess of Salisbury, No 10, Dresden, 2 March 1888

[Received 5 March by post. Qy: ~~The Queen / Berlin for perusal~~; Put by, S[alisbury], 5 March]

Press coverage and public views on German crown prince's illness and the succession; unpopularity of crown princess and anger towards Morell Mackenzie

The press continues to report on the health of the German Crown Prince[141] with an exuberance of painful pathological detail. But absolute reticence is observed, in respect to certain sides of this distressing

---

[138] Latin: 'an event or situation covered by the provisions of a treaty'.

[139] See n. 67 in this section.

[140] This is referring to Bismarck's refusal to recognize Ferdinand I as knyaz (prince) of Bulgaria.

[141] Friedrich Wilhelm; he was suffering from cancer of the larynx.

case which are the daily subject of conversation amongst all ranks of the community.

The current official formula is, that the Prince's illness has thrown the German people into deep affliction. This is only true with limitations. His Imperial Highness may, perhaps, be described as being beloved by the masses; but he is not popular with 'the classes' – being, in fact, the object of dislike of various degrees in many of the Courts, as well as in social and political circles by no means contemptible in influence and numbers.

Those whom I have in view are, no doubt, accessible to feelings of compassion, and the tragic personal aspects of the Prince's malady may draw from them the appropriate Lacrimæ rerum.[142] But, except in this temporary, sentimental, sense, they would not lament the close of a great career, and they would learn with equanimity, or satisfaction, that the reign of the Emperor was to be followed by that of his grandson.

Prince William may not impossibly disappoint the expectations of his partizans: he may be wanting in the wish, as he probably would be in the power, to carry out the reaction which, we are told, is to mark his accession to the throne of Prussia and Germany. Some of those who indulge such hopes, represent the Prince as placing himself in obtrusive hostility to the wishes and ideals of his parents, and as entertaining in particular, towards his august mother,[143] something of those feelings of filial impiety of which the domestic history of the Hohenzollerns offers several examples. According to certain German Conservatives, this reputed antagonism is, under the circumstances, almost meritorious.

The minority which can appreciate the character and talents of the Crown Princess is now nearly silenced by the party of detraction: it is certain that the unpopularity of Her Imperial Highness is extreme. I have even heard the opinion, that it would be very unadvisable for her to return to Berlin,[144] on account of the manifestations which might ensue.

The irritation against Sir M. Mackenzie has not diminished: professional Chauvinism has certainly augmented, or originated, the general anger against our specialist. He is arraigned as a quack, who should never have been consulted, and his systematic employment is called a national scandal and disgrace.[145]

---

[142] Latin: 'tears of things' (Virgil, *Aeneid*, 1.461).

[143] Victoria.

[144] At the time of the dispatch Victoria and Friedrich Wilhelm were staying at San Remo.

[145] For Friedrich Wilhelm's treatment by Mackenzie, see n. 103 in Munich section.

The above views and sentiments, with the malignant stories, or fables, by which they are illustrated, are not back-stair gossip. My information is always necessarily incomplete, but it is never obtained, as Gibbon puts it, 'from the scullions'.[146]

FO 68/173: George Strachey to Marquess of Salisbury, No 11, Dresden, 16 March 1888

[Received 19 March by Berlin. For: The Queen; S[alisbury], 20 March]

Reactions to emperor's death; Wilhelm I's significance in overcoming particularism

The Emperor's death has called forth in this city as much excitement and sympathy as could be expected amongst a race not notable for mobility or depth of feeling.[147] The public grief is not, of course, what it is in Berlin, but official and municipal pressure has imposed complete abstinence from amusements and entertainments, and there is a fair show of mourning, on the part, at least, of the female population of Dresden.

The press notices of the late Emperor are over-sycophantic, even for obituary literature. Much of their language would be only applicable to a ruler who was Solon, Cæsar, Alfred, and Charlemagne, combined. While ascribing to the Monarch achievements in war and peace which, both in conception and execution, were the work of the nation, or of his advisers and generals, the commentators on his life seem to have passed over the following point of view. Any one who was acquainted with Saxony – (and the same applies in various degrees to the other confederated states) – in the years immediately subsequent to the establishment of the new Germany, could see that the hostility of the so-called "enemies of the Empire" was largely mitigated by the conciliating character of His Imperial Majesty who, in later life, joined a certain mild dignity and natural benevolence to a manner of usual [note in margin: 'unusual?'] fascination. Advancing age, which (except in fiction), seldom adds to such advantages, augmented the amenities of the Emperor's individuality and conversation investing him with an irresistible interest and attraction. I have known the bitterness of local malignants (who were not accessible to sentiments of servility, or even of loyalty) melt away under the spell of the Emperor's

---

[146] Quotation ('from one of the scullions') from Edward Gibbon's *The History of the Decline and Fall of the Roman Empire*, Vol. 1, ch. 4 (1776).

[147] Wilhelm I died on 9 March 1888.

presence which, they said, almost reconciled them to the system of which he was the representative. The Empire would, no doubt, have continued to subsist under a less patriarchal and less venerable monarch. But, if the new order of things stands now, 18 years after its foundation, firmly built on the 'Rocher von Bronze',[148] this is in no small degree owing to the peculiar personality of the Emperor William, which was admirably in place as an antidote to the idiosyncrasy of the other principal author and support of German Unity, whose genius was constantly provocative of collisions and resentments calculated to retard the consolidation and development of the Empire.

FO 68/173: George Strachey to Marquess of Salisbury, No 12, Dresden, 30 March 1888

[Received 2 April by Berlin. S[alisbury], 2 April]

Commentary on the emperor's rescripts; Liberal disappointment over new emperor's policy

The comments on the Emperor Friedrich's rescripts continue, the various interpreters reading their own ideas and wishes into the monarch's expressions.[149] The Dresden 'Nachrichten' in which some slight remnant of the spirit of 'Particularism' may still survive, refines on certain distinctions (visible to the Editor)[150] in the Imperial language, according as the reference is to Germany or to Prussia. The Emperor, says the acute publicist, accentuates his relations to the representatives of the people; but the King lays strong emphasis on his Prerogative.

The Conservativism of this journal is often of uncertain sound. For instance, we read the hope that the new sovereign may give reality to the principles assimilated by him in his life as Crown-Prince, which are described as those of his own generation, and not those of his father's, who had one foot planted on the basis of the old autocratic Prussia.

The alleged disappointment, and stifled anger, of the liberal party, at the Emperor's apparent adhesion to the old grooves, furnish the Conservatives with a text for daily vituperation of their opponents.

---

[148] French phrase used in the German language: 'rock of bronze', allegory for the strength and sovereignty of the monarchy, first used by Friedrich Wilhelm I in 1716.

[149] Strachey is referring to the imperial rescript to Otto von Bismarck of 12 March 1887 (see pp. 95–98), the rescript for Alsace-Lorraine of 15 March, and the rescript of 21 March on the participation of the crown prince in the affairs of government.

[150] Julius Reichardt.

Surely, plain words like "maintenance of the authority of the Crown", ought to convince the "freisinnige"[151] of the folly of their absurd expectations that "the Kaiser would abdicate a portion of his sovereign rights, and exert his influence to establish Parliamentary Government".

And on another occasion: – "Fortunately, realities are stronger than" the vain imaginings of these people. What Kaiser Friedrich has promised, will prevail: he walks in the paths of his venerable Father, and does not dismiss the true councillor of the throne to make room for the obedient servants of the International High-Finance. Prince Bismarck may be "trusted to preserve the firm structure of the Prussian Monarchy from the contamination of "English principles". Such allusions to the Empress[152] are frequent: the following hint is less covert: – "With England our Empire is now so nearly connected, that many a German patriot begins to apprehend an excess of English influence".

The assumed mortification of the adverse party may be a suitable peg for these diatribes, which, however, are often open to retort. As a matter of fact, the only visible, or audible, signs of dissatisfaction with the present conjuncture, have come from the Conservatives and the Aristocracy, who are chagrined that the Imperial Crown, contrary to expectations, has fallen to the object of their aversion, while the hopes which they had built on their Marcellus[153] are, for the present at least, deferred.

FO 68/173: George Strachey to Marquess of Salisbury, No 20, Dresden, 27 April 1888

[Received 30 April by Berlin. Qy: X; S[alisbury], 1 May]

Attacks of the Grenzboten *on Queen Victoria and her daughter; German reactions to Queen's visit to Berlin; 'grave-digger' party may be preparing a new political approach*

The article in the Bismarckite 'Grenzboten', headed "Foreign influences in the Empire",[154] was aimed, not only at the Queen, but also at the Empress Victoria. This sarcasm is characteristic. "Her discussions with Prince Bismarck appear to have chiefly turned on money and

---

[151] See n. 3 in Berlin section.

[152] Victoria.

[153] Marcus Claudius Marcellus, who, before his death, was considered presumptive heir of Emperor Augustus. Strachey is referring to Crown Prince Wilhelm.

[154] 'Fremde Einflüsse im Reiche', *Die Grenzboten: Zeitschrift für Politik, Literatur und Kunst*, 19 April 1888.

property questions, which appear to have a special interest for the High Lady". Again: – "the Empress has up to now remained an English woman in a foreign country, and it is a question if she attaches more value to the dignity of German Empress than to the title of Princess Royal of England".

This week the "gravedigger" party[155] is comparatively silent. The 'Anzeiger' is neutral: the semi-official 'Journal' is principally concerned about Rumania and General Boulanger. The 'Nachrichten' continues to mutter distrust of British machinations, but has now spoken in becoming terms of the Queen, pointing out, however, that Prince Bismarck might be trusted to foil any new intrigues, and hinting that the time-table of the royal train was altered on account of the presumed hostility of the local public to the mother of the Empress.[156]

Both the arrival and the visit to Berlin presented different aspects, according as the observer, or writer, was a Conservative, or a 'freisinnig'[157] partizan. The 'Nachrichten' could record a fair reception, and was much struck by the crowd's approval of the Sikhs,[158] and of Her Majesty's dog. Whereas the liberal 'Zeitung' reported, that the hopes of the disloyal faction had been utterly disappointed, the Queen having been received with an enthusiastic and affectionate welcome.

A Berlin 'reptile[']'[159] has been expatiating, on "the singularly touching and devoted love of Prince Bismarck for his all-highest master", with which 'the faithful servant is bowed down when in dumb grief he approaches the Kaiser's bed of suffering.'

The interpretation of this may be, that the Bismarckian parties are beginning to contemplate the possibility of the Emperor's recovery, and are preparing for a change of front.

The "Grenzboten" article has been ascribed by liberals to Dr Roessler, the Director of the official Prussian "Literary Bureau", popularly called "Press Bureau".[160] The 'gravediggers'[161] have hinted that the author is Dr Treitschke, the German Macaulay: the Professor is a violent Anglophobe, but the article is not in his vivid, ornate, style. Both suggestions are probably 'tendentious'.

---

[155] National Liberals.
[156] Victoria visited Berlin from 24 to 26 April 1888 on her return journey from Italy.
[157] *Deutsche Freisinnige Partei*. See n. 3 in Berlin section.
[158] Victoria's servants Abdul Karim and Mohammad Buksh.
[159] An organ of the so-called 'reptile press', see n. 67 in this section.
[160] The author of the article was, on Bismarck's instruction, Moritz Busch.
[161] National Liberals.

FO 68/173: George Strachey to Marquess of Salisbury, No 28, Dresden, 1 June 1888

[Received 4 June in Berlin. Qy: Put by; S[alisbury], 4 June]

Ramifications of libellous article 'No petticoat government' published in Dresdner Nachrichten

Herr Eugen Richter's Philippic in the Prussian Landtag[162] against the authors, avowed and veiled, of the Bismarckite libels on the Imperial Family, and the Prussian prosecutions of certain newspapers for republishing, with the expressions of their disapproval, the article from the 'Dresdner Nachrichten' – 'No petticoat Government'[163] – has made the Dresden Editor the hero of the day. D[r] Bierey is much elated at his 'bad eminence', and he is now vituperating the 'freisinnig'[164] leader with the ferocity which has always been so characteristic of Germany [*sic*] personal discussions.

D[r] Bierey[165] has further raked up afresh the whole conflict, which he has restated with new insults to the Emperor and Empress. He says, that having read over his article – 'Down with Petticoat Government' – he fails to understand why it should have excited so much attention and criticism. The article was moderation itself, and elicited a whole library of letters of approval from all parts of the world! "It was the simple, though fresh, expression of the feelings which, at the time, moved countless German hearts. The resignation of the Reichskanzler was threatened on account of a Bulgarian marriage.[166] We gave utterance to the demand of the nation that the new Emperor should not separate himself from the most approved of councillors." He says further: "at present everything has to be englished [*sic*] – even the royal hounds – although the process gives them the mange" (the reference is to a report that the dogs in the Potsdam kennel had caught disease from some English animals.)

Here I would remark, that to designate a lady as a 'Frauenzimmer' is a gross violation of the proprieties of German speech, and that this insult was assocated with the allusion to the Emperor as 'Friedrich der Britte'.[167] There is a peculiar infamy in the term 'Bulgarian marriage', from the fact that 'Bulgaren-Hochzeit' is necessarily suggestive to Germans of the 'Bluthochzeit', or S[t] Bartholomew.

---

[162] On 26 May 1888.
[163] '*Keine Frauenzimmerpolitik*', published on 11 April 1888. For the 'Bismarckite libels', see previous dispatch.
[164] *Deutsche Freisinnige Partei*. See n. 3 in Berlin section.
[165] In his leader of 1 June 1888.
[166] See pp. 99–100.
[167] Pun: *Britte* (Brit), instead of *Dritte* (third)

I may be allowed to observe, that it is a satisfaction to me that my previous correspondence on this topic should have been, in a sense, anticipatory of many of the statements and arguments in the speech of the German 'Cleon', or 'Catiline',[168] such is the last Bismarckite description of a public man as Conservative as any member of Her Majesty's Government.

[...]

P.S. I find on reviewing Dr Bierey's language that my description on page 2 is altogether insufficient. Going by the rule 'be Kent unmannerly when Lear is mad'[169] – I should substitute for 'ferocity' – 'unmitigated blackguardism' which is not too strong for the occasion. G.S.

FO 68/173: George Strachey to Marquess of Salisbury, No 30, Dresden, 21 June 1888

[Received 25 June by Berlin. X; S[alisbury]]

Remarks on the German Emperor's manifesto to the army

The "undisguised spirit of medieval militarism" which the 'Standard'[170] detects in the manifesto of William II to the Army[171] has not been observed here. The antecedents and tastes of the young ruler made it natural that his official utterances should accentuate the military side of sovereignty, and I do not believe that, even amongst those most disposed to put ill constructions on his words, the manifesto has been criticized for excessive self-assertion, or for professional elation, or that it has been construed as a warning to foreign powers.

The suspicion has certainly not arisen, that Germany will now be 'less anxious than before to avoid quarrels.' The predominant desire of all classes is, that war may be averted. Even the military are pacific, being, as the "nation in arms", destitute of the aggressive instincts proper to a body of Mamertines or Mamelukes.[172] The public expect

---

[168] Cleon became leader of Athenian democracy in 429 BC; he was a politician without noble ancestry and spoke out strongly against the conservatives. Catiline was a Roman senator who promoted the plight of the plebs and attempted to overthrow the Roman Republic and the elite power of the Senate in 63 BC.

[169] William Shakespeare, *King Lear*, Act 1, Scene 1.

[170] *The Standard*, 18 June 1888.

[171] Imperial proclamation to the army, 16 June 1888.

[172] Mamertines were Italian mercenaries who seized the Sicilian city of Messina in 288 BC. Mamluks were members of a military caste with Turkish, Mongol and Circassian slave heritage; they remained powerful in Ottoman Egypt until 1811.

of the Emperor that he will adhere to the conciliatory policy of the preceding reigns, and William II will fall into great unpopularity if this hope is disappointed.

No unfavorable remarks have been made on the Proclamation to the Prussians.[173] In an address to an agnostical people, coming from a quarter not credited with puritanical observance of the personal sanctities of life, pious avowals, and repeated invocations of the Deity, may seem out of place. But such pretences are not displeasing to German taste. Some have welcomed the Emperors language as evidence that he sympathizes with the orthodox camarilla which his august father had in such deep abhorrence. On the whole, the manifesto is thought to be suited to the occasion, and it's religious element is taken for the traditional phraseology of the Hohenzollern's, who have usually "particularized", as has been said, or appropriated, the Supreme Being, for the exclusive benefit of the Prussian house and nation.

FO 68/173: George Strachey to Marquess of Salisbury, No 33, Dresden, 29 June 1888

[Received 2 July by Berlin. Qy: X; S[alisbury]]

Press speculations on omission of England from German Emperor's throne speech

It is characteristic of the German press, that although the Emperor's speech[174] was circulated here in the early afternoon of Monday, the principal journals refrained from comments until the evening of the following day, or till Wednesday. By a very curious coincidence – suggestive of a common source of inspiration – the ultra-Bismarckite National-Liberal 'Anzeiger',[175] and the independent Conservative 'Nachrichten',[176] were simultaneously surprised to find that the speech made no reference to Great Britain. The 'Anzeiger' remarked, that the mystery would probably be unveiled in time. "That special negotiations are in process between Berlin and London is proved by the prolonged presence of the Prince of Wales,[177] and the despatch of confidential persons from each capital to the other. The nature of these negotiations is not quite known, and we are reduced to surmises".

---

[173] Proclamation of 18 June 1888.
[174] Speech from the throne on the occasion of the opening of the *Reichstag* on 25 June 1888.
[175] *Dresdner Anzeiger*, 27 June 1888.
[176] *Dresdner Nachrichten*, 27 June 1888.
[177] Edward arrived at Berlin on 17 June and returned to London on 25 June.

The allusion is to the current story of the removal of the Emperor Frederick's papers by the Queen.[178] According to the Bismarckite organs, General Winterfeldt was to be instructed to demand possession of the documents improperly appropriated, and it was added, in the new German fashion of speaking of Great Britain as if we were Venezuela or Zanzibar, that on this point the Reichskanzler might be trusted to allow no trifling. In the view of the 'Anzeiger', the displeasure of Germany was signified by the omission of our name from the Throne Speech.

The "Nachrichten" apparently refers to the same story, but is principally concerned to find a new opportunity for casting aspersions on the Royal objects of its hatred. That paper says: "we do not regret that England is ignored, for have not we Germans lately had much from England to fill us with rage? At any rate there is no danger that under Kaiser Wilhelm English policy will be allowed the influence and pressure on German interests which Great Britain had begun to claim as a matter of right. England knows now that Germany is governed by A <u>MAN</u>, who has the will to assert his own resolves, and knows no object but the greatness and welfare of his "<u>GERMAN</u> fatherland."

I do not believe that the general public had discovered these inner meanings in the omissions of the Imperial Speech. The strong recognition of the alliance with Austria has given satisfaction in this kingdom, where the connexion with the Danubian Monarchy[179] gratifies traditional feelings. The Prussian speech has made a good impression in Saxony: in Dresden a somewhat more Conservative tone would have been approved.

FO 68/173: George Strachey to Marquess of Salisbury, No 35, Dresden, 2 July 1888

[Received 5 July by post. Qy: Put by; X; C.B.R. [Charles B. Robertson]; S[alisbury]]

Reception at Pillnitz castle for Saxon king upon his return from the opening of the Reichstag

The King's presence at the opening of the Reichstag[180] having struck some citizens of this capital as an important historical event, arrangements were made to offer His Majesty an ovation on his return from

---

[178] The documents in question included Friedrich III's diaries, which had already been transferred to Windsor before his death.

[179] Austria-Hungary.

[180] On 25 June 1888.

Berlin.[181] The initiative was taken by the leader of the Conservative Bismarckites,[182] and the Chief Burgomaster of Dresden,[183] under whose guidance some hundred, or thousand, delegates from the Corporations, Institutions, & Societies, of the residence proceeded in steamers to Pillnitz, where they were met by the King in front of the Château.

The Burgomaster delivered a short address, which (1) dwelt 'on the joy of the German people, and of the universe, at the new Emperor's determination to walk in the ways of his grandfather, which had led Germany to the highest pitch of sublimary honour' and (2) 'with loud jubilees hailed the demonstration just given to the world that the King's fidelity to Kaiser and Reich was immoveable, and that His Majesty was united to the new Monarch by the ties both of duty and of cordial friendship.'

The King replied, shortly, that the greeting of the deputations was very gratifying to him, and that he was well satisfied to learn, that the step which he felt it his duty to take, was approved by the citizens of the Residence.

The Royal answer was received with immense enthusiasm by the delegates and the assembled crowd, when the party returned to Dresden, accompanied by various marks of popular approval as they descended the River.

The local public have ascribed a cosmic grandeur to this affair, and "the note of Provincialism" has been absurdly conspicuous in the gorgeous tropes and hyperboles applied by the press to the scenery, incidents, and personalities involved. The whole proceeding has, however, a value, as illustrating the fact that the 'Particularism' of Saxony, which some years ago was still so active, has been superseded by a genuine national German sentiment. The old "enemies of the Empire" are now, for the most part, its friends, and although there is no sign that loyalty to the local Sovereign is evaporating, indications are frequent that the King's reputed patriotism as a German Prince now constitutes one of his most effective claims on the attachment of his subjects.

Regrets were expressed that the proceedings were seriously deranged by stormy weather; and regrets were also expressed that the storms were not hurricanes, such as to cause the omission of this new 'Declaration of Pillnitz'[184] – a point on which it would not

---

[181] Albert returned on 27 June.

[182] Heinrich von Friesen-Rötha.

[183] Paul Alfred Stübel.

[184] Strachey is referring to the joint declaration of 1791 in which Leopold II and Friedrich Wilhelm II supported Louis XVI against the French Revolution.

be right to enlarge here. Today's 'Anzeiger', copying the 'Kölnische Zeitung', calls the presence of the Sovereigns at the opening of the Reichstag "a voluntary, almost improvised, act," – a characteristic "gravedigger"[185] falsehood.

FO 68/173: George Strachey to Marquess of Salisbury, No 45, Dresden, 19 October 1888

[Received 22 October by post. X; S[alisbury]]

Press reactions to published extracts of Friedrich III's diary; Bismarckian press contemptuous; Saxons tend not to deviate from official Bismarckian view

In the Bismarckian levy of bucklers of last spring against the German Emperor and Empress, the Leipzig 'National-Liberal' 'Grenzboten' was conspicuous for its' scurrility and zeal. I quoted at the time from that periodical a mendacious and vulgar libel on the Empress and the Queen.[186] Being eager, as it seems, to rival the 'Kölnische Zeitung' in sudden tergiversation, the 'Grenzboten' has just turned its' back upon itself in the following manner.

On the appearance of the Emperor Frederick's Diary,[187] it said: "We do not doubt, as some do, the complete authenticity of the Diary, or the contributors' right to make extracts and publish them."[188]

But after the issue of Prince Bismarck's Rescript[189] the 'Grenzboten'[190] wrote: – Very many readers, ourselves amongst the number, did not and could not believe in the authenticity of the "Rundschau publications" &c &c.

Prince Bismarck's parasites in the local press have gone on ringing the changes on his arguments, clamouring against D[r] Geffcken and his English backers, and boycotting the considerations in the late Emperor's favour which some Conservatives have so effectively set forth. Even the Dresden semi-official organ[191] abstains from saying

---

[185] National Liberals.

[186] See pp. 308–309.

[187] On 20 September the *Deutsche Rundschau* – without authorization – published extracts of Friedrich III's diary written during the Franco-Prussian War.

[188] *Die Grenzboten: Zeitschrift für Politik, Literatur und Kunst*, 27 September 1888.

[189] In his report to Wilhelm II of 23 September, Bismarck questioned the authenticity of the diary but nevertheless advised prosecuting the *Deutsche Rundschau*. This report and Bismarck's letter to the Prussian minister for justice of 25 September, in which the latter was instructed to act accordingly, were published on 27 September 1888.

[190] *Die Grenzboten: Zeitschrift für Politik, Literatur und Kunst*, 11 October 1888.

[191] *Dresdner Journal*.

a word in deprecation of the current of obloquy now pouring forth under high auspices against that noble Prince, who, for anything which the 'Journal' suggests, might have been a selfish, mischievous, ruler of the later Lancaster or Valois type.

The exalted virtues of the Emperor Frederick, have, of course, their appreciators, even in this Conservative Kingdom. But the majority are seemingly indifferent to his memory, and appear to acquiesce in the official view. The typical North German, or Saxon, is incapable of judging politics for himself. Unless Prince Bismarck's declared opinions, or wishes, run counter to some plain local interests, to dispute them passes here for sacrilege. The sense of his superiority and of his vindictiveness, have brought a naturally servile race to behave in the 19th Century as if they were under the eye of Tiberius or Alva.

FO 68/173: George Strachey to Marquess of Salisbury, No 46, Dresden, 19 October 1888

[Received 22 October by post. X; S[alisbury]]

Continued attacks on Morell Mackenzie amongst the press and public; base style of German political writing

The publication of Sir M. Mackenzie's book[192] could not fail to give rise to a fresh outburst of the Chauvinism, the contempt of England, and hatred of 'the interregnum',[193] of which Dresden is a hotbed. 'Impostor', 'Knave', 'liar', and the other affronts of the Prussian 'reptiles',[194] have been repeated by the 'Cartel' parties[195] here, with new expletives and aggravations of local coining. In these debates it has, from first to last, been a principal object of their original author, and of his parasites, to extract from the controversy means of throwing odium on the 'freisinnige';[196] who are now overwhelmed with fresh insults and accusations on the ground of their participation in the intrigues of the English quack and his crew, and their sympathy with the phantoms which haunted the unhinged mind of the intrusive Hohenzollern. It is in harmony with the rest of the

---

[192] *The Fatal Illness of Frederick the Noble* (1888); the German edition (enclosure to dispatch) was published as *Friedrich der Edle und seine Ärzte* (1888) on 14 October und subsequently confiscated by the Prussian authorities.

[193] Friedrich III reigned from 9 March to 15 June 1888.

[194] See n. 67 in this section.

[195] See n. 208 in Berlin section.

[196] *Deutsche Freisinnige Partei*. See n. 3 in Berlin section.

Bismarckite indictment of Herr Richter and they that are now charged with stealing the late Emperor's cypher by favour of Sir M. Mackenzie.[197]

I have no doubt that our specialist is generally regarded as a mere impostor and that even apart from his supposed inferiority in diagnosis and manipulation to the native practitioners, his employment has been deeply offensive to German popular instincts. It has been remarked to me that, in like circumstances, the intervention of a foreign doctor would arouse very angry feelings amongst ourselves, and I have replied that in such case we should, at any rate be observant of those decencies of criticism which have been so lamentably forgotten here. However, brutality in discussion is an old German vice, and it is, perhaps, inseparable from that personal infirmity of temper which is so characteristic of the greater part of the race. As regards the press, what Lord Beaconsfield, if I remember right, called "a want of finish in invective",[198] will hardly be corrected as long as editors and writers are derived from the lower social strata, and, in accordance with German Laws of caste, are excluded from association with their betters.

FO 68/173: George Strachey to Marquess of Salisbury, No 48, Dresden, 2 November 1888

[Received 5 November by Berlin. Commercial Department to see; S[alisbury]]

On the semantics of Hamburg's 'incorporation' into the Zollverein

The mendacity of the German 'Cartel'[199] press being what it is, when the topics of the day are under debate, the history of events at a little distance is naturally written by them with wholesale perversions of fact. The incorporation of Hamburg in the Zollverein has given the 'inspired' journals an opportunity for almost surpassing themselves.[200] They have been gravely relating, that this arrang[e]ment was the result of a domestic movement for commercial annexation to Germany, which grew up in the Free City, where the conviction had arisen

---

[197] The Foreign Office cipher book was found in the *Kronprinzenpalais* (crown prince's palace) at the end of October.

[198] 'There is great vigour in his invective, and no want of vindictiveness. I admit that now speaking as a critic, and perhaps not as an impartial one, I must say I think it wants finish.' Beaconsfield, House of Commons Debate, 3 April 1868. This remark was addressed to Salisbury.

[199] See n. 208 in Berlin section.

[200] Hamburg, as agreed in the treaty with the German Empire of 25 May 1881, entered into the Customs Union on 15 October 1888.

that the time was come when the interests of Hamburg required that her exceptional position in the Empire should terminate.

Accordingly the Government of the city opened negotiations with the Imperial authorities, who acceded to their desire, and laid before the Federal Council the plan of the settlement completed this week.

All this is fable. There was no spontaneous local call whatever for the incorporation, which was forced upon the city by Prince Bismarck. The Reichskanzler was of opinion, that the Hanseatic merchants had hitherto pursued personal interests only, but, that if their fiscal isolation ceased, their wealth would be partly diverted from the Hamburg transit trade, and the special refining and finishing manufactures of the Free-Port, into the channel of general German business. So much was the Prince impressed by the importance of this idea, that after his preliminary suggestions of 1879 were declined by the senate of Hamburg, he inaugurated a series of coercive measures, commencing with a new interpretation of the Elbe Navigation-Act,[201] which with other reprisals drove the city into compliance in 1881. The incorporation was very unpopular in Hamburg, (except with the so-called 'Prussian' party there), and it was only under continuous pressure and threats that the Senate accepted the required accession to the Zollverein by a slight majority of votes. In all this there was nothing particularly discreditable, the fact that Hamburg was more or less terrorized was no secret, and it is not clear why the transaction should be related in travesty now.

FO 68/173: George Strachey to Marquess of Salisbury, No 51, Dresden, 9 November 1888

[Received 12 November by Berlin. For: African Department / X; H.P.A. [Henry Percy Anderson]; S[alisbury], 12 November]

Dr Peters's speech on Germany's role in Africa; views on German cooperation with Britain

Dr Peters has been lecturing here,[202] before the Conservative Society, on the events on the Zanzibar coast.[203] After enlarging historically on those transactions, from knowledge or otherwise, Dr Peters

---

[201] Strachey is referring to the incorporation of Altona and the Elbe River below Hamburg into the customs territory, in May and June 1880.

[202] On 5 November in the Dresden *Tivolisaal*.

[203] In his talk Peters discussed the Abushiri revolt, an uprising which had occurred in consequence of the Sultan of Zanzibar leasing areas on the East African coast to the German East Africa Company.

investigated "the psychological connection" between the movement of the Mahdi and that of Tippu-Tipp, which last was the result of Stanley's explorations on the Congo. This new Mahometan efferves-cence is only a particular case of the great 'world-historic' struggle of the crescent and the Cross; the power of Emin Pacha is the wall that prevents the seed of European culture being submerged by the con-verging floods of Arab invasion.[204]

D[r] Peters dilated on the horrors of African slavery and slave-hunts, arguing that Europe must interfere, and that Emin Pacha must be res-cued by an expedition in which Stanley's blunders would, of course, be avoided. England, it might be hoped, would in her own interest, be moved to cooperate. The hegemony in the battle of the culture of Christendom against the un-culture of Africa devolves on Germany.

This was followed by a climax in the style of self-assertion which is so fashionable here now. "Germany, the foremost power of Europe, must plant the banner of civilisation in Africa. A higher power has reserved to us the task of kindling in the desert the taper of culture. We are persuaded that the worthiest of our people are with us, and that we must conquer for the good of the African world, and of Germany."

The "African party" here is very numerous, and cooperation with England would be popular, on the assumption that we should be a convenient catspaw. Politically speaking, an actual joint enterprise would be deprecated, and no Englishman who can gauge the preva-lent German feeling towards us would desire to see Great Britain and Germany in any closer alliance for African objects than that just described by Your Lordship.[205]

The naval men of this Empire are full of professional conceit: they look on our ships, crews, and captains as distinctly inferior to their own: The individual sensitiveness, and the various irascible constitu-ents of the national character, are only partly quenched by discipline. Adding the personal temper to the political, there would be very imperfect cordiality, on their part towards our officers, who, in my

---

[204] At the time of the dispatch the Eastern Congo territory (part of the Congo Free State) was de facto ruled by an elite of Swahili-Arab merchants and local allies. In 1887, thanks to Henry Morton Stanley, the Swahili-Arab merchant Hamed bin Mohamed el Murjebi (alias Tippu Tip) had been appointed governor of the Stanley Falls district. Tippu Tip had also agreed to supply the Emin Pasha Relief Expedition intended to release Emin Pasha (Eduard Schnitzer), who, as governor of the Egyptian province of Equatoria, was besieged by Mahdist forces. At the time of Peters's speech, contradictory news about the fate of the expedition was in circulation. In fact, it had already met with Emin Pasha who initially refused to leave Equatoria.

[205] In his speech in the House of Lords, on 6 November 1888, Salisbury referred to the Anglo-German co-operation with regard to the slave and arms trade in East Africa.

belief, would find in Russians, Italians, or even Frenchmen, more unassuming and less captious comrades.

FO 68/173: George Strachey to Marquess of Salisbury, No 55, Dresden, 23 November 1888

[Received 3 December by Berlin. X; Seen by Lord Salisbury]

Reactions to the emperor's speech in Breslau

Although deep satisfaction has been caused to the Conservatives and National-Liberals by the Emperor's public expression at Breslau of his antipathy to the politicians whose present distinctive mark is their reverence for his parents, the allies are now quarrelling over their respective interpretations of the Imperial oratory.[206] Whether in the press, or in the highest departments of literature and science, the Germans have always been brutal in controversy, and in this instance some of the usual amenities are being exchanged between the confederates so artificially joined by a common hatred and a common enslavement. Each party pretends to monopolize the sympathies avowed in the Breslau speech, stigmatizing the rival claimants to the favour of the Crown with terms like 'liars', 'hypocrites', 'hacks', 'lickspittles', (*sic*), and otherwise vituperating them in the characteristic Bismarckian style.

The discussion is Prussian, not Saxon; but the local feeling, in so far as any independent political opinions can be said to exist here at all, is anti-Frederician,[207] and is therefore gratified by an incident which aggravates a 'freisinnig'[208] defeat. However, it has never been customary here to go to the poll with the cry, just heard in Prussia, of "vote for the king", and many Bismarckites appear to doubt whether in the present age it is desirable for a monarch to adopt the style of an electioneering agent. The question has also been asked, if an Emperor and King ought to have descended to the personal rudeness of making the Burgomaster of Breslau the medium for publishing the royal antipathy to the party to which that civic dignitary belongs.[209]

---

[206] On 16 November 1888 Wilhelm II, upon his reception of deputations of the Evangelical and Catholic workers' associations at Breslau, expressed his satisfaction at the result of the elections to the Prussian chamber of deputies, which had taken place on 6 November.

[207] Strachey is referring to the late Friedrich III.

[208] See n. 3 in Berlin section.

[209] On 16 November Ferdinand Friedensburg, on the emperor's instruction, notified the public that the emperor was content with the 'excellent' elections at Breslau.

Even the 'Nachrichten' abandons on this occasion its complimentary manner, remarking that it has been an easy task for the opposition
press to draw comparisons between the reigning Emperor and King
Frederick William IV of Prussia, who, in the period of Reaction,
used to travel about hectoring, or complimenting, the local authorities
on the results of the elections. The Editor[210] expresses his grave doubts
of the propriety of these royal interferences with the exercise of the
electoral function, saying, with a tinge of sarcasm, that as, according
to Count Douglas, the Emperor considered it his duty to stand
above parties, he must have had solid grounds for the remarkable
departure from his own rule just witnessed in the Breslau incident.

The organ of the municipality, the 'Anzeiger', has reported the
Breslau speech without comment. It reprinted, yesterday, an article
from a Berlin 'reptile',[211] which enlarges on the grandeur of the
Emperor's individuality in language of which the following sentence
is a sufficient sample. "It is his will himself to guide the new era on its
destined road, and to impress it with its distinctive character".

FO 68/174: George Strachey to Marquess of Salisbury, No 5, Dresden, 19 January 1889

[Received 24 January viâ Vienna. X; S[alisbury]]

Germans politically credulous; developments in Morier incident

This nation is in a fever of political credulity similar to the infatuation
of our ancestors on the announcement of the Rye House Plot,[212] or to
the panics which seized on the Parisians at the beginning of the
Revolution.[213] Any loose report published under 'reptile'[214] auspices
in Cologne or Berlin, any libel circulated 'par ordre du mufti',[215] however augmented by such new turpitudes as local mendacity may suggest, at once obtains credence with millions of dupes. The minority
that disbelieves, or doubts, shrinks from open dissent: criticism of
Bismarckian policy, acts, or words, being only whispered, or hinted
in sarcasms and shrugs. Men are in dread of tale-bearers, and they

---

[210] Julius Reichardt.

[211] For the 'reptile' press, see n. 67 in this section.

[212] The Rye House Plot of 1683 was a failed conspiracy to assassinate the pro-Catholic
King Charles II and his brother (the future James II).

[213] French Revolution of 1789.

[214] See n. 67 in this section.

[215] Humorous German figure of speech of French origin: 'by order of the mufti', i.e. by
order of the superior and in this case by order of Bismarck.

are intimidated by the real or fancied consequences of those denunciations for 'treason to the Empire', or complicity in foreign and Frederician intrigues,[216] which are so characteristic a feature of the new Germany.

Sometimes a sudden reflux of feeling occurs, when the assertion is calmly made that the rejected fable had never been current, except in the columns of those infamous journals which are sustained by Jewish and English gold. That this has happened in the case of the Morier incident, has been already reported by me, and I now beg to draw attention to the following surprising paragraphs from the Conservative 'Correspondence for Germany'[217] which exonerate the Ambassador on an entirely new ground, and reopen an old chapter of Bismarckian revilement of England.

'It is gross disloyalty of the representative of a power in friendly relations with the country where he resides to communicate with that country's enemy. But Morier was not in this position. "For England, in 1870, was not a power friendly to us." (spaced in orig.) Had Germany been defeated early in the war,[218] England might with propriety have joined the anti-German coalition. So little did England affect neutrality, that the war office sold guns with the Tower-Mark to the French Government. This is proved by the Memoirs of Count Palikao,[219] and the Protocols of the French National Assembly. In the latter we read, as amplified – "the treaty with M^r van der Weyer, otherwise the English Ministry of War, was concluded by the French Embassy in London".[220] Such was the feeling in England in 1870, and the sentiments of the Court were similar, all forced interpretations of the Queen's Diary[221] notwithstanding.'

The above (condensed) is from the National Liberal 'Anzeiger',[222] which is owned by the municipality of this capital.

[…]

---

[216] See pp. 111–113 and pp. 316–317.

[217] Strachey mistakes the party news sheet *Conservative Correspondenz* for the National Liberal newspaper *Der Korrespondent von und für Deutschland* which is quoted in the dispatch. For the Morier incident, see pp. 114–115.

[218] Franco-Prussian War, 1870–1871.

[219] *Un Ministère de la Guerre de vingt-quatre jours, du 10 août au 4 septembre 1870 par le général Cousin de Montauban comte de Palikao* (Paris, 1871).

[220] This is referring to the treaties drawn up between Great Britain and Prussia (9 August 1870) and between Great Britain and France (11 August 1870) relative to the independence and neutrality of Belgium.

[221] *Der Korrespondent von und für Deutschland* was referring to extracts of Queen Victoria's diary from 1870, which had been quoted by the liberal weekly *Die Nation*.

[222] *Dresdner Anzeiger*, 17 January 1889.

P.S.: The statement of Prince Soms-Braunfels is going through the papers, and the respectable 'Anzeiger' is not ashamed to print in large spaced letters, the insinuation that the question of the forgery is still sub judice.

FO 68/174: George Strachey to Marquess of Salisbury, No 7, Dresden, 30 January 1889

[Received [undated] by Vienna. X; S[alisbury]]

Laudatory press articles about the emperor to mark his birthday; public recognition of the occasion in Saxony

The historian Mommsen, in his academical discourse on the Emperor's birthday,[223] compared the reign of a new ruler to a closed book, whose contents it is not yet permitted to read. The adulatory articles of the Bismarckian press have been describing the book is [*sic*] already open, and as recording the history of a great monarch who, in some circumstances of his accession and career recalls the memory of Charlemagne, Barbarossa and Frederick William II[,] has displayed lofty qualities as a statesman and general: he has given proofs, calculated to fill men with amazement of his acuteness of mind and nobility of character. The verdict of posterity may be anticipated. His grandfather's grandson is a hero, and the heroic style is visible in the grand and majestic language of his public utterances, as well as in that lofty attitude of his that so deeply impressed the admiring nations which lately received the Imperial visitor with their plaudits.

The knowledge and sympathies of the Delight of Germany embrace the entire field of culture. "The Emperor's Majesty" even condescends to such trifles as Operas and Bills of Fare. He is an enthusiast for the music of Richard Wagner, and he has banished from the Imperial table the offensive Ménu, with its foreign title and contents, replacing the unpatriotic French designations of dishes by honest German equivalents &c. &c. &c.[224]

The Byzantine effrontery of the Saxon scribes is not original. The recurrence of the same topics, the similar arrangement of the paragraphs, the identity of illustrations and expressions, prove that the basis of all this fulsome and ridiculous rhetoric is supplied by some

---

[223] Speech held on 24 January at the Königlich Preussische Akademie der Wissenschaften.

[224] Menus written in German were used for the first time at a formal dinner to celebrate the royal parade, on 10 September 1888.

Berlin Press Bureau, official or private. The new Marcellus having unfolded in a moment to the proportions of Caesar and Justinian combined, some credit might have been allowed to those who so well prepared the Imperial paragon for the station on which his powers and virtues cast so much splendour. Far from this, the Bismarckites in the genuine Temper of Friedrichsruhe,[225] pass by the father and mother[226] of William II in a silence as malignant as their former lampoons. It is their hint always to speak of him, not as the son of his parents, but as the grandson of his grandfather.[227] In the chorus of birthday panegyric the noblest of the Hohenzollerns is ignored as if he had never reigned, figuring at best, as a mere shadow of a name accompanied by 'lamentable', 'unhappy', or some similar adjective suggesting a sentiment half-way between compassion and contempt.

Here, as in the provinces, the anniversary was kept with the usual demonstrations of loyalty, and post-prandial military and professional eloquence was even more exuberant and less observant of proportion than in former years. All these excesses of fustian and servility must be taken, of course, with a certain allowance; but, after the due deductions are made, it is certain that there is present, at bottom, much attachment to the Emperor's person, and still more attachment to the Imperial Idea, which has now grown to be a dangerous rival to the local dynastic sentiment,

FO 68/174: George Strachey to Marquess of Salisbury, No 12, Dresden, 18 February 1889

[Received 21 February by Vienna. X; S[alisbury]]

Press speculation on enigmatic article in Hamburger Nachrichten *regarding Bismarck succession*

The minority that takes interest in political topics has been trying to decipher the mysterious article in the Hamburg 'Nachrichten' which is the sensation of the day.[228]

---

[225] Friedrichsruh, Bismarck's manor house.

[226] Friedrich III and Victoria.

[227] Wilhelm I.

[228] 'Die Nationalliberalen und der Reichskanzler' ('The National Liberals and the Imperial Chancellor'), *Hamburger Nachrichten*, 8 February 1889.

Some have translated the enigma as a warning to the National-Liberals to support Prince Bismarck, on pain of punishment by the eventual appointment as Reichskanzler of a "Major-General", under whose reactionary administration they will quickly find that they have exchanged whips for scorpions. According to other interpreters, the bribe is held out to the imperfect allies[229] over whom Prince Bismarck has contrived to lose his hold, that their return to their old connection shall be rewarded, when, in the course of nature, the proper time comes, by the nomination of their leader, Herr von Bennigsen, to the high office in question. A third reading of the puzzle is, that Prince Bismarck, seeing in Count Waldersee, who enjoys the special confidence of the Emperor and Empress,[230] and is reputed to be a malignant Stockerite,[231] his successor designate, now desires to rouse a feeling against that officer and his clique, whose political tendencies the Reichskanzler regards as hardly less pernicious than those of the recognized "enemies of the Empire".

Other commentators have sagaciously observed that, as the debated article bears the mark of the Wilhelmstrasse,[232] it must mean something; but that what that something is, it is not given to an ordinary intelligence to say. Of this party are the Editors of the 'Nachrichten', and the semi-liberal 'Zeitung',[233] who shake their heads in oracular fashion at the riddles of the Hanseatic 'reptile',[234] and at the "authentic" elucidations of "the Burgomaster of Nuremberg",[235] profoundly observing that peculiar forces are at work in this Empire, and that what they are close observers will no doubt ultimately discover, the only present certainty being – that Louvois will refrain from bequeathing his entire functions to Barbesieux.[236] That such serious reasonings on a tissue of sorry nonsense place the nation in a degrading light, people do not see. It does not strike them that dishonour is done to the Reichskanzler when, as is the case in all these speculations and discussions, it is taken for granted that he is an intriguer of the Restoration or the Oeil-de-bœuf school:[237] nor do they remark that Germany is compromised

[229] The National Liberals.

[230] Auguste Viktoria.

[231] Strachey is referring to adherents of Adolf Stoecker's anti-Semitic Lutheran movement.

[232] This refers to the imperial foreign office.

[233] *Dresdner Nachrichten* (editor: Emil Bierey) and *Dresdner Zeitung* (Lippmann Badt).

[234] For the 'reptile' press, see n. 67 in this section.

[235] Otto Stromer von Reichenbach.

[236] The reference to the marquis de Louvois and his son, both seventeenth century French statesmen, is an allusion to Otto von Bismarck and his son Herbert.

[237] Oeil-de-bœuf (French: 'bulls eye'), the name for a small oval window,which, figuratively, also refers to an antechamber to Louis XIV's bedroom at Versailles.

by assumptions which almost sink the Empire to the political level of Turkey or Afghanistan.

Prince Bismarck is a statesman, measured by whom Pericles, Pitt, or Cavour, are utter pigmies. He is the "secular man" who, when certain cycles of time come round, appear on the scenes to rule and dazzle mankind. Nevertheless, instead of forming and controlling parties by the high influences of intelligence, dignity, and eloquence, he governs – so it is believed – by the anonymous machinery of a slanderous, inspired, press, through which he deals his enemies, of whatever station or set, blows in the dark, conveying by the mysterious medium of "ambiguous voices", hints and menaces which unsettle the popular mind, and prevent the growth of that healthy political intelligence which the constitutional leaders of some other countries have done so much to develop and educate.

Not only so, but this "statesman of the ages" in [sic] conceived as disposing of the future of the Empire according to the humour of the moment – as threatening his friends with government (if I may use Pitt's classical remark on Sir T. Robinson) by a "jack-boot":[238] while to this freak, or to anything else which Prince Bismarck, or the Emperor, may ordain[,] 47 millions of Germans would, it is supposed, silently submit, as if they were the helpless fellow-citizens of a Praetorian Guard, or the dumb subjects of Amurath or Aurungzebe.[239] In this last assumption I should quite concur. The institutions of the Empire subsist inviolate, not because of the readiness of the people to maintain their rights, but from the want of a disposition in the rulers to subvert the established order of things.

FO 68/174: George Strachey to Marquess of Salisbury, No 17, Dresden, 28 March 1889

[Received 30 March viâ Leipzig. X; S[alisbury]]

German press speculation on negotiations between Herbert Bismarck and Edward Malet

The semi-liberal 'Zeitung'[240] has been discussing the recent movements of Sir Edward Malet and Count Herbert Bismarck in a series of articles, which exhibit the national capacity for the so-called 'higher criticism' in a very favorable light. Such pretences as an

---

[238] Pitt reportedly made the private remark 'The duke [of Newcastle, the prime minister] might as well send his jackboot to lead us' after Thomas Robinson was appointed leader of the House of Commons, in 1754.

[239] Murad I and Muhi-ud-Din Muhammad.

[240] *Dresdner Zeitung.*

Ambassador's alleged visit to a sick mother,[241] and a Secretary of State's journey to London for pleasure,[242] are too transparent to impose on the 'Zeitung'[.] In the "well informed circles" to which the Editor[243] has access, it is an open secret that the "negotiations of Lord Beresford"[244] led to a preliminary understanding of a particular nature between Germany and England, which has been developed in Sir E. Malet's frequent and protracted 'conferences' with Your Lordship, and will be finally concluded by the personal interposition of Count Bismarck. On the details of the understanding, it is desirable at present to speak with reserve. They relate, however, to the topics on which Prince Bismarck "negotiated" with the Queen last year at Charlottenburg,[245] and their settlement will be followed by the formal adhesion of Great Britain to the Triple Alliance.[246]

Very different is the tone of the 'reptiles',[247] which speak with a certain scorn of these rumours, as if they related to combinations which it would be beneath the dignity of Germany to entertain. The official 'Journal'[248] thinks that the journeys under debate, and that of "the English diplomatist Lord Beresford", have no political signification, and it enlarges on the disadvantages likely to result to Germany from the intrusion of England into the Triple Alliance. A demonstration of this is given, with enormous periphrasis, from the Hamburg 'Nachrichten', which argues that although our accession to the League would be a great reinforcement to the material guarantees of peace, it would arouse the jealousy of Russia to the utmost, so as probably to precipitate the struggle which it is sought to defer. Furthermore, the policy of Great Britain will always be "selfish, trimming, and unreliable". Our participation in the Alliance would probably cause its disruption: it would be our object to make our associates cats-paws, and, in case of their defeat, we should throw them over.

[241] Malet left Berlin for London on 24 February 1889 and returned on 14 March.

[242] Herbert von Bismarck visited London and Epsom – Rosebery's seat – on a special mission from 22 March to 30 March 1889.

[243] Lippmann Badt.

[244] Beresford visited Berlin in early February 1889 where he had an audience with Wilhelm II, on 2 February, and an interview with Bismarck, on 3 February.

[245] Victoria visited Berlin from 24 to 26 April 1888; Victoria's audience with Bismarck was on 25 April.

[246] The diplomatic manoeuvres of early 1889 originated in Bismarck's plan for an Anglo-German alliance. Numerous exploratory contacts had been made since 1887 with regard to an Anglo-German rapprochement, and the defensive treaty was to be of limited duration and directed against France. For the Triple Alliance, see n. 174 in Berlin section.

[247] For the 'reptile' press, see n. 67 in this section.

[248] Dresdner Journal.

The Hamburg organ, or the 'Journal', supports these views by extracts from a new work[249] by the eminent metaphysician E. von Hartmann, which appears to be mainly a deification of the policy of Prince Bismarck. The Fichte of the new Empire protests against reliance on such a broken reed as Great Britain. Whoever associates with 'perfide Albion'[250] says the pessimist sage of Berlin, must prepare to be deserted when war breaks out: at any time that nation of Punic shopkeepers would be likely to leave their ally in the lurch, "especially in the most critical moment". All of which, observes the 'Journal', is so thoroughly well known to the Reichskanzler, that the bruited Alliance may be assumed to have no basis in reality.

As an impostor in philosophy, Hartmann is unmatched, and his politics may be as absurd as his mental science. My knowledge of his present treatise is only indirect; but I can say that his Anglophobia is shared by the majority of the contemporary German professional class, who, unlike their predecessors of the beginning and the middle of the century, have no sympathy with progressive programmes and ideas, and, in some instances, are the advocates of reaction.

FO 68/174: George Strachey to Marquess of Salisbury, No 21, Dresden, 1 May 1889

[Received 3 May. For: The Queen; S[alisbury]]

Emperor and empress visit Dresden on Saxon king's birthday; king's level-headed political stance towards German Empire

The Emperor and Empress came to Strehlen last week[251] to congratulate the King of Saxony on his birthday. To the great disappointment of the inhabitants of this city, the Imperial train proceeded direct to the station at the Villa, and their Majesties did not come into Dresden. The Imperial visit caused however great satisfaction here, as it was interpreted as a sign that the Emperor actually entertains towards the King those sentiments of esteem and confidence which have been spoken of as felt by the younger for the elder monarch.

[249] Eduard von Hartmann, *Zwei Jahrzehnte deutscher Politik und die gegenwärtige Weltlage* (Leipzig 1889).

[250] The anglophobic expression 'perfidious Albion' was a stock phrase in nineteenth-century France and widely used in Wilhemine Germany.

[251] On 23 April 1889.

According to German and English testimony on which it is perhaps justifiable for me to rely, the Emperor has a strong friendship for the King of Saxony, in whom he places such trust that the Imperial decisions may be expected, in critical moments, to be influenced by the King's opinions and advice.

The head of the Empire could not have a more loyal or a more statesmanlike councillor. The temper of Pyrgopolinices and Bobadil[252] can hardly be called a national German vice; but it is not unknown in Berlin, where, besides, the results of personal irascibility, impatience of criticism, and vindictiveness, are sometimes apparent in the acts of Government. To such dispositions the King of Saxony would always, if consulted, be strongly adverse. The chauvinism of the young Bismarckian Germany is the object of His Majesty's contempt: his military experience, which has taught him how incalculable are the hazards of war, has made him a constant advocate of peace: and, what is rare in Germans of high station, he has an English tolerance of opposition, with a preference for conciliation and persuasion before peremptory settlements in politics. It will be fortunate for Germany, and Europe, if the voice of so enlightened an adviser is heard in Berlin when grave resolutions have to be taken.

FO 68/174: George Strachey to Marquess of Salisbury, No 41, Dresden, 6 September 1889

[Received 9 September. Qy: X; S[alisbury]]

Sedan Day celebrations; new nationalist tone

Owing to the demand made on Saxon Enthusiasm at the recent Wettinfeier, and to the Emperor's approaching visit, there was some abatement of the customary popular demonstrations on the anniversary of Sedan.[253] Conformable to the practise here, the observances of the day were of an exclusively voluntary character, the official participation usual in some other parts of Germany having been restricted in Dresden to the display of flags on public buildings, and an outdoor musical performance by order of the Stadtrath.[254]

---

[252] The fictitious characters Pyrgopolynices (*The Braggart Soldier* by Titus Maccius Plautus, *c.* 205 BC) and Captain Bobadil (*Every Man in his Humour* by Ben Johnson, 1598) are known for their boastfulness.

[253] The 800th anniversary of the Wettin Dynasty was celebrated in grand style at Dresden from 15 to 19 June. For Sedan Day, see n. 50 in this section; on Wilhelm II's visit, see the following dispatch.

[254] German: 'municipal council'.

Apart from the casual lowering of patriotic temperature above stated, a certain change may be said to have gradually come over the spirit in which this holiday is kept. I do not say that the rejoicings on the overthrow of France, and the Establishment of the new Germany, are now marked by a temper of offensive chauvinism, or that public modesty and restraint has been effaced by a high degree of pharisaic complacency and self-assertion. I think, however, that these vices, or shadows, of national character are coming into sight, and that it is a question if grounds are not now visible for that complaint of ὕβρίς [255] which one of our political leaders brought (at the time quite unjustly) against the Germans.

Here, as elsewhere, the school ceremonial is a main feature of the day. Leipzig, and the War of Liberation, are no longer texts for professorial and schoolboy declamation, Königrätz [sic], Mars-la-tour, and Sedan,[256] with the subsequent political and industrial evolution, being described as forming one of the most glorious chapters in the history of our race, while the Emperor William I and Prince Bismarck are extolled in Superlatives at which the greatest of mankind might blush as undeserved. An oration at one of the chief town schools was on 'Prince Bismarck in relation to religion, art, and the state'. This style recurs not only at the yearly September function, but in the daily class-room, where, for nearly a quarter of a century, owing to the remarkable transformation which has occurred in the character and ideals of the instructors of German youth, pressure has been constantly maintained, calculated to inculcate servility, sycophancy, and exaggerated national self-esteem.

If the parodists of the ideas and language of Schleiermacher and Fichte are the scholastic majority, there are not wanting those who strive to give the rising generation a worthier educational direction. An example of this occurred in one of the Dresden schools, where a teacher ventured to enlarge on the public worth of the French, and to exhort his pupils not to be misled by vain notions of a German monopoly of wisdom, power, and virtue.

In reproducing these words, the National Liberal 'Anzeiger'[257] was giving the antidote to its own leader which, after ascribing the 19th century conception of German unity to the ages of Wallenstein and Luther, and calling Prince Bismarck the personification of those specifically German qualities – truth, honour[,] circumspection, and strength – deplored the deficiencies of the nation in pride and self-esteem, and denounced the corruption of the German

---

[255] Greek: 'hubris'.
[256] Respectively, the battles of 3 July 1866, 16 August 1870, and 1 September 1870.
[257] *Dresdner Anzeiger*, 2 September 1889.

home, stage, and language by intrusive foreign fashions, dramas, and words.

FO 68/174: George Strachey to Marquess of Salisbury, No 42, Dresden, 13 September 1889

[Received 16 September. Qy: Extract to War Office (as marked), P.L. [printed letter], 18 September; The Queen; S[alisbury]]

Emperor's visit to Saxony

The Emperor has left Saxony for Westphalia.[258] In honor of the illustrious guest the municipality and the public had revived the architectural and other decorations which adorned the city during the ceremonials of last June.[259] New propylæa of imposing dimensions, flanked by colossal statuary, and leading to a richly embellished triumphal way, were erected for the occasion. The monarch was greeted by a civil torch-light procession, with a serenade, in which 12,000 persons took part, while his daily departure, and return from the manœuvres drew from crowds of a density almost new in Dresden experience loud demonstrations of popular enthusiasm and attachment.

I do not think that the visible excitement was inferior to that shewn on the visit of the Emperor's venerable grandfather[260] seven years ago. It indicates a considerable mastery by the young Emperor of the arts of popularity, as well as the progressive extinction of regional sentiment under the growth of the German idea, and, perhaps, the effect of those influences of involuntary conviction which escapes definition in words, that in the second year of his reign, having as yet no particular record to shew, the reception of William II should be comparable in warmth to that accorded in this capital to one of the great figures of German history, towards the close of his long and memorable career.

The circles which were in close contact with the Emperor during his visit were full of praises of his unaffected, cordial manner, and his frank vivacious style of conversation. This language was, I think, less prompted than usual by Byzantine motives.

The Emperor's deferential deportment towards his royal hosts was highly appreciated both in the Palace and by the Public. The

---

[258] Wilhelm II visited Dresden from 5 to 10 September 1889.
[259] Strachey is referring to the Wettin anniversary; see n. 253 in this section.
[260] Wilhelm I visited Dresden from 14 to 20 September 1882 (*Kaisertage*).

prevalent belief respecting the influence of the older over the younger ruler was confirmed by a speech in which the Emperor proposed the King of Saxony's health at one[261] of the State Banquets.

He said "There is a heavy debt which I have to discharge to Your Majesty. For many years Your Majesty has cared for me with unchangeable fidelity and kindness, and taken thought for me. My deceased father especially entrusted me to Your Majesty's heart, with the prayer that I might be the object of Your solicitude if he should be overtaken by his destiny. Your Majesty has generously fulfilled this request, and I have long found a cordial friend and fatherly councillor in Your Majesty. It is a great gratification to me to express my humblest thanks for this." It will be fortunate for Germany and Europe if the ambition of Augustus should be restrained by the mature intelligence of Trajan.[262]

On the manœuvres field, the Emperor was indefatigable. [Note in margin: 'Qy: Extract to War Office'] According to the testimony of the foreign officers present, the Saxon Army is not surpassed in perfection of equipment, or instruction, by any German Corps. I hear that His Imperial Majesty was completely satisfied both with the strategy shewn, and the tactical execution of the various movements. The force collected about Oschatz consisted of 36 Battalions of Infantry, (3 more are in garrison in Strassburg) – 30 squadrons of Cavalry, and 22 Batteries of artillery. These troops form the peace establishment of the Kingdom. At three or four days notice, the Corps can be mobilized, for foreign service, [end of highlighted extract for War Office] in a strength which we should hardly send abroad without preparation for as many months.

FO 68/174: George Strachey to Marquess of Salisbury, No 46, Dresden, 18 October 1889

[Received 21 October. X; S[alisbury]]

Saxon elections; significant Social Democrat gains

The Saxon Landtag meets in biennial sessions, before each of which one third of the members of the lower house vacates their seats. The census is less democratic than that of the German Parliament, the property qualification being imposed of the possession of in real

---

[261] On 7 September 1889.
[262] Strachey is referring to the first and thirteenth emperors of the Roman Empire.

estate, or of the payment of 3 marks in direct taxation. This restriction excludes the lower class of artizans from the suffrage.

In view of the opening of another session of the local legislature, the prescribed renewal took place last Tuesday[263] in 27 vacancies. Previous to the elections, such parliamentary agitation as the lukewarm political temperaments of Germany can sustain was put in scene. In Dresden, for instance, there was a little canvassing for the 'Cartel', or joint party 'of order',[264] two or three meetings of electors, a few newspaper articles, placards inviting support for 'throne and altar', against Social-Democracy and its malignant 'crypto-republican' ally the 'freisinnig'[265] faction. The preparations of the followers of Bebel and Liebknecht were necessarily somewhat subterraneous. Their press is extinguished, and, if they address their friends in public, the Commisary of police gags the speaker at the first audible words of disparagement of official beliefs, policy, or persons, or, perhaps, summarily closes the assemblage.

When the results of the polls were reported, some of the Bismarckite organs spoke as if a great victory had been won all along the line by the parties of 'order'. The fact was quite otherwise. The 'signature' of the day was a large accession to the Social Democratic vote, with a serious subtraction, in places, from the absolute or relative strength of the 'Cartel'.

In Dresden, the aggregate poll of the coalition candidates in the three contested districts shewed an augmentation, compared with 1883, of 15 per cent. The parallel advance of Social Democracy was 30 per cent. In one district the 'Cartel' candidate,[266] a popular member of the municipality[,] was warmly supported by the Conservatives, National Liberals, Progressists and 'Christian Socialists'. His poll was 25 per cent larger than the patriotic vote in 1883, while the poll of Social Democracy had nearly doubled. In these circumstances the Dresden 'Anzeiger' discerned "a proof that in the hearts of our population love and fidelity to Kaiser and Reich, to King and Fatherland, with Law and Order, are still as living realities as before." Of the following polls the arithmetic requires no comment.

[263] 15 October 1889.
[264] For the so-called 'Cartel', see n. 208 in Berlin section.
[265] *Deutsche Freisinnige Partei*. See n. 3 in Berlin section.
[266] Paul Schickert.

Polls		1883	1889
Leipzig 2nd district	National Liberal	1358	3323
	Socialist	305	2379
Leipzig 3rd district	Cartel	3949	4230
	Socialist	1492	7900
Chemnitz	Cartel	1181	2130
	Socialist	2523	4088
Chemnitz country	Cartel	1185	1465
	Socialist	570	7569
Stollberg	Conservative	2321	2727
	Socialist	1688	2235

In other electoral districts the gains of the Social Democrats were less marked, in a few there was some decline. But most of the polls told the same story, the progress of Social Democracy being[,] moreover, visible in constituencies where the industrial population is a relative minimum, which was not so before.

The dislocation of parliamentary strength at these 27 elections was not important. The Social Democrats maintained one severely contested seat, and gained two, thereby raising their contingent in the Landtag from five to seven members. The single 'freisinnig' member[267] was re-elected in the face of a vigorous and unscrupulous opposition, and that party, which seemed to be almost extinct in Saxony, otherwise shewed signs of active rejuvenescence. The Saxon Progressists,[268] still so called, who have apostasized from their old creed, lost two seats out of four.

Looking to the fifteen cases where the Social Democrats contested seats, I find the following figures.

	Votes
Poll of coalesced party of 'Order'	25,040
Poll of Social Democracy	76,477.

I must remark that this great minority is representative, not of 'Her Majesty's Opposition', but of the red republic and the commune.[269] As the political majority, untaught by the portentous consequences of their attempt to stifle ideas by Act of Parliament, and by the failure

---

[267] Friedrich Bönisch.

[268] *Fortschrittspartei.*

[269] Strachey is referring to the revolutionary government of 1871, *La Commune de Paris* (March – May 1871).

of recent Social legislation to mitigate,[270] in the smallest particular, the enthusiasm and resentment of a highly intelligent and fanatical party, or otherwise to act as a sop in the way expected, is favorable to the contemplated renewal of the repressive system, it is satisfactory to think that the dispositions of the army are excellent, the troops being 'ready to fire on their fathers'. The promised fruits of the mixed method of coercion and seduction, so confidently announced as being on the verge of appearance, may, of course, shortly become visible. Those who have to deal with practical politics & who, like myself, do not easily pass from facts to speculation, must be content to say that in Saxony, the centre of German industrial gravity, and especially in Chemnitz – the Manchester of the Empire – the phantom of Social Democracy never yet shewed in the proportions to which it has attained now.

FO 68/174: George Strachey to Marquess of Salisbury, No 48, Dresden, 26 October 1889

[Received 28 October, U.F.S. [Under Flying Seal] to Berlin. X; S[alisbury]]

Press views on German colonial policy

The opinions of the liberal German press on the Reichskanzler's colonial policy are largely shared by the minority amongst the public which takes interest in such comparatively esoteric questions. The prevalent bondage of mind prevents positive criticism of Prince Bismarck's measures; but the question is asked, if his infallibility has been as plainly manifested on the coast of Zanzibar as it has been in Germany and Europe.[271] The colonial party speak with less circumlocution, Shareholders in the African companies complain that they were tempted to invest their money by false official encouragement and pretences, and that they have been abandoned to the diplomatic necessities of the Wilhelmstrasse.

The 'Dresden Nachrichten'[272] which is now nearly as servile as one of the professional reptiles,[273] observes that the colonial enthusiasm is 'gone out'. 'Whose fault is it?' asks the Editor,[274] judiciously adding 'that is a point we will not discuss.' The treatment of Dr Peters, he

---

[270] Strachey is referring to the Imperial Law Concerning Disability and Old-Age Insurance of 22 June 1889.

[271] Strachey is referring to the Abushiri revolt of 1888–1889. See n. 203 in this section.

[272] On 24 October 1889.

[273] For the 'reptile' press, see n. 67 in this section.

[274] Emil Bierey.

continues, "by the Empire" – (the usual German euphemism!) – has thoroughly sobered many patriots. The lost territory in Zanzibar cannot be recovered without great sacrifices in money, and the process of securing it against the Arab slave-dealers is hard. Dr Peters has been disavowed by the German officials. New-Guinea has gone to sleep: its name is never heard. The only good asset in the African property appears to be the Cameroon and Togo Coast. The South-Western Company have sold half their land to the English,[275] because the required capital was not forthcoming in Germany, although Herr Bleichroder – the English Consul General, belongs to the German African enterprises. To throw dust in the eyes of the public, the information is given that the Sovereignty of the Reich is reserved, i.e. Germany pays for the protection of English settlers and traders. The true truth is, that the remainder of the Company's possessions will soon follow the first half.

This language is circuitous, but the drift is plain. The 'Nachrichten' is of opinion that the Great Colonial Empire is a bubble, that it appears to be verging towards collapse, and that the public are tired of it. The specific Colonial party affect a less pessimist tone. And stifling their anger against the author of their delusions and hopes, they maintain their unremitting vituperation of the policy and agents of Great Britain in "the dark continent".

FO 68/174: George Strachey to Marquess of Salisbury, No 51, Dresden, 8 November 1889

[Received 12 November. Seen at Berlin. Qy: Home Office, P.L. [printed letter], 13 November; C.M.K. [Charles M. Kennedy], 12 November; J.F. [James Fergusson]; Mr Strachey does not quite understand the English law, which does not much differ in principle; S[alisbury]]

Declaration by Saxon public prosecutor relating to laws on strikes

In his recent speech on the Social Democracy Bill,[276] the Socialist Liebknecht contrasted the behaviour of our authorities and public to the British workman with the parallel conditions here. He might

[275] The *Dresdner Nachrichten* was referring to the purchase of land (210,000 square kilometres) and of mining rights (290,000 square kilometres), as agreed between the Groll-Syndicate and the *Deutsche Kolonial-Gesellschaft für Südwest-Afrika* (German South West Africa Company) on 19 September 1889. The imperial chancellor ultimately withheld his approval of this contract.

[276] On 5 November 1889, at the first reading of the bill to extend the Anti-Socialist Law of 1878 (see n. 10 in this section).

have added, that while with us intimidation is recognized as <u>part of the inevitable machinery of strikes</u>, [text underlined in pencil; note in margin and above: '? often incidental to'] in Germany the question is debated whether combinations for securing higher wages should be allowed at all. Strikes have been of late frequent in Saxony, so that the time seemed to be come for indirect official intervention on behalf of the capitalist class, whose returns are being menaced by the growing call for a better remuneration of labour. Accordingly the Public Prosecutor of Chemnitz[277] – the Manchester of the Kingdom, and the Empire – has issued a notice declaratory of the law on combinations[278] for obtaining higher wages, especially by strikes. Persons inducing or trying to induce others, by <u>physical force, menaces, or publishing names</u>, [underlined in pencil] to join any such combination, are liable, on conviction, to three months imprisonment, or more. Those who by similar means, hinder or try to hinder, manners of such combinations from retiring, are liable to the same penalties. Anyone who, by violence or threats, compels another to acts, or omission of acts, in the above respects, may be sentenced to a year's imprisonment, with a fine of £30.

In publishing this notice, the representative of the Saxon Minister of Justice[279] refers to certain recent irregularities arising from strikes, and gives warning that every such offence will hereafter be visited with the full rigour of the law.

In a village[280] where a strike occurred, a weaver has recently been sentenced to 10 days imprisonment "for using threatening expressions". This is all the information the German newspapers would give in such a case, and no one cares to be supplied with accurate knowledge of the circumstances of the offence. The probability is, that the remarks inculpated as "threatening" would strike Your Lordship, or Lord Hartington , as language perfectly appropriate for the individual and the incident.

---

[277] Christian Julius Schwabe.

[278] Trade unions and the freedom of coalition were regulated by Sections152 and 153 of the Trade Regulations Act for the North German Confederation of 1869 (adopted as *Reichsgewerbeordnung* in 1871).

[279] Christian von Abeken.

[280] Limbach.

FO 68/174: George Strachey to Marquess of Salisbury, No 53, Dresden, 22 November 1889

[Received 25 November For: Chancellor of the Exchequer; S[alisbury]]

German and Saxon finances under discussion in Landtag; *exceptionally complicated*

The official Reports on the Finances of the Kingdom are now under discussion in the Landtag. The public accounts of Saxony, which follow the usual German pattern, run for such long periods, and the local receipts are so mixed up with revenue collected for the Empire, that the figures are extremely difficult to analyze and appreciate. In the first place, the biennial Reports, and the Explanatory speech, refer to six separate years. The Saxon Landtag has, for instance, now before it: 1st the definite balance-sheet for 1886 and 1887: 2^{ndly} the calculated results for 1888 and 1889: 3^{rdly} the Budget for 1890 and 1891. Further, there is the usual German separation of expenditure and ways and means into Ordinary and Extraordinary, while a portion of the revenue written in the balance-sheet is the property of the Empire, and is finally diverted into the Imperial Exchequer, from which, again, a counter current of subsidy pours into the Treasury of the Kingdom from the surplus receipts of Imperial taxation assigned to the separate states.[281]

Budget speeches like those which in our own Parliament have so often established a Minister's reputation as a financier and an orator, are as unknown in Dresden as they are in Berlin. Financial statements here are a mere inartistic jungle of figures, conveyed in a special vocabulary as unintelligible to the public as terms like Ampères, volts, and ohms. No German newspapers are capable of treating finance in an instructive and attractive manner, so that the public cannot follow the various questions of this class which come under debate in the Landtag. I do not know any book, German or Saxon, which states even the annual expenditure and revenue of the Kingdom.

Official estimates ascribe to the current biennial period (1888, 1889) an apparent surplus of more than £1,000,000, which may, perhaps, be the equivalent of £12,000,000 for our own Chancellor of the Exchequer.[282] Only a few experts would be competent to say (after considerable study) what portion of this sum is veritable surplus, and I will not attempt the problem here. It is, however, indubitable

---

[281] On the financial transfers between the German Empire and the federal states, see n. 55 in Darmstadt section.

[282] George Goschen.

that the Minister's[283] balance is large, and that it shews the momentary financial position of Saxony to be good, if not brilliant.

In Germany, surplus does not indicate remissions of taxation. The practice here is, in the separate states, as for the Empire, not to relax the pressure of the financial screw, but to return part of the excess of revenue to the taxpayers, or to classes of taxpayers by circuitous, indirect, channels, the requirements of the spending departments being so adjusted as to absorb the rest. How this rule has been exemplified in the present instance, I shall report when the discussions in the Landtag have proceeded further.

FO 68/175: George Strachey to Marquess of Salisbury, No 11, Dresden, 14 February 1890

[Received 17 February. S[alisbury]; Printed and circulated to Cabinet]

Emperor's rescript suggesting an international solution to labour problems would be ruinous for Germany

I desire to draw attention to a point connected with the Imperial Rescript which proposes an International discussion of the labor question of the day.[284] The Emperor defines his object as being to attain an International agreement to "limit the demand which may be made on the labour of the workers." The essentials of the problem are: – 1.: a normal work-day: 2[.]: restrictions on the employment of children: 3[.]: prohibitions of Sunday labour.

Now the power of Germany to sustain industrial competition with ourselves, depends entirely (certain specialities excepted), on the following circumstances.

1. The average German work day is 11 hours, while the British work-day is 9 hours, and commands a higher remuneration. 2. The German restrictions on children's labour are less severe than ours. 3. The same is the case with regard to the observance of Sunday.

It is the existence of these conditions, and others subsidiary, which enables Germany to rival, or undersell, us in the markets of the world. Germany can challenge our industrial supremacy because her workers submit to demands on their labour which our workers will not accept. It is plain, then, that if the demands made on labour here are lowered to the British level, the margin of advantage which Germany now enjoys will be abolished. Her exports of staples must

---

[283] Leonce von Könneritz (minister of finance).

[284] For the imperial rescript and the proclamation of 4 February 1890, see n. 249 in Berlin section.

be ruined, the existing customs duties would no longer suffice for the protection of native industry, and capital would migrate to countries where it might command better returns.

A number of official and industrial personages to whom I have stated this difficulty, have remarked in reply, that the idea was new to them, and that they did not know how to escape the conclusion that it was a Reductio ad absurdum[285] of the first of the Imperial Rescripts. The managers of a leading company observe, that although their article, which goes all over the world, is almost a speciality, a limitation of their hours of labour to the english [*sic*] level must at once entail the closure of their works. The only escape would be, by the distribution of the present wage fund amongst an increased number of hands, which would mean more Social Democracy, and prospective Revolution.

FO 68/175: George Strachey to Marquess of Salisbury, No 12, Dresden, 21 February 1890

[Received 24 February via Berlin. Interesting. For: The Queen; Prince of Wales / Circulate / Home Office, P.L. [printed letter], 6 March; S[alisbury][286]

First Reichstag *election results in Saxony; huge increase in Social Democratic vote*

As long as I can remember, the leading personages here, ministerial [,] civic and industrial, with the entire Conservative and National-Liberal majority, and the Government and Bismarckian newspapers without exception, have never ceased reiterating their assurance, that under the admirable system of joint proscription and cajolery devised by the wisdom of the Imperial administration, the working classes of the Kingdom, and of the Empire, were being gradually, but surely, weaned from the Socialist heresy. Dissentients from this belief, or allegation, were set down as sympathizers with the propaganda, and, if too openly expressing their doubts, were liable to suffer in their offices or professions.

Yesterday's polls rudely dispelled the received illusion. Recovering beyond all hope from the discouragements and reverses suffered under

---

[285] Latin: 'reduction to an absurdity'.

[286] Additional note to dispatch: '[To] Sir T. Sanderson. Mr Strachey N° 12 February 21. It is our general habit to mark M[r] Strachey's Despatches with a[n] X only. But the present one in spite of its style, is of more than usual interest. Should it not be circulated to the Cabinet, and sent to the Home Office, for perusal?' W.A.C. [William A. Cockerell], 24 February 1890. 'Certainly. I have marked it ac[cor]d[ingl]y. Strachey though "crusty" is decidedly clear, and when he has something practical to write about, he writes well.' T.H.S. [Thomas Henry Sanderson]

the 'Cartel' coalition of 1887,[287] the Hydra of Social-Democracy has risen again with unprecedented rigor, and with such an augmentation of electoral strength, that some of the polls recorded appear scarcely credible.

Saxony sends 23 members to the Reichstag. In 1887 the Social-Democrats held 7 seats, all of which they lost to the 'Cartel' coalition at the dissolution of that year. They have now apparently regained 4 or 5 of those seats, and have the prospect of adding to their number at the casting elections which may be requisite.[288]

As the combination against them has been well sustained, this result is remarkable. But the real significance of yesterday's polls will be apparent from a few comparisons, which I make in round numbers.

Social Democratic Polls in

	1887	1890
Zittau	1,700	4,860
Leipzig county	19,300	27,280
Zwickau	12,900	19,450
Chemnitz	15,350	24,000
Bautzen	1,550	3,881
Freiberg	5,600	8,037
Dresden Altstadt	9,170	13,126

The press has not yet uttered a word of comment on these figures which, striking as they are, do not tell their whole story unless they are compared with data taken from the General Election of 1884. I find, for instance, that in the parliamentary period 1884–1887, the Social Democratic vote augmented in Chemnitz 6 per cent, while yesterday's poll there shewed an advance on 1887 of no less than 50 per cent. For Leipzig, the growth in the former triennial period was 4 per cent: in the last similar period 27 per cent. In Dresden: 6 per. cent, then, 45 per. cent, now. In Zittau: against a diminution then[,] 180 per. cent. now. Zwickau: instead of 10 per cent, now 35 per. cent. Freiberg: against a diminution in 1887, yesterday an addition to the Socialist poll of 45 per. cent since the last General Election.

There has been in some places a polling off of the 'Cartel' vote, which I conjecturally ascribe to the absence of a good electoral cry like that of 1887. "Vote for your old Emperor and the Military

[287] For the so-called 'Cartel', see n. 208 in Berlin section.
[288] The Social Democrats won a total of six seats in Saxon constituencies.

Septennate"[289] was felt as a more positive actuality than the mere call to defeat, on general grounds, the candidates of Social-Democracy, whose chimeras are not at present within the range of practical politics.

FO 68/175: George Strachey to Marquess of Salisbury, No 14, Dresden, 7 March 1890

[Received 10 March. Qy: Home Office for perusal, 12 March; Returned 21 March; S [alisbury]]

Final Reichstag *election results; political extremes gain at expense of National Liberals; Bismarckite press abusive*

The Saxon casting elections have not brought the Social Democrats any further successes. The scales were turned against them by the 'freisinnig'[290] vote, a portion of which was polled for the 'Cartel', while the Socialists mostly stood aloof where liberals were contesting seats with 'Cartel'[291] candidates. The final electoral results to the kingdom are: the two Conservative parties[292] are at their old strength (13) the single 'freisinnig' member[293] is re-seated while the 3 [in-text annotation: '9?'] National Liberals are reduced to 3, having lost 6 seats to the Social-Democrats.

If these figures are compared with those for the Empire, it is seen that in Saxony the representation of the political extremes, High Conservativism and Social Democracy, is overwhelmingly above the normal, while the repression of the National-Liberals is excessive, and the 'Freisinn' is at a standstill.

In Germany, where society strictly rests on the basis of caste, incitements to class hatreds are doubly foolish. Nevertheless, in emulation of the 'Reptiles'[294] of Berlin, Hamburg, and Cologne, the local Bismarckite press organs are making it their business to envenom and complicate the new situation, by speaking of the victors in insulting and exasperating terms. Threats of a dissolution, of a German Brumaire,[295] and the like, alternate with violent diatribes against the opposition, the principal objects of this vituperation being the 'freisinnig' electorate, whose political beliefs and aims are

---

[289] For the army bill (military septennate), see n. 119 in Berlin section.

[290] See n. 3 in Berlin section.

[291] See n. 208 in Berlin section.

[292] *Deutschkonservative Partei* (10) and *Deutsche Reichspartei* (*Freikonservative*) (3).

[293] Louis Heinrich Buddeberg.

[294] For the 'reptile' press, see n. 67 in this section.

[295] Strachey is referring to the coup of 9 November 1799 (18 Brumaire in the year VIII, French Republican Calendar), when Napoleon overthrew the governing *Directoire exécutif*.

misrepresented, and ascribed to infamy of personal motive, although the party includes something like the majority of the bourgeoisie of Protestant Germany, of the professions, and, in places, of the civil and judicial service, and is, in fact, as loyal and Conservative a class as exist in Europe.

The Ministerial 'Journal'[296] systematically brackets the independent liberals with the Social-Democrats, and treats them, as mere political scum. This organ gravely argues that Socialism has reduced the working-classes by its alluring visions of material ease and enjoyment, and says that the cure for the disease will in due time be vouchsafed, though not through the arm of flesh. The 'Nachrichten'[297] boldly ascribes a certain share in the recent electoral calamities to the Emperor's rescripts,[298] and the Editor[299] says that this opinion is very general. He has reluctantly come to the conclusion that the gagging system has broken down, and is unable to see the beneficial effects which official eyes discern as resulting from the new state Socialism.[300]

FO 68/175: George Strachey to Marquess of Salisbury, No 19, Dresden, 21 March 1890

[Received 24 March. Qy: The Queen; S[alisbury]]

Public indifference with regard to Bismarck's resignation

Prince Bismarck's withdrawal from public life has not given rise to any of those displays of public excitement and consternation which accompanied the occasional announcements of his retirement during the late Emperor's reign.[301] The Germans feel imperfectly and move slowly, and the nation may yet show the great Minister marks of gratitude and sympathy like those paid by races of warmer political and personal temperament to Thiers, Cavour, or Peel. Thus far, however, not a ruffle has disturbed the popular equanimity: there are no meetings, no anxious conversations: and, to borrow the

---

[296] *Dresdner Journal.*

[297] *Dresdner Nachrichten.*

[298] For the imperial rescript and the proclamation of 4 February 1890, see n. 249 in Berlin section.

[299] Emil Bierey.

[300] The term state socialism refers to Bismarck's social policy (to appease the working classes) and the laws on health insurance (1883), accident insurance (1884), and old-age and disability insurance (1889; see n. 270 in this section).

[301] On Bismarck's resignation, see pp. 123–124.

classical remark of Horace Walpole on a somewhat similar occasion, it does <u>not</u> "rain gold boxes."[302] While the German press, two or three personal "reptiles",[303] excepted, writes, as it has written of the entire crisis, in the calm style of narrative suitable for the description of a change of Government in another country or age.

So striking is the general indifference, or submissiveness, that Bismarckite journals have been putting the question – 'how is it that no one is now asking "what next"'? The answer has been, that the German people, though feeling that a statesman of Prince Bismarck's calibre and prestige cannot be quite replaced, are of opinion that a satisfactory termination of the crisis has been attained by the virtual transfer of the late Reichskanzler's principal functions to the Emperor, whose wisdom will be adequate to the solution of the most difficult problems of policy and administration. The employment of an abject, acquiescent, tone, when the acts of those in high authority are discussed, does not here exclude undertones of criticism and disapproval, and, in this particular instance, there seems to be a disposition afloat to ask if the Emperor's behaviour to Prince Bismarck in the late transactions[304] does not need justification. On the whole, opinion is suspended, and I would remark, meanwhile, that the comments of the London press on this topic are, in all respects, (allowances being made for errors of details), as superior in substance to what is written in Germany as they are in literary form.

FO 68/175: George Strachey to Marquess of Salisbury, No 23, Dresden, 17 April 1890

[Received 19 April by post. Qy: Home Office / Berlin for perusal, 23 April / Commercial Department to see; S[alisbury]; Returned from Berlin, 30 April]

Socialist opinions differ regarding 1 May demonstration in favour of eight-hour working day

The leading Social-Democrats have been discussing how effect can best be given to the decision of the "Congress of Paris"[305] in favor

---

[302] Horace Walpole's phrase 'it rained gold boxes' (posthumously published in his *Memoirs of the Reign of King George the Second* (1822)) refers to the support which William Pitt received from several cities after he was dismissed as secretary of state for the southern department, in April 1857.

[303] For the 'reptile' press, see n. 67 in this section.

[304] See previous dispatch and pp. 121–123.

[305] Resolution of the International Workers' Congresses at Paris of 20 July 1889 (to commemorate the Haymarket riot of 1886).

of a universal Labour demonstration on the 1st of May. The journalist Schippel, who represents Chemnitz – the Saxon, or German Manchester – in the Reichstag, pressed his associates to call on the workmen of Germany to keep the day in question as a holiday, and to organize parades, processions, and meetings, calculated to impress the public with the importance of the 8 hour movement.[306]

Social Democracy has its 'Invincibles' and its Parnellites,[307] and, compared with Schippel, those old parliamentary hands, Bebel and Liebknecht, are almost Conservative in feeling and language. Whatever may be thought of Liebknecht's social Utopia, he writes and speaks with unusual force, and, as far as general topics are concerned, he would not, in England, be thought a very subversive politician. In concert with Bebel, he has combated the Schippel programme, arguing that the 31st of April [note in margin: 'The 31st of April does not exist in most Countries. The 30. must be meant.'] is a holiday in Prussia (fast-day) and that few operatives could afford to waste a second day, or even a half day. His advice to workmen was – avoid all tumults, especially street processions: May-day meetings to petition for the eight hours day would be sufficient. Provocative agents were not wanting, and amongst the operatives there were numerous madcaps, who, in the explosive social conditions now existing, might easily produce mischief. "Do not discredit the movement: quiet, steady, progress is wanted, not noisy street "effects"['']."[308]

The question has now been considered at a conclave of the Socialist members of the Reichstag, held in Halle,[309] who have issued a manifesto to the working classes of Germany which shews by its moderate, warning, language, that the counsels of Bebel and Liebknecht have prevailed. A certain concession is, however, made to the Schippel party; for while the 35 parliamentary leaders of Social Democracy dissuade their followers from giving the intended manifestation an identical form, they say, parenthetically that there will be no objection to the Mayday holiday in cases where it can be taken without giving rise to conflicts.

The Schippel programme could not fail to cause great irritation to the employers of labour. Some works have announced that they will reply to a holiday by a lock-out: others, that hands absent on the 1st of May will not be employed further. The tone of the Rescript of Halle has somewhat reassured the public; but the apprehension that

---

[306] The demand was made in the *Berliner Volkstribüne* of 22 March 1890.
[307] 'Parnellites' were Irish nationalist supporters of Charles Stewart Parnell.
[308] Open letter to Schippel, published on 1 April 1890.
[309] On 13 April 1890.

disturbances may occur is not dispelled, and its presence has confirmed the depression of industrial values.

I am informed that the Saxon Government is in communication with Berlin as to the measures of prohibition, or precaution, which it may be desirable to order for the 1st of May. If the Prussian authorities decide on interference with meetings, or other manifestations, their example will be followed with alacrity here. The official caste, in all ranks, talks of strikers and socialists as if they were foreign enemies. The language I hear is: "the time is not far distant when those people must be shot down with artillery". The capitalist and shopkeeper class are equally intemperate.

[...]

P.S. According to the latest accounts, the operatives of this Kingdom, and of the adjoining regions, are disposed to acquiesce in the recommendations of the Parliamentary leaders of the Socialist party.

FO 68/175: George Strachey to Marquess of Salisbury, No 28, Dresden, 27 April 1890

[Received 5 May, U.F.S. [Under Flying Seal] to Berlin. For: Chancellor of Exchequer; S[alisbury]]

Saxon finance minister's views on bimetallism

I have asked the Saxon Minister of Finance his present views on Bimetallism.[310] Herr von Thümmel is an experienced administrator who has a thorough pratical [*sic*] knowledge of monetary questions, but, as usual in Germany, has less of the book-culture of these subjects than would be possessed by a high English or Indian official. He considers that many of the principal problems relating to prices, the circulation, and the like, cannot be stated or solved with mathematical accuracy, and that in currency discussions only approximate, probable, results can be attained.

His Excellency leans to the party which asserts the appreciation of gold; but he admits a recent fall in the costs of production, and, ascribes the prevalent lower prices of commodities to these two causes combined. He is of opinion, that the metallic circulating medium is deficient in quantity. He believes that the relative value of gold and silver might be regulated by international arrangement;

---

[310] Bimetallism is a monetary system based on both gold and silver money as legal tender with a fixed rate of exchange between the two metals.

but thinks that such artificial ratio would only have a temporary stability. The bimetallic league without England, advocated by Herr Arendt, and the extreme German 'Agrarians',[311] the Saxon Minister calls an absurdity. A working silver Union without all the commercial countries he treats as unthinkable, and he considers that the international double-standard is not, at present, within the range of practical politics.

His Excellency also observes, that the silver agitation which was making so much noise in Germany a few years ago is now as good as dead. He knows of no disposition in any official quarter to move in the bimetallistic sense. But if Prussia proposed an international rehabilitation of silver the Governments of the other German states would scarcely offer resistance.

The affinities of the bimetallists with the bucolic, and other parties of the Reichstag, were fully explained in my Currency Report of March 1887. At that time, silver commanded a secure majority, so that a repeal of the Law of 1873,[312] which established the Gold Standard, was attainable. The parliamentary situation has, however, changed since then. The Bimetallism of Germany, unlike that of England and France, is not the esoteric doctrine of a scientific minority. Its main supporters are ignorant junkers and agriculturists with political opinions almost bordering upon lunacy, to whom economic questions are altogether incomprehensible.

FO 68/175: George Strachey to Marquess of Salisbury, No 29, Dresden, 2 May 1890

[Received 5 May, U.F.S. [Under Flying Seal] to Berlin). For: Mr Matthews / Commercial Department; S[alisbury]]

1 May passed largely peacefully; views of governing classes on labour discontent

No traces of the international strike were visible in Dresden,[313] and no disturbances have been reported from the provinces, where, as here, the absentees from work were a minimum.

[311] Arendt was member of the *Deutsche Reichspartei*; the extreme interests of the so-called Junker were represented by the *Deutschkonservative Partei*.

[312] The gold standard was adopted in December 1871; Strachey is referring to the Coin Law of 9 July 1873 which established the *Mark* as the common currency in all German states (from 1 January 1876).

[313] The International Workers Congresses (Paris, 20 May 1889) had called for international demonstrations and strikes on 1 May 1890.

The competent authorities of this capital anticipated, at the worst, a little extra movement in the streets after night-fall. But where we should employ half-a-dozen additional policemen, German precaution calls entire brigades and divisions of troops under arms, and accordingly the garrisons of Dresden, Leipzig and other places, were consigned to barracks all day, and sentries were doubled, by ministerial order. Some prudent Colonels, however, being of opinion that the possibilities of Revolution may still be present, have required their officers to remain ready at call till to-morrow evening.

Open air assemblages and processions were not forbidden by proclamation, except in Leipzig, where it was notified that the police had orders in case of resistance, to "use their weapons." Two meetings of workmen were held here at which Socialists of note delivered harangues on the Eight hour day.

Some of the municipalities of the kingdom, and the State Railway Department, warned the operatives in their pay that absentees on the 1st of May would be dismissed. In Chemnitz, all the employers of labour in the spinning, weaving, machine, tool, and foundry branches, signified a similar determination to their hands. Numerous manufacturers, building societies, metal workers &c &c in Dresden, and elsewhere in Saxony, adopted the same course, or threatened strikers with reprisals in the form of a lock-out.

Certain Radical journals accuse the organs which can no longer be called Bismarckian of intentionally treating the labour-problems of the day in a comminatory style calculated to inflame class hatreds and provoke collisions. The charge is somewhat highly coloured; but these burning topics are, no doubt, discussed in some quarters, in language which, amongst ourselves, would be thought reprehensible. I have from time to time reported that the representatives of capital and industry, and, above all, the official hierarchy, are too apt to think of the operatives of Germany as a 'swinish multitude' which, if recalcitrant, must be brought to reason by bayonets and grape-shot. The following is characteristic of Imperial Germany. I stated to an official who has had high employment in the local civil administration, that I could not understand the Saxon regulations equivalent to our Riot-Act.[314] The answer was, that on this subject legislation was silent: the police and military had to look, not to the law, but to their instructions.

---

[314] The Riot Act of 1714 gave the authorities the power to forcibly disband groups of twelve or more people who were rowdy, or had unlawfully come together and who had ignored pleas to disperse.

FO 68/175: George Strachey to Marquess of Salisbury, No 30, Dresden, 9 May 1890

[Received 12 May, U.F.S. [Under Flying Seal] to Berlin. Qy: X; S[alisbury]]

Emperor's Trade Act speech to Reichstag *popular in Saxony*

The Imperial speech to the Reichstag has been very well received here.[315] The monarchical feeling of the majority, (no where more than in this kingdom), is so delicate, that open animadversion on the policy claimed by the Emperor as personal would be thought to violate the elementary decorums of life. Any written or spoken words relative to Royalty, jarring in the smallest particular on the German conception of the reverence due to the Crown, are likely to be followed by a prosecution for malignant libel. The Emperor's popularity is great, so that, on all grounds, assent and admiration were assured for his speech beforehand, whether he announced an augmentation of military burdens or their restriction – whether his programme of industrial legislation was favorable to capital or to labour.

If confidential criticisms, like those reported by me on previous occasions, are current, I have not heard them. There seems cause for amazement at the confidence with which the Imperial statesman – (some would say D[r] Hinzpeter) – refers to the restrictions in the 'Novel' to the 'Trade Act', so long advocated by the liberal left, as the natural cure for the chronic condition of strike by which Germany is now troubled. It is notorious that the existing agitation amongst the operatives refers to none of the points in which reform is now offered, their demand being for an increased remuneration of labour, to take effect in higher wages for fewer hours of work.

FO 68/175: George Strachey to Marquess of Salisbury, No 32 A, Dresden, 23 May 1890

[Received 26 May. S[alisbury]]

Bismarck's controversial views on German relations with Russia as reported in the press

Prince Bismarck's recent Tusculan Dissertations [*sic*][316] appear to be more approved by his enemies than by his friends. In Germany,

---

[315] At the opening of the *Reichstag*, on 6 May 1890, Wilhelm II announced a Trade Law amendment bill which regulated and extended the protection of workers.

[316] Strachey's reference to the *Tusculanae Disputationes* by Cicero (45 BC) alludes to Bismarck's interviews with the American, French and Russian newspapers, and in

official character, once assumed, is indelible, so that a Lieutenant, or a copying clerk, or a Minister of State, retains, on retirement, his hierarchical designation, and is expected to continue to exhibit, on pain of obloquy, or worse, the behaviour and sentiments of a place-man. Prince Bismarck's radical critics remark that he has done excellent service in defying a stupid superstition, and that it is a matter for congratulation that in a country of low political enlightenment like this the greatest of the national statesmen should decline to wear the traditional gag, and set the example of a new departure on English, French, and Italian lines, by returning to the feelings and assuming the rights of a private citizen.

The Prince's reported views on this Empire's proper attitude towards France are, on the whole, in harmony with average german [*sic*] feeling. Not so his observations to the Russian journalist on Turkish and Balkan politics. It is not true that this nation would "not tolerate a Sultan policy",[317] and in his animosity against the late ruler of Bulgaria,[318] Prince Bismarck stands almost alone. His avowals of sympathy with the guet-apens[319] of Sofia were generally condemned by his countrymen, very few of whom share his preference, declared to M. Loof [*sic*], and shewn in such numerous ways, for that close alliance with Russia which, till recently, has always been a traditional object of Hohenzollern diplomacy since the conclusion of the Seven Years War.[320] The foreign policy of Germany will not, for the present, be decided in the streets; but it is certain that the Czar and his subjects have inspired large portions of the nation with antipathy, which is peculiarly the case here. Prince Bismarck might view a Russian occupation of Constantinople with indifference: the general public would hold, that it was incumbent on Germany to prevent the occurrence of a catastrophe so dangerous to the Empire and to Europe.

---

particular to the interview with Evgenii L'vovich Kochetov (pseudonym L'vov) on 28 April 1890, published in the *Novoye Vremya* on 10 May 1890.

[317] I.e. a pro-Ottoman policy against Russia.

[318] Alexander von Battenberg, prince (knyaz) of Bulgaria.

[319] French: 'ambush', in this context the surprise attackers. This refers to the coup against Alexander of Bulgaria in August 1886; see n. 25 in Darmstadt section.

[320] The Seven Years' War, 1756–1763, which marked the emergence of Prussia as a Great Power.

FO 68/175: George Strachey to Marquess of Salisbury, No 35, Dresden, 6 June 1890

[Received 9 May. Qy: X; S[alisbury]]

Fabrice foresees more temperate parliamentary debates on army bill

Count Fabrice informed me yesterday that the prospects of the new Army Bill in the Reichstag were encouraging.[321] Although the opposition are so much augmented in numerical strength, their temper is less combative that it was in previous Parliaments, and they now shew a certain willingness to consider Government measures on their merits. His Excellency observed, that, in his opinion, there has been too much delay in maturing, and submitting to the legislature, the larger schemes of military reform which will soon be brought forward. Germany must drain her resources to the bottom: the momentary European situation was quiescent, but the continuance of tranquillity would be best secured by the immediate acceptance of the sacrifices which the nation cannot evade.

His Excellency may never have heard of Plato, but he thinks that mankind ought to be governed by "experts"[322] – at any rate in the war department – and he diverged into an excursus on the absurdity of the measures requisite for public defence being controlled by political babblers. However, he is aware that even the Germans will not submit to the rule of "Major-Generals," and on my remarking – that is 'Utopia' –, he assented, and agreed that having got our Parliaments we must stomach them.

I alluded to the improvement in German parliamentary manners, and said that it was a new sensation to read a speech by the Reichskanzler, which did not assume that every one who objected to official doctrines, or proposals, was an insolent, factious, ruffian. Count Fabrice said that, in that respect, no doubt there had been room for increased tolerance and temper, and that General von Caprivi was well adapted, by his personality, for a new departure in that direction. And, added his Excellency, the spirit of moderation is visible all round – a verity which he unconsciously proceeded to illustrate in his own person, by speaking with impartiality, and even with benevolence, of the leaders of the 'freisinnig' party,[323]

---

[321] The amendment bill to the Imperial Military Law of 1887 (see n. 119 in Berlin section) provided for an increase in the strength of the army by 18,577 additional men, taking the total to 486,983. The bill was passed on 28 June 1890.

[322] Strachey is referring to Plato's dialogue *Crito (Κρίτων)*.

[323] *Deutsche Freisinnige Partei*. See n. 3 in Berlin section.

and concluding with superlatives in favour of Bebel, whom he called
the greatest orator of Germany – which was not so before.

FO 68/175: George Strachey to Marquess of Salisbury, No 45, Dresden, 3 October 1890

[Received 6 October. S[alisbury]]

Saxon king a steadying presence in imperial affairs

The King has left for Vienna, where he was to proceed with the
Emperors to Styria for chamois hunting.[324] The ostentatious friendship which at present unites the Habsburgs and the Hohenzollerns
contains a large political element; but the tie between those dynasties
and the house of Wettin is one of genuine personal attachment. King
Albert has inspired with strong feelings of regard the representatives
of the two royal lines whose old antagonisms have forced Saxony into
alliances and conflicts which have cost the kingdom dear.

According to a current legend, the Emperor Frederick formally
appointed the King of Saxony Mentor to his son. As a matter of
fact, those high personages did not entertain for each other the sentiments assumed, and the peculiar and increasing intimacy of the
Courts of Dresden and Berlin has a more natural basis.

No occupant of a throne can be freer than the King from the usual
defects and prejudices of royalty. His Majesty is an agreeable, and,
what is rare here, a humorous, companion. Though not of the professorial calibre, like his father,[325] he has considerable general culture,
and is very strong in history. He is the only German who can confidently be affirmed to be equal, in the modern scientific sense, to the
command of large armies, and he has a thorough knowledge working, as well as intellectual, of the various political and administrative
problems of the day.

Questions of geography and personality have given the Emperor's
relations with the Regent of Bavaria[326] a merely occasional and formal
character. And, in that kingdom, the transformation of the old
Germany to the new has not been so radical, or so cordially accepted,
as the parallel change here. For these and other reasons, the ruler of
the German state which comes next to Prussia in size – (though not in
wealth and industrial importance) has not assumed the second place

---

[324] Albert arrived at Vienna on 1 October, and proceeded to Styria, together with the
two emperors, on the same day. He returned on 11 October 1890.

[325] Johann I.

[326] Luitpold.

in the Imperial hierarchy, and that position has been occupied by the King of Saxony. When grave decisions have to be taken in regard to the foreign policy of the Empire, the King's counsels will carry great weight. They will fall on the side of sobriety, with entire subordination of mere military motives, and with an enlightened regard to the necessities of civilisation and progress. I am glad to be able to say, that in the King of Saxony's 'Weltanschauung',[327] as the Germans say, or 'cosmical conception', sympathy with Great Britain is cardinal. His diplomatic ideal is a Quadruple Alliance[328] which should solve Oriental problems in our sense, and he would see in a Russian advance on India an encroachment of barbarism which ought to be treated as a menace to Germany and Europe. It proves for his largeness of mind, that in spite of the soreness arising from his accumulated grievances against us, and the satisfaction caused him by the courtesies of Russia to Saxony, he continues to take an entirely objective view of the international questions in which we are concerned.

FO 68/175: George Strachey to Marquess of Salisbury, No 54, Dresden, 12 December 1890

[Received 15 December. For: The Queen; Copies to: Education Department, P.L. [printed letter], 22 December / Berlin (in original); S[alisbury]]

Emperor's outspoken views on German education not well-received in Saxony

The Emperor's speech for the Higher Schools Conference[329] has been even less favourably received than his Rescripts on the Industrial Reform and the Army.[330] In Saxony, a single newspaper – the Leipzig semi-official organ[331] – has made a show of approval. In other quarters, there is either the significant silence which is equivalent to condemnation: or it is argued that the Emperor could not have used the language placed in his mouth: or his facts are denied and his deductions refuted, with a bluntness unusual in German discussions of Royal utterances.

In my personal opinion, there is much in this allocution to justify those who maintain that the Emperor's brilliant gifts do not include the qualities which constitute an 'esprit juste',[332] and that he is

---

[327] Literally 'world view' (concept of the world).
[328] Alliance of Austria-Hungary, Germany, Great Britain, and Russia.
[329] On 4 December at the opening of the conference at Berlin.
[330] For the rescripts in question, see n. 249 Berlin section and n. 171 in this section.
[331] *Leipziger Zeitung.*
[332] French: 'just spirit'.

specially given to overhasty generalisation. In his view, the teachers of Germany are imperfectly educated: being half taught, they cannot effectively teach: the masters wrongly treat their work as done when they leave the schoolroom: they teach their pupils book-knowledge, but do not impart education in the higher sense: they have neglected to combat the advances of Social Democracy.

I have seen something of the German tutorial class, and I concur in the view, generally taken, that these animadversions have no real basis. The teachers of the youth of the Empire have thoroughly learned their business as instructors under an elaborate system of pedagogic science, they are an able and meritorious body of men, and they slave conscientiously at their work at all hours. Then, as the typical Higher School of the Empire is a day, sometimes a morning, school not residential like Eton or Harrow, the influence of the German Arnold, or Drury,[333] and his assistants, on their pupils is, in the nature of things, only scholastic. For the rest, the German educational staff of the higher ranks is thoroughly, perhaps excessively, conservative and imperialist. As for preachments against Social-Democracy, besides being contrary to school regulations, they would be absurdly out of place in lecture-rooms where nine tenths of the pupils belong to strata which furnish Bebel and Liebknecht with few or no recruits.

The Imperial indictment complains of the neglect of modern, i.e. recent, history in the schools. His Majesty thinks that if young Germany is taught "how the transition from the French Revolution to the 19th Century" was effected, "growling at the Government" would diminish, and there would be less worship of foreign ideals. On this, even Conservatives and National-Liberals remark, that it is not the business of schools to teach politics, while in the non-Prussian part of the public there is great dislike of those official Hohenzollern interpretations of history which the Emperor is, in fact, recommending. As regards over-work at home, the excessive study of antiquity, and the like, the failure and defects, which the allocution much exaggerates, arise partly from the circumstances and character of the nation, partly from faults of system, by no means, as the Imperial Censor thinks, from the imperfect ideals and practise of preceptors.

The Emperor was ill-advised in describing the journalistic staff of Germany as the refuse of the Gymnasiums.[334] This has given great

---

[333] Strachey is referring to the English educators and headmasters Thomas Arnold and Henry Drury.

[334] German equivalent to a grammar school.

offence; even the 'reptiles'[335] of approved capacity for adulation have strongly resented being called 'Hunger-candidates'.[336] I do not think well of the ability or integrity of the German press, but it is not quite conducted, as the Imperial criticisms imply, by the scum of Grub Street.

These descents of the young Monarch into the area of public discussion may prove his enlightened desire to promote progress; but many good Imperialists consider that the 'new course'[337] is calculated to weaken the authority of the crown, which must lose much of its nimbus if its bearer mixes as a disputant in the controversies of the day.

FO 68/176: George Strachey to Marquess of Salisbury, No 10, Dresden, 21 February 1891

[Received 23 February. X; S[alisbury]]

Newspaper responses to Bismarck's criticism of imperial politics

Here, as in the rest of the Empire, the Friedrichsruhe[338] controversy is being hotly debated by the Press, and by the fraction of the public which is politically inclined.[339] Opinions are not divided along the ordinary party lines. Common to all the disputants is the amazing readiness with which every rumour, or rumour of a rumour, is at once accepted, without criticism, as positive, ascertained, truth. Prince Bismarck's popularity and prestige have scarcely been shaken since his retirement,[340] and as the idea of a statesman out of office going into open opposition is inconceivable to the German mind, and would, if realized be almost held to be indictable offence, the subterranean procedure ascribed to the Ex-Chancellor is treated by many as the mode of action which it is natural for him to adopt.

The 'Nachrichten',[341] which is generally in harmony with the average local bourgeois sentiment, reprobates the manner in which certain intriguers have thrust themselves between the Emperor and "the patriotic party". The nation is pained at the conflict into which Prince Bismarck has been drawn by the contrivance of these malignants. Will none of the German sovereigns set the Kaiser right? It is

---

[335] For the 'reptile' press, see n. 67 in this section.

[336] In his speech Wilhelm denounced journalists as 'candidates destined to starve, [...] being in many cases depraved former grammar school pupils [*Gymnasiasten*]'.

[337] 'New Course' refers to the realignment of policy after Bismarck's dismissal in 1890.

[338] Bismarck's manor house at Friedrichsruh.

[339] For the conflict over Bismarck's interference in imperial politics, see pp. 129–131.

[340] On Bismarck's retirement, see pp. 123–124.

[341] *Dresdner Nachrichten*, 17 February 1891.

well that the warning voice from Friedrichsruhe should be so plainly heard, when the guidance of policy is subject to the instigation of democrats and Jews, when industry and agriculture are menaced with a return to free-trade, Africa is abandoned, the army is irritated, and other disturbances of the system inaugurated by the Paladins of the new Empire are in sight.

I have heard language equivalents, at bottom, to this, from high officials. Its prevalence in other places besides Dresden is established by the fact that the quasi National-Liberal and free-trade 'Zeitung'[342] has been censuring the strong Bismarckian partizanship of 'a large portion of the press', and complaining of the reprehensible want of reverence and submission with which the Emperor's opinions on political and economic topics have been received and discussed. This organ thinks that the Friedrichsruhe fronde,[343] however culpable is not, at present, within the reach of the law; but that the right of a subject, however great his position and antecedents, to resist and discredit the Emperor's policy, has its limits, as would surely be seen if Prince Bismarck thought fit, for instance, to publish state papers, or the like. But, says the 'Zeitung', it is a disgrace to Germany that these scandals,[344] which have partly arisen from the legends circulated by French correspondents (!), should be aired before the European public, and it is to be hoped that Prince Bismarck will not tarnish his name by making serious steps necessary.

The local organ of Social-Democracy[345] exults over the internecine war of its oppressors, and improves the occasion by pointing out that, amidst this crashing of political systems and reputations, the 'rocher de bronze'[346] of the Socialist cause and creed remain unquestioned and intact. The partizans of Bebel have, on the whole, been speaking with decency of their arch-enemy, and they cannot, at any rate, be charged with the infamy of hinting at the propriety of his eventual arrest and imprisonment in a jail.

On the foregoing, I would observe, that it is idle to measure the behaviour of the disputants in this controversy by standards taken from English or French history. The Germans are in the political nursery, and they are now less near to the possession of a recognized constitutional morality, and to the conquest of the virtues of tolerance, magnanimity, and self-assertion than they were 40 years ago. Further, it may suit the sensational necessities of our Berlin

---

[342] *Dresdner Zeitung*, 21 Feburary 1891.

[343] The *Fronde*, a historical term for the violent political opposition to the growing power of royal government and resultant series of civil wars in mid-seventeenth century France.

[344] The *Dresdner Zeitung* was referring to the 'inspired' articles in the *Hamburger Nachrichten* and the *Allgemeine Zeitung*.

[345] *Sächsische Arbeiter-Zeitung*.

[346] See n. 148 in this section.

newspaper correspondents, to talk of "great excitement and anxiety" prevailing, and similar, but the prose and calm of German daily life are, in reality, entirely unruffled by all these transactions. The people are passive, they are submissive, and they are acquiescent in the fact that, although the nation is not quite governed 'par ordre du mufti',[347] it has, at present, no power of popular or parliamentary initiative in policy, or of resistance to the Imperial will.

FO 68/176: George Strachey to Marquess of Salisbury, No 23, Dresden, 15 May 1891

[Received 18 May. X; S[alisbury]]

Cool public reception of emperor's speech praising 'Borussia' student corps

The Emperor's speech to the rowdy section of the students of Bonn,[348] and his appearance at the drinking bout in the costume of the Corps 'Borussia', have not been well received by the German public. When the ultra-Imperialist Dresden 'Zeitung'[349] observes that a deplorable impression has been produced amongst the educated classes, and at the Universities, by the monarch's eulogy on one of the most objectionable features of the German academic system, criticism must have gone very far.

It may be proper to explain, that the so-called 'Corps', which the Emperor extols as nurseries of patriotism, discipline, and courage, include, at most, one tenth, or twelfth, of the youth in Statu pupillari,[350] the large majority of whom belong neither to a 'Corps', nor to a 'Burschenschaft', nor to any of the numerous student corporations.[351] Some of these last named bodies have a useful intelligent, or social, purpose, and they include numbers of steady, reading, men. Whereas the 'Corps' generally absorbs, and represents, the idling, swaggering, bumptious, gambling, spending, fighting elements in student life. Some of the 'Corps' rules, are childish: e.g. the men may not travel on the Railway second-class, or go to a second-rate Hôtel, or sit more than two together in an open carriage To what extent such folly predominates in the code of the 'Borussia', I do not know.

---

[347] See n. 215 in this section.
[348] On 6 May 1891 at Bonn.
[349] *Dresdner Zeitung*, 15 May 1891.
[350] Latin: 'under guardianship'; those at universities who do not hold a master's degree.
[351] Corps were originally regional corporations of students (e.g. Borussia for Prussia); the *Burschenschaft* fraternities dated back to the national movement of 1815 and drew their members from a larger, and less elitist, base.

The 'Corps', then, is the special institution from whose spirit a young German, in the Emperor's opinion "will derive his best education for his future life". His Majesty's devoted partizans in the 'Zeitung' urge, in his defence, the argument that he was led astray by his eloquence, and that whatever meaning his words may seem to bear, it was not his intention to advocate the generalisation of the 'Corps' system, or to express approval of a such a barbarous proceeding as the 'Mensur'[352] or students['] duel!!

On this last point the Socialist 'Arbeiter Zeitung'[353] remarks that criticism of Imperial oratory is a dangerous thing and that they do not feel equal to any more prosecutions for libel. But that as a matter of fact language like "I hope You will joyfully use Your swords", is a recommendation to break the law. For the Supreme Court of the Empire has formally declared students['] duels to be as criminal as any other form of personal combat,[354] and cases of conviction and punishment for the offence are, from time to time, reported from the 21 German University towns.

It will be interesting to see if the Imperial doctrine checks the ardour of the Leipzig Police, who are notable for their intolerance of students['] duels. Their watchfulness is such, that University combatants now seldom venture to fight within the city. A few days ago, some student duellists, and their seconds, were arrested on their return from a 'Mensur' at Halle, brought to trial, and sentenced to 3 months imprisonment.

FO 68/176: George Strachey to Marquess of Salisbury, No 27, Dresden, 5 June 1891

[Received 8 June. For: Commercial Department; 'I think it might instruct Sir J. Crowe to read this.' T.H.S. [Thomas Henry Sanderson]]

Responses to Caprivi's speech on grain duties

The Reichskanzler's speech on the grain duties has given unbounded satisfaction to the Protectionist classes.[355] The Conservatives, the

---

[352] 'Academic' fencing.

[353] *Sächsische Arbeiter-Zeitung*, 8 May 1891.

[354] Decision of the *Reichsgericht* of 6 March 1883; duels were prohibited under Section 15 of the Imperial Penal Code of 1871.

[355] In his declaration in the Prussian house of deputies, on 1 June 1891, Caprivi – despite widespread concerns about a meagre harvest and rising food prices – announced that taxation on corn would remain unaltered.

Anti-Semites, the larger land-owners, the holders of industrial papers, and the corn lobby, are enthusiastic in praise of the policy which he announces. They are not quite pleased with his admission of the fact, that cereals are dearer here than in the free markets by the full amount of the German import duty. But they are gratified by his adhesion to the monopolist dogmas that cheap corn does not make cheap bread, and that the extra ten or eleven schillings a quarter, which the Tariff enables the German farmer to add to the natural cost of his wheat, is partly, perhaps entirely, paid not by the German consumer, but by the growers of the Punjab and the Ukraine.

On the Dresden Stock Exchange, General Caprivi's declaration caused a general fall of values. The decline began with the paper of the Austrian and Russian railways and institutes principally affected by the state, or prospects, of the traffic in cereals. It developed under the influence of the pessimism of a part of the Commercial class, in regard to the high food prices now prevailing in Germany, which, in their view, are calculated to impair industrial progress, and to pro-long the uncertainties of the present economic situation.

The behaviour of the Corn Exchange suggests an interesting com-mentary on the Reichskanzler's theories of price. Some time since, the local quotation of wheat had reached 250 Marks the metrical ton. A confident assertion having appeared in the Press, that the Imperial Government would shortly propose a reduction of the duties on cereals, a sudden fall of 7 to 10 Marks ensued. On the report of General Caprivi's speech being known, there was an instant recovery, and both wheat and rye have now taken a start near the previous maximum, while further additions to the cost of the loaf have been announced by the bakers.

Highly characteristic of Germany is the reserve which a large por-tion of the press maintains on the whole subject. In Dresden, the semi official paper devotes daily leaders to the politics of Servia, Bulgaria, Rumania and Russia; but to the discussion of food supplies, and their cost, the 'Journal'[356] does not descend. The National-Liberal 'Anzeiger'[357] quotes, but does not criticize. The Socialist organ,[358] however, which writes Political Economy of the pure English type takes the situation as a text for fresh assaults on capital and its agrar-ian allies. The Conservative 'Nachrichten'[359] thanks General Caprivi for his manly stand against the Hebrew operators from whose satur-nalia the Empire has now been saved, and for his profound remark,

---

[356] *Dresdner Journal.*
[357] *Dresdner Anzeiger,* 3 June 1891.
[358] *Sächsische Arbeiter-Zeitung,* 3 June 1891.
[359] *Dresdner Nachrichten,* 3 June 1891.

that "under lowered duties Germany would be so flooded with for-eign grain, that our next harvest would be compromised, and our farmers would be unable to obtain a remunerative price for their products". The Generals repudiation of the chatter of Adam Smith and Mill is not however, uncomprising [*sic*] enough for the 'Nachrichten', which fears that surprises may still occur. But, adds the writer, the Reichskanzler's speech is 'an arsenal of weapons, from which the "patriotic parties" will be able to borrow invaluable arguments when the Treaty with Austria comes on for discussion'.

[...]

P.S. Last night's 'Arbeiter Zeitung' publishes an appeal from the Central Council of the Social-Democratic party to the workmen of Germany,[360] to organize anti-Cornlaw meetings all over the Empire.

FO 68/176: George Strachey to Marquess of Salisbury, No 38, Dresden, 22 August 1891

[Received 24 August by post. X; T.V.L. [Thomas Villiers Lister]

Highly misinformed German press article on Gladstone's friendly disposition towards Russia and France

The Official 'Journal',[361] which is notable for exhaustive ignorance of the facts and personalities of English politics, has had a leader on the visit of the French fleet to Portsmouth.[362] The writer gives a surprising picture of the Slavophil[e] tendencies, and Gallomania, of the Gladstonian party and their chief. According to the Dresden publi-cist, 'the English liberals prior to the rupture of 1886,[363] were in close alliance with the Russian Nationalists, and to this policy, of which the famous "Hands-off"[364] was the watch-word, they have con-stantly adhered when all great European questions have been in debate. Owing to the sympathy of the Gladstonians with Russia, the presence of the French fleet is producing in their camp effects like those lately witnessed at Cronstadt'.

---

[360] The proclamation is dated Berlin, 1 June 1891.

[361] *Dresdner Journal*, 20 August 1891.

[362] A French naval squadron visited Portsmouth from 19 to 26 August 1891 on its return from Kronstadt (see n. 340 in Berlin section). On 20 August the Queen received French naval officers at Osborne House; on 21 August she reviewed the fleet.

[363] This is referring to the accession of the conservative government in 1886.

[364] See n. 63 in this section.

'Their specific object is the succession of England to the unwritten Franco-Russian alliance, and their Courtship of the war-party in France must act as a stimulus to Chauvinist aspirations'.

After developing these ideas at length, from the resources of his moral consciousness, the writer analyzes Mr Gladstone's motives for coming so prominently to the front at this particular moment with his worship of France! 'Are his obtrusive oglings, and professions of friendship, inspired by the hope that they may encourage the Republic to attack Germany, and so draw Russia into a war which would make England mistress of the situation, and enable her to dictate to Russia on her Indian frontier? Perhaps not, unless he sees in such complications a ladder by which he could mount to power again.'

The article further describes the entire English liberal press as 'endeavouring to bring the recent visit of the German emperor[365] into contempt, and to discredit the friendly feelings of Her Majesty's Government for Germany in favour of the obsequious Gallomania of which the Gladstonians are now making such ostentatious display.'

The writer may have confounded Mr Gladstone with Mr Labouchere, and the 'Daily Chronicle' with the 'Daily News'.[366] Or he may have hoped to recommend himself to official notice and protection, by warning the readers of the 'Journal' – a very select minority – against the hallucinations and ineptitudes into which, all the world over, men necessarily fall, when they are led, not by Conservative principles, but by the unpatriotic dogmas of the liberal creed.

FO 68/176: George Strachey to Marquess of Salisbury, No 48, Dresden, 27 October 1891

[Received 29 October. X; T.V.L. [Thomas Villiers Lister]]

Responses to the emperor's bestowal of honours on Professor Helmholtz but not Professor Virchow

The Bismarckians' are jubilant at the bestowal of the title of 'Excellenz' on Professor, Helmholtz the seventh instance,[367] it is

---

[365] Wilhelm II visited Great Britain from 4 to 13 July 1891.

[366] The *Daily Chronicle* was largely supportive of Gladstone; the *Daily News* was partly owned by Henry Labouchère who belonged to the radical wing of the Liberal party.

[367] On 18 October 1891, in honour of Helmholtz' 70th birthday (31 August), Wilhelm II made him *Wirklicher Geheimer Rat* (*Geheimrat;* privy councillor) with the grade (*Prädikat*) *Exzellenz.*

said, of the descent of that honour on a German not holding civil or
military rank. Of the Professor's invention of the Augen-Spiegel,[368] or
of his great contributions to the doctrine of the Conservation of
Energy, and to physiological optics and acoustics, only a minority
of the enthusiasts have heard: and of his new admirers in the
upper classes, scarcely one would stoop to meet a mere philosopher
on equal social terms. All this exultation has arisen because Professor
Virchow has been dignified by no similar mark of his sovereign's
favour. The chief European representative of the new pathology
and anthropology has for thirty years been one of the leaders of
the 'progressist' party[369] which he helped to found. As a 'Whig of
the Revolution',[370] whose attitude in the 'Conflict Time', especially
in the incident of his challenge from the Minister-President
Bismarck,[371] did so much to repress the 'Major-General' style of discussion in the German parliament, Virchow has been obnoxious to
the governing powers and their allies, and the ovations just paid to
him in Berlin, in which there was some admixture of political colour,
revived antipathies which had been slumbering.[372]

   The anti-'freisinnig' camp is therefore highly gratified at the distinction made between the two great Germans, the more so as
they have discovered in the Rescript to Helmholtz a side thrust
against the member for Berlin. Still, the feeling is very general,
that taking sides in politics is not a proper function of the Crown,
and this incident will be quoted as confirmatory of the opinion maintained by many loyal & Conservative Germans, that one of the family virtues of the Hohenzollerns – tact – has not been inherited by
the Emperor William. How little the supposed manifestation of the
monarch's displeasure has availed to 'dash in pieces'[373] the most influential of the members for the capital, is apparent from the professor's speech at the Banquet of the Municipality of Berlin,[374] some

[368] German: 'eye mirror'; the ophthalmoscope was invented in 1851.

[369] *Deutsche Fortschrittspartei*, founded in 1861; known as the *Deutsche Freisinnige Partei* from
1884 (see n. 3 in Berlin section).

[370] Virchow participated in the March Revolution of 1848.

[371] Strachey is referring to the Prussian constitutional conflict of 1859–1866, which
revolved around plans for the reorganization of the army and parliamentary rights against
the monarchy and its executive. The incident he mentions happened in the Prussian house
of deputies, on 2 June 1865, when Bismarck, in the course of a fierce political debate, challenged Virchow to a duel (which was declined by the latter).

[372] Strachey is referring to the festivities on the occasion of Virchow's 70th birthday (13
October).

[373] In his toast at the banquet of the provincial diet of Brandenburg, at Berlin, on 5
March 1890, Wilhelm II said 'I will smash those who are in the way of this work'
[Work =Wilhelm II's duty as sovereign].

[374] At the Berlin town hall on 21 October 1891.

expressions of which had a flavour of Guildhall oratory in the days of Lord Mayor Beckford. All this, the Bismarckian organs suppress. Continuing my parallel, I would say that in the opinion of some good Conservatives here, the Emperor will do well, like his august ancestor in England, to "have nothing more to do with that devil Wilkes."[375]

FO 68/176: George Strachey to Marquess of Salisbury, No 55, Dresden, 4 December 1891

[Received 7 December. For: The Queen / Prince of Wales; S[alisbury]]

German feelings vis-à-vis Caprivi's leadership and political course of action

General Caprivi's defence of his policy has excited a certain interest here. As far as I can judge, the general public is in a somewhat pessimist temper; but is not dissatisfied with "the new course",[376] and is not looking for help from Friedrichsruhe.[377] "The present discontents" are mainly felt by Conservatives, National-Liberals, Colonials, Anti-Semites, Protectionists, Bimetallists, Agrarians, and other adherents of the 'Cartel'.[378] With them, the new Chancellor is unpopular, because he treats liberal opinions as a permissible form of political belief: because he appears to be unsound on Africa, the Tariff, Poland, and the Jesuit Laws: because he will not revive the Guilds, or legislate against the Jews; or place the Stock-Exchange under Police control, or tamper with the Gold coinage.

With their own sentiments on such matters, they consider Prince Bismarck to be more or less in touch, and his return to power would further be acceptable to them, as ensuring the revival of that hectoring, browbeating, manner in politics, on which, although in Germany its use gives great weight to the authority of public men, General Caprivi has turned his back.

These malcontents have numerous allies in the civil service, especially in Prussia, and amongst the officers of the Army, whose grievances, form however, a chapter apart. Under "the old course", orders were obeyed in silent submission, and the discussion of

[375] George III, 1771 (as quoted in a letter by John Calcraft to William Pitt, 1st Earl of Chatham, 24 March 1771).
[376] See n. 337 in this section.
[377] Friedrichsruh, Bismarck's manor house.
[378] For the so-called 'Cartel', see n. 208 in Berlin section.

Government personages and measures was a freedom on which no one in the public pay liked to venture. The gag has now been removed, and something like an English license of criticism has been growing up, which is called an anarchical and dangerous condition of things, due to the disappearance of the former "Olympian elements" in German statesmanship. If General Caprivi were to be a little brutal in official business, if he could have his Arnim, Geffcken, and Morier incidents,[379] his Royal Interregnum,[380] his 5000 actions against libellers and defamers, the complaint would not be heard from his subordinates that he is a Minister without a policy, a mere Newcastle or Addington, coming after Chatham or Pitt.

The opposition so constituted is a formidable phalanx, which has its academic and 'reptile'[381] supporters; but it is not the people of Germany. The parties of the Catholic centre, of Progress, of Constitutional and Social Democracy with the Guelphs, Poles, Danes, and Alsatians, form nearly two thirds of the active Electorate. Prince Bismarck's resignation[382] removed an Alp from the minds of all of these, and it is their feeling that under his successor there has been a marked improvement in administrative aims and methods.

Looking to the above arithmetic, it may then be said, that a German plebiscite – (of Dresden I am not speaking) – would give General Caprivi a vote of confidence, a view which the results of recent bye-elections, Imperial and local, would seem to confirm.[383]

Leaving the future undiscussed, I would venture on the statement that this nation does not, at present, desire Prince Bismarck's return to office. Uneasiness exists; but it arises from a prevalent suspicion regarding the intentions of France and Russia, or from vague feeling which cannot be analyzed. And, unless I mistake, in respect both to domestic and foreign affairs, a certain disquietude has been recently growing amongst patriotic and loyal Germans because their faith in the wisdom and discretion of the Crown has, of late, been so frequently and so rudely shaken.

---

[379] For the incidents in question, see n. 261 in Berlin section (Arnim affair of 1874), n. 224 in Berlin section (prosecution of Geffcken in 1888), and pp. 114–115 (Morier incident of 1888–1889).

[380] Strachey is referring to the ninety-nine day reign of Friedrich III.

[381] See n. 67 in this section.

[382] See pp. 123–124.

[383] By-elections for the *Reichstag* were held in the electoral districts Stolp (Pomerania; 27 October), Rastenburg (East Prussia; 18 November), and Hall (Württemberg; 23 November). By-elections of federal states were held, among others, in Kaiserslautern (Bavaria, 7 November) and Trier (Prussia, 21 November).

FO 68/176: George Strachey to Marquess of Salisbury, No 57, Dresden, 14 December 1891

[Received 16 December. For: Commercial Department]

Local indifference towards commercial treaties and proposed tariff changes; political parties about-turn on free trade has lost them credibility

The Treaties of Commerce have been received here with character-istic indifference and reserve.[384] The dominant local interest is the industrial, and it does not appear that the makers of the metallic, tex-tile, and industrial, staples regard the proposed Tariff changes with either enthusiasm or apprehension. Before 1879, the administrative hierarchy of the Kingdom professed belief in Free-trade.[385] In that year, the governing body, from the highest to the lowest, had to adopt Protection as a cardinal official doctrine from which it was not permissible for a public servant to dissent. They have now to exe-cute another change of front, and a certain modification of their lan-guage is already perceptible.

The 'Free' Conservatives and the National-Liberals are again con-spicuous for the servility which has brought their parties into such contempt with the electorate. Turning their backs on themselves, they are defending the Treaties by arguments which flatly contradict their previous opinions. The Municipal 'Anzeiger'[386] – always an adept in trimming – thinks that the Treaties should be adopted because it is doubtful if an appeal to the Constituencies would give a Protectionist Reichstag. This organ now allows that customs duties may have some slight effect on the cost of imported produce; but it denounces the doctrine, promulgated with such success by a deplor-able democratic agitation, that such duties raise the price of bread.

On the other hand the Social-Democrats, with whom are united the small Saxon 'freisinnig'[387] party, applaud General von Caprivi's policy which, they hope, may prove to be the precursor of a further advance in the direction of the cheap loaf and free-trade. The reactionary and 'Agrarian' Conservatives, to whom belong the courtly and aristocratic sections of opinion, are equally outspoken in their allegation that the Treaties are a betrayal of the agricultural interest, which it is the first

[384] Commercial treaties based on a most-favoured-nation clause were concluded with Austria-Hungary, Italy, Belgium, and Switzerland. They were passed by the *Reichstag* on 18 December 1891 and came into effect in February 1892.

[385] New (protective) German tariffs had been introduced by the Imperial Tariff Law of 15 July 1879.

[386] *Dresdner Anzeiger*, 12 December 1891.

[387] See n. 3 in Berlin section.

duty of sound statesmanship to uphold. Their views are stated, with an exaggeration amounting to caricature, in the 'Nachrichten',[388] which reiterates the old contentions that import duties do not raise the price of corn, and that if the 'International Hebrew Mammon' were laid under proper restrictions, there would be cheap bread. This organ's wholesale repudiation of the most elementary notions of Political Economy suits the ignorance, and anti-Semitic jealousies, of the average 'Philistine', and it has a large Saxon and German circulation. Absurd as the 'Nachrichten's['] opinions frequently are, they are, at least plain-spoken – an unusual merit here.

FO 68/177: George Strachey to Marquess of Salisbury, No 9, Dresden, 26 February 1892

[Received 29 February. Seen at Berlin. For: The Queen; S[alisbury]]

Negative reception of the emperor's speech to the provincial diet at Brandenburg

The Emperor's speech to the States of Brandenburg[389] may have suited his special audience; but it has been no better received by the general public than the Monarch's previous allocutions. Political Emancipation, and personal self-respect are very imperfectly matured here. Still, the Germans are no longer in the phase of Byzantine subjection described in the words quoted by Burke – "our Prince tells us to eat straw, and we eat straw."[390] They have an unequalled veneration for the function of Government; but the time is past for telling them that it becomes loyal subjects to hold their tongues and pay taxes, and that the critically disposed had better emigrate to countries with institutions more congenial to their tastes.

If the theory of "the Intelligent Despot", to which the Emperor keeps so persistently recurring, is altogether out of date, so is his family theology. This is not the age of the Grand Elector[391] or Frederick William I, and to the average German, or Prussian, the notion of the Providential mission of the Hohenzollerns is a mere superstition. Saxons, Bavarians, Hanoverians and others, would argue that the achievements of

[388] Strachey is referring to the editorials of 10 to 13 December 1891 in the *Dresdner Nachrichten*.

[389] The speech was held at the banquet of the provincial diet of Brandenburg at Berlin, on 24 February 1891.

[390] Thomas Paine, in his *Rights of Man: Being an Answer to Mr. Burke's Attack on the French Revolution*, part one (1791), quotes a Brunswick soldier as saying 'If the prince says, eat straw, we eat straw'.

[391] Friedrich Wilhelm.

Frederick the Great, and of some of the ancestors and successors, if due to superior guidance at all, were the work of the powers of evil. In particular, they would call the battle of Rossbach,[392] by which the Emperor illustrates the alliance between Prussia and heaven, as an instance of the triumph of the bad principle, and they would decline to glorify a victory in which Germans were in the defeated ranks.

His Imperial Majesty's popularity has declined within the last two years. His public utterances have shaken the belief in his prudence. The dismissal of Prince Bismarck[393] has raised against him a party of unforgiving enemies. The army is dissatisfied. The terrors of the law of libel may again prevent the open expression of disapprobation, but they cannot stifle the general regrets and dislike aroused by the reiteration of unconstitutional doctrines and exploded claims.

[…]

P.S. The tone of the notices of the speech just published in the local newspapers is uniformly unfavorable. They contain no direct censure; but shew the usual dexterity of a faltered press in applying the precept "and without sneering, others teach to sneer".[394]

FO 68/177: George Strachey to Marquess of Salisbury, No 14, Dresden, 26 March 1892

[Received 28 March. For: The Queen; S[alisbury]]

Saxon views on political crisis in Berlin

The crisis in Berlin caused some anxiety in ministerial circles here.[395] The belief is entertained that the pacification first concluded will prove to be only an armistice. It is thought that the division of the offices of Reichskanzler and Prussian Premier will be a source of constitutional and personal friction. And it is argued that Count Caprivi cannot, without loss of dignity and prestige, entirely turn his back on his own uncompromising advocacy of the Prussian Education Bill,[396] the opposition to which he characterized as grounded in atheism.

---

[392] In the Battle of Rossbach (5 November 1757) Friedrich II led Prussian forces to a victory over a Franco-Imperial allied army. The battle marked a turning point in the Seven Years' War.

[393] For Bismarck's dismissal, see pp. 123–124.

[394] From *Epistle to Dr Arbuthnot* by Alexander Pope (1735).

[395] For the ministerial crisis and Caprivi's resignation as Prussian minister president, see pp. 138–140.

[396] See n. 296 in Berlin section.

According to my informant, Count Caprivi does not look forward to a privileged occupation of the post of Reichskanzler. No fundamental differences, political or personal, separate him from the Emperor. But he cannot persuade himself that he enjoys that full measure of trust which, under a Constitutional regime, the Crown should accord to its responsible adviser. He knows, or suspects, that the Imperial policy and decisions are affected by concealed influences behind the throne, and on these terms he would not consent to continue at the head of the Government of Germany.

Count von Caprivi inspires entire confidence here. He has not tried to Prussianize the Empire. He is thought to possess many of the best attributes of statesmanship, while none of those to whom his succession might be expected to fall have any outdoor reputation whatever, marking them out for the place. Most of the maxims which our own public philosophy affirms are repudiated here. In Germany it is thought natural that the higher political functions should be entrusted to persons without political knowledge – to a "Major-General", a desk-official, an Ambassador. Parliamentary experience and popular influence, are not reckoned among the qualifications which should be exacted from a Prime Minister.

FO 68/177: George Strachey to Earl of Rosebery, No 29, Dresden, 8 October 1892

[Received 10 October. X; R[osebery]]

Saxon views on Kálnoky's speech regarding British foreign policy

Count Kalnoky's remarks to the Deputations on the continuity of our Foreign policy have been read with satisfaction here.[397] It has not been the assumption of official circles, or of the fraction of the German public which has political interests, that Her Majesty's late Government had entered into partnership, even in a qualified and conditional manner, with the Triple Alliance.[398] There has, however, prevailed a belief, that a Conservative administration would be disposed, at a critical moment, to lend a certain degree of moral

[397] Strachey is referring to the sitting of the Hungarian Delegations at Budapest, on 3 October 1892, in which Kálnoky expressed his conviction that future British foreign policy would undergo no important modification under the Gladstone administration. This had replaced Salisbury's conservative government on 18 August 1892.

[398] Rumours of Britain's accession to the Triple Alliance (see n. 174 in Berlin section) had been prevalent since its renewal in May 1891 and Wilhelm II's visit to Britain in July 1891.

support to a combination which is directed against powers with whom we ourselves are in something like chronic diplomatic conflict. While, on the other hand, it has been thought that, with a liberal Cabinet in office, Great Britain would lean more towards Republican France than towards Monarchical Germany, and that our antagonisms to the designs and encroachments of Russia would be less accentuated than before.

The Saxon Minister for Foreign Affairs[399] is absent. In his department I was told, on my return to Dresden, that your acceptance of office has been welcomed in Germany as a sign that Mr Gladstone's programme did not include the abdication of British international responsibilities by 'scuttle', or otherwise.

FO 68/177: George Strachey to Earl of Rosebery, No 39, Dresden, 10 December 1892

[Received 12 December. X; 'Curious', R[osebery]]

Anti-Semitism roused by the Ahlwardt case

To day's "Nachrichten"[400] remarks that Rector Ahlwardt is probably the most popular, and Judge Brausewetter the best hated, man in the Empire.[401] This is the natural exaggeration of an anti-Semitic organ: the nation is not sunk so low that, for instance, a plebiscite would declare in favour of "The Headmaster of all the Germans." What is true is, that the monomania of Ahlwardt infects, in one shape or other, almost the entire Conservative electorate, whose jealousy of the Jews as unbelievers, as capitalists controlling the Stock-Exchange, as middlemen intruding between producer and purchaser, as liberal journalists and parliamentary leaders, is not without ramifications in the National-Liberal party. In this Kingdom, the unintelligent classes – I mean the Aristocracy and gentry, and Court, (the Royal Family excluded) – with the military and civil services, and no small number of traders and peasant proprietors, are in complete sympathy with the "Jew-Bait". Allowance being made for the comparative humanity of 19th Century feelings and ideals, the

---

[399] Georg von Metzsch.

[400] *Dresdner Nachrichten.*

[401] The trial conducted by Brausewetter at the Berlin *Landgericht* dealt with two pamphlets in which Ahlwardt accused the armament company Ludwig Loewe & Co. of selling defective rifles and being part of a Franco-Jewish conspiracy against Germany. On 9 December 1892 Ahlwardt, headmaster of a Berlin primary school and member of the German *Reichstag*, was found guilty of libel and sentenced to five months' imprisonment.

temper of the Anti-Semites of the New Germany towards "the cir-cumsied [*sic*] dog"[402] may be said to be that of the contemporaries of Richard the 1st and Simon de Montfort. In the social circles to which I properly belong here, approval of the 'Jew-Bait' is absolutely universal: I have just heard from a representative of the very highest local official enlightment [*sic*], the opinion that, after all, "there is probably something in it".

This trial has given prominence to a social peculiarity which modern Berlin, Dresden, and Munich possess in common with the Rome of Tiberius. Count Hohenthal, Saxon Minister at Berlin, and Member of the Bundesrath[403] (who is a very favorable specimen of his order) being examined, deposed, that he had formally reported to the Prussian War Office a private conversation between three pensioned officers, to which he had listened in a Restaurant.[404] The ground was, that some of the remarks made were "not calculated to inspire confi-dence" in the Army. The particulars the Count said, were of a trivial nature: he attached no importance to them, and did not know if they bore on the Ahlwardt case. This was confirmed by the officials who received the information: The details had made no impression on them. The Court treated all this as "vague" talk, and a subpoena which had been sent to Countess Hohenthal was accordingly cancelled. That a Minister Plenipotentiary and Member of the Bundesrath, who was formerly in the Saxon Regiment of Garde-Reiters, should assume the functions of a <u>delator</u>, surprises no one, and the natural English com-ment on the incident would be unintelligible to an average German.

FO 68/177: George Strachey to Earl of Rosebery, No 40, Dresden, 17 December 1892

[Received 19 December. For: Commercial Department; 'Amusing', R[osebery]]

Recent debates about bimetallism have not reinvigorated German interest despite changed political landscape

At the date of the Paris Monetary Conference,[405] and when our Royal Commission[406] was sitting, the silver question was one of the German

---

[402] William Shakespeare, *The Tragedy of Othello, the Moor of Venice*, Act 5, Scene 2.

[403] Federal Council.

[404] On 6 December 1892 Hohenthal testified that in February 1889 he had overheard a conversation between two of the plaintiffs, Isodor Löwe and Oberstleutnant Kühne, and a third person, on supply of weapons to the army. According to Hohenthal the conversation also contained derogatory remarks about military officers.

[405] The international monetary conference was held at Paris in 1881.

[406] The Royal Commission was appointed to inquire into the changes in the relative val-ues of precious metals (Gold and Silver Commission), November 1886 to October 1888.

topics of the day. Bimetallism[407] was then frequently under debate in the Reichstag, in Chambers of Commerce and other public bodies, and it was the theme of a cloud of pamphlets, articles, and manifestoes [*sic*], which formed a literature apart. So that an abbreviated Report on the Currency Discussion of the Empire, addressed by me to the office in 1887, covered 40 pages of print.[408]

The arguments recently heard in Germany for and against the rehabilitation of silver – (the speeches on Count Mirbach's parliamentary interpellation of last Monday excepted)[409] –would hardly fill a short dispatch. This revived interest in a subject which, as regards financial and official circles, is as good as buried.

In my Report of 1886,[410] I explained the alliance of Bimetallism with the 'Agrarians' and Protectionists of the German Legislature, and I stated that, according to my belief, the silver party numbered 190 members, or nearly half the House. The parliamentary constellation of 1892 differs, <u>toto caelo</u>,[411] from that of 1887. It is very doubtful if the present Reichstag would grant the Imperial Government powers to join an International Silver League. The elements of the situation now include an important personal factor. Some years ago Prince Bismarck, who was exhaustively ignorant of economic science, began to dabble in currency questions, and some of his <u>obiter dicta</u>[412] were significant of sympathy with the protectionist crusade against foreign wheat and general low prices. The present Reichskanzler has delivered a declaration of war against Bimetallism, identifying the advocates of the doctrine that "the earth is flat" with the friends of Rector Ahlwardt.[413] His personal equation points, therefore, to the maintenance of the established monetary system of Germany,[414] and he would, besides, be hardly disposed to raise up a fresh swarm of antagonisms by posing as the advocate of "currency-mongering", and dear bread.

---

[407] See n. 310 in this section.

[408] Strachey's report to the Marquess of Salisbury of 16 February 1887 was printed as *Report on the Recent Currency Discussions in Germany*, March 1887.

[409] In the interpellation, dated 9 December 1892 and discussed in the *Reichstag* on 12 December, Mirbach enquired about the intended German course of action at the Brussels Monetary Conference (22 November to 17 December) with regard to the depreciation of silver.

[410] Commercial Report to the Earl of Rosebery, Dresden, 21 May 1886.

[411] Latin: 'diametrically'.

[412] Latin: 'something said in passing'.

[413] Strachey is referring to Caprivi's reply to Mirbach's interpellation on 12 December 1892. On the anti-Semite Ahlwardt see the previous dispatch.

[414] See n. 312 in this section.

The 'Nachrichten'[415] – (almost the only newspaper in Germany with thoroughly well written 'leaders' in the English style –) argues that it is just like Count Caprivi's prejudiced mind to lump together Bimetallists and Anti-Semites, as if these were convertible terms. Whatever Dresden partizans of the Jew-Bait may say, the Reichskanzler's identification was sufficiently exact. The Anti-Semites are, as a rule, enemies of the "International Gold Standard Swindle", which they denounce as a creation of Jews and liberals, and as the origin of the fall of agrarian values under the pressure of the produce of India and Russia.

In illustration of a previous paragraph I will mention, that one of the Saxon Ministers tells me that he is "at heart, a decided 'Agrarian' only it would not do to say so"[.] He has a lively faith in Herr von Arendt, the German agitator now in Brussels, and supposes that Bimetallism would perhaps prove a panacea for some of Germany's troubles – "but," adds His Excellency, "I do not know what it is".

FO 68/178: George Strachey to Earl of Rosebery, No 1, Dresden, 4 January 1893

[Received 7 January by post. R[osebery]]

Prevailing pessimism in Saxony

The New Year has opened amidst a chorus of universal discontent. Nearly everybody is dissatisfied with everything – industrial, commercial, social, political. Whether in private discussions, or in editorial retrospects of 1892, the local tone is one of unmixed lamentation. Ministers, members of the Bundesrath,[416] Generals, bankers, tradesmen, journalists – all appear to be under the influence of a helpless pessimism. The characteristic belief of the Germans, that the remedies for men's evils lie not in themselves, but in their rulers, is reflected by the press. For instance, the Municipal 'Anzeiger'[417] remarks that 'the mass of the people want to feel that they are under the protection of a reliable ruler'. 'The smile of the peace-goddess is no adequate consolation for the loss of the pillar of the Empire, for the collapse of the ideal enthusiasm of the nation.' The Germans crave for ideals.

---

[415] *Dresdner Nachrichten*, 16 December 1892.
[416] Federal Council.
[417] *Dresdner Anzeiger*, 1 January 1893.

"The ideal of our people's soul is still the aged Reichskanzler,[418] that type of the grand, self-reliant, German nature." 'But we are now in danger of losing our confidence in ourselves, and in the sound vitality of the nation' – a curious result of the possession of the qualities of steadfastness and self-assertion.

All the comments which I hear on the 'present discontents', and their causes, may be summed up in the classical remark – 'Si Choiseul avait été içi'![419] The disturbed condition of public and commercial affairs is laid to the charge of 'the New Course'.[420] Count Caprivi has very few supporters in Saxony; but the clamours against his policy have no foundation in intelligent political dissent.

FO 68/178: George Strachey to Earl of Rosebery, No 2, Dresden, 14 January 1893

[Received 16 January. Qy: Intelligence Department, E.F.C. [Edward Francis Chapman]; R[osebery]]

Widespread disapprobation of army bill likely to be short-lived

If there were any stability in German public and parliamentary opinion, the Army Bill would have to be described as dead.[421] Dislike of the measure is hardly a maximum in Saxony: but the local newspapers indicate, some by their silence, others by their arguments the extreme unpopularity of the proposed reform. As far as I can see, repudiation of the Bill is nearly universal in all classes, the Military excepted: I have it from unimpeachable sources, that the peasant proprietary of the Kingdom protest against the increased taxation which is in sight. The Minister of Foreign Affairs admits this, and believes that a similar spirit prevails in other parts of the Empire. He remarks, however with justice, that in Germany public opinion is not a serious political quantity, and he expects that the parliamentary opposition to the Bill will shortly evaporate. That is to say, the bulk of the Conservative and National-Liberal parties, and sections of the Catholic centre, will, at the last moment, not from motives like those which sway our House of Commons, but from their servile instincts, and terror of authority, turn their backs

---

[418] Otto von Bismarck.

[419] This French dictum is ascribed to Louis XV and refers to the First Partition of Poland, in 1772, which would not have taken place 'if only Choiseul [French foreign minister 1766–1770] had been here'.

[420] 'New Course' refers to the realignment of policy after Bismarck's dismissal in 1890.

[421] For the army bill (Imperial Military Law), see nn. 312 and 322 in Berlin section.

on all their late protestations, after the fashion of which the recent history of the Reichstag offers so many amazing examples. This line is to day recommended, or predicted, by the National-Liberal 'Anzeiger'[422] – (always an advocate of Byzantine proceedings) which argues, that as the Reichskanzler persists in his demands, the public must give way.

Herr von Metzsch and his colleagues would regret the development of a German parliamentary deadlock, like the Prussian 'Conflict' period of 1860–66.[423] But, if the Legislature proved intractable, Saxony would support an arbitrary solution of difficulties, even to the extent of a breach of the constitution. In this kingdom, resistance to an invasion of popular rights, whether by material or moral force, is utterly unthinkable. If Germany is not now in the hands of 'Major-Generals', the credit is due to the rulers of the 26 states of the Empire, and not to their subjects, who, at present, are incapable of firing a shot in defence of their liberties and laws.

FO 68/178: George Strachey to Earl of Rosebery, No 11, Dresden, 25 February 1893

[Received 27 February. For: Commercial Department; R[osebery]]

No agitation in Saxony with regards to agrarian political affairs

The demonstrations of the 'Agrarians' at the Berlin 'Tivoli', and in the Prussian Landtag and the Reichstag, have had no echo here.[424] The agricultural situation of the Kingdom is unlike that of the Provinces of Pomerania and Preussen, in which the strength of the Prussian 'Agrarians' lies. Saxony is an industrial country, it has no latifundia,[425] the large estates are a mere minimum, the soil being mainly held by "peasant" proprietors and urban holders of allotments. Possessors of less than 15–20 acres are not effective sellers of produce, so that the agricultural majority have hardly suffered much from the fall of prices, like the holders of property on lease, or the possessors of large estates. They are thus little disposed to agitate for high corn duties, or to denounce Commercial Treaties, or to

---

[422] *Dresdner Anzeiger.*

[423] See n. 371 in this section.

[424] Strachey is referring to the constitutive meeting of the *Bund der Landwirte* (Agarian League) at the Berlin Tivoli brewery on 18 February 1892, and the debates in the German *Reichstag* (28 January to 17 February) and the Prussian house of deputies (14 to 16 February).

[425] Latin: 'landed estates'.

call for bimetallism,[426] or for restrictions on personal liberty and on the stock-exchange.

The owners of the 'Rittergüter',[427] and the larger "peasants" (with more than, say, 20 acres) have of course, to complain of loss of income. But many of them paid exorbitant prices for their estates in past years, when land was at a high premium: some have been extravagant, and are mortgaged beyond their means (not a common fault in Saxony): few, (at any rate in the higher class), have fallen into reduced circumstances, like so many country families in England. The local landlords of this class may be almost as reactionary in politics as the agitating class in Prussia. But they are not such irreconcilable Bismarckites and some of the remedies demanded by their neighbours, e.g. cheaper railway freights in the Eastern Provinces – would be injurious to the agricultural interests of the Kingdom.

Certain Saxon aristocratic landlords are prominent in the Reichstag on the side of monopoly and reaction: some have joined in the recent proceedings at Berlin. On the other hand, the Agricultural Council of Saxony[428] discountenances collective 'Agrarian' agitation, either in the political or the economic direction. A manifesto just issued, from some "farmers['] friends" connected with that semi-official institution, advises the landlords of this kingdom to hold aloof from Agricultural Leagues of the political type, which are reducing the landed gentry and peasantry to pursue phantoms, instead of attending to those realities of economy, industry, and scientific culture, by help of which, assiduously followed, fair returns may still be drawn from the soil.

FO 68/178: George Strachey to Earl of Rosebery, No 16, Dresden, 27 April 1893

[Received 1 May viâ Berlin. For: The Queen / Prince of Wales / Paris; R[osebery]]

French feelings vis-à-vis Alsace-Lorraine

The first French Delegate to the Sanitary Conference[429] was M. Barrère, who has filled the various positions of member of the

---

[426] See n. 310 in this section.

[427] Manors.

[428] *Landeskulturrat für das Königreich Sachsen.*

[429] The International Sanitary Conference took place at Dresden from 11 March to 15 April; it dealt with the prevention of epidemic diseases.

Commune,[430] convict sentenced to Cayenne, and Minister Plenipotentiary. This young Diplomatist's merits are well known: they include the possession of our language in a degree almost unique in a foreigner, and he professes marked English sympathies. I asked him to tell me "the true truth" on the subject of Elsass-Lothringen: was the "study of revenge" deeply planted in the French mind? M. Barrère replied that there could be but one answer to my question. The feeling that the lost provinces must, and would, be reconquered, was universal. You might say, without abuse of language that the names Metz and Strassburg were deeply written in every French heart. A lost battle – a dozen lost battles which were "mere thrashings", like Waterloo – might leave behind them a rancour, which would be dissipated in time. But the bitter sense of ignominy that attends the conquest of large integral portions of national soil, is not so easily lost: in France, the hatred and hopes left by the disasters of 1870[431] are as vivid as they were twenty years ago, and, according to present appearances, they will not subside within any assignab[l]e limits of time.

It is not in my power to test M. Barrère's opinions on the topic. If they are as sound as his judgments on German things and persons, they must have considerable value.

FO 68/178: George Strachey to Earl of Rosebery, No 17, Dresden, 11 May 1893

[Received 13 May by post. X; R[osebery]]

Unpopularity of army bill; its rejection by the Reichstag; subsequent dissolution of this body

On the publication of the proposals for the increase of the Army, nowhere in Germany was their reception more unfavorable than in this Kingdom.[432] They were condemned as imposing burdens, personal and fiscal, in excess of the requirements of the Empire, a judgment nearly identical with that of the heads of the Saxon administration, who assented with reluctance to the adoption of the intended reform as a Government measure.

As the discussion of the Bill advanced, its unpopularity grew. Except in the barracks, it seemed to have no supporters at all.

---

[430] Strachey is referring to the revolutionary government, *La Commune de Paris* (March to May 1871).

[431] Franco-Prussian War of 1870–1871.

[432] For the army bill of 1893 (Imperial Military Law), see nn. 312 and 322 in Berlin section.

Even the local official press did not venture to write in its favor. In a country with a serious constitutionalism, no ministry could have withstood the outcry which arose.

After a time, symptoms of change became perceptible. Amongst officials, editors, politicians, private persons, the national alacrity in tergiversation began to assert itself. The reason was to be found, not in Count Caprivi's parliamentary arguments, to which very little weight was attached, but in the mixed influence of indifference and fear and, above all, of that Byzantine servility which is one of the most striking characteristics of the Bismarckian era.

By degrees advocacy of the Bill became general. Soon there were heard ambiguous voices which recalled the Prussian 'Conflict-Time' (relative to the Army organisation) of thirty years ago,[433] and hinted that, in the new Germany, popular resistance to the monarch's will would prove as futile as it did in the old. Such warnings were understood to foreshadow the eventuality of a coup d'état, a form of settlement to which, it was universally allowed, the Emperor and his advisers would, if other methods failed, probably resort. In numerous confidential discussions of the subject, I found it to be universally admitted as an axiom, that a violation of the constitution of the Empire would meet with no obstacles on the part of the confederated Governments, or with any resistance, however faint, even in the way of protest, from the German public. That Saxony and Dresden are actually in the condition of political impotence thus implied, is unquestionable. Here, as in the east of North-Germany, authority would command implicit obedience by a few strokes of the pen.

Now that the Bill has been rejected, its merits and demerits are perhaps less discussed than its side issues. The Dresden 'Journal' sees in the late parliamentary proceedings, proofs that the time is come for a retrogade [*sic*] constitutional Reform, and that stern means must be found for compelling members to renounce the scandalous practice of voting with specific parties, instead of following the plain indications of Government experts. Other newspapers are chiefly lamenting the measures of reactionary legislation under debate by the late Reichstag,[434] the reappearance of which, they fear, must be uncertain. Some are harping as what they call the fresh proofs of the political incompetency of Count Caprivi, and of

---

[433] See n. 371 in this section.

[434] Amongst other things, this is referring to the so-called *Lex Heinze* which stipulated the prosecution of 'pimping' and the censorship of 'immoral' publications, artwork, and depictions. After its first reading, on 3 and 15 December 1892, the amendment bill to the Imperial Criminal Code was transferred to committee.

the necessity of recalling Prince Bismarck or, at any rate, of constituting him grand referee to be consulted as often as complications arise.

Of the present feelings of the general public – whether they now regret the rejection and the dissolution – it is impossible to speak yet with certainty. The situation will not be much affected by the Emperor's address to the Military at the Tempelhof review.[435] His language (which is marked by the usual maximum of imprudence) may please the parties of "Throne and Altar", but may be interpreted by the Opposition as an attempt to dictate to the electorate by the Crown.

FO 68/178: George Strachey to Earl of Rosebery, No 19, Dresden, 20 May 1893

[Received 23 May by post. X; R[osebery]]

Electoral preparations and publicity; activity of Social Democrats; many Reichstag factions represented in Dresden

The outward signs of popular excitement visible after a Dissolution of the House of Commons are almost unknown in Germany.[436] There is no general absorption in the one overpowering interest: the public seem rather to be playing at elections. Except in some of the larger towns, meetings are not held, and there is no systematic issue of addresses, or canvassing. The press notices of electoral preparations and incidents are very meagre; leading articles are heavy and uninstructive, and, above all, where persons are discussed, full of the timidity natural to journalists who have to write with one eye on the Libel, and 'Hatred and Contempt', paragraphs of the Criminal Code.[437]

To all this the Social-Democrat[s] offer an honorable contrast. Their activity is praised by their opponents, who wonder at their perfect organisation, their devotion to their flag, and their intrepidity in calling things and individuals by plain names.

In each of the 23 constituencies of the Kingdom the Socialists have their man ready for the contest; while, on the side of "order"[438] the

---

[435] In his address of 9 May 1893 Wilhelm II stated that, if the newly elected *Reichstag* was to reject the army bill again, he would be prepared to make every effort to see it through.

[436] The German *Reichstag* was dissolved on 6 May 1893 and new elections were scheduled for 15 June.

[437] Strachey is referring to Sections 130–131 and Sections 185–200 of the Imperial Criminal Code of 1871.

[438] For the '*Kartell der Ordnungsparteien*', see n. 208 in Berlin section.

hunt for willing and capable candidates is still proceeding, and, in places, under very adverse conditions.

The 'freisinnig'[439] leader, Barth, lately argued that there would be no enlightened public opinion in Germany as long as there was no parliamentary Government.[440] It would be more accurate to say that such Government cannot exist where the parliament is split up into above a dozen parties.

Nearly all the factions of the late Reichstag have their equivalents here; for instance the Dresden electorate have before them ten separate programmes. According to present announcements, the local candidate of 'Throne and Altar' will be a master-glazier,[441] who belongs to the 'Tivoli' wing of the Conservatives,[442] and therefore combines reactionary German Toryism and anti-Semitism in their most malignant forms. The liberals must support Herr Wetzlich, or the representation will fall into Social-Democratic hands. But, as above explained, the various platforms are not yet fully organized, and I need hardly add that the results of the Saxon polls of next Thursday three weeks are altogether beyond calculation.

FO 68/178: George Strachey to Earl of Rosebery, No 31, Dresden, 16 September 1893

[Received 18 September. X; [Rosebery]]

Impending British naval demonstration incites press ruminations on British accession to Triple Alliance; general dislike of British foreign policies

The newspapers are publishing confident and detailed descriptions of the naval demonstration on the coasts of Italy, by which we are to reply to the visit of the Russian squadron to France.[443] The articles and paragraphs on this subject have revived the old assertions and speculations relative to our connection with the Triple Alliance, and in language that can hardly be called complimentary. There is

---

[439] See n. 3 in Berlin section.

[440] Strachey is probably referring to Barth's article 'Die Sackgasse' (The Deadlock), published in *Die Nation: Wochenschrift für Politik, Volkswirtschaft und Literatur*, No 32, 6 May 1893.

[441] Eduard Wetzlich (*Konservativer Landesverein*).

[442] This refers to the 'Tivoli Programme' named after the Berlin Tivoli brewery where, in 1892, the party conference of the *Deutschkonservative Partei* (German Conservative Party) adopted an anti-Semitic programme.

[443] Strachey is referring to the plans of the British Mediterranean Squadron to visit Taranto (16 October) and La Spezia (23 October). The Russian visit to Toulon (a return of the French visit to Kronstadt in 1891) was scheduled for 13 October. For the Triple Alliance, see n. 174 in Berlin section.

nothing new in this. At times a radical or a socialist organ may publish a friendly estimate of our motives and our strength, but the
prevalent tone of the leading newspapers of the Empire expresses
that sentiment of half contemptuous dislike which, however much
decorous official language may mask the fact, is the feeling that predominates in Germany towards us.

I quote, as typical, the 'Anzeiger'[444] – a moderate and sensible
National-Liberal journal owned by the municipality of Dresden –
which remarks that although the cooperation, a passive sympathy
of a British fleet in the Mediterranean would be invaluable to
Germany, our formal accession to the Triple-Alliance would be an
evil. Germany cannot guarantee the British status quo, India
included, while the effect of a British military diversion on the
continent would be nil: it would not take France half an army
corps to keep us at bay: England would be as embarrassing an ally
as Turkey. Very desirable for Germany would be the abandonment
of the old British trick of playing the benevolent neutral for your own
pocket – a change of habits not to be expected from a Government
presided by Mr Gladstone. Their recent attitude in the Siamese
difficulty[445] shews that effective recognition of Great Britain's true
interest, with vigorous action in support, which characterized the
statesmanship of Lord Salisbury, is hardly to be looked for at present.

On these and other topics there is usually a suggestive monotony of
language in the German press. Very little independence is shewn:
Even the best journals being satisfied to reproduce the articles of
the Correspondence circulars[446] lithographed in Berlin.

FO 68/178: George Strachey to Earl of Rosebery, No 40, Dresden, 3 November 1893

[Received 6 November by post. X; R[osebery]]

Saturday Review *wildly exaggerates international implications of Saxon king's military jubilee*

The 'Saturday Review'[447] writes – "something of an additional
counter-note to Toulon and Paris was also (i.e. besides Spezia)[448]

---

[444] *Dresdner Anzeiger*, 16 September 1893.
[445] This is referring to the lack of British support for Siam in the Franco-Siamese War of
1893.
[446] *Nationalliberale Korrespondenz*, Berlin.
[447] *The Saturday Review of Politics, Literature, Science, and Art*, 28 October 1893.
[448] See n. 443 to previous dispatch.

sounded at Dresden, where the "Military Jubilee"[449] of the King of Saxony was celebrated in the presence, and with the assistance, of the Emperor, not without some talk of "drawing-swords", and some presentation of Marshals' bâtons".

I have neither heard nor read a single remark from a German source calculated to justify, in however faint a degree, this acute suggestion. Both to the public, and to the high personages concerned, the proceedings in question were absolutely devoid of international significance. I am confident that the King and his advisers would have treated as childish the idea that the Dresden festivities might be taken as a counterblast to Toulon. As regards the Emperor, it is within my knowledge that, as far back as last Christmas, His Majesty having been casually told of his neighbour's approaching Jubilee, desired his informant to convey in the appropriate quarter, that he should not fail to offer his congratulations in person on that interesting occasion.

FO 68/179: George Strachey to Earl of Rosebery, No 4, Dresden, 4 January 1894

[Received 8 January by post. Seen at Berlin. 'Print(ed) & then ask me as to circulation', R[osebery]; Proofs annexed in print][450]

Explanation of Irish Home Rule analogy previously used to describe German Empire; outlines forces of centralization at work in the empire

Your Lordship has requested me to report on "the gradual extinction of Home Rule" in Germany, to which I referred in the final paragraph of my Despatch[451] on the Saxon political situation. The term Home-Rule was employed by me in the sense which it bears when

---

[449] Fiftieth anniversary of military service, 22 October 1893.

[450] Note in file: 'Mr Strachey, No 4, 4 January 1894. This is an interesting Despatch. I think Strachey used the word Home Rule rather loosely – but there is no question that the tendency in Germany has been towards centralization. Whether there is not a certain equilibrium and whether we are not on one side of it and the Germans on the other and both tending towards it is another question.' T.H.S. [Thomas Henry Sanderson], 8 January 1894; 'Is there not something more to be said? (and as to this I should take to ask Strachey.) Is there not a first reaction against this centralization, and have these not been very distinct signs of State individualism of late in Bavaria, & to a less [*sic*] degree in Wurtemberg? Has not, to put it another way, the attempted legislative & administrative centralization awakened the independent nations among the populations of the smaller [note in margin: 'the Southern'] German nationalities?' R[osebery].

[451] FO 68/178: George Strachey to Earl of Rosebery, No 45, Dresden, 9 December 1893 (not included in this volume); Rosebery's request is dated 23 December.

our domestic discussions of the affairs of Ireland[452] receive illustration from foreign precedents, that is, as a general expression for the Constitutional systems established in Hungary, Finland, Norway, Iceland. To these instances high authority has added the case of the German Empire, where, however, Home Rule is not a stable principle, but an element of Government which is suffering gradual abridgment, and is surely, if slowly, approaching the condition of a vanishing constitutional quantity.

To demonstrate this in detail, would be to write the history of German legislation from the year 1867 downwards, or, at least, to give a catalogue of the laws passed by the Reichstag since that date.[453] Within the circumscribed space available here, I can only note the salient points of the centralizing process by which a number of the principal prerogatives of local sovereignty have been, by degrees, lost to their original possessors, and absorbed into the Imperial power. The statutory law of Germany now determines the regulation of trade and industry, limited liability, usury, the hours of work, holidays, the liabilities of employers, national insurance, and the entire range of labour questions. Again, under Imperial law are colonisation, emigration, nationality, settlement and domicile: banking, the currency, coining, weights and measures, patents, trademarks, copyright: treaties, the consular service (except in Germany), posts,[454] telegraphs, lighthouses: also, medical, sanitary, and veterinary regulation. Further, railway management and control, ports, maritime and internal navigation. Imperial, also, is the press law, the restrictive legislation on religious societies, the law of marriage and on civil registration. There is uniform organisation of judicature and procedure, of legal practice, fees, and costs: an Imperial Court of appeal[,] a bankruptcy law, complete Criminal and Commercial codes. The Army and Navy are Imperial institutions: there is Imperial taxation which includes the Customs duties, stamps, the excise and consumption duties on beer, brandy, sugar, salt, and tobacco.

In the case of a single item of this list – beer – Bavaria, Wurtemberg and Baden, with Elsass-Lothringen are nominally exempt.[455] These

---

[452] The Government of Ireland Bill (Second Home Rule Bill) was defeated in the House of Lords on 8 September 1893.

[453] The German *Reichstag* was first established as the *Reichstag* of the North German Confederation in 1867.

[454] With exception of Bavaria and Württemberg.

[455] Taxation on beer belonged to the reserved rights (*Reservatrechte*) retained by Baden, Bavaria and Württemberg in the November (Versailles) Treaties of 1870 (for Bavaria, see n. 220 in Munich section). The taxation on beer in the Imperial Territory of Alsace Lorraine – which had its origins in French legislation – was regulated by decree of 10 March 1875.

exceptions made, it may be said that the faculty of legislating on the subjects just enumerated has been entirely withdrawn from the individual Confederated States. Moreover, the force of the centralizing movement is far from being exhausted. A German Civil Code has been drafted,[456] the movement in favour of a German Income Tax challenges the autonomy of the separate Exchequers, and there are premonitory signs of Imperial Legislation in other directions, whereby state prerogative will be further curtailed. More obscure than the action of the Reichstag is that of the Imperial Executive, which exerts pressure on the local administrations calculated to augment their dependency on Berlin.

Conformably to the gradual abatement of Home Rule in Germany, a visible change has come over the programmes and debates of the separate Parliaments. Now that German Unity is nearly full-grown, politics proper have almost dropped from their horizon. The King of Saxony's speech from the throne,[457] at the recent opening of the Landtag, affords an average illustration of this fact. First, there are threnodies on the industrial and agricultural depression, on the scarcity of fodder, and on the embarrassments entailed on the Treasury of the Kingdom by the existing financial relations of the Allied Governments and the Empire. Next follows a statement of the question of the school-grants, described in my previous correspondence. Thereupon are named two subjects for new legislation: protection of fields and gardens against marauders: railway improvement, extension of light lines, and purchase of rolling-stock. Furthermore, an Appendix to the Royal speech enumerated twenty laws passed by the last Landtag, and sanctioned in 1892. Of these a third relate to finance, the remainder dealing with such subjects as the slaughter tariff, discipline of domestic servants, fire insurance, fees to judicial attendants, and the like.

The foregoing statement is, I need hardly say, not an exhaustive report, but a rapid sketch of the subject such as I have been able to give without constitutional works, lists of the Laws of the Empire and so forth. Competent local authorities might correct some of my facts; their fundamental appreciations would, I believe, be identical with those submitted in this Despatch.

[...]

---

[456] A first draft of the German Civil Code (*Bürgerliche Gesetzbuch*) was presented in 1888; the code was finally, passed by the *Reichstag* on 1 July 1896 and became effective 1 January 1900.

[457] On 15 November 1893.

P.S. In the paragraph which alludes to the Customs Duties, I have omitted to mention the incorporation of Hamburg and Bremen in the Zollverein.[458]

FO 68/179: George Strachey to Earl of Rosebery, No 9, Dresden, 26 January 1894

[Received 29 January by post. X; R[osebery]]

Saxon views on reconciliation between emperor and Bismarck

The Bismarck incident has caused an extraordinary commotion here.[459] It is the sole subject of conversation. All the telephonic news in the press relative to the great event of to day have been printed in extra-spaced type: a large number of sympathizers have shewn their enthusiasm by hanging flags from their houses. The prevailing excitement could hardly be more intense if, in the course of a war with Germany's neighbours, announcement were made of the capture of Warsaw and Belfort.

The newspapers have almost surpassed themselves in minute hypothetical investigations of the more frivolous aspects of the affair, such as the place of origin, and particular vintage of the wine sent to Friedrichsruh,[460] the quantity – whether a bottle or a cask – , the "psychological moment" (i.e. motive) in the choice of Count Moltke as the bearer of the message of peace,[461] the nexus between the reconciliation and the Bismarckian sentiments of the German Ambassadress at Vienna,[462] and other trivialities, all elucidated at length, and on grounds mostly supplied by the moral-consciousness of the respective writers.

The cry of the Bismarckites <u>sans phrase</u>,[463] of the agrarians, and other partizans of reaction, now is, "Bismarck is coming". And they talk as if their enemies Count Caprivi, and the Liberals, had already collapsed, and were retiring, panic-stricken, from the scene. The organ[464] of the Conservative Anti-Semites, which represents,

---

[458] See n. 200 in this section.

[459] Strachey is referring to Otto von Bismarck's visit to Wilhelm II on 26 January 1894.

[460] Friedrichsruh, Bismarck's manor house.

[461] Wilhelm's conciliatory letter to Bismarck was delivered – together with a bottle of old Rhine wine – on 22 January 1894.

[462] Princess Marie von Sachsen-Weimar-Eisenach, wife of Heinrich VII , Prince Reuß zu Köstritz.

[463] 'Outright Bismarckite'. The term was used for the pro-Bismarckian *Deutsche Reichspartei (Freikonservative)*.

[464] *Dresdner Nachrichten*, 26 January 1894.

or inspires, the views of the lower Dresden middle-class, says that Prince Bismarck's visit to Berlin probably means 'Check to Caprivi'. This paper hints that there will next be a solution of the existing crisis in terms of a return to the approved national programme of the "Old Reichskanzler", which will cause a recovery from the political, commercial, and industrial chaos that followed the adoption of the "New Course".[465]

The moderates do not use the language of positive illusion; but they express a certain vague hope, or belief, that Prince Bismarck may hereafter stand behind Count Caprivi, as supreme adviser to the Crown, to be consulted as grand referee in moments of special perplexity.

A quasi-liberal (not 'freisinnig')[466] journal avoids the hyper-refined speculations and servility of its colleagues. The 'Zeitung'[467] dismisses the idea just named as unconstitutional nonsense, and treats the reconciliation as a mere personal incident, highly creditable, no doubt to those concerned, and calculated to fill the German public with profound gratitude and satisfaction, but as quite devoid of political importance except in so far as it may check the prevalent misuse of Prince Bismarck's name and influence. This system is not tortuous enough to suit the average local mind, to which the 'camarilla' interpretation is more congenial.

FO 68/179: George Strachey to Earl of Rosebery, Confidential, No 11, Dresden, 9 February 1894

[Received 12 February. For: The Queen; 'One would like to know the sources of the information in this despatch', R[osebery]; 'I will write', T.H.S. [Thomas Henry Sanderson]; Done, 15 February]

Saxon king's views on Bismarck's recent audience with the emperor

The King of Saxony visited Prince Bismarck during his stay at Berlin, when the conversation turned on the ex-Reichkanzlers's meeting with the Emperor.[468] Prince Bismarck spoke with much feeling of the kindness of His Imperial Majesty, who, he said, had treated him with surprising cordiality, and with marks of honour in excess of his due. At their interview, only general and personal topics had been discussed, his august host refraining from all political allusions.

[465] See n. 337 in this section.
[466] See n. 3 in Berlin section.
[467] *Dresdner Zeitung*, 26 January 1894.
[468] Albert visited Berlin from 25 to 28 January 1894 on the occasion of Wilhelm II's birthday (27 January); he met with Bismarck on 26 January.

The King followed the Emperor's example as regards reticence on public affairs. Prince Bismarck equally remarked, that he thought it desirable that the Reichstag should sanction the Commercial Treaty with Russia.[469]

The King of Saxony was struck by the change in the Prince's appearance, but found that the outward signs of increased age were not accompanied by an iota of decline in the great Minister's conversational vivacity and vigor of mind.

The King has a strong regard for Prince Bismarck, partly founded on his interference, after the battle of Sadowa,[470] to prevent the annexation of Saxony to Prussia. To myself, His Majesty said many years ago, "c'est le Prussien que j'aime le mieux".[471] But he would deprecate the exertion of a Bismarckian influence on policy, of which, in his opinion, the possibility is excluded, both at present and for the future. A Saxon Conservative lately said in a debate in the Reichstag on the new taxes – 'if all our wisdom fails us, we must take counsel at Friedrichsruh'.[472] In official quarters here, this language is treated as mere drivelling.

FO 68/179: George Strachey to Earl of Kimberley, No 16, Dresden, 10 March 1894

[Received 12 March. For; The Queen / Lord Rosebery; K[imberley]]

German public feeling with regard to Gladstone's resignation

The comments of the local press on the recent Ministerial changes at home have been similar to those reported from the other capitals of the Empire.[473] While refraining from the malevolence customary in German appreciations of the late head of Her Majesty's Government, the various organs have not concealed the public satisfaction at his withdrawal from office.

For nearly a quarter of a century that illustrious statesmen has been, in Germany, one of the most unpopular figures of contemporary European politics. On this antipathy I need not enlarge. Originating during the Franco-German war, it has been augmented

---

[469] For the commercial treaty, see n. 354 in Berlin section.

[470] Battle of Königgrätz (3 July 1866; part of the Austro-Prussian War) in which Austrian and Saxon troops were defeated by Prussia.

[471] French: 'It's the Prussian that I like the best'.

[472] Arnold von Frege-Weltzien on 31 January 1894.

[473] Gladstone resigned as prime minister on 2 March 1894; his administration was succeeded by that of the Earl of Rosebery.

by some of the subsequent developments of British Liberal policy, the recent Irish legislation included,[474] which have been judged to be antagonistic in direction to the new German ideals. These feelings have not been confined to the retrograde Junker class. They have nowhere been stronger than amongst the National-Liberals who, with all their serious shortcomings, are not a party of prejudice and darkness. I have ground[s] for the belief that the dislike in this quarter was largely stimulated by Prince Bismarck, whose animosity against the late Premier is a matter of history.

On the other hand, the adherents of the 'freisinnig', or democratic, programme have always declared to general sympathy with Gladstonian principles and practise: it is true that in respect to Home Rule, and certain foreign questions, their approval has been subject to considerable qualifications. The great German radical party is now, since last year's collapse, broken up into two weak fractions, one of them represented by the Berlin 'Nation', which sees ground[s] for congratulation in the transfer of power from "the great figure, half finance-artist, half theosoph", to the hands of so admirable a successor.[475] As regards my special Saxon horizon, I can say that Lord Rosebery's assumption of the Premiership has made a very favorable impression, and that it is calculated to give German feeling towards England the opportunity for a new departure, for which, here as in the rest of the Empire, there is some room.

FO 68/179: George Strachey to Earl of Kimberley, No 17, Dresden, 22 March 1894

[Received 24 March. Qy: X; Commercial Department to see; K[imberley]]

Saxon vote in Reichstag *on treaty with Russia not representative of local population; Saxons more mild-mannered than other German states in political affairs*

Of the 23 Saxon members of the Reichstag, 12 voted for, 11 against, the first paragraph of the Treaty with Russia: this was the division on which the calculations of the imaginary majority have been based.[476]

---

[474] Strachey is referring to the Second Home Rule Bill; see n. 452 in this section.

[475] *Die Nation: Wochenschrift für Politik, Volkswirtschaft und Literatur*, 10 March 1894. *Die Nation* was edited by Theodor Barth, who belonged to the *Freisinnige Vereinigung* (Free-Minded Union; founded by moderate members of the *Deutsche Freisinnige Partei* in May 1893). The left wing of the former *Deutsche Freisinnige Partei* (see n. 3 in Berlin section) henceforth constituted the *Freisinnige Volkspartei* (Free-Minded People's Party).

[476] Article 1 of the commercial treaty between Russia and Germany (see n. 354 in Berlin section) granted German and Russian subjects equal rights to trade and industry in the

So close a balance of opinion does not correspond with the feelings of the electorate. The population of the Kingdom is, in its essential character, industrial and commercial. The Rittergüter, or estates of the aristocracy and middle-class, are a mere fraction of the soil, their individual acreage is very small, and they are invariably leased to farmer-capitalists for long terms. Of the owners of the minor holdings, (75 per cent of the whole) many pursue agriculture, or gardening, as an accessory business, so that they have no surplus produce for the market. There is no sufficient basis for a strong territorial party, and the Saxon 'Agrarians' would have little importance but for their alliance with the local Anti-Semites of both fractions,[477] who are represented in the German Parliament by 6 members, or more than one fourth of the entire Saxon contingent.

I am told by a high official who has just been to Berlin, that the Prussian partizans of "Throne and Altar" are venting their discontent with the Treaty and the 'New Course'[478] in strong language. The ornamental classes of Saxony are far more submissive than the Junkers of Pomerania and Brandenburg, and their disinclination to censure official policy and persons, in however private a manner, is always very marked. On the present occasion, their irritation against "the Master Builder" and his "Clerk of the Works"[479] is expressed in a very diluted form, and some Agrarians are remarking that, with rye selling at 130 Marks per ton, an import duty of 35 Marks per ton is not a despicable amount of protection. Of the larger landlords, a few disapprove the Agrarian agitation, and argue that the state has to care for other interests besides those of agriculture.

On the attitude of the intelligent circles of the Kingdom, I wrote in a former Despatch. Their Press organs contain nothing on this subject worth notice. The Anti-Semitic 'Nachrichten'[480] has been neutral as regards the Treaty, but never the less makes it a text for such attacks on the Reichskanzler as the risks of prosecution allow. 'The Empire is now governed by the aid of demagogic influences, and between the leaders of the 'New Course' and the true pillars of conservative and monarchical feeling a chasm is yawning. The "Old Course" dictated policy to the world – the "New Course" has to purchase peace by the payment of subsidies and tributes abroad. In his

---

territory of the other contracting partner. This article – as with all 21 articles of the treaty – was passed by the *Reichstag* on 16 March 1894.

[477] *Deutsche Reformpartei* (German Reform Party) and the *Deutschsoziale Partei* (German Social Party).

[478] 'New Course' refers to the realignment of policy after Bismarck's dismissal in 1890.

[479] Leo Graf von Caprivi and Karl Heinrich von Boetticher.

[480] *Dresdner Nachrichten*, 18 March 1894.

four years of office, General Caprivi has not uttered a word calculated to warm the Idealismus of the nation: it is his talent to beat their aspirations and ideals to the ground'.

FO 68/179: George Strachey to Earl of Kimberley, No 22, Dresden, 25 May 1894

[Received 28 May. X; K[imberley]]

Saxon press views on miners' congress

The local journals have taken notice though not in detail, of the Miners' Congress at Berlin.[481] Their reports have been altogether tendentious, the object being, to exalt the English delegates at the expense of their foreign colleagues. While the representatives of German, Austrian, French and Belgian mining industry – such was the argument – were so enslaved by their Utopian dreams of the socialistic State of the Future as to be incapable of comprehending, or discussing, the actual wants of the moment, our countrymen suggested practical solutions of the labour problems which the Congress had been convoked to discuss. The gulf between the insular and the continental conceptions political and economic, was seen to be irremediably deep, there were numerous personal collisions, the result of the antagonisms displayed being, that the English delegates abruptly took their departure,[482] leaving the rump Congress to continue its deliberations at its pleasure.

Such was the gist of the comments in question, which not only placed Mr Burt, Mr Pickard, and their associates, in a very advantageous light compared with the German Social-Democrats; but also spoke of them, directly or impliedly as standing in the front of the new English labour movement. It is hardly necessary to say, that the English and the German Delegates of the Congress belonged to entirely different political platforms, the opinions of Messrs Burt and Pickard being, as far as a parallel can be drawn at all, analogous to those of Herr Richter and Herr Rickert. The proper English equivalents for Singer and Liebknecht would be Mr Burns and Alderman Tillett, and all comments on the situation which ignore

---

[481] The Berlin International Miners' Congress was held from 14 to 19 May 1894.

[482] The majority of British delegates left Berlin on 18 May and 19 May before the congress closed.

this fact, must misrepresent the significance of the debates of the Miner's Congress.

FO 68/179: George Strachey to Earl of Kimberley, No 25, Dresden, 13 June 1894

[Received 15 June. For: Lord Rosebery; X]

Negative Saxon views on British treaty with Congo; general German animosity towards Britain

The National-Liberal 'Anzeiger'[483] has reproduced the Radical Frankfort Zeitung's report of M. Deloncle's remarks to their interviewer on our treaty with the Congo State.[484] The Dresden writer's[485] preface is this – "Deloncle pleads for a joint action of Germany and France against England, an idea which, it is true, is more and more gaining ground in Germany also, where people have got heartily tired of the eternal English chicanery." And further: "Deloncle's low estimate of the worth of the English alliance to Germany needs no confirmation. The untrustworthiness of England is no secret, and German politicians are complaining that her unreliable friendship has been bought by a system of undue connivance at British encroachments."

These remarks would meet with few contradictions, either here or elsewhere in the Empire. Such popular feeling as exists towards England (of a "public opinion" in Germany it is absurd to speak), is largely tinctured with ill-will. The age of Bismarck has dropped that admiration for our institutions and statesmen, which marked the men of '48[486] without distinction of party or class. The parliamentary chiefs of the new Germany, the publicists, the professors of history, the teachers of youth, youth itself, have grown to regard us with dislike, and to talk of 'perfide Albion'[487] after the manner customary in France in the beginning of the Queen's reign. Anglomania still survives; but it is not a national creed, only the persuasion of certain crowned heads, of a few ministers, of a minority of liberal politicians, of a portion of the commercial as distinguished from the industrial class, of some Social Democrats. Lately there have been signs of

---

[483] *Dresdner Anzeiger*, 11 June 1894.

[484] The interview, dated Paris 6 June, was published in the *Frankfurter Zeitung* on 7 June 1894. For the Anglo-Congolese (Anglo-Belgian) agreement of 12 May 1894, see n. 365 in Berlin section.

[485] Name not traceable.

[486] The Revolution of 1848.

[487] See n. 250 in this section.

defection amongst our 'freisinnig'[488] friends. Even the Berlin 'Voss' the 'Nation' and other democratic organs,[489] partly under the African influence, have begun to modulate their old key of admiration into a carping tone. In discussing this topic with our enemies, our friends, or neutrals, I never heard an opinion differing to an appreciable extent from that just submitted.

The 'Anzeiger' is a sensible paper, the organ of the Municipality, not a mere trumpet of Boulevard folly and prejudice. The article quoted ridicules the idea, or pretence, of M. Deloncle, that the sea-power of Great Britain is not superior, in efficiency, perhaps not equal to the young navy of the German Empire.

FO 68/179: George Strachey to Earl of Kimberley, No 29, Dresden, 11 September 1894

[Received 13 September. X]

Press views of Antwerp peace congress

It is customary in this Empire to treat the proceedings of the International Peace Society with profound contempt. The reports of their recent meeting have drawn forth comments of the usual description. The National Liberal Dresden "Anzeiger"[490] observes that the discussions and resolutions of the Antwerp Congress have met with general disapproval in the German Press, and calls it supporters ignorant, clamorous, subversive idealists.[491]

This may seem strange in a country where all classes are radically pacific, not even the Army being bellicose. One reason lies in the prevalence in Germany of the Platonic belief that for the higher inspirations in politics mankind ought to look to trained experts, and not attend to the unofficial chatter of laymen. As the 'Anzeiger', trying to be sarcastic, puts it: 'to hear the peace-mongers, the Government, which is appointed by the Monarch, and the Parliament, the body elected by the people, have no comprehension

---

[488] See n. 3 in this section.

[489] The daily *Vossische Zeitung (Königlich privilegirte Berlinische Zeitung von Staats- und gelehrten Sachen*) and the weekly *Die Nation*.

[490] *Dresdner Anzeiger*, 6 September 1894.

[491] The sixth Universal Peace Congress met at Antwerp from 29 August to 1 September 1894. The main resolutions concerned duelling, the inviolability of human life, the abolishment of death penalties, free activity of all countries in new colonies, the necessity of permanent treaties of arbitration, the truce of armaments, the freezing of naval budgets, and the institution of a Peace Sunday on the continent.

of the true interests of the nation, this being exclusively possessed by the gentlemen who participate in the Peace Congress'.

On the other hand, a minority denies the esoteric character of public affairs, declining, in particular, to admit that competency in international problems is monopolized by Ambassadors and other high functionaries of state. But, between this party and the "peace-mongers", there interposes the question of Elsass-Lothringen.[492] Suggestions of European disarmament and arbitration indirectly involve eventual discussion before the Areopagus[493] of the future of the claims of the Empire to the continued possession of the Reichsland. On this point, absolute unanimity of feeling prevails throughout the nation. For the defence of the ancient "avulsa imperii"[494] reconquered in 1870, every German who deserved the name is as ready to die in the last ditch as we ourselves should be if Anglesea [*sic*] and the Isle of Wight were threatened. It was a note-worthy utterance of Bebel in the Reichstag, that if Metz and Strassburg were endangered, the followers of Social-Democracy would show that they knew their duty.[495]

FO 68/179: George Strachey to Earl of Kimberley, No 40, Dresden, 31 October 1894

[Received 1 November. For: Lord Rosebery; K[imberley]]

Saxon press on the fall of Caprivi

An event so sensational and unexpected as the Ministerial Crisis could not fail to arouse the German public from their normal polit-ical torpor.[496] In this city where, as I have often had occasion to report, Bismarck worship has always been a maximum, there is a vis-ible disposition to exult over the fall of Count Caprivi. The anti-semitic and Free Conservative "Dresdner Nachrichten",[497] which is generally a fair index to the opinions of a large portion of the local middle-class, administers severe kicks to the dead lion, calling

---

[492] The territory of Alsace-Lorraine was annexed by the German Empire in 1870–1871. It was known as the *Reichsland* (imperial territory) *Elsaß-Lothringen*.

[493] The council of elders in pre-classical Athens; named after the rock north-west of the Acropolis.

[494] Latin: 'cut off from the empire'.

[495] Strachey is referring to Bebel's speech of 15 July 1893.

[496] On Caprivi's resignation and Hohenlohe's succession as imperial chancellor, see pp. 164–168.

[497] *Dresdner Nachrichten*, 28 October 1894.

him a mere soldier, ignorant of politics, who, in passive obedience to orders, assumed an office which he was quite unqualified to fill. The Ex-Reichskanzler's record is the Colonial collapse, the Russian treaty fiasco, the famous declaration in the school debate, "Atheism versus Christianity", and the discreditable despatch on the occasion of Count Herbert Bismarck's marriage.[498] His successors are not likely to be his equals in supple readiness to submit to that 'sacrifizio dell' intelletto'[499] which appears to be a growing requirement for the occupiers of the post of Reichskanzler, now, under the new system, losing its political dignity, and threatening to sink to the level of a mere military command.

The 'National Liberal' "Anzeiger"[500] (organ of the Municipality) has no original articles on this topic, but betrays, in various ways, a certain satisfaction at General Caprivi's removal from office. Positively venemous [*sic*] is the tone of the leading National Liberal journal of the Kingdom, the Leipzig 'Tageblatt',[501] which gives a spicilegium[502] [note in margin: 'Qy'] of Berlin extracts tending to prove that the Reichskanzler was fairly turned out of office, thanks to the impatience caused by his shilly-shally system, and colourless policy, and to the resentments [*sic*] aroused by the behaviour of his "reptile press".[503]

In the chorus of Bismarckian sentiment the 'Zeitung',[504] a paper more liberal than the preceding, does not join, using language fairly sympathetic, & hinting that the statesman's fall has been the result of palace intrigues. Very suggestive is the reserve of the 'Journal',[505] which does not even venture on a single valedictory compliment to the retiring Minister. The official mouthpiece says, that the crisis at Berlin is not a subject for comment, in its columns, adding that Count Caprivi did not obtain from the Emperor, or from his colleagues, the support requisite to enable him to carry out his programme.

---

[498] The *Dresdner Nachrichten* was referring to the Heligoland-Zanzibar Treaty of 1890 (see n. 436 in Berlin section), Caprivi's speech in the Prussian house of deputies of 29 January 1892 concerning the elementary school bill (see pp. 138–140), the controversial German–Russian commercial treaty of 10 February 1894, and Caprivi's instruction to the German ambassador to Vienna of 9 June 1892 not to attend Herbert Bismarck's Viennese wedding.

[499] Italian: 'sacrifice of the intellect' (a concept of Christian devotion, here subjugation to the authority of the emperor).

[500] *Dresdner Anzeiger.*

[501] *Leipziger Tageblatt.*

[502] Latin: 'anthology'.

[503] For the 'reptile press', see n. 67 in this section.

[504] *Dresdner Zeitung.*

[505] *Dresdner Journal*, 27 October 1894.

What reaches me personally is in the direction of the opinions of the 'Nachrichten'. I need hardly say that the 'Agrarians' are jubilant at the unexpected removal from power of their grand enemy. It is no part of the German character to behave with generosity to a fallen foe.

FO 68/179: George Strachey to Earl of Kimberley, No 44, Dresden, 15 November 1894

[Received 19 November: For: Lord Rosebery; K[imberley]]

Public feeling in Saxony with regards to subversive political parties

There was lately published at Leipsic a pamphlet[506] on the subversive parties by Dr Rössler, formerly director of the Berlin 'Literary Bureau', the Government Office through which Prince Bismarck inspired the 'reptile' press of Germany, as for instance, in his campaign against the Emperor and Empress Friedrich.[507] Foreseeing that the Reichstag might be indisposed to comprehensive, effective, legislation against Social Democracy, the pamphleteer proposed a simple expedient by which coercion would be available in any desired degree. The constitution would be suspended, the Parliament, if recalcitrant, would be turned out of doors, and the Emperor, in conjunction with the Federal Council would assume supreme power for a term of years, when the edicts neccessary [*sic*] for the defense of society would be promulgated.

The Leipzig 'Grenzboten'[508] (Free-Conservatives) has ridiculed this as chimerical, observing that the fact that such suggestions had been solemnly discussed by a portion of the German press proved the existence of a degraded state of feeling, and was a national disgrace. The Dresden public must, I presume, be well aware that the impending proposals of the Imperial Government relative to Social Democracy exclude exceptional legislation on the pattern of the old Bismarck law.[509] Nevertheless there is here a strong current of opinion in favour of policy which would, in effect, involve the perpetration of a coup d'État. At a local meeting which was largely attended by the aristocracy, military, civil officials, and private

[506] Constantin Rössler, *Die Sozialdemokratie* (Berlin 1894).

[507] For the 'reptile press', see n. 67 in this section. For Bismarck's 'relationship with' and 'campaign' against Friedrich I and Victoria, see pp. 99–100, 104–106, and 111.

[508] *Die Grenzboten: Zeitschrift für Politik, Literatur und Kunst*, 18 October 1894.

[509] Strachey is referring to the 'subversion bill' (*Umsturzvorlage*), see n. 381 in Berlin section. For the Anti-Socialist Law which had expired in 1890, see n. 10 in this section.

burghers, a Prussian Kammerherr resident here,[510] and well known as a rabid enthusiast on behalf of 'throne and altar', delivered an address on the lines of the above named pamphlet.

His ranting rhetoric was received with enormous applause throughout, which reached a maximum, when he recommended that all Socialists condemned under his prospective legislation should, after their punishment by imprisonment of home, be transported to the Bismarck Archipelago or the Cameroons, and kept under supervision there.

A petition from Dresden urging drastic measures against the internal enemy, their deprival of constitutional rights included, has received 80,000 signatures in the kingdom.[511] To this, objections have been raised in National-Liberal quarters, and the declaration made, that the party will not countenance reactionary plans. It is, however, significant of Dresden feeling, that the National-Liberal 'Anzeiger',[512] the organ of the Town Council, calls the speech just quoted a very statesmanlike and important manifesto.

[...]

P.S. Since the above was written, the Prussian Kammerherr named has repeated his lecture at Leipzig,[513] before a large assemblage of the partizans of Order, when a resolution was passed, declaratory of the determination of those present to support the Crown in its campaign against the propagators of subversive doctrines.

FO 68/179: George Strachey to Earl of Kimberley, No 45, Dresden, 24 November 1894

[Received 26 November. For: Lord Rosebery; K[imberley]]

German press widely subscribe to Anglophobia

The Berlin correspondent of the 'Standard' has been at his old trick of persuading his employers that their editorials are creating a 'sensation', or 'surprise', in Germany.[514] This public does not read English newspapers, hardly knows them even by name, and the

---

[510] Werner von Blumenthal, on 10 November 1894.

[511] The petition to the *Reichstag* and the Federal Council was drawn up by the Dresden *Konservative Verein* on 3 July 1894.

[512] *Dresdner Anzeiger*, 12 November 1894.

[513] On 12 November 1894.

[514] Strachey is referring to Emil Witte's article, dated 19 November, on the German reaction to the *Standard's* editorial of 12 November (see pp. 169–170).

idea of its being excited by their opinions is ludicrous. What has happened is, that the entire German press, whether originating, or copying from the party Circular correspondence sheets, is labouring under an acute attack of Anglophobia. If their diatribes against our greed, treachery, and weakness, appear less venomous than the attacks of the 'Figaro' and its consorts, the reason is that the literary hacks of Berlin, Cologne, and Dresden, trained as they are under the daily pressure of the gag, have not acquired the art of effective journalistic writing.

The bitterness of spirit to which I allude has been recently manifested by a rain of articles, paragraphs, and allusions, referring to the affairs of China and Japan, Samoa, New Guinea, Madagascar, Delagoa Bay, the African boundaries, the Suez Canal, the Temple of Philae, and so forth. A special gravamen has been suggested by the Prime Minister's speech at the Guildhall,[515] which is called a bid for the foundation of an anti-German Triple Alliance, and by the language used in England on the death of the Czar,[516] in which our German critics profess to discover servilities of language that surpass the worst excesses of French prostration in that quarter. Our domestic politics are in an equally discreditable groove. All parties are absorbed in the desire to win the favour if the Demos, the honour and safety of the Empire are disregarded – all of which is worse under a Radical administration.

These sentiments may be found in the representative organs of the daily and periodical press of the Empire, Conservative and Liberal, and even in the Radical Berlin 'Voss'.[517] A particularly heavy blow against the enemy has been suggested by the Leipzig 'Grenzboten',[518] which, after a fashion, is the German "Nineteenth Century". That magazine has worked out the idea of a German-French alliance to be directed against our present colonial and maritime supremacy, which is to be ["]crushed by the French and German navies of the future." Great Britain is a country which "in the insatiable voracity of its territorial appetite swallows whatever it can get, and grudges others that which it cannot itself absorb". 'Germany has everywhere to encounter in all their hateful nakedness the Polyp-arms of the envy and malevolence of her British enemy.' This article is quoted at length by the Dresden official 'Journal',[519] which signifies its approval.

---

[515] See n. 391 in Berlin section.

[516] Alexander III died on 1 November 1894.

[517] *Vossische Zeitung (Königlich privilegirte Berlinische Zeitung von Staats- und gelehrten Sachen).*

[518] *Die Grenzboten: Zeitschrift für Politik, Literatur und Kunst,* 1 November 1894.

[519] *Dresdner Journal,* 3 November 1894.

FO 68/179: George Strachey to Earl of Kimberley, No 48, Dresden, 15 December 1894

[Received 17 December. For: Lord Rosebery; K[imberley]]

Criticism in Saxony of proposal to prosecute Socialist Reichstag *members*

The request to the Reichstag to permit the prosecution of Herr Liebknecht has been widely disapproved here, except in quarters where official decorum prevents the expression, or formation, of personal judgments.[520] It is to the credit of the local newspapers that none of them have separated themselves on this occasion from the press of the Empire: not even the subsidized Government 'reptile', the 'Journal',[521] has ventured to advocate the prosecution, or to pretend that a majority of the Reichstag was likely to decide in its favour. I have been surprised to find the ornamental classes indisposed to accept the principle of the assimilation of parliamentary offences to common crimes.

By the German aristocratic and official castes, Socialists and Liberals are habitually spoken of as dogs, or worse: I lately heard the Reichstag described, as an assemblage composed, if the Conservatives were excepted, of "mere blackguards". – Still, such feelings do not exclude the recognition of the truth that if a Parliament is to exist, its discipline ought not to rest with the police.

Of the intelligent circles, the knowledge of a Diplomatist is never perfect, nor quite direct. I am assured, however, that the enlightened majority of the citizen class of this capital see with regret that the opening of "the newest course"[522] has been marked by an unfortunate political blunder. A Minister[523] with no party at his back, without imposing antecedents or striking personal qualities, allows the Government to be drawn into a constitutional conflict calculated to divide the supporters of "throne and altar" into hostile camps, and to "bring water", as the Germans say, "to the mill"[524] of the

---

[520] Liebknecht, together with other members of the Social Democratic faction, remained seated during cheers for the emperor in the *Reichstag* sittings of 6 December 1894. In a letter of 9 December the imperial chancellor requested the *Reichstag* to give its approval to Liebknecht's prosecution for lèse-majesté. This was rejected on 15 December.

[521] *Dresdner Journal*. On the so-called 'reptile press', see n. 67 in this section.

[522] This refers to the new administration under Hohenlohe and is an allusion to Caprivi's 'New Course'.

[523] Ernst von Köller, Prussian minister of the interior.

[524] The German proverb '*Wasser auf seine Mühlen bringen*' translates as 'That's all grist to his mill'.

subversive parties! Such a beginning, it is urged, bodes no good. So many difficulties lie ahead – (some of them, for instance, the financial, are likely to prove insoluble on the terms proposed by the Imperial Government) – that the Reichskanzler's proper course was to calm antagonisms not to permit them to be roused.

To the gag the Germans are accustomed, and they accept it as a fundamental national institution. But to the classes here in question, its application to the Legislature is an absurdity against which they protest – as the German manner is, in silence.

In the face of the proposed "arrest of the six members", the utter absence of an active public opinion may seem strange. If existing, it could attain, in Saxony at least, to no open expression, for meetings to discuss such a burning question would not be permitted. As regards the offence with which the Socialists are charged, I would say that German legal theory and practice afford a general basis to the view of the Berlin Public Prosecutors.

Schoolboys of ten or twelve years of age have been arrested for lèse-majesté: a person who good humouredly spoke of the Imperial babies as "little chaps" (Bengel) was recently indicted for the outrage. Not long since, some individuals who did not rise at a dinner when the Emperor's health was drunk, were prosecuted and sentenced: this occured [*sic*] in Saxony.

FO 68/180: George Strachey to Earl of Kimberley, Confidential, No 8, Dresden, 7 February 1895

[Received 11 February. Seen at Berlin. For: Lord Rosebery; K[imberley]]

Dismal view of Saxon ministerial changes

The Ministerial changes of the secondary German states have as a rule, a mere personal origin, in which politics have no part, and are scarcely more discussed by the local public than junior appointments in the Army. The previous possession of superior administrative, courtly or diplomatic rank is the sine qua non for high office, large scope being allowed to palatial considerations, which may give the wrong man the place. Pari passû and with the growing transfer of authority to Berlin, there has been a progressive deterioration in the Saxon Cabinet Ministers of the last twenty years, especially at the Foreign Office, where, within my time, there has been a descent from positive statesmanship to the very minimum of bureaucratic intelligence.

The department of Finance is shortly to be vacant by the retirement, from ill-health, of Herr von Thummel, a capable expert. His successor will be Herr von Watzdorf, at present keeper of the Privy Purse, personal Secretary to the King and Queen, and acting Lord Chamberlain. For the exercise of such functions this gentleman is well fitted; but for high administrative work his only qualifications are, that he is <u>persona grata</u> at Court, and is connected by marriage with the Minister of Foreign Affairs.[525]

Herr von Watzdorf will have to manage the State Railways, Woods, Forests, Mines, Domains, and the like, and he will have to contribute to the evolution of the German financial problems which now perplex the statesmen of the Empire. Yet his appointments has been received here in silence: neither press nor public have uttered a word of praise or blame. On my asking a leading financier what was said on the subject, the reply was "nothing is, or will be, said at all: the matter is not discussed on grounds of politeness." Another middle-class informant answered in the same sense – "in regard to such topics, our population, as you know, is muzzled:"– "and of course, the Finanzraths[526] will prevent any mischief being done." All of which may be appropriately summed up in the classical phrase "il fallait un calculateur, un danseur l'obtint"[.][527]

FO 68/180: George Strachey to Earl of Kimberley, No 11 Dresden, 31 May 1895

[Received 3 June. X; K[imberley]]

Spectator *article misrepresents German Emperor's role in crisis over amendment of Criminal Code*

According to a recent article in the London 'Spectator' the Emperor William has been in conflict with "his people", and has suffered "defeat" at their hands, by the rejection of "his" fiscal plans, and "his" proposed legislation against the Subversives.[528] As commentary on the late Parliamentary situation in Berlin, this language is altogether unmeaning. On some other occasions when the calm of Germany has been disturbed by political cyclones, the Emperor has been identified, and on solid grounds, with a particular line of legislation. And there have been times when his opinions and wishes

---

[525] Watzdorf's wife was a distant cousin of Georg von Metzsch.

[526] Senior civil servants in the ministry for finance.

[527] French: 'a schemer was needed, a dancer was chosen' from Beaumarchais' play *La Folle Journée, ou Le Mariage de Figaro (1884)*.

[528] 'The German Emperor's Defeat', *The Spectator*, 18 May 1895. Amongst other things, the article discussed the implications of the *Reichstag's* rejection of a surcharge on tobacco (13 May) and of the 'subversion bill' (*Umsturzvorlage*; see n. 381 in Berlin section) on 11 May.

have been the subject of guesses and assertions often founded on irresponsible gossip, or positive frictions. During the late events, nothing of this sort happened. As far as was known, the Emperor kept silence on the topic of the day: and the public refrained from the customary conjectures. Earlier remarks of His Imperial Majesty on the necessity of combating the internal enemies of society, and certain phrases from his addresses to the recruits, were not forgotten.[529] But it was thought that between such expressions and the Bill for the Amendment of the Criminal Code no visible connexion existed and the responsibility for that measure was laid on the Imperial Government and not on the Crown. Still less was the Emperor accused of sympathy with the amendments of the Catholic Centre.[530] Far from it, the current opinion was, that his consent as King of Prussia would never be given to the application to Germany of a gag of that description. On the whole it may be said, that the Germans are entirely unconscious of the existence of the state of things on which the 'Spectator' has been philosophizing with so much acumen.

FO 68/180: George Strachey to Earl of Kimberley, No 13, Dresden, 29 June 1895

[Received 1 July. For: The Queen; S[alisbury]]

Emperor's dignified role in celebrations to mark the opening of the Kiel Canal; press moderate towards less dignified performance of the French

The Minister for Foreign Affairs has returned home deeply impressed by the festivities and functions of Hamburg and Kiel.[531] Speaking to me on the subject, he remarked that the Emperor had played his part through'out with remarkable tact and success, sustaining to the full his dignity as head of Germany, both by his general demeanour, and by his imposing delivery of his speeches at Hamburg and Kiel, the latter of which was, for prudence sake, read, after it had been submitted to the editorship of Herr von Böttcher.

---

[529] Strachey is referring, in particular, to Wilhelm's speech of 23 November 1891, in which he – in the face of subversive socialist activities – demanded army recruits to follow his orders without grumbling, even if he ordered them to shoot their own relatives.

[530] Instigated by the Catholic *Zentrum* faction, the bill was extended to protect recognized religious institutions and their doctrines from sacrilege along with incitement to blasphemy.

[531] For the opening of the Kiel Canal, see pp. 177–179.

Herr von Metzsch observed, that the conduct of the French, had caused much amusement: their perversities were remarkable, and an absurd effect was produced when their ships remained dark during the illumination of the fleet. Their arrival at Kiel with the Russians was comical, and the Grand Duke Alexis expressed his dissatisfaction at his own forced share in the manoeuvre.

I remarked that the interest and enthusiasm aroused by all this pageantry must leave a mark on the imagination of the German people: the opening of the Canal was another nail in the coffin of 'Particularism'. Of that sentiment, which only survives here in the minds of an obscure minority of microscopic proportions and importance, Herr von Metzsch is not a devotee, and he replied with emphasis, that my estimate of the effect of the recent proceedings was the same as his own.

The Press has spoken of the apparent discourtesy of the French visitors in very mild terms, throwing the blame on the incurable chauvinism of the Boulevards. The complaint is, that in France the "study of revenge" – in itself a perfectly legitimate and even laudable end – is pursued in an ignorable, malignant, childish spirit, which brings daily discredit on the Republic. In the same way, there is no impeachment of the alliance with Russia, only of the ignominious, grovelling devices by which it has been purchased, and is sought to be maintained.[532]

FO 68/180: George Strachey to Marquess of Salisbury, No 17, Dresden, 12 July 1895

[Received 15 July. Seen at Berlin. X; S[alisbury]]

Absence of German interest in changes to British cabinet

It is the habit of some of the representatives of the London press abroad to colour their correspondence with sensational pictures of continental feeling on English topics. These reports are expanded into editorials in which foreign popular opinion is further falsified and caricatured, until a climax of exaggeration is reached, like, for instance, the assertion (in a very sober weekly quarter) that Lord Rosebery's resignation caused "keen excitement" all over Europe", "made the nations quiver", and in fine gave rise to "emotion in every quarter of the globe."[533]

[532] For the Franco-Russian rapprochement, see pp. 153–154.

[533] Strachey is referring to the *Spectator* article of 29 June 1895 ('Effects of the English Crisis Abroad') which reported on international reactions to Rosebery's resignation, on 22 June 1895, and the succession of Salisbury as prime minister.

Speaking of Germany, I may safely affirm that such language misrepresents the plainest facts of the situation. To any one with the slightest varnish of acquaintance with this Empire, there is something ludicrous in the idea of a German sentiment on the ministerial revolutions of London. There have been here no speculations in that direction at all. Neither "excitement" nor "emotion" have been visible – only the usual feeling of passive national dislike, associated, in the case of politicians, with the belief that our power and prestige are in a decrescendo course, and that Germany need not fear us as enemies, or court us as allies.

The tone of the press has, on the whole, conformed to this. The current argument has been, that there is a continuity in the diplomatic policy of England, by whichever party governed, which makes it certain that, though the sympathies of the successive advisers of the Crown may oscillate between Paris and Berlin, our foreign programme will, in essentials, always remain the same. In a few instances, satisfaction has been expressed on the ground that under the new Government our relations with France and Russia may possibly become more strained, in which Germany would find her account.

After verifying the above in various ways, I told Herr von Metzsch what I was writing to Your Lordship on the subject. His Excellency said the facts could not be more correctly stated, although, for his part, he took an accidental personal interest in these changes, as they had brought his brother-in-law, Mr Goschen, into power.[534] A highly acute financial personage tells me, that having last week had good opportunities for observing the drift of Prussian and Hanseatic opinion in circles friendly to us, he can say that our political vicissitudes are there regarded as matters in which Germany has no direct concern.

FO 68/180: George Strachey to Marquess of Salisbury, No 21, Schweizermühle, 10 August 1895

[Received 12 August by post. X; S[alisbury]]

Storm of press protest in response to Standard's *critical leader on German Emperor's visit to Cowes*

The leader in the 'Standard' on the Emperor William's visit to Cowes has raised a hurricane of protests in the German press.[535]

---

[534] Goschen was appointed First Lord of the Admiralty. His sister Marian was married to Georg von Metzsch.

[535] Wilhelm visited England from 5 to 15 August 1895 to attend the Cowes Week regattas. The article in question, published on 5 August, criticised Wilhelm's inexperience in foreign affairs and Germany's policy towards Russia, France and East Asia. Enclosure: newspaper clipping from *The Standard*, 5 August 1895.

Prominent in bitterness are the leading National-Liberal journals e.g. the "Kölnische Zeitung", "National Zeitung", with, of course, Prince Bismarck's Hamburg "reptile".[536] Specially venomous is a long article in the Anti-Semitic Dresden 'Nachrichten',[537] a newspaper with a large local and general circulation. There is the familiar picture of British arrogance, cupidity, and cunning, and of that sense of military impotence which makes us glad to cringe at times to "the b~y Germans" and "their mushroom Empire" (the terms in which we speak of our neighbours). There is also the old axiom that Germany deprecates alliance with us – . "Between England & Germany politeness may exist; but, on grounds national, psychological, and political, friendship – never."

Of similar purport, though less acrid in style, are leaders in the Dresden municipal 'Anzeiger', and the official 'Journal': the last named boils over with anger at the notion of an English publicist daring to lay hand on the sacred person of the German Emperor.[538]

It is noteworthy that the "Tageblatt" and "Voss",[539] which, as representatives of the enlightened middle-class radicalism of Berlin and Germany, give little or no encouragements to Anglophobia, have taken umbrage at the 'Standard' editorial. As even the 'Tageblatt' calls the London Unionist journal Your Lordship's "officious" organ, and ascribes its language to Downing Street inspirations, it is not wonderful that the entire German press should systematically see in almost every article in the 'Standard' on foreign affairs a 'communiqué' from your hand. For this once, the 'National Zeitung' leaves the question of authorship undecided: the Dresden opinion is that the source of the incriminated 'Standard' leader is doubtful.

FO 68/180: George Strachey to Marquess of Salisbury, No 23, Dresden, 24 August 1895

[Received 26 August by post. For: ~~Mr Balfour~~ / Commercial Department; T.H.S. [Thomas Henry Sanderson]; '? No action required'; H.F. [Harry de la Rosa Burrard Farnall]; G.N.C. [George N. Curzon]]

Press complaints about British 'spies' gaining access to German iron foundries

The statements of the Berlin 'Voss' regarding the "spies" sent by the British "Iron Trade Association" to the metallurgical centres of

---

[536] Strachey is referring to the *Hamburger Nachrichten* . For the 'reptile' press, see n. 67 in this section.

[537] *Dresdner Nachrichten*, 8 August 1895.

[538] *Dresdner Anzeiger*, 9 August 1895, and *Dresdner Journal*, 8 August 1895.

[539] *Berliner Tageblatt* and *Vossische Zeitung* (*Königlich privilegirte Berlinische Zeitung von Staats- und gelehrten Sachen*).

Germany are going the round of the press of the Empire.[540] A Dresden newspaper quotes the disgraceful imputations thrown upon the so-called "spies" and their principals, aggravating them by what is perhaps an addition of its own. The 'Zeitung'[541] alleges that the English emissaries came with introductions from Downing Street, and remarks that details must be supplied, in order that on the recurrence of similar recommendations the German parties interested may know how to take their precautions.

The 'Voss' article is dated from London – a very familiar device. It derides the low scientific training of our iron-masters, who did not know how to take advantage of the Thomas-Gilchrist process,[542] from the intelligent use of which Germany has reaped such great benefit. The writer is ignorant enough to confound converters with blast-furnaces. He is equally unaware that the 'acid' process was adopted on the large scale by the German makers of malleable iron and mild steel, because that invention enabled them to utilize the phospuretted ores and white pig of the country, thus freeing them from their dependence on our hematite iron.

The industrial evolution in question is, I need hardly say, nothing new. Its metallurgical and statistical aspects were minutely examined by myself about ten years ago, in a Report, laid before Parliament, on the working of the Protective German Tariff.[543]

FO 68/180: George Strachey to Marquess of Salisbury, No 24, Dresden, 3 September 1895

[Received 5 September. For: The Queen / Mr Balfour; S[alisbury]]

Saxon and German commemorations of Sedan jubilee

The anniversary of Sedan has been kept throughout this kingdom with enthusiastic popular demonstrations and rejoicings.[544] Of the

---

[540] Strachey is referring to an article which appeared in the *Vossische Zeitung* (21 August 1895) concerning a delegation comprising seven employers' representatives and seven representatives of workmen's associations, which had been sent by the British Iron Trade Association to Belgium and Germany in July and August 1895. According to the article the delegation gained access to German iron works under the pretext of investigating the conditions of labour; instead it focussed on the technical details of production and thereby infringed business ethics.

[541] *Dresdner Zeitung*, 23 August 1895.

[542] Method of converting pig iron into steel without the consumption of fuel, named after Sidney Gilchrist Thomas.

[543] *Report on the Effects of the German Customs Tariff Reform and on the Revision in 1885*, 10 September 1885.

[544] On Sedan Day (2 September), see n. 50 in this section.

processions and other open-air ceremonials, the displays of patriotic emblems and decorations, the musical performances, the addresses, the banquets, the illuminations, it may be said that they commemorated in a suitable manner the men and events to whom honour was to be paid. These jubilee proceedings had in no respect an official origin or character. From first to last they were organized by municipal and parochial bodies, private military societies, and mixed committees of management. No troops were present: the army was only represented by the veterans of the great war, for whom new charitable foundations were instituted. At one of the out-door functions in this city the King was present; but he came without escort, less in his personality as sovereign, than as the comrade of the survivors of St. Privat and Beaumont,[545] to whom he addressed a few sentences of suitable sympathy and recognition.

The attitude of the Saxon public has again demonstrated what, perhaps, required no further proof – namely, than in none of the 26 States of the Empire is the new pan-Germanic spirit stronger than it is here. Particularism is dead: the people may almost be described as Germans first, Saxons afterwards. Of the large German jubilee literature I have seen enough to be able to say, that its characteristic has been, reasonable reserve and self-restraint, the infatuations of the 'Roi. Soleil'[546] style in history having been laudably absent, as well as all provocative and recriminatory language. There is truth in some remarks of the Dresden 'Anzeiger', that the "note" (sit venia verbo)[547] of this commemoration is: – 'Deutschland über alles'.[548] – Germany, that is, great in the glories of war, but greater in the conquest of her long desired "ideal good", the Unity of the nation.

FO 68/180: George Strachey to Marquess of Salisbury, No 25, Dresden, 16 September 1895

[Received 23 September. Seen at Berlin. For: The Queen / Mr Balfour; S[alisbury]]

Emperor's indictment of Social Democracy with regards to Sedan jubilee; German prosecutions for lèse-majesté abound

Although the Emperor's habit of participating in political controversy is generally thought to be prejudicial to the interests and authority of

---

[545] Battles of Gravelotte (18 August 1870) and Beaumont (30 August 1870).
[546] French: 'Sun King' (i.e. Louis XIV).
[547] Latin: 'pardon the expression'.
[548] German: 'Germany above all'; first line of *Das Lied der Deutschen*, by Hoffmann von Fallersleben (1841).

the Crown, His Imperial Majesty's Stettin arraignments of Social-Democracy,[549] with the subsequent confiscations and arrests in Berlin, Leipsic, and other places, have been approved in Conservative and National-Liberal circles. It is characteristic of Germany, that the imputability of the articles of the "Vorwärts" is taken as proved, although of their particular contents not a word is known. As usual in such cases, the truth will never reach the public. Copies of the incriminated newspapers cannot be obtained. the [sic] Editors and printers will be tried and condemned in secret sittings, of which no record will be divulged except a bare statement of the sentences passed. The republication of defamatory matter, even in the form of a liberal report of the proceedings in a Court of Justice, is not privileged here, but is equivalent to the original libel.

The language of the "Vorwärts" on the "high-holy"[550] William I may have been reprehensible: so may that of the philosophical Berlin weekly, "Moral Culture", seized yesterday for reference to the recent utterances of the reigning monarch.[551] It is equally likely that the expressions used were such as in Italy, or England, or the United States, would, in similar circumstances, give no umbrage. Mere levity in speaking of a royal personage may constitute lèse-majesté, even when malicious intention is absent. What may be called Star-chamber trials[552] for that crime are as frequent in Germany, or, at least, in Prussia, as they were in Rome under Tiberius. Schoolboys have been prosecuted for 'Majestas':[553] a familiar though friendly remark in the intimacy of private conversation on Princes in the nursery has set the law in motion: an eminent historian[554] has been tried for scientific strictures on the policy of the Emperor's remote ancestor, the "Great Elector".[555] The Public Prosecutor's task is, in one respect, easy. The 'Delator'[556] of Tacitus is well-known here: the duty of "informing" is taught in the nursery

---

[549] In the imperial rescript issued at Stettin on 8 September 1895 Wilhelm II referred to the socialists and their press as 'unpatriotic enemies' who, during the course of the celebrations for the 25th anniversary of the Franco-Prussian War and Sedan Day, had insulted the memory of Wilhelm I and thus offended the German people.

[550] 'Sacrosanct' (*hochheillig*).

[551] *Ethische Kultur* of 14 September 1895; the article in question was entitled 'Der Kaiser und die Sozialdemokratie'.

[552] Strachey is referring to the Court of Star Chamber, an early modern English court of law, which became notorious for arbitrary decisions.

[553] Law of *majestas*; this refers to the ancient Roman laws on treason.

[554] Name not traceable. Possibly Strachey is referring to Heinrich von Treitschke.

[555] Friedrich Wilhelm, Elector of Brandenburg.

[556] Latin: "denouncer'. In his *Annales* Tacitus describes the role and abuse of *delatores*, during the reigns of Tiberius, Cladius and Nero.

and schoolroom, and is imposed, or, at any rate, not disapproved by the national codes of social and professional honour.

FO 68/180: George Strachey to Marquess of Salisbury, No 34, Dresden, 30 November 1895

[Received 2 December. X; S[alisbury]]

Interview with editor of Dresdner Journal*; its Anglophobic tone and misrepresentation of British foreign policy addressed and remedied*

Some time since I remarked to Herr von Metzsch that the 'Journal' was in the habit of discussing our policy and affairs in a tone which, for a Government organ, seemed unusual. Shewing him the article on "the Armenian bloodbath", I said that such language was not calculated to promote the friendly feelings towards us which the King and his Government always appeared so desirous to maintain.[557] As a newspaper the 'Journal' might have little political weight; still, as it was published by the Department of the Interior, of which His Excellency was head, its contents, even in the non-Ministerial portion, might be said to carry the mark of official approval.

Herr von Metzsch having looked over the corpus delicti observed, "this is exceedingly strong", adding, that he did not know why such a line was adopted, and that he should send for the responsible editor,[558] and make him explain.

After a certain interval that personage called on me, under instruction, he said, from the Minister. He intimated that the leaders of the 'Journal' on foreign affairs were not, properly speaking, original, being more or less transcripts, from various sources, with local alterations. Neither he nor his subordinates were actuated by hostility or disrespect towards England, and he was sorry if the articles had suggested a different idea.

The Editor's tone was courteous and apologetic throughout, and I replied in a friendly manner, arguing that English statesmen and policy would be better understood in Germany, if the press would deal with our feelings and motives in a direct, simple, manner, instead of making them the subject of deep interpretations and

---

[557] The article in the *Dresdner Journal* (21 November 1895), which insinuated that Britain had adopted a conciliatory course towards the Porte, had been prompted by the Hamidian massacres against the Armenian population. These had spread throughout the Ottoman Empire after a rally of 2,000 Armenians, petitioning for reforms at Constantinople, on 1 October 1895, had been violently broken up.

[558] Johannes Poppe.

constructions. Further, I remarked on the german [*sic*] trick of ascribing mere newspaper utterances to high official inspiration, and said that the 'Journal' might set a useful example by discarding this mischievous habit.

Since the date in question, a decided change has come over the 'Journal'. The old insensate Anglophobia has been dropped, our "isolation" is no longer a standing text, and ministerial authorship is not read into the 'leaders' of the 'Standard' or 'Observer'. In some other press organs similar signs of improvement are visible.

FO 68/180: George Strachey to Marquess of Salisbury, No 35, Dresden, 9 December 1895

[Received 11 December. For: Mr Balfour; S[alisbury]]

Disapproval of emperor's political orations

The Emperor's address to the military at Breslau provoked in loyal circles a renewal of the criticisms to which his speeches almost invariably give rise.[559] The press refrained from passing judgement on the utterances of "All Highest the Same":[560] a liberal journal vented its' disapproval by the familiar German device of printing the Imperial menaces [*sic*] in special type. But in private conversation, there was less restraint, when, at least, good security was present that the remarks exchanged would not be carried for the Public Prosecutor. To myself, the regret was expressed in more than one high quarter, that the Emperor seemed as far as ever from recognition of the fact that the functions of his station are not those of a party orator, and that while his descents into the arena of political strife tend to hinder the solution of the problems of the day, they strengthen the hands of his enemies, and derogate from the proper reserve and dignity of the Crown.

The medieval element in the Monarch's "Weltanschaung"[561] is in itself calculated to arouse sympathy here. But then, as the extreme partizans of "Throne and Altar" observe, His Imperial Majesty's emphatic assertion of his "cosmical conception" unfortunately miss the mark. Germany, or, to be exact, Prussia, is no longer in the age of the Great Elector,[562] or of the Great Frederick, and is not to be

---

[559] In a speech of 2 December 1895 Wilhelm II expressed his expectation of support from his army, especially in times of political catchphrases and party considerations.

[560] Translation of *Allerhöchstderselbe*, a pronoun which used in official writing instead of *er* (he), roughly equivalent to 'the aforesaid all-highest'.

[561] Literally 'world view' (concept of the world).

[562] Friedrich Wilhelm, Elector of Brandenburg.

governed by 'Major generals' so that the Emperor's menaces fall as mere <u>bruta fulmina</u>,[563] and, in no one instance have they hit the mark. Whether his persuasions or threats are addressed for the "horde" of Social Democracy, or to the Agrarian nobles of East Preussen and Brandenburg, not a single recalcitrant obeys, not a vote at the elections is affected. No one is "smashed up", but prestige is lost to the throne.

I may take this opportunity of saying, that some recent speculations, or assertions, of the London 'Spectator' regarding an eventual resort by the Emperor to extra-constitutional methods of Government betray ignorance of the elements of the German political vocabulary and situation.[564]

FO 68/181: George Strachey to Marquess of Salisbury, No 3, Dresden, 10 January 1896

[Received 13 January. Seen at Berlin. X; S[alisbury]]

Press controversy over Transvaal incidents reinvigorated; meeting at Leipzig expressing sympathy with Boers and in support of a German fleet

The German press was dropping the controversial elements of the Transvaal incident,[565] when the fresh vituperations of the 'Times' & 'Standard' provoked a renewal of the strife from this side. The palm in these deplorable outbursts of invective may, perhaps, be assigned to our own journals: the meaner social standing, education, and influence, and the vast inferiority of argumentative and stylistic power of the publicist of Berlin or Dresden, make him a weaker and less responsible agent of international mischief than his London rival. The drift of the last German rejoinders is, that the strength and prestige of the British Bobadil[566] are not commensurate with his arrogance and bluster, which have isolated him amongst the powers: that, in spite of certain transparent pretences of political apology and regret, the sympathies of England are on the side of

---

[563] Latin: the full phrase '*bruta fulmina et vana*' means 'thunderbolts that strike blindly and in vain' and is attributed to Pliny the Elder.

[564] Strachey is referring to the article 'The Threat of Repression in Germany', published on 30 November.

[565] For the crisis in the South African Republic, the failed 'Jameson Raid' and Wilhelm II's subsequent Kruger telegram, see pp. 188–195.

[566] Character in Ben Jonson's comedy *Every Man in his Humour* (1598); a cowardly braggart.

the late filibusters: that the marauder-in-chief[567] was acting under orders from the Cape, and that the attitude of Her Majesty's Government, if formally correct, has by no means been above suspicion. I have not observed any resuscitation of the old trick of ascribing the Editorials of the 'Standard' to Your Lordship, the radical press has refrained as a rule, from the extreme conclusions of the parties of 'Throne and Altar'; but its tendency to go against the current is weaker than before. Exceptional is the attitude of the Berlin weekly, the 'Nation', which almost amounts to partizanship for us: but in the Prussian Capital the flame of German patriotism never burns as fiercely as in Dresden. The 'Zeitung' argues that, scandalous as our newspaperian language may be, we have been paid back as we deserve: if driven to bay, we may find means, especially through our influence with Italy, of disturbing and countervailing the Triple-Alliance.[568]

The Pan Germanic Union of Leipsic[569] has held a meeting to sympathize with the Boers, when a collection was made on their behalf. Speeches with suitable denunciations of England were delivered by Professors and others, a Telegram of gratitude was sent to the Emperor, and a subscription opened for a fund wherewith Germany is to build a fleet which will make 'Rule Britannia' a legend of the past. The sum handed in was £150: The 'Leipzig' periodical 'Grenzboten' had previously[570] recommended a move of this description on the ground that the Reichstag had refused the funds requisite for the establishment of the naval supremacy of the Empire.[571] It has been proposed by certain 'Africans' to hold a meeting here with a similar programme. But this project has not yet assumed a definite shape.

[...]

P.S: Although I was educated in the belief, or prejudices, of the Palmerstonian age and school, I must express my opinion that none of the German Expectorations are comparable for spite, contemptuous insolence, and brag, with certain leaders, letters, and news-reports in the 'Standard' of the 9th Instant just come to hand.[572]

---

[567] Leander Starr Jameson.

[568] For the Triple Alliance, see n. 174 in Berlin section.

[569] The nationalist *Alldeutscher Verband* held its meeting on 7 January.

[570] On 28 November 1895, in a review of Georg Wislicenus' *Unsere Kriegsflotte* (*1895*).

[571] In March 1895 the *Reichstag* approved eighty per cent of the navy estimates for the fiscal year 1895–1896. As in previous years the budget guaranteed the maintenance of the existing fleet, but not its extension.

[572] Amongst other things, the articles and letters in question referred to German intrigues in South Africa.

FO 68/181: George Strachey to Marquess of Salisbury, No 6, Dresden, 17 January 1896

[Received 20 January. Seen at Berlin. For: The Queen; S[alisbury]]

Transvaal affairs remain a press matter rather than inciting a public response; Englishmen not subjected to ill treatment

Conformably to my habit of collecting typical opinions on the more urgent topics of the day, I have been asking a large number of German personages of various classes and positions, courtly, ministerial, parliamentary, military and private – from the very highest downwards – to inform me what language was being; or had been, held within their respective spheres of observation on the Anglo-German feud. In almost every instance the answer was this. 'The Transvaal affair[573] has not come under discussion, or remark, in my hearing: the whole dispute has passed for an international newspaper quarrel of secondary interest, to which no attention need be paid'. Of the nature of the various English manifestations against Germany and the Emperor, I found as good as no knowledge: the accounts of our preparations, actual or supposed, had excited, at the utmost, feelings of curiosity.

General business circles have preserved a similar calm. Our newspaper pictures of the eventual destruction of German commerce by our fleets have only caused amusement, or suggested the remark that, after all, "these are hardly the days of Queen Bess[574] and Nelson". Bankers have been more agitated, their daily business being affected by every new fact or rumour: according to their reports, only their English and American clients have manifested an interest in the Transvaal conflict. Of anti-english [*sic*] feeling in financial quarters I hear nothing. I understand that the proposed call to the public on behalf of the Boer wounded has been dropped, on the ground that such appeal might be thought to bear a provocative character.

In Leipzig, both the new pan-Germanic patriotism and colonial sentiment always run high. I learn from a reliable source, that traces of irritation may be discerned there; but they are, in part, only the signs of the commercial dislike of England always present in that trade metropolis. A reliable English informant writes to me from Chemnitz, that the permanent anti-English industrial jealousies of that great manufacturing center are perceptible, but, he adds, – "nothing special has been called forth by late events": "the matter

[573] See pp. 188–195.
[574] Elizabeth I.

(the Transvaal affair) is treated with comparative indifference; and I have heard no unpleasant remarks".

A Leipzig house has just published an insulting letter from their London correspondents, cancelling business orders given some weeks ago. The German Anglophobia has been altogether Platonic, no english-man having suffered from the brutality, or patriotism, of German mobs or employers. At the Dresden 'Theatre des Varietés' some english artists were lately accorded an unusually enthusiastic reception.

[...]

P.S. Fresh opinions, just taken enable me to confirm the first two pages of this Despatch, and to describe their contents as applicable to some other parts of the Empire.

FO 68/181: George Strachey to Marquess of Salisbury, Most Confidential, No 8, Dresden, 24 January 1896

[Received 3 February. Seen at Berlin. For: Print (South Zambezi) / The Queen / Mr Balfour / Duke of Devonshire / Mr Chamberlain; S[alisbury]]

King of Saxony's remarks on the Kruger telegram

On my bringing under the King's notice, one evening at the Palace, the newspaper statement that he had telegraphed approval of the Emperor's congratulations to President Krüger, His Majesty said that the story was without foundation, adding – "I had nothing what-ever to do with that business."[575]

On a subsequent occasion, when I had adverted to the Transvaal topic, the King observed that he 'had disapproved of the Telegram which gave rise to the Anglo-German estrangement: it was an injudi-cious move which should not have been made. And, he continued, "you may be certain that no such message would have been sent by me".

I replied that this last utterance was superfluous; but how could the Emperor have fallen into such an unhappy error? The King rejoined, that the Emperor was only the apparent, not the virtual, author of the Telegram. 'I understand', His Majesty said, 'that the idea of the mes-sage originated with Prince Hohenlohe, who represented that it would be politic to make a demonstration of that sort. 'The Emperor was the complying; not the originating, party: he might, however, have made stylistic alterations in the Telegram sent in his name'.

[575] On the Kruger telegram and the Transvaal conflict, see pp. 188–195.

I remarked that the Imperial message had been read in England as a challenge to our plain rights, and had provoked ebullitions of patriotic sentiment of which the German newspapers had hardly given a sufficient account. I was afraid that the abatement of the anger of our public against the Emperor might be a somewhat slow process. The King answered that my point was quite intelligible to him, and that, at any rate, it would be some time before His Imperial Majesty could resume his visits to the Isle of Wight.[576]

The King proceeded to say that one person had come out of these transactions with flying colours – Mr Chamberlain had faced the situation with energy and tact: he had done exactly the right thing, and his timely interposition had prevented the crisis from assuming an acute shape.[577]

[…]

P.S. January 31. A high official personage here speaks of the origin of the German demonstrations in similar terms to the above, and he states that, according to his Berlin news, the Telegram was drafted by Baron von Marschall on the lines settled by the Emperor and his advisers.

FO 68/181: George Strachey to Marquess of Salisbury, No 13, Dresden, 19 February 1896

[Received 22 February. For: Mr Balfour; African Department; S[alisbury]]

Press hostility to England now less bitter over Transvaal incident

The English and German official publications, and the parliamentary debates in London and Berlin, have led to a certain limited revival here of the press discussions on the Transvaal question.[578] But the German controversial tone is now far less bitter than before, and much of the acrimonious language employed may be traced to the belief that there is an absence of conciliatory dispositions on our side of the Channel. It is remarked that the charge of duplicity brought by us against others has now recoiled on ourselves, while the attitude of the Imperial Government has been as correct and

---

[576] Wilhelm had visited the Isle of Wight annually since 1889 to attend the Cowes Week regattas.

[577] Albert was referring to Chamberlain's immediate repudiation of the 'Jameson Raid', on 1 January, his subsequent communications with the Transvaal government and the announcement of an investigation.

[578] For the Transvaal question, see the previous dispatches and pp. 188–195.

loyal as it has been firm. The praise of Herr von Marschall is unanimous: he is held up as a pattern of diplomatic integrity and skill, and extolled as a worthy exponent of the rule that when national claims are vindicated foreign rights and interests must also be respected – a principle of which, it is argued, there is no corresponding recognition in the English Blue Book.

The general public is sated with the African Topic, and is glad to learn that the official relations of Berlin and London were not disturbed by the recent press clamours, which no one here took seriously. Few would dissent from the opinion of a Dresden journalist,[579] who says that the two countries should now renew their former friendship, seeing that they have multifarious interests in common, and that the further accentuation of minor differences can only serve to unchain those spirits of European discord which, while England and Germany are in agreement are condemned to inaction. I need hardly say that to these sentiments the Court and Government of Saxony would cordially subscribe.

FO 68/181: George Strachey to Marquess of Salisbury, No 25, Dresden, 30 May 1896

[Received 1 June. For: Mr Balfour; S[alisbury]]

Recent anti-Socialist legislation enacted in Saxony; its effects; comparison with Baden

I have reported the circumstances under which the Saxon Government laid before the Landtag of the Kingdom a Bill for the modification of the suffrage by the adoption of the system of indirect election.[580] A minority of the constitutional left, which had some support in industrial circles, and amongst the Professors of the University of Leipsic, continued to denounse [*sic*] the Bill. But their attempts to rouse the constituencies to effective protests against interference with the existing electoral system were unsuccessful, and it was plain that approval of the proposed change was by no means confined to Conservative politicians. Finally, the Bill was carried, in a slightly amended form, through the lower Chamber of the Diet by a large majority – (56 against the 15 Social Democrats & 7 other members) – in the upper house by an unanimous vote.

---

[579] Name not traceable.

[580] The bill stipulated the introduction of an indirect three-class franchise based on tax revenue. It was passed on 6 and 18 March and enacted on 28 March 1896; it replaced the Electoral Law of 1868.

On the side of Social-Democracy, there was wide divergence of opinion as to the course which it might be advisable to pursue. A conclave held at Leipsic[581] recommended that the party should, by way of protest, resign all its seats in the Landtag, and likewise entirely abstain from the polls at the next election. The policy of mere negation was, however, rejected by a general congress[582] held in Dresden, which adopted resolutions opposed to the Leipzig vote, and pledged the Social-Democratic leaders and electorate, to maintain their political activity on the old lines. It was further agreed that the programme of the party must henceforth include systematic agitation for the recovery of the popular rights infringed by the abolition of the direct suffrage.

There seems no certainty how the change will work. According to some prominent Conservatives, the Social-Democracy of the Kingdom has received a blow from which it will not recover. On the other hand one of the ministerial personages who introduced the Bill told me privately that he should be satisfied if its result was to prevent the extreme left from receiving accessions to their actual parliamentary strength. Of the Social-Democrats, some take an optimist, some a pessimist view of the new situation. Many of them argue that the so-called reform, being a measure of persecution must have the usual moral effect of oppressive legislation, that is, there will be a reaction in favour of the party which it is intended to crush.

It may be of interest to compare the above with the situation in the Grand Duchy of Baden, where, according to the public journals, the Government desires a change, in the Conservative direction, of the existing representative system, but sees no prospect of the apposite measures being adopted by the Diet.

FO 68/181: George Strachey to Marquess of Salisbury, No 38, Dresden, 30 September 1896

[Received 13 October. S[alisbury]

Press views of tsar's visit to Balmoral, and recent events in the Bosphorus

Before and during the Czar's visit to Balmoral,[583] a number of the leading newspapers of the Empire gave vent to their Anglophobia

---

[581] On 30 March 1896.
[582] Held on 7 and 8 April 1896.
[583] Nicholas II visited Britain from 22 September 1896 to 5 October. On 27 and 29 September he met Salisbury at Balmoral where they discussed the situation in the Near

in articles and notes full of the familiar estimates of our national character and policy. A maximum of ill-will was displayed by the Dresden 'Journal', which affected to entertain the suspicion that the recent events on the Bosphorus, like those of last year, might be traced to British instigation. However, our duplicity had now been unmasked, and the isolation of the universal mischief-maker was complete. No compliments or arguments at Balmoral would induce the Emperor of Russia to accept our Turkish programme, with its transparent political pretences and humanitarian cant.

A voice crying in the wilderness was that of the local 'Zeitung',[584] which, almost day-by-day called our motives laudable, our proposals wise, and our national attitude worthy of our great strength. Moreover the visit to Balmoral, unlike such merely ornamental episodes as the meeting at Breslau,[585] might have a serious influence on the affairs of Europe, and would, at any rate, bring the Czar into contact with the representatives of statesmanship of an experienced, enlightened and disinterested type.

Strongly tinctured as the 'Zeitung' is with benevolence towards us, it has not ventured to suggest that an Armenian agitation like ours should be started here. A move in that direction would obtain no support from the general public. Even in quarters where I should have expected the recitals of the massacres to have roused, if not anger, at least, compassion, I have found complete indifference to prevail. According to those who should be competent to judge, there are more traces of a disposition to sympathize with the Turk than of a tendency to pity his victims, whose protection, it is thought, is a mere transcendental object for the attainment of which Germany has no call to sacrifice "the Pomeranian Grenadier".[586]

FO 68/181: George Strachey to Marquess of Salisbury, No 43, Dresden, 2 December 1896

[Received 3 December. X; S[alisbury]]

Hamburg dock strike blamed on English intrigues

According to certain appearances, the conviction was lately beginning to spread in the German press, that the malignant tone in

East and the Ottoman Empire, following recurring outbreaks of violence against Armenians at Constantinople, which had started in August 1896.

[584] *Dresdner Zeitung.*

[585] Wilhelm II and Nicholas II met at Breslau on 5 and 6 September 1896.

[586] Bismarck used this expression in a speech he made in 1888 when he stated that the 'whole of the Balkans is not worth the bones of a single Pomeranian grenadier.'

which the relations of this Empire with England have been discussed during the past year by the newspapers of both countries ought to be dropped. A recent leader in the Berlin 'National Zeitung'[587] was an indication of a readiness here to "bury the hatchet", and the existence of the hope that our press would be disposed to join in a new departure. The Hamburg Dock-strike seems to have crossed, for the present, all chances of a move in that direction.[588] At once, ambiguous voices, apparently inspired from Friedrichsruh,[589] suggested that the strike was the result of the machinations of envious British capitalists: (how the intrigues of the enemies of labour came to be furthered by Tom Mann was not explained).

The original hint has now swelled into a formal indictment, which even the comparatively moderate Dresden 'Anzeiger'[590] does not hesitate to support. That journal is arguing that the strike is "a shabby English trick", put in hand "to damage Liverpool's successful Elbe rival, Hamburg". This idea is being ventilated in detail in various quarters, and the diatribes against our mean shipowners, and also against our dockers, have no end. The London 'Globe' has been named as containing a letter which gives some of the German charges a plausible sound. An English employer has written to express his pleasure at the German labour movement, and to state that he had proposed to a member of Parliament the formation of a large subscription fund, to be collected from masters and men, which would be employed for getting up strikes on the Continent. Again – the 'Shipping Telegraph' is quoted as openly declaring that the Hamburg strike is an English manoeuvre.

The 'Anzeiger' articles on foreign topics, and leading German questions, are usually taken from the lithographed Berlin National-Liberal fly-sheets:[591] and it may be noticed that a member[592] of that party yesterday spoke in the German Parliament in the above sense. The liberal 'Zeitung', as was to be expected from its antecedents, has elaborately suppressed all references to Anglophobian interpretations of the Hamburg strike.

---

[587] *National Zeitung*, 22 November 1896.

[588] On the Hamburg dock strike, see pp. 206–207.

[589] Friedrichsruh, Bismarck's manor house.

[590] *Dresdner Anzeiger*, 1 December 1896.

[591] *Nationalliberale Korrespondenz*.

[592] Hermann Paasche.

FO 68/182: George Strachey to Marquess of Salisbury, [private], Holmhurst, East Twickenham, 30 June 1897

['Acknowledge receipt in suitable terms', 8 July, Private Secretary; S[alisbury]]

Strachey's retirement; reports on his farewell audience with Saxon king and expresses regret at leaving the service

I beg to report that, before quitting my post, I explained to Herr von Metzsch that, as my letters of recall would be presented by my eventual successor, my audience of the King on departure could not be conducted with any official ceremonial.[593] His Majesty thereupon received me at the Palace "en visite",[594] when he repeated, in the most gracious manner, the assurances of esteem on public and private grounds which had fallen from him from time to time during my protracted residence at his Court. Excluding all other topics, the King spoke with deep sympathy of the disruption of old ties now imposed on my family and myself, of his regrets at our departure, and of his anxious hope that our eventual life in our own country might be a happy one. The King of Saxony exhibited some emotion, and, for my own part, I was unable to do more than thank His Majesty, in such imperfect manner as I could, for the unremitting kindness and, I may say, championship, of which I had been the object on his part for more than twenty-three years. Finally, I offered my acknowledgments for the honour previously done me by the sovereign, in sending me a fine vase of porcelain from the Royal Factory as a mark of his friendship and approbation.

Of the Queen, I had taken leave at an earlier date. I likewise paid visits to the Princes of the Royal Family, and Mrs Strachey also went through the appropriate forms on our departure.

On this occasion I beg to add, that the termination of my 45 years work under the Crown, which commenced before the Crimean War, gives me feelings that I cannot adequately describe. The taedium vitae[595] consequent on the cessation of useful public employment, and the pressure of circumstances,[596] which, as I have explained to the Private Secretary,[597] have made somewhat heavy demands on my strength, are not lightened by the thought that my connection with the highest branch of the Imperial Service is severed. To the

---

[593] George Strachey left Dresden for London on 29 March 1897; he retired on a pension on 1 July.

[594] French: 'to pay a call'.

[595] Latin: 'weariness of life'.

[596] Strachey is referring to health and financial problems.

[597] Eric Barrington.

Staff of the Office my acknowledgements are due for nearly half a century of tolerance and good-will: to Your Lordship I owe promotion to the representative rank abroad which no Englishman can fill without pride. In these directions my regrets, and also my thanks, lie: and trusting that my expression of them may not be found out of place.

WÜRTTEMBERG

(STUTTGART)

STUTTGART

FO 82/169: Henry Barron to Earl Granville, No 19, Stuttgart, 5 May 1884

[Received 7 May by messenger. 'This does not seem to call for any action. I cannot say I feel much sympathy for these inebriates.' J.P. [Julian Pauncefote], 7 May; G[ranville]]

Three British men tried for drunken offences and infractions of Imperial Criminal Code

I have the honor to report that three British subjects have been tried and convicted here under the following circumstances.

During the night of the 9th–10th of February a drunken affray took place at the Stuttgart railway terminus between four young foreigners (three of them English) and some railway porters. No one was much hurt.

Another disturbance occurred in the night of 1st–2^d of March, in which two[1] of the same Englishmen and three others of different nationalities were implicated. This time lamps, windows, trees and other property were damaged.

Six young men were now arrested, of whom three, Francis Baker, Alexander Fraser and Gerard Anderson were British subjects. The two first have been kept in prison ever since; the last named was released on bail.

On the 30th of April all six were brought to trial before the "Strafkammer" (Correctional Chambers) of the "Landgericht",[2] and all pleaded guilty.

The indictment comprised thirty seven separate counts. The proceedings lasted eleven hours. Messrs Baker and Fraser were sentenced to five months and three months imprisonment respectively, for "Resistance" and "Damage to property". Mr Anderson was sentenced to 14 days for "Resistance". Their long detention of nearly two months was credited to Baker and Fraser as one month in reduction of their respective terms. All were condemned jointly to pay the costs.

This case now calls for some short observations.

[1] Francis Baker and Alexander Fraser.
[2] 'District Court'.

In the first place the rank of the Tribunal and the cumbrous nature of the proceedings have tended to magnify the importance of and probably also the penalties for these drunken frolics. I have ascertained that some of the offenses committed are by the German Code classified as "Vergehen" (délits)[3], and could not therefore be tried by the Police court.

Secondly the Crown Prosecutor[4] very improperly denounced the accused as aliens, who should therefore be treated with special severity.

Thirdly the damages have been fully paid for. No one appeared to claim compensation, a fact which aroused the indignation of the Crown Prosecutor. The compensations paid and the costs of the trial must form a heavy addition to the penalties imposed.

It is highly probable that, under the advice of their advocate M[r] Kaulla, Mess[rs] Baker and Fraser will pray for a mitigation of their sentence, and will ask me to support their petition.

In such an event I should, considering all the circumstances, consider myself bound to support their appeal to the clemency of the Crown, and at the same time to call the attention of the Government to the improper language of its' Crown Prosecutor.

[…]

P.S: I beg to include a summary of reports of this trial taken from a newspaper.[5] Being alone I am not able to prepare a translation in time for tonight's messenger. H[.]B.

FO 82/169: Henry Barron to Earl Granville, No 31, Stuttgart, 3 November 1884

[Received 6 November by messenger. For: The Queen / Gladstone / Berlin; G[ranville]]

Reichstag elections; strong performance by National Liberal and Free Conservative coalition

The elections of Deputies to the Reichstag took place as throughout all Germany on the 28th of October. In Wurtemberg they have produced much excitement and many surprises.

Of the 17 seats assigned to this Kingdom, (one for 116000 inhabitants) only 14 were definitively filled up at the first poll. The constituencies, where an "absolute majority" was not polled by any

---

[3] French: 'misdemeanours'. Article 1 of the German Penal Code of 1871 differentiates between indictable offences (*Verbrechen*), non-indictable offences (*Vergehen*) and infringement (*Übertretung*).

[4] Karl Schönhardt.

[5] Enclosure: original (cutting) 'Gerichtssaal', *Neues Tagblatt*, 2 May 1884.

candidate, will have to proceed to a second election between the two candidates who at the first election had polled the greatest number of votes. This "ballottage" must take place within 14 days from the declaration of the poll.

Of the 6 organized political parties, only 4 were represented by Wurtemberg deputies in the late Reichstag, viz; the Conservative party by 5 deputies; the Centre[6] by 4, the Volkspartei (Democratic) by 6, the Freisinning (Progressist) by 1, Unenumerated (Wild) 1.

The most conspicuous feature of the present struggle had been the alliance of the "Conservative" and "National-Liberal" parties, with a view of forming a working majority for supporting the present Imperial policy.

The general result of the elections in Germany may be somewhat disappointing to the Chancellor.[7] But in Wurtemberg they have brought him an unexpected accession of strength. The new so-called "middle party"[8] has already wrested three seats from the two Democratic parties, and will probably gain two of the three still in suspense.

As compared with the rest of Germany, the Socialist party has made little progress in Wurtemberg, having polled in all 8100 votes, as against 6,150 in 1881.

In all 240,000 votes were recorded, of which 112000 were given to the 2 Allied parties, an increase of 21800 above 1881; 66,157 to the two democratic parties,[9] a decrease of 7,552; 53,490 to the Centre candidates, (Catholic party) a decrease of 6,780.

FO 82/170: Henry Barron to Earl Granville, No 5, Stuttgart, 7 February 1885

[Received 12 February by messenger. Qy: War Office, copy – what answer?; Done; To Sir H. Barron No [no number given], 28 February; T.V.L. [Thomas Villiers Lister]

Recruitment of foreign nationals to British army

A M[r] Wilhelm Steller requests me to inform him on what conditions he would be admitted to serve in the British army. Having served three years and risen to the ranks of sub-officer in the German army, he is anxious to utilize his military knowledge by active

---

[6] *Zentrumspartei* (Catholics).

[7] Otto von Bismarck.

[8] A contemporary name for the coalition of the National Liberal Party and *Deutsche Reichspartei* (Free Conservatives).

[9] *Württembergische Volkspartei* and the *Deutsche Fortschrittspartei*.

employment in the service of a Colonial Power, more especially, if possible, in the present Egyptian campaign.[10]

Applications of this nature are frequently addressed to me. I believe that, as a rule, aliens are not enlisted in Her Majesty's military service. But exceptions certainly are or have been made to that rule.

I have the honor therefore to request that Your Lordship will enable me to answer similar applications on official authority, and to refer applicants if need be, to the proper Department for further particulars.[11]

FO 82/170: Henry Barron to Earl Granville, No 8, Stuttgart, 6 March 1885

[Received 11 March by messenger. For: The Queen; G[ranville]]

Appointment of a new minister for worship and education

I have had the honor to report a slight change in the Wurtemberg Ministry. By a Royal Decree of the 28th ultimo D^r von Gessler Minister of Worship and Education has at his own request been allowed to retire, and Dr Otto von Sarwey has been appointed Minister in his place.

Dr Gessler has held the above office since 1870. His retirement is no doubt connected partially with the rejection of his bill on Church Temporalities.[12] [Note in margin: 'vide my N° 39 of 1884'] As however Dr Sarwey was the author of the Committee Report of the First Chamber highly favorable to the above measure, he is committed on this essential point to the policy of his predecessor.

Dr Sarwey[,] once a practicing advocate, has made himself known by a standard work on the political laws of Wurtemberg,[13] and has risen by his ability to the Council of State, to the Privy Council and to the First Chamber.

[10] Barron is referring to the continued British war against the Mahdist Sudanese after the fall of Khartoum in January 1885 (see n. 32 in Berlin section).

[11] In his dispatch No 3 of 28 February 1885 Granville acquainted Barron with the information provided by the secretary of state for war on the matter, 'that foreigners are only allowed to be enlisted for the British Army in special cases, where their services are required with Regimental Bands & that each case is submitted for the approval of the Secretary of State for War before the enlistment takes place.'

[12] On 22 December the Württemberg chamber of deputies resolved not to proceed with the reading of the bill on administration of property and possessions of Catholic parishes, and asked the government to introduce an amended bill.

[13] *Das Staatsrecht des Königreichs Württemberg*, 1883, 2 vols.

Like the Ministry as a whole, he is not classified under any political party. Party affiliations and party spirit do not prevail in the Upper or indeed in either Chamber of the Landtag. The Government, though responsible to the Legislature, is not held bound to retire on every defeat. Each measure is therefore considered solely on its' own merits, not on its' party bearings.

FO 82/170: Henry Barron to Marquess of Salisbury, Treaty, No 7, Stuttgart, 21 November 1885

[Received 28 November by messenger. S[alisbury]][14]

Extradition treaty with Russia declined by Württemberg chambers

A treaty for the mutual surrender of criminals was in 1884 [*sic*] signed between Germany and Russia, was approved by the Bundesrath[15] and laid before the Reichstag, but owing to its' bad reception in this Body was allowed to drop. In its' stead a similar treaty was signed during the present year by Prussia with Russia, and afterwards (on the 17th of October) another by Bavaria.[16] These treaties, not requiring the sanction of the Prussian and Bavarian Parliaments, have, I believe become law.

In the debate on the Bavarian budget of Foreign Affairs the Russo-Bavarian treaty was severely criticized by two speakers,[17] and defended in a long speech by the responsible Minister.[18] The objections urged against it were twofold; firstly that it was unconstitutional on the part of one Confederate State to negotiate separately with a foreign Power; secondly that the provisions of the new treaty were dangerous and monstrous. The chief stumbling block, but also the very essence of these treaties, consists in the clause providing that political offences shall not be pleaded as a bar to extradition.

---

[14] Note on docket: 'It is clear that the plan by which it is proposed if possible to nullify the rejection of the Russo German Extradition Treaty by the Reichstag, is, conclusion of separate treaties to the same effect between Russia and the component states of the Germany Empire. Copy to Home Office for perusal', J.H.G.B. [John Henry Gibbs Bergne].

[15] Federal Council.

[16] After the Federal Council declared its consent for the measure on 12 February 1885, the Russo-German Extradition Treaty was signed on 20 March of that year. It was based on the treaty concluded between Prussia and Russia (13 January 1885) and presented to the *Reichstag* on 6 May 1885 where it stalled. The Russo-Bavarian treaty was signed on 1 October 1885, and published on 17 October.

[17] Wolf Frankenburger and Joseph Egid Geiger, on 12 November 1885.

[18] Friedrich Krafft von Crailsheim.

I have thought it necessary to recapitulate thus briefly the above facts, before reporting to Your Lordship that overtures have been made here by Russia for the conclusion of a similar treaty. I am informed that those overtures have hitherto been declined on the ground that the Wurtemberg Chambers would disapprove of such a treaty.

There is no formal text of law, as in Belgium,[19] requiring the sanction of the Legislative Chambers to a treaty. It would however evidently be difficult to put it into execution in the face of their opposition.

FO 82/170: Henry Barron to Marquess of Salisbury, No 37, Stuttgart, 21 September 1885

[Received 24 September by messenger. For: The Queen; T.V.L. [Thomas Villiers Lister]]

Emperor and other dignitaries visit Württemberg in honour of army manoeuvres

I have the honor to report that His Majesty the German Emperor, accompanied by the Crown Prince[20] and the Princes William and Albert of Prussia and Arnulph of Bavaria, arrived in Stuttgart by special train from Carlsruhe on the 18th.

His Imperial Majesty was received at the railway station by the King of Wurtemberg, the Princes of the Royal Family now here and Prince Herrmann [*sic*] of Saxe-Weimar. There were also present at this reception the Cabinet Ministers, the Royal Household, the Prussian Legation, the General Officers, the Burgomaster[21] and Municipal Colleges &c.

After most cordial greetings the Royal Personages proceeded to the Palace amidst the applause of a vast multitude. There they were received by the Queen and the Princess of the Royal Family.

These fine illustrious guests, together with their numerous suites, including Field Marshal Count Moltke Chief of the General Staff, are accommodated in the Royal Palace to the number of 41 persons. 46 foreign and German officers deputed to attend the manoeuvres are accommodated in an hotel as the Kings guests. Thus 87 guests, besides their servants, are being entertained by the King during 5 days.

The manoeuvres of the Wurtemberg army (forming the 13th German Army-corps) began on the 19th instant by a grand review

---

[19] Barron is referring to Article 167 of the Belgian constitution of 1831.
[20] Friedrich Wilhelm.
[21] Theophil Friedrich von Hack.

near Ludwigsburg, which was attended by the Emperor and the King. Their Majesties drove in a "daumont"[22] phaeton along the front of the army, followed by a numerous and brilliant Staff representing most European countries. They then took separate carriages and witnessed the first "défilé"[23] in a standing position. The Queen[24] and the Princesses were also present in open carriages. An immense concourse of spectators had assembled from all parts of the Kingdom. A remarkable feature of this review was the large muster of "Kriegervereine", voluntary societies of old soldiers.

Yesterday the Emperor attended a fête given to him by the City in the Stadtgarten, Prince William of Wurtemberg, and assisted at a "gala" performance at the Court theatre.

His Majesty has held no reception of the Diplomatic Body, but desired that I should be presented to him at the theatre. He proposes to attend the field manoeuvres for three days and to leave for Baden on the 23rd instant.

I beg to inclose an official programme of the festivities and proceedings proposed to be carried out during his Majesty's stay.[25]

The Emperor has been everywhere received with the greatest enthusiasm. This visit is certainly calculated to display, probably to strengthen, the attachment of the Wurttemberg People to the Imperial Throne.

FO 82/171: Henry Barron to Earl of Rosebery, No 8, Stuttgart, 24 February 1886

[Received 1 March by messenger. For: The Queen / Gladstone; R[osebery], 1 March]

Second chamber rejects constitutional amendment to increase the number of peers in first chamber; demands for revision of constitution

The chief political measure of the present session, viz; the constitutional amendment brought in by the Government for increasing the number of Peers has been rejected by the Chamber of Deputies.[26]

The Constitution of Wurtemberg[27] provides that the Chamber of Peers shall consist of:

---

[22] A carriage without a coach box driven by outriders or jockeys.
[23] French: 'march past'.
[24] Olga.
[25] Enclosure: 'Programme of festivities during the presence of His Majesty the German Emperor, King of Prussia in Stuttgart, 18–23 September 1885'.
[26] On 18 February 1886.
[27] Articles 129–132 of the constitution of 1819.

1.$^{\underline{o}}$ The Princes of the Royal Family; (there are now 6);

2.$^{\underline{o}}$ The Heads of the Mediatized Houses ("Standesherren") who were formerly endowed with votes in the Imperial or Provincial Diets; (there are now 20);

3.$^{\underline{o}}$ Of members appointed by The King, hereditarily or for life. (there are now 9)

The aggregate number of these appointed under the 3rd category is not to exceed one third of the number of the other two categories.

It has now come to pass from various causes that the number of those qualified to hold seats under the two first categories has fallen from 40 to 26. Consequently the number of seats at the disposal of the Crown has now fallen from 13 to 8, and the whole number of Peers to 35, of whom many are incapacitated by infirmity or absence. This Chamber contains not one trained jurist.

It is now admittedly necessary to increase the strength of the Upper chamber. The measure proposed by the Government,[28] and unanimously accepted by that Chamber,[29] consisted of a law in the following article, to be substituted for the original article 132 of the Constitution. "The number of Members named by The King for life cannot exceed the third part of the other members of the First Chamber. The number of Hereditary Members named by the King shall not exceed the fourth part of those included in the two first categories."

The result of this measure might have been to increase the chamber by 6, thus raising its number to 41 members. In reality the Government only intended to create two more life Peers from amongst experienced State Functionaries, but by no means to create any new hereditary members. This measure was rejected, not on its own demerits, but on strategical party considerations.

The object of the two socalled "German" and "Democratic" parties[30] is to remodel thoroughly not one Chamber alone but both. A revision of the constitution in this sense has been long demanded by a majority of the Chamber, and even promised by the Crown. Many partial amendments of the Constitution have been enacted since its original promulgation in 1819. In the present state of public indifference on the subject it was felt that the promised reforms might be postponed till the Greek calends unless some means were found of bringing pressure to bear on the Government. This useful leverage was discovered in the present critical condition of the Chamber of Peers, which urgently calls for a remedy.

[28] On 4 May 1885.
[29] On 15 May 1885.
[30] *Deutsche Partei* (National Liberals) and *Volkspartei.*

The Chamber of Deputies is now composed of the following six categories: amounting in all to 92 members: –

1. 13 deputies of the "Ritterschaft" (the minor Nobility) owning certain estates;
2. The 6 Protestant "Superintendants-General";
3. 2 Catholic Dignitaries including The Bishop;
4. The Chancellor of the University;
5. One deputy elected by each of the 63 "Oberamts" (administrative districts).

The object of the opposition is to form this Chamber exclusively by universal suffrage, ejecting The Nobility and Clergy. Their tactics have so far entirely succeeded. The Committee of the Chamber reported against the bill, mainly on the ground that a more complete reform was necessary and should be introduced without delay.

In a masterly speech D^r von Mittnacht[31] the Prime Minister finally announced that the Cabinet had resolved to seek the Royal permission to bring in before the next elections (in 1888) a comprehensive measure amending Chapter IX of the Constitution, that affecting the Legislative Chambers. He carefully guarded himself against promising a popular chamber to be elected solely by universal suffrage, as such a Body might be dangerous to the Crown and to the State. He announced that the new measure would be drawn on the lines of the electoral law proposed by him and Baron Varnbüler in 1867,[32] therefore on the principle of a tax-paying franchise combined with indirect elections.

Notwithstanding this pledge the Chamber rejected the Government measure before it by 53 to 31 votes.

FO 82/172: Henry Barron to Marquess of Salisbury, No 9, Stuttgart, 24 February 1887

[Received 28 February by messenger. For: The Queen / Circulate; S[alisbury]]

Reichstag election results; government parties gain support

I have the honor to report that the elections for the Reichstag in Wurtemberg have resulted in a success surpassing all expectations for the two combined Government Parties.

---

[31] On 17 February 1886.
[32] The bill – part of a comprehensive plan to revise the Württemberg constitution – was submitted to the Württemberg chamber of deputies on 19 December 1867.

The Opposition has lost five seats viz; Stuttgart, Heilbronn, Tübingen and Mergentheim previously held by the "Volkspartei", and Rottweil previously held by the "Freisinnig"[33] Party. The "Centre"[34] has preserved its four seats; but two of its' members will certainly vote for the military bill,[35] while two will probably follow Mr Windthorst.

The proportion of the two so-called "National" Parties to the Opposition is now as 13 to 4 instead of 8 to 9 as before. In the division of January 14th 8 Wurtemberg deputies voted for and 8 against the "Septennat." The Democratic Party previously numbering 8 votes in the Reichstag will now disappear entirely from that Assembly, a singular result of universal suffrage!

The numbers of votes recorded were unprecedented. In Stuttgart alone out of 32 000 electors 29 000 recorded their votes. The closest contest was that for the 15th district (Ehingen-Blaubeuren) where of 20,650 electors 18,974 went to the poll and gave a majority of 1379 to the "Centre" candidate.[36]

The Wurtemberg Deputation now consists of 8 National-Liberals Messrs Veiel, Leemann, Fischer, Adä, Siegle, Grub, Keller, Bayha; of 5 Conservatives (Reichspartei) Messrs Neurath, Ow, Stälin, Ellrichshausen, Burkhardt [sic]; of 4 "Centre" members, Counts Neipperg and Adelmann, Messrs Göser and Gröber.

The Socialists have progressed in numbers (in Stuttgart from 3346 to 4590) but have not carried any seat in Wurtemberg.

The evident cause of this great wave of public opinion shown by the elections of the 21st has been the late war panic.[37] It has been loudly inculcated by the highest Authorities that the only chance of avoiding war lay in strengthening the army to the utmost.

FO 82/173: Henry Barron to Marquess of Salisbury, No 10, Stuttgart, 23 February 1888

[Received 27 February by post to Darmstadt. For: The Queen / Berlin for perusal, P.L. [printed letter], 29 February; P.C. [Philip Currie]]

Landtag session prorogued; issues at heart of debate on constitutional change

I have the honour to report that the Landtag has been prorogued from the 18th instant sine die[38] by a Royal

---

[33] *Deutsche Freisinnige Partei* (see n. 3 in Berlin section).
[34] *Zentrumspartei* (Catholics).
[35] For the seven-year the army bill (Imperial Military Law), see n. 119 in Berlin section.
[36] Adolf Gröber.
[37] For the war panic of 1887, see pp. 231–232 and 491–492.
[38] Latin: 'without a date (for a future meeting)'.

Rescript.[39] It is expected that it will be convoked again about November.

Of the three measures which necessitated the holding of this short session two have been passed, that on the insurance of Agricultural labourers and that on the compulsory expropriation of land for public purposes.[40] That on agricultural boundary rights was lost in consequence of differences between the two Chambers.

Informal discussions have proceeded between the Government and the delegates of the three Parties[41] with a view to a revision of the Constitution[42] without however having as yet led to an agreement.

A revision of the IXth Chapter, that concerning the composition of the Legislative Chambers,[43] has been promised ever since 1848; but it is doubtful whether any proposal whatever would secure the necessary majority of two thirds in both Chambers.

On the main principle viz; the transfer of the 28 representatives of the privileged classes from the lower to the upper Chamber, no serious difference exists. It is on the two subsidiary questions viz; the future composition of the lower Chamber, and the future enlarged powers necessarily claimed by the upper Chamber, that an agreement has hitherto been found impossible.

The Constitution of Wurtemberg, now unique in Europe, and resting on a combination of the feudal and Democratic principles, has hitherto worked fairly well. Nothing however will satisfy the Democratic Party but a Popular Chamber emanating solely from universal suffrage.

This is what the Government is firmly determined to resist.

It is probable that a compromise will be effected on the following lines. The new Chamber of Deputies to consist of 90 Deputies, of whom 73 to be elected, as at present, by ballot and universal suffrage, 1 by each of the 63 Oberamts[44] and 10 by the cities. The 17 remaining deputies to be elected by the highest tax-payers.

---

[39] The rescript was dated 16 February 1888.

[40] The Württemberg chamber of deputies met from 26 January to 18 February 1888; the bills in question were passed on 9 and 16 February.

[41] *Deutsche Partei* (National Liberals), *Demokratische Volkspartei* (Progressives), and *Landespartei* (Catholics).

[42] Constitution of 1819.

[43] See pp. 429–431.

[44] Administrative districts.

FO 82/173: William Conyngham Greene to Marquess of Salisbury, No 32 Stuttgart, 19 June 1888

[Received 20 June by post. For: The Queen / Mr Bergne; S[alisbury]]

Death of emperor; commemorative actions in Stuttgart

The painful news of the death of the Emperor Frederick reached Stuttgart soon after midday on Friday last.[45]

The bells of all the churches in the town were immediately tolled, and flags were displayed at half mast on the principal buildings. In the brief interval which elapsed between the receipt of the sad intelligence and the time fixed for the funeral commemoration the whole town assumed a mourning aspect. The main streets, including both shops and private residences, were decked with black flags, and the blinds were drawn down in the principal houses of business. Special editions of the Newspapers were issued from time to time and eagerly purchased by the passers by, and the latest particulars from Berlin perused with sorrowful interest. Expressions of condolence in the bereavement of The Widowed Empress Victoria were general, and the regret of the public was very sincere.

His Majesty The King at once deputed His Royal Highness Prince William to proceed to Berlin as His representative at the funeral of The Emperor, but subsequently countermanded the order on learning that the ceremony was to be confined to the nearest relatives of the deceased Sovereign.

A commemorative Service was held yesterday in the Schloss Capelle[46] here which was attended by Their Royal Highnesses Prince and Princess[47] William, representing The King and The Queen,[48] by Prince and Princess[49] Hermann of Saxe Weimar and Their daughter The Princess Olga, The Grand Duchess Wera, Duke Albrecht of Wurtemberg, The Duke of Urach, the Corps Diplomatique, and the Dignitaries of the Court and State.

I have the honour to enclose a copy the form of service used on the occasion.[50]

Similar services were held in the Churches of all confessions in the Capital.

[45] Friedrich III died on 15 June 1888.
[46] Palace chapel.
[47] Charlotte.
[48] Olga.
[49] Auguste.
[50] Enclosure: programme of service ('Zum Trauergottesdienst für Seine Majestät den deutschen Kaiser Friedrich'), Königliche Schlosskapelle, 18 June 1888.

FO 82/173: Henry Barron to Marquess of Salisbury, Confidential, No 50, Stuttgart, 31 October 1888

[Received 3 November by messenger. X / See Mr Cadogan's No 63; S[alisbury]

Woodcock affair; defamatory press article about the King of Württemberg

Much sensation has been caused here by a clever article in the Münchner Neueste Nachrichten [note in margin: 'No 488 of 23^{d} Oct.'] which professes to describe a neighbouring Court, evidently that of Wurtemberg. As this paper has been seized I am not yet able to inclose a copy, but I have prepared a summary of the article in question and I will add a few comments. It is headed;

Unpleasant discussions.

§1 [Note in margin: 'The divisions are my own.'] There are things which run from mouth to mouth in saloons and taverns, but which never appear in the Press. Such a state of things we have long known in Bavaria. For a newspaper to discuss the affairs of its' own Court is like handling a hot iron. But we think that an open discussion of principal facts is better than irresponsible and secret scandal-mongering.

§ 2 The Sovereign of a neighbouring State stands honorably by the great German cause. The long years of his reign have been fruit-ful for trade and Industry, Art and Science. But increasing years and infirmities have gradually estranged him from his people. He passes but a short season in his Capital, spending the summer at the extremity of his dominions, the winter on the French Riviera or in Italy. His delicate health makes him shun intercourse with others than his immediate surroundings. He transacts business only thro' his Secretary[51] even with his own Ministers. As these are honorable and able men the Government has hitherto worked smoothly and efficiently.

§ 3 But a painful impression is now gaining ground that all is not as it should be. The People, thoroughly monarchical as it is, misses the personal presence of it's Sovereign and the sight of a brilliant Court. It would submit patiently to these ills if they were owing to the malady of it's Sovereign. But it is believed that there are men who exploit that malady for their own selfish purposes, to the injury of the Benefactor and the State. That these persons are foreigners makes the matter worse.

---

[51] The *Münchner Neueste Nachrichten* was probably alluding to Karl's *Kabinettschef*, Albert Julius Freiherr von Griesinger.

§ 4 The first one of these persons [note in margin: 'M^r R Jackson.'] made his appearance about 7 years ago, having been employed in a foreign Consulate. The invalid Monarch took an interest in this intelligent foreigner, appointed him to be his reader, and loaded him with orders, titles and presents. Other Courts also conferred distinctions upon him. The Emperor William alone refused him the desired Order. The parvenu soon became the inseparable companion of the Sovereign, while the life-long devoted friend of the latter [note in margin: 'Baron Spitzemberg.'] was thrust aside. It must be admitted that this foreigner did not abuse his influence and abstained from all interference in personal or political affairs.

§ 5 Suddenly[52] there appeared on the scene two new figures[,] compatriots of the previous favorite. [Note in margin: 'Mr C. Woodcock. Mr D. Hendry.'] These gentlemen were less moderate in their pretensions. They obtained large gifts of money and a house in the Capital. The Sovereign appears here almost daily. Busy tongues speak of mysterious "spiritist séances", at which the ancestors of this illustrious race are made to appear. These performances have exercised a most pernicious effect on the health of the Sovereign. A celebrated physician[53] insisted on the immediate banishment of the two adventurers. These actually did depart for a time after receiving a considerable "douceur" in money, but re-appeared again after the doctor's departure.

§ 6 Since this event these two strangers have more and more captured the confidence of the illustrious invalid. They gambled away and squandered his money to such an extent that the Court establishment had to be reduced. The expenditure for the last sojourn in Italy was so enormous that it has not yet been liquidated.[54]

§ 7 The population of the Capital makes these aliens responsible for all these evils and shows its' ill humor in various modes. Employés of the State have been known to avoid their accustomed evening beer tables in order not to have to listen to unpleasant remarks. The collection for the approaching Jubilee[55] of the Monarch has given rise to painful debates.

---

[52] In 1883.
[53] Carl Liebermeister.
[54] Karl stayed in Italy, near Florence, from December 1887 to May 1888.
[55] The 25th anniversary of Karl's reign was in July 1889.

§ 8 The recent promotion of one of these adventurers to the Nobility[56] is most warmly discussed in the Public, tho' not in the Press with the sole exception of a democratic organ[57] which adds that this mark of favor will probably not appear in the Staatsanzeiger.[58]

§ 9 The Nation, devoted as it is to its' ruling Dynasty, is now doubly anxious at seeing that the Heir Presumptive[59] exhibit a strong tendency towards seclusion. Moreover after a second marriage he has no male issue, so that the Crown will probably pass to the Catholic branch of this reigning family, who are almost strangers to this chiefly Protestant country.

§10 All this reminds one involuntarily of the state of affairs in Bavaria which ended in such a fearful catastrophe.[60] If the Clique should drive things to extremities, the People asks whether it will find such a wise and strong head as we have found to steer the vessel into port. We hope that this patriotic revelation of the work of these dark beings may lead to a change for the better.

I have sought information from the best and most impartial sources, and can assure Your Lordship that the real facts are very different from those recorded in the above indictment.

As to § 2. that the King shuns intercourse with others and even with his own Ministers is the reverse of the truth. He is when at Stuttgart and Friedrichshafen in daily personal communication with his Prime Minister Baron Mittnacht, who also passes the summer in the latter town. He gives daily audiences all the year round with readiness and constant dinner parties wherever he resides. His malady certainly has not affected his temper or bearing which are quite the reverse of morose and misanthropic.

As to §§ 3 and 4, it is true that he has promoted two American gentlemen to positions of friendship and honor. The first of these M[r] Jackson Vice Consul of the United States in 1880 first attracted the King's notice by his musical talents. He was appointed first a reader, then (in 1881) the title of Hofrath[61] and the order of the Crown.[62] He generally accompanies the Court on its' travels. He is a quiet

---

[56] Woodcock was elevated to Freiherr von Savage on 5 October 1888.

[57] *Der Beobachter: Ein Volksblatt für Schwaben*, 21 October 1888.

[58] *Staatsanzeiger für Württemberg* was the official Württemberg newspaper.

[59] Wilhelm.

[60] See pp. 480–487.

[61] Court councillor.

[62] The Order of the Crown (*Ritterkreuz erster Klasse*) was bestowed on Richard Jackson in September 1881.

unassuming person well spoken of by all. He had nothing to do with the resignation of Baron Spitzemberg[,] late Grand Chamberlain.[63]

(§5) M[r] Charles Woodcock seems to have ingratiated himself with the King by his literary and musical accomplishments, also, according to rumor by his powers as a medium or "spiritist". He is described as a highly educated and intellectual person. He is not an inmate of the Palace but inhabits a house which has been lent (not given to him) by the King. He has lately been ennobled under the title of Baron von Savage. The third person alluded to, M[r] Hendry, is only a relative and companion of Baron Savage.

All the statements under paragraphs 6 and 7 are mere guesses or absolute falsehoods. No such interference of D[r] Liebermeister is believed or has ever been before been heard of. Neither is there any sign or rumor of a reduction or embarrassment of the Royal Household.

It is quite true that people grumble at the King's protracted absences from his Capital, and that this is attributed partly to the influence of the "Americans". This is the real grievance which is impairing the King's popularity. As for the tendency to seclusion attributed to Prince William I have seen or heard no sign of it. On the contrary both Their Royal Highnesses contribute largely to and take a constant part in the social gaieties of Stuttgart.

§ 10. These doleful forebodings and comparisons are simply ridiculous and perfidious. The King is a man of good intellect and abilities, both quite unimpaired by age or illness. Thro['] a long and eventful reign he has evinced undoubted wisdom in the choice of his counsellors and in the Government of his Kingdom during most critical periods.

I can assure Your Lordship that the "patriotic revelation" is a list of exaggerations and inventions founded on a slight basis of fact, somewhat in the manner of the Paris Figaro.[64] It is in fact a kind of romance or ~~rather~~ more properly it may be called a "novel with a purpose". That purpose becomes clear enough after a little consideration.

The King's real crime is that he selects France for his winter residence, which we know on high authority [note in margin: 'Norddeutsche Allg. of Oct. 24.'] to be "a nation of savages"; and to make the matter worse, he resides at the very town where a Prussian spy has just been sentenced to 5 years imprisonment![65] Here is in my opinion the secret cause of all this virtuous indignation.

---

[63] Spitzemberg retired due to ill health in April 1886.

[64] *Le Figaro* published a lewd article on the Woodcock affair on 28 October 1888.

[65] Barron is referring to Fritz Kilian who was sentenced under the provisions of the French Law of Espionage at Nice, on 26 October 1888.

This mysterious article is evidently intended as a warning to the King that the eyes of the "National" party are upon him. What makes it more ominous are the hints thrown out in § 9, which clearly show that not only the King but the Dynasty is threatened.

[...]

P.S. I have at last procured from Munich and beg to inclose a copy of the article in question.[66]

FO 82/173: Henry Barron to Marquess of Salisbury, Confidential, No 55, Stuttgart, 14 November 1888

[Received 17 November by post. X][67]

Cabinet and court reactions to press article implying scandalous relations between King of Württemberg and Baron Savage

The Staatsanzeiger of today publishes an announcement (copy and translation inclosed,)[68] [note in margin: 'No 267. 14 Nov. Translation'] relating the proceedings which have taken place in the Cabinet in consequence of the recent notorious article dated 23rd ultimo in the Münchner N.[eueste] Nachrichten.

It is here recorded that a Cabinet Council[69] presided by Prince William unanimously agreed to address an information to the King recommending a prosecution for libel, and respectfully warning His Majesty of the dangers which might arise from further exciting utterances of the Press;

that the King[70] answered by thanking his Ministers for their "good intentions and loyal feelings";

that the Minister-President[71] had travelled to Nice by the King's desire and had found Baron Savage already departed of his own free will;

---

[66] Enclosure: article 'Unliebsame Erörterungen' ('Unpleasant discussions'), *Münchner Neueste Nachrichten*, 23 October 1888.

[67] An additional note to No 55 in FO 82/173 reads: 'The previous despatches respecting the "unpleasant discussions" were not sent to the Queen. I have not therefore suggested sending either of these 2 despatches to Her Majesty.' H.H. [Henry Hervey], 17 November; S[alisbury]].

[68] For the 'Woodcock affair', see the preceding dispatch. Enclosures: original (article), 'Wiederholt aus letzter Nummer' ('Repeated from the last issue'), *Münchner Neueste Nachrichten*, 13 November 1888; original and translation of announcement in *Staatsanzeiger für Württemberg*, 14 November 1888.

[69] On 24 October 1888.

[70] Royal decree of 29 October 1888.

[71] Hermann von Mittnacht; he arrived at Nice on 6 November 1888.

that the said gentleman has never taken a part in "spiritist" experiments;

that the Ministers have no reason to complain of his interference in affairs of State;

that they have not offered or hinted at their resignation;

that they have never demanded the removal of any person from the "entourage" of the Sovereign;

finally that the King had ordered all criminal proceedings initiated or projected to be dropped.

Thus apparently ends this deplorable crisis, which seems to have been most humiliating to all the parties concerned. The dignity of the Crown and the harmony of the State have been certainly compromised by the evident pressure put on the Sovereign in consequence of a mendacious newspaper article, which pressure it is vainly attempted to disguise.

FO 82/174: Henry Barron to Marquess of Salisbury, Confidential, No 17, London, 23 May 1889

[Received 23 May by hand. This matter has not hitherto been dealt with officially. Qy: Private Secretary. For: The Queen; P.C. [Philip Currie]; S[alisbury]; 'I think it would be best avoided', V.R. [Victoria Regina];[72] Draft Sir H. Barron, 10 June 1889]

Rumoured amalgamation of British legations at Stuttgart and Munich meets with King of Württemberg's disapproval

I have the honor to inclose the copy of a note which I have received from Baron Mittnacht[73] alluding to a rumor which had reached his ears that Her Majesty's Government proposed to incorporate the British Legation at Stuttgart with that of Munich.

His Excellency is instructed to express the deep regret which such a transfer would cause to the King of Wurttemberg. He requests me to convey to Your Lordship those apprehensions and the anxious desire that Her Majesty's Legation should continue to reside at Stuttgart.

This step on the King's part has taken me by surprise. I certainly knew that he would feel hurt by such a project being carried out, but I did not suppose that he attached so much importance to the matter.

---

[72] An additional note to No 17 in FO 82/174 reads: 'The Queen writes on it [the dispatch] "I think it would be best avoided" i.e. better keep the Mission.' S[alisbury], 26 May 1889.

[73] Enclosure: copy of Mittnacht to Barron, Stuttgart, 17 May 1889. For the amalgamation of the missions at Stuttgart and Munich, see pp. 5–8.

I have for obvious reasons kept this project entirely secret, and have no means of knowing how it reached the Wurttemberg Government. Under these circumstances, I am sure that Her Majesty will feel that a withdrawal of her Mission during the present reign, but especially in the present year, would be ill timed. In the ordinary course of nature a suitable opportunity for carrying out such a measure must arise before very long.

In this view I am not moved by any personal considerations, being convinced that, if the two Missions were to be united, my claims to hold the new united Mission are such as could not be passed over.

If economy be the object in view, I may mention that my Legation has already suffered diminution at my expense by the withdrawal of the Secretary, which ought to satisfy the demands of the Treasury.[74]

FO 82/174: Henry Barron to Marquess of Salisbury, No 36, Stuttgart, 24 October 1889

[Received 26 October by post. For: The Queen; S[alisbury]]

Dubious background of the man accused of attempting to assassinate Prince Wilhelm

The searches instituted by the Ludwigsburg Tribunal have cleared up the mystery which surrounded the recent outrage, and have given it a different complexion from that which it assumed from the prisoner's declarations.[75] These have proved to be false in every particular.

He is not Klaiber a saddler from Ulm, but Martin Müller from Oethlingen in the Oberamt[76] Kirchheim, a member of the Evangelic[al] Church, son of a highly respected wool spinner once Landtag Deputy[77] now deceased, and nephew of a well known Stuttgart Prelate.[78]

His antecedents are very unfavorable. He has been employed in various trades and places, and lost two of these situations through acts of swindling. He returned lately from Munich to Oethlingen and was received by his brothers who have kept up their father's business. He showed such signs of mental derangement that he was placed under medical observation.

---

[74] Conyngham Greene, second secretary, was transferred to The Hague in April 1889.
[75] Barron is referring to the attempted assassination of Prince Wilhelm at Ludwigsburg on 20 October 1889.
[76] Administrative district.
[77] August Müller.
[78] Gottlob von Müller.

An anonymous letter lately received by the Princess Charlotte warning her of some impending misfortune is now proved to have emanated from Müller.

On the day of the crime he was visited in the prison by Prince William, who said: "Why did you try to kill me"? He answered that he bore no ill will to His Royal Highness personally, but that he wanted a Catholic King for Wurttemberg.

The next day Monday he changed his story and boasted of being the agent of some secret "anarchist" society.

All this is evidently empty braggadoccio. The man seems to be really demented, and affected with the "vainglorious" as well as the "homicidal" forms of mania.

Strange to say; this is the first instance recorded in history of an attempt to murder one of the reigning family in Wurttemberg.

[…]

P.S. The King has ordered a Prayer of Thanksgiving to be read in all the Evangelical churches on Sunday next the 27th of October.

FO 82/174: Henry Barron to Marquess of Salisbury, No 40, Stuttgart, 26 November 1889

[Received 29 November by messenger. Qy: Private Secretary; T.V.L. [Thomas Villiers Lister]; 'Lord Salisbury will allow him to remain until the end of the financial year. This hardly seems to require an answer.' E.B. [Eric Barrington]; S[alisbury]]

Personal objections to proposed amalgamation of Stuttgart and Munich legations

In compliance with the instruction conveyed in your N° 5 of June 10th I duly acknowledged Baron Mittnacht's note of May 17th and informed him that his observations would receive the careful and respectful consideration of Her Majesty's Government.[79] In that note Baron Mittnacht stated that the King and the Government of Wurttemberg regretted deeply the proposed removal of Her Majesty's Legation from Stuttgart, adduced several arguments favoring the maintenance of this ancient Legation, and adverted to the excellent mutual relations which had existed between us during my tenure of this office.

Since that time the appointment of a Secretary[80] to this Legation has confirmed the Government in its' confidence that the Legation would be maintained.

---

[79] Salisbury's No 5 conveyed these instructions to Barron, but no further details about amalgamating the British missions at Munich and Stuttgart. See also p. 000.

[80] Baron Vaux of Harrowden, was transferred to Stuttgart on 1 November 1889.

Nevertheless it would now appear that the above measure is still contemplated, "in view of a pledge of long standing to the Treasury". That pledge is in the annual Estimates worded as follows: "it is proposed on the occurrence of vacancies to amalgamate the Missions at Munich, Darmstadt and Stuttgardt so as to reduce the cost."[81]

This pledge is indeed of such long standing that it seems to have been till now quite forgotten. It was certainly overlooked in 1883 and 1885, when, on the occasion of vacancies at Stuttgart and at Munich, it might have been carried out without any injustice. The above pledges, so far from threatening existing rights, forms their strongest guarantee! On the faith of it I accepted my present office. It clearly does not apply to the present conjuncture when there is no vacancy. Moreover my pension, added to the provision necessary to be made in some shape for carrying on the business of the suppressed Mission, would certainly absorb all the saving expected. Therefore the proposed measure would, during my life at least, not tend "to reduce the cost."

I have therefore the honor to submit respectfully that Her Majesty's Legation should not be removed under present circumstances; firstly in deference to the strong feeling on the subject by the King of Wurtemberg. Secondly because the alleged saving would prove to be illusory; Because the "pledge to the Treasury" constitutes an equally valid pledge of fair treatment to the holders of the offices concerned; and of respect to vested rights; Because the Treasury might possibly not sanction the grant of a pension to a person in fairly good health five years before the appointed age for retiring;[82] Because it is certainly not intended by the Regulations (clause XVII)[83] and would be against all precedent that the career of a Minister, after his having served a long and expensive apprenticeship with a view of attaining that rank, should be compulsorily closed after five years tenure; Because the Queen, whom I have served faithfully for 49 years without a censure and with scanty reward cannot allow my long unblemished career to be thus terminated in apparent disgrace.

A vacancy or other opportunity must arrive before long in the ordinary course of nature. Meanwhile there is no apparent urgency

---

[81] This recommendation was first made in the *Estimates for Civil Services for the Year Ending 31 March 1885*, which was printed by order of the House of Commons on 25 February 1884 and repeated in subsequent financial years up to that of 1889–1890.

[82] Retirement age was seventy years.

[83] Barron is referring to the *Regulations for Her Majesty's Diplomatic Service* (as revised in 1872) according to which, after five years (or less), 'the question of reappointment [...] or a transfer to another mission shall be open for consideration'.

for carrying out the above measure in the face of so many serious objections.

FO 82/175: Henry Barron to Marquess of Salisbury, No 8, Stuttgart, 4 March 1890

[Received 7 March by messenger. For The Queen / ~~Circulate~~, P.L. [printed letter], 13 March / Home Office for perusal; S[alisbury]

Reichstag election results; changes in political representation for Württemberg; lesser turnout at the polls in comparison to 1887

With reference to my No 7 of the 21st ultimo I now have the honour to enclose a statement showing the final result of the late general election for the Reichstag in Wurttemberg as compared with that for 1887.[84]

The nine second ballots have resulted in a great success for the Democratic party, which has now carried nine of the 17 seats allotted to this Kingdom.

The so-called "Volkspartei" is a speciality of Wurttemberg and has it's head-quarters at Stuttgart; (vide my No 38 of Nov.r 3rd 1889.).[85] It has put forward a few candidates in other parts, but without success, excepting alone in the adjacent town of Pfarrheim. It will enter the Reichstag with 10 members under the leadership of Mr Payer. But if, as is probable, it should coalesce with the "Freisinnig" party under Mr Richter, it would form a strong Fraction of 79 members.

The aggregate numbers polled at this election viz: 299,243 votes show a decrease of 21.300 as compared with those of 1887.

The two Parties belonging to the Coalition termed "Kartell"[86] have been the principal sufferers, having lost nine seats and 85.170 votes. The National-Liberal candidate[87] however finally retained his seat for Stuttgart against a Socialist competitor[88] by 16.349 to 13.458 votes. The "Centre"[89] has lost 6224 votes, this probably because it's four seats were known to be safe, and because no others could be seriously contested by this party.

[84] Elections were held on 20 February 1890; run-off elections in Württemberg were held on 1 March. Enclosure: comparative statement of results regarding the two general elections of deputies to the *Reichstag* in Württemberg, Stuttgart, 4 March 1890.
[85] Not included in this volume.
[86] See n. 208 in Berlin section.
[87] Gustav Siegle.
[88] Karl Kloß.
[89] *Zentrumspartei* (Catholics).

The Socialist party has not yet conquered a seat here, but has increased its numbers from 11.013 to 26.669 votes. It will number 37 members in the new Reichstag. This rapid and alarming growth now forms the chief danger threatening Germany. It is evidently the result of the Direct Universal Suffrage rashly given to the Empire in 1871.[90] The only remedy would seem to consist in some gradual reform of that institution.

FO 82/175: Henry Barron to Marquess of Salisbury, Treaty, unnumbered, Stuttgart, 13 April 1890

[Received 18 April by messenger. For: The Queen; S[alisbury]]

Letter of recall received by Queen of Württemberg in a special audience; her dismay at closure of legation

I have the honor to report that the Queen of Württemberg[91] received me yesterday in a special audience for the purpose of my delivering to Her the Letter from Her Most Gracious Majesty announcing the termination of my mission at this Court.[92]

Her Majesty expressed to me most emphatically the sense of mortification which She experienced at the withdrawal of this ancient Mission from residence at Stuttgart, especially now in Their Majesties' declining years. This expression of feeling was evidently intended to be reported.

FO 82/175: Baron Vaux of Harrowden to Marquess of Salisbury, No 31, Stuttgart, 14 October 1890

[Received 17 October by messenger. For: The Queen / Berlin for perusal, 23 October; S[alisbury]]

Remarks on political sensitivities associated with command of Württemberg army corps; German Emperor and Prince Wilhelm discuss Alvensleben's successor

I have the honour to report that His Royal Highness Prince William of Wurttemberg returned on Saturday from a short visit which he had been paying to the German Emperor in Berlin.[93]

---

[90] Universal male suffrage for citizens over 25 years of age was introduced in the North German Confederation in 1866. It was enacted as imperial law in 1871.

[91] Olga.

[92] Despite his protest to the Foreign Office, Barron officially retired on a pension on 1 April 1890. He presented his letter of recall to the King of Württemberg on 9 April.

[93] Prince Wilhelm visited Wilhelm II at Potsdam on 9 October 1890.

I met His Royal Highness shortly after his return and in the course of conversation he informed me that there was no truth in the newspaper reports that he had gone to Berlin to join a shooting party of the Emperor's, but that on the contrary he had been summoned there at very short notice, and at considerable inconvenience to himself, in order that the Emperor might have an opportunity of discussing with him the question of the appointment of a successor to General von Alvensleben, who is shortly to resign the command of the Wurttemberg army, which forms the 13th Army Corps of the German Imperial army.[94]

Since the conclusion of the military convention between Wurttemberg and Prussia,[95] nearly 20 years ago, the General Commanding the Wurttemberg army has invariably been a Prussian.

Of late years considerable friction has arisen between the Prussian Commanding Officers with the members of their staff, who have generally been Prussians, on the one hand, and the native officers of the army on the other hand. This has been especially marked during the last 2 or 3 years of General von Alvensleben's tenure of the Command, and some eighteen months ago a very serious quarrel occurred between Prince William and the General, which resulted in His Royal Highness refusing to serve any longer under General von Alvensleben and resigning the command of the Brigade which he then held.

Since that time Prince William has taken no active part in military affairs here. Now however that the removal of General von Alvensleben has been decided on, a very general wish has been expressed throughout the Country, that Prince William may be appointed to the command of the Wurttemberg Army Corps. The appointment would be very popular both in the army itself and amongst the people generally.

The officers of this army are appointed and commissioned by the King of Wurttemberg, but the Convention to which I have already referred provides that the appointment of the General commanding the 13th Army Corps must also receive the consent of the German Emperor. Up to the present time the result of this has been that a Prussian officer has always held the Chief Command here.

At the present moment the appointment of Prince William would probably be the best way of arranging matters, but unfortunately

---

[94] Alvensleben was recalled on 19 October 1890; his successor was the Württemberg general Wilhelm von Wölckern.

[95] Military convention signed between the North German Confederation and Württemberg at Versailles, 25 November 1870.

there are some objections to the appointment which make it unlikely if not impossible.

In the first place His Royal Highness himself is personally averse to taking the Command, and moreover during the King's repeated absences during the last few years in France and Italy, Prince William has acted as Regent, and would probably do so again under similar circumstances. It is considered that it would be very difficult if not impossible for one person to combine the office of the Command of an Army Corps as intimately connected with Prussia as this one is, with the independent position which ought to be occupied by the Regent. The further minor objection that as Prince William is not yet a General of Division, he is not eligible for the Command of an Army Corps, would probably not prove an insuperable bar to his appointment.

If, as appears to be generally expected, Prince William is not given the Command, great hopes are entertained here that the German Emperor may be induced to give his consent to the appointment of a Wurttemberg officer[.]

Active negotiations are at present in progress with a view to this object. General von Caprivi recently paid the King a visit at Friedrichshafen,[96] where Prince William was also present, and the recent journey of His Royal Highness to Berlin was undertaken in consequence of the desire of the German Emperor to converse personally with him on the subject.

The relations between the two Courts are very friendly. Prince William assured me that he parted on excellent terms with the Emperor. The recent appointment by the Emperor of his most intimate personal friend, Count Philip zu Eulenburg as Minister at this Court,[97] is sufficient evidence that no strained relations are likely to exist, and that any questions that may arise will be settled in the most amicable manner.

No appointment to the Command of this Army Corps has yet been made, it is sincerely to be hoped that it will be found possible to appoint an officer who will succeed in avoiding the friction which has been the cause of so much ill feeling of late years.

---

[96] On 3 and 4 October 1890.
[97] Count Philip zu Eulenburg was appointed in March and accredited on 31 May 1890.

FO 82/178: Victor Drummond to Earl of Rosebery, No 23, Munich, 15 March 1893[98]

[Received 17 March by bag. X; R[osebery]]

Speech by Friedrich Ludwig Gaupp on constitutional revision in Württemberg; minimal immediate effect but likely to aid those seeking reform of upper chamber; limited prospects for reform

A meeting of the "German party"[99] was lately held at Tubingen in Wurttemberg when a well known Wurttemberg Jurist delivered a discourse of some importance on Wurttemberg constitutional revision, a translation of which I have the honour to enclose herewith taken from the published account in the Wurttemberg newspaper the "Beobachter" or "Observer"; –[100] and although Dr Gaupp's conclusions have not been much noticed in the Wurttemberg Press they open the road later to agitation in favour of at least reforming the Upper Wurttemberg Chamber and the remarks made from the Wurttemberg Working class newspaper the "Beobachter" show that a revision of the Wurttemberg constitution in this sense would be favourably received by the party it represents, although it acknowledges that several years must elapse before such a reform could be obtained.

Dr Gaupp wishes nothing less than the abolition of the First Wurttemberg Chamber; he bases his arguments on the fact that it no longer acts as a Bulwark against revolutionary attempts of the Chamber of Deputies, as the German Empire is the only guarantee against revolutionary movements, all political questions being now decided by the "Reichstag" and are not brought before the Wurttemberg parliament which was no defence against the Revolution of 1848 nor would be now.

The Wurttemberg Upper Chamber is dead. For 300 years from 1514 to 1806 there was only one Chamber, and King Frederick included but one Chamber in his Draft Constitution. The Congress of Vienna forced the present two Chambers on Wurttemberg.[101]

---

[98] From 1890, dispatches on Württemberg were mostly sent from Munich and are filed both in the FO 82 (Württemberg) and FO 9 (Bavaria) series.

[99] *Deutsche Partei* (Württemberg National Liberals). The meeting took place on 8 February 1893.

[100] Enclosure: translation of article entitled 'Revision of the Wurttemberg Constitution', *Der Beobachter: Ein Volksblatt für Schwaben*, undated.

[101] The Württemberg *Ständeverfassung* (representation of the estates whose rights were regulated by the Tübingen contract of 1514) was revoked by King Friedrich on 30 December 1805. In November 1815 Friedrich, after a failed attempt to impose a new constitution, presented a new draft which was subsequently also rejected by the Assembly of

Dr Gaupp condemns both the Nobles of the Wurttemberg Upper Chamber, many of them youths whose votes can counterbalance those of the most valued statesmen, and the system of voting by proxy. The Life Members he says are turned into forced labourers and spend their lives in doing the work of the nobility.

Dr Gaupp however, in the latter part of his discourse declaims against universal suffrage, showing that he holds not only Radical but Conservative opinions, declaring that it leads to mob rule and caesarism or electoral corruption.

The "Beobachter" criticizes these remarks upon universal suffrage, showing that the evils pointed at by Dr Gaupp can be overcome by the continued political education of the masses by associations and the press, but agrees that the abolition of the Upper Chamber is a necessity, although not believing in the 'German party' giving the effect to its good intentions.

I have taken some trouble to inform myself upon the effect caused at Stuttgardt by Dr Gaupp's discourse. The person to whom I addressed myself for information states that it has made some impression, but he does not believe that the proposed Reform will ever be accepted, although there has been continued complaint that the Members of the Upper Chamber did not interest themselves much in questions which interested the Württemberg people but only in those where their own interests are concerned.

Dr Gaupp's idea to form one Chamber and to permit a portion of the First Chamber to enter it will probably never be realized. There is much more probability that the First Chamber will be reformed by obtaining a number of new members, representatives of the lower nobility, the clergy, trade and industry, and such fresh elements as it is considered would be certainly advantageous; but at all events this change will not take place at present; it will take time to bring in a Reform Bill in this sense and to induce the First Chamber to accept Reform of any kind which would curtail its privileges which the majority, the "Standesherren" or higher nobility by birth have enjoyed for so long. These Reforms may be greatly needed, but as Württemberg is so well governed and great abuses nowhere exist, the present state of things will remain probably for a long time in their actual condition.

the Estates. The bicameral system was finally introduced by the Württemberg constitution of 1819. Article 13 of the Act of the German Confederation included the Final Act of the Congress of Vienna of 1815, to which Drummond refers, and which promised each German state a constitution (*Landständische Verfassung*). It did not, however, specify the type of representation to be established by the individual states.

FO 82/178: Victor Drummond to Earl of Rosebery, Treaty, No 3, Munich, 28 March 1893[102]

[Received 1 April by bag. For: Western Department / X; R[osebery]]

Impressive speech by Mittnacht in favour of maintaining Württemberg's diplomatic representation at Munich; abolition of legations at St Petersburg and Vienna

With reference to my Despatch N° 21 Treaty of the 8th December last upon the Württemberg diplomatic posts at Vienna and St Petersburg I have the honour to inform Your Lordship that on the 23rd instant the Estimates for the Wurttemberg Diplomatic Service were debated in the Chamber of Deputies.

On the estimate for Legations and Consulates, Baron Mittnacht the Minister for Foreign Affairs spoke in defence of some Legations whose existence was attacked by the "Deutsche"[103] and "Volks"[104] parties on economical and other grounds.

The Petersburg mission whose raison d'être was to a great extent lost since the deaths of the late King and Queen of Wurttemberg,[105] was dropped by the Government from the estimates, but the Munich and Vienna missions were defended by them, and the Munich mission after a weighty speech by Baron Mittnacht was agreed to without a division. The Vienna Legation on the other hand was only voted for one year, so that after the year 1894 it will be abolished. The Berlin Legation was not attacked, all parties agreeing as to its necessity.

Baron Mittnacht, in reviewing the history of this question, pointed out that the necessity for Wurttemberg of having Legations at Munich and Vienna stood on a different footing from what might be called the 'family post' at S[t] Petersburg. There were numbers of Germans in Austria, many of them Wurttembergers, all of whom could look to the Wurttemberg representatives for assistance and advice. Much valuable information came to the Wurttemberg Government, through its representatives at these neighbouring and important posts, which would otherwise be wanting. In Baden for instance there was no Wurttemberg Legation, and the consequence was that the Wurttemberg Government failed to receive much valuable information respecting Baden, obtaining only imperfect and

---

[102] From 1890 dispatches on Württemberg were mostly sent from Munich, and are filed both in the FO 82 (Württemberg) and FO 9 (Bavaria) series.

[103] *Deutsche Partei* (Württemberg National Liberals).

[104] *Württembergische Volkspartei.*

[105] Olga was the daughter of Nicholas I of Russia. Olga died in October 1892; Karl in October 1891. The mission at St Petersburg was abolished from 1 April 1893.

inaccurate accounts of important matters through the Press. No respectable Government could confine its information to mere newspaper reports. Prussia found this, and, in spite of the existence of the Bundesrath[106] in Berlin, Prussia kept up Legations in all the German States of any importance, which furnished her with very valuable information. It was not true that official personages sent occasionally in special missions could replace regular Ministers.

They had not the same local knowledge, nor the same intimate relations with the Government of the country, and could not therefore do the same work.

Regular reports made by an intelligent regular representative on the spot were of the greatest use to his own Government.

Baron de Mittnacht went on to say that the influence of the Bavarian Government in the affairs of the Empire was undoubtedly an important one. Bavaria was the second German State in size and importance, and was fully recognized and respected as such especially in Berlin, – perhaps more so than is agreeable to many Prussians. Whenever Prussia and Bavaria were agreed on any common course of action in any Imperial question, different proposals from any other quarter would hardly be of any account at all; the question would then in fact be settled out of hand. Wurttemberg again had many interests in common with Bavaria. North and South German interests did not always and everywhere exactly tally even when the most correct attitude in the transaction of the affairs of the Empire was observed. Wurttemberg had thus every interest to maintain a very accurate understanding with Bavaria, and for this purpose a permanent Envoy was necessary. Then again there was the question of the reserved rights (of the separate States).[107] Baron Mittnacht referred to his experience of more than twenty years and assured the house that important interests of the country would be injured if the Legation in Munich were abolished. In Bavaria, where so many Wurttemberg subjects resided, a Wurttemberg representation was especially necessary to advise and assist them in their needs, and to keep the Wurttemberg Government regularly informed. The regular representative of Württemberg in Munich[108] had many opportunities of obtaining interesting information from his colleagues of the Corps Diplomatique. The just influence of Bavaria in Germany was very great and even on this ground alone Wurttemberg required a Legation in Munich.

---

[106] Federal Council.
[107] For the so-called *Reservatrechte*, see. n. 220 in Munich section.
[108] Oskar von Soden.

After Baron Mittnacht's impressive speech, all further objection to the Legation at Munich was withdrawn.

FO 82/178: Victor Drummond to Earl of Rosebery, Confidential, No 84, Munich, 9 December 1893[109]

[Received 20 December by post. For: The Queen / Berlin; R[osebery]]

Resignation of Württemberg's envoy to Berlin; political friction between Prussian and Württemberg governments

It is reported from Stuttgart, that, Herr von Moser, the Wurtemberg Minister at Berlin, has sent in his resignation,[110] and that this resolution on his part has been taken, owing to his position there becoming embarrassed from the unsatisfactory relations existing between the Prussian and Wurtemberg Governments.

With respect to this matter, I am enabled, through a confidential source, to bring to Your Lordship some of the reasons which have led to Herr von Moser's retirement.

First. The Wurtemberg Manœuvers last September.

His Imperial Majesty The German Emperor gave instructions[111] that the Wurtemberg and Baden Troops should fight for several days against each other, that Wurtemberg should call out its' "Landwehr" Militia, and that the Baden Troops should enter Stuttgart after beating back the Wurtemberg army. The drought, however, in Wurtemberg last summer, was very severe, and the Wurtemberg Chambers agreed unanimously,[112] that it would be a heavy tax on agriculturists, if Manœuvers on as large a scale as proposed should be carried out. The Government was, therefore, invited to take measures to have the programme curtailed.

Baron de Mittnacht[,] President of the Council and Minister of foreign affairs, then instructed Herr von Moser to bring this proposal to the notice of the Chancellor of the Empire,[113] expressing the hope that His Imperial Majesty would give it His favorable consideration, and if possible, reduce the Manœuvers to two days; it appears that The Emperor very graciously acceded to this, but His Imperial

---

[109] From 1890, dispatches on Württemberg were mostly sent from Munich and are filed both in the FO 82 (Württemberg) and FO 9 (Bavaria) series.

[110] Moser handed in his resignation in early December whilst on leave of absence from Berlin; he retired on 19 February 1894.

[111] Imperial order (*Cabinetsordre*) of 14 February 1894.

[112] On 2 June 1893. The motion was carried by 39 to 35 votes.

[113] Moser notified Leo von Caprivi on 19 July 1893.

Majesty was offended at the request being made through the Wurtemberg Minister, instead of through the General commanding in Wurtemberg, General von Wölckern, who ought to have reported directly to The Emperor as his Commander in Chief; however, on reviewing the Wurtemberg Troops on the 20th of September last,[114] His Imperial Majesty expressed His entire satisfaction with their appearance, and with the officers who led them; but, from that time The Emperor has shown His dissatisfaction with Baron de Mittnacht and the Wurtemberg Military Authorities, owing, it is said, to reports made to Him at Stuttgart, that He had been deceived as to the necessity of curtailing the Manœuvers through the dearth of fodder; I am told that His Imperial Majesty spoke very shortly to General Caprivi, whom he reproached for having induced Him to consent to a reduction in the Manœuvers.

Second.

Baron de Mittnacht's visit to Prince Bismarck at Kissingen.[115] It was a very natural thing that Baron de Mittnacht should wish to see his old friend once more, whose illness at the time caused his friends considerable anxiety, but The Emperor, it is said, believed that the visit was made to annoy Him, and Baron de Mittnacht was afterwards made aware of His Majesty's displeasure.

The King of Wurtemberg availed Himself of the opportunity presented, by requesting Baron de Mittnacht to use his influence, when with Prince Bismarck, to bring about a reconciliation between the Prince and the Emperor; The King of Wurtemberg expected that the Negotiation would be successful, and that The Emperor would then have been grateful for the Service rendered Him; Prince Bismarck, however, refused a reconciliation, and when His Imperial Majesty arrived at Stuttgart[116] to attend the Manœuvers, neither Baron de Mittnacht, nor General von Schott Minister of War, nor General Wölckern met with a graceful reception. It was very different with The King of Wurtemberg, whose relations with The Emperor are most friendly.

Third.

The Wurtemberg Government's strong opposition to the proposed Imperial Tax on Wine in the Federal Council,[117] and their having

---

[114] The emperor viewed the manoeuvres of the XIII (Royal Württemberg) Corps on 15 and 16 September 1893, not on 20 September as stated in the dispatch.

[115] On 25 and 26 August 1893. At the time Bismarck was suffering from shingles and pneumonia.

[116] On 14 September 1893.

[117] Württemberg voted against the majority of the Federal Council on 20 November 1893. The wine tax bill was eventually dropped in January 1894 after its first reading in the *Reichstag*.

persuaded the Baden Government to join in their protest, met with General Caprivi's displeasure, apparently shared in by the Emperor, for on His Imperial Majesty's recent visit to Babenhausen[118] to shoot with The King of Wurtemberg, He could not be induced to discuss the matter.

Four.

I am informed that on the abovementioned visit to Babenhausen, His Imperial Majesty pointed out to The King the great inconvenience arising out of the actual state of things with respect to the army and asked whether it was not advisable to alter the Versailles agreement[119] by a new Military Convention, abolishing the Wurtemberg Ministry of War, and forming instead a Military Cabinet in its' place, the same as in Baden;[120] it is believed, that The King was personally satisfied with the reasons for this alteration at the time, but, to carry out such an arrangement, it must be remembered that it must be presented to both Chambers, and to carry it through a two thirds majority is necessary, now it is very improbable that this majority can be obtained, a Dissolution of the second Chamber is out of the question, neither would such a course be advisable; for it is confidently believed that the next Elections[121] will bring in more Members of the opposition, already well represented in numbers. There is a great amount of discontent amongst all classes, and Public opinion in Wurtemberg is a great Factor, the late Kings William and Charles of Wurtemberg carefully avoided any conflict with it, and in consequence the Wurtembergers are used to utter freely their sentiments. They cling to their reserved rights,[122] and it will be difficult to induce them to surrender them, or give up their peculiarities, one is a dislike to Strangers and the preference which has been lately shown for North Germans engenders many bitter remarks. It is possible, however, that His Majesty The King of Wurtemberg seeing the present temper of His Subjects, and who is most patriotic in His feelings, may, through a personal friendly understanding with The Emperor prevent for the present any

---

[118] From 6 to 11 November 1893.

[119] Military convention between the North German Confederation and Württemberg of 25 November 1870. It was one of the 'November Treaties' of Versailles, by which the South German States joined the North German Confederation to form the basis of the German Empire.

[120] The *Militärkabinett* was an advisory body under the command of the German Emperor; its jurisdiction included officers from Baden. Following the military convention, and the complete integration of the Baden army into the Prussian army, the Baden ministry of war was abolished in December 1871.

[121] The next elections were held on 1 February 1895.

[122] On the *Reservatrechte*, see n. 220 in Munich section.

attempt to alter the Versailles agreement, and it looks as if this had happened, if the reports which are now circulated in the Press are correct, namely, that a large interchange of Prussian and Wurtemberg officers in both armies, is to take place in the near future.

It is impossible to say exactly how far the Prussian proposals have gone,[123] but very likely the answer given from Stuttgart was not satisfactory, and that Her von Moser who is a rich man and who only accepted the Post at Berlin under great pressure, feeling that his position was one which he could no longer sustain owing to the differences between the two Governments, at once declared his intention to resign, and it will be very difficult to find anyone with all the necessary qualifications to replace him.

FO 82/178: Victor Drummond to Earl of Rosebery, Confidential, No 87, Munich, 23 December 1893[124]

[Received 26 December by post. For: The Queen; R[osebery]]

Plans to change Versailles military agreement abandoned after popular outcry; Württemberg retains reserved rights over her military for the time being

With reference to my Despatch N° 84, confidential, of the 9th instant, respecting the resignation of Herr von Moser,[125] Wurtemberg Minister to Berlin, and the causes which induced him to retire, namely, difficulties between the Prussian and Wurtemberg Governments, one of those related to the desire of His Imperial Majesty, The German Emperor[,] to have the Versailles Military Agreement altered in favour of a Military Cabinet at Stuttgart, abolishing the Ministry of War there;[126] I have now the honour to inform Your Lordship that the Wurtemberg Minister of War, General Schott von Schottenstein has just returned to Stuttgart from making an official Visit to Berlin,[127] and that it appears that all idea of altering

---

[123] See the following dispatch.

[124] From 1890 dispatches on Württemberg were mostly sent from Munich, and are filed both in the FO 82 (Württemberg) and FO 9 (Bavaria) series.

[125] See n. 110 in this section.

[126] See preceding dispatch.

[127] Schott, carrying out a royal order of 1 December 1893, visited Berlin from 15 to 22 December to establish the definitive terms of exchange between Württemberg and Prussian officers, as stipulated in the military convention of 25 November 1870. The intended harmonization also included recognizing the length of service of Württemberg officers seconded to the Prussian army (as compared to Prussia officers of the same rank) and details of their uniform.

the Versailles Agreement is for the present abandoned, and that the Military privileges of The German Emperor and The King of Wurtemberg remain undisturbed as regards appointments and promotions in their respective armies, the pending negotiations concern only the regulations for an interchange of Officers, particularly with regard to the quota of Senior Officers (Captains) they do not relate to changes in the highest grades.

There is no doubt, that an agreement had been arranged between the Prussian and Wurtemberg Governments, with the view of placing the Wurtemberg Troops under the direct control of the Prussian War Office and for abolishing the Wurtemberg Ministry of War, neither is there any doubt, that if the suspicion of such an arrangement had not leaked out, which enabled the voice of public opinion to protest vehemently against such an infringement of Wurtemberg's reserved rights,[128] the agreement would have been effected.

It was Baron de Mittnacht who used his authority with The King and who pointed out to His Majesty the serious consequences which would ensue from an infringement of the Versailles agreement, and thus determined His Majesty to address Himself to The Emperor to prevent the proposed change, it is said, through the mediation of the Adjutant-General, General von Franckenstein who is a "persona gratissima"[129] with The Emperor, it appears, that His Imperial Majesty was pleased to yield to the arguments used against the proposal, which has probably saved The Emperor from a serious conflict with the South German States and Saxony, for I am informed confidentially, that the Governments of these States were all prepared to bring their influence to bear, to uphold the reserve[d] rights of Wurtemberg.

FO 9/269: Victor Drummond to Earl of Kimberley, No 19, Munich, 7 June 1894[130]

[Received 2 July by messenger. X; K[imberley]]

Bill to revise Württemberg constitution withdrawn; heated debate on amendments to electoral law; closure of chambers until after elections will affect political business

With reference to my despatch No. 14 of the 12th ultimo, I have the honor to inform Your Lordship that after five days'[131] Debate on

---

[128] On the *Reservatrechte*, see n. 220 in Munich section.

[129] Latin: 'a highly favoured person'.

[130] From 1890 dispatches on Württemberg were mostly sent from Munich, and are filed both in the FO 82 (Württemberg) and FO 9 (Bavaria) series.

[131] 29 May to 2 June 1894.

the question of the Revision of the Constitution to amend the Würtemberg Electoral law, Baron de Mittnacht yesterday informed the Wurtemberg Chamber of Representatives that by His Majesty The King's Royal Order, the Bill as presented to their consideration in regard to this matter, has been withdrawn, and that the Sittings of the Chamber were now closed.[132]

The real cause for this proceeding has been occasioned by the great divergence of views which separated the different parties in the Chamber, and which showed that it was very doubtful if the Government could obtain the $\frac{2}{3}^{rds}$ majority necessary to pass such a measure.

During the Debate the Democrats insisted on reform, in favour of a Representative Chamber of the People, the abolition of the Upper Chamber, and declared that they will persist in this determination as long as the Party exists.

The Centrum (Ultramontane) party[133] declared against privileged members being allowed in the Lower Chamber, upheld the Upper Chamber with modifications, and advocated Proportional representation.

The German Liberal Party[134] could come to no general agreement, all holding different views.

Several Members spoke in favour of the modifications proposed in Committee, those referred to in my abovementioned despatch.[135]

In fact the different parties were so thoroughly disunited that it was no use continuing the debate, and the withdrawal of the Bill (which was not unexpected) became necessary.

On the other hand the closing of the sittings of the Chambers was hardly a wise proceeding, there were two important matters which had been assented to by the Chamber, one, a new Law for reforming the Würtemberg Public School system to bring it more in agreement with that of the other German States, and which was, at the time, being carried through the Upper Chamber with

---

[132] The bill to revise the composition of the chambers of the Württemberg *Landtag* (chapter 9 of the Württemberg constitution of 1819) was presented to the *Ständischer Ausschuss* (joint committee of both chambers) on 8 April 1894. Mittnacht's notifications to withdraw the bill and close the sittings were dated 4 June 1894; they were read to the second chamber on 5 June 1894.

[133] At the time of the dispatch the Württemberg *Zentrumspartei* (Catholics) had not yet been founded; however it had been represented de facto in the Württemberg *Landtag* since 1889. On 14 May Deputy Gröber proposed to form a *Zentrum* faction. See also n. 145 in this section.

[134] *Deutsche Partei* (Württemberg National Liberals).

[135] In its report of 8 May 1894 the commission of the second chamber requested an increase in the number of cities represented in the second chamber. This was instead of the proposed inclusion of six representatives from the regional agricultural associations (*Landwirtschaftliche Gauverbände*) and the chambers of trade and commerce.

very slight modifications,[136] this Law cannot now be passed before next year, after the Elections in January;[137] again, at the beginning of the late Parliamentary Session, a matter which caused a good deal of sensation last year in Würtemberg (a reported modification of the Military Convention of 1871 [sic][138] between Prussia and Würtemberg, in regard to the interchange of officers)[139] was strongly commented on by one of the Democratic party, Herr Payer, who moved[140] that the Chamber should be informed what truth there was in the rumour; Baron de Mittnacht declared that the agreement relating to this point in no way modified the Convention; upon which, Herr Graber [sic], a member of the Centrum party, moved that the Chamber be informed whether the number of officers sent to serve in Prussian Regiments did not surpass the limit of the Convention and whether the Imperial Treasury did not gain at the expense of Würtemberg?[141] These motions were referred to a Committee to give their judgement thereupon, but, now, of course their decision cannot be presented.

It is not likely that the Chambers will be again convoked before the general Elections in January 1895, when it is believed that the Democrats will gain two or three more seats from their political opponents, they are a united party with capable and clever Leaders; at the same time, Baron de Mittnacht has great influence and will undoubtedly use it to try and obtain a Government Majority, he has already pointed out that a Reform of the Electoral law as demanded by the Democrats could not be acceded to for fear the peace of the land and the Monarchy itself might suffer, and he will probably, at the proper time, bring this view prominently before the electors to prevent them voting for that party.

---

[136] On 16 May 1894. The reform of the elementary schools was eventually delayed until the *Volksschulgesetz* of 1909.

[137] Elections took place on 1 February 1895; the *Landtag* was opened on 20 February.

[138] See n. 119 in this section.

[139] See n. 127 in this section. The debate took place on 26 May 1894.

[140] On 23 May 1894.

[141] Article 8 of the military convention between the North German Confederation and Württemberg of 25 November 1870 did not set a limit on the number of seconded officers. With regard to the second part of his motion Gröber referred to the fact that savings resulting from the exchange were paid to the imperial treasury.

FO 9/269: Arthur George Vansittart to Earl of Kimberley, Confidential, No 52, Munich, 1 November 1894[142]

[Received 5 November by messenger. For: Lord Rosebery; K[imberley]]

Assessment of political parties and their prospects ahead of Württemberg general elections

With reference to my despatch No. 46 of the 19th ultimo, in view of the approaching general elections in Würtemberg,[143] perhaps the following information, which I have been able to procure from a private and confidential source may prove of interest.

Of the different factions in the field it may be asserted that, at the present moment, the Würtembergische Volkspartei[144] stands very good chances. After a long period of stagnation, there are visible symptoms of considerable movement amongst its partisans, and the number of adherents to this party has of late increased. Its most dangerous adversaries would seem to be in the first place the Conservatives of all kinds, behind whom stand the Government with their large staff of functionaries.

In Würtemberg, where the Government has no small amount of power, their influence is considerable. The army of functionaries of all kinds are assisted by the Evangelical clergy and there is no doubt they will, when the time comes, offer considerable resistance to the designs of the Volkspartei in obtaining seats in the Chambers.

In addition to the Conservatives the Volkspartei must count with the new Centrumspartei,[145] which is the outcome of the Catholic reaction since 1870, and is now led by Herr Gröber, the Deputy. In religious, political, and social relations the new Centrum faction hold the same views as the German Centrumspartei.

In former years the Catholics and Democrats assisted each other against the Government candidates, and it was not uncommon for them to vote together against the Ministers, more especially when the latter were assisted by the strictly Conservative Evangelical party.

But, of late, this policy has ceased, and the above-mentioned alliance cannot now be said to exist any longer.

Finally, the Social Democrats, who find that the Volkspartei is too moderate in its views, promise to become a dangerous adversary.

---

[142] From 1890, dispatches on Württemberg were mostly sent from Munich and are filed both in the FO 82 (Württemberg) and FO 9 (Bavaria) series.

[143] Elections took place on 1 February 1895.

[144] Left liberal party; part of the *Deutsche Volkspartei* at imperial level.

[145] After the initiatives of July 1894 (when a provisory committee was established and a party program was drafted) the Württemberg *Zentrumspartei* was officially founded on 17 January 1895. See also n. 133 in this section.

Taking into consideration all the above circumstances it is quite possible that the Government adherents, although they have of late greatly diminished, may ultimately obtain a majority. The Prime Minister Herr von Mittnacht, who is a Catholic, may possibly succeed in gaining over the Centrum faction. Should he succeed in this, it will be extremely difficult for the Volkspartei to obtain a majority, for it must be remembered that in the Chambers there are about twenty privileged members[146] who chiefly vote for the Government. In the above event it may safely be prophesied that things will go on as at present, and remain as they are. But it will be necessary for the Evangelical party, which certainly enjoys the King's protection, to be careful not to hurt the feelings of the Catholic fraction; otherwise the Catholics would soon be driven over to the opposition.

As regards the press, the "Beobachter", which is the favourite Democratic organ, is at present engaged in warfare with the "Deutsche Volksblatt" (organ of the Centrum party) and the "Schwäbischer Merkur" (organ of the National liberal party).

I might mention here that, in spite of meetings, propaganda, etc... the cause of Social Democracy has not advanced quite so quickly in Würtemberg, as it perhaps has in Bavaria. The Würtemberg populace is distinctly shrewd, and rather attaches itself to the Volkspartei, which party contents itself with reasonable reforms.

It is the opinion of some persons of high rank and standing that Social Democracy could be most successfully combated by the real Liberal fraction, but this belief is certainly not shared by the governing powers who, invariably, endeavour to subdue the Moderate-Democrats, and by so doing, they, in reality, further the designs of the Socialists.

In conclusion it may be added that Würtemberg, on the whole, is a well governed and thriving country; that public opinion has considerable influence, and that really abuses cannot be said to exist.

As long as Herr von Mittnacht continues at the head of affairs serious troubles need not be anticipated. His Excellency is extremely moderate in his ways and speeches, and he possesses the gift of reconciling people, and disarming his opponents. But he has aged of late, and is beginning to show signs of being weary of his long term of office. In Berlin he undoubtedly has powerful adversaries of his Württembergische policy, and it is perhaps there where the danger lies.

---

[146] The privileged members were the representatives of the *Ritterschaft* (noble landowners, of which there were thirteen), the churches (eight) and Tübingen University (one). Altogether the second chamber consisted of ninety-three deputies.

FO 9/270: Victor Drummond to Earl of Kimberley, No 8, Munich, 20 February 1895[147]

[Received 27 February by messenger. For: ~~Lord Rosebery~~; K[imberley]]

Remarks on Württemberg election results; democrats in the ascendant

With reference to my despatch No. 7 of the 16th instant upon the elections in Wurtemberg,[148] I have the honour to make the following remarks: –

The Government parties have been defeated. His Excellency Baron de Mittnacht, President of the Council and Minister for Foreign Affairs, still represents Mergentheim a seat he has held for thirty years. He was opposed by an Ultramontane.[149]

The Socialist members for Stuttgart and Canstatt,[150] who now for the first time enter the Wurtemberg diet, owe their debut entirely to the democrats who voted for them in the 2nd balloting.

Will the democrats, now, being the strongest party show themselves as moderate in their political aims as has been suggested? may they not develop a socialist tendency? if so, this must result in either more demands being made by the proletariat, or by widespread alarm in the classes holding more conservative views.

The democrats in the last Parliament declared that their stand point was, that there should be no privileged members in the 2nd chamber,[151] and in favour of a single chamber. Baron de Mittnacht[152] said the Government would never consent to such a measure, as it would be a danger to the tranquillity of Wurtemberg, and even a danger to the Monarchy. The democratic programme is now the same, including administrative reforms, School, direct taxation, and railway reforms, state economy, the amelioration of the middle and lower classes, and a progressive income tax.

I hear the Würtemberg Minister of Finance[153] will present to the diet a Bill in this sense. There is a question still unanswered remaining over from the last session made by the Leader[154] of the democrats.

---

[147] From 1890 dispatches on Württemberg were mostly sent from Munich, and are filed both in the FO 82 (Württemberg) and FO 9 (Bavaria) series.

[148] Elections took place on 1 February 1894, second ballots on 14 and 15 February.

[149] Johann Hofmann.

[150] Karl Kloß and Menrad Glaser.

[151] See n. 146 in this section.

[152] On 2 June 1894.

[153] Karl von Riecke. A tax reform bill was presented to the Württemberg *Landtag* on 14 May 1895; the bill was finally rejected in January 1899.

[154] Friedrich von Payer; on 23 May 1894. See p. 000.

Was the royal order of the 1ˢᵗ December 1893 in agreement with the military convention of 1870, and with the Würtemberg Constitution?[155] this question will again be asked and lead probably to some burning remarks as to Prussian demands concerning the interchange of Wurtemberg Prussian officers.

With respect to the demeanour of the democrats and the Centrum party towards the Wurtemberg Government in the coming session, I have every personal reason to believe that if Baron de Mittnacht grants certain concessions and conciliatory treatment to both parties, the current legislative measures of the Government may run smoothly.

I have the honour to refer Your Lordship to my despatch No. 14 of the 12ᵗʰ of May 1894,[156] giving a summary of the Bill proposed in the last session of the Wurtemberg diet for the revision of the Constitution to amend the electoral Laws, and to my despatch No. 19 of the 7ᵗʰ of July [sic], 1894, showing what led to its withdrawal.[157]

FO 82/182: Victor Drummond to Marquess of Salisbury, Confidential, No 9, Munich,[158] 13 March 1897

[Received 22 March by messenger. For: Mr Chamberlain / Duke of Devonshire / Mr Balfour / Mr Goschen; T.H.S [Thomas Henry Sanderson]]

Negative feelings amongst Württembergers and Germans towards Britain and her policies

With reference to my Despatch Nᵒ 5 of the 15ᵗʰ Ultimo, I have the honour to state that during my stay at Stuttgart I made inquiries in regard to the feelings in Wurtemberg towards England and whether it was as hostile as during the past year; I regret to say that from my conversations with Gentlemen who I knew were not unfriendly to us that there can be no doubt that the undercurrent of unfriendliness still exists, in proof of this one Gentleman showed to me a letter he had just received from a friend who holds a prominent position in one of the Wurtemberg provinces, a person of culture and refinement, in this letter referring to the German Emperor's proposal for a Blockade of the Piraeus and which Her Majesty's

---

[155] See n. 119 in this section.
[156] Not included in this volume.
[157] For the dispatch of 7 June 1894, see pp. 456–458.
[158] After the amalgamation of the missions in Stuttgart and Munich most dispatches on Württemberg were sent from Munich.

Government did not assent to,[159] the writer declared that it was a rudeness on England's part which was constantly being shown towards Germany and that his hatred for France had now been transferred to England, he added that the time would come when Germany would have a fleet capable of fighting England and that then Germany would wipe out England's insults and rudeness to Germany.

I found also a general feeling that our Navy is not considered to be in an efficient state, there is the same feeling in Bavaria.

The feelings that pervades [sic] the Germans is that it is impossible that England can do any thing for honestys' sake and without any pecuniary or political design.

<hr />

[159] On 14 February 1897 Wilhelm II proposed to Austria, Britain, and Russia a joint naval blockade of the Piraeus to prevent the Greeks further assisting the Cretan revolt against Ottoman sovereignty. Salisbury, in his circular of 17 February, stated that any blockade should be preceded by an understanding on the future status of Crete.

BAVARIA

(MUNICH)

MUNICH

FO 9/252: Hugh Guion MacDonell to Earl Granville, No 22, Munich, 24 April 1884

[Received 26 April by post. For: The Queen / X, Ch.W.D. [Charles Wentworth Dilke] / Berlin for perusal, P.L. [printed letter], 14 May; G[ranville]]

Remarks on Federal Council resolution to establish an imperial ministry responsible to parliament; wariness of various German states; Bavaria not averse to it

The Munich journals have lately reproduced a note published by the official Journal of the Empire[1] regarding a resolution taken by the Bundesrath[2] in its' session of the 5th instant on the subject of the probable establishment of an Imperial Ministry responsible to the Parliament.

Nobody here would have suspected that this question, which only figured in the programme of the new secessionist-progressist Party[3] could have become the subject of a debate in the Bundesrath.

The note published by the official Journal appeared incomprehensible; and the somewhat embarrassed terms in which it was worded have tended in no small degree to awaken public curiosity – in as much as the credit of the initiative seems, by the note, to be attributed to Prussia, while the other states are represented as having done no more than adhere to the proposal.

The result of the information which I have been able to obtain is that as soon as the secessionist programme had been made public, the Government of Saxony felt alarmed at the danger which would threaten the so-called autonomy of the Federal States, if Prussia should happen to favour the application of the ideas adopted by the new party. It is said therefore that Saxony instructed her delegate[4] to the Bundesrath to sound his co-delegates as to the views of the other states.

---

[1] *Deutscher Reichsanzeiger und Königlich Preußischer Staatsanzeiger*, 6 April 1884. For the debate and resolution in the Federal Council, see pp. 33–34.

[2] Federal Council.

[3] *Deutsche Freisinnige Partei*; see n. 3 in Berlin section.

[4] Oswald von Nostitz-Wallwitz.

The King of Saxony who happened to be in Berlin when the secessionist-progressist-programme was published,[5] fearing that the idea of a responsible Imperial Ministry would menace the interests of the other states, at once broached the subject with Prince Bismarck, and finding the chancellor somewhat doubtful as to the course to be pursued, the King lost no time in instructing his delegate to treat the matter in conjunction with his colleagues in the Bundesrath.

The President of the Council of Wurtemburg [sic],[6] on the other hand, who likewise was in Berlin at that moment, felt the same apprehensions and resolved with the approval of the Governments of several of the Federal states, to bring forward a motion with the object of drawing from the Bundesrath a declaration that the establishment of an Imperial Ministry was contrary to the spirit of the Constitution – in as much as it rests exclusively on the principle of federation, and not on that of the fusion of the German people.

Unfortunately for the promoters of this scheme Bavaria did not deem it necessary to follow them in that direction.

The Government of this Country thought that it was giving too much importance to the aims of a purely parliamentary group, to bring forward such a motion in the Federal Council. The Bavarian Government would have liked to set it aside, but "having learnt that the Prussian Government saw no objection to accepting it, the Bavarian Government no longer hesitated to adhere to it". These are the terms used by the Bavarian Foreign Minister.[7]

At all events it was only after the step taken by the Bavarian Minister that the Berlin Cabinet was able to take the initiative in the proposal mentioned by the official Journal and of which doubtless Your Lordship has already been informed.

It would perhaps be unfair to conclude from this incident that the Bavarian Government will prove itself ready, if necessary, to abandon the Federal party in favor of the policy of unity. The incident simply affords one more proof of the state of subordination to the Imperial Chancery in which the Bavarian Government now finds itself – the special reasons for which I have already had the honor to lay before Your Lordship.

However, if I may venture to offer an opinion, I believe that Prussia would not have been sorry to keep her secret intentions in complete obscurity, but in presence of the determined attitude of Saxony, Baden and Wurtemburg and several of the other minor

---

[5] On 5 March 1884.
[6] Hermann von Mittnacht.
[7] Friedrich Krafft von Crailsheim. The statement is not datable.

states, the Prussian Government was forced to lead the way and assume to itself the credit of being the first to maintain the Constitutional principle of the autonomy of the Federal states.

FO 9/252: Hugh Guion MacDonell to Earl Granville, Confidential, No 26, Munich, 1 May 1884

[Received 7 May by messenger. For: The Queen / X, Ch.W.D. [Charles Wentworth Dilke] / Prince of Wales; G[ranville]]

King's absence from installation of Knights of St George due to financial discomfiture

The absence of the King from the ceremony of Installation of the Knights of St George[8] – which took place on the 25th ultimo – has again given rise to strange reports regarding the mental condition of His Majesty.

The fact of the King deputing his uncle, Prince Luitpold, to perform the duties of grand master on that occasion, was a direct violation of the statutes of the order.

His absence from the ceremony is said to have been due to His Majesty's financial embarrassments, which are daily increasing; but I have also been privately informed that the King declined to appear in public lest the discontent of the smaller tradesmen might induce them to seize that opportunity for making some sort of demonstration. This supposition I believe to be groundless for the Bavarians are, as I have already had occasion to remark, thoroughly devoted to their Sovereign, a fact amply shown by the indulgence they have hitherto given to his excentricities. His Majesty is, it appears, now determined that the subject of money shall not stand in the way of his whims and fancies; in consequence of which his ministers, it is sad to relate, think it right to deceive him as to the real state of things. They have even gone so far as to invent excuses for the stoppage of the works at his numerous country palaces, inducing him to believe that the stones requisite for the buildings are too heavy for transport by train. The only person admitted to His Majesty's presence is his personal attendant,[9] through whom he transacts all the business of the State. In spite of the mask of confidence – when his temper has been roused – he does not hesitate to descend to acts of violence against him.

[8] Royal Military Order of Saint George.
[9] MacDonell is referring to *Hofsekretär* Philipp Pfister; Ludwig's private secretary was Richard Hornig.

With regard to His Majesty's Debts, his Private Secretary has, it appears, found it impossible to procure the funds, necessary for meeting the Kings liabilities, either from the Frankfort Bankers or with the assistance of the Imperial Government at Berlin, – Prince Bismarck having peremptorily declined to countenance any transaction of the kind. The only course at present open to them, therefore, is either to form a Syndicate of Bankers here, or to accept the offer of a London firm (Messrs Baring & C°, I believe)[10]; but in both cases nothing can be done unless the consent of the "Agnates"[11] is absolutely guaranteed.

FO 9/252: Hugh Guion MacDonell to Earl Granville, No 33, Munich, 9 July 1884

[Received 16 July by messenger. For: The Queen / Lord Derby / Prince of Wales / X, Ch.W.D. [Charles Wentworth Dilke]; G[ranville]]

Allgemeine Zeitung *reports appreciative sympathy shown by British press towards imperial colonial policy*

Enclosed herewith I have the honor to transmit to Your Lordship the translation of an article which has recently appeared in the "Allgemeine Zeitung"[12] on the subject of the sympathy manifested by the English Press with the colonial policy of the Empire.

The persistent animosity formerly displayed by this Journal – when treating of matters connected with England – justifies, no doubt, the value which is here attached to the Article in question.

The "Allgemeine Zeitung" is the most important newspaper in South Germany and carries great weight especially with the middle and upper classes. Consequently it is to be hoped that the sound advice it now tenders, viz- that the Germans must henceforth moderate their ill-founded aversion for England, may be heeded and be the means of restoring friendly feeling which the "Allgemeine" itself has helped to disturb.

[10] In March 1884 the London merchant bank Baring Brothers & Co. offered a loan of six million marks.

[11] Otto, Ludwig's brother, and Luitpold, Ludwig's uncle.

[12] On 1 June 1884 *The Fortnightly Review* published an anti-Bismarckian and pro-French article entitled 'England's Foreign Policy', signed 'G'. The speculation over its authorship, which *The Times* attributed to Gladstone, led to general assessments and comments on foreign policy and Anglo-German relations in the British and German press. Enclosure: translation of article entitled 'Germany, England, and the "G" article in the Fortnightly Review' ('Deutschland, England und der G-Artikel der "Fortnightly Review"'), *Allgemeine Zeitung*, 6 July 1884.

FO 9/252: Hugh Guion MacDonell to Earl Granville, No 37, Munich, 4 August 1884

[Received 13 August by messenger. For: The Queen / X, Ch.W.D. [Charles Wentworth Dilke] / Copy to Paris / Prince of Wales; G[ranville]]

Kölnische Zeitung *echoes call in French press for re-establishment of friendly Franco-German relations; Bavarian public opinion remains anti-French*

The extraordinary articles which have lately appeared in the Paris "Figaro" would probably have passed unnoticed here had not the Kölnische Zeitung given undue importance to the idea, put forward by the French Journal, of the necessity of a friendly understanding if not an alliance, between Germany and France.[13]

I shall not examine how far the opinion of the "Figaro" may be taken as the faithful echo of the present tone of public feeling in France, nor to what degree the sentiments expressed by the Cologne Gazette represent the views of the (north) German people or of the Imperial Government, but, if I may venture to offer an opinion, I think that the majority of Bavarians look upon the idea of closer relations with the French Republic, at the present moment and under the present circumstances, as the fancy of a disordered mind.

The animosity professed by this part of the Empire towards France, certainly appears as keen as ever, and an understanding with the Republic would, to all appearances, be most unpopular; but, it is difficult to overlook the fact that the aversion at one time felt for Austria was perhaps stronger and more deep-rooted than the antipathy hitherto manifested towards France, – and yet no trace whatever of that illfeeling is now apparent.

I have already had the honor to state to Your Lordship that public opinion in Bavaria – especially as regards the foreign policy of the Empire – is almost exclusively governed by the Press, which in its turn seeks its inspirations at Berlin; consequently if, at any moment, it was deemed necessary to convert the Bavarians to a different way of thinking, I do not believe much difficulty would be experienced in convin[c]ing them that a cordial agreement with France is necessary for the interests and security of the Empire.

---

[13] MacDonell is referring to the articles in *Le Figaro* of 25 and 27 July 1884 entitled 'Anglais contre Français et Allemands' and 'Nos amis les Anglais, nos ennemis les Allemands' which proposed to make common cause with Germany against British predominance, and to an article in the *Kölnische Zeitung* of 29 July 1884.

FO 9/252: Hugh Guion MacDonell to Earl Granville, No 54, Munich, 19 November 1884

[Received 3 December by messenger. For: The Queen / X, Ch.W.D. [Charles Wentworth Dilke]; G[ranville]]

Reichstag *election results in Bavaria*

With reference to my Dispatch N° 45 Confidential of the 19th ultimo, I have the honour to inform Your Lordship that the result of the Bavarian Elections for the Imperial Parliament, which has only now been made public, leaves no doubt, as I had been led to anticipate, that the position of the Centre (clerical) party remains unchanged.[14]

The following table will perhaps show more clearly the changes which have taken place amongst the various parties since 1881.

	1881	1884	gain	loss
Catholics	32.	33.	1.	
National Liberals	9.	10.	1.	
Progressists	4.	2[.]		2.
Socialists	1.	2.	1.	
Democrats	1.	1.		
Conservatives	1.	0.		1.

The success of the Socialists in Bavaria, as in other states of the Empire, is an unquestionable fact; and has certainly caused a deep sense of uneasiness thro'out the Country – in Munich especially where of two electoral districts, hitherto represented by Catholics, the one has passed, by a small majority, to the hands of the Socialists, whilst the other has, with the aid of the latter, fallen to the lot of the Liberals[.]

Notwithstanding that the Socialists and the Liberals have loudly proclaimed their intention to act independently, no doubt seems now to be entertained that their double success was due to their joint action, if not to a compromise suggested, it is said, from Berlin; the latter supposition being based upon the support which the Socialist candidate[15] received from officers on half-pay and Government employés. – That the success of the Socialists was due to some such scheme is all the more evident from the fact that in Bavaria but especially in Munich, there only exists two distinct and

[14] Elections to the *Reichstag* were held on 28 October 1884.
[15] Georg von Vollmar.

important political parties, viz: the Catholics and Anti-Catholics, into which are blended – through a feeling of mutual hatred – the various groups of every political shade and colour.

The progress of the Socialists is all the more remarkable considering the legal disadvantages they have had to contend with.[16] It may therefore be fairly admitted that they owe their success to their own exertions and to the extraordinary activity displayed by their leaders, who have succeeded in gaining some 20,000 votes in the stronghold, so to speak, of Catholicism.

As to the Clericals, they have, relying on their former success, shown less activity, and have limited their efforts to proclaiming that they were ready to vote for any candidate, regardless of party, who was willing to oppose the May Laws.[17]

It is perhaps worth noting that the partisans of Prince Bismarcks' new economic ideas, i.e. the Protectionists, have likewise enlisted a fair number of supporters; this is perhaps due to the general feeling prevalent in Germany, as indeed in many other Countries, that native industry, more especially agriculture, is suffering from the effects of foreign competition.

FO 9/254: Hugh Guion MacDonell to Earl Granville, Confidential, No 15, Munich, 15 June 1885

[Received 17 June by Messenger. For: The Queen / Berlin for perusal; G.Dl. [George Dallas], 1 July; Prince of Wales / Duke of Cambridge; G[ranville]]

South German press denounce Bavarian support for Prussian motion to exclude Duke of Cumberland from Brunswick succession

The decision taken at Berlin, with reference to the Brunswick succession has necessarily been the subject of general comment in south Germany, but nowhere has it been so keenly resented as in Bavaria.[18] – The Conservative Journals have denounced it as an act of violence, whilst the liberal organs – ever ready to "contribute" to the consolidation of the Empire – have not, on this occasion,

---

[16] MacDonell is referring to the Anti-Socialist Law of October 1878 (see n. 10 in Dresden section).

[17] The Prussian May Laws of 1873–1875, amongst other things, transferred the training and appointment of clergy to state authority, reformed disciplinary authority over church members, regulated the civil aspects of disaffiliation and curtailed various ecclesiastical rights. See also n. 37 in this and n. 131 in Berlin section.

[18] At the time of the dispatch the Prussian motion on the question of the Brunswick succession (see n. 65 in Berlin section) had been referred to the judiciary committee (*Justitzausschuss*) of the Federal Council.

ventured to display their German patriotism to the prejudice of their Bavarian nationality.

Owing to the prominent and exceptional position held by Bavaria, she has – notwithstanding the manifest submission, of the King and of his Ministers, to the behests of the Chancellor – been hitherto looked upon, both by her own people and by the other Federal states, as the only member of the Confederation which could venture to take the lead in offering some sort of resistance to the encroachments which Prussia is steadily making on their autonomous rights. It is due to this circumstance that the eyes of South Germany have lately been turned towards Bavaria – in the hope that she would, at last, make a stand against the Imperial decision which so closely threatens her very existence as an independent state. The result, however, has only furnished a fresh proof of the pliability of this Government, and of the complete control which Prince Bismarck exercises over His Majesty and His Ministers.

One of the immediate consequences of the action of Bavaria, in the Brunswick question, is that some of the newspapers of this country are already discounting the effect which the new principle proclaimed at Berlin, must have in the succession in Coburg and in Wurtemburg. If so frivolous a pretext is admitted – they say – the Federal Council may now, if it pleases, declare that a Foreign Prince[19] in Coburg or a Protestant Prince[20] in Wurtemburg are incompatible with the peace of the Empire; and as regards Bavaria, should the Chancellor consider it necessary to maintain an insane King on the Bavarian throne or retain the aid of an imbecile and accommodating Government, he may, by the stroke of his pen, set aside the Wittelsbach Dynasty as dangerously ultramontane and force this country to pander indefinitely to the vices and follies of a demented Sovereign.

Furthermore – it is argued – the Federal Council, according to the constitution of the Empire, can only interfere between two states in cases of conflict which are not within the jurisdiction of an ordinary tribunal; – how can the Minister, therefore, of a Prince, who represents legitimacy itself, advise the dispossession of another Prince, equally legitimate, for state reasons.

One of the newspaper articles, to which I refer above, boldly calls the attention of its readers to the unconstitutional proceedings of the Prussian Government – "An Act", it says, "hitherto considered in all countries as the work of violence and revolution"; and adds "well may the Liberal press turn its attention to the effect it will produce when the succession in Wurtemburg and Coburg comes to be discussed. If the Federal states tacitly countenance the Prussian Veto, and thereby

[19] Alfred, Duke of Edinburgh. See pp. 148–149.
[20] The heir presumptive, Prince Wilhelm.

invest the leading state with the power to interfere in matters of hereditary succession, they do not deserve to be leniently dealt with – the acceptance of so dangerous a doctrine will inevitably make them a prey, sooner or later, to the all-absorbing power – Prussia."

Notwithstanding the urgent appeals of Saxony and Wurtemburg, the Bavarian Ministers decided to furnish their Representatives at the Bundesrath[21] with instruction,[22] so framed, as to meet the wishes of Prince Bismarck, without, if possible, wounding the susceptibilities of the Bavarians. To attain that object they have imagined that the easiest way was to abandon altogether the Duke of Cumberland, and to make no reference to the article of the Constitution[23] which the Imperial Chancellor invokes.

The following, therefore, is the form of declaration which the Bavarian Representatives have been instructed to propose: –

"The Confederate states declare that the taking of possession, by the Duke of Cumberland, of the Duchy of Brunswick is inadmissible, due to his being in a state of war with Prussia, one of the Federal states; and that in consequence of the existing Treaty which unites the said confederate States between them, it is recognised that a state of war between members of the union may imperil the territorial power of the individual states".

This form of declaration, if not suggested by Prince Bismarck, has already met with approval.

The declarations suggested by Saxony and Wurtemburg are, I believe, in the same sense – without however admitting that a state of war exists between Prussia and the Duke of Cumberland. This difference is of no importance since the form suggested by Bavaria may be considered as accepted.

FO 9/254: Hugh Guion MacDonell to Marquess of Salisbury, Confidential, No 22, Munich, 4 July 1885

[Received 6 July by post. For: The Queen / Earl of Iddesleigh / Berlin for perusal; G.Dl. [George Dallas]; Prince of Wales / Duke of Cambridge; S[alisbury]]

Bavaria's proposal to resolve Brunswick question accepted by Federal Council; state governments uneasy about future Federal Council intervention in other matters of succession

I endeavoured in my N[os] 15 and 20 Confidential of June 15th and 29th last, to describe the part taken by Bavaria in the Brunswick

---

[21] Federal Council.
[22] On 9 June 1885.
[23] Article 76 of the imperial constitution; see n. 66 in Berlin section.

Succession question.[24] The objection raised, by the Southern States of Germany to the Prussian proposal, was one of principle, but it was easy to foresee that Bavaria, on this as on former occasion, was ready to lend herself to any arrangement which the Chancellor thought fit to suggest, however detrimental it might prove to the interests of the other autonomous states. Obliged, therefore, to agree in dispossessing the Duke of Cumberland of the Throne of Brunswick, the Federal Governments, with Bavaria as their leader, endeavoured to seek safety in the form – rather than in the substance – of an act which threatens their own existence. The Bavarian amendment to the Prussian proposal having found favor with the Chancellor, Bavaria is necessarily reproached with having deserted the Federal camp – but it is doubtful whether any of the other states, in her position, would have ventured to act differently.

The difficulty experienced by the Federal Governments in uniting to resist the encroachments of Prussia on their privileges, no doubt proceeds from the very embarrassing part which this Government is called upon to play. The ministers are not allowed to perform a single act or affix a single signature without the sanction of the King, who lives in absolute seclusion and with whom they can only treat through the medium of his private Secretary or his favorite valet;[25] being in a minority in the chamber they are invariably defeated and if any serious question has to be negotiated with the Imperial Government they generally discover at the last moment that it has been settled by His Majesty privately and directly with Prince Bismarck. In most cases therefore the President of the council[26] is only guided by what he may hear from Berlin or by the indiscretions of the King's Private Secretary. It may fairly be said therefore that it was due to this state of things that notwithstanding the gravity of the question the Bavarian Ministers did not deem it prudent on this occasion to abandon their usual reserve, by acting in concert with or advising the other states to adopt a more resolute course. – From the first, therefore, Bavaria openly avoided her intention to reject as far as possible the interpretation set by Prussia on Art. 76 of the Imperial constitution,[27] but, at the same time to arrive at a direct understanding, subject to the approval of the Chancellor,

---

[24] For Bavaria's conduct in this matter, see the preceding dispatch. For the Brunswick succession question and the Federal Council's resolution of 2 July 1885, see also n. 65 in Prussia.

[25] Philipp Pfister and Richard Hornig.

[26] Johann von Lutz.

[27] For Article 76 of the imperial constitution, see n. 66 in Berlin section.

as to the form in which the Federal Council was to set aside the claim of the Duke of Cumberland. The difficulty of the task was to find a formula applicable to the case of the Duke which would at the same time leave the principle of legitimacy unscathed.

The Governments of Stuttgardt and of Saxony, having been kept ignorant of the progress of the negotiations between Prussia and Bavaria, agreed to draw up separate counter-proposals.[28]

The Saxon Government was of opinion that Art[.] 76 of the Constitution invoked by Prussia only aims at an existing conflict between two states, consequently the Federal Council is not competent to decide as to the merits of a conflict in anticipation, though, by the spirit of the Constitution it has the right to prevent the breaking out of such a conflict. As the Empire rests on a Federation of German Princes, which Federation was constituted by the Federal Princes themselves for the protection of their respective States; in joining the confederation they recognised and reciprocally guaranteed the integrity of their respective territories. It is difficult therefore, according to the views of the Saxon Government, to admit to the Government of one of the states of the Empire, a Prince who has not unreservedly accepted the act of recognition or of guarantee. The Duke of Cumberland has, it is true, declared his readiness to govern Brunswick according to the Constitution, but he also maintains his claim to the Kingdom of Hanover. So long as this contradiction exists in the Duke's declarations[29] the Saxon Government was of opinion that He could not be placed in possession of the Duchy.

In framing the above, which I am told was the purport of the counter proposal prepared by Saxony with the approval of Wurtemburg, the two Governments entertained, it is said, the hope of bringing the Duke to declare his intention with regard to Hanover; but either it has been ascertained that the Duke is bound by certain engagements not to abandon his claim to that Kingdom, or the two Governments hesitate to assume an independent attitude, the fact is that they have since adhered to the Bavarian proposal.

It is interesting to follow the many opinions expressed in South Germany with regard to this question – though everyone seems to agree that the Chancellor has gladly availed himself of the

---

[28] On 4 and 5 June the Saxon and Württemberg representatives to the Federal Council communicated their position with regard to the original Prussian proposal of 18 May; however, they did not file counterproposals.

[29] See pp. 56–57.

opportunity with a double object; – first, with a view to securing the power of dealing with those Dynasties which he deems objectionable; and secondly with a view to retaining the funds belonging to the late King of Hanover, which sum it is whispered is destined to ransom one or more of the Federal states.[30]

In any case Prince Bismarck has on this occasion obtained a further proof that even in matters of sovereignty, the Federal states are no longer in a position to uphold their autonomous Rights.

At an interview I had yesterday with the Minister for Foreign Affairs, His Excellency informed me that the Bavarian proposal had definitely been accepted by the Federal Council.[31] He assured me, however, that as it aims at preserving intact the principle of legitimacy, and was simply framed with a view to excluding the Duke of Cumberland from Brunswick, no fear need be entertained that this decision can ever, hereafter, be invoked as a precedent. I took the liberty of pointing out to His Excellency that according to his own sta[te]ment, he had a few days before quoted the opinion of Prince Bismarck as regards the value of the word "precedent" – "a word", which His Excellency had represented the Prince as having said, "did not exist in the political Dictionary"[.] Whatever Bavaria may think of the declaration, His Excellency could not deny that the Federal states had now recognised the competency of the Federal Council to interfere in questions of legitimate Succession in the various states of the Empire; and on the same grounds that the Duke of Cumberland is said to have forfeited his right to Brunswick, the son[32] may be likewise find himself some day dispossessed of that throne. Though His Excellency would not admit the force of this argument the Saxon and Wurtemburg Ministers[33] here are of opinion that he fully realises the error which has been committed.

I may here observe that this is the first occasion upon which the Chancellor is supposed to have given way to one of the Federal states by withdrawing his proposal.

[30] The 'Guelph fund' consisted of the confiscated assets of King Georg V of Hanover. It was administered by a Prussian commission. See also n. 67 in Dresden section.

[31] Friedrich Krafft Freiherr von Crailsheim was referring to the modified proposal adopted by the judiciary committee on 1 July 1885 and passed by the Federal Council the following day.

[32] Prince Georg Wilhelm.

[33] Oswald Freiherr von Fabrice and Oskar Freiherr von Soden.

FO 9/254: Hugh Guion MacDonell to Marquess of Salisbury, No 26, Munich, 14 July 1885

[Received 21 July by Mr MacDonell. For: The Queen; S[alisbury]]

Circular of Vicariate of Paderborn on required qualifications for those wishing to enter ecclesiastical profession; criticism from liberal and Catholic parties

A German Newspaper[34] has lately published a circular which the Vicariate General of Paderborn has confidentially addressed to the "curés" of that Diocese,[35] requesting them to inform all those who destine themselves to the Ecclesiastical profession that they must, before entering a seminary, follow the University classes of Theology, Philosophy and History and obtain a so-called, certificate of assiduity. This Circular said to be dated the 27th of February last was made public at about the same time as Archbishop Melchers was called to Rome and replaced, in the see of Cologne, by Monsignor Cremens[36] – a prelate, known to be well thought of by the Imperial Chancellor.

The spirit of the Circular in question, and that which prompted the selection of the new Archbishop for Cologne, has led public opinion to conclude that the Holy See was by these means seeking to conciliate the Imperial Government and thus give tangible proof of the earnestness of its intentions.

The Liberal Journals at once seized the opportunity to proclaim the defeat of the clericals; whilst the Catholic journals, almost without exception observed the most marked silence as to the cause and origin of the circular. Whether due to the painful impression created amongst the Roman Catholics, or due to such remonstrances as may have been addressed to it from Rome, the Vicariate General deemed it prudent to address a note to the papers, on the 1st instant, stating that the Confidential Circular in question, was simply intended to guide theological Students in the most practical way of pursuing their vocation; by so doing no recognition of the prescriptions contained in the May Law was ever intended, on the contrary the true spirit of the Circular was in opposition to those Laws.[37] Their

---

[34] *Kölnische Volkszeitung*, 24 June 1885.

[35] The directive was addressed to the deans (*Landdechanten*) of the Paderborn diocese; it was dated 17 February 1885.

[36] Philipp Krementz. News of his succession as Archbishop of Cologne circulated from early April 1885 and he was officially appointed on 30 July 1885. Melchers, having been dismissed by verdict of the Prussian Royal Court for Church Affairs for violating the May Laws, had been in exile in the Netherlands since 1876. He arrived in Rome on 13 July 1885 and was created cardinal on 27 July.

[37] Amongst other things, the Prussian law of 11 May 1873 introduced state supervision for the training of clergy. These provisions were attenuated by the law of 31 May 1882

only object was to relieve the seminaries of the expense of maintaining the younger Clergy. Consequently the Vicariate considers that it has conscientiously observed the respect due to the Laws of the Church and maintained intact its devotion to the Holy See and its ties with the Roman Catholic Episcopate.

This declaration has, of course, been severely criticized by the organs of both parties. The Catholics thought it constituted a withdrawal of the ill-imagined circular; whilst the liberals accepted it as an explanation, the object of which was to cover the differences which exist between the Bishop[38] and the more intolerant of his co-religionists. Alarmed however, at the discussion of one of the points upon which the Catholics rest their objections to the May Laws, the ultramontane organs now demand a clear and unequivocal withdrawal of the Confidential Circular of the 27th of February. As yet, no such document has appeared and it remains to be seen whether the Bishop of Paderborn will, by so bold a proceeding, succeed in conciliating the German Catholics to the objectionable Laws of May, or whether Germany is to witness a renewal of the "Kulturkampf"[.]

Whatever may result from this incident, it is now clear enough that the Holy See can no longer charge the Prussian Government with interfering in the education of the Clergy, by means of those special prescriptions which the May Laws provide, since one of its most prominent Bishops can cast a doubt on what has hitherto been considered as an essential principle of the Roman Catholic Doctrine, and with regard to which the Pope[39] has repeatedly proclaimed he could make no concession.

FO 9/257: Victor Drummond to Marquess of Salisbury, Treaty, Confidential, No 3, Munich, 28 January 1886

[Received 15 February. For: The Queen / Prince of Wales ('abroad – not sent') / Gladstone / Western Department: 'This ought not to have been marked in the Treaty section', J.H.G.B. [John Henry Gibbs Bergne]; 'Tell him so', J.P. [Julian Pauncefote]; Berlin for perusal; R[osebery]]

Rumours of a regency in Bavaria; ministerial representations to the king concerning his financial situation

Various rumors respecting the extravagance of His Majesty The King of Bavaria have lately appeared in the Continental Press and

---

which, granted exemption from the compulsory state exams for non-theological subjects (*Kulturexamen*). This was reflected in the Paderborn circular. For the Prussian May Laws of 1873–1875, see also n. 17 in this section and n. 131 in Berlin section.

[38] Franz Kaspar Drobe; Bishop of Paderborn.

[39] Leo XIII.

hints are therein given that if this continues it may lead to a Regency being appointed in the person of Prince Luitpold the King's uncle and Heir presumptive to the Crown; further, that the Bavarian Executive have considered it their duty to make certain representations to the King with the intention that His Majesty should allow His monetary affairs to be put in order, this it is said would probably lead to a Ministerial crisis causing the present Ministers to be replaced by others belonging to the Ultramontane party under the leaderships of Baron Frankenstein a well known leader of the Center[40] in the Reichstag and in the Chambers.

These reports are certainly founded on fact, and as far as I learn from my Colleagues and others I am led to believe at the present moment events may be preparing which may later prove of serious importance to the Royal Family of Wittelsbach.

The King's extravagance, caused by His craze for building Castles and His complete retirement, becomes more and more a source of uneasiness not only to His Ministers but to the Royal Family of Bavaria who three years ago assisted His Majesty to procure a Loan of eight millions of marks or four hundred thousand pounds, and who are no longer inclined to make themselves responsible as security for any fresh loans. The Ministers cannot advance money from the Treasury, neither dare they bring forward a measure in the Chambers to tax the people for the King's Debts or to raise a Loan.

I have asked Baron von Crailsheim as to the truth of the report that the Ministry had remonstrated with The King as stated in the Press; His Excellency replied that they had considered it necessary to forward a statement to His Majesty[41] concerning the state of the Civil List and Finances of the Country and that some advice had been offered for their reputation in the future; He added, "of course I cannot say whether The King will accept the advice or even make any reply thereto neither is it necessary that He should do so; what had been carried out could only be viewed as placing before His Majesty a sketch of the state of the Finances of the Country in regard to the interests of The King".

It is to be remarked that the sensational news respecting King Louis is always originated at Frankfort or in Paris, possibly under Ultramontane influence, by the adherents of Prince Luitpold or Prince Ludwig who are known to be closely attached to that Party, (although they may have no knowledge of the intrigue) a party

---

[40] *Zentrumspartei.*

[41] Crailsheim was referring to the memorandum of 6 January, addressed to the court secretary and *Vorstand* of the *Hof- und Cabinettskasse*, Ludwig von Klug.

which, luckily, has never been able to gain any influence over The King, and which would therefore be glad for their own purposes to see a Regency established.

It is also significant that the Vienna "Fremdenblatt",[42] which is in the habit of receiving inspirations from the Imperial Foreign Office, has lately published a letter from Rome, saying that Pope Leo XIII has repeatedly expressed his entire satisfaction and gratitude for the present liberty and protection granted to the Church in Bavaria, this the "Vienna Neue Freie Presse"[43] considers is put forward to clear the Bavarian Ultramontanes from the suspicion that if the reins of Government should pass into their hands they would try to unsettle the relations of Bavaria to the German Empire and adds that if this interpretation is correct it is evident that the party wish to prove their ability of taking the power into their hands at the right time.

The respectable "Bavarian Press" is very shy of writing upon the vagaries of The King and the Vulgar Press is afraid of the Procureur Général[44] and is thus kept in order, but so much prominence has lately been given to the matter that The Munich Press has at last been led to make some remarks.

The "Neuesten Nachrichten"[45] a Liberal Paper says with reference to what is stated to have occurred.

"We are not in a position to control the accuracy of the statements made, but according to our own information it is not only possible but probable that a remonstrance in some such form has taken place"; whilst the "Fremdenblatt"[46] an Ultramontane Paper says: "if this is so it is the newest bit of Paulprying into the private affairs of His Majesty to which the Foreign papers kindly treat us – Should the Ministry, however, have ventured to take such a step we may depend upon hearing of the nomination of other Ministers within a short time".

I am informed, however, that although The King may be irritated on account of His Ministers' representations He is not in the least likely to change them and they certainly have no intention of resigning their posts.

Another report lately presented to the Public was that King Louis had gone to Paris to Baron Hirsch with the object of obtaining a Loan, there is not a word of truth in this, His Majesty is residing in one or other of His Castles in the Tyrol.

---

[42] On 15 January 1886.

[43] On 21 January 1886.

[44] French: 'attorney general'.

[45] *Münchner Neueste Nachrichten*, 11 January 1886; it was referring to a report in the *Frankfurter Zeitung*.

[46] 'Nichts als Gerüchte', *Münchner Fremdenblatt*, 16 January 1887.

The results which are likely to follow from the steps taken by The Bavarian Government in respect to His Majesty are not yet clear enough for me to report upon to Your Lordship, but I shall probably in a few days again refer to the critical state of the King's position.

FO 9/256: Victor Drummond to Earl of Rosebery, Confidential, No 10, Munich, 25 May 1886

[Received 2 June by Mr Vickers. For: The Queen / Prince of Wales / Gladstone / Confidential to Berlin for perusal, No 322; R[osebery], 3 June]

Remarks on king's finances and ministerial actions; Bismarck's private address to king; possible regency

With reference to my previous Despatches on the King of Bavaria's extravagance and the difficulty of the Government to find means of obtaining an assurance from His Majesty that He will curtail His expenses in building, I have the honour to inform Your Lordship that the Press now generally pronounce on the question; the Ultramontane portion blame the present Bavarian Ministry for not having taken measures, sooner, to impress on The King the absolute necessity to live within His means; but the Liberal Press deny this, and show that as early as 1877 the King's attention was drawn to the matter by His Secretary[47] and strongly supported by the King's Ministers, and again two years ago the Minister of Finance[48] presented a statement to the King showing how it was possible for him to arrange with his Creditors, but no attention has ever been paid to these humble remarks, made with a desire of preventing such a crisis as is now presented to the public.

The King's father, King Maximilian, had not such a large allowance as King Ludwig has, nevertheless, He managed not only to give an allowance to His Father,[49] but also built many useful state Buildings (even if not of great architectural beauty) and at his death left several millions of marks. The present King if He would, could also, after a few years find himself in an equally favorable position; His Ministers, however, are evidently of opinion that the chance is small, for a short-time ago they arranged to meet in Conference[50] the leading Members of Parliament, Ultramontane, Liberal and Conservative, they sought together in confidence a means of solving the problem, but after more than one sitting the Conference broke

---

[47] Lorenz von Düfflipp.
[48] Emil von Riedel.
[49] Ludwig I.
[50] The meeting took place on 30 April 1886.

up with no result. One thing, however, was proved that no one was inclined to have recourse to a Vote of the Chambers to pay the King's Debts and it was shown that the Opposition, if the occasion offers, is not inclined to accept office until the King consents to allow himself to be governed by the advice of His Ministers.

Since the Conference last month a very humble address[51] has been again transmitted to His Majesty signed by each one of His Ministers showing how His Majesty's most importunate creditors may be satisfied and how easily His Debts may be paid by the Privy Purse without having recourse to a Loan, by, I am told, deducting yearly an eighth part; again an appeal was made to The King to curtail his building expenses.

This address has been treated in the same manner as that sent to His Majesty last January,[52] namely, by taking no notice of it.

It appears that Prince Bismarck has also addressed The King privately,[53] and that His Majesty has taken means to show his discontent with the remarks made in the Letters which the Chancellor of The Empire wrote to Him, and now Count Lerchenfeld, Bavarian Minister at the Court of Berlin, who arrived in Munich a few days ago,[54] has, it is said, been summoned here conveying a confidential communication from Prince Bismarck to the Bavarian Government, which it is hoped may assist them in finding a means to terminate the present state of affairs.[55]

I learn that nothing will be done until after the closing of the Chambers, which will probably happen this week. We may then expect serious events, if, as I am informed, the Government will insist on a reply to the two Messages sent by them to His Majesty, and it is possible that in case His Majesty does not submit to their conditions, the Chambers will be convoked and the whole matter brought before the Representatives of the Bavarian people; abdication is then possible and a Regency under Prince Luitpold. From the cursory remarks made to me by my German Colleague[56] I imagine such a result would not be disagreable [*sic*] to Prince Bismarck, who very likely

---

[51] Report of the ministry (*Gesamtstaatsministerium*) to Ludwig, 5 May 1886.

[52] See n. 41 in this section.

[53] In a letter dated 14 April 1886, Bismarck advised Ludwig to request that the ministry should apply for the necessary sums in the Bavarian *Landtag*. In a further letter of 19 May, after the ministry's refusal, Bismarck advised Ludwig, once again, to cut his spending drastically.

[54] At the time of the dispatch Lerchenfeld was not in Munich.

[55] Drummond is referring to Lerchenfeld's conversations with Bismarck at Friedrichsruh on 23 and 24 May 1886. The report to Crailsheim mentioned in the dispatch, dated 24 May, was received on 26 May.

[56] Drummond is referring to the Prussian envoy, Georg von Werthern.

believes that if this scandal continues, the little surface cloud of social-ism in Bavaria may by its' use grow larger. There is no doubt, harm in this sense has already been done, as the people, who formerly never paid any attention to the matter, make it now a perpetual sub-ject of discussion and stories respecting the King's eccentricities true and untrue are bandied about.

The hearing of the demands on the King's Privy Purse before the Courts in this capital has been postponed until next month.

FO 9/256: Victor Drummond to Earl of Rosebery, No 16, Munich, 12 June 1886

[Received 16 June by post. For: The Queen / Prince of Wales / Gladstone; R[osebery]]

King of Bavaria resigns himself to medical care; medical problems declared incurable

I have the honour to inform Your Lordship that His Majesty the King of Bavaria, has submitted Himself to the care of the Doctors[57] appointed by the Government to take charge of His Majesty, who arrived this morning at Schloss Berg, from Hohenschwangau.[58] Schloss Berg is a small Castle, very prettily situated on Starnberg Lake, with about one hundred acres of wooded Park, and one hour from Munich.

Many people it appears waited on the road to greet His Majesty on His departure from Hohenschwangau.

It is said that He thanked them in a few touching words.

I regret to state, however, that it is reported that Experts declare His Majesty's malady incurable, and He is now it is stated watched by four ordinary Keepers, under a head Keeper.[59] Two of these,[60] have already been in personal attendance on His Royal Highness, Prince Otto of Bavaria.

It is, I assure Your Lordship a very sad duty to me, to be obliged to report what has happened, for not only do I feel that the King of Bavaria's subjects have (even if only for a time) lost, by the will of God, one who they respected and were devoted to, but I am con-vinced that if His Majesty's mind had not been affected, He, from His extraordinary intelligence, His liberal views, and enlightened

---

[57] Bernhard von Gudden and Franz Carl Müller.

[58] On 9 June 1886, on the basis of a psychiatric report of 8 June, Ludwig was declared insane and placed under tutelage. On 11 June, after he was informed of the ministerial decision to appoint Luitpold as Prince Regent, Ludwig was placed in custody.

[59] *Oberpfleger* (head nurse) Barth.

[60] Nurses Braun and Mauder; the two other nurses were called Hack und Schneller.

ideas, would have been one of the most popular Monarchs of Modern times. All my Colleagues, who have had the honour of conversing with His Majesty, tell me that He is so well informed and entertaining, that however long their audience had lasted, they always left His Majesty's presence, feeling that it had been one of pleasure; only, too abreviated [*sic*].

The story I have reported is made still sadder, by Her Majesty the Queen Mother's illness,[61] since the occurrence has been broken to Her.

Baron de Malsen, was commissioned by the Government to fulfill this sorrowful duty. Her Majesty has lived to see both her sons under restraint.

For such a calamity Her Majesty will assuredly receive the sympathy of all classes, especially those who have the honour to know Her and appreciate Her beautiful qualities.

The Bavarians are a most loyal, and devoted people to their Sovereign, and their Princes, and they certainly will not refuse themselves this opportunity of showing their commiseration for Their Majesties, for whom they entertain so much reverence.

FO 9/256: Victor Drummond to Earl of Rosebery, No 18, Munich, 14 June 1886

[Received 16 June by post. For: The Queen / Prince of Wales / Gladstone / Treaty Department; Her Majesty's condolences have been telegraphed to Mr Drummond together with the sympathies of Her Majesty's Government; R[osebery]]

King of Bavaria and Dr Gudden found drowned in Lake Starnberg

I have been staying these last few day, in a Country Inn, on Lake Starnberg, one hour from Munich, the Inn is only twenty minutes from the Schloss Berg, where the King of Bavaria has been, since he left Hohenschwangau, as I have already reported to Your Lordship in my Despatch N° 16 of the 12th Instant.

Yesterday, a friend of mine who had come to pass the day with me, walked over to the Schloss, to enquire in what state the King was, after His journey. He saw there, D' Gudden and Baron Washington, in attendance on His Majesty. They both said that His Majesty had passed a good night, and was as well as could be expected under the circumstances, they added that His Majesty

---

[61] Marie.

had no intention of going to Munich this week, as had been gossiped. At seven this morning, as I was about to go to Munich my servant rushed in, and told me that he had just heard, that His Majesty had last evening committed suicide. On enquiring I could only find, that this was a rumour, I sent my servant off in a boat, with a note to Baron Washington, in attendance on the King, requesting him to be good enough to inform me what truth there was in the report, and in case it was correct, I begged to express my sincere sympathy, with those who were in attendance with His Majesty.

In an hour after, I received a letter (copy herewith inclosed)[62] in reply to mine, from Count Töerring, verifying the rumor.

Your Lordship will see that it is not only a suicide, but a tragedy, for it appears that a tremendous struggle, must have taken place between the King and poor Dr Gudden, whom His Majesty must have dragged into the Lake with Him.

I have just learned that some time after the King and Doctor Gudden had gone out, their absence being prolonged, search was made for them, and not finding any trace of them in the Park, a Gendarme was despatched to this Inn, (which is just outside the Park) to enquire of the Proprietor, if by chance, the King had come here, the Gendarme ascertaining that there was no news of Him here, returned, and the alarm was raised, and search made in the Lake, where the Bodies were discovered.

I cannot give any further details at present, but it seems extraordinary, that no precautions were taken by Doctor Gudden, for he must have known how violent the King had been at times, and it is curious that he should have suspected nothing, in the King's expressing a wish to take a walk in the Park, at that time of night, in a pouring rain.

Curious also, that whereas in the daytime Gendarmes were all round the grounds, that at night, there was not one within hailing distance.

I feel sure that popular feeling will declare itself in a very pronounced manner against the Ministry, and I must say, I think, with some reason, for their manner of proceeding has not been one which could possibly find favour with the late King's subjects, who consider that His treatment was very harshly carried out.[63]

---

[62] Enclosure: copy of letter (in French) from Count Toerring to MacDonell, Berg, 11 June 1886.

[63] For Ludwig's deposition, see n. 58 in this section.

FO 9/256: Victor Drummond to Earl of Rosebery, No 40, Munich, 26 July 1886

[Received 29 July by post. For: The Queen / Prince of Wales; R[osebery], 30 July]

Ultramontane dissatisfaction at prince regent's decision to retain liberal ministry

Although it is well known that the Ultramontane party in Bavaria has for years shown its' animosity towards the Liberal Government under Baron de Lutz, on account of the leanings of the Government towards old Catholicism[64] and remaining so long in office in spite of the repeated majorities against them in the Chambers, yet, they have now surpassed themselves in giving vent to their animus; they thought that long suffering would bring its' reward sooner or later, and on the death of King Louis II, knowing that the Government would be then obliged to place their resignation in the hands of The Prince Regent they fully believed that Baron de Lutz would disappear and Baron de Franckenstein the leader of the opposition and the Ultramontane party take his place; they were the more convinced that this would happen as they believed that The Prince Regent of Bavaria was as bigoted as themselves and that He would be glad to rid Himself of a Government who had no sympathy with the extreme Catholics.

In this they have been sadly deceived, as I made Your Lordship aware of in my Despatch N° 37 of the 7th instant,[65] The Prince Regent not only refused to accept the resignation of the Lutz administration, but eulogized their services to the Country and stated that the Highest Church Dignitaries had frequently expressed satisfaction as to the condition of the Roman Catholic Church in Bavaria.[66]

These clear expressive words of His Royal Highness have exasperated the Ultramontane Party and their Newspapers evidently feel sorely the thrust, for every day they show their indignation and rage at The Prince Regent's praise bestowed on The Lutz Ministry, they even throw doubt on the truth of the statement He made that any expressions favorable to the Ministry had been used by either The Pope[67] or His Bishops. They have even threatened

---

[64] The Old Catholic Church came into existence in 1871 in opposition to the First Vatican Council (1869–1870), and especially the dogma of papal infallibility. Despite political support by government officials it was not formally recognized.

[65] Drummond is referring to his No 36 of 7 July 1886.

[66] Luitpold rejected the Bavarian ministry's resignation of 5 July in his own letter the following day.

[67] Leo XIII.

The Prince Regent, that, unless He takes care [of] the Bavarian Roman Catholic subjects of The King will distrust Him and that this will be made apparent at the Elections which take place next year, that the veil will then be lifted and it will be shown who has the majority in the Country.

The Ultramontane cry is assured. "Down with Lutz".

The liberal party will, however, try to weaken their adversaries by using and endeavoring to prove the Prince Regent's words respecting the satisfaction of the Church Dignities with the conditions of their Church in Bavaria, and they will trust to the loyalty and devotion of the People to Their King and the Prince Regent to stultify the present cry of hatred against the Government.

The present Press War against the Ministry it is believed has its' initiative in Munich, its' object is now to raise a determined struggle for mastery at the Elections[68] in the hopes of securing the majority and thus forcing the Prince Regent to call upon some one of their party to form a Ministry; in this again I believe they will be deceived, for the majority of the Bavarian people, as far as I can learn, are favorable to a liberal Government which has kept the finances of Bavaria in a sound condition without a deficit and is tolerant to all confessions of faith, neither do the People desire to see a religious question sprung upon them.

The Prince Regent who has retained the services of the Lutz Ministry is what He has declared Himself to be,[69] a good Catholic and Patriot, with a desire to use all His efforts to strengthen the Bond of Union and friendship between Bavaria and Germany, to do all He can for the advancement and prosperity of His Country as concerns its' domestic and commercial interests and to use His authority to secure peace in the different religious denominations.

On account of the great popularity His Royal Highness enjoys in the hearts of the people and the army I think we shall see a change in the present Ultramontane tirades, which are only doing harm to their own cause, and as the Bishops in Bavaria show no signs of moving in the angry wave of party, the Electors will probably not pay any more attention to the matter.

---

[68] Elections for the second chamber of the Bavarian *Landtag* were held in July 1887.

[69] Drummond is probably referring to Luitpold's letter to the ministry of 6 July 1886.

FO 9/256: Victor Drummond to Earl of Iddesleigh, Very Confidential, No 56, Munich, 20 December 1886

[Received 24 December by Messenger Lumley. For: The Queen / Lord Salisbury; I [ddesleigh]]

Austrian army not ready for war with Russia; Crailsheim hopes England would ally with Germany in such a war

I have the honour to inform Your Lordship that I hear from a good source that Prince Bismarck and the Military Authorities in Berlin have every reason to believe that the Austrian army is not at present in a position to fight Russia single handed, [note in margin: 'See Sir E. Malet's N° 455 Confidential confirming this statement']⁷⁰ in fact that she is not prepared for a great war, neither is the opinion formed of the intelligence of Austrian Superior officers of such a nature as to give Germany much confidence in her Ally.

These facts may partially account for the determination shown by Germany not to offend Russia and for the German Official Press again trying to throw dust in the eyes of the Public, by declaring that Germany has no fault to find with Russia, that there is no reason that the two Countries should not continue to be good friends.

This time, however, the veil is too thin after the remarks in the Reichstag made by Field Marshal von Moltke and Baron de Bronsart.⁷¹ Is it not rather to give time to Austria to put on her armour?

In a conversation I lately had with Baron de Crailsheim, on the present state of affairs, knowing he must be aware of what part Germany would take in a War between Russia and Austria, I remarked that it was hardly possible Germany would leave Austria in the field alone, he replied, oh Germany has nothing to do with Bulgaria,⁷² and she would in that question let Austria fight her own battles, but I said, supposing Austria was defeated, in such a case, His Excellency said, and if Russian troops were on Austrian Territory then Germany would certainly interfere she will never allow the Russians to subdue Austria. This, as the Bavarian Government's policy is that of Prince Bismarck[,] I imagine to be the real truth.

Bavarians hope that in the next war England will be fighting on the side of Germany, fancying that we shall be fighting Russia, whilst they are fighting France, and that in such a case an Alliance between Russia and France would ensue and bring about an Alliance between

---

⁷⁰ See pp. 70–73.

⁷¹ Drummond is referring to the speeches of 3 December (Bronsart von Schellendorff) and 4 December 1886 (Moltke) on the occasion of the first reading of the army bill (see n. 119 in Berlin section).

⁷² For the Bulgarian Question, see pp. 70–73 and 75–77.

England and Germany, but man is born to be deceived and the hidden mysteries of Prince Bismarck are still undeveloped.

FO 9/256: Victor Drummond to Earl of Iddesleigh, No 57, Munich, 21 December 1886

[Received 24 December by messenger: For: The Queen / Lord Salisbury; Seen by Lord Iddesleigh]

Münchner Neueste Nachrichten disappointed in German government's harsh words on British Bulgarian policy

Little did I think when writing yesterday my Despatch N° 56 very confidential, that my last words therein would be verified so speedily, but the article which has appeared in the "Nord [*sic*] Allgemeine Zeitung"[73] has quite astonished everyone who has read it.

This Evenings "Neueste Nachrichten" which is the semi official paper says: it is an enigma which has yet to be unravelled, it cannot understand how at the moment – that England is showing great energy in the Bulgarian question[74] as regards Russia that Germany should choose that very moment to say hard words respecting her policy. This is sufficient for the moment to show that the feeling in this quarter is one of surprise and disappointment. The words of "Neuestes [*sic*] Nachrichten" are to the point. "und gerade in diesem momente die absage Deutschlands an England"! or "and just at this moment to throw over England"!

FO 9/258: Victor Drummond to Earl of Iddesleigh, No 5, Munich, 4 January 1887

[Received 17 January by messenger. For: The Queen / Prince of Wales / Mr Smith / Mr Goschen / Mr Stanhope / Lord G. Hamilton / ~~Intelligence Dept~~, H.B. [Henry Brackenbury]; Copy to Paris and then to Berlin for perusal, 19 January; Qy: Tell Mr Drummond to send despatches on similar subjects under Flying Seal through Paris; 'done privately', 19 January; S[alisbury]]

Bavarian public opinion believes war with France to be imminent

Although this week there are more hopeful signs of Peace being maintained this year,[75] as given to the Public by the Press,

---

[73] *Norddeutsche Allgemeine Zeitung*, 20 December 1886. The article stressed the need for understanding between the German and Russian governments with regard to the Bulgarian Question – in which German interests 'are not at stake' – and that the 'continued concord' between the three imperial powers was 'inconvenient from an English point of view'.

[74] See pp. 70–73 and 75–77.

[75] Drummond is referring to the assurances of peace given at two New Year's receptions in Paris by the French president, Jules Grévy, and the French prime minister, René Goblet.

nevertheless, doubts are still expressed by the community in general in this capital whether the spring will pass without a conflict between Germany and France; a friend of mine who was formerly in the German Diplomatick services and who is well informed on German Political matters is of opinion that war is certain next spring; in the Military element their conversation shows that they expect to fight the French shortly. Certainly everything that foresight can justify is being carried out to be ready for the day War is declared.

I find that the general opinion in Bavaria is that war cannot be postponed much longer, the Imperial taxes are so high and weigh so heavily on the people that any further imposts would become unbearable, in proof of this I may mention that a Gentleman employed in Trade tells me that in 1870 he paid one hundred marks on his business, that now for exactly the same, he pays seven hundred marks; the Tradespeople are at present living in a state of uncertainty and are loth to give orders; respectable people do not purchase more than they find absolutely necessary; the general feeling therefore is, how long is this to last? rather than continue in this state of suspense and with the impression that to postpone War is to play into the hands of our enemies affording them time to become stronger than we are, is it worth while hesitating longer when we are at the present moment more powerful than our opponents? of course Bavaria is only a portion of the German Empire but if the same reasoning is developed throughout Germany, then I surmise that War is probable in the Spring, in which case, I am told, there is a possibility of the German army advancing before the declaration of War reaches France, that the artillery in force will be the first to attack, for until two or three of the frontier forts are taken, it will be a difficult undertaking to push in between them, the Germans are confident of blowing up these forts with ammunition which they have had for some time, and of such a character, that, as my informant said, "not a man will come out alive from the forts", what the secret is of the explosive matter, the nature of the gun or the shell I am unable to find out and I expect very few officers in the German army know!

I am informed also that in case of War Germany will be able to produce two million five hundred thousand men, including all forces; this is, if true, a considerable higher figure than given in the official German estimates.

FO 9/258: Victor Drummond to Marquess of Salisbury, Confidential, No 15, Munich, 8 February 1887

[Received 16 February by messenger. For: The Queen / Rome for perusal, 25 February / Berlin for perusal, 1 March; J.P. [Julian Pauncefote]]

Press publish letter from Leo XIII to papal nuncio at Munich respecting political actions of the Centre Party; tension amongst Catholic factions over whether to vote for imperial army bill

In my Despatch N° 11 of the 27th Ultimo, I had the honour to inform Your Lordship that the Battle of Elections for the new German Parliament, is, in Bavaria, between the Centre or Ultramontane party and the National Liberal party, and the former believe they will have the same majority of Members as in the last Parliament.[76] Right or wrong they are determined to uphold their Leader Prince Bismark's clever antagonist, Herr von Windhorst [*sic*].

The organ of the National Liberal Party in Munich the "Neuestes [*sic*] Nachrichten" has on several occasions hinted that a Letter was in the hands of Prince Bismark from His Holiness The Pope which expressed the hope that the Centre party would vote for the Military Septennate.[77]

The Centre Press pretended that it was doubtful whether such a letter existed, and so the matter remained until the 4th instant, when a Letter, a copy and translation of which, in French, I have the honour to inclose herewith,[78] from Cardinal Secretary of State Jacobini to Monseigneur de Pietro, the Nonce[79] to the Court of Bavaria, was published in the Press.

This very important Letter has naturally caused astonishment in the ranks of the Centre party, particularly, as it showed the reservation of their Leader in Bavaria, Baron de Frankenstein, who has not made it known to them.

This letter explains that it has been written on account of one addressed by Baron de Frankenstein to the Nonce[80] in which he requested to be informed whether "the Pope considered that the existence of the Centre party in the German Parliament was no longer necessary in which case he and many of his Colleagues would no longer ask for re-election."

[76] Elections to the *Reichstag* were held on 21 February 1887. In the elections of 1884 the *Zentrumspartei* won twenty-eight of forty-three seats in Bavaria.

[77] For the army bill, see n. 119 in Berlin section.

[78] Enclosures: newspaper cutting (uncited, undated) which reproduces the original dispatch (in French) from Cardinal Jacobini to the nuncio at Munich, 21 January 1887; cutting (uncited, undated) of the dispatch in German translation.

[79] French: 'nuncio'.

[80] Franckenstein to de Pietro, 16 January 1887.

To this controversial question the present Letter is a reply; His Holiness answers in words of peace, "eulogising the Centre for their services, stating that entire liberty of action has been always accorded it in political questions, but that He cannot accord to the party the right to choose their own line of proceeding in questions concerning the interests of the Church, that the Military Septennate affects matters of religious and moral importance, and His Holiness believes if the Centre had voted for the Government on this question that they would have favorably decided for the revision of the May Laws.[81] The Pope is therefore disposed to take every means to conciliate the friendly sentiments shown by the powerful Empire of Germany, with the view towards the amelioration of the future position of the Holy See". These wishes the "Pope requests should be made known to Baron de Frankenstein, so that he may bring them to the knowledge of the Members of the Centre."

This Papal Letter may be considered as a mild rebuff to Baron de Frankenstein, as it would appear that Baron de Frankenstein's Letter to the Nonce must have been written in consequence of a previous Letter on the part of His Holiness and which has been forwarded to Baron de Frankenstein by The Nonce,[82] expressing the wish that the Centre party should vote in favor of the Military Septennate, and is probably the Letter originally hinted at, in the "Neuestes Nachrichten", as above stated, and before the Vote on the army Bill was taken in the German Parliament; the contents of this Letter were, it is said, withheld from the Members of the Centre, who are already expressing some feeling at this treatment, and it will doubtless have its' effect on the Electors at the coming Election, who can save their conscience with the help of the Ballot.

The organ of the Centre party in Munich the "Munchener Fremdenblatt"[83] commenting upon the Letter shows but little signs of repentance, it says: "The centre values the wish expressed by His Holiness with all due reverence, but their decision to vote a three years Military Bill cannot be shaken, the Centre has voted according to its' conscience and it will continue to act so in future. The Pope's letter," it says, "is a warning to elect resolute Catholics

---

[81] For the May Laws, see n. 17 in this section.

[82] Drummond is referring to Lodovico Jacobini's telegraphic instructions to Angelo Di Pietro of 1 January, which were forwarded to Franckenstein on 2 January, and to Jacobini's more detailed dispatch to Di Pietro of 3 January. In a further letter of 12 January Di Pietro reminded Frankenstein of the wishes of the Holy See.

[83] 'Papst und Septennat', *Münchner Fremdenblatt*, 6 February 1887.

to the "Reichstag", this is "easy". It rudely finishes by adding that "the Candidates for election must be asked three questions."
"Will you vote against the Septennate?"
Will you vote against all Monopolies?
Will you vote against the restriction of the ordinary and direct elective rights?
Only he who answers, Yes! to these questions can be a Candidate for the Centre."

The opinion I have formed, is, that The Pope has used His influence on this occasion in the interests of Peace, as He did in the difficulties which arose between Germany and Spain in the Caroline Island's question;[84] but, naturally the real reason is to show that He has yet Power in Europe and for the purpose of gaining more influence with the German Government to regain what He considers are His sacerdotal rights in Germany.

All Parties are interested to know what the first Letter contained, for it is now acknowledged that it is in existence; In conversation with Baron de Crailsheim this morning I asked him if this was so, he replied, certainly, and that it had been shown to him when he lately visited Berlin,[85] I inquired then, whether he thought it would be made public, he said, yes, and before long, he added, that it was to the same effect as the Letter which has caused so much sensation.

I may here mention that Baron de Soden, the Minister for Wurtemberg, who had seen Baron Crailsheim two days before told me that His Excellency was then of opinion that the letter would not be promulgated, so he must have only-just been informed that it would appear when I saw him.

This first letter will in one sense be of more interest than that just disclosed, as it is evident that it is the one referred to in Prince Bismark's speech on the 24th of January last, when he said: "he believed that the action of the Centre would not be approved of in Rome and that before the Elections the voters would be enlightened as to whether and how far they enjoyed the countenance of the Roman Curia in the revolutionary attempts against the German Empire which they favored."

---

[84] The conflict between Germany and Spain was resolved by the arbitration of Pope Leo XIII, whose verdict of 24 October 1885 acknowledged Spanish sovereignty over the Caroline Islands and granted the freedoms of trade and settlement to Germany.

[85] Crailsheim visited Berlin from 18 to 22 January 1887.

FO 9/258: Victor Drummond to Marquess of Salisbury, Confidential, No 23, Munich, 25 February 1887

[Received 28 February by messenger. For: The Queen / Berlin for perusal, 30 March / Rome for perusal, P.L. [printed letter], 11 March; S[alisbury]]

Press dispute over motives for publishing Leo XIII's letter advising Centre party to vote for imperial army bill

With reference to my Despatches N°s 15 and 18 marked confidential of the 8th and 10th instant, inclosing translations of two Letters from Cardinal Jacobini to Monsignor The Nonce in Munich,[86] showing that The Pope desired the Centre Party in the Reichstag to vote for the Military Septennate Bill, I have the honour to inform Your Lordship that no sooner were these letters published, when remarks appeared in the Ultramontane Press, accusing the Prussian Government of having published them; thereupon, the "Nord Allgemeine Zeitung"[87] [sic] declared this observation to be a "grobe luge"[88] or "clumsy lie" and stated that, on the contrary, the order for publication of the letters was sent from Rome to show the Pope's annoyance at the attitude of the Leaders of the Ultramontane Party in not carrying out the wish expressed by His Holiness.

I have been assured to day that the Bavarian Government had the letters published, doubtless, with the knowledge of The Chancellor of The Empire.

With respect to this matter I may here mention that Baron de Frankenstein, the Leader of the Centre party in Bavaria, sent a letter on the 15th instant to the "Augsburg Postzeitung",[89] in which he makes a declaration that Cardinal Jacobini's letter of the 3rd Ultimo, mentioned in my Despatch N° 18, had never been communicated to him, that the first time he saw it, was, when it appeared in the "Münchener Allgemeine Zeitung";[90] This pleading may be expressed as "throwing dust in the eyes of the public" for although the letter itself may not have been communicated to him nor to Herr von Windhorst [sic], nevertheless, both leaders were informed of the "wish", expressed in the letter, on the part of The Pope, that they should influence their followers to vote for the

---

[86] For the letters of 3 and 21 January addressed to the papal nuncio at Munich, Angelo Di Pietro, see previous dispatch.

[87] *Norddeutsche Allgemeine Zeitung*, 10 February 1887.

[88] *Grobe Lüge*: 'gross untruth'.

[89] Published on 15 February 1887.

[90] On 9 February 1887.

Septennate. Baron de Frankenstein therefore, may be considered to have committed "une indiscretion superficielle"[.][91] The "Liberal Press"[92] have been insisting that a third letter would be addressed by The Pope to the German Catholic Bishops requesting them to point out to the new Members of the Center [*sic*],[93] elected to the Reichstag, the importance of their now voting in favor of the Military Septennate Bill when again presented to the German Parliament; this letter is a stretch of "Press" imagination for I hear on the highest authority that there is no reason for such a statement and as Monsignor The Nonce said to me lately, "Why should a third letter be found necessary if two have no effect, and when it is clear that Prince Bismarck has already a sufficient majority to pass the Bill in question.["]

FO 9/259: Victor Drummond to Marquess of Salisbury, Treaty, No 58, Munich, 22 June 1887

[Received 27 June. For: The Queen; J.P. [Julian Pauncefote]]

Queen Victoria's Golden Jubilee celebrations in Munich

I have the honour to inform Your Lordship that yesterday, on the occasion of the Queens Jubilee, the following Programme was carried out in this Capital to show the rejoicings of Her Majesty's Subjects resident in Munich[.][94]

In the morning, at 11 a.m., a special service was held in the English Church which was honoured by the presence of His Excellency Baron de Crailsheim, Minister of the Royal Household and Secretary of State for Foreign Affairs and the Diplomatic Body, all appearing in Uniform, like myself. "God Save the Queen" was heartily sung by the whole Congregation.

In the daytime I received visits from the Marshal of the Court[95] of His Royal Highness Prince Leopold as also from the Lady[96] in waiting to Her Royal Highness Princess Leopold,[97] to present their felicitations; also from the Court Dignitaries, the Diplomatic Body, The Bürgermeister of Munich,[98] and members of the Court society[.]

---

[91] French: 'minor indiscretion'.
[92] Drummond is referring to the *Allgemeine Zeitung* of 25 February 1887.
[93] *Zentrumspartei*.
[94] The 50th anniversary of Victoria's accession as queen was on 20 June 1887.
[95] Max du Jarrys Freiherr von La Roche.
[96] Klementine Freiin von Limpöck.
[97] Gisela.
[98] Alois von Erhardt.

In the evening at 9 pm Her Majesty's Legation was beautifully illuminated on the street side, the piece in gas jets consisting of the letters V.R. with the Royal Crown above surrounded by stars, while all the windows of the Legation were lit up with Candles.

In the same hour I invited His Excellency Baron de Crailsheim, the Diplomatic Body and all the British Residents in Munich to an illuminated Garden Party and supper. The Garden was lit with Coloured Fires, the Band of the "Erstes Leib Regiment[''], one of the finest on the Continent, played during the whole evening, which was fresh and still rendering the entertainment a complete success[.]

At 10 p.m. Baron de Crailsheim in a few but very graceful[,] touching and courteous words proposed the health of our Gracious Queen, the Band playing "God Save the Queen".

I immediately acknowledged the compliment to Her Majesty by proposing the health of the Prince Regent[99] of Bavaria the Band playing the Bavarian National Anthem, and continuing afterwards with the "British Grenadiers" and "Rule Britannia".

Dancing then took place until midnight at which hour the Band played the English and Bavarian National Anthems and so ended one of the most lovely entertainments of rejoicing given in honour of our Beloved Queen.

Crowds remained in the street until the last moment the Police however kept the street clear for the arrival and departure of my guests in their usual exact but amiable manner.

Great interest has been taken in the success of The Queen's Jubilee rejoicings by all classes in Munich and the Bavarian Press generally have published articles laudatory of the Queens public and private life during Her Majesty's Reign.

FO 9/258: Victor Drummond to Marquess of Salisbury, Confidential, No 63, Munich, 11 July 1887

[Received 14 July by post. For: The Queen / Prince of Wales; S[alisbury]]

Rumours of change to constitution regarding regency; government measures to increase popularity of prince regent

With reference to my Despatch N° 59 Confidential of the 22nd Ultimo relative to the State of King Otto's Health and my observations thereupon I have the honour to state further in respect of these

---

[99] Luitpold.

that I have for some time heard rumours that in the Court Circles here it was considered possible that in the next Parliamentary session a proposal might be made for altering the wording of the articles of the Constitution concerning the Regency, modifying them so as to admit of the Prince Regent being named to the throne in the place of his nephew, as it is disadvantageous to the interests of the kingdom to have a King only in title who does not govern, whose state of health, is hopeless and whose reign is unreal.[100]

A change such as above indicated has been since mentioned in the North German and Austrian Press, causing comment on the part of the Bavarian Press: curiously the latter, in expressing their doubts as to the feasibility of carrying out such a substitution, base them chiefly on the open secret that His Royal Highness The Prince Regent being opposed to such a proceeding, it is not likely that his desire will be interfered with.

This I believe; but certainly everything has been done to impress upon the Bavarians that The Prince Regent is their Ruler and friend. His visits to the cities in the provinces have been carried out in the greatest state, he has showered decorations in profusion, large sums of money have been distributed to the poor and different institutions, immense enthusiasm was excited, no doubt partially caused by the amiable[,] charming and frank manner with which all classes were received by His Royal Highness. All Court Ceremonies are now carried out with every possible magnificence, His Royal Highness attends constantly solemnities both in the City and Country such as processions of the shooting or other societies, the unveiling of statues etc.

On the other hand since the Prince Regent has assumed the reins of Government orders have been given by the Authorities that on King Otto's Birthday and Nameday[101] a Te Deum alone is permitted; no holiday is allowed as is the case on the Prince Regent's fête Days.

The Government indeed, it would appear, take every means to make the people forget their real king and feel that the Prince Regent has alone authority over them.

Whatever the rumours, which I have brought to Your Lordship's notice, may signify, the events of last year still remain in the People's mind,[102] and therefore whatever the wishes of some may be in respect

---

[100] Otto suffered from severe mental illness. From the first day of his reign (13 June 1886) Luitpold, under the provisions of the Bavarian constitution of 1818 (*Titel* II, Articles 9–22), continued to serve as regent, a position which he had already assumed on 10 June 1886 under Ludwig II.

[101] On 27 April and 30 June.

[102] Drummond is referring to the end of Ludwig II's reign.

to a change in the Constitution it is, in my opinion, one which cannot be ventured upon for yet some time; however I am informed by several persons of position that such a result may be reached, that the Government and those surrounding His Royal Highness desire that it should take place, while on the other hand others who speak with authority think that nothing will be attempted, although if certain circumstances should arise, favourable to such an event, it might be practicable[.]

An observation made to me this day is to the point; on asking the opinion of a person of high standing belonging to the Commercial Community he said "It is possible but not probable, for is not His Royal Highness to all intents and purposes King already?"

I attach no importance to the existing rumours but at the same time I have thought it right to present them to Your Lordship as foreshadowing an unlikely but not impossible event.

FO 9/258: Victor Drummond to Marquess of Salisbury, Confidential, No 80, Munich, 29 October 1887

[Received 5 November. Qy: X; S[alisbury], 6 November]

German press resentful of crown prince being attended by Morell Mackenzie; observations on German character and reliance on prejudiced press articles for information about Britain

The German Press has lately shown extreme sensibility respecting the treatment of their Crown Prince by an English Physician, and I am sorry to notice that not only is the Press guilty of this jealous feeling, but many German doctors and other intelligent persons.[103]

To an unbiassed [*sic*] mind, it appears strange that a great people should give way to such feelings, instead of rejoicing in the fact that the most learned authority on the special disease from which the Crown Prince Imperial is suffering, (although a foreigner) should be employed to destroy it, but a rational mind cannot understand the German character, the little generosity and the small amount of reasoning power that is to be found in the German nature, this may appear inexact, but, it is in my humble opinion, really true, in as far as regards the body of the German people, and to bring a case besides the present unwarrantable envy at seeing Sir Morel [*sic*] Mackenzie attending their Prince Imperial, this is also shown in a remarkable manner by the false views held by the German

---

[103] Friedrich Wilhelm, who suffered from laryngeal cancer, had been treated by Morell Mackenzie since May 1887. Mackenzie's initial assessment indicated a benign tumour. In October Mackenzie attended the crown prince at St Remo.

Press and by the German people in regard to England's Home and Foreign Policy, its' administration and social life. This impression, I humbly submit, should always be taken into account by Her Majesty's Government, and I will offer a few observations in respect to it.

Constantly, I notice in the German Press the blame attached to Her Majesty's Government by the Irish Nationalist and British opposition Press,[104] but arguments in favor of the policy of her Majesty's Government hardly ever appear. Why is this? and why has German feeling generally been and apparently is not generous to England? the reason is not far to explain, the "Kolnische Zeitung" is perhaps the chief source which nourishes this feeling, for information respecting English affairs is generally quoted by the German Provincial Press from that Paper, it never tires of showing its' unfriendliness for England except when it is necessary for Germany's own advantage to gain England's goodwill, then, its' remarks become toned down, but this never lasts long. Neither Editors of the German Provincial Press, as far as I learn, nor do Germans in general, (outside of the principal Trade Centers) read the English Newspapers, so that the German Public may be said to have their ideas of what concerns England formed from extracts from Papers which give a one sided view, thus, the public, even some of the most rational and intelligent, only see the course of events in one light, as they never see the true light in the evidence of the other side. The consequence is (outside of Berlin and Trade Centers) ignorance and incapacity for Germans to master the true position of our affairs.

I apprehend, from conversation with Germans, that they are not so logical as we believe them to be, they abide by what they happen to have read or heard; to argue with them and explain that their opinion is erroneous is of no avail, nothing will turn them out of the path they have taken, until you show them in black and white that they have only a Knowledge of one side of the question and that the wrong one.

In illustration of their pertinacious and confined views, I mention the following story.

Some years ago, Müller, a German was sentenced to death and hung in England for the murder of Mr Briggs.[105] I remember it

---

[104] Drummond is referring to the reportage on the Irish Home Rule movement.

[105] On 9 July 1864 Thomas Briggs was robbed on a train journey and died after being thrown out of the carriage. The suspect, Franz Müller, who maintained his innocence, was convicted for murder (the first British railway murder) and publicly hanged on 14 November.

caused a great sensation at the time, as the German Press argued the case in favor of their Countryman and that they roundly abused the English Courts of Justice.

A friend of mine in Munich tells me, that then as now, the Professors of the University here attended a Debating Club every Saturday Evening; the Wife of one of the Professor's in conversation with my informant spoke very harshly at the time respecting the English Judge[106] and Jury by whom Müller was condemned, insinuating it was owing to Müller's nationality; my friend expostulated and being very angry at not making any impression on the Lady in his exposé of what really had happened, and of the justice of the sentence, said to her, "I can clearly see that you are merely repeating what your husband has told you, now, I am sure he can never have read the Judge's summing up nor the speech of the Prosecuting Counsel[107] or the evidence proving Müller's guilt for he is too clever and honorable a man to speak as he does if he had done so, I will give you a Newspaper containing these facts, on the condition that you will promise that your Husband will read them and bring them before his Colleagues at their next meeting" – the lady promised, the consequence being, that a message was sent to my friend on the part of the Professors, stating "that they had been grossly deceived by the Newspapers which had only given a onesided version, that they all agreed after reading the evidence against Müller and the Judges summary, that the Verdict and the hanging of Müller was a most just sentence and that no trial could have been fairer".

This one case is good for all cases.

In anything which concerns England the German Press are always ready to expose her shortcomings, whatever the matter may be, such as the bursting of a gun, defective bayonets, the remarks made in England that German Commercial Houses are ousting British trade from distant lands where it has been hitherto supreme, etc. It is pleasant to feel, however, that the German Press is now handicapped in one item of news; which it was always so pleased to make much of. I refer to that where Naval officers were obliged to bombard native Villages of Savages who had murdered our people on the African Coast or the Islands of the Pacific, this was boldly set forth as an uncivilized act, now, since Germany has a strong Navy and has been forced to perform similar punishment, such necessary operations are no longer condemned. Germany's Naval policy has become nearly assimilated to ours.

[106] Sir Jonathan Frederick Pollock.
[107] William Ballantine.

The Moral to be drawn from what I have stated and from the present case of envy and jealousy of Sir Morel Mackenzie being entrusted with the case and treatment of the malady from which His Imperial Highness suffers, shows that the German people in general are not generous in their nature, and that they never will accept anything to be right except from a German point of view which is in most cases prejudiced.

FO 9/260: Henry Cadogan to Marquess of Salisbury, Confidential, No 3, Munich, 20 January 1888

[Received 24 January by post. For: The Queen / Berlin for perusal, P.L. [printed letter], 3 February; S[alisbury], 24 January]

Remarks on publication of papal encyclical to bishops of Bavaria; relations between church and Bavarian state since 1817

The Papal Encyclical[108] to the Catholick Bishops of Bavaria having attracted general attention in this Country and caused much comment, I venture to point out to Your Lordship the causes which, as far as I can ascertain, have led to its publication[.]

In order to do this, it is necessary to remind Your Lordship that in October 1817 a Concordat was drawn up and signed between King Maximilian I of Bavaria and The Pope.[109] Its clauses were however considered by the King's advisers to be so incompatible with the internal Government of the Country, that its publication was temporarily withheld, and it was not till the following year that it appeared in the form of an appendix to the New Constitution, which had meanwhile been drawn up.[110]

This course considerably diminished its importance, as its provisions – which went in some cases beyond the articles of the Constitution – were no longer final, but rather formed an integral part of an act which could only be altered by the joint decision of the Crown and Parliament, and the question of its independent validity gave rise to continual Parliamentary conflicts between the Liberal and Catholick Parties.

---

[108] Pope Leo XIII's encyclical *Officio sanctissimo* (On The Church in Bavaria), dated 22 December 1887, was published in Bavaria on 3 January 1888.

[109] Pius VII.

[110] The Concordat of 24 October 1817 was published as an appendix to the *Religionsedikt*, which itself formed part of the Bavarian constitution of 26 May 1818.

Four years later – in 1821 – King Maximilian issued a Royal decree, better known as the "Tegernsee Declaration"[111] by which the Concordat was declared independent of the Constitution, and the Catholick cause was still further strengthened in 1852 by King Maximilian II who issued a Decree[112] in which still further concessions were granted to the Church of Rome.

During the long period in which the "Culturkampf" raged in Prussia, Bavaria was the scene of a Liberal movement which, though it did not take the form of legal repressive measures, was directed with much persistence against the pretensions of the Ultramontane Party. Of this Liberal or "Old Catholic"[113] party Baron Lutz, the then Minister of Public Worship was a strong partisan.

The Ministry were constantly accused in Parliament of having broken the Concordat, and disregarded the Royal Decrees of 1821 and 1852.

Baron Lutz however maintained that the Concordat had been incorporated with the Constitution, and that the former could only be valid so long as its provisions coincided with the articles and stipulations of the latter; that the King alone had no power to alter the Constitution, and that the Decrees were only worth the paper they were written on.

This occurred in 1882; but since that time the relations between Church and State have much improved. The Government have made several concessions, notably with regard to school matters, and the education of the Clergy, and it appears that His Holiness has frequently expressed his sense of the improved state of things.

When the late King died in 1886, the Ministers sent in their resignation in consequence of the great difficulties which lay in their way owing to the growing opposition which was manifested to them by the ultramontane Party.[114]

The Prince Regent refused to accept their resignation, and embodied the refusal in a manifesto[115] in which His Royal Highness maintained that his confidence in them remained unbroken, and that he was confident that they would continue to guard the interests of his subjects both in civil and spiritual matters: with respect to the latter he was glad to be able to remind them that "the highest authority of the Catholick Church has repeatedly declared himself <u>completely satisfied</u> with the position of the Catholick Church in Bavaria."

---

[111] On 15 September 1821 Maximilian I Joseph declared that the Concordat was to be regarded as state law.

[112] Royal decree of 8 April 1852.

[113] See n. 64 in this section.

[114] See pp. 488–489.

[115] Letter from Luitpold to the Bavarian ministry (*Gesamtministerium*), 6 July 1886.

This utterance of the Prince Regents is, my Lord, the probable reason for the publication of the Encyclical.

It is true that Baron Crailsheim hardly admitted this when talking to me on the subject, and maintained that not only had the Pope repeatedly expressed himself in the above sense, but that His Holiness had never protested against the accuracy of the statement. The whole tone of the Liberal Press coincides with Baron Crailsheims view, that the Pope has been urged to this course by the "Intransigeant" Party for purely party purposes.

On the other hand Monsignore Guidi, Auditore of the Nuncio,[116] assured me that the Pope, while expressing his pleasure at the improved position of the Church in Bavaria, had never said anything which could be construed in the above sense; that His Holiness had privately protested through The Nuncio, against the accuracy of the Prince Regents manifesto, and had only been prevented from doing so publicly out of consideration for the difficult position of the Ministers at the time of the crisis in 1886.

From what I hear it is extremely doubtful whether The Pope would ever have gone the length of expressing himself entirely satisfied: His Holiness had already considerably weakened the cause of the Ultramontane Party by his interposition at the time of the Septennate Bill,[117] and such an utterance as above would not only have precluded them from seeking any further assistance from Rome, but would be entirely inconsistent with the purpose of the Encyclical.

The general opinion is that the Encyclical is intended as an answer to, if not a protest against the Prince Regents manifesto.

The Encyclical, which I have the honour to forward to Your Lordship here with, together with a précis translation,[118] is very moderate in tone, being for the most part a historical retrospect of the Church in Bavaria, and containing general advice and instruction as to the education of the Clergy. The only allusion to the Concordat expresses a regret that its provisions have been abrogated, and a hope that the Prince Regent will soon take measures for the well being of the Church.

On the question of the education of the laity the Encyclical is more precise, and mentions the Pope's regret that "children are still forced to attend schools where the name of God is either never mentioned, or where false instructions concerning Him is given".

[116] Fulco Luigi Ruffo-Scilla.
[117] See pp. 493–497.
[118] Enclosures: original encyclical (*Sendschreiben Unsers Heiligsten Vaters Leo XIII durch göttliche Vorsehung Papst and die Erzbischöfe und Bischöfe Bayerns*), 1888; précis translation of the papal encyclical addressed to the Catholic episcopacy of Bavaria, 22 December 1887.

This Paragraph shews that His Holiness has been misinformed on the subject as the day schools in Bavaria are not "religion-less" (confessionslos) but mixed – that is to say that even in cases where Protestants[,] Catholicks and Jews attend the same Day school, then each obtain religious teaching from a priest or clergyman of their own confession.[119]

Baron Crailsheim told me that His Excellency had at first feared that the Publication of the Encyclical would cause difficulties to the Ministry. But since the full text has become known its moderate character has become apparent to everyone, and as the Ultramontane Party have allowed the Estimates for Public Worship and Schools to pass without opposition[120] it is clear that their line of action has not been much influenced.

Its inaccuracy as regards the schools is regretted by the Catholicks themselves who admit that its value has been thereby diminished.

As the Encyclical is addressed to the Bishops Baron Crailsheim told Monsignore Guidi that the Government did not propose making any official answer to it. Monsignore Guidi hinted that perhaps the Bishops would draw up and present a petition to the Prince Regent on the subject.

Baron Crailsheim informed him however that this would probably do more harm than good; that the present relations of Church and State in Bavaria were more favourable than they had been for some time, and that if the Government who had already made several concessions were to make further ones under compulsion, they had better at once resign and make way for an Ultramontane Ministry – a course which they do not contemplate.

FO 9/260: Victor Drummond to Marquess of Salisbury, No 5, Munich, 7 February 1888

[Received 13 February by post. For: The Queen; S[alisbury, 14 February]]

Publication of terms of Austro-German alliance; patriotic speech by leading member of National Liberals illustrates Bavarian devotion to German Empire

The publication of the terms of the German-Austrian alliance of October 7. 1879 has been welcomely received in Bavaria.[121] The

---

[119] The establishment of non-denominational schools was enabled by Royal Ordinance of 29 August 1873 which introduced the formation of school districts on the basis of municipality rather than parish. However, a revision of the ordinance on 26 August 1883 reinstated confessional schools as the norm.

[120] Crailsheim was probably referring to the deliberations in the finance committee of the second chamber (*Finanzausschuss*); the reading of the budget of the ministry for church and school affairs began on 24 January 1888.

[121] For the secret treaty of 7 October 1879 (published on 3 February 1888), see n. 489 in Berlin section.

Bavarian Press agree that owing to the present threatening attitude of Russia on the German Austrian Frontier[122] it was necessary to show that Power what the conditions of that alliance are with respect to their position in case of an attack.

It is hoped that Russia may now be induced to withdraw a portion of her forces and give a guarantee of her peaceful intentions which she so prominently sets forth in words not in deeds.

There is no doubt that the publication of the Treaty is for the purpose of ensuring Peace, but it is here believed at the same time that in any case it will force Russia to show her hand and declare what her real views are and enable Germany and Austria to decide on their future policy.

In my Despatch N° 47 of November 9. 1886 I informed Your Lordship of the complete state of Bavarian Military organisation, nothing being wanting for the Bavarian army to march at twelve hours notice.

The German and Austro-Hungarian armies are now no longer two armies but one army for the present.

Everyone here is quite calm owing to this feeling of security and from the knowledge that everything that foresight can determine upon is provided for in the present and future.

This feeling has been strengthened by the Chancellor's recent speech in the German Reichstag[123] and the Bavarian press is unanimous in the assertion that, come what may, Bavaria will be in the front rank in its devotion to the Cause of the Empire.

During a debate, in today's sitting of Parliament,[124] on the vote for national school teachers[,] a handsome tribute to The German Chancellor was paid by D^r von Schauss, a leading member of the Liberal Party, who ended his speech with the following words: –

"A Teachers profession is at all times full of responsibility, and is now doubly so in Germany, as none of us can foretell what is in store for the coming generation. Yesterday Germany witnessed a day which, though peaceful, yields in importance to no national event of the last twenty years."

"The unity of German's princes[,] peoples, and political parties was yesterday displayed in – I may say – an emotional manner."

---

[122] Drummond is referring to the movement of troops from the interior of Russia to Russian Poland (Vistula Land) and the Austro-Hungarian frontier.

[123] In the speech of 6 February, to which Drummond is referring, Bismarck famously stated 'We Germans fear God and nothing else in the world'.

[124] Second chamber of the Bavarian *Landtag*; Schauß delivered his statement during the reading of the budget for elementary schools.

"Foreign Countries should know that in questions which concern the preservation and power of our Fatherland Bavaria is unanimous."

"We all agree with the German Prince in wishing for peace, but if war be inevitable, Bavaria – conscious of her historical traditions – will yield to no other German race in patriotism and selfsacrifice."

"Love for the Fatherland unites us all: Love for the Fatherland is the battle cry which, if war be inevitable, will preserve that unity."

FO 9/260: Victor Drummond to Marquess of Salisbury, Very Confidential, No 14, Munich, 20 March 1888

[Received 23 March by post. For The Queen / Prince of Wales / Berlin / Treaty Department; S[alisbury], 23 March]

Public sensibilities offended by prince regent's discourteous attitude towards past and present German emperors

I regret to report to Your Lordship a sudden irritation in public feeling in Munich towards His Royal Highness The Prince Regent,[125] this feeling has even taken possession of a portion of the army in garrison here, this makes it of more importance.

The causes arise from, first, that His Royal Highness did not attend at the Railway Station to greet The Emperor Frederick on His way to Berlin from San Remo.[126] Secondly, that He gave no orders for the proper observance throughout Bavaria of the day of the late Emperor's funeral;[127] no Flags were hoisted at half mast on the public Buildings, no Church Bells were tolled, no minute guns fired, no orders were given to the Troops.

Thirdly, His Royal Highness did not attend the Emperor's funeral.

The excuse given officially for the Prince Regent not appearing at the station, is that He requested The Emperor by telegraph to allow Him to present His respects on His Majesty's arrival at Munich but that The Emperor replied begging Him not to appear, people, however, ask why His Royal Highness should telegraph? as it was almost an invitation for a refusal on account of the early hour 8.20 a.m[.] when the train arrived. As Ruler of the Kingdom He had a perfect right to do what He liked under the circumstances; the Queen

---

[125] Luitpold.

[126] Upon hearing the news of Wilhelm I's death, on 10 March, Friedrich III, accompanied by his wife Victoria, left San Remo for Berlin and arrived at Munich the following day.

[127] On 16 March 1888.

Mother of Bavaria[128] went to the station and was received by their Imperial Majesties, this led the Press to make The Queen Mother a pretty speech, saying, that "the thanks of the Bavarian people were due to Her for Her attendance"; Her Majesty had, however, telegraphed requesting permission to be present which The Emperor had graciously acceded to on account of Her Majesty being an own Cousin.

No excuse is given to the public for the second cause I mention. The reason given for the third, is that The Prince Regent believed that although Bavaria as a German State ranked next to Prussia He would have had to accept an inferior position to the King of Saxony and this He was not inclined to do. I am, however, informed that delicate points of precedence had been carefully arranged at Berlin and that His Royal Highness would have been in line with the Sovereigns present, how far this statement is correct I cannot say. The displeasure of the people and officers in garrison in Munich towards The Prince Regent is confirmed to me by my Colleague of Wurtemberg[129] who has a Son[130] in the Cavalry.

Next Thursday night there is to be an imposing Torch light Funeral Procession in memory of the late Emperor William at which all the Societies of Munich will be represented, they are to finish their programme by presenting themselves before the Palace where they will sing the Bavarian National Hymn ending with a thundering Cheer "ein donnerndes Hoch" for The Prince Regent.

This performance will possibly show the real feelings of the Munich population towards their Ruler, a fine moonlight night and good Bavarian Beer, it is to be hoped, may divert the feelings of displeasure in the breasts of those who have been expressing their disapproval of His Royal Highness, who has always shown the Bavarian people His consideration and a sincere desire to please them.

FO 9/262: Victor Drummond to Marquess of Salisbury, No 5, Munich, 14 February 1889

[Received 18 February by post. For: The Queen; S[alisbury]]

Prince regent modifies regulations for Bavarian court balls with respect to rank of British and French chargés d'affaires

In his Despatch N° 3 of February 4, 1875 Sir R Morier, at that time Her Majesty's Representative at the Court of Bavaria, addressed to

---

[128] Marie.
[129] Oskar von Soden.
[130] Heinrich von Soden.

Lord Derby his remarks on a point of etiquette, respecting his position and that of his French Colleague[131] who, as Chargés d'Affaires, were not permitted to sit, at the Royal Supper Table at the Court Balls, with their Colleagues, who all held the rank of Envoys. They were thus put on the same footing as Second Class Bavarian Officials.

Sir R Morier informed the Minister for Foreign Affairs, Baron de Pfretschner, that, as a permanent accredited Chargé d'Affaires and Representative of Great Power, he would never consent to such an arrangement, and stated that he should in future, after attending the Royal Circle, absent himself from the Ball.

This he carried out, as did also his French Colleague, with or without the excuse of indisposition.

The Earl of Derby, in his Despatch N° 4 of February 11, 1875 approved of the course Sir R Morier had adopted.

A Court Ball was given here a short time ago,[132] and two days before Baron de Crailsheim called upon me and said, "I have come to give you some good news: The Prince Regent[133] has in future consented to the Representatives of Great Britain and France having seats at the Royal Table at Supper at the Court Balls."

His Royal Highness had done this on his advice and after consulting with our Colleagues. It was only natural, he said, that the Representatives of such Great Powers as Great Britain and France should not be separated or any occasion from their Colleagues, and His Royal Highness had fully concurred; but, His Excellency added, the line must be drawn between permanent Chargés d'Affaires and Chargés d'Affaires 'ad interim'.

In thanking Baron de Crailsheim for his communication I said that I was delighted to be freed from the annual excuses for not attending the Court Balls and that it pleased me much that he should have been the author of the new Regulation.

His Royal Highness The Prince Regent afterwards requested The Master of the Ceremonies[134] to tell me how pleased His Royal Highness was to see me at His Table.

I have troubled Your Lordship with this account of the favour so graciously granted by His Royal Highness The Prince Regent as shewing the good position Her Majesty's Representative and his French Colleague[135] hold at Court, and to record it as a precedent in future.

---

[131] Édouard de Lefebvre.
[132] On 21 Janaury 1889.
[133] Luitpold.
[134] Maximilian Joseph Pergler von Perglas.
[135] Camille Barrère.

FO 9/262: Victor Drummond to Marquess of Salisbury, No 40, Munich, 28 July 1889

[Received 1 August by post. Print (Western Europe); For: The Queen / Circulate / Copies to: Berlin / Vienna; S[alisbury]]

Prince Ludwig's speech at inaugural dinner of gymnastic festival (Deutsches Turnfest)

I have the honour to inform Your Lordship that His Royal Highness Prince Ludwig – eldest son of The Prince Regent,[136] and Heir Presumptive to the throne of Bavaria – made a speech at the inauguration dinner of the German Athletic Associations which has attracted general attention in the German and Austrian Press.[137]

His Royal Highness, in the course of his speech, recapitulated the events in German history since the beginning of the Century and pointed out how essential it was that the German Unity which had been gained should be maintained 'by keeping true to Emperor and Empire'.

Turning to the Austrian associations who were present His Royal Highness dwelt on the firm friendship of Germany for the House of Hapsburg and said "Hold fast to Your German language and Your German Sentiment."

This speech has been much applauded by the German press who hold it as a good omen that the Heir Apparent to one of the largest German States should proclaim his Imperial and German sentiments in such an outspoken manner.

FO 9/262: Victor Drummond to Marquess of Salisbury, No 49, Munich, 26 September 1889

[Received 30 September by post. For: The Queen; Qy: Copy to Rome; Berlin for perusal, 9 October; S[alisbury]]

Bavarian Catholic Convention at Munich

Referring to my Despatch N⁰ 16 of the 12th of April last, respecting the Memorial of the Bishops' of Bavaria addressed to His Royal Highness the Prince Regent[138] and the reply thereto by Baron de Lutz in the name of His Royal Highness, which I stated was not satisfactory to the Ultramontane party,[139] I have the honour to inform

---

[136] Luitpold.
[137] The speech was held on 27 July 1889 at the opening of the seventh *Deutsches Turnfest* at Munich.
[138] Luitpold.
[139] In a memorandum of 14 June 1888 the Bavarian bishops compiled their grievances regarding the state of the Catholic Church in Bavaria. Minister president Lutz replied on

Your Lordship that a proof of their dissatisfaction has just been shown at a Congress[140] held in Munich on the 23rd instant, under the authority of the Bavarian Catholick Church Committee, about ten thousand persons drawn from Munich & the different Provinces attended the Congress.

The object of the Congress as set forth by the various speakers and by the resolutions, ultimately carried, was to clear away the obstacles which prevent the Church of Rome exercising its' authority in all religious-political and school matters such as those mentioned in my Despatch referred to above, the Catholick Members of Parliament being requested to use their best endeavors to force the Bavarian Government to accede to their demands.

A protest was made against the late manifestations at Rome in honor of Giordano Bruno,[141] with expressions of deep sympathy and sorrow with the Pope's[142] present position and declaring that the temporal Power in His Holiness must be reaffirmed,[143] indignation was expressed with the reply of Baron de Lutz to the Bishops' Memorial; the Liberal Press was much abused and all true Roman Catholicks were advised to boycott it from their homes as it insulted the Church.

The proceedings were brought to a close with cheers for His Holiness The Pope and His Royal Highness the Prince Regent[144] of Bavaria.

FO 9/262: Victor Drummond to Marquess of Salisbury, No 58, Munich, 18 November 1889

[Received 15 November. For: The Queen; Rome for perusal, No 257; S[alisbury]]

Debate on motion by Centre Party to change interpretation of placet regium; attacks on government policies towards the Catholic Church

Referring to my previous Despatch I have now the honour to report more fully on the Debate mentioned therein and which causing the

---

28 March 1889, and, while making various concessions, insisted on the precedence of state law over ecclesiastical law and the continued practice of the *placetum regium* (royal approval; see n. 146 in this section). He also repudiated the demands for compulsory daily school masses and the introduction of confessional middle schools (as a rule).

[140] *Bayerischer Katholikentag* (Bavarian Catholic Convention).

[141] A statue of Giordano Bruno was unveiled at the Campo de' Fiori in Rome on, 9 June 1889 (Whit Sunday). The festivities included a procession, a gala dinner and conferences (which had started on the previous evening and ended on 10 June).

[142] Leo XIII.

[143] Temporal papal sovereignty ended in September 1870 when the Italian army entered Rome.

[144] Luitpold.

defeat of the Government has given rise to much comment in Bavaria.

The Leader of the Centrum party in the Chambers Herr Geigner [*sic*][145] opened the Debate, he made a long speech, in which he stated that his party desired no change in the Constitution itself but only that it should be carried out as it was before 1870 when the Crown of Bavaria in regard to the "placet regium"[146] showed its' benevolence in favor of the Pope and the Church. He attacked Baron de Lutz severely saying, that he was the cause of the present controversy and held him responsible for the withdrawal of the Church privileges. He referred to Prince Bismarck who had made concessions to the Roman Catholick Church,[147] he had made them on a large scale and Baron de Lutz might have made them on a small scale, but he had not even met them half way, he was responsible for the decrease in faith and morals in Bavaria.

Respecting the old Catholics he said, we wish to shake off that association altogether, for have they not separated themselves from us?[148]

Calling on all Catholics to vote for the motion, given in full in my previous Despatch, he finished by declaring that his party wished the authority of the Church to be equal to that of the State, adding, damaging the authority of the Church damages that of the State.[149]

Baron de Lutz[150] replying to the accusation that he had been the cause of the difficulties between Church and State said, there are others who have brought the Church into antagonism with the State, it is a very old story and no one will live long enough to see it finished.

The "placet" relates to all matters of Faith of all Confessions. It is Law and the oath of the Constitution is Law and in matters of Law one has no will of his own but only the word, must. ("muss").

To believe you and your Press it is I who have invented the present state Laws in regard to the Church, but they have existed long before I was a Minister, I am not the author but the Executor. Why am I

---

[145] Joseph Geiger, on 6 November 1889.

[146] The requirement for a *placetum regium* ('royal approval') of the publication of ecclesiastical laws and ordinances was stipulated by the constitutional edict of 1818. In 1870 (rescript of 9 August) the *placetum regium* was extended to the decrees of the Vatican Council.

[147] See 000–000.

[148] The Bavarian government formally regarded the Old Catholics (see n. 64 in this section) as part of the Catholic Church.

[149] The motion was dated 19 October 1889. It requested the Prince Regent, Luitpold, to instruct his ministry, firstly, to declare that the *placetum regium* as defined in section 58 of the constitutional edict of 1818 did not extend to religious dogmas and ethical doctrines, and, secondly, not to treat the Old Catholics as part of the Catholic Church. The motion was passed on 8 November with a majority of 81 to 78 votes.

[150] On 6 November 1889.

reproached because you find the "placet" intolerable? That should have been considered when it was added to the Constitution.

In negotiations with Rome the rights of the State in regard to the Church have always been upheld and Rome has never acknowledged them and never will.

In regard to the motion that a petition shall be presented to the Regent, according to the rules of the Constitution He cannot answer it. The Regent must interchange His views with His responsible Ministers. If the motion is passed here and even in the Upper house and a dissolution should result what will happen then? Nothing! "Nichts". It will only cause a still further breach between Church and State. Baron de Lutz finished by declaring that the "placet" in Church affairs had never been abused and as to the Old Catholics, nothing had ever been done to favour them, neither did he believe that he was in favor with them.

The Minister of Finance[151] followed stating that he and his Colleagues in the Ministry agreed with Baron de Lutz in all he had spoken and done as Minister of Public Worship.

Dr Daller, rector of Freising College, closed the Debate in a violent speech,[152] saying, he could understand the enunciations set forth by Baron de Lutz as a Professor but not in his position as a statesman, who had trampled on the rights of three million of his countrymen and brought agitation amongst the people. He lost his temper on being interrupted and used the following words which caused great excitement in the Chamber, "We saved the existence of the Royal House of Bavaria in 1886"[153] these words were received with shouts of indignation from the supporters of the Government and by the public in the Gallery.

Dr Daller continued, the position of affairs is so serious that we on our side have determined to make a Declaration, the terms of which I gave in my Despatch N° 57 of yesterdays date.[154]

The reasons for this vehement attack on Baron de Lutz I have every reason to believe arise from the Prince Regent's Manifesto after the King's death in 1886 in which He stated that the Highest Authority of the Church has repeatedly said that he was entirely satisfied with the position of the Church in Bavaria, this was not relished

---

[151] Emil von Riedel, on 6 November.

[152] On 8 November 1889.

[153] In reaction to an interruption from the left side of the chambers, Daller said that, if provoked, he might 'speak about the year 1886, when we [i.e. the Right] saved the material existence of the Bavarian royal house'.

[154] Daller declared that the *Zentrum* faction could not accept Lutz' interpretation of the constitutional edict of 1818 and would retain this position in the reading of the budget for the ministry of cultural affairs.

by the intransigent party who succeeded in making their views known to the Pope,[155] and it is said, this was the cause of the Encyclical addressed in 1887 to the Archbishops of Bavaria, and mentioned in Mr Cadogan's Despatch N° 3 confidential of January 20th 1888.[156] Another reason is the answer made by Baron de Lutz in the name of The Prince Regent to the Memorandum of the Bishops of Bavaria, as reported in my Despatch N° 16 of the 12 April last, and particularly the Prince Regents' letter to Baron de Lutz "approving" what he had written.[157] This has not been forgiven by the Intransigents and it led, I am told, to the Catholic Congress in Munich, reported in my Despatch N° 49 of the 26th September last,[158] when a resolution was passed to urge the Deputies of the Centrum to bring forward the motion which has now been presented to the Chambers, and which will from its' result, reach on their own too impetuous zeal, as assuredly the Prince Regent cannot retreat from His approval of Baron de Lutz' Letter to the Bishops, even were the petition passed by the Upper Chamber and presented to Him, which it is allowed on all sides cannot happen.

On Wednesday the 13th next the second motion mentioned in my last Despatch will be brought forward in the Chambers by Herr Geigner, thus; that "a petition he presented by the Chambers to The Prince Regent urging His Royal Highness to request His Ministers to arrange that in the Council of the Empire[159] means shall be taken to repeal the Law of the 4th July 1872 relating to the order of Jesus in favor of the Congregation of The Redemptionists."[160]

This motion, likewise, I believe, even if voted by the Lower Chamber[161] will be thrown out by the Upper Chamber.

My own belief is that the Centrum party were determined to show The Pope that He may count upon them in any emergency and with the view to show His Holiness their devotion and zealous attachment for Him in His present wounded position. In this they have succeeded and in showing their durable animosity to Baron de Lutz but in their endeavour to make an impression on the Bavarian people

[155] Leo XIII.

[156] See pp. 503–506.

[157] Luitpold approved of Lutz' reply (of 28 March 1889) to the Bavarian bishops on 24 June 1889. See n. 139 in this section.

[158] See pp. 511–512.

[159] *Bundesrat* (Federal Council).

[160] The Jesuits Law of 4 July 1872 banned the Jesuit Order in the German Empire. It was amended in 1904 and repealed in 1917. On the Redemptorist question, see pp. 534–535.

[161] On 8 November 1889 the motion, dated 19 October 1889, was carried with 81 to 74 votes.

to influence them in the next Elections I doubt their obtaining any success.

FO 9/263: Victor Drummond to Marquess of Salisbury, No 22, Munich, 11 March 1890

[Received 14 March by post. For: The Queen; S[alisbury]]

Catholic Centre Party rejects budgetary estimates for the arts following dispute with government over placetum regium; *anti-*Centre *protests by students and press*

With reference to my Despatch N° 15 of the 19th ultimo, in which I pointed out the manner in which the Centrum party showed their discontent with the Government for not agreeing to their views on the interpretation of the "Placetum Regium", and on the Old Catholic and Redemptorist Questions,[162] I regret to say that although Baron de Crailsheim Acting Minister for Public Worship and Instruction has been very conciliatory to the opposition they have nevertheless continued their irritant policy of, at intervals, rejecting credits demanded for necessary purposes, such as heating the National Picture Galleries, the maintenance of the annual Exhibition of Pictures, for the purchase of pictures for the National Galleries etc.[163] This unfortunate policy was commented upon in the National liberal paper the "Münchener neueste Nachrichten" of the 6th instant in an article headed "Little pigs in their sty", – insulting to the Leaders of the Centrum who made a request to the Government in the Chambers that the article should be suppressed and the Editor[164] punished.

The anger of the Professors and students of the Academy of Art has also been aroused and the latter on the night of the 8th instant made a demonstration before the house of Dr Orterer one of the Centrum leaders; they were dispersed by the Police after serenading the Doctor with "cats' music",[165] and they then retired to a Brewery and drank the health of His Royal Highness The Prince Regent[166] and the Ministers, ending with 'Pereats'[167] for the Centrum Leaders.

---

[162] For the dispute over the *placetum regium* and the Old Catholic question, see the previous dispatch. On the Redemptorist question, see pp. 534–535. The Old Catholic question was partly resolved by a ministerial regulation of 15 March 1890, which denied Old Catholics the right to be recognized and treated as Catholics.

[163] Drummond is referring to the decisions of the finance committee of the second chamber of the Bavarian *Landtag* on 5 March 1890.

[164] Georg Hirth.

[165] Noisy protests, discordant singing (charivari).

[166] Luitpold.

[167] Latin *'pereat'*: 'down with'.

Dr Orterer the next day requested explanations from the Government and what protection would be afforded to him, blaming the Police Authorities for permitting demonstrations which the Law declares are not permitted during the sitting of the Chambers within a distance of six hours from the Capital.

Baron de Crailsheim in his reply[168] regretted the incident, declared that Members would be protected and that such scenes as had taken place would not be permitted and that the Authorities of the Academy and University had been requested to take measures to prevent any excesses on the point of the Students, – and with respect to the article in the "Münchner neueste Nachrichten" – "Schweinchen in den Stall" – and an appeal in that paper to the people of Munich to make a great demonstration in favour of His Royal Highness The Prince Regent on his birthday tomorrow, Baron de Crailsheim remarked that the Minister of Justice[169] had already taken measures to prosecute it.

I am informed that it is possible that some arrangement may be made in a day or two conducive to an understanding between the Government and the Centrum party which will facilitate the business of the Chambers, and prevent the existing controversy.

FO 9/263: Victor Drummond to Marquess of Salisbury, No 33, Munich, 23 April 1890

[Received 2 May by bag. For: The Queen; T.V.L. [Thomas Villiers Lister]]

Bavarian Reichsrath *propose increased budget for purchase of works of art*

With reference to my Despatch N° 22 of the 11th ultimo[170] on the debates in the Bavarian Chambers as to the refusal of the majority, formed of the Ultramontane party, to vote the amount demanded by the Government for Art purposes, I have the honour to inform Your Lordship that when the Reichsrath[171] had before them yesterday for their consideration the Bills passed in the Lower House,[172] that for buying works of art which had been cut down from 120,000 to 60,000 marks was debated and a proposal for its' increase to 100,000 marks was agreed to.

---

[168] On 10 March 1890.
[169] Leopold Freiherr von Leonrod.
[170] See preceding dispatch.
[171] First chamber of the Bavarian *Landtag*.
[172] On 28 March 1890.

Curiously enough His Royal Highness Prince Louis whom the Ultramontanes have always considered as favourable to their views made the most effective speech in favour of the larger amount. His Royal Highness, forcibly laying stress upon the importance of having an annual Exhibition of Pictures and Works of Art, showed that thus the Munich artists would be enabled to see the best pictures of their rivals and, learning from them, perceive their own defects and improve their knowledge and talent, but, for this purpose, His Royal Highness said, a building specially adapted should be erected, – plans had already been before the Artists Committee for a long time, but on account of want of Funds the foundation stone had not yet been laid.

It remains now to be seen whether the Ultramontane party, the majority in the lower House, will retreat from the ground they have taken up and assent to the proposal of the Upper House.

There is a satisfactory indication in the Speech of His Royal Highness Prince Louis, which is, that He shows Himself independent in character and free from the prejudices of the Ultramontanes, who are always inclined to determine State matters by permeating them with an overflow of religious dogma.

FO 9/263: Horace Augustus Helyar to Marquess of Salisbury, No 53, Munich, 19 June 1890

[Received 23 June by post. Print; A.G. [Anglo-German] neg[otiatio]ns; S[alisbury]]

Heligoland-Zanzibar Treaty

I have the honour to transmit herewith to Your Lordship Extracts [note in margin: 'Translation'] from the Allgemeine Zeitung[173] relating to the Anglo = German Convention and expressing the view taken here of the weighty concessions made by Germany therein.[174]

At the usual reception today of the Minister for Foreign Affairs, Baron de Crailsheim in the course of conversation remarked that the Convention must be regarded with satisfaction by the Bavarian Government as a settlement of difficulties always pending and as a guarantee for the future. He added that while Heligoland was no doubt precious in the eyes of all Germans, there could be no doubt about the very serious and highly valuable concessions in Africa made by Germany.

---

[173] Enclosure: translated extracts from the *Allgemeine Zeitung* of 18 and 19 June 1890.
[174] For the Anglo-German agreement of 1 July 1890, see n. 436 in Berlin section.

FO 9/263: Victor Drummond to Marquess of Salisbury, No 66, Munich, 4 September 1890

[Received 8 September by post. X; T.H.S. [Thomas Henry Sanderson]]

Death of Johann von Lutz

With sincere regret I have the honour to inform Your Lordship that the Minister of State Baron de Lutz, until lately Minister of Public Worship and Education and President of the Council of State, died yesterday after a long illness, which began with Inflammation of the Lungs, and severe attacks of Asthma.

Baron de Lutz was born in 1828, he was named in 1867 by the late King Louis II, Minister of Justice and afterwards Minister of Public Worship.

Friendly to the Roman Catholic Church, of which he was a member, he still incurred the displeasure of the Ultramontane party by not conceding to all their demands in Church matters.

From the moment the German Empire was proclaimed, and as long as he was enabled to serve his Country he used all his influence to strengthen and secure German unity. He was a clever statesman, charming in conversation, full of humour, and very amiable. His loss will be much felt by His Royal Highness, The Prince Regent of Bavaria,[175] and outside the Ultramontane party, by all Bavarians.

FO 9/264: Victor Drummond to Marquess of Salisbury, No 2, Munich, 5 January 1891

[Received 9 January by messenger. For: The Queen / Prince of Wales / Mr Stanhope / Berlin for perusal, No 15; S[alisbury]]

Wilhelm II to attend Bavarian army manoeuvres

The Newspapers here have lately been engaged in controversy, respecting the German Emperor's intention to inspect, next September, the two Bavarian army Corps at the time of their Manoeuvres.[176]

The first statement given in the Press mentioned these Manoeuvres as Imperial, thereupon, the Ultramontane Press commented as to

---

[175] Luitpold.
[176] The manoeuvres were planned from 9 to 11 September.

this appellation, declaring that there could be no such thing in Bavaria, as the Bavarian army was under the orders of The King, and at present under those of the Prince Regent[177] acting for His Majesty.

The Liberal Press followed, explaining that Imperial Manoeuvres meant merely that His Imperial Majesty would honour the Manoeuvres with His presence, which He has the Authority to do at all times in accordance with article LXIII paragraph 3 of the German Constitution of April 16th 1871, wherein, it states that it is the right and duty of the Federal Commander in Chief[178] to inspect the different armies of the Empire and convince Himself as to their fitness and capacity deciding the result of the Inspection with the Sovereigns of the respective armies.

The late Emperor William I never assisted at the Bavarian Manoeuvres out of regard for the late King Louis of Bavaria who had a dread of meeting His Brother Sovereigns and had no sympathy with Military spectacles neither had He any skill or the necessary Knowledge in Military matters. The Crown Prince Frederick was, therefore, at that time[179] named Inspector General of the Bavarian army which He had often led to victory in the war of 1870[180] and to whom that army was devoted, on His death after He came to the Throne, Field Marshal Count von Blumenthal was entrusted[181] with the Inspector Generalship, he had also fought with the Bavarians when he was Chief of the Staff of the 3rd Corps d'armée and his appointment was thoroughly appreciated by the Bavarian army.

The Liberal Press endeavour to show that The German Emperor's visit next September is owing to an invitation from His Royal Highness The Prince Regent, but from what I learn from one of my German Colleagues, The Emperor informed the Bavarian Minister at Berlin[182] that He had the intention of attending the Bavarian Manoeuvres to inspect the two army Corps and on this decision of His Imperial Majesty being announced to The Prince Regent, He, immediately sent word to The Emperor that it would give Him the greatest pleasure to receive His Imperial Majesty.

---

[177] Luitpold.
[178] Article 63 refers to the Emperor.
[179] On 16 June 1871.
[180] As commander of the III German Army Corps.
[181] On 12 April 1888.
[182] Hugo Graf von Lerchenfeld.

FO 9/264: Victor Drummond to Marquess of Salisbury, No 13, Munich, 10 February 1891

[Received 12 February by post. X; S[alisbury]]

Allgemeine Zeitung opinions on foreign policy; remains ill-disposed towards Britain

I have the honour to enclose a Précis, in translation, of an article from the Allgemeine Zeitung of February 8th which as usual shows its unfriendliness to England.[183]

It certainly has not failed on the present occasion to do so, as also to make splenetic remarks in respect to Your Lordship's policy towards Germany, bestowing at the same time a thrust at General Caprivi for not taking into account the national feeling of Germany (the Allgemeine Zeitung's) in respect to her African Colonies. But the most important remark is that Germany should draw closer to Russia and encourage friendly relations between Russia and Austria-Hungary so as to leave England isolated in case of war with Russia.

FO 9/264: Victor Drummond to Marquess of Salisbury, No 44, Munich, 12 September 1891

[Received 15 September by post. For: The Queen / Mr Matthews; S[alisbury]]

Foreign press overstate tension between Prussia and Bavaria; conversation with Crailsheim on integration of Bavaria within empire; emperor's visit to Munich

English[,] French and Russian Newspapers have lately commented upon a certain friction between Prussia and Bavaria as shown by the German Northern and Southern Press; this is said to have arisen by certain Prussian papers advocating the assimilation of the Bavarian exceptional Laws to those of Prussia. It did not appear to me to be of any importance for a skirmish of this kind is of old date and is renewed from time to time, but, as the English and French Press still give the matter more importance than it deserves I have made enquiries of my German Colleagues as well as of Baron de Crailsheim whether it is a matter in which the Prussian and Bavarian Governments are seriously concerned or whether it

---

[183] Enclosure: précis translation of article in *Allgemeine Zeitung* of 8 February 1891. The article provided a commentary on the *Reichstag* debates which took place from 3 to 6 February, concerning colonial and African affairs. It criticized Caprivi's remarks about British sympathies towards Germany as being detrimental to German interests.

is only newspaper effervescence. The former say there is nothing in it [,] that they have not given any attention to the matter. Baron de Crailsheim says that its origin was through insignificant newspapers both in Prussia and in Munich; – those in Munich he had never heard of – and it was astonishing how newspapers of high standing should have paid any attention to their bickerings.

In reply to certain questions I asked, Baron de Crailsheim said that no demand had lately been made by Prussia to assimilate Bavarian postage stamps to those of Prussia,[184] – that the Bavarian Government would endeavour to bring about a Reform in the Bavarian marriage Laws in the sense of the proposal mentioned in my despatch N° 43 of this day's date;[185] – that as to the negotiations to have the same rules throughout the Empire in the Military criminal procedure,[186] this matter had not up to the present been brought before the Bavarian Government, – that it was a personal matter between the Prussian and Bavarian Ministers of War,[187] – that if any alteration of the present procedure is advised by the Prussian Minister of War it will have to be laid before the Federal Council, and there the opinion of the Bavarian Government would make itself heard. His Excellency added, Bavaria has no exceptional privilege in respect to the military Law and if it is necessary to change it there is no infringement of Bavaria's rights. Baron de Crailsheim further said that when the Chancellor[188] of the Empire passed some time with him on last Wednesday night, he had purposely avoided asking him any question concerning the negotiations between the Ministers of War. He had mentioned to His Excellency the foolish remarks of the Press, but the Chancellor said he had paid no attention to the articles published, – in fact the matter is one to which I may say Her Majesty's Government need not give any attention, and which I have only reported to Your Lordship to expose the hollowness of these exaggerated newspaper reports.

In any case, the Emperor's visit to Munich[189] will still further strengthen the bond of union between North and South as it has

[184] The right to maintain a separate postal system and to issue stamps was stipulated in the November (Versailles) Treaties of 1870.

[185] Dispatch No 43 is not included in FO 9/264.

[186] The question of a German Military Penal Code, which had already been under discussion between 1871 and 1881, was taken up by the imperial government in 1890. At the time of the dispatch the draft code, developed by a commission of the Federal Council, was put on hold. The new Military Penal Code was ultimately passed in 1898; it replaced the Bavarian code of 1869 and the Prussian code of 1845. See also p. 525.

[187] Hans Karl von Kaltenborn-Stachau and Benignus von Safferling.

[188] Leo von Caprivi.

[189] Wilhelm II attended the manoeuvres of the first and second Bavarian army corps at Munich from 7 to 11 September.

the personal relations between their respective rulers, which as the *Allgemeine Zeitung* remarks,[190] proves the actual unity of the whole of Germany; and this shows how insignificant is the quarreling of certain newspapers about this and that detail of the relations between Northern and Southern Germany.

FO 9/264: Victor Drummond to Marquess of Salisbury, Confidential, No 60, Munich, 8 December 1891

[Received 7 [*sic*] December by post. Private Secretary; T.H.S. [Thomas Henry Sanderson]; (Seen by Lord Salisbury)]

French government intend to promote their diplomatic representative to rank of envoy

Referring to my telegram of this date, I have the honour to inform Your Lordship that Monsieur Barrère my French colleague sent me word last night that as he was unwell he wished me to call upon him, having a communication to make to me. I accordingly saw him this morning when he said "I think it only fair to you to inform you that I have received a Note from Monsieur Ribot stating that if agreeable to His Royal Highness The Prince Regent,[191] the French Government intend accrediting me to His Royal Highness as Envoy Extraordinary and Minister Plenipotentiary.[192] I have seen Baron de Crailsheim who appeared much pleased and said that he would bring the matter to His Royal Highness' consideration immediately on his arrival from the country today."

Mr Barrère added "You have been here so much longer than I have that I feel in fairness to you that you should have the precedence, and I therefore thought it proper to inform you of what is to take place in order that you might inform Lord Salisbury in case your Sovereign is disposed to have Her Representative of equal rank to that of your colleagues, in which case and that Letters of Credence are sent to you before the end of the year I would delay presenting my letters before yours to enable you to have the precedence."

Monsieur Barrère is going to Paris where he intends to study the question of Egyptian sanitary matters and take the instructions of his Government before attending the Egyptian International

---

[190] *Allgemeine Zeitung* of 10 September; the article in question was an excerpt from the *Norddeutsche Allgemeine Zeitung* of the same day (morning edition; transmitted by telegram).
[191] Luitpold.
[192] Barrère was accredited as permanent chargé d'affaires from 1888; Drummond held the rank of minister resident at Munich and Stuttgart.

Conference for the reorganization of the Alexandrian Sanitary Commission which is to meet at Venice on the 5th of December and to which Monsieur Barrère has been appointed as French Delegate.[193]

Your Lordship will learn from the above the good terms existing between the French and English Legations, I am happy to say that as far as Her Majesty's Legation is concerned they are the same existing with other foreign Legations in Munich.

I thanked Monsieur Barrère very heartily, for the confidence he had shown me.

FO 9/265: Victor Drummond to Marquess of Salisbury, No 10, Munich, 15 March 1892

[Received 18 March by bag. For: The Queen; S[alisbury]]

Munich press advocates press freedom

The German Emperor's speech at the Banquet of the Brandenburg Chamber of Deputies has been much commented upon in the Bavarian Press, and I have the honour to give herewith the opinion of the most important newspapers published in Munich.[194]

The "Allgemeine Zeitung[''][195] declares that the articles of those newspapers confiscated for "Lèse Majesté" are not treasonable, but express the critical opinions of many classes of the Nation, which have also been expressed before in a vigorous manner among members of the Reichstag and Landtag, adding that magnanimity and disregard of personal amour propre in a Monarch are among his greatest claims to respect, and of this Wilhelm I German Emperor was a brilliant example. To protect the freedom of the Press, legislation is necessary, but at present it is not believed that it would have any chance of passing the Reichsrath[196] and the Bundesrath;[197] the

---

[193] The Sanitary, Maritime and Quarantine Council in Egypt (successor to the Sanitary Administration of Egypt) was founded in 1881 and consisted of fourteen European and nine Egyptian members. Following the international conference at Venice just four Egyptian members remained on the council and an international convention for the protection against cholera was adopted.

[194] Wilhelm II's speech at the banquet of the Provincial Diet of Brandenburg on 24 February 1892 was criticized for its neo-absolutistic stance. He depicted opponents to the imperial government as grumblers and ended with the remark, 'My course is the right one, and I shall continue to steer it'.

[195] On 13 March 1892.

[196] First chamber.

[197] Federal Council.

remedy for the present undesirable confusion of affairs is the responsibility of the Ministry as representing the Throne.

The Munich Neueste Nachrichten[198] considers that the articles complained of were certainly not treasonable, but may be described as sharp but well meant criticisms; the Press ought to be given free course to do its' duty, and express itself as its conscience directs it. The trials now pending will have to undergo the verdict of public opinion.

In general in South Germany the feeling is widespread that the Monarch should be kept above and apart from the strife and personalities of parties.

FO 9/265: Victor Drummond to Marquess of Salisbury, No 41, Munich, 20 July 1892

[Received 22 July by bag. For: Mr Stanhope; Intelligence Department: War Office, E.F.C. [Edward Francis Chapman]]

Bavarian Military Penal Code to be subsumed into that of Prussia; press predict widespread discontent

In my despatch N° 55 of the 11th of November last I informed Your Lordship that the Bavarian Chambers voted an address to the Prince Regent of Bavaria to maintain the present Bavarian Military jurisdiction.[199]

It now appears that the project for a general assimilation of German Military jurisdiction is to be brought forward in the next German Parliamentary Session and it is reported that this will be in the form of the present Prussian Military jurisdiction.

The Bavarian Press show that if this is carried out it will cause a very deep and painful impression in Bavaria, and a very unfavourable impression amongst the people.

A surrender of this kind to Prussia will be too dearly bought with the nomination of His Royal Highness Prince Leopold as Inspector of the Fourth German Army Inspection and will be a rebuff to the Bavarian House of Representatives.[200]

---

[198] On 8 March 1892.
[199] The second chamber made an address on 4 November 1891 in which it asked Luitpold to advise the Bavarian plenipotentiaries to the Federal Council to consent only to a German Military Penal Code if the principles of the Bavarian Military Penal Code of 1869 were maintained.
[200] Leopold was appointed on 27 June 1892.

FO 9/265: Horace Augustus Helyar to Marquess of Salisbury, No 43, Munich, 28 July 1892

[Received 1 August by post. For: The Queen / Prince of Wales; S[alisbury]]

Kissingen demonstration in honour of Bismarck; Bismarck's speech; mixed response from South German press

I have the honour to enclose herewith to Your Lordship a translation of the full text of the speech made by Prince Bismarck on Sunday at Kissingen[201] at the large and enthusiastic popular demonstration made in his honour by thousands of admirers from all parts of South Germany and especially from Baden[,] Hesse, Thuringia and the Palatinate.

The demonstration passed off without a hitch, and the language used by the Prince was more guarded and less calculated to give offence in high quarters than that of some of his recent speeches.

Prince Bismarck's visit to Kissingen has not passed without comment in the South German Press.

The 'Allgemeine Zeitung'[202] a short time since attacked in no measured terms the organs of General Caprivi for their criticism of Prince Bismarck especially as to the latter's alleged 'want of patriotism', stating that the South German people have known and appreciated Bismarck's patriotism these last thirty years and asking if gratitude is only the duty of the people, and not also the duty of the Government?

On the other hand the Wurttemberg 'Beobachter' a leading Stuttgardt paper concurs in and emphasises the attacks upon Prince Bismarck while at Kissingen,[203] whom it accuses of being the cause of Social Democracy, Clericalism (sic); and Antisemitism, and ends by saying "He was a misfortune to our Fatherland"[.][204]

On the whole however, the attitude of the South German Press towards Prince Bismarck while at Kissingen may be described as sympathetic and respectful.

The Prince leaves Kissingen on the 30th instant for Jena.

---

[201] Enclosure: translation of Prince Bismarck's speech at Kissingen on 24 July 1892.
[202] On 12 July 1892.
[203] Bismarck stayed at Kissingen from 26 June to 30 July 1892.
[204] *Der Beobachter: Ein Volksblatt für Schwaben*, 12 July 1892. The article in question ended with the remark, 'It was misfortune for our Fatherland, that Prince Bismarck had not been removed from the helm of the state long ago.'

FO 9/265: Victor Drummond to Earl of Rosebery, No 51, Munich, 29 October 1892

[Received 2 November by post. For: Mr Campbell Bannerman / Intelligence Department War Office, E.F.C. [Edward Francis Chapman]; Berlin for perusal, 9 November; R[osebery]]

Press reaction and public opinion on imperial army bill; Catholic voters follow individual political instincts rather than obey instructions

With respect to the Provisions of the new German Army Bill now before the Federal Council of the Empire,[205] I have the honour to state that until their publication by the "Cologne Gazette"[206] the Bavarian Press although supplying Columns of Extracts from the North German Press have furnished but few comments upon the possibilities of what the hitherto assumed provisions of the New Army Bill might lead to, leaving the Public to draw their conclusions; acknowledging, however, the benefit which would be rendered to the Empire if two years service with the colours was adopted instead of three years as is now the case.

The Provisions of the Army Bill as now published have produced an uneasy impression in Bavaria, as it is believed that the estimated expenditure will be far exceeded.

The following Extracts from the National Liberal and Ultramontane Press demonstrate the present unfriendly attitude towards the New Army Bill. The Socialist Organs also are opposed to any increase to the present strength of the army.

I. Neueste Nachrichten of October 19, 1892.
II. " " of " 26, 1892.
III[.]Fremdenblatt of " 26, 1892. s[207]

With respect to the feeling evinced against the New Army Bill I may mention a very important incident as regards the Roman Catholic or "Centrum" Party, which has taken place at Kelheim in lower Bavaria at an election there a few days ago[208] of a new Member for the Bavarian House of Representatives.

Two candidates offered themselves, both being Roman Catholics of the Ultramontane party which led to disunion in the ranks of

---

[205] On the army bill presented to the Federal Council on 20 October 1892, see pp. 143–144.

[206] *Kölnische Zeitung*, 24 October 1892.

[207] Enclosures: précis translations of articles in *Münchner Neueste Nachrichten* of 19 October and 26 October 1892 and *Münchner Fremdenblatt* 26 October 1892.

[208] On 19 October 1892.

their party, for Dr Sigl, who offered himself in opposition to the clerical candidate Herr Rauchenecker, was only defeated by a few votes in a constituency having 11,000 voters; and this happened owing it is stated from the fact that Herr Sigl is opposed to the New Military Bill. That Roman Catholic voters should have voted in such large numbers in disregard of the advice of their party leaders tends to show that at the General Election next year[209] it is not impossible that many of the Roman Catholic Working class voters will give their votes in a more liberal sense, and in accordance with their own personal interests, and not at the dictation of those who consider themselves their advisers. If this happens it will be a revolution in the records of Ultramontane chronicles, one which would greatly agitate the Holy See, and heartily grieve and displease His Holiness.[210]

There is no doubt that since the death of Dr Windthorst, and Baron de Franckenstein the loss of their extraordinary influence (especially that of Dr Windthorst) over the Roman Catholic bourgeoisie and working classes is seriously felt by the Ultramontane party and that those who have succeeded them have not the authority their predecessors had on the hearts of their coreligionists in those classes mentioned above.

The affection of the people for Dr Windthorst and the admiration for his courage in his political battles (the Culturkampf) with Prince Bismarck inspired the Roman Catholics throughout Germany. They have now no leader who can produce these feelings. The election at Kelheim proves this, and now Roman Catholic voters have had the courage to vote in accordance with the dictates of their own consciences, at the General Election many may follow the example given; if this should take place it might eventually lead to a breach in the unity of the 'Centrum' party and cause the present majority they hold in the Imperial Parliament to be divided on any important political or administrative questions brought forward by the Government although on religious questions they would in all probability be united.

FO 9/267: Victor Drummond to Earl of Rosebery, No 39, Munich, 11 May 1893

[Received 15 May by post. For: The Queen / St Petersburg / Berlin; R[osebery]]

Münchner Neueste Nachrichten *on russification of Baltic provinces*

Since 1876 Europe has witnessed the gradual Russification of the Baltic Germans in Courland Livonia and Esthonia, who had from

---

[209] The *Reichstag* elections were held on 15 June 1893.
[210] Leo XIII.

the year 1800 enjoyed exceptional privileges retaining their old manners and customs with the free use of their language.[211]

The continued oppression pursued by Russia has at different times been severely animadverted upon by the German Press and hints have been thrown out that Germany might be in the position some day to annex the persecuted provinces.

Upon this subject a very interesting article appeared in the "Münchener Neueste Nachrichten" of the 6th instant, a précis of which I have the honour to annex herewith in translation.[212] The article is headed "The future of the Baltic provinces in Russia", and is interesting as it not only produces historical facts to prove that neither the late Chancellor of the Empire Prince Bismarck nor the present Chancellor General Caprivi have countenanced or would countenance under any circumstances the annexation of these Provinces, but it also furnishes a statement made by a Livonian Nobleman[213] now settled in Austria who formerly played a prominent rôle in Livonian affairs, and who declares that the Baltic Germans have always been and are true and loyal subjects of the Emperor of Russia and that though undoubtedly feeling they are suffering from through the changes now being carried out in order to Russianize them, they will never offer any resistance, beyond endeavouring to carry out their old German customs and ways of living in their own homes; and that if the Russians publish[214] a belief that Germany is inclined, if the opportunity offered itself, to annex the Russian Baltic provinces, it is only a pretence for further persecution and for their more complete Russification.

FO 9/267: Victor Drummond to Earl of Rosebery, No 40, Munich, 15 May 1893

[Received 19 May by post. For: The Queen / Prince of Wales; R[osebery]]

Impending Reichstag *elections; uncertain future of army bill; anti-Prussian sentiments dominate Bavarian political scene*

The Dissolution of the German Parliament at Berlin owing to the rejection of the Huene compromise in the German Army Bills has

---

[211] Curonia, Livonia, and Estonia were Baltic governorates of the Russian Empire. In 1876, as a prelude to the russification measures of the 1880s, the office of the Baltic Governor-General, established in 1800, was abolished.
[212] Enclosure: translation of article 'The Future of the Baltic Provinces of Russia', *Münchner Neueste Nachrichten*, undated.
[213] Name not traceable.
[214] The article was referring to the Russian press in general and in particular to the *Novoye Vremya*.

not at present produced any excitement in Bavaria, although each party is preparing for the coming struggle at the elections on the 15th of June for the new Parliament.[215]

What the result of the elections will be it is quite impossible to foresee; it is doubtful whether they will be decided on the Huene compromise of the Army Bill, for it must be remembered that the Parliament is elected for a term of five years, and there are other internal questions of State of importance which will have to be decided, considered by many to be of more importance than new Army Bills, matters concerning the economic interests of the Empire.

With respect to the recent Votes given by the Centre party against the Huene compromise it is to be observed that there is in the Ultramontane ranks a certain amount of antipathy to Prussia, in fact this feeling pervades more or less the Bavarian people. This has been lately shown in a speech made by D[r] Daller the leader of the Bavarian Centre fraction just before the rejection of the German Army Bill.

He said "If the Bavarian Members of the Prussian Centre voted for the Army Bill the Members of the Bavarian Centre must separate themselves from them.[216] The Bavarian people were dissatisfied with the measures of the Imperial Government. Imperial Finances were so exhausted that if it were anything but the Empire in question it would have to be put in wardship and guardians appointed. Were we not right to defend ourselves in 1866?[217] Prussia is a Military State and has no mercy for its' subjects certainly none at all for us Bavarians".

Again, D[r] Sigl proprietor of the Munich newspaper "Vaterland" a few days ago[218] issued an article in which he says that in the next war Bavarian millions and the sacrifice of Bavarian lives will cause Prussia to become more powerful than she is, and will determine the future of Bavaria, if Germany is defeated there is an end to the German Empire, although the victors probably would spare Bavaria; if Germany is victorious then Bavaria will become a Prussian Province and Bavaria will cease to exist as an independent kingdom. Thereupon the "Kreuz Zeitung"[219] put forth a statement that D[r] Sigl is on very friendly terms with the Bavarian Ministry, thus, as Baron von Crailsheim has remarked to me, insolently insinuating that they

---

[215] The *Reichstag* was dissolved on 6 May 1893. For the rejection of the army bill and the compromise proposal, see nn. 312 and 322 in Berlin section.

[216] In his speech at Neubeuern of 16 April 1893, Daller was referring to the Bavarian members of the *Zentrum* faction of the *Reichstag*.

[217] Daller was referring to the Austro-Prussian War of 1866.

[218] On 5 May 1893.

[219] *Neue Preußische Zeitung* (*Kreuzzeitung*), on 10 May 1893.

were responsible for the article. Dr Sigl has indignantly replied that there is not a word of truth in the insinuation.

The causes of Bavarian dislike of Prussia (in Wurttemberg it also exists) arise from the idea that Prussia wishes to extinguish Bavaria's reserved rights,[220] religious differences, the late endeavours of Prussia to oust Bavarian Military Jurisdiction,[221] assimilating it to the Prussian; and the German Commercial Treaties with Austria and Italy and the proposed Commercial Treaty with Russia,[222] emanating from Prussia, are not regarded with any favour by the agricultural population of Bavaria (i.e. the majority); – complaints are made that Bavarian officers in garrison with Prussian officers are looked down upon by the latter; neither are the people contented with the Old Age Insurance Laws;[223] – these are some of the causes which do not fail to make an impression on the Bavarian people unfavourable to their Prussian kinsfolk.

This anti Prussian feeling in Bavaria however must not be regarded as showing any opposition to German Unity which is upheld as strongly as ever.

There is also a gradual democratic spirit showing itself in the ranks of the peasantry and the small farmers of Bavaria. Agrarian meetings have lately been held in several of the Bavarian Provinces where the Speakers have had the courage to speak against the Bavarian nobility and the clergy. One speaker[224] last week declared that "agriculturists were no longer properly represented by Priests or Nobles in Parliament. Religion is sacred to us, and in fact there is more religion and morality with us than in the Castles".

Another speaker[225] compared "the Nobility to Drones in the Beehive who live on the rents extracted from the labour of the farmers.["]

The Ultramontane party have taken alarm at the views expressed at these meetings by forming Christian Farmers meetings, and are endeavouring to counteract in every possible way their effect.

The coming elections therefore for the Federal Parliament next June are looked forward to with much interest and fears are expressed that many Votes which have been given to the

---

[220] Bavaria's sovereign rights were upheld in the November (Versailles) Treaties of 1870. These *Reservatrechte* included the maintenance of separate postal and railway systems, military command to be retained by the king in peacetime, property insurance regulations, citizenship laws, and beer and brandy taxes.

[221] See nn. 186 and 199 in this section.

[222] On the commercial treaties, see nn. 319 and 354 Berlin section.

[223] Law concerning Disability and Old-Age Insurance of 22 June 1889.

[224] Benedikt Bachmaier at the peasant's meeting in Poigham on 8 May 1893.

[225] Name not traceable.

Ultramontane Party will be given to the Democratic or Socialist Party; certainly some members of the aristocracy who held seats in the late Parliament have refused to seek reelection as they are afraid of not being reelected.

There is an uneasy feeling amongst the better classes. The speech of His Majesty The German Emperor a few days ago to His Staff has not assisted to allay this feeling, the Bavarian Press express regret at the words used towards certain members of the Federal Parliament as to their want of patriotism and to expressions made use of not worthy of cultivated men.[226]

It is impossible to foretell what the result of the elections in Bavaria will bring forth but my own personal opinion is that there will be but little change in the different parties, for the Ultramontane leaders have a great hold on the peasantry, and where a second ballot is necessary they will be almost certain to obtain a majority of votes.

FO 9/267: Victor Drummond to Earl of Rosebery, No 61, Munich, 15 August 1893

[Received 18 August by bag. For: Rome for perusal, No 155, 1 September / Eastern Department; 'This is the best thing we have had from Munich', R[osebery]; Returned from Rome, 2 October]

Bavarian press comments on relations between France, Russia, England, and the Triple Alliance

When France a few days ago sent her ultimatum to Siam,[227] a portion of the German Press endeavoured to impose on the German Public by demonstrating that England would be glad to see Germany remonstrate with France against her annexationist policy in Siam and against her declaration that if her ultimatum to Siam was not accepted, Siamese ports would be blockaded, as Germany was interested in preventing such measures owing to her holding the most important position after England in the Siamese trade and the same newspapers declared that Germany would certainly not pull the chestnuts out of the fire for England – on the contrary it was a pleasure to Germany to see France occupied in the East, in China and Siam, and Germany would certainly do nothing to prevent her carrying out such a policy. The Munich "Allgemeine

---

[226] Drummond is referring to Wilhelm II's speech of 9 May in which he criticized the rejection of the army bill.

[227] The Franco-Siamese War took place in 1893. On 20 July 1893, at Bangkok, the French presented Siam with an ultimatum, demanding that she renounce her claims to the left bank of the Mekong River.

Zeitung"[228] upon this remarked that England will certainly keep clear of being drawn into a war with France, and Germany has no reason to spill the blood of her sons to compensate England for her military weakness, adding that it is not for Germany to seek English sympathy and popularity by being drawn into conflict with France; and other newspapers have hinted that England's true policy is to join the Triple Alliance.[229]

There has now appeared in the Ultramontane newspaper the "Bayerischer Kurier"[230] published in Munich, a communiqué stated to be from a valuable source, a former diplomat[231] being hinted at. It is of some interest as it pretends to expose the intrigues of Baron de Mohrenheim the Russian Ambassador in Paris in his endeavours to bring Austria into more friendly relations with Russia with the view probably of a "rapprochement" later between the two Empires, and of loosening the Triple Alliance. Baron de Mohrenheim, it is surmised, believes England may later be drawn nearer to the Triple Alliance and Austria drawn away from it. The writer of the communiqué therefore proposed that Germany should take the steps to insure the friendship of England for the Triple Alliance for the reasons he sets forth.

Again with reference to the Triple Alliance a statement has been lately made in the Munich "Allgemeine Zeitung"[232] that Italy has concluded a separate convention with Russia, which, however, has been denied by the "Agenzia Stefani";[233] whereupon the "Allgemeine Zeitung"[234] publishes a statement that the denial gives no ground for doubting the truth of the report. It explains that it is in the form of a mediation of Russia in a particular case, a step, it says, which Italy sees itself impelled to by the absolute unreliability of military aid to be given her by England.

I enclose translations herewith of the abovementioned communiqué, together with the article on the assumed Convention between Italy and Russia.[235]

May it not be that Italy has granted some Italian port for the Russian Fleet or Squadron to make use of when cruising in the Mediterranean in the summer?

---

[228] On 2 August 1893.
[229] On the Triple Alliance, see n. 174 in Berlin section.
[230] On 7 August 1893.
[231] Name not traceable.
[232] On 26 July 1893.
[233] On 8 August 1893.
[234] On 10 August 1893.
[235] Enclosures: translation of an article entitled 'Behind the scenes' [*Hinter den Coulissen*], *Bayerischer Kurier*, undated [7 August 1893]; translation of an untitled article from the *Allgemeine Zeitung*, undated [26 July 1893].

FO 9/269: Victor Drummond to Earl of Kimberley, No 25, Munich, 27 July 1894

[Received 30 July by messenger. X; K[imberley]]

Ultramontane press incensed by Federal Council decision to allow Order of Redemptorists but not Jesuits; Ultramontane party tactics in religious and political matters

The decision taken by the German Imperial Federal Council on the 9th instant permitting the return of the order of Redemptorists, or White Fathers, whilst retaining the Imperial Law of 1872 excluding the Jesuits, has been received very coldly by the Bavarian and Würtemberg Ultramontane Press, for although it expresses itself thankful for a small instalment of what the Roman Catholic party have demanded for several years, it still declares that the agitation will continue until the Law of 1872 is entirely abolished, and hints that the party will know how to make itself disagreeable to the Imperial Government in the next session of the Imperial Parliament at a time convenient to itself to push forward its claims, in a renewed demand for the return of the Jesuits.[236]

The Bavarian Government is blamed for not voting in favour of the abrogation of the Law of 1872. This shows the spitefulness of the Ultramontane party, for, although the Bavarian Government promised to use its best endeavours to induce the federal Council to vote for the return of the White Fathers, they have never expressed their desire to see the return of the Jesuits; they carried out their promise honourably and successfully, and instead of showing their gratitude the Ultramontane party show their displeasure.

A short time ago, I enquired of my Colleague The Nuncio[237] what was the present position of the Ultramontane party in regard to its adherence to its Leaders, in religious and political matters. His Excellency replied, that it had been decided that the Members of the party would follow their Leaders' views and act together in all religious questions, but in political and social questions, they could act and give independent votes according to their own views.

The Catholic Congress to be held next month at Cologne[238] will show what policy will be pursued to obtain the abrogation of the

---

[236] The Anti-Jesuit Law of 4 July 1872 banned the Jesuit Order in the German Empire. It was extended by implementing the ordinance of 20 May 1873 to the missionary order of the Most Holy Redeemer (Redemptorists). The White Fathers (*Societas Missionariorum Africae*) were not affected by the Anti-Jesuit Law. In his dispatch Drummond refers to the Congregation of the Holy Ghost, the ban on which was likewise lifted by the Federal Council on 9 July 1894.

[237] Andrea Auiti.

[238] From 26 to 30 August 1894.

above-mentioned Law of 1872; the language made use of by Members of the Ultramontane party at Catholic meetings held this month, show[s] great irritation and angry feeling. If the same indignation is shown at the Congress, the Cultur Kampf may be revived.

FO 9/269: Arthur George Vansittart to Earl of Kimberley, No 63, Munich, 22 November 1894

[Received 24 November by post. X; K[imberley]]

Split between Prussian and Bavarian factions of Social Democratic Party

With reference to my despatch No. 48 of the 26th ultimo, I have the honour to report that the split, which has now evidently occurred between the Socialist deputy Bebel, on the one hand, and the Deputies Vollmar and Grillenberger on the other, is being watched with interest here.[239]

In answer to Bebel's accusations, recently made in Berlin,[240] the deputy Grillenberger has published in his Organ the "Fränkische tagespost",[241] an article defending his policy, and stating that the Social-Democratic party is not Russia, and its' members will simply not put up with an autocratic rule. The article though makes allowances for Bebel's temperament, and finishes up by saying that when he has exhausted his anger it is to be hoped he will acknowledge having brought accusations which, had they been made by any other member of the party, he would have been the first to condemn himself.

The principal points in Bebel's utterances against Vollmar are that he is in the first place an Aristocrat,[242] and that, as such his movements must be viewed with suspicion: that in the next place his policy of winning over the peasants at any price is a wrong one. The proper course would be to win over the rural artizans, workmen, etc … who were much more disposed to adhere to a communistic programme.

The "Bayerischer Kurier",[243] in a recent review on the Socialistic situation, sums up as follows:

---

[239] The differences originated in Bebel's criticism of the SPD deputies of the Bavarian *Landtag* which, on 1 June 1894, had approved the state budget, containing ameliorations for lower-grade civil servants.

[240] At a Berlin party meeting, on 14 November 1894.

[241] On 17 November 1894.

[242] Georg von Vollmar's family was elevated to the nobility in 1790; his full name was Ritter von Vollmar auf Veltheim.

[243] On 20 November 1894.

"One thing is certain, that there is a split between the North and South of the Social-democratic party. The aristocrat Vollmar with his partizans on the one hand, and Bebel at the head of the Prussian Socialists on the other hand. In one word the Prussian understands how to impose himself with his love of command, and to make himself the most cordially detested German everywhere."

The Social-democratic Organ of Munich,[244] in an article just published, entitled "Bebel's raising of the Colours" accuses him of having thrown down the torch of dissension in the ranks of the party, and states that his recent appearance can only be called a Pronunciamiento[245] directed against the results of the "Frankfurter Parteitag".[246]

It is needless to quote any further, for the split is now in active progress, and mutual vituperations between the different leaders of the Social-democratic party are likely to be the order of the day for some considerable time to come.

FO 9/269: Victor Drummond to Earl of Kimberley, No 65, Munich, 29 November 1894

[Received 3 December by post. X; K[imberley]]

Anti-Bebel speech made by Deputy Vollmar at Social Democrat meeting

With reference to Mr Vansittart's despatch No. 63 of the 22nd instant, I have the honour to report that a Social-democratic meeting, which was very numerously attended, was held in Munich on the 26th instant.[247]

The Deputy Vollmar in his speech, which lasted two hours, and which was warmly applauded, attacked Bebel's recent attitude and utterances: Vollmar, in qualifying Bebel by the name of "The Dictator" called out "it is not with myself here one has to reckon with, but with the whole Bavarian Social-democratic party. I shall do my duty as long as the Party requires me, but as long as I enjoy its' confidence I shall not allow myself to be intimidated, and least of all through such menaces."

At the close of the meeting two Resolutions were passed, one protesting against Bebel's attitude and utterances with respect to the Bavarian Social-democrats; and the other containing a vote of Confidence in Vollmar.

[244] *Münchner Post*, 22 November 1894.
[245] Spanish: 'public declaration'.
[246] Bebel's initiative to compel *Landtag* deputies to vote against state budgets was dismissed at the Frankfurt party congress (21 to 27 October 1894).
[247] See previous dispatch.

FO 9/270: Victor Drummond to Earl of Kimberley, No 3, Munich, 10 January 1895

[Received 14 January by messenger. For: The Queen / Lord Rosebery / Copy to Berlin for perusal; 'Ask Mr Drummond to send originals of newspaper articles', K[imberley]]

South German and Prussian particularism; Bavarian parties condemn imperial subversion bill; petition to Reichstag; socialist meeting and contempt for the same

Much irritation has been lately shown by the German Press against Prussia, chiefly owing to Prussia's reactionary policy; the new Project of Law, the "Umsturz Vorlage", now under discussion in the Imperial Diet being received in the South German States with marked disfavour.[248]

With respect to Particularism in the South German States, it has hitherto been forgotten that there is also Prussian Particularism, the two are antagonistic to one another, but this Particularist feeling concerns the ideas and requirements of each particular State; it is in no way inimical to the Empire.

The German people are as strong in their fidelity to the Unity of the Empire as hitherto, there is nothing to prevent them, however, from showing discontent with their own internal affairs; the idea, therefore, as given in the French Press, that the present dissatisfaction of the South Germans with Prussia may loosen the strings which hold the German Empire together, is erroneous.

With respect to the "Umsturz Vorlage", or project of law to combat Socialism, Bavaria and Würtemberg raise their voices against it, for there are measures proposed in the Project of Law which affect others besides the Socialists.

At a meeting held by the Democratic party in Munich on the 5th instant, but at which all political parties were represented, the "Umsturz" proposal was unanimously condemned. Professor D[r] Quidde said article 130[249] punishes attacks on Religion, the Monarchy, family life, and property severely, but does not punish attacks on the rights of the People, and the Constitution.

The project of Law was specially directed against Social Democracy, but not against The Chief of the Press Bureau[250] viz; – Mr Rössler.

In alluding to article 131,[251] Dr Quidde said, as it stands, not only would those persons be punished who purposely misrepresented

---

[248] For the 'subversion bill' (*Umsturzvorlage*), see n. 381 in Berlin section.

[249] Article 130 of the Imperial Criminal Code of 1871 concerned incitement of the people (altered on 20 March 1876).

[250] The Prussian *Literarisches Büro*; see also n. 67 in Dresden section.

[251] Article 131 of the Imperial Criminal Code of 1871 concerned contempt of government.

facts, but likewise those would be punished who know, or who must take for granted, that facts have been misrepresented. Besides the Press, every one reproducing an article, facts, etc … would be punished. In his opinion the whole paragraph should be removed. Under the new law, half the population of Munich would come under accusation for all that was said in the recent "Fuchsmühl" affair.[252] [Note in margin: 'See Mr Vansittart's despatch No. 56 of the 8th November [18]94]

Dr Quidde further stigmatized article III.[253] Under its' provisions, plays from the great national Poet Schiller, such as "Tell" and the "Robbers", would be condemned, because Schiller glorified in these pieces certain crimes.

Other speakers also gave their views strongly condemning the project of law.

D[r] Conrad (a professor of literary note) said German Culture should not become the plaything of an absolute Ruler, or of his chamber servants.

D[r] Sigle [sic], editor of an anti-Prussian newspaper,[254] said that he wished it to be known that the Ultramontane Party would reject the Project of Law, which was directed against every party, which did not run as a slave after the all Powerful one at Berlin.

After various other speakers of all kinds of politics had spoken, the following Resolution was unanimously voted: –

That the 1000 Citizens (or more) present declare the "Umsturz Vorlage" to be a most dangerous menace to civil Freedom and culture. They expect the Reichstag to reject the Project of Law with an overwhelming majority, and that, on their part, they will take into consideration the necessity for ameliorating the present penal code in a more liberal and national spirit.

After the above Resolution was passed, the meeting addressed the following petition to the Imperial Diet (Reichstag) –

1. That the Reichstag be pleased to reject the proposal submitted by the Federal Council, for altering the Penal, Military, and Press Codes, as being a most dangerous menace to civil Freedom and German Civilization.

---

[252] On 30 October 1896 a legal dispute between inhabitants of Fuchsmühl (Upper Palatinate) and the local lord of the manor escalated when a detachment of 50 soldiers forcibly intervened against a crowd of 180 people who were insisting on their long-honoured right to cut wood in a forest. Two peasants were killed, some thirty people were wounded.

[253] Article 3 of the bill adjusted to Article 23 of the Imperial Press Law, of 7 May 1874, to the proposed amendments to the Imperial Criminal Code. It concerned confiscation of publications without court order.

[254] *Das Bayerisches Vaterland.*

2. That the Reichstag be pleased to take into consideration the necessity of a Reform in the present Penal Code in a Liberal, and national Sense of the Word.

Again a great Socialist meeting was held in Munich yesterday, when Herr Volmar [*sic*], Socialist member of Munich, spoke against the reactionary policy at Berlin, and against the "Umsturz Vorlage". He said "the project of Law has been presented, and is the production of a non responsible Government which sees the mountain high increasing discontent without knowing how to stop it. It must be thrown out. The German people who have been sleeping now begin to move, and the leader to Victory in this fight is Socialism. The meeting unanimously passed a Resolution condemning the Project of Law, which is for the purpose of destroying the small rights of the people remaining to them."

I have the honour to inclose herewith translation of an Extract from the "Munich Bavarian Courier",[255] [Note in margin: 'Précis translation'] taken from a letter of the Correspondent[256] of the "Frankfurter Zeitung",[257] giving his opinion on the present discontent in South Germany. In it he mentioned that there is a disposition to blame the Bavarian Government for not having withstood in the Federal Council, the Prussian Reactionary policy.

FO 9/270: Victor Drummond to Earl of Kimberley, No 9, Munich, 21 February 1895

[Received 27 February by messenger. For: The Queen / Lord Rosebery; K [imberley]]

Cautionary press comments on German Emperor's personal will transcending the will of the people

The extraordinary activity of mind of His Imperial Majesty The German Emperor as well as the activity of His Majesty's movements and his strong will have made a great impression upon the German people. The words written by His Majesty in the Golden Book in the Munich Guildhall "Suprema lex regis voluntas"[258]

---

[255] Enclosures: original (cutting) from *Bayerische Kurier*, 5 January 1895 and précis translation.

[256] Name not traceable.

[257] The correspondent's report, dated Munich 1 January, was published on 3 January 1895.

[258] 'The king's will is the highest law'. Wilhelm signed the Golden Book on 8 September 1891 upon his visit to Munich.

have been interpreted as signifying the Emperor's own personal will which is considered shown, by His dispensing with the services of the two Chancellors of the Empire without consulting the Federal Council.[259]

Upon the relations between the Emperor and the German Nation, I have the honour to inclose herewith Précis translations of two remarkable Articles[260] which have lately appeared in the "Munich latest news"[261] of the 8th and 11th ultimo. The first is headed "the highest law" and comments upon the phrase "Suprema lex regis voluntas", and says that the Emperor should remember that the Empire was made with the blood of the People, and points out that the will of the Prince concerns the Imperial legislature which can only be executed by the help of the Federal Council and Imperial Parliament.

The Emperor is praised for wishing to do only that which is good in the service of the German Nation, but a hint is given to His Majestys' Counsellors that they should have the courage to say to His Majesty that when he acts upon the "Suprema lex regis voluntas" He should be told that this is not the highest Law, but that of the Welfare of the People.

The second Article headed the "German people and their Emperor" shows the German Empire is an eternal Confederation, in regard to which, The Emperor is only a Chief with His equals, their relations of the Emperor and the people being founded on mutual esteem and love: the people do not wish to be ruled by Him but loved. Is this the case? let this question remain unanswered says the writer,[262] who then presupposes a rupture between the Emperor and the people and supplies its probable results, giving three ways, adhering to the second, consisting in a return to the old traditions of the Imperial Constitution. The Emperor and His people must mutually respect each other, and His Majesty should be thus counselled.

These Articles have probably been instigated on account of the late reactionary policy at Berlin,[263] and on account of the general belief

---

[259] For Bismarck's and Caprivi's dismissals, see nn. 252 and 298 in Berlin section.

[260] Enclosures: original (cutting) 'Das höchste Gesetz', *Münchner Neueste Nachrichten*, 8 January 1895 and précis translation ('The Highest Law'); original (cutting) 'Das deutsche Volk und sein Kaiser', *Münchner Neueste Nachrichten*, 11 January 1895 and précis translation ('The German People and their Emperor').

[261] *Münchner Neueste Nachrichten*.

[262] Name not traceable.

[263] Drummond is referring, amongst other things, to the 'subversion bill' (see n. 381 in Berlin section).

that the entourage of the Emperor never have the courage to offer advice to His Majesty, and it is feared therefore that there is a possibility that His Majesty may some day carry out some measure, or do something antagonistic to the feelings of the people.

FO 9/270: Victor Drummond to Marquess of Salisbury, Confidential, No 38, Munich, 24 August 1895

[Received 26 August by messenger. S[alisbury]]

British press articles have stirred up German animosity towards England; other causes of resentment

Certain articles which have lately appeared in the English newspapers, the "Standard" and the "Globe", have again stirred up German irritation against England, their publication is declared to be a great want of tact and have increased England's unpopularity in Germany, which is to be regretted.

The cause of Germanys displeasure, with England has been, I consider, brought about in the first instance, by the German Colonial party, jealous of our great success in Africa and by the Bismarck party who were annoyed, at the time of the death of the late Emperor of Russia[264] to see signs of a friendly "rapprochement" between Russia and England which would be inimical to their own policy, which is, to further a policy of discord between the two nations as also between England and France, in order to distract attention from Germany; then, there is always, outside of Government quarters, a soreness that England will not join the Triple Alliance[265] and, not so long ago, annoyance at New Zealand's proposal in regard to Samoa,[266] again the Congo agreement and the idea that we wished Germany to protest against French proceedings in Siam.[267]

German jealousy and selfishness are the actual causes of Germany's irritation. England is always the "perfide Albion" if she does not conform to Germany's wishes. England it is declared is always trying to make a catspaw of Germany.

---

[264] Alexander III died on 1 November 1894.

[265] For the Triple Alliance, see n. 174 in Berlin section.

[266] Drummond is referring to New Zealand's proposal to annex Samoa under a British protectorate, which was put forward in April 1894.

[267] For the Anglo-Congolese (Anglo-Belgian) agreement, see n. 365 in Berlin section; for the French proceedings in Siam, see n. 227 in this section.

I may be permitted to refer, with reference to my above remarks, to my Despatches N° 80 confidential of the 29th October 1887 and N° 61 of August 15th 1893.[268]

FO 9/270: Victor Drummond to Marquess of Salisbury, No 39, Munich, 30 August 1895

[Received 9 September by messenger. X; S[alisbury]]

Forty-second Roman Catholic Convention in Munich; little change in political agenda except willingness to work with state and Protestants to combat socialism; measures in this regard

The forty second annual Congress of the German Roman Catholics assembled at Munich on the 26th instant, it was formally opened on the 27th instant[269] by the President, Count von Preysing, who commenced proceedings by reading a letter from The Pope[270] laudatory of the objects the Congress had in view.

Telegrams of loyalty were sent to the Pope, His Imperial Majesty The German Emperor and His Royal Highness The Prince Regent of Bavaria,[271] and gracious replies were received.

There is little of real novelty to be reported on from the results of the Congress, it was chiefly, a yearly repetition of old annual phrases; but, a remarkable change in one point must be noticed, which is, that the Roman Catholic Party appear disposed no longer to look upon the State or The Protestants as enemies, but declare their readiness to act with them to combat atheism and revolutionary principles.

Count von Preysing referred in his speech to the growing indifference of the people towards Religion which, he said, must be combated by religious school teaching, by Confessional schools, and by particular attention to religious education in the middle and high schools; other speakers insisted on every means being taken to combat Socialism, (on this point I may remark that it is reported that four thousand people attended the Roman Catholic Congress and that 20,000 [*sic*] Socialists attended a Socialist meeting held in Munich a few weeks ago,)[272] they declared Christian workmen's associations were essential to assist religious feeling among the working classes, that Christianism is combined in Christ, The Church and The

---

[268] See pp. 500–503 and 532–533.

[269] On 26 August; the 42nd *Katholikentag* took place from 25 to 29 August.

[270] Leo XIII to Count von Preysing, president of the organizing committee, dated Rome, 30 July 1895.

[271] Luitpold.

[272] Drummond is referring to the workers' summer fete at Holzapfelkreuth on 18 August 1895.

Pope, and that all Christian sects should be drawn into one fold, (of course the Roman Catholic.)

Referring to The Pope's position in Rome, one of the speakers, Baron von Hertling, said, that the 20th September 1870 had brought no solution, but only conflict, the Roman Catholics must fight on until it is closed, this can only be done by the return of the Italian people to The Pope, who is still a Prisoner, but who must sooner or later be set free, as it cannot be suffered that His Holiness should be the Subject of any Prince, the restoration of The territorial Sovereignty is necessary to put an end to the Conflict.[273]

Among other things advocated by the speakers were, liberty for all religious Orders, more Sunday recreation for Soldiers, abolition of Duelling, erection of cheap houses for workmen's homes, free Roman Catholic Universities; all these measures have, already, on other occasions been proposed.

Special mention was made of The Pope's exertion in favour of Peace between all classes and races, and of The German Emperor's desire for Peace, also The Prince Regent of Bavaria was mentioned as "a true Son of the Church, who showed His love for and His duty to His people."

The Congress was closed yesterday, when the archbishop of Munich[274] delivered His blessings.

I may add that the Roman Catholic party are undoubtedly very earnest in their work to combat Socialism and with this object they have several Societies, the most important is the People's Union,[275] this society held its annual meeting at Munich on the 27th instant, when it was shown that the Society had been formed to enable the people to assist the Bishops and Priests in their combative work, to uphold and show the advantages of religion as opposed to socialist doctrines. In 1893, there were one hundred and forty thousand members of the Union, in this year they number one hundred and eighty thousand. The Membership costs one shilling. The result of the Society's work, in its' attempt to attract the working classes into its' fold will be matched with much interest; there is no doubt of the extraordinary power being exercised by The Pope[,] His Bishops and Clergy to convert the world into the Roman Catholic haven, a civilizing but aggressive policy which cannot be too carefully taken into consideration by the leading Ecclesiastical Authorities of other Creeds.

---

[273] The 'Capture of Rome' of 20 September 1870 marked the incorporation of the Papal States into the Italian kingdom. The rights and prerogatives of the Pope and the Holy See and its relationship with Italy were regulated by the Law of Guarantees of 13 May 1871.

[274] Anton von Steichele.

[275] *Volksverein für das katholische Deutschland*, founded in 1890.

FO 9/270: Brooke Boothby to Marquess of Salisbury, No 53, Munich, 10 November 1895

[Received 18 November by bag. X; S[alisbury]]

Landtag *debates on imperial subversion bill and social democracy; complaints of emperor's growing power over smaller states*

I have the honour to report that the Social Democratic party in the Bavarian Diet have availed themselves of the Debates on the Estimates for the Ministry for Foreign Affairs to make a violent attack on the Government for their support of the anti Revolution Bills and for their generally subservient attitude towards Prussia in the Federal Council.[276]

Their leader, Dr Grillenberger complained also that the German Emperor was assuming the position of an absolute ruler rather than that of President of the Federal Council;[277] that the state of affairs in the Empire was tending more and more to a military dictatorship; that the Governments of individual States were becoming daily more powerless; and that the Bavarian people were lapsing into slavery.

Baron Crailsheim, the Minister for Foreign Affairs replied. After justifying the attitude of the Bavarian Representatives in the Federal Council, – where their lack of Opposition was due to the unanimity which prevailed there – His Excellency declared that their support of the Anti-Revolution Bill was necessitated by "the Anarchist Movement, which had recently spread to Bavaria", and the elements of which had shown themselves in Social Democratic Assemblies. He made an urgent appeal to the great 'bourgeois' parties to rouse themselves from their lethargy, and instead of exhausting their strength in combating each other, to combine against the common enemy, namely Social Democracy.

This appeal had unfortunately the very opposite effect, as each party in the effort to justify itself, was led to throw the blame on the other. Hence there ensued, contrary to a previous agreement, a prolonged general discussion on the causes of and remedies for social democracy, and the general state of political affairs in Bavaria. Although in this discussion the doctrines of the Socialists were strongly condemned, yet the complaints made against the growing predominance of Prussia and the Emperor's attitude towards the several

---

[276] The debates in the second chamber of the Bavarian *Landtag* took place on 28 and 29 October. On the 'subversion bill' (*Umsturzvorlage*), see n. 381 in Berlin section.

[277] The German Emperor, as King of Prussia, held the presidency of the confederation (*Bundespräsidium*); he was not president of the Federal Council, which, according to the imperial constitution of 1871, was chaired by the imperial chancellor.

States found an echo in other parts of the House – Dr Daller, a leader of the Clerical Party, agreed with Dr Grillenberger that "the King of Prussia is President of the Federal Council, and only as such bears the title of German Emperor; we must hold fast to that." "It seems" he continued "that efforts are being made to stretch the power and influence of the President far beyond the limits of the Imperial Constitution." – Dr Orterer and other speakers also urged that Bavaria should more carefully maintain her independence.

As regards the general discussion on Social Democracy, the Clerical and the Liberal Party each made use of the old arguments, the former attributing its origin to the scientific instruction of the University Professors, which had undermined the religious convictions of the people, and taught them to regard the duties of brotherly help and support of their poorer neighbours as unnecessary; the latter retaliating that, in works of benevolence and philanthropy, the Liberals as a party were equally active, and that the real cause, that divided the two parties and prevented any combined action against Social Democracy, was to be found in the direct and indirect attacks of the Clericals for many years past on the Constitution of the German Empire.

At the close of the discussion, the vote was declared to be agreed to on a show of hands without a division.

The Social Democratic movement does not appear to be making any serious advance in this part of Germany.

FO 9/271: Victor Drummond to Marquess of Salisbury, No 2, Munich, 9 January 1896

[Received 17 January by bag. For: ~~The Queen~~ / Mr Balfour / Mr Chamberlain / African Department; S[alisbury]]

Anti-British attitude manifested by Bavarian press following Transvaal incident

I have the honour to inform Your Lordship that the Bavarian Press in its comments on recent events in the Transvaal has shown itself to the full as hostile to England and as violent and contemptuous in the language employed as the most extreme of the Prussian Organs.[278] While admitting the correctness of the attitude assumed by Her Majesty's Government at the actual moment of the inroad made by Mr Jameson's followers, the Bavarian newspapers nevertheless maintain that this invasion had the moral support and sanction of the Colonial Office, and was carried out with the full knowledge of M^r

---

[278] On the Transvaal crisis and the 'Jameson Raid', see pp. 188–195 and n. 450 in Prussian section.

Cecil Rhodes, and that it was only the failure of the attempt which forced Her Majesty's Government to disavow it. In every fresh Article on the subject the complaint is reiterated that England has the deliberate intention of establishing a Protectorate over the Transvaal, and of finally annexing it. This, it is urged would be the most flagrant and unheard of breach of the law of nations, but in accordance with Great Britain's course of action in every quarter of the world. The "Allgemeine Zeitung" in its issues of yesterday and today has somewhat moderated the offensiveness of its tone, but the "Neueste Nachrichten", which has a still larger circulation continues, to use the same expressions of hatred and contempt.

I quote in the Inclosure in this Despatch, a few extracts in translation from the leading Munich papers.[279]

FO 9/271: Victor Drummond to Marquess of Salisbury, Confidential, No 15, Munich, 2 April 1896

[Received 6 April by messenger. For: ~~The Queen / Duke of Devonshire / Mr Balfour~~ / Confidential to Berlin / ~~Colonial Office~~; S[alisbury]; Copy, 2 April]

Emperor's congratulatory telegram to President Kruger following 'Jameson Raid' attributed to royal sympathy with Boers and a diplomatic tactic to elicit Dutch friendship

With respect to the raid made by Dr Jameson and his followers into the Transvaal last December and the German Emperor's telegraphic message to President Krüger congratulating him on the Boers' victory, which caused general indignation throughout the whole English race, but which gained His Imperial Majesty great popularity with his people, who consider themselves the natural protectors of the Boers, the message was, according to information I have received from a confidential source, not only sent to President Krüger on account of His Majesty's sympathy with the Boers, but possibly with the view to assist Germany in obtaining Holland's friendship.[280]

Germany's sympathy is given to the Boers for the following reasons; – in the belief that the Transvaal and Orange Republic and even the Cape dominion are really Dutch possessions, and that the Dutch should be the Paramount Power in South Africa; also Germany desires to save the Boers from what they call British tyranny, and last not least to obtain great commercial advantages in opposition to us. This sympathy for the Boers was particularly

---

[279] Enclosures: translations of articles in *Münchner Neueste Nachrichten* of 4, 5 and 8 January 1896.

[280] On the 'Jameson Raid' and the ensuing Kruger telegram, see pp. 188–195.

noticeable at the time of the Jameson raid, when the "ouitlanders"[281] of German origin declared their willingness to act with the Transvaal Government against the English.

With relation to what I mention above of Germany's desire to have Holland's friendship, it must be remembered that until late years Holland had no friendly feelings towards Germany, fearing nothing more than amalgamation with the German Empire, as since it has been erected, hints had been expressed from time to time that Holland should form a part of it. This idea was not regarded with any favour by the Dutch, but since Germany has given its moral protection to the Boers, who have always preserved their attachment to the Mother Country, the Dutch have altered their sentiments, and the Germans are now much more liked, and recent events have added to this feeling.

The German Government is, I am told, aware that there is an influential party in Holland, not perhaps at present very numerous which upholds the maxim that where the Dutch element is in South Africa, the colonies there should belong to Holland; they are supported by certain German elements which covet a great German Colonial Empire, their influence is becoming daily stronger, their aim being to unite the Netherlands with Germany, and to acquire the Dutch Colonies.

German demonstrations of late years in favour of the Boers and Dutch in South Africa may therefore be looked upon as a Diplomatic means of drawing Holland in time into the folds of Germany with the prospective view above-mentioned, losing no opportunity to win the friendship of the Dutch.

Dr Jameson's raid gave the German Emperor the ideal chance of accentuating this policy at our expense with the best possible results for furthering Germany's views in regard to Holland.

FO 9/271: Brooke Boothby to Marquess of Salisbury, No 29, Munich, 12 June 1896

[Received 17 June. For: The Queen / Mr Balfour / Berlin, P.L. [printed letter]; S[alisbury]]

Speech by Prince Ludwig at German dinner in Moscow; asserts independence of Bavarian state and loyalty to empire; reflects anti-Prussian sentiment in Bavarian public opinion

I have the honour to report that the news which reached Munich on Tuesday last – through the channel of the Vienna "Neue Freie

---

[281] 'Uitlanders', foreign residents of the South African Republic.

Presse"[282] – of the speech of Prince Louis of Bavaria at Moscow, at the dinner given by the German colony on the 6th instant, has been the subject of general interest and discussion here during the past few days. – His Royal Highness is reported to have protested against the words "Prince Henry and all the Princes in his suite", used by the President[283] in the toast which he proposed, declaring that they were "not vassals, but the allies of the German Emperor"; that as such – as the Emperor William I had always admitted – they had stood 25 years ago at the King of Prussia's side; that as such they would again stand together, should the safety of Germany be in danger. The latest accounts received direct from Moscow state that Prince Louis concluded by exhorting all Germans to stand always together and to remain firm in their fidelity to the Empire.

The vast majority of the people of this county are in entire agreement with the views expressed by Prince Louis both as to the independence of Bavaria and as to the desirability of German unity. Many, however, regard the speech as unfortunately ill-timed and calculated to convey to foreigners the erroneous impression that there is internal disunion in the Empire. On the other hand there are many who, though staunch supporters of a "United Germany" and appreciating the advantages to be derived therefrom in case of war, are nevertheless not too well disposed to Prussia, and view with great uneasiness the growing tendency to centralisation; these latter rejoice in the accidental circumstance which called forth Prince Louis's emphatic protest. This anti-Prussian sentiment has been specially evident during the past year in the Reports of [the] Chamber of Commerce, which complain that Bavarian interests are neglected in Commercial Treaties, and in the speeches of some influential deputies in the Diet: it is also very generally noticeable in the conversation of the people.

The "Allgemeine Zeitung",[284] the most influential of the Munich daily newspapers, expresses its opinion of the Moscow incident as follows "Prince Louis has correctly stated the Constitutional position, and at the same time has so insisted on the advantages of German kinship and German unity, that all misconstruction, even for the most malevolent is rendered impossible. It is not the Prince's words which can create a false impression abroad, but the commentaries which have been made on them in one part of the German Press."

---

[282] Issue of 8 June 1896.
[283] Karl Camesa-Sasca.
[284] On 11 June 1896.

When a Berlin paper seeks to bring the Bavarian people as "thorough Germans"[285] into opposition with their Royal Family, this hopeless attempt can only result in producing the greatest indignation. The Wittelsbach dynasty is no less "thoroughly German" than our people, and well has the dynasty proved it – and not least Prince Louis."

FO 9/272: Victor Drummond to Marquess of Salisbury, No 23, Munich, 29 July 1897

[Received 9 August by messenger. X; S[alisbury]]

Speech by Johann Baptist Sigl at Peasants Union meeting critical of Catholic Centre Party and in favour of Bavarian national party; peasant movement gaining ground

I have the honour to report an incident which has created some sensation in Bavaria.

At a meeting of a "Peasants Union" "Bauernbund", Dr Sigl a democratic Leader, formerly Representative in the Imperial Diet as Member for Kelheim and now elected Member for Regen in Franconia,[286] has lately[287] made a Speech at Pfaffenhofen denouncing the Centrum or Ultramontane party and Prussian particularism. He said, "we must now have a real Bavarian party which will know how to do its duty, the Centrum party must cease to exist as a Bavarian party for it follows slavishly the lead of the Prussian Centrum, if we succeed in crushing the Centrum[,] if we can form a Bavarian party whose Representatives will appear at Berlin then I am authorised to declare publicly that this event will be received with favour and with thanks in a high[,] very high place. This party, however, exists already[,] it is to be found in the Peasants party the real Bavarian the people's party."

Dr Sigl's observation that this would give gratification to a person in a very high place has mystified the Public, some believed it had reference to the Bavarian Minister[288] at Berlin others to Baron de Crailsheim who it is declared by the Centrum party lately mentioned to a leader of the Peasants party, Dr Rassinger [*sic*],[289] that he foresaw that the future of Bavaria, the solving of Bavarian questions and the strengthening of Bavarian interests in Berlin could only be brought

---

[285] The original article used the expression '*kerndeutsch*'.
[286] Regen is located in Lower Bavaria.
[287] On 22 August 1897.
[288] Hugo Graf von Lerchenfeld.
[289] Georg Ratzinger.

about by the formation of a Bavarian party in the Reichstag, however, this has been officiously denied.

Baron Crailsheim told me only a short time ago that he viewed the advancing successful movement by the Peasants party with some concerns for it would have to be reckoned with at the Elections next year and that it would probably add another fraction to the Chambers which might cause difficulties to the Government on Government questions, this confirms me in my opinion that Baron de Crailsheim never could have made use of the words said to have been delivered by His Excellency in conversation with Dr Rassinger.

This new Peasant movement, however, is gaining ground throughout Bavaria inimical to the Centrum party, the Roman Catholic Priests, the Nobles and Prussian Particularism.

FO 9/272: Victor Drummond to Marquess of Salisbury, No 42, Munich, 13 October 1897

[Received 18 October by messenger. For: War Office (Intelligence Division) / Berlin for perusal (P.L.) [printed letter]; S[alisbury]; Seen at Berlin [stamped]]

Bavarian opposition towards proposed reforms of German imperial military judiciary procedures; upholds reserved rights

Interpellations were made yesterday in the Bavarian Diet as to the attitude of the Bavarian Government on the question of the impending Reforms of the German Imperial Military Judicial Procedure, which is looked forward to with distrust by Bavaria who wishes to maintain her own Military Laws, carried out publicly, whereas Prussia's are secret.[290] The Minister of War, Baron von Asch, replied that the proceedings in the Federal Council were secret and, therefore, he could not give any information respecting them but that he would consult his Colleagues as to what further answer he could give; to day, His Excellency made a statement in the Chamber that he is authorised to say that the Imperial Federal Council has not yet come to an understanding, but that the Bavarian Government adheres to its' position already declared in 1891 and 1892 that they uphold the Bavarian Military Law of Publicity in its' proceedings and not less they are determined to uphold the Bavarian reserve rights; His Excellency, however, did not specially mention those as to Military Judicial Procedure, and with regard to this I have the honour to refer Your Lordship to

---

[290] For the German Military Penal Code, see n. 186 in this section.

my Despatch N° 54 of the 30th of October 1891, in which I mention a conversation I had with Baron de Crailsheim, when he stated that, in regard to Military Judicial Procedure, Bavaria had no reserved rights and that it was a matter that must be finally decided by the Imperial Federal Council.²⁹¹

It is said, that The Prince Regent of Bavaria spoke very seriously to His Majesty The German Emperor during the Military Manoeuvres last month,²⁹² showing, that it would be impossible for Bavaria to change her Military Laws which she had maintained for so many years, and that The Emperor accepted the arguments set forth by The Prince Regent.

FO 9/272: Victor Drummond to Marquess of Salisbury, No 57, Munich, 31 December 1897

[Received 10 January by messenger. For: Mr Balfour, A.J.B. [Arthur James Balfour] / Duke of Devonshire / Mr Goschen, G.J.G. [George Joachim Goschen] / Admiralty / Commercial Department; S[alisbury]]

Views of Bavarian political parties regarding increase in size of German fleet; economic assessment of German shipping needs; statistical illustration of growth in merchant shipping

With reference to my despatches N°s 47 and 48 of the 5th and 13th ultimo, upon the proposed increase of the German Fleet, and to the Bill produced to the German Reichstag in this sense, I have the honour to report that meetings have been held in Bavaria and Wurtemburg which shew the views of the different parties.²⁹³ The Colonial, National Liberal and Conservative party is entirely in favour of [the] Septennate arrangement; the Socialist and Democratic against it, although not opposed to a moderate increase of the fleet, and the Centrum party are in favour of a fleet sufficient to protect German citizens abroad and the German coasts but not for a fleet which would be a menace to others. The "Munich General News"²⁹⁴ has obtained the views of the Wurtemburg National Economist, Dr Schaffle, who in a very long and able report sums up with the expression that the present German fleet must be made more efficient in numbers of battle ships and cruizers to prevent a blockade of Germany's ports and to assist German merchant

---

²⁹¹ For the *Reservatrechte* (reserved rights), see n. 220 in this section.
²⁹² Wilhelm II met Luitpold at Würzburg and Nuremberg on 1 and 2 September 1897.
²⁹³ For the imperial naval bill, see n. 536 in Berlin section.
²⁹⁴ Schäffle's four-part article 'Ein Votum für die Marinevorlage' ('A vote for the navy bill') was published in the *Allgemeine Zeitung* on 23, 29, 30, and 31 December 1897.

ships from being captured in case of war and enable them to reach
their own or neutral ports in safety.

Dr Schaffle agrees with Admiral Tirpiz [*sic*] as to the composition
of the German fleet necessary for German requirements even in time
of peace, but that this must be the minimum.

Dr Schaffle closes his remarks with the following observations on
English and Commercial interests, "that the immense strides
Germany has made in her commercial affairs since these last ten
years has astonished her rivals, and England would if possible be
too glad to take any opportunity to destroy this on account of her
jealousy of our progress."

For the first time in this century our ships' tonnage last year surpassed
that of England in the Port of Hamburg. Since 1873 our trade with
England has only increased 88% (in the last ten years 35%) – whereas
with Sweden it has increased 97%, Austria-Hungary 341%, United
States of America 128%, Mexico and South America 317%, East
India and Eastern Asia 488%, Australia 475%, the Cape 270%, the
Levant 2261%.["]

Dr Schaffle shows that "whilst Germany's trade has increased
exceptionally by 55 millions sterling, [note in margin: '55,000,000']
that of Russia, France and England have diminished. The slur on
Germany's goods – "made in Germany" – has not damaged
German industries but those of England." "Yes!", says, Dr Schaffle,
"we have emancipated ourselves from England which is the cause
of her rancour and animosity – and we must be prepared to protect
the trade we have gained by having a strong fleet."

The National-Liberal, Colonial and Conservative Press use daily
arguments not only to show that Admiral Tirpiz' plan must be carried out, but also rightly or wrongly that no Power is opposed to this
except Great Britain.

ANNOTATED INDEX OF NAMES

Page numbers in italic type refer to sender/address of dispatch.

Arendt, Otto (1854–1936), publicist and conservative politician. Member of the Prussian house of deputies (1886–1918) and the *Reichstag* (1898–1918). 347, 372

Arnim-Suckow, Harry Graf von (1824–1881), Prussian diplomat. Envoy extraordinary and minister plenipotentiary at Lisbon (1862), Kassel (1863), Munich (1863), to the Holy See (1864), and Paris (1871; 1872–1874 as imperial ambassador); fled to Switzerland to avoid prison sentence (1875). 127, 130, 165, 364

Arnold, Thomas (1795–1842), English educationist; headmaster of Rugby School (1828–1841). 354

Arnulf (1852–1907), Prince of Bavaria. General. 428

Asch zu Asch, Adolf Freiherr von (1830–1906), Bavarian general and minister of war (1893–1905). 550

Augusta (1811–1890), Princess of Sachsen-Weimar-Eisenach. Married Wilhelm I in 1829; Queen of Prussia from 1861; German Empress from 1871. 38, 40, 101

Augusta (1843–1919), Princess of Saxe-Meiningen. Married Prince Moritz of Saxe-Altenburg in Meiningen in 1862. 40

Auguste (1826–1898), Princess of Württemberg. Married Hermann of Saxe-Weimar-Eisenach in 1851. 434

Auguste Viktoria (1858–1921), Princess of Schleswig-Holstein-Sonderburg-Augustenburg. Married Wilhelm II in 1881; German Empress and Queen of Prussia, 1888–1918. 141, 212, 259, 325, 328

Auiti, Andrea (1849–1905), Italian archbishop. Apostolic nuncio in Munich (1893–1896) and Lisbon (1896–1903); cardinal priest (1903). 534

Bachmaier, Benedikt (1852–1912), Bavarian farmer and politician (Bavarian Peasants' League). Member of the second chamber of the Bavarian *Landtag* (1893–1904) and the *Reichstag* (1893–1912). 531

Badt, Lippmann (dates unknown), bookseller and editor of the *Dresdner Zeitung*. 325, 327

Balfour, Arthur James (1848–1930), politician and statesman. MP (1874–1922); secretary for Scotland (1886), chief secretary for Ireland (1887), first lord of the treasury (1891–1892; 1895–1905), lord privy seal (1902), prime minister (1902–1905), first lord of the admiralty (1915–1916), foreign secretary (1916–1919), lord president of the council (1919–1922; 1925–1929); created Earl of Balfour and Viscount Traprain (1922). 140, 179, 183, 185, 194, 199, 201–203, 206–207, 209–210, 213–215, 257, 259–260, 403–405, 408, 412–414, 462, 545–546, 547, 551

Ballantine, William (1812–1887), English lawyer and serjeant-at-law. 502

Barrère, Camille (1851–1940), French diplomat. Consul general at Cairo (1882); envoy extraordinary and minister plenipotentiary at Stockholm (1885), Munich (1891; from 1888 permanent chargé d'affaires), and Berne (1894); ambassador to Rome (1897–1924). 375–376, 510, 523–524

Barrington, Eric (1847–1918), British civil servant. Principal private secretary to the secretary of state for foreign affairs (1885–1892; 1895–1905); assistant under-secretary of state for foreign affairs (1906–1907). 418

Barron, Sir Henry (1824–1900), British diplomat. Secretary of legation at Lisbon (1858) and Brussels (1861; 1871); secretary of embassy at Constantinople (1866); again secretary of legation at Brussels (1871); minister resident at Stuttgart (1883–1890). 6–7, 20, 24, *423–433*

Barth, Theodor (1849–1909), lawyer and liberal politician. Member of the Prussian house of deputies (1898–1903) and the *Reichstag* (1881–1898; 1901–1903). 379

Barthélemy-Saint-Hilaire, Jules (1805–1895), French statesman, journalist and philosopher. 291

Bashford, John Laidlay (1852–1908), British author and journalist. Berlin correspondent of the *Daily Telegraph* (1885–1903), then of the *Manchester Guardian, Daily Graphic, Pall Mall Gazette*, and *Westminster Gazette*. 69–70, 195–196

Battenberg, Franz Joseph von (1861–1924), German prince, youngest son of Prince Alexander of Hesse and by Rhine and Julia von Battenberg. 229–230

Battenberg, Ludwig von (1854–1921), eldest son of Prince Alexander of Hesse and by Rhine and Julia von Battenberg. British naval officer from the age of 15; admiral 1904; First Sea Lord, 1912, resigned 27 October 1914. From 1917 Louis Alexander Mountbatten, 1st Marquess of Milford Haven. 229

Baur von Breitenfeld, Fidel (1835–1886), Württemberg diplomat. Envoy extraordinary and minister plenipotentiary at Karlsruhe (1869), Vienna (1872) and Berlin (1881–1886; at the same time plenipotentiary at the Federal Council). 33

Bayha, Friedrich (1832–1902), innkeeper and politician. Member of the second chamber of the Württemberg *Landtag* (1868–1870; 1890–1894) and the *Reichstag* (1887–1890). 432

Bazaine, François Achille (1811–1888), French general. Marshal of France (1864). 114–115

Beaconsfield, *see* **Disraeli, Benjamin**

Beauclerk, William Nelthorpe (1849–1908), British diplomat. Third secretary at Athens (1876), Berne (1877), and St Petersburg (1879); second secretary at Rome (1880), Washington (1887), and Berlin (1888); secretary of legation at Peking (1890); consul general at Budapest (1896); minister resident at Lima (1898–1908). *111–113, 117–119*

Bismarck, Herbert von (1849–1904), German diplomat and politician; son of Otto von Bismarck. Worked at the Berlin foreign office from 1873; *Botschaftsrat* in London (1882); envoy to The Hague (1884); under-secretary (1885) and state secretary for foreign affairs (1886–1890). *Reichstag* member (1884–1886; 1893–1904). 16, 46, 49n, 59–60, 68–69, 81, 83, 87–88, 93–95, 105, 114–116, 121, 124–125, 155, 205–206, 275, 283n, 325n, 326–327, 393

Bismarck, Otto von (1815–1898), Prussian statesman. Envoy to the Federal Diet at Frankfurt (1851–1859), ambassador to St Petersburg (1859) and Paris (1862); Prussian minister president and foreign minister (1862–1872; 1873–1890); chancellor of the North German Confederation (1867-1871); *Reichstag* member (1867; 1891–1893); from 1880 also Prussian minister of trade (1880–1890); imperial chancellor (1871–1890); Graf 1865; Fürst 1871. 8–10, 13–17, 20, 22, 33, 36, 41–54, 56–65, 67, 70–80, 84–85, 92, 94–106, 108, 111, 115, 120–133, 135, 141–142, 145–146, 165–166, 174–177, 201–202, 204–206, 222, 231, 238, 248, 254–256, 265, 272, 274–276, 285n, 288–289, 295, 301–304, 307n–310, 313, 315–316, 318, 321, 325–328, 330, 335, 343–344, 348, 349–350, 355–356, 361–364, 367, 371, 373, 378, 384–387, 390, 392–394, 416n, 417, 425, 453, 468, 470, 473, 474–476, 478, 484–485, 490–491, 493, 496–497, 507–508, 513, 526, 528–529, 540–541

Bissing, Walter Freiherr (b.1855), journalist. London correspondent of the *Kreuzeitung* from 1888 to 1900. 180

Bleichröder, Gerson von (1822–1893), German banker. From 1855 head of the banking firm of S. Bleichröder. 102, 336

Blokland, Jonkheer Gerard Beelaerts van (1843–1897), Dutch jurist and South African diplomat. From 1884 representative (minister resident) of the South African Republic at Berlin, Lisbon and Paris; from 1889 as envoy extraordinary and minister plenipotentiary. 173, 180

Blumenthal, Leonhard Graf von (1810–1900), Prussian field marshal. 520

Blumenthal, Werner von (1847–1928), Prussian military officer and chamberlain. Master of ceremonies under Wilhelm I 395

Boetticher, Karl Heinrich von (1833–1907), Prussian civil servant, politician and statesman. State secretary of the imperial office of the interior (1880–1897) and vice chancellor (1881–1897). 124, 186, 217n, 388, 400

Bönisch, Friedrich (1832–1894), Saxon jurist and liberal politician. Second mayor of Dresden (1884–1894); member of the second chamber of the Saxon *Landtag* (1875–1894). 334

Boothby, Sir Brooke (1856–1913), British diplomat. Second secretary at Vienna (1889), Munich (1895), and Paris (1896); secretary of legation at Rio de Janeiro (1898), Tokyo (1901), and Brussels (1902); councillor of embassy at Vienna (1905–1907). 544–545, 547–549

Boulanger, Georges (1837–1891), French general and politician. Minister of war (1886–1887). 2n, 87, 89–90, 135, 282n, 290, 309

Brackenbury, Henry (1837–1914), British army officer. Private secretary to the viceroy of India (1880), acting military attaché at Paris (1881–1882); director of military intelligence (1886–1891). 69, 491

Brausewetter, Georg Robert (1836–1896), judge. From 1888 director of the Berlin district court. 369

Briggs, Thomas (1795–1864), British banker, murdered by Franz Müller on a train. 501

Bronsart von Schellendorff, Walther (1833–1914), Prussian general. Prussian minister of war (1893–1896); adjutant general to Wilhelm II (1896). 177, 183–184, 186, 209, 490

Bruno, Giordano (1548–1600), Dominican friar, philosopher, and astronomer. 512

Buchanan, Sir George William (1854–1924), British diplomat. Secretary of legation and chargé d'affaires at Darmstadt and Karlsruhe (1893); agent on the Venezuela boundary arbitration tribunal in Paris (1898); secretary of embassy at Rome (1900) and Berlin (1901); consul general at Sofia (1903); envoy extraordinary and minister plenipotentiary at The Hague (1909); ambassador to St Petersburg (1910) and Rome (1919–1921). 8, 18–19, 249

Buchner, Max (1846–1921), German physician, ethnographer and colonial explorer. 36

Buddeberg, Louis Heinrich (1836–1925), Saxon merchant and liberal politician. *Reichstag* member (1881–1898; 1907–1912). 342

Bülow, Bernhard von (1849–1929), German statesman and diplomat. Envoy extraordinary and minister plenipotentiary at Bucharest (1888); ambassador to Rome (1893); imperial state secretary for foreign affairs (1897–1900); imperial chancellor and Prussian minister president (1900–1909). 154, 213–214

Bülow, Maria von (1848–1929), née Beccadelli di Bologna, married to Karl August von Dönhof from 1867 to 1882; married Bernhard von Bülow in 1886. 154

Bulwer-Lytton, Edward Robert (1831–1891), British statesman, diplomat and poet. Secretary of legation at Copenhagen (1863), Athens (1864), Lisbon (1865), and Madrid (1868); secretary of embassy at Vienna (1868), and Paris (1868; from 1873 minister); envoy extraordinary and minister plenipotentiary at Lisbon (1874); viceroy and governor general of India (1876–1880); ambassador to Paris (1887); 1st Earl of Lytton (1880). 102

Bunsen, Christian Karl Josias Freiherr von (1791–1860), Prussian diplomat. Chargé d'affaires at the Prussian legation to the Holy See (1823), minister resident (1827), and envoy extraordinary and minister plenipotentiary (1834–1838); envoy extraordinary to Berne (1839–1841) and London (1842–1854); also the provisional central government's envoy to London (December 1848–May 1849); member of the Frankfurt National Assembly (May 1848–January 1849) and the Prussian upper house (1858). 295

Buol-Berenberg, Rudolf von (1842–1902), jurist and Catholic politician. Member of the second chamber of Baden (1881–1896) and the *Reichstag* (1884–1898; its president 1895–1898). 175

Burkardt, Germain (1821–1890), farmer and Württemberg politician. *Reichstag* member (1887–1890). 432

Burke, Edmund (1729–1797), Anglo-Irish politician, statesman, philosophical and political thinker. 302, 366

Burkhardt, Theodor Otto (b.1846) wood-block cutter and socialist agitator. 270

Bürklin, Albert (1844–1924), jurist and National Liberal politician. Member of the second chamber of Baden (1875–1881), the *Reichstag* (1877–1898), and the first chamber of Baden (1905–1918). 175

Burns, John (1858–1943), English politician and trades unionist. MP (1892–1918); president of the Local Government Board (1905–1914) and the Board of Trade (1914). 389

Burt, Thomas (1837–1922), British trades unionist and politician. MP (1874–1918); parliamentary secretary to the Board of Trade (1892–1895). 389

Busch, Clemens August (1834–1895), German diplomat. Consul general at Budapest (1878); acting secretary of state at the Berlin foreign office (1881); under-secretary of state (1881); envoy extraordinary and minister plenipotentiary at Bucharest (1885), Stockholm (1888), and Berne (1892–1895). 39–41

Cadogan, Henry George Gerald (1859–1893), British diplomat. Third secretary at Berlin (1883); second secretary at Munich (1885); secretary of legation at Teheran (1890). 435, *503–506*, 515

Camesa-Sasca, Karl (dates unknown), German merchant. President of the German club in Moscow. 548

Campbell-Bannerman, Sir Henry (1836–1908), British politician and statesman. MP (1868–1908); chief secretary for Ireland (1884–1885); secretary of state for war (1886; 1892–1895); prime minister (1905–1908). 143, 527

Caprivi, Leo von (1831–1899), German general and statesman. Imperial chancellor (1890–1894) and Prussian minister president (1890–1892). 16–18, 124, 126–127, 132, 136, 138–144, 146, 157, 162–168, 182, 186, 201, 203, 205, 248n, 358–360, 363–365, 367–368, 372–374, 377, 384–385, 388–389, 392–393, 447, 452–455, 521–522, 526, 529, 540

Carew-Hunt, Henry Thomas (1846–1923), British consular agent. Consul at Port-au-Prince (1883), Königsberg (1886), and Danzig (1889); consul general at New Orleans (1903–1915). 90–91

Carnot, Marie François Sadi (1837–1894), French statesman. President (1887–1894). 153, 161–162

Cockayne-Cust, Henry (1861–1917), English politician and author. Editor of the Pall Mall Gazette (1892–1896); MP (1890–1895; 1900–1906). 191

Cockerell, William A. (1840–1919), civil servant at the Foreign Office from 1860; assistant clerk (1877); senior clerk (1893–1906). 170, 340

Conrad, Michael Georg (1846–1927), German publicist and naturalist writer. *Reichstag* member (1896–1898). 538

Corbett, Sir Vincent Edwin Henry (1861–1936), British diplomat. Attaché at Berlin (1885); third secretary at Berlin (1886), The Hague (1887), and Rome (1888); second secretary at Constantinople (1891), Copenhagen (1894), and Athens (1895; from 1900 secretary of legation); British commissioner at the *Caisse de la Dette Publique* in Cairo (1903); minister resident at Caracas (1907) and at Munich (1910–1914). 60

Courcel, Alphonse Chodron de (1835–1919), French diplomat. Ambassador to Berlin (1881–1886) and London (1894–1898). 40

Cousin-Montauban, Charles, comte de Palikao (1796–1878), French general and statesman. Prime minister and minister of war (August–September 1870). 322

Crailsheim, Friedrich Krafft von (1841–1926), Bavarian statesman. Minister of foreign affairs (1880–1903), minister president (1890–1903); member of the first chamber of the Bavarian *Landtag* (1895–1918). 427, 468, 478, 481, 484n, 490, 495, 497–498, 505–506, 510, 516–518, 521–523, 530, 544, 550–551

Crawford, James Adair (dates unknown), British colonial civil servant. Under-secretary to the foreign department of the government of India (1892); chief political resident of the Persian Gulf (1893); acting chief commissioner of Baluchistan (1895). 197n

Crispi, Francesco (1818–1901), Italian politician and statesman. Prime minister of Italy (1887–1891; 1893–1896); minister of the interior (1877–1878; 1887–1881; 1893–1896); foreign minister (1887–1891). 128–129, 140, 155

Cross, Richard Assheton (1823–1914), British statesman and politician. MP (1857–1862; 1868–1886); home secretary (1874–1880; 1885–1886); secretary of state for India (1886–1892); lord privy seal (1895–1900); created Viscount Cross (1886). 279

Crowe, Sir Joseph Archer (1825–1896), British diplomat, art historian, and journalist. Consul general at Leipzig (1860) and Düsseldorf (1872); commercial attaché at Berlin (1880); commercial attaché for Europe at Paris (1882–1896). 358

Currie, Philip Henry Wodehouse (1834–1906), British diplomat. Senior clerk (1873), principal private secretary to the foreign secretary (1878–1880); assistant permanent under-secretary of state (1882), permanent under-secretary (1889); ambassador to Constantinople (1894) and Rome (1898–1903); 1st Baron Currie (1899). 6, 432, 440

Curzon, George Nathaniel (1859–1925), British statesman. MP (1886–1898); parliamentary under-secretary of state for India (1891–1892) and for foreign affairs (1895–

1898); viceroy and governor general of India (1899–1905); secretary of state for foreign affairs (1919–1924). Created Baron Curzon of Kedleston (1898), 5th Baron Scarsdale, (1916); Marquess Curzon of Kedleston and Earl of Kedleston (1921). 202, 403

Dallas, Sir George E. (1842–1918), civil servant (Foreign Office). Assistant clerk (1881), senior clerk Western Department (1890), chief clerk (1896–1900) 274, 277, 473, 475

Daller, Balthasar von (1835–1911), Catholic priest and politician. From 1864 professor at the Freising Lyceum, from 1886 its rector; member of the second chamber of the Bavarian *Landtag* (1871–1911). 514, 530, 545

Davis, Edmund (1861–1939), British businessman, mining financier and art collector. 168

Degouy, Robert (1862–1912), French naval officer. 163

Deimling, Ludwig von (1833–1906), military officer from Baden. From 1870 in Prussian service. 240

Deines, Adolf von (1845–1911), Prussian officer. Military attaché at Madrid (1885) and Vienna (1887–1884); from 1888 aide-de-camp to Wilhelm I; commanding general of the VII imperial army corps at Koblenz (1902–1906). 114–115

Delbrück, Hans (1848–1929), German historian and politician. Tutor to Prince Waldemar of Prussia (1874–1879); professor at Berlin University (1885); member of the Prussian house of deputies (1882–1885) and the *Reichstag* (1884–1890). 185

Delguey de Malavas, Jacques (1852–1942), French naval officer and military historian. 163

Deligiannis, Theodoros (1820–1905), Greek statesman. Minister of foreign affairs (1863; 1864–1865; 1869–1870; 1878) and prime minister (1885–1886; 1890–1892; 1895–1897; 1902–1903; 1904–1905). 260

Deloncle, François (1856–1922), French politician and consul. Member of the Chamber of deputies (1889–1898; 1902–1914). 390–391

Derby, *see* **Stanley, Edward Henry**

Déroulède, Paul (1846–1914), French writer and politician. Co-founder of the nationalist *Ligue des Patriotes* (1882). 134, 290

Detring, Gustav (1842–1913), German civil servant. Customs offical at Tientsin (1875–1905). 202

Devonshire, *see* **Cavendish, Spencer Compton**

Dilke, Charles Wentworth (1843–1911), 2nd baronet (1869), English politician. MP (1868–1885; 1892–1911); parliamentary under-secretary of state for foreign affairs (1880–1882); member of the privy council (1882); president of the Local Government Board (1882–1885). 7–8, 33–34, 36–37, 39, 47, 49, 222, 265, 267, 271, 274, 467, 469–472

Disraeli, Benjamin (1804–1881), British statesman. MP (1837–1876); chancellor of the exchequer (1852; 1858–1859; 1866–1868); prime minister (1868, 1874–1880); created Earl of Beaconsfield (1876). 56–57, 317

Dönhoff, Karl August Graf von (1833–1906), Prussian diplomat. Envoy extraordinary and minister plenipotentiary at Dresden (1879–1906). 154

Douglas, Hugo Sholto Graf (1837–1912), German entrepreneur, writer, and politician. Member of the Prussian house of deputies (1882–1912). 321

Dreesbach, August (1844–1906), carpenter, journalist, and socialist politician. Member of the Baden *Landtag* (1891–1902) and the *Reichstag* (1890–1893; 1898–1906). 242

Drobe, Franz Kaspar (1808–1891), Catholic priest. Bishop of Paderborn from 1882. 480

Drummond, Sir Victor (1833–1907), British diplomat. Secretary of legation at Rio de Janeiro (1873) and Washington (1877); secretary of embassy at Vienna (1882); chargé d'affaires at Munich (1885); minister resident at Munich and at Stuttgart (1890–1903). 6–8, 19, 23, *448–458, 486–503, 506–543, 545–547, 549–552*

Drury, Henry (1778–1841), English scholar and educator; master at Harrow School (1801–1841). 354

Dufferin, *see* **Hamilton-Temple-Blackwood, Frederick**

Düfflipp, Lorenz von (1821–1886), Bavarian civil servant and court secretary to Ludwig II (1866–1877). 483

Durège, Max (dates unknown), British consular agent. Vice consul at Danzig (1883–1895). 91

Eckhard, Carl (8922–1910), jurist, entrepreneur and National Liberal politician. Member of the second chamber of the Baden *Landtag* (1861–1863; 1865–1873) and the *Reichstag* (1871–1874). 248

Edward (1841–1910), Prince of Wales. Crowned Edward VII, King of the United Kingdom of Great Britain and Ireland, and Emperor of India in 1901. 33, 41, 54, 56, 60, 63, 68–69, 73, 75, 77, 81, 85–86, 89, 91, 93, 94–95, 98, 100, 102, 104, 113–114, 121, 124–126, 128–129, 131, 138, 141, 143, 145, 147–148, 162, 174, 176, 185, 199, 201, 203, 207, 209, 212–213, 215, 235, 246–247, 254–256, 260–261, 279, 288, 290, 295, 299, 301, 312, 340, 363, 375, 469–471, 473, 480, 485–486, 488, 491, 498, 508, 519, 526, 529

Eisenlohr, August (1833–1916), Civil servant and statesman. *Ministerialdirektor* (1883), *Staatsrat* (1890) and president (1892–1900; from 1893 with the title of minister) of the

Baden ministry of the interior. Member of the second chamber of the Baden *Landtag* (1866–1870) and the *Reichstag* (1877–1878). 246–247, 251, 253

Eissenstein-Chotta, Arthur Ritter von und zu (1846–1911), Austrian diplomat and writer (pseud. Max von Essen). Secretary of embassy at Berlin (1887–1892). 92

Elizabeth I (1533–1603), Queen of England and Ireland from 1558. 411

Ellrichshausen, Joseph Freiherr von (1832–1906), estate owner and politician. Member of the second chamber of the Württemberg *Landtag* (1882–1895) and the *Reichstag* (1887–1890). 432

Ellstätter, Moritz (1827–1905), Civil servant and statesman. Baden minister for finances (1868–1893); from 1871 also plenipotentiary at the Federal Council. 241, 246

Emin Pasha (Eduard Schnitzer) (1840–1892), German physician and naturalist. Explorer of Africa and governor of the Egyptian province of Equatoria. 319

Erbach-Schönberg, Marie von (1852–1923), née Marie von Battenberg, German princess. Translator and writer. 229

Erhardt, Alois von (1831–1888), Bavarian jurist and politician. Mayor of Munich (1870–1887). 497

Ernst August (1845–1923), Duke of Cumberland and Teviotdale; last Crown Prince of Hanover (from 1851). Followed his father, Georg V, into exile in Austria in 1866. 55–57, 473–478

Eulenburg, Botho Graf zu (1831–1912), Prussian statesman. *Oberpräsident* of the province of Hanover (1873–1878) and the province of Hesse-Nassau (1881–1892); minister of the interior (1878–1881; 1892–1894) and minister president (1892–1894). From 1899 member of the Prussian upper chamber. 164, 166–167

Eulenburg, Graf Philip zu (1847–1921), Prussian diplomat and close friend of Wilhelm II. Envoy extraordinary and minister plenipotentiary at Stuttgart (1890) and Munich (1891); imperial ambassador to Vienna (1894–1902). 447

Eyschen, Paul (1841–1915), Luxembourg statesman, and diplomat. Prime minister (1888–1915). 150

Fabrice, Alfred Graf von (1818–1891), Saxon general and statesman. Minister of war (1866–1891); minister president (1876); and from 1882 also foreign minister. 267–268, 276, 279, 284, 351, 478

Farnall, Harry de la Rosa Burrard (dates unknown), civil servant (Foreign Office). Junior clerk (1873); assistant clerk (1894); senior clerk (1900). 403

Fergusson, Sir James (1832–1907), 6th baronet of Kilkerran (1849), British politician and colonial administrator. MP (1854–1857; 1859–1868; 1885–1906); governor of South

Australia (1869–1873), New Zealand (1873–1874), and Bombay (1880–1885); parliamentary under-secretary of state for India (1867–1868), home department (1867–1868), and for foreign affairs (1886–1891); postmaster general (1891–1892). 336

Ferry, Jules (1832–1893), French politician and statesman. Mayor of Paris (1870–1871); prime minister (1880–1881; 1883–1885). 64

Fichte, Johann Gottlieb (1762–1814), German philosopher. 304, 328

Finger, Jakob (1825–1904), jurist and Hessian statesman. Minister president and grand ducal minister of foreign affairs, of the interior, and of justice (1884–1898). Member of the second chamber (1862–1865) and the first chamber (18991903) of the Hessian *Landtag*. 232, 236, 243–244

Fischer, Ludwig von (1832–1900), politician. Mayor of Augsburg (1866–1900); member of the second chamber of the Bavarian *Landtag* (1863–1900) and of the *Reichstag* (1871–1874; 1884–1884; 1898–1900). 432

Fleck, Franz Ludwig (François Louis) (1824–1899), Bishop of Metz. 150

Förster, Paul (1844–1925), teacher, politician and anti-Semitic publicist. *Reichstag* member (1892–1898). 211

Fort, George Seymour (1858–1951), British colonial administrator and author. Resident magistrate at Umtali (1893). 196

Franckenstein, Georg Freiherr von und zu (1825–1890), landowner and politician. Member of the first chamber of the Bavarian *Landtag* (1847–1890) and the *Reichstag* (1872–1890). 481, 488, 493–494, 496–497, 528

Frankenburger, Wolf (1826–1889), lawyer and Bavarian politician. Member of the second chamber of the Bavarian *Landtag* (1869–1884) and the *Reichstag* (1874–1878). 427

Franz Joseph I (1830–1916), Emperor of Austria and Apostolic King of Hungary from 1848. 248n, 352

Fredericks, Vladimir Alexandrovich (1837–1892), Russian diplomat. Minister plenipotentiary and envoy extraordinary to Stuttgart (1884–1892; at the same time accredited to Baden).

Frederik VIII (1843–1912), King of Denmark from 1906. 154

Frege-Weltzien, Arnold von (1841–1916), estate owner, publicist, and conservative politician. Member of the first chamber of the Saxon *Landtag* (1893–1916) and the *Reichstag* (1878–1903). 386

Friedensburg, Ferdinand (1824–1891), Prussian jurist and mayor of Breslau (1870–1891). 320

Geiser, Bruno (1846–1898), German journalist and socialist politician. *Reichstag* member (1881–1887). 272

Georg V (1819–1878), Crown Prince of Hanover (1837); King of Hanover (1851–1866). 55n, 285n, 478

Georg Wilhelm (1880–1912), hereditary Prince of Hanover. 478

George (1819–1904), British prince, 2nd Duke of Cambridge (1850). British army officer. 54, 56, 473, 475

Gessler, Theodor von (1821–1886), Württemberg jurist and statesman. Professor at the University of Tübingen (1857), from 1863 its chancellor. Minister for church and school affairs (1870–1885); member of the second chamber of the Württemberg *Landtag* (1862–1870). 426

Gibbon, Edward (1737–1794), British historian and MP (1774–1784). 306

Giers, Nikolai (1820–1895), Russian diplomat and statesman. Minister of foreign affairs (1882–1894). 53n, 71, 82n, 92–93

Gisela (1856–1932), Archduchess of Austria. Married Prince Leopold of Bavaria in 1873. 497

Gladstone, William Ewart (1809–1898), British statesman and politician. MP (1832–1845; 1847–1890); chancellor of the exchequer (1852–1855; 1859–1866; 1873–1874; 1880–1882); prime minister (1868–1874; 1880–1885; 1886; 1892–1894). 51–52, 72–73n, 283n–284, 286–287, 291, 299, 360–361, 368n–369, 380, 386, 470n

Glaser, Menrad (1853–1896), typesetter and socialist politician. Member of the second chamber of the Württemberg *Landtag* (1895–1896). 461

Goldbeck, Bernhard (dates unknown), British consular agent. Vice consul (1880) and consul (1886–1893; repeatedly acting consul general) at Frankfurt. 227–228

Gönner, Albert (1838–1909), jurist, civil servant and politician. Mayor of Baden Baden (1875–1907) and member of second chamber of the Baden *Landtag* (1883–1908; 1893–1906 its president). 252

Görtz-Wrisberg, Hermann Graf (1819–1889), Brunswick civil servant and statesman. State minister president and plenipotentiary at the Federal Council (1883–1889); president of the council of the regency (1884–1885). 56

Goschen, George Joachim (1831–1907), British statesman and politician. MP (1863–1900); chancellor of the exchequer (1887–1892); first lord of the admiralty (1871–1874; 1895–1900); 1st Viscount Goschen (1900). 298, 338, 346, 402, 462, 491, 551

Göser, Johannes (1828–1893), priest and Württemberg politician. *Reichstag* member (1887–1893). 432

Gosselin, Martin le Marchant Hadsley (1847–1905), British diplomat. Third secretary at Berlin (1873); second secretary at St Petersburg (1874), Rome, St Petersburg (1880), and Berlin (1882); secretary of legation at Brussels (1885); secretary of embassy at Madrid (1892), and Berlin (1893); minister at Paris (1896); assistant under-secretary of state for Foreign Affairs (1898–1902); envoy extraordinary and minister plenipotentiary in Portugal (1902–1905). 49, *149–154*, 159–159, *160–169*, *174–177*, *179–186*, 187, *195–199*

Granville, *see* **Leveson-Gower, Granville George**

Greene, William Conyngham (1854–1934), British diplomat. Third secretary at Stuttgart (1883); second secretary at Stuttgart (1887), The Hague (1889), Brussels (1891); secretary of legation at Teheran (1893); H.M.'s agent at Pretoria (1896); envoy extraordinary and minister plenipotentiary at Berne (1901), Bucharest (1906), and Copenhagen (1911); ambassador to Tokyo (1912–1919). *434*, 44n

Grierson, James (1859–1914), British army officer. Military attaché at Berlin (1896–1900). 194

Griesinger, Albert Julius Freiherr von (1836–1899), Württemberg civil servant. From 1883 private secretary to Karl I, then to Wilhelm II 435

Grillenberger, Karl (1848–1897), journalist and socialist politician from Nuremberg. Member of the *Reichstag* (1881–1897) and the second chamber of the Bavarian *Landtag* (1892–1897). 535

Gröber, Adolf (1854–1919), jurist and politician. Member of the second chamber of the Württemberg *Landtag* (1889–1919) and of the *Reichstag* (1887–1918). 432, 457–459

Grub, Friedrich (1833–1908), farmer, entrepreneur and Württemberg politician. *Reichstag* member (1887–1890). 432

Gruner, Hans (1865–1943), German explorer and colonist. From 1892 to 1914 colonial official in the German protectorate Togoland. 182, 187

Gudden, Bernhard von (1825–1886), psychiatrist and personal physician to King Ludwig II 19, 485–487

Guidi, Giovanni Battista (1852–1904), Catholic priest and diplomat of the Hoy See; uditore at Munich (1887). Secretary of state to Leo XIII (1890–1892); titular Archbishop of Stauropolis (1902). 505–506

Gurko, Iosif 231; *see also* **Romeiko-Gurko, Count Iosif Vladimirovich**

Haberkorn, Ludwig (1811–1901), Saxon jurist and politician. Mayor of Kamenz (1856) and Zittau (1857–1886); member of the second chamber of the Saxon *Landtag* (1849–1893; its president 1859–1870; 1875–1890); *Reichstag* member (1867). 266, 302

Hack, Theophil Friedrich von (1843–1911), head of the Stuttgart municipality (*Stadtschultheiß*) from 1872 to 1892; member of the second chamber of the Württemberg *Landtag* (1882–1884). 428

Haffner, Paul Leopold (1829–1899), Catholic priest. Vicar general (1866–1877) and from 1886 Bishop of Mainz. From 1899 member of the first chamber of the Hessian *Landtag*. 228–229

Hahnke, Wilhelm von (1833–1912), Prussian general; chief of the military cabinet of the King of Prussia and German Emperor (1888–1901). 177

Hamed bin Mohammed el Murjebi (1832–1905), Swahili-Arab merchant and slave trader; known as Tippu Tip. Governor of the Stanley Falls District in the Congo Free State (1887–1891). 319

Hamilton, Lord George Francis (1845–1927), British statesman and politician. MP (1868–1906); first lord of the admiralty (1886–1892), secretary of state for India (1895–1903). 491

Hamilton-Temple-Blackwood, Frederick (1826–1902), British diplomat and statesman; Irish peer. Created Earl of Dufferin in British peerage (1871) and Marquess of Dufferin and Ava (1888). Governor general of Canada (1872); ambassador to St Petersburg (1879), and Constantinople (1881); viceroy of India (1884); ambassador to Rome (1888) and Paris (1891–1896). 59, 151

Harcourt, Sir William Vernon (1827–1904), British statesman. MP (1868–1904); home secretary (1880–1885); chancellor of the exchequer (1886; 1892–1895). 60, 156, 160–161, 165, 222, 271

Hardinge, Arthur Henry (1859–1933), British diplomat. Consul general at Zanzibar (1894); commissioner of the East Africa Protectorate (1895); envoy extraordinary and minister plenipotentiary at Teheran (1900), Brussels (1906), and Lisbon (1911); ambassador to Madrid (1913–1919). 196–197n

Hartmann, Eduard von (1842–1906), German philosopher. 328

Hatzfeldt, Paul Graf von (1831–1901), German diplomat. Envoy extraordinary to Madrid (1874); ambassador to Constantinople (1878); secretary of state in the Berlin foreign office (1881); minister of state without portfolio (1882–1885); ambassador to London (1885–1901). 39, 51–53, 179n, 188–189, 199–201

Heine, Karl (1819–1888), entrepreneur and National Liberal politician from Leipzig. Member of the second chamber of the Saxon *Landtag* (1869–1888) and the *Reichstag* (1874–1877). 272

Heinrich (1862–1929), Prussian prince and German admiral. 40, 177, 209n, 548

Helena (1846–1923), Princess of the United Kingdom, third daughter of Queen Victoria. Married Prince Christian of Schleswig-Holstein in 1866. 40

Helmholtz, Hermann von (1821–1894), German physicist and physician. Professor of physiology at Königsberg (1849), Bonn (1855), and Heidelberg (1858); professor of physics at Berlin (1871). 361–362

Helyar, Horace Augustus (1853–1893), British diplomat. Third secretary at Madrid (1878) and The Hague (1879); second secretary at The Hague (1881) Washington (1884), St Petersburg (1888), and Munich (1890–1893). *249, 518, 526*

Hendry, Donald (*c.*1854–1935), companion of Charles Woodcock; from 1879 to 1888 on continental tour in Europe; from 1883 at Stuttgart; from 1910 librarian at Pratt Institute Free Library in Brooklyn, New York. 436, 438

Heneage, Charles (1841–1901), British diplomat. Third secretary at the Hague (1867), and Munich (1869); second secretary at St Petersburg (1872–1874). 237

Heneage, Edward (1840–1922), British politician. MP (1865–1868; 1880–1892); Chancellor of the Duchy of Lancaster (1886); 1st Baron Heneage (1896). 237

Herbette, Jules (1839–1901), French diplomat and foreign office official. Ambassador to Berlin (1886–1896). 81, 83, 133–134, 141, 161–16, 162, 178

Herbette, Marie Mathilde (b.1845), née Sibert. Married Jules Herbette in 1867. 133

Hermann (1825–1901), Prince of Saxe-Weimar-Eisenach. Württemberg general. 428, 434

Hertling, Georg von (1843–1919), Catholic politician and statesman. Bavarian minister president (1912–1917); imperial chancellor and minister president of Prussia (1917–1918); member of the first chamber of the Bavarian *Landtag* (1887–1891) and *Reichstag* (1875–1912). 543

Hertslet, Sir Edward (1824–1902), Foreign Office librarian and author of reference works. 160

Hervey, Henry (1832–1898), civil servant (Foreign Office). Junior clerk (1854); 1854; assistant clerk (1871); senior clerk (1877–1896). 293n, 297, 439

Heuduck, Wilhelm von (1821–1899), Prussian general. Commander of the XV imperial army corps at Strasbourg (1885–1890). 231

Hill, Sir Clement Lloyd (1845–1913), British diplomat and politician. Junior clerk (1867); acting second secretary at Munich (1875–1876); private secretary to the under-secretary of state for foreign affairs (1885–1886); assistant clerk (1886); senior clerk (1894–1905); MP (1906–1913). 160n, 179n, 187, 196–197n

Hinzpeter, Georg Ernst (1827–1907), teacher. From 1867 tutor to Prince Wilhelm of Prussia (Wilhelm II); from 1904 member of the Prussian upper house. 115, 349

Jacobini, Lodovico (1832–1887), Italian cardinal from 1879. Apostolic nuncio to Austria (1874–1880) and cardinal secretary of state (1880–1887). 493–494, 496

Jagemann, Eugen von (1849–1926), Baden jurist and diplomat. Envoy extraordinary and minister plenipotentiary at Berlin (1893–1903). 166

Jameson, Sir Leander Starr (1853–1917), British colonial administrator and politician. Chief magistrate of Mashonaland (1891–1893); administrator of Matabeleland (Southern Rhodesia; 1894–1896); for his involvement in the raid against the South African Republic sentenced to fifteen months' imprisonment (June 1896). From 1900 member of the assembly of the Cape Colony; prime minister of the Cape Colony (1904–1908). 171–173, 188–189, 190n, 192, 196n, 410, 413n, 545–547

Jarrys, Freiherr von La Roche, Max du (1834–1888), military officer. Marshal of the court of Prince Leopold of Bavaria. 497

Jocelyn, William Nassau (1832–1892), British diplomat. Secretary of legation at Stockholm (1868) and Berne (1873); secretary of embassy at Constantinople (1874–1878); chargé d'affaires to Hesse and Baden at Darmstadt (1878–1892). 19, *221–248*, 249

Johann Albrecht (1857–1920), German prince. Regent of the Grand Duchy of Mecklenburg-Schwerin (1897–1901) and regent of the Duchy of Brunswick. (1907–1913); president of the *Deutsche Kolonialgesellschaft* (1895–1920). 181

Johnston, Sir Henry Hamilton (1858–1927), British explorer, diplomat, and colonial administrator. Consul in Mozambique (1889); commissioner and consul general for the British Central Africa Protectorate (1891); consul general at Tunis (1897); commissioner, commander in chief and consul general for the Uganda Protectorate (1999–1901). 196

Joost, Wilhelm (1860–1917), German business man and consul at Lourenço Marques (Maputo) (1893–1895). 180

Jöst, Franz (1851–1921), socialist politician. Member of the second chamber of the Grand Duchy of Hesse (1885–1896) and the *Reichstag* (1890–1896). 242

Kálnoky, Gusztáv Zsigmond gróf (1832–1898), Austro-Hungarian diplomat and statesman. Minister plenipotentiary and envoy extraordinary to Copenhagen (1874); ambassador to St Petersburg (1880); minister of foreign affairs (1881–1895). 76, 368–369

Kaltenborn-Stachau, Hans Karl von (1836–1898), Prussian general and statesman. Minister of war (1890–1893). 522

Karl Alexander (1818–1901), Grand Duke of Saxe-Weimar-Eisenach from 1853. 262

Karl I (1823–1891), King of Württemberg from 1864. 7, 19–20, 428–429, 434–440, 442–443, 446–447, 450, 454

Katkov, Mikhail (1818–1887), Russian journalist and from 1863 editor of the *Moskovskiye Vedomosti* (Moscow News). 67, 82n, 288

Königsmarck, Carl Graf von (1839–1910), Prussian estate owner. Member of the *Reichstag* of the North German Confederation (1867) and the Prussian upper house (from 1877). 40

Könneritz, Léonçe Robert Freiherr von (1835–1890), Saxon landowner and statesman. Member of the second chamber of the Saxon *Landtag* (1866–1876) and the *Reichstag* (1874–1877); *Oberhofmarschall* (1873–1891); *Kreishauptmann* of Zwickau (1874) and Leipzig (1876); minister of finance (1876–1890). 339

Krementz, Philipp (1819–1899), Archbishop of Cologne (1885–1899). Created cardinal in 1893. 479–480

Kruger, Paul (1825–1904), South African politician. Member of the executive triumvirate (1881–1883) and president of the South African Republic (Transvaal) (1883–1900); from 1900 in exile. 15, 18, 171n, 172n, 181, 190–193, 412–413, 546

Kusserow, Heinrich von (1836–1900), Prussian diplomat. Secretary of legation at Washington (1865–1868); *Legationsrat* in the Berlin foreign office (1874); Prussian envoy extraordinary and minister plenipotentiary at Hamburg (1885–1890); *Reichstag* member (1871–1874). 49

Labouchère, Henry Du Pré (1831–1912), English journalist, writer, politician. Attaché at Washington, Munich, Stockholm, Frankfurt, St Petersburg, and Dresden (1854–1862); second secretary at Constantinople (1862–1863); MP (1865–1868; 1880–1906). 361

Ladenburg, Ferdinand (1835–1899), German banker. From 1884 British vice consul at Mannheim. 237

Lascelles, Sir Frank Cavendish (1841–1920), British diplomat. Consul general at Cairo (1879) and Sofia (1879); envoy extraordinary and minister plenipotentiary at Bucharest (1887) and Teheran (1891); ambassador to St Petersburg (1894) and Berlin (1895–1908). 9–10, 18, *187–195*, 197n, *199–217*

Lassalle, Ferdinand (1825–1864), socialist politician and writer. Founding president of the *Allgemeiner Deutscher Arbeiterverein* (1863). 279

Launay, Edoardo de (1820–1892), Italian diplomat. Envoy extraordinary and minister plenipotentiary at Berlin (1853–1861 for Sardinia; 1861–1864; 1867–1892) and St Petersburg (1864–1867); from 1875 ambassador to Berlin. 40, 103

Leemann, Julius (1845–1905), farmer and politician. From 1891 professor for agriculture at Tübingen. Member of the of the second chamber of the Württemberg *Landtag* (1888–1891) and of the *Reichstag* (1884–1891). 432

Lefebvre de Béhaine, Édouard Alphonse, comte de (1829–1897), French diplomat. Chargé d'affaires at Munich (1871); envoy extraordinary and minister plenipotentiary at The Hague (1880); ambassador to the Holy See (1882). 510

Lister, Thomas Villiers (1832–1902), civil servant (Foreign Office). Assistant under-secretary of state for foreign affairs (1873–1893). 34, 86, 236–237, 297, 360–361, 425, 428, 442, 517

Louis Viereck (1851–1922), socialist journalist and politician. *Reichstag* member (1884–1887); emigrated to the USA in 1896. 272

Löwenstein-Wertheim-Rosenberg, Karl Fürst zu (1834–1921), Catholic politician, friar and priest (from 1908). Hereditary member of the first chambers of Bavaria (1856), Baden (1860), Württemberg (1861), and Hesse (1863); president of the central committee of German Catholics (1868) and co-founder of the *Zentrum* party (1870). *Reichstag* member (1871–1872). 80

Lucanus, Hermann von (1831–1908), Prussian civil servant; chief of the privy council (*Geheimes Zivilkabinett*) of Wilhelm II (1888–1908). 177

Lüderitz, Adolf (1834–1886), German merchant and colonist in South West Africa. 34n, 36n, 40–41

Ludwig I (1786–1868), King of Bavaria (1825–1848). 483

Ludwig II (1845–1886), King of Bavaria from 1864. 19, 469–470, 474, 480–488, 499n, 504, 514, 519–520

Ludwig III (1845–1921), Bavarian prince. Prince regent (1912–1913); reigned as last King of Bavaria (1913–1918). 481, 511, 548

Ludwig III (1806–1877), Grand Duke of Hesse-Darmstadt from 1848. 518

Ludwig IV (1837–1892), Grand Duke of Hesse-Darmstadt from 1877. 243–245, 249, 254, 259

Luise (1838–1923), Prussian princess. Grand Duchess of Baden from 1856. 261n–262

Luitpold (1821–1912), Prince of Bavaria. Prince regent from 1886. 352, 469–470n, 481, 484–485n, 488–489, 498–500, 504–506, 508–511, 513n–517, 519–520, 523, 525, 542–543, 551

Lutz, Johann (1826–1890), Bavarian statesman. Minister of justice (1867–1871) and of cultural affairs (1869–1880); head of the council of ministers (1880–1890); ennobled in 1880 and given the title Freiherr in 1883. 476, 488–489, 504, 511–515, 519

Lyons, Richard Bickerton Pemell (1817–1887), British diplomat. Baron Lyons (1858), created Viscount Lyons (1881); envoy extraordinary and minister plenipotentiary at Washington (1858–1865), ambassador to France (1867–1887). 10, 64, 82

Lytton, *see* **Bulwer-Lytton, Edward Robert**

Macaulay, Thomas Babington (1800–1859), British historian and politician. MP (1830–1847; 1852–1856); secretary at war (1839–1841); created 1st Baron Macaulay (1857). 309

MacDonell, Sir Hugh Guion (1832–1904), British diplomat. Secretary of embassy at Berlin (1875) and Rome (1878); chargé d'affaires at Munich (1882); envoy extraordinary to Rio de Janeiro (1885), Copenhagen (1888), and Lisbon (1893–1902). 8, 55, 181, *467–480*

Mackenzie, Sir Morell (1837–1892), British physician. 18, 112, 305, 316–317, 500, 503

Malcolm, Ian Zachary (1868–1944), British diplomat and politician. Honorary attaché at Berlin (1891–1893) and Paris (1893); assistant private secretary to the secretary of state, Salisbury, (1895–1898); MP (1895–1906; 1910–1919). 151

Malet, Sir Edward Baldwin (1837–1908), British diplomat. Secretary of legation at Peking (1871), Athens (1873), and Rome (1875); secretary of embassy at Rome (1876) and Constantinople; consul general in Egypt (1879); envoy extraordinary and minister plenipotentiary at Brussels (1883); ambassador to Berlin (1884–1895). 9–10, 13, 15–16, 21, *41–47, 48–49, 53–54,* 61, *65–80,* 82, *84–86,* 91, *93–106, 110–111, 114–117, 119–128, 131–140, 143–145, 147–149, 151–152, 154–159, 161–162, 169–173, 177–179,* 180–181, 287, 326–327, 490

Malsen, Ludwig Freiherr von (1828–1895), Bavarian diplomat and court official. *Oberhofmarschall* from 1868. 486

Maltzahn, Helmuth Freiherr von (1840–1923), Prussian statesman. State secretary in the imperial treasury (1888–1893); *Oberpräsident* of the province of Pommerania (1810–1911). *Reichstag* member (1871–1888). 241

Mann, Tom (1856–1941), British trades unionist, socialist politician and activist. 203, 417

Manteuffel, Edwin Freiherr von (1809–1885), Prussian general. Military governor of Schleswig (1864); commander during the Austro-Prussian War and the Franco-Prussian War; governor general of Alsace-Lorraine (1879–1885). 276–277

Margherita (1851–1926), Princess of Savoy. Queen consort of Italy (1878–1900). 141, 155n

Maria Alexandrovna (1849–1926), née von Adlerberg. Married Niko Dadiani. 71

Marie (1825–1889), Princess of Prussia. Married Maximilian of Bavaria in 1842, Queen of Bavaria from 1848. 486, 508–509

Marie (1849–1922), Princess of Sachsen-Weimar-Eisenach. Married Prinz Heinrich VII Reuß zu Köstritz in 1876. 384

Marschall von Bieberstein, Adolf Freiherr (1842–1912), jurist and diplomat. Baden envoy to Berlin and plenipotentiary at the Federal Council (1883–1890); imperial state secretary for foreign affairs (1890–1897); German ambassador to Constantinople (1897) and London (1912). Member of the first chamber of the Baden *Landtag* (1875–1883) and the

Mill, John Stuart (1806–1873), English philosopher and economist. 360

Minghetti, Marco (1818–1886), Italian statesman. Prime minister of Italy (1863–1864; 1873–1876). 154

Miquel, Johannes von (1828–1901), jurist, National Liberal politician and Prussian statesman. Mayor of Osnabrück (1865–1870; 1876–1880) and Frankfurt am Main (1880–1890); Prussian minister of finance (1890–1901). Member of the second chamber of the Hanoverian *Landtag* (1864–1866), the Prussian house of deputies (1867–1877), the upper house (1882–1890; 1901), and the *Reichstag* (1867–1877; 1887–1890). 146, 233

Mirbach-Sorquitten, Julius von (1839–1921), jurist, estate owner and conservative politician. Member of the Prussian upper house (1874–1918) and the *Reichstag* (1878–1881; 1886–1898). 371

Mittnacht, Hermann Freiherr von (1825–1909), Württemberg jurist and statesman. Member of the second chamber of the Württemberg *Landtag* (1861–1900); minister of justice (1867–1878), foreign minister (1873–1900) and minister president (1876–1900). 431, 437, 439–440, 442, 450–453, 456–458, 460–462, 468

Möbius, Kurt (dates unknown), secretary at the German general consulate in London. 36

Moeller, Eduard von (1814–1880), Prussian civil servant. *Oberpräsident* of Hesse Nassau (1867) and Alsace-Lorriane (1871–1879), 276–277

Mohrenheim, Arthur Pavlovich (1824–1906), Russian diplomat. Envoy extraordinary and minister plenipotentiary at Copenhagen (1867–1882); ambassador to London (1882–1884) and Paris (1884–1897). 533

Moltke, Helmuth Graf von (1800–1891), Prussian general. Chief of staff of the Prussian army (1858–1888); member of the *Reichstag* (1867–1891) and the Prussian upper house (1872). 131, 428, 490

Moltke, Helmuth Johannes von (1848–1916), Prussian general; aide-de-camp to Wilhem II (1891); chief of the imperial general staff (1906–1914). 384

Mommsen, Theodor (1817–1903), historian, classical scholar, and politician. Member of the Prussian house of deputies (1863–1866; 1873–1879) and the *Reichstag* (1881–1884); Nobel laureate in literature (1902). 323

Monson, Sir Edmund (1834–1909), British diplomat. Consul general and minister resident at Montevideo (1879); envoy extraordinary and minister plenipotentiary at Buenos Aires (1879), Copenhagen (1884), Athens (1888), and Brussels (1892); ambassador to Vienna (1893) and Paris (1896–1905). 10, 64

Morier, Sir Robert Burnett David (1826–1893), British diplomat. Attaché at Vienna (1853) and Berlin (1858); second secretary at Berlin (1862); secretary of legation at Athens (1865), Frankfurt (1866), and Darmstadt (1866); chargé d'affaires at Stuttgart (1871) and

Munich (1872); envoy extraordinary and minister plenipotentiary at Lisbon (1876) and Madrid (1881); ambassador to Russia (1884–1893). 9, 18, 93, 114–115, 322, 364, 509–510

Moser, Rudolf von (1840–1909), Württemberg diplomat and civil servant. Deputy plenipotentiary (1875–1879; 1882–1890) and plenipotentiary (1890–1894) at the Federal Council; from 1890 also envoy extraordinary and minister plenipotentiary at Berlin. 452–455

Mostyn, Hubert George Charles (1860–1935), 7th Baron Vaux of Harrowden (1883), British diplomat. Third secretary at Stuttgart (1889); second secretary at Stuttgart (1891; also acted as chargé d'affaires at Darmstadt in 1891 and in 1892), at Belgrade (1892), Berne (1893), and Brussels (1895–1898). 442, *445–447*

Mozaffar ad-Din Shah Qajar (1853–1907), Qajar shah of Iran from 1897. 261

Mpande kaSenzangakhona (1798–1872), king of the Zulu people (1840–1872). 46

Muhi-ud-Din Muhammad (1618–1707), known as Aurangzeb, Mughal emperor (1658–1707) 326

Müller, August (1825–1877), Württemberg village official (*Schultheiß*) in Güglingen. Member of the second chamber of the Württemberg *Landtag* (1861–1862). 441

Müller, Franz (1840–1864), German tailor; convicted murderer of Thomas Briggs. 501–502

Müller, Franz Carl (1860–1913), psychiatrist and personal physician to Prince Otto of Bavaria. 486

Müller, Gottlieb von (1816–1897), Priest and prelate from Stuttgart. 441

Müller, Martin (b. c.1854), would-be assassin of Prince Wilhelm of Württemberg. 441–442

Münster, Georg Herbert Graf zu (1820–1902), German diplomat. Hanoverian envoy extraordinary and minister plenipotentiary at St Petersburg (1856–1865); imperial ambassador to London (1873) and Paris (1885–1900). Member of the first chamber of the Hanoverian *Landtag* (1846–1866), the *Reichstag* (1867–1874), and the Prussian upper house (1867–1902). 36, 43, 45–46, 48, 116, 134, 274

Murad I (1326–1389), Ottoman Sultan from 1362 to 1389. 326

Muraviev, Mikhail Nikolaevich (1845–1900), Russian diplomat and statesman. Envoy extraordinary and minister plenipotentiary at Copenhagen (1893–1896); foreign minister (1897–1900). 154

Nachtigal, Gustav (1834–1885), German physician, explorer, and colonist. Consul general at Tunis (1882); imperial commissioner for West Africa (1884). 13, 35–36, 45n, 50

Napoleon I (1769–1821), Emperor of the French (1804–1814; 1815). 244, 303, 342n

Napoleon III (1808–1873), Charles Louis, later Louis Napoléon Bonaparte. President of the French Second Republic (1848–1851); assumed dictatorial powers in December 1851; Emperor of the French (1852–1870). 42

Natal'ia Obrenovich (1859–1941), née Keschko; known as Natalie of Serbia. As wife of Milan I, Princess consort (1875) and Queen consort (1882–1889) of Serbia. 110–111

Ndumbé Lobé Bell (1839–1897), also known as King Bell; leader of the Duala people (South Cameroon) from 1858, businessman, and politician. 275

Neipperg, Reinhard von (1856–1919), estate owner and politician. Member of the first chamber of the Württemberg *Landtag* (1880–1887) and the *Reichstag* (1881–1890). 432

Nelson, Horatio (1758–1805), British admiral. 1st Viscount Nelson (1801). 411, 442

Neurath, Konstantin Sebastian Freiherr von (1847–1912), jurist, estate owner and Württemberg politician. Member of the *Reichstag* (1881–1890). 432

Newcastle, *see* **Pelham-Holles, Thomas**

Nicholas II (1868–1918), Tsar of Russia (1894–1917). 18–19, 183, 259–262, 415–416

Niko I Dadiani (1846–1903), last Prince of Mingrelia (Samegrelo) from 1853 to 1867. 71

Northcote, Stafford (1818–1887), British statesman and politician. MP (1855–1885); president of the Board of Trade (1866–1867), secretary of state for India (1867–1868); chancellor of the exchequer (1874–1880); first lord of the treasury (1885–1886); 1st Earl of Iddesleigh from 1885; foreign secretary (1886–1887). 56, 57, *65–73*, *229–231*, 278–279, *285–288*, 293n, 475, *490–492*

Nostitz-Wallwitz, Hermann von (1826–1906), Saxon statesman. Minister of the interior (1866–1891), the royal house (1869–1871; 1882–1895), and foreign affairs (1876–1882); member of the second chamber of the Saxon *Landtag* (1857–1866) and the *Reichstag* (1874–1877). 268–270, 291–292, 300–301

Nostitz-Wallwitz, Oswald von (1830–1885), Saxon diplomat. Envoy extraordinary and minister plenipotentiary at Berlin (1873–1885). 33, 467

Novalis (1772–1801), German poet and author. 304

Olga (1869–1924), Princess of Saxe-Weimar-Eisenach. 434

Ol'ga Nikolaievna (1822–1892), Grand Duchess of Russia. Married Karl of Württemberg in 1846, Queen Olga of Württemberg from 1864. 428–429, 434, 445, 450

Oppenheimer, Sir Charles (1836–1900), merchant and British consular agent. Consul (1880) and consul general (1882–1900) at Frankfurt. 227–228

Orterer, Georg (1849–1916), Bavarian teacher and Catholic politician. Member of the second chamber of the Bavarian *Landtag* (1883–1916; from 1899 its president) and the *Reichstag* (1884–1892); styled Ritter von Orterer (1901). 516–517, 545

Osten-Sacken, Nikolai von der (1831–1912), Russian diplomat. Minister resident at Darmstadt (1870); envoy extraordinary and minister plenipotentiary at Munich (1880); ambassador to Berlin (1895–1912). 204

Otto (1848–1916), King of Bavaria (1886–1913). 470n, 485, 489, 498–500, 520

Ow-Wachendorf, Hans Freiherr von (1843–1921), estate owner, civil servant and politician. Member of the second chamber of the Württemberg *Landtag* (1876–1906) and the *Reichstag* (1878–1890). 432

Paasche, Hermann (1851–1925), German statistician, economist, and politician. Member of the *Reichstag* (1881–1884; 1893–1918). 417

Palmerston, Henry John Temple (1784–1865), 3rd Viscount Palmerston (1802), British statesman. MP (1807–1865); secretary at war (1809–1828); foreign secretary (1830–1841; 1846–1851); home secretary (1851); prime minister (1855–1858; 1859–1865). 286

Parnell, Charles Stewart (1846–1891), Irish politician. MP (1875–1891), leader of the Home Rule League (1880) and the Irish National Land League (1882). 299, 345

Pasteur, Jean Baptiste (1851–1908), French diplomat. Secretary of legation at Copenhagen (1891–1894). 154

Pauncefote, Julian (1828–1902), British diplomat. Assistant under-secretary of state for the colonies (1874) and foreign affairs (1876); permanent under-secretary of state for foreign affairs (1882); envoy extraordinary and minister plenipotentiary (1889) and ambassador to the United States of America (1893); created 1st Baron Pauncefote (1899). 234, 277, 279, 293n, 295, 423, 480, 486, 493, 497

Payer, Friedrich von (1847–1931), lawyer and democratic politician. Member of the second chamber of the Württemberg *Landtag* (1894–1912) and the *Reichstag* (1877–1878; 1880–1887; 1890–1917). 444, 458, 461

Peel, Sir Robert (1788–1850), British statesman. MP (1809–1850); home secretary (1821–1830); prime minister (1834–1835; 1841–1846). 289, 343

Pelham-Holles, Thomas (1693–1768), Duke of Newcastle upon Tyne, British statesman. Prime minister (1754–1756; 1757–1762); 1st Duke of Newcastle under Lyme. 364

Pergler von Perglas, Maximilian Joseph (1817–1893), Bavarian diplomat. Minister resident at Athens (1847) and Hanover (1854); envoy extraordinary and minister plenipotentiary at St Petersburg (1860), Paris (1866), and Berlin (1868–1877; from 1870 also plenipotentiary at the Federal Council); from 1877 royal chamberlain (with duties of master of ceremonies). 510

Peter, Clemens (died 1891), priest at the Dresden Johanneskirche. 293

Peters, Carl (1856–1918), German explorer, politician, and colonist. Founder of the *Deutsch-Ostafrikanische Gesellschaft* (1884); imperial high commissioner for the Kilimanjaro Region (1891–1892); for his cruel treatment of the local people dismissed from his post at the Imperial Colonial Office for misuse of official power (1897); until 1914 resident in England. 34–35, 182, 318–319, 335–336

Pfeil, Markus Graf (1859–1916), German consular official. Vice consul and commissary consul at Lourenço Marques (1895–1897); consul at Bombay (1898–1903) and Kiev (1903–1905). 180

Pfister, Philipp (1832–1889), Bavarian civil servant. Court secretary to Ludwig II (1884). 469, 476

Pfisterer, Georg Philipp (1837–1915), farmer and anti-Semitic politician. Member of the second chamber of the Baden *Landtag* (1895–1899). 256–257

Pfretzschner, Adolph Freiherr von (1820–1901), Bavarian statesman. Minister of trade (1865–1866) and finances (1866–1872); minister president and minister of foreign affairs (1872–1880); member of the first chamber of the Bavarian *Landtag* (1872–1897). 510

Pickard, Benjamin (1842–1904), British coal miner, politician and trades unionist. MP (1885–1904). 389

Pickenbach, Wilhelm (1850–1903), businessman and politician. Co-founder of the *Deutscher Antisemiten-Bund* (1884). *Reichstag* member (1890–1893). 243

Pietro, Angelo Di (1828–1914), apostolic nuncio to Munich (1882) and Madrid (1887). Cardinal (1893) and prefect of the Congregation of the Council (1893–1895). 493–494, 496–497

Pitt, William (1708–1778), known as Pitt the elder, British statesmam. Prime minister (1766–1768); 1st Earl of Chatham (1866). 326, 364

Pitt, William (1759–1806), known as Pitt the younger, British statesman. Prime minister (1783–1801; 1804–1806). 286, 289, 364

Pius VII (1742–1823), born Gregorio Barnaba Chiaramonti. Cardinal 1785; pope from 1800. 503

Pius IX (1792–1878), born Giovanni Maria Mastai-Ferretti. Pope from 1846. 80

Plessen, Ludwig Freiherr von (1848–1929), German and Prussian diplomat. Secretary of embassy at St Petersburg (1883), Vienna (1884), and London (1884); consul general at Budapest (1888–1890); envoy extraordinary and minister at Athens (1894–1902); Prussian envoy extraordinary and minister plenipotentiary at Darmstadt (1890–1894) and Stuttgart (1902–1907). 41, 170

Polignac, Jules de (1780–1847), French diplomat and statesman. Minister president (1829–1830). 289

Pollock, Sir Jonathan Frederick (1783–1870), British lawyer, judge, and politician. MP (1831–1844); attorney general (1834–1835; 1841–1844); chief baron of the exchequer (1844–1866); 1st baronet (1866). 502

Poppe, Johannes (dates unknown), journalist and editor of the Dresdner Journal. 407–408

Powerscourt, *see* **Wingfield, Mervyn**

Preißer, Max (1853–1925), carpenter and socialist agitator from Lindendau. 270

Preysing-Lichtenegg-Moos, Conrad Graf von (1843–1900), Bavarian nobleman and Catholic politician. Member of the *Reichstag* (1871–1893; 1900–1903) and the first chamber of the Bavarian *Landtag* from 1881. 542

Primrose, Archibald (1847–1929), 5th Earl of Rosebery (1868), British statesman. Lord privy seal (1885); foreign secretary (1886; 1892–1894); prime minister (1894–1895); created Earl of Midlothian (1911). 17, *63–64*, 142n, *143–156*, 169n, *228–229*, *249–250*, *282–284*, 327n, *368–386*, 387, 396, 401, *429–431*, *448–456*, *483–489*, *527–533*

Puttkamer, Robert von (1828–1900), Prussian statesman. Member of the *Reichstag* (1874–1884; 1890–1891), the Prussian house of deputies (1879–1885), and the upper house (from 1889); *Oberpräsident* of Silesia (1877) and Pomerania (1891–1899); minister of cultural affairs (1879–1881) and of the interior (1881–1888). 57n, 109–110

Quidde, Ludwig (1858–1941), German historian, liberal politician and pacifist. Executive secretary of the Prussian Historical Station at Rome (1890–1892); member of the second chamber of the Bavarian *Landtag* (1907–1918) and the Weimar National Assembly (1919); Nobel Peace Prize laureate (1927); emigrated to Switzerland (1933). 537–538

Racke, Nicola (1847–1908), wine merchant and Catholic politician. Member of the second chamber of the Hessian *Landtag* (1875–1893) and the *Reichstag* (1884–1890). 242

Radolin, Hugo Graf von (1841–1917), Prussian and German diplomat. Secretary of legation at Dresden (1874–1876); secretary of embassy at Constantinople (1876–1881); envoy extraordinary and minister plenipotentiary at Weimar (1882–1884) and at Constantinople (1892–1894); ambassador to St Petersburg (1895–1900) and Paris (1901–1910). *Oberhofmarschall* to Friedrich Wilhelm (Friedrich III) and Princess Victoria (1884–1888). 40

Radziwill, Anton von (1833–1904), Prussian general. Adjutant general and aide-de-camp to Wilhelm I and Friedrich III 40

Raesfeldt, Ferdinand von (1835–1914), civil servant in the Bavarian ministry for finance; deputy plenipotentiary at the Federal Council (1877–1884; in 1880 plenipotentiary). 34

Ranke, Leopold von (1794–1886), German historian. 304

Ratzinger, Georg (1844–1899), Catholic priest, publicist and politician. Member of the second chamber of the Bavarian *Landtag* (1875–1881; 1893–1899) and the *Reichstag* (1877–1878; 1893–1899). 549–550

Rauchenecker, Johann (1853–1903), brewery owner and Catholic politician. Member of the *Reichstag* (1892–1893). 528

Reichardt, Julius (1826–1898), publisher and founding editor of the *Dresdner Nachrichten*. 307, 321

Reuter, Paul Julius Freiherr von (1816–1899), entrepreneur, journalist, and founder of Reuter's Telegram Company. Naturalized British subject (1857). 59–60

Rhodes, Cecil (1853–1902), British business man, colonist and South African politician. Founder of the British South Africa Company (1889); prime minister of the Cape Colony (1890–1896). 170–173, 180, 192, 546

Ribot, Alexandre (1842–1923), French statesman. Prime minister (1892–1893; 1895; 1914; 1917); minister of foreign affairs (1890–1893; 1917), of the interior (1893), of finance (1895; 1914–1917), and of justice (1914). 523

Richard I (1157–1199), King of England from 1189. 370

Richter, Eugen (1838–1906), publicist and liberal politician. Member of the *Reichstag* (1867–1906) and the Prussian house of deputies (1869–1905). 50, 97, 214, 216, 299, 310–311, 316, 389

Rickert, Heinrich (1833–1902), journalist and liberal politician. Member of the *Reichstag* (1874–1903) and the Prussian house of deputies (1870–1902). 389

Riecke, Karl von (1830–1898), civil servant and Württemberg statesman. Head of the Württemberg statistical bureau (1873–1880) and the *Steuerkollegium* (1880–1891); minister of finance (1891–1898); plenipotentiary at the Federal Council (1871–1872; 1892–1898); member of the first chamber of the Württemberg *Landtag* (1872–1891). 461

Riedel, Emil von (1832–1906), Bavarian jurist and statesman. Minister of finance (1877–1904). 483, 514

Ripon, *see* **Robinson, George**

Robertson, Charles Boyd (d.1905), British diplomat and civil servant (Foreign Office). Acting third secretary at Washington (1871); acting second secretary at Stuttgart (1879);

acting assistant clerk (1882); assistant clerk (1882); superintendent of the treaty department (1894–1903). 152, 312

Robinson, George (1827–1909), Earl de Grey and Earl of Ripon (1859), British statesman. Secretary of state for war (1863–1866), for India (1866), and for the colonies (1892–1895); lord privy seal (1905–1908); 1st Marquess of Ripon (1871). 171

Robinson, Sir Hercules (1824–1897), British colonial administrator. Governor of Hong Kong (1859), British Ceylon (1865), New South Wales (1872), Fiji (1874), and New Zealand (1879); high commissioner for Southern Africa and governor of the Cape Colony (1881–1889; 1895–1897); created 1st Baron Rosmead (1896). 37

Robinson, Sir Thomas (1703–1777), English politician and architect. 326

Romeiko-Gurko, Count Iosif Vladimirovich (1828–1901), Russian field marshal. Governor of St Petersburg (1879–1880); governor general of Poland (1883–1894). 231

Roos, Johann Christian (1828–1896), Catholic priest. Bishop of Limburg (1885); Archbishop of Freiburg (1886). 235, 242

Rosebery, *see* **Primrose, Archibald**

Rößler, Constantin (1820–1896), German publicist and journalist. From 1877 head of the Prussian *Literarisches Büro*; secretary of legation in the Prussian ministry of foreign affairs (1892–1894). 309, 394, 537

Rotenhan, Wolfram Freiherr von (1845–1912), German diplomat. Envoy extraordinary and minister plenipotentiary at Buenos Aires (1884–1890), Berne (1897), and the Holy See (1897–1907); under-secretary of state in the Berlin foreign office (1890). 149–150, 213

Rudini, *see* **Starabba, Antonio**

Ruffo-Scilla, Fulco Luigi (1840–1895), Catholic priest and apostolic nuncio to Munich (1887–1889); elevated to cardinal in 1891. 505

Russell, Emily (1843–1927), née Villier; British courtier. Married Odo Russell in 1868; Baroness Ampthill (1881). 38–40

Russell, Francis Shirley (1840–1912), British army officer. Military attaché at Berlin (1889–1891). 119

Russell, Odo (1829–1884), British diplomat. Attaché at Paris, Vienna, Constantinople, Washington, and Naples; from 1860 on special service at Rome (as unaccredited envoy to the Holy See); on special mission to the German headquarters at Versailles (November 1870–March 1871); ambassador to Berlin (1871–1884); styled Lord Odo Russell from 1872, created Baron Ampthill (1881). 08–10, 13–15, 25n, *33–37*, 38–40, 49

Safferling, Benignus von (1836–1898), Bavarian general and statesman; minister of war (1890–1893). 522

Said Pasha Kurd (1834–1907), Ottoman statesman and diplomat. Governor general of the Archipelago (1881); minister of foreign affairs (1882; 1885–1896); ambassador to Berlin (1883–1885). 53

Saldern, Conrad von (1847–1908), German diplomat. Acting consul in Ragusa (1882) and acting consul general in Sofia (1884); temporarily in charge of the imperial legation at Tangier (1887); acting consul general at Warsaw (1887) and Odessa (1888); consul at Tbilisi (1889), Basel (1893), and Stockholm (1897). Minister resident in Bangkok (1899) and Seoul (1903–1906). 230

Salfeld, Siegmund (1843–1926), German rabbi and scholar. Preacher at Dessau (1870); rabbi in Dessau (1878) and Mainz (1880). 243

Salisbury, Robert Arthur Talbot Gascoyne-Cecil (1830–1903), 3rd Marquess of Salisbury (1868), British statesman. MP (1853–1868); secretary of state for India (1866–1867; 1874–1878); secretary of state for foreign affairs (1878–1880; 1885–1886; 1887–1892; 1895–1900); prime minister (1885–1886; 1886–1892; 1895–1902). *54–63*, 65, 73n, *75–143*, 170, *179–217*, *226–228*, *231–248*, *256–262*, 284, *288–368*, 368n, 380, *401–419*, *427–447*, *462–463*, *475–483*, *493–526*

Sanderson, Thomas Henry (1841–1923), civil servant (Foreign Office). Junior clerk (1859); private secretary to the foreign secretary (1866–1868; 1874–1878; 1880–1885); assistant clerk (1876); senior clerk (1885); assistant under-secretary (1889), then permanent under-secretary of state for foreign affairs (1894–1906); created Baron Sanderson (1905). 76, 144, 340n, 358, 381n, 385, 403, 462, 519, 523

Sarwey, Otto von (1825–1900), Württemberg civil servant and statesman. Minister for church and school affairs (1885–1900); member of the Württemberg *Landtag* (1856–1864; 1866–1876) and the *Reichstag* (1874–1876). 426

Schäffle, Albert (1831–1903), political economist. Professor at the universities of Tübingen (1860) and Vienna (1868); Austrian minister for trade (February to October 1871), then publicist in Stuttgart; member of the Württemberg *Landtag* (1862–1865). 269, 551–552

Schauß, Friedrich von (1831–1893), jurist, banker and National Liberal politician. Member of the second chamber of the Bavarian *Landtag* (1869–1892) and the *Reichstag* (1871–1881). 507–508

Schickert, Paul (1827–1906), Saxon railway official and politician. *Stadtrat* in Dresden and member of the *Landtag* (1888–1894). 333

Schiller, Friedrich (1759–1805), German poet and playwright. 538

Schippel, Max (1859–1928), Saxon journalist and socialist politician. Professor for *Staatswissenschaften* at Dresden (1923–1928); *Reichstag* member (1890–1905). 345

Schmidt, Reinhardt (1838–1909), German businessman and liberal politician. Member of the Prussian house of deputies (1890–1909) and the *Reichstag* (1881–1907). 175

Schmits, August (1838–1921), journalist and from 1872 to 1901 editor of the *Kölnische Zeitung*. 115

Schnæbelé, Guillaume (Wilhelm Schnäbele) (1831–1900), French railway police officer, originally from Alsace. 83–84, 86–87, 296

Schönhardt, Karl (1833–1916), jurist. Attorney general at Stuttgart. 424

Schorlemmer-Alst, Burghard Freiherr von (1825–1895), estate owner and Catholic politician. Member of the Prussian house of deputies (1870–1889), the *Reichstag* (1870–1871; 1874–1885; 1890), and the Prussian upper house (1890–1895). 147–148

Schott von Schottenstein, Maximilian Freiherr (1836–1917), Württemberg general and statesman. Minister of war (1892–1901) and minister president (1900–1901). 453–455

Schütte, Ernst Wilhelm (1848–1919), from 1885 chief of the political police in Berlin. 111

Schwabe, Christian Julius (dates unknown), Saxon public prosecutor. 280, 337

Schweinfurth, Georg August (1836–1925), botanist, ethnologist. Explorer of Africa, and promoter of German colonialism. 182

Schweinitz, Hans Lothar von (1822–1901), Prussian general and diplomat. Envoy extraordinary to Vienna (1869); imperial ambassador to Vienna (1871) and to St Petersburg (1876–1892). 71

Scott, Sir Charles Stewart (1838–1924), British diplomat. Second secretary at Mexico (1866), Lisbon (1868), Stuttgart (1871), Munich (1872), Vienna (1873), St Petersburg (1874), and Darmstadt (1877); secretary of legation at Coburg (1879); repeatedly acting chargé d'affaires at Darmstadt from 1877 to 1883, and at Stuttgart in 1881; secretary of embassy at Berlin (1883); envoy extraordinary and minister plenipotentiary at Berne (1888) and Copenhagen (1893); ambassador to St Petersburg (1898–1904). *37–41, 47–57, 60–68, 81–84, 86–93, 106–110*

Senden-Bibran, Gustav von (1847–1909), German admiral. Chief of the imperial naval cabinet (1889–1906); adjutant general to Wilhelm II (1901–1909). 177, 206

Sharpe, Alfred (1853–1935), British colonial administrator. Commissioner and consul general for the British Central Africa Protectorate (1896–1907); governor of Nyasaland (1907–1910). 196

Shuvalov, Count Petr Andreievich (1827–1889), Russian diplomat. Ambassador to London (1874–1879). 94, 131–133

Shuvalova, Countess Elena (1830–1922), née Chertkova. Married Pyotr Shuvalov in 1864. 133

Siegle, Gustav (1840–1905), industrialist and Württemberg politician. *Reichstag* member (1887–1898). 432, 444

Sieveking, Ernst Friedrich (1836–1909), German jurist. Member of the Hamburg *Bürgerschaft* (1874–1877) and senate (1877–1879); from 1870 president of the common court of appeal of the Hanse towns. 187

Sigl, Johann Baptist (1839–1902), Bavarian journalist and politician. Founding editor of the *Bayerisches Vaterland* (1869); member of the *Reichstag* (1893–1898) and the second chamber of the Bavarian *Landtag* (1897–1899). 528, 530–531, 538, 549

Simon de Montfort, 6th Earl of Leicester (1208–1265), Franco-English nobleman. 370

Singer, Paul (1844–1911), factory owner and socialist politician from Berlin. *Reichstag* member (1884–1911). 389

Smith, Adam (1723–1790), Scottish philosopher and economist. 360

Smith, William Henry (1825–1891), British bookseller, newsagent, politician, and statesman. MP (1868–1891); first lord of the admiralty (1877–1880); secretary of state for war (1885–1886; 1886–1887); first lord of the treasury (1887–1891). 89, 491

Soden, Heinrich Freiherr von (1864–1941), Württemberg military officer. 509

Soden, Oskar Freiherr von (1831–1906), Württemberg diplomat. Chargé d'affaires at Karlsruhe (1866); envoy extraordinary and minister plenipotentiary at Munich (1868–1906). 451, 495, 509

Solms-Sonnenwalde, Eberhard Graf zu (1825–1912), German diplomat. Envoy extraordinary and minister plenipotentiary at Rio de Janeiro (1872), Dresden (1873), and Madrid (1878); ambassador to Rome (1887–1893). 155

Spaarmann, Adolf (1837–1911), German publisher at Styrum. 112

Spahn, Peter (1846–1925), jurist and Catholic politician. Prussian minister of justice (1817–1918); member of Prussian house of deputies (1882–1888; 1891–1898; 1904–1907), the *Reichstag* (1884–1917; vice president 1895–1898; 1909–1911), the Weimar National Assembly (1919/20), and the Weimar *Reichstag* (1920–1925). 175

Spitzemberg, Wilhelm Freiherr Hugo von (1825–1888), Württemberg general. Grand chamberlain, and aide-de-camp to King Karl I. 436–437

Spring-Rice, Sir Cecil (1859–1918), British diplomat. Second secretary at Brussels (1891), Washington (1893), Berlin (1895), and Constantinople (1898); secretary of legation at Teheran (1898); British commissioner at the *Casse de la Dette Publique* in Cairo (1901);

secretary of embassy at St Petersburg (1903); envoy extraordinary and minister plenipotentiary at Teheran (1906) and Stockholm (1908); ambassador to Washington (1913–1918).
187, 195, 202

Stablewski, Florian (1841–1906), Polish priest and Archbishop of Gniezno and Poznan
(1891–1906). Member of the Prussian house of deputies (1876–1891). 137–138

Staelin, Julius (1837–1889), businessman, manufacturer, and politician. Member of the
second chamber of the Württemberg *Landtag* (1876–1889) and the *Reichstag* (1877–1889).
432

Stanhope, Edward (1840–1893), British politician and statesman. MP (1874–1893); president of the Board of Trade (1885–1886); secretary of state for the colonies (1886–1887);
secretary of state for war (1887–1892). 491, 519, 525

Stanley, Edward Henry (1826–1893), styled Lord Stanley prior to 1869, 15th Earl of
Derby (1869), British statesman. MP (1848–1869); parliamentary under-secretary at the
Foreign Office (1852); secretary of state for the colonies (1858; 1882–1885); first secretary
of state for India (1858–1859); foreign secretary (1866–1868; 1874–1878). 37, 191, 470, 510

Stanley, Henry Morton (1841–1904), British-American explorer and journalist. 319

Starabba, Antonio, marchese di Rudini (1839–1908), Italian statesman. Prime minister of Italy (1891–1892; 1896–1898). 129, 140

Starke, Wilhelm (1824–1903), German jurist and civil servant. From 1873 to 1896 official
in the Berlin ministry of justice; member of the Prussian house of deputies (1859–1861;
1866–1867). 199

Stauffenberg, Franz August Freiherr Schenk von (1834–1901), jurist and politician.
Member of the Bavarian second chamber (1867–1877; 1879–1899; president 1873–1875);
Reichstag member (1871–1893; vice president 1876–1879). 73

Staveley, Thomas G. (1825–1887), civil servant (Foreign Office). Junior Clerk (1843),
assistant clerk (1857), senior clerk (1860). 37, 39

Steichele, Anton von (1816–1889), Catholic priest and church historian. From 1878
Archbishop of Munich and Freising. 543

Stephan, Heinrich von (1831–1897), Prussian civil servant. General post director (1870),
postmaster general (1876), and state secretary of the imperial post office (1880–1897);
Prussian minister of state without portfolio. Member of the Prussian upper house from
1872. 195–196

Stephen, Sir Alexander Condie (1850–1908), British diplomat and translator.
Secretary of legation and chargé d'affaires at Coburg (1893–1897); minister resident at
Dresden (1897–1901). 148

Stoecker, Adolf (1835–1909), Lutheran theologian, publicist, and politician. Founder of the anti-Semitic *Christlich-Soziale Arbeiterpartei* (1878); member of the second chamber of the Prussian *Landtag* (1879–1898) and the *Reichstag* (1881–1893; 1898–1908). 97, 109n, 325

Stoilov, Konstantin (1853–1901), Bulgarian politician and statesman. Minister of foreign affairs (1881; 1883; 1896–1899); minister of justice (1883–1884; 1886–1888; 1894–1896); prime minister (1887; 1894–1899). 233–234

Strachey, Catherine (1841–1920), née Doveton. Married George Strachey in 1862. 418

Strachey, George (1828–1912), British diplomat. Secretary of legation at Copenhagen (1867), Berne (1873), and Dresden (1873, with additional role of chargé d'affaires); minister resident (1890–1897). 7–8, 11, 17, 21, 23–26, *265–419*

Strenge, Karl Friedrich von (1843–1907), jurist and statesman. State minister of Saxe-Coburg-Gotha (1891–1900). 152

Stromer von Reichenbach, Otto Freiherr von (1831–1891), jurist and mayor of Nuremberg (1867–1891). 325

Stübel, Paul Alfred (1827–1895), lawyer and politician. Mayor of Dresden (1877–1895); member of the second chamber of the Saxon *Landtag* (1877–1884) and the *Reichstag* (1881–1884). 302, 314

Swaine, Leopold (1840–1931), British army officer. Military attaché at St Petersburg (1878), Constantinople (1879–1881), and Berlin (1882–1889; 1891–1896). 38, 58–59, 81–82, 86, 91–93, 116–117, 144–145, 149–150, 165

Széchényi, Emmerich Graf (1825–1898), Austrian diplomat. Envoy extraordinary and minister plenipotentiary at Stockholm (1849–1850) and Naples (1860–1864); ambassador to Berlin (1878–1892). 40

Tauffkirchen-Guttenberg, Carl von (1826–1895), Bavarian diplomat. Envoy extraordinary and minister plenipotentiary at St Petersburg (1867), the Holy See (1869; from 1871 also accredited for Prussia), and Stuttgart (1874–1895). 79n–80

Tausch, Eugen von (1844–1912), policeman; from 1887 superintendent of the Berlin political police. 209, 213

Tcherevin, *see* **Cherevin, Pyotr Alexandrovich**

Tessendorff, Hermann (1851–1895), Prussian jurist. Public prosecutor in Burg (1864), Magdeburg (1867), and Berlin (1873); *Senatspräsident* at the higher regional courts in Königsberg (1879), Naumburg (1884), and at the Berlin *Kammergericht* (1885); from 1886 *Oberreichsanwalt* in Leipzig. 86

Thielmann, Max von (1846–1929), German diplomat. Secretary of legation at Washington (1875) and Brussels (1878); first secretary at Paris (1880), Constantinople (1883). Consul general at Sofia (1886); Prussian envoy extraordinary and minister plenipotentiary at Darmstadt (1887), Hamburg (1890); and Munich (1895); ambassador to Washington (1895); secretary of state of the imperial treasury (1897–1903). 70

Thiers, Adolphe (1797–1877), French statesman and politician. President of the Third Republic (1871–1873). 289, 343

Thil, Friederike Freifrau du Bos du (1811–1891), née Freiin v. Rotsmann. From 1855 mistress of the robes at the grand ducal court of Hesse. 244–245

Thil, Karl Wilhelm Heinrich Freiherr du Bos du (1777–1859), Hessian statesman. Minister of foreign affairs (1821–1847), minister for finance (1821–1829), and minister president (1829–1848); member of the first chamber of the Hessian *Landtag* (1820–1847). 244

Thümmel, Hans von (1824–1895), Saxon jurist and statesman. Minister of finance (1890–1895) and minister president (1891–1895). 346–347, 398–399

Tillett, Ben (1860–1943), British socialist politician and trades unionist. Alderman on the London County Council (1892–1898); MP (1917–1924; 1929–1931). 389

Tirpitz, Alfred von (1849–1930), German admiral, statesman and politician. State secretary of the imperial naval office (1897–1916); member of the Weimar *Reichstag* (1924–1928). 214, 552

Toerring-Jettenbach, Clemens Maria zu (1826–1891), Bavarian civil servant and chamberlain to Ludwig II; hereditary member of the first chamber of the Bavarian *Landtag* (1866). 487

Trafford, William Henry (1833–1910), English jurist and justice of peace for Norfolk; friend of Randolph Churchill. 287

Treitschke, Heinrich von (1834–1896), historian and publicist. Professor at the universities of Freiburg, Kiel, Heidelberg and, from 1873, Berlin; *Reichstag* member (1871–1884). 309, 406n

Trench, Power Henry Le Poer (1841–1899), British diplomat. Second secretary at Washington (1870), the Foreign Office (1879), and Rome (1881); secretary of legation at Tokyo (1882–1889); secretary of embassy at Berlin (1889–1893); envoy extraordinary and minister plenipotentiary in Mexico (1893–1894) and Japan (1894–1896; also consul general). *128–131, 140–143, 145–147*

Tschirschky und Bögendorff, Heinrich von (1858–1916), German diplomat. Private secretary to Herbert von Bismarck (1885); secretary of legation at Vienna (1886), Athens (1888), and Berne (1890); first secretary at Constantinople (1893) and St Petersburg (1894); envoy extraordinary and minister plenipotentiary at Luxembourg (1900); Prussian envoy to Hamburg (1901); secretary of state for foreign affairs (1906–1907); ambassador to Vienna (1913–1916). 69–70

Victoria (1840–1901), Princess Royal of the United Kingdom. Married Friedrich Wilhelm (Friedrich III) in 1858; German Empress and Queen of Prussia from 1888. Known as Empress Frederick after her husband's untimely death in 1888. 20, 39–40, 86, 99–100, 111, 131, 133–135, 205, 259, 305, 308–309, 315, 324, 394, 434, 443

Viktoria (1866–1929), Princess of Prussia. Married Adolf of Schaumburg-Lippe in 1890 and, secondly, Alexander Zoubkoff in 1927. 20, 99n, 101

Villers, Hippolyte de (1843–1920), Luxembourg diplomat. Chargé d'affaires at Berlin (1889–1916). 150

Villiers, George (1847–1892), British army officer; military attaché at St Petersburg (1880), Berlin (1881) and Paris (1882–1889). 39, 64

Virchow, Rudolf (1821–1902), German pathologist, anthropologist, and liberal politician. Professor at Würzburg (1849) and Berlin (1856); member of the Prussian house of deputies (1862–1902) and the *Reichstag* (1880–1893). 362

Vittorio Emanuele III (1869–1947), Prince of Naples; King of Italy (1900–1946). Emperor of Ethiopia (1936–1941) and King of the Albanians (1939–1943). 150–151

Vivian, Hussey Crespigny (1834–1893), 3rd Baron Vivian (1886), British diplomat. Envoy extraordinary and minister plenipotentiary at Berne (1879), Copenhagen (1881), and Brussels (1884); ambassador to Rome (1892–1893). 155

Vladimir Alexandrovich (1848–1909), Grand Duke of Russia and army officer. 71, 185

Vohsen, Ernst (1853–1919), German colonist and publisher. Agent of the French Senegal Company (1875–1887); German consul at Sierra Leone (1881–1887); head of the *Deutsch-Ostafrikanische Gesellschaft* (1888–1892). 187

Vollmar, Georg von (1850–1922), politician and socialist publicist. Chairman of the Social Democratic Party in Bavaria from 1894; member of the second chamber of the Saxon *Landtag* (1881–1889), the Bavarian *Landtag* (1893–1918), and the *Reichstag* (1881–1887; 1890–1918). 266, 279, 472, 535–537, 539

Waddington, William (1826–1894), French statesman and diplomat. Minister of public instruction (1873; 1877); minister of foreign affairs (1877–1879); prime minister (1879); ambassador to London (1883–1893). 76

Wagner, Richard (1813–1883), German composer. 297, 323

Waldersee, Alfred Graf von (1832–1904), German general. Chief of the imperial general staff (1888–1891); commander of the IX imperial army corps (1891–1898); inspector general of the 3rd army inspectorate (1898–1904); commander of the international relief expedition in China (1900). 131–132, 206, 325

Waldersee, Georg Graf von (1860–1932), Prussian army officer. 117

Wölckern, Wilhelm von (1827–1905), Württemberg general. Commander of the XIII (Royal Württemberg) imperial army corps (1886–1895). 453

Wolkenstein-Trostburg, Anton von (1832–1913), Austrian-Hungarian diplomat. Envoy extraordinary and minister plenipotentiary at Dresden (1880); head of the trade department in the Austrian foreign office (1881); ambassador to St Petersburg (1882) and Paris (1894–1903). 92

Woodcock, Charles (1850–1923), American pastor. From 1879 to 1889 on continental tour in Europe; from 1883 at Stuttgart where, while royal chamberlain, lover of King Karl of Württemberg; created Freiherr von Savage in 1888. 19–20, 436–440

Wyndham, Percy (1864–1944), British diplomat. Third secretary at Berlin (1892) and Teheran (1895); second secretary at Teheran (1895), Vienna (1897), and Constantinople (1897); secretary of legation at Brussels (1906); secretary of embassy at Rome (1808); envoy extraordinary and minister plenipotentiary at Bogota; special mission to the Republic of Poland (1919). 151

Xylander, Emil von (1835–1911), Bavarian general. Plenipotentiary at the Federal Council (1884–1890). 34

Zedlitz und Trützschler, Robert Graf von (1837–1914), Prussian civil servant and statesman. Minister for cultural affairs (1891–1892). *Oberpräsident* of the Prussian provinces of Poznań (1886), Hesse-Nassau (1898) and Silesia (1903–1908); member of the Prussian upper house from 1910. 138–139

Zimmermann, Oswald (1859–1910), journalist, publicist, and anti-Semitic politician. Member of the second chamber of the Saxon *Landtag* (1903–1908) and the *Reichstag* (1890–1898; 1904–1910). 243

SUBJECT INDEX